# Nigeria

## THE BRADT TRAVEL GUIDE

## PUBLISHER'S FOREWORD

The first Bradt travel guide was written in 1974 by George and Hilary Bradt on a river barge floating down a tributary of the Amazon. In the 1980s and '90s the focus shifted away from hiking to broader-based guides covering new destinations – usually the first to be published about these places. In the 21st century Bradt continues to publish such ground-breaking guides, as well as others to established holiday destinations, incorporating in-depth information on culture and natural history with the nuts and bolts of where to stay and what to see.

Bradt authors support responsible travel, and provide advice not only on minimum impact but also on how to give something back through local charities. In this way a true synergy is achieved between the traveller and local communities.

*

What's special about this book? It's the way Lizzie Williams paints the picture of Nigeria, warts and all, while making serious travellers long to go there. She emphasises the fact that all the scare stories about Nigeria's corruption and crime-rate are of concern to expats and business people but that travellers getting off the beaten path will meet nothing but kindness and hospitality. Indeed, it seems to be that rarity, a country untouched by tourism, with all the advantages that this bestows: no beggars, no tourist-related crime, no expectations of a bribe.

Through this book, and her belief that future visitors will share her enthusiasm for this 'unique and compelling country', Lizzie has paid a great compliment both to Nigeria and to the open-minded people who decide to see it for themselves.

*Hilary Bradt*

23 High Street, Chalfont St Peter, Bucks SL9 9QE, England
Tel: 01753 893444   Fax: 01753 892333
info@bradtguides.com   www.bradtguides.com

# Nigeria

## THE BRADT TRAVEL GUIDE

### Lizzie Williams

Bradt Travel Guides Ltd, UK
The Globe Pequot Press Inc, USA

**First edition 2005**

Bradt Travel Guides Ltd
23 High Street, Chalfont St Peter, Bucks SL9 9QE, England
Published in the USA by The Globe Pequot Press Inc, 246 Goose Lane,
PO Box 480, Guilford, Connecticut 06475-0480

**British Library Cataloguing in Publication Data**
A catalogue record for this book is available from the British Library

ISBN-10: 1 84162 124 2
ISBN-13: 978 1 84162 124 1

**Photographs**
Darren Humphrys
*Front cover* Muslim schoolchildren in Katsina

**Illustrations** Carole Vincer
**Maps** Alan Whitaker; regional maps based on ITM *Nigeria*

Typeset from the author's disc by Wakewing
Printed and bound in Italy by Legoprint SpA, Trento

# Author/Photographer

## AUTHOR

Lizzie Williams (lizziebx1@yahoo.com) is a travel writer and tour leader based in Cape Town, South Africa. Originally from London, she has notched up ten years to date on the road in Africa and the Middle East, firstly as an expedition leader on overland trucks for four-and-a-half years, and now is something of an expert on border crossings and African beer. She has led numerous trips throughout eastern and southern Africa, between Istanbul and Cairo, and has spent some time working in South America. In Harare, Zimbabwe , she has worked as a manager of an overlanders' lodge and travel agency specialising in Mozambique, and has established and managed a lodge in Cape Town equipped to receive overland trucks. She has written numerous magazine articles and brochures on African travel, contributed to books on working abroad, is author of the current *Footprint Handbook to South Africa*, and updated the present edition of the *Rough Guide to Turkey*. She has worked as content editor for the website www.go2africa.com – a leading online travel agency for travel all over Africa – and wrote www.overlandafrica.com, a comprehensive website on the overland industry. Her next project is a coffee-table book on overlanding, and she is scheduled to update several Africa guidebooks in 2005. She has visited 20 African countries, none of which were quite as absorbing as Nigeria.

## PHOTOGRAPHER

Darren Humphrys (dchphotos@yahoo.com), who took the photographs for this book and contributed to the research, is a freelance photographer and tour leader. Born in Perth, Australia, where he worked as a newspaper photographer before arriving in Africa eight years ago, he worked as an overland expedition leader for several years before settling in Cape Town. He has travelled extensively throughout eastern and southern Africa and has led numerous tours, taking photographs wherever he has been. He spent a year in Morocco establishing a new programme for a UK–based overland company, and has worked for stints in the Middle East. His photographs are widely sold through various photographic agencies and he was runner up in the Wildlife Photographer of the Year competition in *Geographical* magazine in 2003.

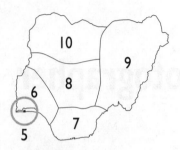

# Contents

## LIST OF MAPS

For key to map symbols, see page 114

# Acknowledgements

Right from the off, I'd like to thank my dad, Lewis Williams, for his continued support, and for giving great advice such as 'get yourself to Nigeria before someone else writes this book'. Thanks to Richard Pieterse for the books and maps, and his first-hand reports on working in Nigeria. Thanks to Tricia Hayne of Bradt for her patience and understanding on how huge and impracticable this project was, and her enthusiasm in seeing it through despite all the difficulties. Thanks to Dan Isaacs, the BBC correspondent in Lagos for his encouragement. In Nigeria, Darren and I would like to sincerely thank Sharon and Paul Fay for their exceptional hospitality in Lagos – enjoy the rest of your contract! Thanks also to their friends, Mave and Conner, and all the other people we met in Lagos who entertained us with stories and anecdotes and gave me an insight into expat life. A sincere thank you to Alan Parke, a long term expat in Nigeria, for his invaluable advice and useful comments after being the first person in Nigeria to read the book. Victoria Soluade of Soltan Travel and Tours in Lagos was extremely helpful, as were the staff at the Kano tourist office. Thanks to Peter Jenkins and Liza Gadsby from Pandrillus in Calabar for all their information, and Sam who was such a special host at the Drill Ranch in Afi. The same goes to Nicola Pulman of Cercopan, and to Tunde Morakinyo of Environmental Resources Management who gave me invaluable information on Nigeria's national parks. Thanks to Andie, Grant and Steve from Oasis Overland for their route notes. Also thanks to the hundreds of Nigerian people that greeted us and chatted to us throughout Nigeria, and who taught us so much about what Nigeria is all about. Finally, a huge thank you to Darren Humphrys (Crusty to his friends) for joining and inspiring me in Nigeria, for taking the wonderful photographs, and for sharing that 'most obscure moment of the day'.

## HELP US UPDATE NIGERIA: THE BRADT TRAVEL GUIDE

Given that there is little on-the-ground information available about Nigeria, this was an enormously difficult book to write, and a lot of it is based on first-hand experiences rather than on written information. The Nigerian people are hugely hospitable and charmingly humorous and I hope many more travellers go to Nigeria to meet them. I would like to hear about any experiences that could enhance the next edition of this book. Things change, though much more slowly in Nigeria than in other places in the world, so if a hotel or restaurant has closed down, if a destination is no longer accessible, or if you feel that an increasingly dilapidated sight is no longer worth the effort of getting there, I want to know. On a positive note, if the tourist office suddenly decides to print brochures and information for visitors, or if the National Parks office decides to count how many animals are left in Nigeria's parks, I want to know that as well. Write to me at info@bradtguides.com.

# Introduction

Nigeria is Africa's most populous country and Lagos is the world's second-largest city. Since 1999, it has been the world's fourth-biggest democracy, and as the sixth-biggest supplier of crude oil on earth, by rights it should be Africa's economic giant. Nigeria has also had the reputation for centuries as being one of the world's most chaotic and dangerous places. A warning to early sailors to the region was 'beware, take care of the Bight of Benin. Few come out though many go in'. To put it plainly, as travel destinations go, Nigeria is far from the most pleasant West African country to travel in – it's impoverished and the majority of the population lives on under US$2 a day; it's dirty and an environmental nightmare, with piles of rubbish literally everywhere, and its natural resources have been stripped bare; nothing works and everything is seriously dilapidated, and the infrastructure is totally inadequate; there are frequent shortages of fuel, electricity and water, and vehicle traffic and human congestion are tremendous. It has a history of despot military dictators, and corruption at all levels of society; it has witnessed overwhelming political upheavals, and there's an ongoing religious and ethnic conflict that has already killed 10,000 people since 1999 and is so volatile it could feasibly be regarded as a civil war – a conflict that is so primal that Nigerian people are killing each other in hand-to-hand fighting and mob violence. To the international community, Nigeria is still sometimes regarded as a pariah nation, run by a government that is largely incapable of controlling the largest population in Africa. In his Ghana guide, my colleague at Bradt, Philip Briggs, describes Ghana as 'Africa for beginners'. Well by the same token, I would describe Nigeria as 'Africa for the very experienced'. It is simply one of the world's most difficult places to travel in. The notion of travelling here conjures up a horrific reaction – as I found out when Bradt first offered me the commission to write this book. When I told people I was going to Nigeria they were appalled. Those I spoke to who had been to Nigeria (mostly on business with hefty Sheraton-accommodating expense accounts, I might add), agreed. I even got the same reaction from colleagues in the travel industry who had taken passengers through Nigeria on overland trucks. It's far from a holiday destination, there's very little to see in the way of conventional sightseeing, and it's an environmental disaster. Nigerians themselves have no interest in conserving and preserving their natural or historical legacies, and there is no tourism industry to support the national parks or historic sites. One of the directors of the wholly ineffective Nigeria Tourism Development Board told me that for 16 years before the present civilian government was elected, in 1999, the secretive military discouraged tourism so foreigners wouldn't see what was going on in the country.

Everywhere in Nigeria, contrasts abound. Step outside the Meridian Hotel in Port Harcourt, easily the most luxurious hotel in Nigeria, and you'll see people selling yams from wheelbarrows at the gate; outside the Virgin airline offices, you'll see goats in the car park. From 24-hour internet cafés to dead bodies in the street; from roadblocks where the policemen wear bandanas and mirrored sunglasses to the ladies going to church in the most beautiful dresses you've ever seen; from plane-loads of wealthy Nigerians going to Dubai on shopping trips to people so poor they resort to eating rats and maggots; from black-magic markets full of unexplainable fetishes and charms in a country where there are still rumours of human sacrifice going on, to more people carrying modern cellphones that take photographs than perhaps anywhere else in the world. It's appalling and awful, fascinating and appealing, and funny and sad, all at the same time; Nigeria is that extreme.

So why go to Nigeria? Well, it's impossible to deny its pride of place amongst the potential travel destinations of the world, and there are undeniably few of these left as the world gets increasingly smaller. For the adventurous traveller, Nigeria offers the opportunity to see the country in its raw and naked state. Travel is challenging and exciting and your experiences will be memorable and educational. Alternatively, you may have picked up this book because you intend to work there. Nigeria has wide market opportunities, and there are many foreign companies operating in industries such as pharmaceuticals, oil, roadbuilding and telecommunications. There is a huge expat community, especially in Lagos, that has successfully made Nigeria its home. And if you are going to work there, you will find that there are effectively two Nigerias – one is the expat world of Lagos with its yacht clubs, societies, posh restaurants and supermarkets selling imported items, and the other is the rest of the country. I encourage you also to explore the latter.

Love it or hate it, Lagos has to be seen to be believed: nowhere on earth will you experience such mind-boggling, vibrant chaos as in this mass of humanity. In the waterlogged south of the country are deltas and lagoons where people's lives haven't changed for hundreds of years, and in the north are ancient kingdoms and walled cities, even today ruled by sultans and emirs. Nigeria has a fascinating and turbulent history, and the cultural assets of the nation are universally recognised, with more than 250 rich and diverse ethnic groups, several religions, and the warm-hearted hospitality of almost 140 million people. The highlight of travelling in Nigeria is meeting these culturally rich people; practically any person in any corner of Nigeria will offer a moment of their time to say 'welcome'. For the traveller with an open mind and friendly demeanour, meeting the people is an overwhelming experience – they are colourful, intelligent, curious, creative, imaginative, and generous.

My colleague Darren, who travelled with me in Nigeria, advises: 'Nigeria isn't easy. Everywhere we go, without exception, the Nigerians are absolutely dumbfounded to see two *oyibos* (whites) walking along the streets, sitting in the local bush taxis, and eating in the local restaurants or food stalls. It just doesn't happen here. Having said that, we have always been treated with friendliness and helpfulness. I think because we have both travelled a bit, and are therefore not totally overwhelmed or intimidated by some of the situations, we remember to remain friendly and calm (most of the time!).'

Travel in Nigeria can sometimes be stressful and is frequently stalled by inconvenience and inefficiency; not every experience will be pleasant, and away from the expat suburbs of Lagos, westerners are a rare sight indeed. But if you're up to the challenge, it's one of the most exciting and engaging countries in the world. Whilst I have written for other guidebook publishers before, the joy of writing for Bradt is that their authors are encouraged to write much more personally. Quite frankly there is no other way to write about Nigeria than personally. It's a destination that's not about Eiffel Towers or Serengeti Plains, but about a conversation or a unique moment. Every traveller to the country will experience a very personal and distinctive trip. I hope this book will greatly assist any travel to Nigeria and help to quell its awful reputation as a travel destination. It's a unique and compelling country with an enormous personality.

# Part One

# General Information

## NIGERIA AT A GLANCE

**Location** Between tropics of Cancer and Capricorn, on Gulf of Guinea
**Neighbouring countries** Benin, Niger, Chad, Cameroon
**Area** 923,768km$^2$
**Altitude** Rising to 2,419m at Chappal Waddi, on Cameroon border
**Terrain** Southern lowlands merge into hills and plateaux in centre; mountains in southeast; plains in north
**Climate** Tropical in south; arid in north
**Status** Federal republic
**Government** Bicameral presidential system
**President** Olusegun Obasanjo (since 1999)
**Capital** Abuja (moved from Lagos in 1991); population 2 million approx
**Other major towns** Lagos (population 13 million approx), Port Harcourt, Kano
**Administrative regions** 36 states and 1 Federal Capital Territory, further divided into 774 local government authorities
**Population** 137,253,133 (2004)
**Birth rate** 38.24 births per 1,000 population (2004)
**Life expectancy at birth** 50.49 years (2004)
**Age structure** 0–14 years, 43.4%, 15–64 years, 53.7%, over 65, 2.9% (2004)
**Population living with HIV/AIDS** 5.8% (2001)
**Literacy** 68% (2003)
**GDP per head** US$800 per annum (2003)
**Natural resources** Predominantly oil and natural gas; also tin, columbite, iron ore, coal, limestone, lead, zinc
**Official language** English
**Major local languages** Yoruba, Igbo, Hausa, Edo, Efik, Kanuri
**Religion** Muslim 50%, Christian 40%, indigenous 10%
**Currency** Nigerian naira (N)
**Exchange rate** £1 N234, US$1 N138 (2004; used to research this guide); £1 N256, US$1 N133, €1 N175 (April 2005)
**International airports** Lagos, Abuja, Port Harcourt, Kano
**International telephone code** +234
**Time** GMT +1
**Electricity** 220 volts at 50HZ; three-pin British-style plug
**Weights and measures** Metric
**Flag** Three equal vertical bands of green (representing agriculture), white (for unity and peace), green
**National motto** Unity and Faith, Peace and Progress
**Public holidays** Jan 1, May 1, Oct 1; Christian and Muslim holy days

# Background Information

## FACTS AND FIGURES
### Location and size
The Federal Republic of Nigeria is located between the tropics of Cancer and Capricorn, on the Gulf of Guinea on the western coast of tropical Africa. It lies between latitudes 4° and 14° north of the Equator and longitudes 3° and 14° east of the Greenwich Meridian. It is part of West Africa, though borders Central Africa on its frontier with Cameroon to the southeast. Nigeria's total land area covers 923,768km² and it's one-and-a-half times the size of France, or one-third larger than the US state of Texas. It is five times larger than Ghana, 13 times as large as Sierra Leone and occupies one-seventh of West Africa. It is bordered by an 853km stretch of Atlantic Ocean coastline to the south, a 1,690km border with Cameroon to the east, a 773km border with Benin to the west, a 1,497km border with Niger to the north, and has a small 87km border region across Lake Chad, which it shares with Chad in the extreme northeastern corner of the country. Nigeria is roughly 1,600km from north to south and 1,100km wide.

### Population
The size of its population is one of Nigeria's most significant and distinctive features. When Nigeria became independent in 1960, the population was 35 million. At the time of writing, the population was put at a staggering 137,253,133 (2004 CIA Factfile) – a figure that represents over 4% of the world's entire population. It's the largest population in Africa and, at the country's current 2.45% rate of growth, one that could reach 200 million by 2020. Statistics put one in six Africans as being Nigerian, and the country is home to a quarter of all sub-Saharan Africans and half of all West Africans. It has the largest city in Africa: Lagos, with an estimated population of 13 million, overtook Cairo in 2001 to become the second-largest city in the world after Mexico City. Several of Nigeria's 36 states have populations greater than those of entire African countries. And these figures in reality are very likely to be much higher – there hasn't been a population census in Nigeria since 1991, and there are several million Nigerians living overseas (for example three million in the US and one million in South Africa).

Some of the reasons why the population is so high are that Nigeria has one of the lowest levels of modern family planning use in the world, coupled with a very high fertility rate – the average woman has over five pregnancies. Quality health services are hard to find throughout the country, and cultural and social pressures also limit access to family planning. In Muslim-dominated regions, where having many children is highly valued, some women need their husband's permission to seek medical care. And one man may have several wives, all producing children, so any man who is even an averagely successful trader supports perhaps up to 20 children. Some 40% of this colossal population is under 14 years of age. Population growth not only has an adverse effect on the health of Nigerian families, but

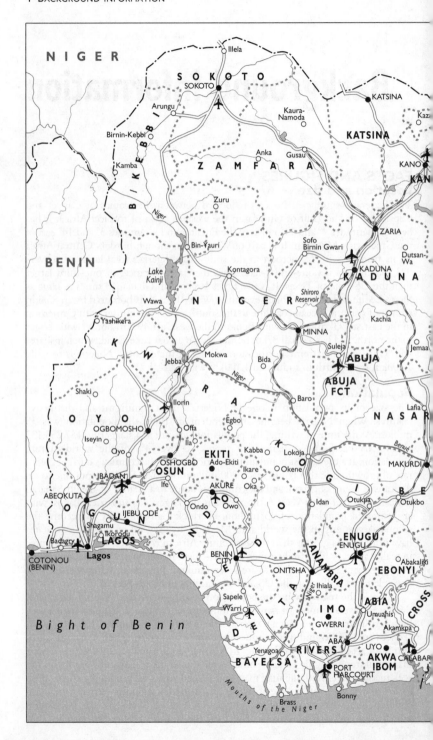

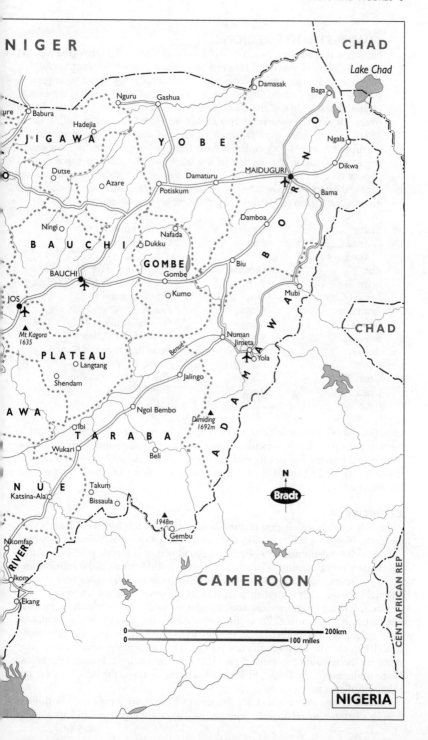

## ADMINISTRATIVE REGIONS

Nigeria is divided into 36 states and 1 Federal Capital Territory (see map on pages 4–5), all of which are referred to by their own rather unique titles that you will notice on car number plates throughout the country. Nigeria is governed by the Federal Capital Territory (FCT), of which Abuja is the capital, located in the middle of the country just north of where the Niger and Benue rivers converge. However, it only took over from Lagos as official capital in 1991, and is much smaller than Lagos, and many of the governmental departments and big organisations have been slow to relocate their offices to the new capital. In this edition of the book we still refer to Lagos, with a population of over 13 million, as Nigeria's overwhelmingly principal city. After Lagos, the largest of the cities are the state capitals, with Kano (roughly 10 million) and Ibadan (6 million) being the next largest respectively.

| State | Capital | State mottoes |
|---|---|---|
| Federal Capital Territory | Abuja | Centre of Power |
| Abia | Umuahia | God's Own State |
| Adamawa | Yola | The Highest Peak of the Nation |
| Akwa Igbom | Uyo | Promised Land |
| Anambra | Akwa | Home for All |
| Bauchi | Bauchi | Pearl of Tourism |
| Bayelsa | Yenagoa | Pride of the Nation |
| Benue | Markurdi | Food Basket of the Nation |
| Borno | Maiduguri | Home of Peace |
| Cross River | Calabar | The People's Paradise |
| Delta | Asaba | The Big Heart |

stretches the availability of food, services and infrastructure. Merely to remain at current per capita levels, agricultural production, industrial and other economic output, and provision of health, education and other social services would all need to double within 25 years. This situation will be a challenge of historic proportions for Nigeria.

## Ethnicity

Nigeria has a rich and diverse cultural history that extends back to at least 500BC, when the Nok people first inhabited the area. The ethnicity of Nigeria is so varied that there is no definition of a Nigerian beyond that of someone who lives within the borders of the country. The ethnic variety is both dazzling and confusing, and there are more than 250 ethnic groups with their own language and distinct cultural heritage, each with their own very strong sense of ethnic allegiance.

The following groups are the country's largest and most politically influential: the Hausa in the north (21% of the population), the Yoruba in the southwest (21%), the Igbo, also referred to as the Ibo, in the southeast (18%), the Ijaw in the east (10%), and the Fulani in the north (9%). The larger of the minor groups that make up the remaining population are the Tiv, Kanuri, Igala, Idoma, Igbirra and Nupe in the north; the Ibibio, Efik and Ekoi in the east; and the Edo, Urhobo and Itsekiri in the west.

In an area one-and-a-half times the size of France, with nigh on 140 million people all trying to retain their identity in 250 cultural groups, and speaking a

| State | Capital | State mottoes |
|-------|---------|---------------|
| Ebonyi | Abakaliki | Salt of the Nation |
| Edo | Benin City | Heartbeat of Nigeria |
| Ekiti | Ado Ekiti | Fountain of Knowledge |
| Enugu | Enugu | Coal City State |
| Gombe | Gombe | Jewel of the Savanna |
| Imo | Owerri | Land of Hope |
| Jigawa | Dutse | The New World |
| Kaduna | Kaduna | Liberal State |
| Kano | Kano | Centre of Commerce |
| Katsina | Katsina | Home of Hospitality |
| Kebbi | Birnin Kebbi | Land of Equity |
| Kogi | Lokoja | Confluence State |
| Kwara | Ilorin | State of Harmony |
| Lagos | Ikeja | Centre of Excellence |
| Nassarawa | Lafia | Home of Solid Minerals |
| Niger | Minna | Power State |
| Ogun | Abeokuta | Gateway State |
| Ondo | Akure | Sunshine State |
| Osun | Oshogbo | State of the Living Spring |
| Oyo | Ibadan | Pace Setter |
| Plateau | Jos | Home of Peace & Tourism |
| Rivers | Port Harcourt | Treasure Base of the Nation |
| Sokoto | Sokoto | Seat of the Caliphate |
| Taraba | Jalingo | Nature's Gift to the Nation |
| Yobe | Damaturu | The Young Shall Grow |
| Zamfara | Gusau | Home of Agricultural Products |

different language, it's not hard to imagine the difficulties and ensuing chaos of governing such a vast variety of people. The boundaries of the former British colony were drawn up to serve commercial interests, largely without regard for the territorial claims of the indigenous ethnic groups, and the country's unity has been consistently under siege from alternating dominant groups that have wanted to take control of the whole country. Between 1914 and 1977 there were eight attempts at secession, the Biafran War being the last of the secessionist movements within this period. Even today, underlying tension continues between the Yoruba and Hausa, though it is predominantly religion, and not ethnicity, that divides the nation.

## Language

English is the country's official language, and is taught in schools and spoken with varying degrees of fluency by nearly 50% of the population, making Nigeria the largest English-speaking country in Africa. Those Nigerians that don't speak it consider English a foreign language, but Pidgin or 'broken' English, a mixture of English and indigenous Nigerian words, is often used in casual conversation and has been spoken and understood by almost all Nigerians for more than a century. It's a complete Nigerian fabrication (although local versions of Pidgin are found throughout the world) and a language in its own right, spoken with a lot of spirit and gesticulation. Hausa, Igbo, Yoruba, Fulfulde and Kanuri are spoken by millions of first- and second-language speakers. Three languages other than

English are accepted in government: Yoruba, Hausa and Igbo, and a total of nine are broadcast on television and radio. Each of the 250 ethnic groups has their own distinct language, with scores of dialects within each group, and the *Index of Nigerian Languages* published in 1992 records over 500 languages spoken in modern Nigeria. Some have developed written traditions but most are pre-literate, with only a small number of speakers, and some of the minority languages are endangered, simply due to lack of use. Educated Nigerians are often fluent in several tongues, and the more widespread languages are taught in schools and universities in Nigeria and abroad. Indeed, the BBC news website gives the option of presenting the world news in Hausa, proving that many millions worldwide speak it. (Also see *Appendix 1* on page 329).

## HISTORY

Before beginning any account on Nigeria's history, it should be stressed that modern Nigeria, like much of Africa, is a product of European colonial rule.

### NIGERIA'S FOUR DOMINANT ETHNIC GROUPS

The **Hausa** inhabit northern Nigeria and southern Niger. In Nigeria, they live predominantly in the northern states, especially around Kano, Sokoto and Kaduna, a region referred to as Hausaland. There is no Hausa race as such, but a great many people speak the language, and are historically a fusion of nomadic people from North Africa, the Chad Basin and from present-day Sudan, that were absorbed, long ago, into Hausaland. According to legend, the Hausa trace their origins to Berber immigrants from Tripoli and Baghdad, and the Hausa rulers descended from a 'founding hero' named Bayinjida, supposedly the son of the king of Baghdad. In the 10th century he became *sarki* (king) of Daura, a dot on the map near Katsina, after killing a big snake at the Kusugu well that was terrorising people and only allowing them to fetch water once a week. He married the queen of Daura, and their children founded the other Hausa towns, which became known as the Seven Hausa States (see box on page 304). The Hausa Empire controlled much of the northern region from the end of the 11th century, and converted to Islam in 1350. The Seven Hausa States were centered on *birni*, or walled cities, where the Hausa developed techniques of efficient government, including a carefully organised feudal system and a highly learned judiciary that gave them a reputation for integrity, and the ability to administer Islamic law.

The **Fulani** people are scattered throughout West Africa from Senegal to Cameroon, including Nigeria. Over time, a number of African states, including ancient Ghana and Senegal, have had Fulani rulers. The Fulani also converted to Islam and were known to have arrived in Hausaland in the early 13th century, though their origin is more of a mystery. Once a pastoral nomadic people, theories and legends abound; descendants of gypsies or Roman soldiers who became lost in the desert, a lost 'tribe' of Israel, or relatives of the Tuareg who inhabit the southern edge of the Sahara. More realistically, it's believed the Fulani originated from Mauritanian shepherds who were looking for new pastures. Whatever their origin, the Fulani, with their olive skin and straight hair, settled in the cities and mingled freely with the Hausa, and mostly adopted the latter's customs and language. Historically, they have been a devoutly religious, educated elite who made themselves indispensable to the Hausa kings as government advisers, Islamic judges, and teachers. Between 1750 and 1900,

Nigeria is a creation of the British Empire builder who, in search of new markets, raw materials and the need to exert political influence overseas, laid down borders at the end of the 19th century. Before this time, Nigeria wasn't called Nigeria, and in the centuries leading up to colonialism all of West Africa was divided into smaller areas with different names, occupied by varying ethnic groups. Empires, kingdoms and states flourished, died, moved, or changed identity in the geographical space that we know today as modern Nigeria. Even as recently as the 1850s, when Lagos became a British colony, few would have foreseen a political state with borders roughly matching modern Nigeria, and a whole lot of history had happened before then. It is usually presumed that Nigeria got its name from the River Niger, but it was actually a colonial officer's wife, a Flora Shaw, who in 1898 joined together the word *niger*, meaning 'black', with the word 'area', creating Nigeria. The following account of the historical development of the northern and southern regions in pre-colonial Nigeria, which follow distinctively different paths, is roughly based on modern Nigeria's Muslim/Christian divide (see map on page 34).

they engaged in many holy wars in the name of Islam, and during the first part of the 19th century, the Fulani carved out two important empires. One, based on Massina, for a time controlled Timbuktu; the other, centred at Sokoto, included the Seven Hausa States and parts of western Cameroon. The sultan of Sokoto continued to rule over northern Nigeria until the British conquest in 1903. Other Fulani retained their traditional lifestyle and remained aloof from the Hausa and in some measure from Islam as well, herding cattle outside the cities and seeking pastures for their herds.

The **Yoruba** in the southwest of Nigeria and parts of the Benin Republic are made up of numerous smaller collections of people, united by a common belief that the spiritual city of Ile-Ife (today in Osun State) was their place of origin and 'Garden of Eden,' and that the *alafin* (king) of Ile-Ife was their spiritual leader. The Yoruba are unusual in Africa in their tendency to form urban communities. It is assumed that their primary antecedents, the Odudua, came from Egypt, based on the resemblance of sculptures found in Ile-Ife to those in Egypt. Yoruba society was organised into kingdoms, the greatest of which was called Oyo from the 14th century, which extended as far as Ghana in the west and the banks of the Niger in the east. At one time of considerable power and importance, the Oyo Empire collapsed in the 1800s through a series of wars for which the slave trade was largely responsible. Today many of the large cities in Nigeria (including Lagos, Ibadan and Abeokuta) are in Yorubaland. Christianity has been the dominant Yoruba religion since the mid-19th century, whilst some have converted to Islam and others retain their traditional spiritual religion. Vestiges of Yoruba culture are also found in Brazil and Cuba, where Yoruba people were imported as slaves.

The **Igbo,** also referred to as the Ibo, in the southeast, are again a synthesis of smaller ethnic groups. Their origins are completely unknown, as they claim to be from about 20 different places. Traditionally the Igbo have inhabited inaccessible areas and live in the Niger Delta and forested southeast of the country where they were forced to retreat into the forest to escape the Fulani's slave raids. Their largest societal unit was the village, where each extended family managed its own affairs without being dictated to by any higher authority. Like the Yoruba, the Igbo were greatly influenced by Christian missionaries in the mid-19th century.

There are several dominant themes in Nigerian history that are essential in understanding contemporary Nigerian politics and society. Firstly, the **spread of Islam** in the north a millennium ago and later the creation of the Sokoto Caliphate in the jihad (holy war) of 1804–08, that brought most of the northern region and adjacent parts of Niger and Cameroon under a single Islamic government (discussed under *Religion*, page 30). This history helps account for the religious divide between north and south that has been so strong during the colonial and post-colonial eras. Secondly, the **slave trade**, both across the Sahara Desert and the Atlantic Ocean, had a profound influence on virtually all parts of West Africa. Slavery was widespread, and many ethnic distinctions were reinforced because of slave raiding and trading, and the conversion to Islam and the **spread of Christianity** were intricately associated with issues relating to slavery. Thirdly, the **oil boom** that since independence in 1960 has unleashed such rapid change and expansion in the economy, has caused a severely distorted economic growth that subsequently collapsed in the 1980s. The social consequences of a declining economy and the internal movement of populations between regions and to the cities necessitated the reassessment of ethnic loyalties. This in turn was reflected in politics and religion, and led to a number of successful and failed military coups, a brutal civil war, and let corrupt governments siphon off billions of dollars of oil profits. As the most populous country in Africa, Nigeria has a history that bears scrutiny if for no other reason than to understand how and why this nation remains so divided today.

## West Africa before AD1000

Very little is known about the history of West Africa before AD1000, though a 1960s archaeological dig at Akure in the forest area of today's western Nigeria unearthed stone artefacts dating back to 9000BC, indicating very early human habitation of the region. As for archaeological sites, West Africa doesn't have anything anywhere near as spectacular as Luxor in Egypt, Leptis in Libya, Great Zimbabwe in Zimbabwe, or the Olduvai Gorge in Tanzania to give us any clues. Only a little archaeological study has been undertaken in the region over the last 30 years or so, throwing but a few flashes of light into the dark centuries of West Africa's past. Generally, history can be pieced together by tracking the movement of West African people and defining its cultural groups.

The first inhabitants of pre-colonial Nigeria were thought to have been the Iron-Age Nok people, skilled artisans who lived in the Jos region from 500BC to around AD200. It's a culture that takes its name from the village where the first archaeological discoveries were made during open-cast mining in the region in recent decades. Remarkable terracotta figures of men and animals of such technical detail were unearthed that they proved that the Nok must have achieved a level of material development not repeated in the region for another 1,000 years.

Information is lacking from the 'silent millennium' (1st millennium AD) that followed the Nok ascendancy, apart from evidence of iron smelting on Dala Hill in Kano from about AD600–700. It is assumed, however, that trade linking the Niger region with North Africa played a key role in the continuing development of the area. Certainly by the beginning of the 2nd millennium AD, there was an active trade along a north–south axis from North Africa through the Sahara to the forest, with the savanna people acting as intermediaries in exchanges that involved slaves, ivory, salt, glass beads, coral, cloth, weapons, brass, and other goods. In the 8th and 9th centuries, Arab geographers from as far away as Spain and Baghdad provided the earliest documentation of what are now the northern states of pre-colonial Nigeria, based on descriptions received from returning traders.

By AD1000, it is assumed that the majority of West Africans were no longer living in the Stone Age and were using iron instruments and food-producing techniques. Important resources like the yam and the camel were influencing the lives of people in large areas and undoubtedly there must have been a substantial increase in population. West Africa's pattern of population must have already been one of considerable complexity with a great variety of groups differing in language, economy and culture. Nothing definite is known about the political organisation of these early communities, but it is assumed that they lived in small groups tied by kinship and presided over by a chief or spiritual leader.

## The northern states from AD1000

Trade was the key to the emergence of organised communities in the northern savanna regions, and by the beginning of the second millennium, the first trans-Saharan trade routes had been established from West Africa to the Mediterranean and Arabia. The routes established an avenue of communication and cultural influence that remained open until the end of the 19th century. The Hausa States developed into walled cities that engaged in trade and serviced caravans, as well as manufacturing cloth and leather goods, their wealth founded on the trade routes. By these same trade routes, Islam made its way south into West Africa. The Muslim traders arriving from north of the Sahara converted the early Hausa rulers to Islam. Acceptance of Islam was thought to have been gradual and was nominal outside of the walled cities, where traditional religion continued. Nevertheless, the Seven Hausa States – Hadejia, Daura, Katsina, Kano, Rano, Gobir and Zaria – with their famous mosques and Koran schools came to participate fully in the intellectual life of the Islamic world, and there was a blossoming of Islamic learning and culture. Over the next few centuries, they continued to have good relations with North African Muslim rulers.

A severe drought and famine struck the savanna region from Senegal to Ethiopia in the middle of the 18th century. There had been periodic droughts before, one of seven years' duration in the 17th century, but the great drought of the 1740s and 1750s probably caused the most severe famine that West Africa has known, including that of the 1970s during the Biafran War. The environmental and political instability provided the background for the momentous events of the first decade of the 19th century, when the jihad (holy war) of Usman dan Fodio revolutionised the whole of northern Nigeria. The strongly Muslim Fulani people in the far north moved into Hausaland to escape areas where drought conditions were even worse, and conducted a violent Islamic revolution to create a single Islamic state, known as the Sokoto Caliphate (see *Religion* on page 30). Ever since then, the northern states have adopted a staunch Islamic regime and the two ethnic groups are linked, and are often referred to as one, the Hausa-Fulani.

## The southern states from AD1000

At the beginning of the 2nd millennium, Nigeria's southwest region was occupied by many small communities lost in the forests, swamps and bush, the most significant being the Yoruba who possessed the longest traditions, possibly going back a further 800 years. A number of Yoruba empires flourished in the southern region from the 14th and 15th centuries, and the Yoruba cities of Ile-Ife and Oyo became major trading centres. These were ruled by traditional *alafins* (kings) with the *alafin* of Oyo being head of all Yorubaland, and Ile-Ife being their sacred city. The *alafins* ruled successfully until the early 19th century, when their powers began to crumble, partly through fighting with the Fulani over slaves and the spread of Islam, before the British stepped in and quelled the violence.

Meanwhile, further to the southwest, the Benin Empire, centred on the city of Benin, emerged as the region's most powerful state in the 15th century. The kingdom was to dominate the Yoruba, Igbo and Edo in the south of pre-colonial Nigeria, as far west as Lagos and as far east as the lower Niger, and went unchallenged for the next few hundred years. Ultimate rule lay with the oba (king) of Benin whose line dates from 1170 to the present day. The obas of Benin traditionally had good relations with the Europeans and in the 16th century no other kingdom in West Africa was on such cordial terms with the Portuguese. They even set up an embassy in Lisbon, allowed Portuguese missionaries to build a church in their capital, and requested Portuguese firearms for their army. As early as 1553 the oba of Benin could read, write and speak Portuguese. During this period, Benin City itself was reputedly very magnificent, with walls, gates and wide streets, and may have housed 100,000 inhabitants at its height, spread over 25km². It was known for its grand palace and artisans who worked for the obas, producing many pieces of fine art, including the famous bronze-casting plaques and statues that adorned the palace walls and altars. Benin lost its authority over the region in 1897 when the British arrived, who, after finding evidence of human sacrifice, burnt the city down and looted the palace of its many treasured artefacts.

## The West African slave trade from 1471

A desire for global glory, profit from trade, and missionary zeal brought Portuguese navigators to the West African coast in the late 15th century. Locked in a seemingly interminable crusading war with Islamic Morocco, the Portuguese concluded that maritime expansion might bypass the Islamic world and open up new commercial markets. They hoped to tap into the fabled Saharan gold trade, establish a sea route around Africa to India, and link up with the mysterious Christian heartland. The Portuguese achieved all these goals. They accessed the gold trade on the Gold Coast (modern Ghana), explored the Indian Ocean securing a monopoly of the spice trade, and discovered the roots of Christianity in Ethiopia. Portugal's lasting legacy for present-day Nigeria, however, was its initiation of the transatlantic slave trade.

The outline history of the slave trade can be told simply enough. The first Portuguese sea captains captured unwary Africans whose sale for use as domestic servants elsewhere helped to defray the expenses of the voyage. But the trade soon began to assume a larger scale when labour was needed for the sugar plantations on the recently colonised Caribbean Islands and tropical American coast. After the pope gave permission for slaves to be taken from Africa in 1513, the number of Africans sent to the Americas steadily increased, and slaves were taken from an area that at its widest point stretched from Senegal to the Zambezi River in Angola. In the 16th century the annual export of slaves rose to about 13,000; in the 17th century 27,000; in the 18th century 70,000; and in the first decades of the 19th century, when slavery was finally abolished, numbers of slaves exported each year sometimes reached over 100,000. These figures indicate that at least 15 million slaves were transported across the Atlantic. But the loss of manpower to Africa was far greater, since many lost their lives in the wars that accompanied the trade, and many more died because of hardship, cruelty and hunger during transportation. A ship of slaves would take around five weeks to reach the Americas. Conditions were so cramped and unhygienic it wasn't unusual for half the human cargo to die en route. For every slave that landed in America, another one may have died because of the trade, putting the number of people lost to Africa nearer to 30 million. From pre-colonial Nigeria alone, some 3.5 million slaves were shipped across the Atlantic over the period of the whole slave trade.

White men were not the only criminals in the slave trade: the sale of Africans to other Africans had been practised for centuries in just about every ancient African society. Transportation of slaves had been going on since the earliest days of the trans-Sahara caravans when people captured in the sub-Saharan regions were taken to North Africa and sold into domestic bondage. In his 1826 book, *Travel and Discoveries in Northern and Central Africa*, Captain Clapperton records: 'Slavery, of course, had existed since time immemorial, but the Fulani made a business of it on a scale hitherto unknown. Parts of the road to Tripoli were almost truly white with human bones. Major Denham, in 1822, counted a hundred rotting skeletons round a well, and when he expressed horror the Arabs laughed, prodded the bones with their musket-butts and remarked that they were only blacks'.

The slave trade is singularly one of the most important events in human history, because it operated on such an unprecedented scale and its effects have been so shatteringly widespread. Leopold Senghor, a Senegalese poet and statesman, poignantly called the slave trade 'a bush fire, ravaging Black Africa, wiping out images and values in one vast carnage'. But it is worth noting that the trans-Saharan slave trade went on twice as long as the Atlantic slave trade. When the Europeans first arrived in West Africa and decided that they would transport slaves by ship to the New World, the slave trade in West Africa already existed, and the Europeans who conducted the trade had come from an environment where they were still burning witches and holding public hangings.

In 1471, Benin and the Niger Delta was the first region in tropical Africa to be reached by the Portuguese. Gwatto, the port of the Benin Kingdom, became a depot to handle peppers, ivory, and increasing numbers of slaves offered by the Benin oba in exchange for coral beads, textiles from India, and tools and weapons from Europe. The Portuguese initially bought slaves for resale on the Gold Coast, where slaves were traded for gold. For this reason, the southwestern coast of pre-colonial Nigeria, neighbouring parts of the present-day Republic of Benin (not to be confused with the Kingdom of Benin), and present-day Ghana became known as the 'Slave Coast'. When the African coast began to supply slaves to the Americas in the last third of the 16th century, the Portuguese continued to look to the Bight of Benin as one of its main sources of supply.

Although the Portuguese were the first Europeans to take advantage of this human commodity, their monopoly on trade was broken at the end of the 16th century, when Portugal's influence was challenged by the rising naval power of other European states. The Slave Coast attracted an increasing swarm of foreign ships from Holland, Denmark, Sweden, France, Prussia and Britain. The British arrived in 1562, when John Hawkins took the first British boat of slaves to the West Indies. In exchange for slaves, they traded textiles, metalware, alcohol, tobacco, and later, firearms and also a variety of crops and vegetables imported from America that the Europeans had only just become familiar with themselves — tomatoes, pineapple, papaw, cassava and maize, food items that were to change the African diet forever.

Lagos and Badagry grew into important slave markets and ports, and inevitably, the rich profits to be gained from the trade stimulated intense rivalry between not only the Europeans but among the local African ethnic groups. After the introduction of firearms in the mid-17th century, when Britain alone supplied some 100,000 guns to West Africa annually, the Europeans did not recognise cowries as currency and instead brought gin and guns,. Even the most unwilling chief became embroiled in the trade because to be able to defend his people he needed firearms, and to procure firearms in the first place he needed to find slaves. (Even today, bright blue empty bottles of British-distilled gin are pulled up from the riverbeds around the Niger Delta.)

## The breakdown of the slave trade from 1772

In the first decade of the 19th century, two unrelated developments that were to have a major influence on virtually all of the area that is now Nigeria ushered in a period of radical change. Firstly, between 1804 and 1808 the Islamic jihad (holy war) of Usman dan Fodio established the Sokoto Caliphate (see *Islam*, page 33), a great Islamic empire in the northern states that had a profound influence on much of Muslim Africa. Secondly, in 1807 Britain declared the transatlantic slave trade to be illegal, an action that occurred at a time when Britain was responsible for shipping more slaves to the Americas than any other country.

As the 18th century drew to a close, the anti-slave lobby became an increasingly powerful voice in Britain, brought on by strengthening liberal thinking that emerged after the Industrial Revolution, and by greater public awareness of the atrocities caused during the handling of slaves. In Britain, slavery was challenged by the humanitarian movement, which owed its origins to the Christian Church, and to the theories of equality and fraternity spread by the French Revolution. Already by 1772, British legislation decreed that no slave could be kept on British soil, and in 1807, the anti-slave lobby persuaded the British government to abolish slavery in West Africa altogether. Other countries hesitantly followed the British lead. The US officially abolished slavery in 1808, followed by Holland, Spain, Portugal and France between 1814 and 1817. (Denmark actually was the first country to declare the trade illegal in 1792.) Also in 1817, many of the above countries signed the Reciprocal Search Treaty that permitted the British navy to search boats captained by other nationalities. For several decades, as much as one-sixth of all British warships were assigned to this mission, and a squadron was maintained at the Spanish colony of Fernando Po off the Nigerian coast from 1827 until 1844. British naval crews were permitted to divide cash derived from the sale of captured slave ships, and rescued slaves were usually taken to Sierra Leone where they were released. Apprehended slave runners were tried by naval courts and were liable to capital punishment if found guilty.

This considerably subdued the slave trade but by no means stopped it, and despite the British blockade, almost one million slaves were exported from pre-colonial Nigeria in the 19th century. A flood of captives taken in wars among the Yoruba in the 1830s were shipped from Lagos to meet the demand for slaves in Cuba and Brazil. The risk involved in running the British blockade obviously made profits all the greater on delivery. Britain soon recognised that it needed to do more and abolished slavery in all her colonies in 1833. Finally, Britain was determined to halt the traffic in slaves fed by the Yoruba wars, and responded to this frustration by annexing the port of Lagos in 1861, making it a British colony and ousting the last of the slave traders. The slave trade bought about its own demise when greater public awareness about its brutalities was provoked in Europe, which instigated the emergence of some dedicated European political and religious groups determined to compensate Africa for its sufferings. To do this they wanted to give to Africans the 'blessings of civilisation', therefore justifying increasing interference into African affairs. This was the main force behind European imperialism on the African continent.

## Exploration of the interior in the 1800s

Although the Europeans occupied the coast during the slave trade, they had no incentive to travel inland and knew nothing about the interior of West Africa. But the campaign to eradicate the slave trade and substitute it for trade in other commodities increasingly resulted in the British needing to look inland. They knew that there was a great river, but did not know even the course of its flow, for the many openings of the Niger Delta were thought to be separate streams. Then, in 1788 a group of learned Englishmen got together and formed the 'Association for Promoting the Discovery of the Interior Parts of Africa', more simply known as the 'African Association', financed by the British government.

In 1794, the African Association commissioned Mungo Park, an intrepid Scottish physician and naturalist, to search for the source of the Niger and follow the river downstream. Park reached the upper Niger in Sierra Leone by travelling inland from the Gambia River, and reported on the eastward flow of the Niger. He was forced to turn back when his equipment was lost to Muslim slave traders, but in 1805 he set out again to follow the Niger to the sea. He failed to complete the journey but covered more than 1,500km, passing through the western portions of the Sokoto Caliphate, before being drowned in rapids (near today's Kainji Dam). On a subsequent expedition to the Sokoto Caliphate, Captain Hugh Clapperton learned where the Niger River flowed to the sea. But he also died and it was his servants, brothers Richard and John Lander, who canoed down the Niger River in 1830 from its source in Bussa in Sierra Leone to its mouth in present-day Nigeria. The course of the Niger had been traced. Unfortunately for them, the Lander brothers couldn't enjoy their glory as they were seized by slave traders and sold down the river to a waiting European ship.

Then, in 1841, at the behest of the slavery abolishment lobby, the British government sent a larger expedition up the river by steamship – the most technically advanced piece of equipment the West Africans had yet seen. From then on, the British became masters of the navigable stretches of both the Niger and Benue rivers, and by 1870 there were 14 British steamships operating on the rivers, and amicable contacts had been made with Nupe, one of the southern provinces of the Muslim north.

With the slave trade winding down, and using their newfound knowledge of the interior, the British began to look for other ways to exploit the region's resources. They took over the Jos tin mines, and discovered palm oil, which gradually took over from slaves as pre-colonial Nigeria's biggest export. It was used to lubricate machinery before petroleum products were developed for that purpose, and for making soap, and demand rose rapidly in Britain, which was caught up in the first grimy stages of the Industrial Revolution. The boom in palm oil preserved the prosperity of the Niger Delta where it was farmed, as much as it did of the British port of Liverpool to where it was sent and sold. Ultimately the transition from the slave trade to legitimate commerce was made without causing any economic disaster in the region, and palm oil exports were worth £1 million a year by 1840.

## Expansion of the British 1849–1902

This new wave of commerce and British interest in the area led to the appointment of a full-time consul, John Beecroft, to 'the Bights of Biafra and Benin' in 1849, and the first British consulate opened in Calabar in 1851. Meanwhile, the slave trade was still being practised illegally along the coast, and the British were resorting to gunboat diplomacy to persuade local rulers to sign treaties renouncing the slave trade. This resulted in the complete annexation of Lagos by the British in August 1861, and Lagos became a British colony. Over the next few decades, the city was administered under a British governor and a small legislative council of British officials, and the city's infrastructure developed rapidly. As the colony strengthened economically, trade links improved with the other regions in the interior. Over time, these other regions also came under the protection of the British, although all for different reasons.

During the 19th century, the Yoruba to the north of Lagos had experienced a series of continual spats amongst themselves, and against the Fulani, mostly fighting over slaves or the encroachment of Islam from the Sokoto Caliphate to the north. Missionaries in Yorubaland appealed to the British in Lagos to help restore order, and in 1881, the *alafin* (king) of Oyo requested the governor of Lagos to step in to stop the fighting. There was also a need to protect commerce disrupted by this fighting. The governor answered his appeal, and in 1883 concluded a round of treaties with the big Yoruba chiefs that inevitably led to further British annexations.

Along the coast, east of Lagos, the Kingdom of Benin was still independent despite the establishment of a British consulate in Calabar in 1851. The conquest of Benin in 1897 was sparked by the massacre of the British consul and his party, who were on their way to investigate reports of ritual human sacrifice in the city of Benin. In reprisal the British promptly stormed the city and destroyed the oba's palace, sending the reigning oba into exile. A British Protectorate was established over what were referred to as the Niger districts – the area running along the coast from Lagos to the Cameroons, together with the banks of the Niger and Benue rivers as far inland as British traders were operating at Lokoja, the headquarters of the National African Company. It was first called the Oil Rivers Protectorate, after palm oil, the main commodity in the area, before being changed to the Niger Coast Protectorate. The essential purpose of the protectorate was to control trade coming down the Niger.

In 1886, the British government issued a royal charter to the National African Company, a major trading company in the Niger Delta formed by George Goldie, through an amalgamation of British firms in 1879. The charter gave the company the rights to govern the Niger districts north of Lokoja extending along the Niger and Benue rivers above their confluence, on behalf of the British, and it became known as the Royal Niger Company. The company negotiated trade treaties with Sokoto, Gwandu and Nupe. Meanwhile, the French were making progress in a southerly direction down the Niger from the French colonies in the northwest. The Royal Niger Company employed a Captain Frederick Lugard (who in later years became governor-general of Nigeria) to form a military force known as the West Africa Frontier Force to protect the northern states from possible invasion by the French. These military operations against a rival European colonial power soon proved too expensive for a private company and in 1897 the British government ended the charter, and by 1900 had taken control of the north, and Lugard became High Commissioner of the Protectorate of Northern Nigeria. His clear intent was to occupy the Sokoto Caliphate. Expansion continued towards Lake Chad, and after armed assault, Sokoto and Kano were occupied in 1902.

Lugard's success in northern Nigeria was attributed to his policy of indirect rule, which called for governing the protectorate through the rulers who had been defeated. If the emirs accepted British authority, abandoned the slave trade, and co-operated with British officials, then Lugard was willing to keep them in office. The emirs retained their caliphate titles but were answerable to British district officers, who had the final say over their administrations. One consequence of indirect rule was that Hausa-Fulani domination was confirmed, and in some instances imposed, on smaller ethnic groups, some of them non-Muslim, in the so-called middle belt.

Whilst Lagos retained its title as the British Colony of Lagos, these new areas inland were amalgamated and became known as the Northern and Southern British Protectorates of Nigeria. People living in the colony of Lagos passed for British subjects whilst those living in the protectorates were referred to as British protected persons.

## Unification of Nigeria 1914

Lugard left Nigeria for six years to be governor of Hong Kong, but returned in 1912 as governor-general of Nigeria to set in motion the merger of the northern and southern protectorates with the colony of Lagos. Finally, in January 1914, on the eve of World War I, the British officially joined the regions together as the Federation of Nigeria, with Lagos as its capital, though effectively they were administered separately until 1946. In 1916, Lugard formed the Nigerian Council to represent all of Nigeria, on which sat six traditional leaders, including the oba of Oyo, the sultan of Sokoto, and the emir of Kano. The principle of indirect rule administered by traditional rulers was applied throughout Nigeria, and colonial administrators were instructed to interfere as little as possible with the existing order. In practice, however, the system of indirect rule was modified to fit the needs of the distinctively different northern and southern regions. In the north, the colonial governor avoided any challenge with the local emirs over religion that might incite resistance to British rule, banned Christian missionaries from visiting the region, and permitted Islamic education to go on unhindered. In the south, meanwhile, the British promoted Christianity and Western education because the traditional beliefs of the Yoruba and the Igbo were not seen as contemporary enough. Hausa was recognised as the official language of the north but only English was taught in the south. The development of the infrastructure differed enormously too, with Christian missions contributing financially to schools and healthcare in the south, and the north quickly lagging behind in facilities, relying only on sparse government funds. In contrast, the north benefited from the railways and roads built to transport tin from the Jos mines, whilst people living in the Niger Delta in the south were still using ancient canoes as their only form of transport.

Lugard stepped down as governor-general in 1918, and was succeeded by Hugh Clifford, who had previously been governor of the Gold Coast. In contrast to Lugard, Clifford argued that Nigeria could only benefit from Western experience and was not an advocate for indirect rule. He was indifferent over what he thought was a backward north whilst in the south he saw great potential for building an elite through European-style schools and universities. He even argued for the division of Nigeria into two separate colonies. Whilst Britain did not permit this move, the 1922 constitution was modified to include Clifford's other recommendations, and a new legislative council taking in the southeast and southwest was established, replacing the Nigerian Council and the Lagos Legislative Council, while administration in the north was left untouched. By 1931, strong nationalist sentiments had begun to emerge against Britain's transparent neglect of the northern states. Despite increasing economic development in both regions, there was little political interchange and absolutely no pressure for further unification until after World War II. Interestingly, unlike other African colonies such as Kenya, the British granted access to very few white settlers, and those that did emigrate to Nigeria had to have proven skills essential for the country. By 1938, all of Nigeria was only governed by 380 British officials who administered indirectly through appointed local leaders.

## Path to independence 1920–60

British colonialism created Nigeria, joining diverse peoples and regions in an artificial political entity, and inconsistencies in British policy reinforced regional animosities. The nationalism that rose during the inter-war period was derived not from any sense of country allegiance but from an older political allegiance to region, ethnicity, and a broader feeling of pan-Africanism. In the north, nationalism, based on the foundation of Islam, was pointedly anti-Western, while the nationalists in the south, an elite influenced by European education, were opposed to indirect rule as it formed an unfair class system of government. For once, the country agreed on its sentiment: they wanted self-government, and all nationalists were critical of colonialism for its failure to appreciate the antiquity of indigenous cultures.

A new constitution in 1922 gave the opportunity to a handful of representatives to be elected on to a Legislative Council, giving politically conscious Nigerians something concrete to work on. One of these was Herbert Macaulay, the grandson of the legendary Bishop Samuel Crowther, Africa's first black bishop and a repatriated slave. Macaulay was often dubbed 'the father of Nigerian nationalism', and he aroused political awareness in Lagos through his newspaper, the *Lagos Daily News*.

The nationalist movement splintered into the National Council for Nigeria and the Cameroons (NCNC), led by Nnamdi Azikiwe, the political party that dominated the Igbo east; The Action Group (AG), led by Obafemi Awolowo in the Yoruba west; and the Nigerian People's Congress (NPC), led by Ahmadu Bello in the Hausa north. Meanwhile, after World War II weary Britain was beginning to regard Nigeria as a costly addition to the empire and expressed amenity in granting it more economic and political power. The first step towards de-colonisation was in 1946, when Britain devised a new constitution and a federal system with powers shared between a central authority and three regional legislatures, simply called the Eastern Region, Northern Region and Western Region. (A fourth region, the Mid-West Region, was added in 1962.) The three new regions were to choose representatives to sit on the Central Legislature in Lagos.

The 1951 constitution, in terms of population, gave over half the seats in the central parliament to the Muslim Northern Region. Despite holding the majority, however, the NPC were less advanced politically than the southerners and were still reluctant to have closer links with the other regions. By now, it was very clear that the introduction of democracy had promoted strong north–south regional loyalties that could potentially pull the country apart. If Nigeria was to achieve independence as a single nation, the regional governments were to be given more of the powers they wanted, and the responsibilities of the national government needed to be restricted to national affairs. In 1957, the Eastern and Western Regions were given internal self-government. The Northern Region continued to resist but finally faced the fact that if they wanted to retain access to the coast through the other two regions for trade, they needed to be part of the Federation of Nigeria. They were granted internal self-government in 1959, only after they agreed to direct elections.

Elections were held for a new and greatly enlarged House of Representatives in December 1959. Bello became premier of the Northern Region, Azikiwe premier of the Eastern Region, and Awolowo premier of the Western Region, and official leader of the opposition in the House of Representatives. The deputy leader of the NPC, which had the most seats in the federal parliament, Balewa, became prime minister, while Azikiwe, after aligning his party, the NCNC, with the NPC, assumed the role of governor-general. The government was answerable to a parliament composed of the popularly elected 312-member House of Representatives and the 44-member Senate, chosen by the regional legislatures.

When the federal government met for the first time in January 1960, in the presence of the British Prime Minister Harold Macmillan, they adopted a formal resolution for independence and admission to full membership of the Commonwealth. On October 1 1960, Nigeria gained independence from Britain, and became a member of the Commonwealth of Nations and the United Nations. Queen Elizabeth II gained a new title – the Queen of Nigeria – and was represented at Nigeria's independence celebrations by Princess Alexandra, who formally handed over the Independence Constitution to Prime Minister Balewa. In his speech, he said that the Nigerians had known the British 'first as masters, then as leaders, and finally as partners, but always as friends.' A week after independence, Nigeria was admitted to the UN Security Council.

## The first civilian government 1960–66

The British could never have dreamed of the political chaos that was going to grip Nigeria over the next few decades. The British colonial system had done little to unify Nigeria or prepare it for independence. It was a vast country that had absorbed a block of Africa with a bewildering variety of people, all forced to co-exist within artificial boundaries drawn up by the British. The new government faced an overwhelming task of unifying 250 ethnic and linguistic groups and a persistent historical religious conflict between north and south, a task, as it had transpired by 1966, that was unworkable, at least not without the influence of the military. The new government was a short-lived one, and right from the start it was characterised by political antagonisms, increasing corruption and a fear of Nigeria breaking up into several minor countries based on regions and ethnic groups.

The first crisis occurred in 1962, with the Yoruba objecting strongly to the shape and location of both the Western Region and the newly formed Mid-West Region, because they split their people into different regional governments. Disagreements between Awolowo's Action Group and central government paralysed the Western Region and central authorities assumed control for ten months, when bloody rioting broke out and many members of the Action Group were put under house arrest. This loss of stability in one region gradually undermined the political structure of the whole country. Chief Samuel Ladoke Akintola, prime minister of the Western Region, managed to wrestle the position of Western premier from Awolowo, and immediately organised a new party, the United People's Party, which pursued a policy of collaboration with the NPC–NCNC government in the federal parliament. Then, in late 1962, investigations by the federal government found that Awolowo had funnelled several million pounds of public funds to the Action Group in the 1950s. In the course of the financial investigation, police uncovered evidence of a conspiracy to overthrow the government, and of 200 Action Group activists – who had received military training in Ghana – smuggling arms into Nigeria in preparation for a coup. Awolowo and other Action Group leaders were charged with treason and sentenced to 15 years in prison.

In 1963, Nigeria became a republic within the Commonwealth of Nations. The change in status meant that a president elected for a five-year term replaced the crown as head of state and Azikiwe, who had been governor-general, became Nigeria's first president.

The next crisis occurred during the 1964 general elections, which witnessed widespread electoral boycotts and violent and lawless protest against blatant vote-rigging. The elections were contested by two political alliances incorporating all the major parties: the Nigerian National Alliance (NNA), composed predominantly of the northern NPC, and Akintola's western NNDP; and the United Progressive Grand Alliance (UPGA), which joined the eastern NCNC and the remnants of the western Action Group. The NPC-dominated NNA coalition won 108 seats in the House of Representatives and President Azikiwe asked Balewa to form a government with the NNA majority. The UPGA became the official opposition. But the new government wasn't sitting comfortably in the

House of Representatives. After the elections accusations continued against vote-rigging and electoral abuse. In the six months after the election an estimated 2,000 people died in violent protests in the Western Region, events that set the stage for the end of civilian rule, but that were nothing compared to what was going to happen next.

## Military coups 1966

In January 1966, more rioting broke out, and the military, mostly eastern Igbo army officers, staged a coup, taking Nigeria and the rest of the world by surprise and shattering the political foundations of the country. The coup, led by Major General Johnson T U Aguiyi-Ironsi, overthrew the federal government, wiping out many of the main players. His officers assassinated Prime Minister Balewa in Lagos, Akintola in Ibadan, and Bello in Kaduna, as well as senior officers of northern origin. Azikiwe escaped assassination as he was in London for medical treatment. Major General Ironsi was named president of a new military government, and placed military governors in each of the regions, suspended the constitution, dissolved all political parties, and proclaimed martial law as a solution to Nigeria's problems.

The new government announced itself as a source of national political cleansing to replace the corrupt, discredited civilian rule. It also announced plans to move away from the federal system that had forced politicians to play on tribal passions, and replace it with a unitary state. Surprisingly, despite the bloody character of the coup, these sentiments appealed directly to younger, educated Nigerians in all parts of the country. But the Hausa in the north did not see the coup as a bid for a 'clean' government, but as an Igbo plot to take over Nigeria and a Christian attempt to undermine the emirate states. Troops of northern origin became increasingly restless and fighting broke out between them and Igbo soldiers in garrisons in the south. In June, mobs in the northern cities massacred several hundred Igbo people living in the north and destroyed Igbo-owned property.

To try and prevent further chaos, in July 1966, four months after the first coup, northern army officers staged a second military counter-coup. Ironsi and some of his senior officers were killed. The Muslim officers declared 31-year-old Lieutenant Colonel (later Major General) Yakubu 'Jack' Gowon, a Christian from a small ethnic group (the Anga) in the middle belt, as chairman of the federal military government. His first moves were restoring federalism and releasing Awolowo from prison.

## Biafran War 1967–70

A return to a civilian government was negotiated between September and November 1966 but the regions failed to reach an agreement, in part because the representatives of the Eastern Region failed to appear after the first conference for fear of their safety. The tempo of violence increased, and chaos continued to reign in many of the northern cities, where some 20,000 Igbo living in the north were massacred by the Hausa, leading to a mass migration of over one million Igbo people to their native Eastern Region. The Igbo retaliated and began to kill Hausa living in Port Harcourt and other eastern cities, resulting in the military governor of the Eastern Region, Lieutenant Colonel Odemugwu Ojukwu banishing all non-Igbo from his region.

More negotiations took place in 1967, when Gowon initiated a move to replace the four legislatures of Nigeria with 12 states (three of them in the east). This provision broke up the Northern Region, undermining the possibility of continued northern domination, but Ojukwu feared that Gowon desired to divide the Igbo into these new smaller states, and thus deprive the Igbo of its control over the oil fields and access to the sea. The situation quickly deteriorated, and in an attempt at secession, Ojukwu declared the Eastern Region as the Republic of Biafra on May 30 1967, citing as the predominant cause for this action the Nigerian government's inability to safeguard the lives of the Igbo people. Gowon retaliated by declaring a state of emergency.

The most influential of the Igbo activists that protested during this time was the political dissident Wole Soyinka, one of Nigeria's foremost political campaigners and a prolific writer. Like Ojukwu, Soyinka spoke out against human rights violations and the right-wing policies of Gowon and his predecessor Ironsi. Troubled by the prospect of Nigeria's imminent war with Biafra, Soyinka went to Gowon's regime with the intention of making a personal appeal for peace, but Gowon reacted by jailing Soyinka without charges in solitary confinement for nearly two years.

The federal military government of Nigeria declared war against the new Republic of Biafra, a civil war that lasted three years and left behind an estimated 1–3 million dead and established 'Biafra' as a byword for mass destruction and famine. The Biafran army was an ill-equipped, undermanned, and under-trained rebel force up against a Nigerian army 250,000 strong, but nonetheless had the benefit of superior leadership and superb morale. The bulk of Biafra's military supplies were homemade (see box page 209), but they also got unofficial assistance from France. Only four other African nations recognised Biafra as a republic: Tanzania, Ivory Coast, Gabon and Zambia. No doubt there was sympathy for the Biafran cause, but few African states dared to side with Biafra for fear of giving encouragement to secessionist movements within their own countries. The federal government of Nigeria gained official support from Britain and the Soviet Union (who supplied arms and warplanes to the Nigerian forces) and effectively accepted assistance from the east and the west during the Cold War. The United States remained neutral. It's worth remembering at this point that this was the first real era of television news broadcasting, when Biafra, like Vietnam, was flashed across TV screens worldwide, causing international uproar over disturbing images of widespread massacre and starvation. Some food and medical aid from international aid organisations got into Biafra by way of night-time drops from warplanes, but it wasn't nearly enough and the famine that ensued from the outbreak of war was deathly and determined.

At first the Biafran forces did well and advanced into the Mid-West Region. But by early October 1967, the Biafran side was weakening and the federal forces had already captured their capital Enugu. Despite attempts by the Organization of African Unity (OAU) to end the war, and an appeal by Ojukwu in October 1969 to the UN for mediation, the war raged on until 1970. The federal government insisted on Biafra's surrender, and Gowon observed at the time that 'rebel leaders had made it clear that this is a fight to the finish and that no concession will ever satisfy them.' On January 12 1970, after 31 months of civil war, the Biafran forces surrendered at Owerri, the last major town in Biafran hands, and the Nigerian military government led by Gowon reasserted control and enforced the 1967 constitutional arrangement of dividing Nigeria into 12 states. Ojukwu had fled the country the day before and sought refuge in the Ivory Coast (he was pardoned a few years later and returned to Nigeria, and years later was a candidate in the 2003 elections). At the end of the war, Biafra was no more than 60km wide and just a few kilometres deep, crowded with some three million Igbo refugees. There were severe shortages of food, medicine, clothing and housing, and the region was shattered and in ruins. The cost in terms of human and material resources of the civil war – perhaps the worst civil strife experienced on the African continent at the time – was immense. The actual fighting was bitter enough but the worst sufferers were the civilian population. The federal forces had literally starved the Biafran population into submission.

After the war, Gowon assured the Igbo survivors that they would not be treated as defeated enemies, and a programme was launched to reintegrate them into a unified Nigeria. The federal government granted funds to the eastern states and much of the war damage was repaired. There were no war trials and few imprisonments, and it was Ojukwu, in exile, who was made the scapegoat. Relations were also mended with African states that had recognised Biafra during the war. One of the Igbo survivors was the writer Soyinka, who was released from prison and went on to write *A Shuttle in the Crypt*, a book of poetry that contemplates his time in jail and the critical period between 1966 and early 1971. Around this time he was also quoted as saying, 'as far as the regime is concerned, well, the play is sheer terror for them. Because they feel, how dare – how dare anybody lift his or her voice in criticism against us? We have the guns. Their level of paranoia and power-drunkenness is unbelievable.'

## 1970s oil boom and Gowon's six–year plan

In the post-war period, all significant political power remained with the federal military government and none of the three major, undoubtedly exhausted, ethnic groups had much of a political voice. In an environment where his role was unlikely to be challenged, Gowon announced in October 1970 that he intended to stay in power until 1976, which was set as the target year for the return to civilian rule. He headed the Supreme Military Council, a formidable bunch of military state governors, top-ranking policemen, and heads of the armed forces, that proposed a political plan for the country over the next six years until civil rule was reinstated. The plan was to include a national census, rebuilding of the war-torn east, a new constitution, an attack on corruption, the establishment of even more states, economic development, and organisation of political parties. Criticism of the six-year plan was widespread because the agenda was so broad, and many Nigerians feared that Gowon's programme was so ambitious that it would take much longer than six years to complete, keeping the military in power indefinitely.

Gowon conducted a national census in 1973, which produced some staggering results. Despite a loss of well over a million people during the Biafran War, the population was up 44% in ten years, a growth bigger than in any other developing country. On a more political issue, the north contained 64% of the total population, compared with 53.7% in 1963. The census, on which representation in a new elected parliament would be based, revived fears that one ethnic group would permanently dominate the others.

Gowon's government also made an effective attack on corruption. A damning anti-corruption police department dubbed, rather sinisterly, the 'X squad', made a number of investigations outing scams and extortion rackets in government and public departments and private industry. The list of offenders was endless: from state agencies and contractors who took bribes for sub-standard construction materials bought overseas, to hospitals that were buying expired medical drugs on the international black market for resale to the Nigerian people.

Gowon's economic plan charted Nigeria's transition from an essentially agricultural economy to a mixed economy based on both agriculture and industrial growth. In 1972, the government issued a decree that prevented foreign companies from investing in certain industries in order to stimulate home-based industry. At the time, some 70% of Nigerian industry was foreign-owned or managed, but by

1975, the federal government had bought 60% of the equity of the major oil companies operating in Nigeria. And the timing couldn't have been better for the economy. By the late 1960s, oil was the country's biggest foreign-currency earner, and in 1971 Nigeria was the world's seventh-largest oil producer, and joined the Organization of Petroleum Exporting Countries (OPEC). A heady rise in oil prices caused an instant economic boom in Nigeria, when between 1973 and 1974 the influx of oil revenue increased 350%. Later, in 1975, with Nigeria's full support, OPEC stepped in to regulate prices and Nigeria's exports were dominated by oil for the rest of the 1970s, until the bubble burst in 1981. Given that Nigeria had just emerged from a civil war and one of the worst famines the world had yet to encounter (at least in televised history) the country's excessive prosperity came as a huge surprise. Rocketing oil prices provided the Nigerian government with a chance to go on a spending spree of reckless proportions and industrialisation boomed throughout the rest of the 1970s.

Whilst the six-year plan had some successes, inevitably Gowon came up against obstacles that ultimately led to his downfall. Whilst the military had a grip on government, it didn't have a grip over the urban populace who lived in increasing unemployment, poverty and lawlessness. Crime began to rear its ugly head as a threat to internal security and had a seriously negative impact on economic development. Armed gangs, often composed of former soldiers, roamed the countryside engaging in robbery, extortion and kidnapping, and pirates raided cargo ships awaiting entry to ports. Drug trafficking and smuggling were rife, and all crime was susceptible to the indifference of the police under the blanket of corruption at every level. The government used public executions by firing squads to curb crime but this had little impact on reducing the crime rate, instead promoting a callous public attitude toward violence.

With all these problems to contend with, Gowon, as expected, announced in January 1975 that he was backing off from the 1976 date scheduled for return to civilian rule. This announcement led to mass strikes throughout the country by an already agitated work force, and yet another bloodless coup ending Gowon's nine-year rule. The coup was led by Army Brigadier Murtala Mohammed, who became new chief of state. Gowon wasn't there at the time, but at an Organisation for African Unity (OAC) conference in Uganda, and soon after he swiftly exiled himself to the UK, where he remained on a Nigerian pension.

## The regime of Mohammed and Obasanjo 1975–79

Murtala Mohammed was a 38-year-old Hausa-Muslim northerner, who had received military training at Sandhurst in the UK. In an attempt to restore public confidence in the federal government, he purged more than 100,000 employees in the civil service, police and armed forces, and the diplomatic corps and judiciary, citing malpractice and corruption as means for dismissal. Some were brought to trial, with one former military state governor executed for gross misconduct. His administration created a few more states, raising the number from 12 to 19, led by newly appointed military governors expected to administer federal policies handed down by the Supreme Military Council. The government took over the country's two largest newspapers and TV and radio stations, and took delivery of Soviet-built aircraft for the Nigerian air force.

But Mohammed didn't have the chance to do anything else, as his fellow army officers, disgruntled by his sweepingly harsh policies, assassinated him in 1976. He was replaced by army chief of staff General Olusegun Obasanjo (today's Nigerian president). A Yoruba, Obasanjo had been Mohammed's deputy and retained the support of the military. He pledged to continue the programme towards a civilian government now set for 1979, and to continue the reform of the public service sector. He drafted a new constitution that was adopted in 1979, based on the Constitution of the United States, with provision for a president, a Senate and a House of Representatives. Nigeria was ready for local elections, to be followed by national elections, which would return the country to civilian rule. Plans were made to move the federal capital to Abuja, a location chosen for its central location and because it didn't identify with any ethnic group. Obasanjo set the 1979 elections in motion, after which he retired from the military to set up a farm in his home state, before emerging again years later to win the 1999 elections.

## Return to civilian rule 1979

The 1979 elections were held on schedule in July and August, and attracted many of the key players from the parties that had existed prior to the 12-year-long ban on political activity. Just as the northern NPC had dominated the first civilian government of 1959, its successor, the National Party of Nigeria (NPN), dominated the second, and won the majority of the seats in the House of Representatives and the Senate, and its leader, Shehu Shagari became president. The Yoruba United Party of Nigeria (UPN) came in second and formed the opposition, just as the Action Group had done the first time round.

The new civilian government was born amid great expectations. Oil prices were high and it appeared that unlimited development was possible. But it was all to be short lived. The world recession in the early 1980s sent oil prices plummeting and by 1981 the proverbial bubble had burst. Nigeria quickly sank into a cycle of massive debt, soaring inflation, large-scale unemployment and widespread corruption. The recession put severe strain on the new government, though government spending continued, mostly heavy investment in steel, and Nigeria increased its foreign debt almost five-fold between 1978 and 1982. In addition, the half-hearted attempts to license imports and to control inflation encouraged smuggling, which became a major crime that went virtually unchecked. There were many signs of tension throughout the country and the lack of confidence in their government by Nigerians was more than evident. In Sokoto in 1979, police killed or wounded hundreds of protesting farmers and burned their crops and villages, and in 1980, almost 4,200 people died in religious riots in Kano and Kaduna. The wealthy business community demonstrated their dissatisfaction by leaving, and an estimated US$14 billion of capital left the country between 1979 and 1983. The government responded by finding a scapegoat and expelled two million foreign workers, mostly from Ghana and Niger, that had come to Nigeria for jobs during the oil boom. As the 1983 elections drew near, the economy was in chaos, political despondency was at an all-time low, and the government was in sad shape. It was a perfect atmosphere for the military to step back in and exert control.

## 1980s wave of military coups

Shagari was re-elected for a second term in 1983, but after only a few months army officers seized power on December 31 1983 citing mismanagement and corruption on the part of the civilian government. Army chief Mohammed Buhari, a Hausa who had been Federal Commissioner for Petroleum and Mines during the height of the oil boom, led the coup. But he didn't last long and was largely ineffective during his two-year role as head of state. In August 1985, he was overthrown by General Ibrahim Babangida. The latter was assisted by one Sani Abacha, an army chief who remained valuable to Babangida throughout his presidency, and who Babangida appointed Minister of Defence in 1990. The Babangida regime had a rocky start. He survived several attempted counter-coups led by rival army officers, and serious opposition from unions and student bodies.

The economic crisis deepened further when, in 1986, there was heavy devaluation of the naira, causing a drop in real income, with per capita income falling below US$300, while unemployment was at 12%. Also by 1986, 44% of export earnings were being used to service the foreign debt. On October 1, the government declared a National Economic Emergency, which lasted for 15 months. Wages were cut in the army and public service sectors, import tax was increased to 30%, and petroleum subsidies were cut back. Despite these drastic moves, a drop in world oil prices further compounded Nigeria's situation and the government finally conceded that they could not alleviate their foreign debt without an International Monetary Fund (IMF) loan. In 1988, the World Bank stepped in and provided US$4.2 billion over three years.

Babangida announced that the country would be returned to civilian rule, though this promise was largely delivered to mollify the international community and the World Bank. Transition from military to civilian rule was originally planned for 1989, but scheduled elections were postponed. State elections finally happened in 1991. In preparation for democracy, the official capital of Nigeria was moved from Lagos to Abuja in December 1991 and the number of states increased to 30.

A presidential election was held on June 12 1993, though the military did everything they could to ensure their favoured candidate was elected. However, much to their surprise the vote went in the opposite direction and the election was comprehensively won by Moshood Abiola, a former publisher promoted as a token opposition candidate. Enraged by the result, Babangida reneged on his promise, annulled the elections and returned the country to military rule, throwing Abiola in jail. However, Babangida did resign as self-proclaimed president in August 1993 and his senior aide and former defence minister General Sani Abacha became the new military strongman who, over the next five years, presided over an increasingly oppressive regime.

## Abacha's iron-fisted rule

Corruption, governmental inefficiency and harsh military rule dominated Abacha's term. He was notoriously authoritarian, and was never seen without his trademark sunglasses and a surrounding throng of soldiers from his 3,000-strong bodyguard unit. He immediately dissolved the national and state assemblies, putting generals and police officials in power, banned political parties, abandoned the not-yet-implemented 1989 constitution, and threw opponents of his regime into jail or out of the country. Abacha presented a budget that abandoned market reforms instituted in 1986, making it impossible to negotiate for aid from the IMF. Foreign debt deepened further and industrial output was at an all-time low. Meanwhile, Abacha's opponents maintain that he embezzled some US$4 billion of public funds into private bank accounts in Europe and the Persian Gulf. In the 1970s, Nigeria was the 33rd-richest country in the world – by 1997, it had dropped to the 13th poorest. (In 2002, it was ranked 26th-poorest country in the world.)

His government attracted much international condemnation, particularly through its treatment of the Ogoni people located in the oil-rich southeast of the country. Here, a peaceful campaign of opposition, led by the well-known political dissident and journalist Ken Saro-Wiwa, was violently suppressed by the military and nine prominent Ogoni leaders, including Saro-Wiwa himself, were executed in 1995 on trumped-up charges. Saro-Wiwa had been an outspoken critic of the

Nigerian government and the incident sparked widespread rioting and civil unrest across Nigeria. International human rights groups claimed the charges against Saro-Wiwa were unfounded and that he had had an unfair trial without adequate defence. Many countries withdrew their ambassadors from Nigeria to protest the executions, the Commonwealth suspended Nigeria's membership until 1998, and the European Union (EU) imposed oil sanctions until 1998.

President Nelson Mandela of South Africa orchestrated much of the diplomatic isolation. This could have been in response to Mandela at the time calling for 'quiet diplomacy' over Saro-Wiwa's situation, a move he later deeply regretted, as he was as surprised as any by Saro-Wiwa's execution. Saro-Wiwa's son, Ken Wiwa heard the news of the death of his father whilst he was imploring the world's leaders to do something about his release at the 1995 Commonwealth Heads of Government Meeting (CHOGM) in Auckland, New Zealand. A few years later, Wiwa wrote a brilliant book about what happened to his father called *In the Shadow of a Saint* (see *Appendix 3, Further Reading*).

In 1996, a UN fact-finding mission reported that Nigeria's 'problems of human rights are terrible and the political problems are terrifying.' The prominent Nigerian writer Chinua Achebe wrote an essay relating to this critical period entitled *The Trouble with Nigeria*. 'The trouble with Nigeria is simply and squarely a failure of leadership. There is nothing basically wrong with the Nigerian character. There is nothing wrong with the Nigerian land or climate or water or air, or anything else. The Nigerian problem is the unwillingness or inability of its leaders to rise to the responsibility, to the challenge of personal example, which is the hallmark of true leadership.'

Then, on June 8 1998, Abacha died very suddenly of a heart attack. He was succeeded by another military ruler, General Abdulsalam Abubakar who initially made positive moves to shed the country's pariah status and began to tackle Nigeria's neglected and now desperate economic situation. Like many of his military predecessors, he pledged to step aside for an elected leader, and provisionally predicted a general election for May 1999. Abubakar provided some early signs of hope of easing military rule when he released some political prisoners from jail – including Olusegun Obasanjo who Abacha had thrown in jail in 1995. However, the suspicious and unexplained death of Abiola, the man who had been imprisoned ever since he legally won the 1993 civil presidential election, was a crushing blow to democratic progress.

Despite this, there were concerted efforts towards a civil election and Abubakar drafted a new constitution in late 1998 proposing a US-style of political system. Under the provisions of this new constitution, executive power was to be vested in the president of the republic, and legislative responsibilities were to be entrusted to the National Assembly, comprising the 360-member House of Representatives and the 109-member Senate. The president and members of both houses were to serve a four-year term. Several political parties stepped forward claiming allegiance over the electorate from geographically based constituencies, though only three were permitted to contest the election – the People's Democratic Party (PDP), the Alliance for Democracy (AD), and the All People's Party (APP). The favourite in the presidential campaign was the former military ruler of the 1970s – Olusegun Obasanjo – who was only released from prison eight months before the February 1999 elections. Representing the People's Democratic Party (PDP), he won the elections with just less than two-thirds of the vote, and the PDP secured an absolute majority in both houses of the newly established parliament. Following nearly 16 years of military rule, the new constitution was adopted in 1999, and the transition from military rule to civilian government was finally completed.

## Obasanjo's government

After lurching from one military coup to another, Nigeria now had an elected leadership, and Nigerians were euphoric that they were finally free from military rule. Obasanjo's commitment to democracy and his pledges to fully restore Nigeria's international position after years of ostracism, and to tackle the country's endemic corruption that was crippling the economy, initially gained him high praise from the populace as well as the international community, as did his desire to recover more than US$1 billion allegedly stolen from Nigeria by the family and cronies of Abacha. Abacha's eldest son, Mohammed Abacha, was arrested on charges of fraud, money laundering and embezzlement, and for the murder of the wife of Moshood Abiola, who was mysteriously assassinated in Lagos during Abacha's term. She had been at the forefront of the campaign for the release of her husband and was vocal in her support of efforts to restore democracy in Nigeria. Later, a deal was struck between the Nigerian government and the Abacha family, in which all criminal proceedings against Mohammed were dropped in return for 80% of the family's liquid assets. By mid-1999, at least US$770 million of the stolen state cash had been recovered. Today, the remaining millions remain in Swiss bank accounts and there are ongoing negotiations to get it back.

Despite these successes, the inexperienced civilian government was criticised over its general handling of the economy (symbolised by the building of the US$330 million National Stadium in Abuja for the 2003 All Africa Games, a cost that exceeded the combined budget for both health and education), its failure to halt the widespread corruption at all levels of government, and the spiralling violence between Muslims and Christians – an ongoing conflict that after 1999 was no longer threatened by army intervention. The worst of the fighting has been over the controversial implementation of the Islamic legal code – or Sharia law (see page 35) – introduced in 2000 by regional governments in the northern states. This is an issue that remains highly contentious today between Muslims and Christians, and since military rule ended in 1999, more than 10,000 people have been killed in these clashes, many of which are set off by the most trivial of disputes.

To date the country's government has been ineffective at stopping the warring religious groups, and the population remains nervous about the military once again stepping in and enforcing strict control. Indeed, there was a disastrous incident one night in January 2002 when most people in Lagos thought that was exactly what was happening. On January 28, a fire ignited an army ammunitions dump at the Ikeja army barracks in Lagos causing sporadic explosions, and a wave of artillery shells and mortars rained down over thousands of homes. The number of deaths reportedly ran to more than 1,000, but in reality was probably much higher. The first reaction of people living near Ikeja was to presume that the pop of ammunition marked the start of yet another military coup and thousands streamed on to the streets in panic – not an unreasonable assumption as a number of coups had been launched from the Ikeja base in the past as it was home to an elite parachute brigade. In an attempt to calm things down, politicians and army officers, including President Obasanjo himself, appeared on television insisting that the blast was not an attempt by the military to seize power – small comfort to many in the area.

## Build up to the 2003 elections

As Nigeria approached fresh elections in 2003, there were growing fears for the country's stability in the face of ethnic and religious tension. Nigeria had, after all, never held a successful transition from one elected government to another since independence more than 40 years ago. During the 1999 elections, only three parties were allowed to contest and they had to prove that they had support from

## NIGERIAN POLITICS SINCE INDEPENDENCE

**1957** Oil is discovered in the Niger Delta.

**1960** Independence, with Prime Minister Sir Abubakar Tafawa Balewa leading a coalition government.

**1962–63** A controversial census fuels regional and ethnic tensions.

**1966** January – Balewa is killed in a military coup. Major General Johnson Aguiyi-Ironsi heads up a military administration. July – Ironsi is killed in a counter-coup, and is replaced by Lieutenant Colonel Yakubu Gowon.

**1967** Three eastern states secede as the Republic of Biafra, sparking a bloody civil war that lasts for three years and leaves up to three million dead from fighting or famine.

**1970** The Biafran leaders surrender and the former Biafran regions are reintegrated into the country.

**1975** Gowon is overthrown and flees to Britain, and is replaced by Brigadier Murtala Mohammed, who begins the process of moving the federal capital from Lagos to Abuja.

**1976** Mohammed is assassinated in a coup attempt, and is replaced by Lieutenant General Olusegun Obasanjo, who helps introduce a US-style presidential constitution.

**1979** Elections bring Alhaji Shehu Shagari to power.

**1983** Major General Mohammed Buhari seizes power in a bloodless coup.

**1985** Ibrahim Babangida seizes power in a bloodless coup, and bans all political activity.

across the country in order to prevent parties based on region or ethnicity from running. However, this wasn't the case in 2003, and 30 political parties registered to contest that year's poll.

At the beginning of 2003, Obasanjo and the People's Democratic Party launched their bid for re-election in a poll scheduled for April 19. It was a tightly fought contest against his closest rival, Mohammed Buhari of the All Nigeria People's Party (both Buhari and Obasanjo led military governments in the 1970s–80s). Another presidential candidate was Emeka Odumegwu-Ojukwu of the newly registered All Progressive Grand Alliance (APGA) – none other than the former leader who tried to secede from Nigeria in the 1967 Biafran War. It seemed that Nigeria's 2003 elections were to attract the very same political players of the previous 20 years. The election pitted Obasanjo, a Christian, against Buhari, a Muslim, and some observers feared that the elections could trigger more religious violence. The government made a plea to Muslim leaders not to mix religion with politics, though Obasanjo had lost the support of many Muslims because of his opposition to the introduction of Sharia law.

Obasanjo embarked on a gruelling two-month campaign, appearing at rallies across the country citing electricity, water and unemployment as the main election issues, and making high-profile jaunts into international politics (notably his involvement in negotiations between the UN and Zimbabwe's Robert Mugabe). There were an estimated 60 million people eligible to vote, (over 40% of the population is under 14 years of age) and the process of identifying them was dogged by controversy. In September 2002, the electoral commission distributed 70 million registration cards, more than enough for every one of the country's eligible voters, but unaccountably, large numbers of these disappeared. Then in February 2003, the

| 1993 | Babangida allows elections, but when civilian Moshood Abiola wins, he reneges, annuls the elections and throws Abiola into jail. |
|------|--------------------------------------------------------------------------------------------------------------------------------|
| 1993 | General Sani Abacha comes to power, and begins a dictatorship that suppresses all opposition. |
| 1995 | Ken Saro-Wiwa, a writer and campaigner against damage to his Ogoni homeland by the oil companies, is executed following a hasty trial. In protest, the European Union imposes sanctions until 1998, whilst the Commonwealth suspends Nigeria's membership until 1998. |
| 1998 | Abacha dies suddenly and is succeeded by Major General Abdulsalam Abubakar. Chief Abiola is found dead in his prison cell a month later. |
| 1999 | Parliamentary and presidential elections for a civilian government are finally held, and Olusegun Obasanjo is sworn in as president. |
| 2000 | Sharia law is adopted by several northern states in the face of opposition from Christians. Tension over the issue results in more than 10,000 deaths to date in clashes between Christians and Muslims. |
| 2001 | Nigeria is rated the second-most corrupt country in the world after Bangladesh by Transparency International. |
| 2003 | The second civilian elections since the end of military rule in 1999 take place though polling is marked by delays, corruption and allegations of ballot-rigging. The People's Democratic Party wins for a second time and Obasanjo begins a final (according to the constitution) term of presidency. Violence in the Niger Delta kills about 100, injures 1,000, and displaces tens of thousands. |

police in Lagos uncovered a scam to print as many as five million fake voters' cards – an unidentified man placed a US$800,000 order in a Lagos print shop for the cards – a retired general was the reported suspect. This was a vote-rigging scheme of huge proportions that could easily have swung the elections, representing 8.3% of the projected registration figure of about 60 million.

This was not the only controversy hanging over the elections. There was more violence. In February, ethnic fighting broke out in the northeastern state of Adamawa leaving 110 dead, 500 injured and 21,000 people displaced from their homes. Then, in March, a senior opposition politician was assassinated; Harry Marshall, a senior figure of the All Nigeria People's Party who had been organising Buhari's first campaign rally, was shot dead at his home in Abuja.

## 2003 elections

On April 12 2003, Nigerians went to the polls to elect their next national assembly. 3,000 candidates competed for 360 seats in the House of Representatives and 109 seats in the Senate. Obasanjo's party was the clear favourite, but accusations of vote rigging were thrown around, and 12 people were killed around the country during protest riots on election day. Turnout on April 12 was around 50%, and Obasanjo's ruling party secured an outright majority in both the House of Representatives and the Senate. Then, on April 19, the electorate went to the polls for a second time to vote for the governors of the 36 states and their next president, for which 20 candidates competed. The electoral commission maintained that for a candidate to win the presidential election, he must have gained votes countrywide – at least 25% in two-thirds of the 774 local government areas. This was to ensure that the president did not only represent one region or ethnic group but had nationwide support. Obasanjo got 60% of the vote with a difference of some 12 million, almost twice as much as Buhari, and was inaugurated as Nigeria's president for a second four-year term, marking the first successful transition from one civilian government to another since the country's independence in 1960.

During his first four-year term, Obasanjo had had to manage Nigeria's transition from a military state to a civil society. (Though clearly not all of its people had behaved civilly.) In a country where a small group of soldiers held a tight grip on the reins of power for as long as most Nigerians can remember, he has since been successful in steering the country to a point where few now believe the military have any serious plans to take over. But now that the democratic process has been entrenched in Nigeria, the issues that the country now has to tackle are enormous. His first major obstacle at the end of June, only a few weeks after the elections, was a general strike that ran into a second week. The strike was called to protest an increase in fuel prices of more than 50% in June and the unions had been demanding a complete reversal of the price rise. The government said the fuel hikes were necessary to end shortages and curb the smuggling of cheap Nigerian fuel to neighbouring countries. But many Nigerians regard cheap fuel as a birthright, the only tangible benefit they get from their country's vast oil reserves. Oil workers threatened to block exports of crude oil, and protesters took to the streets burning barricades and smashing car windscreens, and a reported ten people died in clashes with police. And the crisis happened just a few days before George Bush visited Nigeria. Finally, on day nine the government reduced the price increase from 50% to 35% and the strike was called off.

Today there is also an ongoing violent dispute between communities in the Niger Delta and the oil companies. Some ethnic groups, namely the Ijaw, are demanding more political representation and compensation from oil companies operating in the area. The oil industry has polluted their fishing communities and created health risks for the people of the Delta, and as such they are demanding a greater share of the oil wealth that comes from their traditional lands. Oil facilities are constantly being shut down and reopened because of sporadic violence. At times during 2003 and early 2004 Nigeria lost up to 30% of its oil output as installations were closed in the Rivers and Delta states, the two states that produce 85% of Nigeria's total oil. Scores of people have been killed in fighting between different ethnic groups and the Nigerian navy, whose gunboats and troops have been blockading and firing on their villages from the rivers and creeks south of the town of Warri. In April 2004 two US oil workers and a number of Nigerian workers were kidnapped and killed.

On a personal note, I spoke to many people in Nigeria who were predictably unhappy with Obasanjo's government, and said that things were 'better under the military'. Since military rule ended in 1999, the average man on the street has become significantly poorer thanks to Nigeria's dire economic state. One taxi driver I was talking to about the amount of street hawkers there were in Lagos, told me, 'People didn't sell things in the traffic before the poverty came.' When I asked him when this was, he replied, 'When Obasanjo got in.' Yet whether a civilian or military administration is in power, Nigeria's economy is on such a downward spiral that more and more people will unfortunately be resorting to selling their wares in the traffic.

## RELIGION

To fully appreciate how Nigeria's complex religious character shapes and affects all walks of life in Nigerian society, religion needs to be looked at in a little more depth than in the average guidebook. I have never visited a country where almost all of its inhabitants are so fervently religious. A rough line divides Nigeria in an east–west direction between the predominantly Muslim north and the Christian south (see map on page 34). Around 50% of the population are Muslim, and 40% are Christian (the remaining 10% follow indigenous beliefs), and churches and mosques are prolific around the country. Islam was introduced to West Africa from the 11th century onwards via the trans-Saharan trade routes, and European missionaries spread Christianity when they arrived on the coast in the 18th century. Many Christians and Muslims also incorporate some traditional worship into their daily lives that pays homage to gods and spirits. These practices play an important part in Nigerian culture and pre-date the introductions of both Islam and Christianity. While most traditional religions coexist, there has been a historical and recently increasingly violent conflict between the imported religions, Islam and Christianity, which continues to separate the country religiously, politically and socially between the north and the south. Over the last few years, violent religious clashes have intensified since Sharia law was introduced in the northern states. Nigerian politics is plagued by escalating religious rivalries and public unrest over the issue of Islam versus Christianity and under whose rules people in different areas should live. Despite most of the north being Muslim, there are pockets of communities who are Christian, just as there are Muslims living in the south. This is the root of the problem.

## Ethnic Nigerian religions

Nigeria's people worship a variety of complicated traditional religious beliefs, and terms such as fetish or *juju* have produced much confusion. While ancestral spirits and membership of cults still exist, the main object of worship remains a common belief in a supreme being; Olorun or Olodumare (names given to God in Yoruba belief), Chineke or Chukwu (God amongst the Igbo) and Obangiji (God in the Hausa language). Of the three major groups of people, the traditional religion of the Yoruba is God-worship; the Igbo ancestral spirit-worship; whilst the Hausa-Fulani have been Muslim for almost a thousand years. The other traditional religions are too numerous to mention.

There are some 400 Yoruba gods each with a specific role. As might be expected in a culture with only oral records of the past, the same god may be male in one village and female in the next, and have a variety of names, differences that probably arose as myths were passed by word of mouth over the centuries. They serve under one all-powerful god who is variously known, among other names, as Olorun ('the owner of the sky') or Olodumare (roughly translated as 'the almighty'). He or she was creator of the world and had the ability to shape human bodies. The Yoruba explained to early missionaries that the 400 or so minor gods descended from this single god, and all are thought to have been once human, if not mythical, characters in ancient Yoruba history. Traditionally, the Yoruba pay homage to their gods at shrines, some of which still exist, and at certain festivals make animal sacrifices and pray to the gods to look over them. During the 19th century, the traditional religion of the Yoruba altered significantly because of missionary-inspired Christianity, and again in the early 20th century under the dominance of colonial rule, when the British put restrictions on their religious practices, many of which, such as human sacrifice, they thought were barbaric. The British also insisted upon burying the dead in communal graveyards rather than allowing the traditional Yoruba practice of burying them in the house.

The Igbo people traditionally believe in worshipping karma and spirits, and that they have two souls; their eternal soul or Maw, and one that belongs to an ancestor that is always watching over them, the Nkpuruk-Obi. Both souls leave the body when it dies but it is the Maw that goes on to form a shadow or ghost and becomes an Nkpuruk-Obi for somebody else. For this reason, the Igbo consider it bad luck to step on a shadow as they could be trampling on somebody's soul. As in the God-worship of the Yoruba, there is a hierarchy in the Igbo spirit world. This is headed by the ghost king or Eze Ala Maw and the ghost messenger or Onwu, who appear as skeletons and bring death upon a person by striking him at the base of the skull with a large staff. A ferryman or Asasaba brings good souls across the river of death to be reincarnated into a Nkpuruk-Obi or other spirit representing humans or living things such as trees or animals. The living pray to the deceased to look after them and provide a secure future. Death and the afterlife play a large role with elaborate funeral ceremonies and continued pilgrimage to the dead person's grave, though several types of deaths such as suicide are considered shameful.

## Christianity

The arrival of missionaries in the 18th and 19th centuries on the coast made their impact on the southern regions, though they failed to penetrate the Muslim north. Roman Catholic priests accompanied the first Portuguese slave traders to the West African coast and introduced Catholicism to the Kingdom of Benin in the 15th century. Several churches were built to serve the Portuguese traders and a small number of African converts, but the influence of Catholicism dwindled when the Portuguese withdrew, and had all but disappeared by the 18th century. Although churchmen in Britain had been influential in the drive to abolish the slave trade, missionaries only arrived again on Nigeria's coast in the 1840s. Mostly British Protestants, they set up the first mission stations in Calabar, and in Abeokuta, just north of Lagos, and by 1850 had made a considerable impact on the people they were working with. The Roman Catholics arrived again in the 1880s, by which time Christianity was a force to be reckoned with in the southern states. Other European and American missionaries subsequently arrived, as well as a considerable number of African Christians – returning slaves who had been exposed to Christianity elsewhere. There were some 3,000 returned slaves from Sierra Leone and from Brazil in Lagos by 1870. Among them was Samuel Crowther, a Yoruba by birth, who had been rescued as a boy from a slave ship by a British warship and taken and educated in Sierra Leone. He came to Yorubaland to concentrate on the mission stations along the Niger, and at the beginning of the 19th century was the first West African to be ordained an Anglican bishop. (He was the grandfather of Herbert Macaulay, one of Nigeria's leading nationalists in the 20th century.) With the arrival of colonialism at the end of the 19th century, which the missionaries supported, some African Christian communities formed their own independent churches because many European missionaries were racist, and because European Christianity refused to incorporate their local practices and traditions. The number of Nigeria's independent Christian churches grew steadily, and today, Christians make up over 96% of the population in the east and southeastern states, which is where Nigeria's largest concentration of churches are found, ranging from Orthodox to Pentecostal.

In these regions, *everybody* goes to church. Southern Nigeria is a place where millions and millions of people, every Sunday, dress up, pick up their Bibles, and go to church, and on weekday nights there are additional services and Bible study groups. Sunday is the day that Nigerian ladies wear their best and biggest shiny headdresses, men wear their full traditional robes, and children are dressed in their smartest clothes. Many churches have their own sort of uniforms and you'll see several women dressed in the same fabric. There is much hymn-singing and praising the lord, and preachers (male and female) are mostly self-styled evangelists; traditional clergymen are found only in the traditional Roman Catholic churches. Any makeshift building can become a church, stuffed to the gills with plastic seats or wooden benches, sometimes with a microphone system or electric organ or guitar. Whole streets are closed off on Sundays for open-air church services, and outside of the big cities you will see what are termed as 'campgrounds'. These are not for camping at all, but are vast areas used for evangelistic gatherings that often go on until dawn. There is one outside Lagos that can reputedly hold three million people! All over the south you will see billboards advertising well-known preachers and events. Some are even black evangelists from the US, who come to Nigeria to tap into this monumental thirst for religion that Nigerian Christians seem to have.

Society in the south is shaped by God. It is a region where people frequently break out into impromptu hymn-singing; where conversations are peppered with plenty of amens and praise-the-lords; where women in minibuses sing religious songs under their breath for their entire journey; where lay preachers wander motor parks with a microphone and The Word; where cassette stalls in markets belt out never-ending religious tunes; where hundreds of thousands of how-to pamphlets are published on how to live life through the eyes of God; and where businesses are named in the name of God – God's Will Motors and Vote for Jesus Motors (both bus companies); Thank the Lord Bakery; Let God be my Witness Tyre Menders; Pray Harder Hairdressers; Praise the Lord Optical Services; or Jesus Loves You Nursery School. It is quite remarkable, and nowhere else in the world have I seen such a deep and revered attitude to Christianity.

## Islam

Northern Nigeria was the southernmost outpost for the sweep of Islam that was carried from North Africa across the Sahara between the 10th and 19th centuries, but the penetration stopped before it reached southern Nigeria. It was practised unchallenged for some 500 years, though before the 19th century it was the religion of the elite few. Then, from the beginning of the 19th century, whilst the British were embroiled in the slave trade on the coast, other significant events were occurring in the north that had nothing to do with European intervention.

There were a series of spats between the flexible and easygoing Hausa and the more religiously devout Fulani, both living in the northern states. In 1802, one of the Fulani chiefs, Usman Dan Fodio, raised the standard of revolt against the Hausaland rulers, calling for a jihad or Holy War. Whilst the Hausa were predominantly Muslim, many were not so strict and some still practised traditional religions. Dan Fodio campaigned for the purity of the Islamic faith and against the evil ways into which many of its followers had fallen. He intended the jihad to protect and expand the faith, to denote that the authority of local rulers was shaped in religious terms, and to stress that the imam was the local leader for religious prayer and study.

Dan Fodio became known as *sarkin musulmi* or 'Lord of the Muslims', and was leader of what became known as the Sokoto Caliphate, the religious heartland of his movement in the extreme northwest, with the city of Sokoto as its capital. The Caliphate was a loose confederation of emirates that recognised the regime of the commander of the faithful, the sultan. His supporters rallied around him in such numbers that he found himself head of a formidable army of warriors all burning with religious fervour and intent on jihad, which eventually resulted in a series of wars between the Fulani and the Hausa. By 1808, the jihad had invaded the Hausa states of Kano, Zaria and Katsina, and the jihad war-bands went about conquering neighbouring pagan communities and built up a string of new states – Bauchi,

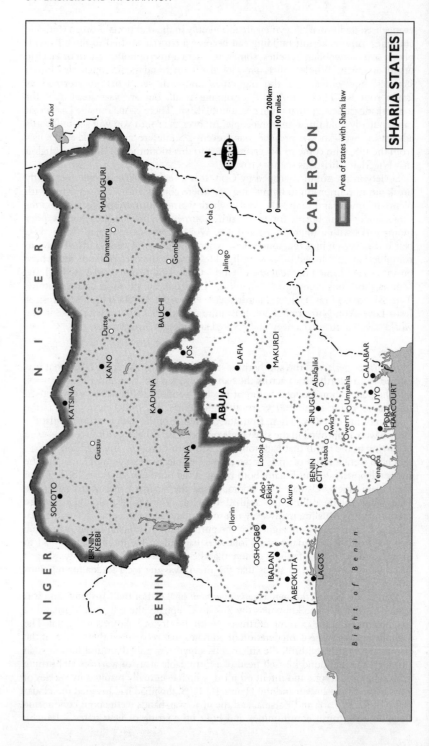

SHARIA STATES

Area of states with Sharia law

Gombe, Adamawa, and others – which all became tributaries to the Sokoto Caliphate; an empire founded by Muslim-reforming zeal. They moved further south, deep into non-Muslim Yorubaland as far as the city of Oyo, shattering the relatively peaceful relationship that had existed in the past between the various Yoruba states. Thousands of Yoruba refugees retreated south and built new cities, where they carried on their resistance to the Caliphate and fought amongst themselves as well. One of these cities was Ibadan, founded as a war camp in 1829 by a group of soldiers from Oyo, which became the largest city in Black Africa during the 19th century.

The movement retained its momentum well into the second half of the 19th century, when the Sokoto Caliphate stretched 1,500km from Dori in modern Burkina Faso, across what is now Nigeria, and into southern Cameroon. In addition, Dan Fodio's jihad provided the inspiration for a series of related holy wars far beyond Nigeria's borders that led to the foundation of Islamic states in Senegal, Mali, Ivory Coast, Chad, Central African Republic and Sudan. An analogy has been drawn between Dan Fodio's jihad and the French Revolution in terms of its widespread impact. Just as the French Revolution affected the course of European history in the 19th century, the Sokoto jihad affected the course of history in Africa from Senegal to the Red Sea. It introduced new forms of political and religious organisation and succeeded in planting deep-rooted Islam, irrevocably affecting the way of life of the region's inhabitants. Today, of the 50% of Nigerians that practise Islam, almost all live in the northern states.

Again, like Christianity in the south, Islam is practised with devoutness and fervour, particularly as many northern states have now adopted Sharia law (see below). Northern Nigerians are strict Muslims and live their lives to the Islamic letter. The north is scattered with mosques and open prayer compounds, and most males pray every few hours. Nigerian Muslim women live their lives as most Muslim women do around the world, though they are not expected to completely cover up. Most wear headscarves and flowing robes but their faces are not covered. Unlike other Islamic areas such as Turkey and the Middle East, but like more staunch regions such as Iran, the female children from walking age (and not puberty) wear headscarves and long clothes.

## Sharia law

Sharia law was first introduced in Nigeria's Zamfara State in January 2000, and is now practised, to a greater or lesser extent, in 12 other northern states. But what exactly is it? To Muslims, Sharia is a God-given code for how life ought to be lived. Calling it 'law' can be misleading, as Sharia extends beyond law, and governs all aspects of religious, political, social, domestic and private life. It's often dubbed Islamic law, but this is arguably incorrect as only part of it is based on the text in the Koran. The Sharia law system is thought to be the work of Muslim scholars during the early centuries of Islam, who fused the messages in the Koran with older Arabic, and other, law systems. There are similarities with ancient Bedouin law, commercial law from Mecca in the 7th–8th centuries, and laws from conquered or conquering countries over the millennia, such as Roman and Jewish law. Despite this, most Muslims believe it to be based on the Koran and hence think of it as the 'will of God'.

Used in varying degrees, for most Muslims it governs their religious way of life. Beyond that, many Islamic countries have adopted Sharia as their civil law. Then there are the countries that use Sharia as their criminal law, applying its judgements and penalties to offences such as adultery or theft, known in Sharia as Hadd offences. These are Saudi Arabia, Sudan, Iran, perhaps most famously

Afghanistan under Taliban rule, regions of Pakistan, and now practically one half of Nigeria, where an estimated 65 million Muslims find themselves faced with criminal sentences that differ greatly to those handed out to non-Muslims. (In the northern cities, you'll see regular federal court houses, Sharia courts, and Sharia appeal courts.)

In Nigeria, Sharia courts impose strict penalties, including floggings for gambling and consumption of alcohol, amputations for theft, and even death for crimes such as adultery. For a first-time theft, it's amputation of the right hand; for a second theft, amputation of the left foot; for sex outside marriage, 100 lashes; and for a person who commits adultery, burial up to the neck and stoning to death. In 2000, Buba Jangebe was the first person to have an amputation carried out since Sharia law was introduced in Nigeria after being found guilty of stealing a cow. Since then, many men and boys have had their hands amputated for theft (reputedly, the minimum value prescribed for amputation is the price of a goat; about US$8); at least one man has been hanged for murder; and a number of women have been given 100 lashes for fornication. Then there is the infamous story of 30-year-old Amina Lawal, who was sentenced to death by stoning for committing adultery. The story brought worldwide condemnation, and for the first time, an outside glance at how horrific these punishments are. Amina Lawal was sentenced to death in 2002, after she was seized from her home by volunteer Islamic vigilantes. The man identified as her lover was released, because the court said there was insufficient evidence against him and he swore on the Koran that he had never had sex with Lawal. But a baby was enough evidence for them to convict Lawal. The sentence was later reversed in the wake of international pressure.

Northern politicians and religious leaders say that crime has dropped sharply in the Sharia states, that floggings are symbolic, not barbaric, and that a fear of punishment promotes lawfulness. But human rights' groups have complained that these religious laws are archaic and unjust. They also represent a constitutional threat because they undermine the national, secular legal system. The gulf continues to widen between, on one side, northern leaders who say they implemented Sharia because of divine intervention and because most Muslims wanted it, and on the other side, mainly Christian southern critics who say it was a move by the political élite to tighten control over what is Nigeria's poorest region, and therefore the one most vulnerable to the country's endless corruption. To the poor, Sharia produces instant results, whereas Nigeria's civil penal system introduced by the British during the colonial days hinges on unaffordable lawyers and judges demanding bribes. The federal government has declared such Sharia punishments unconstitutional but, in direct defiance of this, northern leaders have pressed ahead, resisting what they have described as undue pressure from non-Muslims in the Nigerian government. President Obasanjo has so far failed to defuse these religious tensions.

## Religious clashes

Islam and Christianity both gained momentum throughout Nigeria in the 20th century at the expense of the smaller, increasingly unfashionable indigenous religions. Since 1980, there have been several outbreaks of religious or ethnic-driven violence, resulting in thousands of deaths, injuries, or arrests. The first dramatic religious disturbance was in 1980, incited by a Muslim sect known as the Maitatsine Movement. They demanded absolute obedience to Islam, and violent riots broke out in Kano, killing more than 4,000. After 11 days, the army and air force eventually suppressed the riots after the surprised police had failed to restore any order. Muslim extremists sparked further riots in 1981, and destroyed several

## BLOODSHED OVER BEAUTY QUEENS

Nigeria was due to host the 2002 Miss World beauty pageant in Abuja, when the then current Miss World, Nigeria's Agbani Darego, was scheduled to hand over her crown to her successor in December. But the arrival of the beauty queens ignited a violent response from the already volatile Muslim/Christian divide. In September, rioting broke out between Muslims and Christians in Kaduna killing at least 200 people, injuring another 1,000, and leaving some 11,000 homeless. Angry mobs raged through Kaduna's streets, setting fire to buildings, specifically churches and mosques, and there were even reports of bystanders being stabbed. Young Muslim men chanted 'Down with beauty' and 'Miss World is sin'. The riots were triggered by an article in the Lagos-based newspaper, *This Day*, that suggested Mohammed, Islam's prophet, would have approved of the Miss World competition. Isioma Daniel, a 21-year-old fashion journalist wrote 'The Muslims thought it was immoral to bring 92 women to Nigeria to ask them to revel in vanity. What would Mohammed think? In all honesty, he would probably have chosen a wife from one of them.' After the incident, the government of Zamfara State issued a *fatwa* against her – a religious injunction calling for her death. Mamuda Aliyu Shinkafi, the deputy governor of Zamfara, said at the time 'It is binding on all Muslims wherever they are, to consider the killing of the writer as a religious duty' (she remained unscathed and is still in hiding outside of Nigeria to this day, though the *fatwa* still stands against her). The beauty contest also drew protests from other parts of the world, and contestants from five countries boycotted the event because Sharia courts in Nigeria had sentenced Amina Lawal to death by stoning for adultery in early 2002. Whilst the Miss World organisers had hoped the show would brighten the image of Africa's most populous nation, media coverage instead focused on a death sentence and vicious mob violence. The Miss World contest was moved to London after the riots.

of Kano's state government buildings. Then, in Kaduna in 1982, fighting broke out between the Maitatsine Movement and the police, during which an estimated 500 were killed. The government then banned the sect and many of its leaders were arrested. Nevertheless, the Maitatsine sect continued to demonstrate violently, and in 1984 struck again, this time in northeast Nigeria at Yola, the capital of Adamawa State. The army used artillery to quell the disturbances, but was ill-equipped for riot control and another 700 people died and some 30,000 were left homeless. Then again in 1985, Maitatsine riots claimed more than 100 lives in Gombe and dozens of suspected sect members were arrested. Until this point in what is a very recent history, the lives lost were either of rioting sect members or of those in the police or army. But the violence took on a new dimension in 1987 when unprecedented violence broke out in several high schools and universities. Muslim and Christian students attacked each other, and 12 died in rioting at one college in Kaduna. Within a few days the violence had spread to Zaria, Katsina and Kano, where some 50 Kano churches were torched and many students were injured. All universities and schools were closed in Kano and a curfew was imposed in Kaduna State.

More recently, Sharia has exacerbated differences between the predominately Christian south and the Islamic north. Although the punishments prescribed by

Sharia law apply only to Muslims, Christians living in or visiting the north feel threatened, and tensions between the two communities have led to major outbreaks of inter-religious violence since 1999. In February 2000, more than 2,000 people were killed in religious unrest in Kaduna. In 2001, at least 500 were reported to have died in Jos, and in 2002, another 200 died in Kaduna over the Miss World controversy (see box). There were further sporadic deaths during the 2003 elections. Then on May 11 2004, while we were in Kano, we witnessed the start of riots that subsequently left 30 people dead and were in response to another massacre a few weeks earlier in a village near Jos that killed a reported 200 Muslims.

This slice of violent history is so recent for Nigeria it's difficult to envisage how it will be resolved. Various explanations, some bordering on applied sociology, have been offered to explain this crisis, though many of the underlying causes are probably as old as the nation itself, even if they only simmered beneath the surface before. There are suggestions that it is a passing phase in a nation that has found its freedom after many years of dictatorship, a freedom that Nigeria's people are unequipped to deal with, leading to a heady demonstration of that very same freedom, which unfortunately has chosen the path of violence.

## ECONOMY

Much of Nigeria's economic history has already been documented in the above historical account, simply because the health of the economy is directly linked to the character of those people that govern the country. Today, Nigeria's economy is one of the largest in Africa, with a variety of natural resources and a massive labour force. But despite great potential for high productivity and diversity, the country's historical political turmoil, years of economic mismanagement and corruption, as well as fluctuations in the world oil price, have left the economy close to collapse. Nigeria is heavily in debt, poverty and unemployment are real problems, and foreign investment is thin on the ground. Despite being the world's sixth-biggest oil producer, Nigeria is a developing nation in the lowest 25% of the world's economies, and in 2002, was rated the world's 26th-poorest country. (In the 1970s, Nigeria was rated the 33rd-richest country in the world.) With all the wealth that it 'should' have, Nigeria is a Third-World country, where the real standard of living has fallen sharply in recent decades.

### Before oil

The British replaced indigenous food crops such as cassava with crops of palm oil, as well as groundnuts (peanuts) and cocoa, all intended for export. During the colonial period, Nigeria basically survived on its agriculture for its economy, and for its food. At independence in 1960 agriculture accounted for well over half of GDP, and was the main source of export earnings and public revenue. But since the British left, agriculture has suffered from years of mismanagement, inconsistent and poorly conceived government policies, and the lack of basic infrastructure. And above all the sector has been dwarfed by oil, discovered in the Niger Delta in the 1950s. By the late 1960s oil had replaced cocoa, groundnuts and palm oil as the country's largest foreign-currency earner, and with an injection of oil money, Nigeria's manufacturing industry grew into its own from 1950 to the 1970s – before the discovery of oil there had been very few industries. Nigeria started importing raw materials from other countries, and manufacturing became established. Industries included food processing and the manufacture of vehicles, textiles, pharmaceuticals, paper and cement. One of the effects of the oil and industry boom was that there was a significant rural-to-urban migration that took a lot of the labour force away from the rural areas. Not surprisingly, the largely subsistence agricultural sector declined, and failed to keep up with rapid population movement and growth. Nigeria, once a large net exporter of food, had to import food. Today, Nigeria still needs to import most of its food and only about 12% of the land is cultivated.

Other than oil, Nigeria is considerably rich in mineral resources. Nigeria was once the world's largest producer of tin, with huge deposits in the highland district around Jos. But production collapsed from an average of 10,000 tons per year in the 1970s to 300 tons in the late 1990s, with only an estimated 16,000 tons of tin reserves left. And whilst the reserves of tin have been exploited, other mineral resources have hardly been touched. Some estimates place iron ore reserves at over 800 million tons, but Nigeria's output is only around 50,000 tons per year. Deposits of uranium, lead, zinc, tungsten and gold have also not been exploited to their full potential. Gold has been located in some 65 sites around Nigeria though mining as yet hasn't begun.

## The discovery of black gold

Since 1957, when Shell-BP discovered oil in Nigeria's Delta region, Nigeria's economy has overwhelmingly been dominated by oil. The majority of oil reserves are located in the Niger Delta but newer reserves have been discovered in deeper waters offshore. Today, production exceeds two million barrels per day, or 60.3 million per month, making Nigeria, a member of OPEC, the world's sixth-biggest oil provider. The majority of Nigeria's crude oil is exported to Europe, Asia and the United States. The low-sulphur content of much of Nigeria's oil makes it especially desirable in a pollution-conscious world. At present, oil revenues constitute over 95% of Nigeria's export earnings, 90% of foreign-currency earnings, and 65% of total government revenue (over US$20 billion in 2002). Today, Nigeria's largest joint venture oil company is Shell, which produces nearly 50% of Nigeria's crude oil, with the Nigerian National Petroleum Company (NNPC), the state-owned oil firm, having a 55% interest in Nigeria Shell. The extent of this heavy dependence on oil is signified by the fact that the country has earned in excess of US$250 billion from oil exports from 1970, and OPEC's 2003 estimate of Nigeria's proven oil reserves is put at another 31.5 billion barrels. At today's production rate, that's another 430 years of oil production.

By rights, these figures should indicate a wealthy country with a healthy economy. But since oil was discovered in Nigeria more than four decades ago, this hasn't been the case at all. The problem has been Nigeria's over-dependence on oil in the economy, and the allure of great wealth that has spawned other economic distortions. The 1970 boom in world oil prices, and to a smaller extent the period after 1990 brought on by the Gulf War, led Nigeria to neglect its agricultural and manufacturing bases in favour of an unhealthy dependence on crude oil. This didn't help Nigeria's millions who needed jobs, and it fuelled a massive migration to the cities, which in turn led to increasingly widespread poverty, especially in rural areas. Domestic production costs became excessively high, due in part to erratic electricity and fuel supplies, and today's industrial capacity is a fraction of what it once was, resulting in mass unemployment and high inflation. With the near collapse of the manufacturing industry, the country's necessity to import goods has resulted in high prices for basic commodities. Added to this is the squandering of oil income by the various military leaders and government officials – Abacha alone squirrelled away around US$4 billion – and the corruption and abuse of power at all levels that reached mind-boggling proportions in the 1990s. According to the present Obasanjo government, between 1993 and 1998 Abacha reputedly spent over US$12 billion of oil revenue on 'non-priority items and without proper accounting'. And then, thanks to a thriving black market for oil products, there is the revenue that has simply been lost through crime – from illegal siphoning from pipelines, to stolen oil being freighted out of Nigeria on ships. The government estimates that as much as 300,000 barrels per day of Nigerian crude oil is illegally 'bunkered' (freighted) out of the country, and the Nigerian navy is under orders to capture any ship with oil aboard that is not accounted for. Pipeline theft has increased the number of explosions in recent years, with the most serious disaster being in 1998 at Jesse, when a fire killed over 1,000 people. In 2000 alone, the Nigerian National Petroleum Corporation (NNPC) reported 800 cases of pipeline vandalism, causing a loss of about US$4 billion in oil revenue.

The culture of crime, kickbacks and embezzlement has encouraged mismanagement and wasted huge amounts of national resources – resources that by rights should have filtered through the system from the oil wells in the Niger Delta to the man on the street. GDP per head today is put at about US$800, while roughly 66% of the population lives below the poverty line (compared to 43% in 1985). Another problem in recent years has been ethnic violence from people living around the oil installations in the Niger Delta. Despite the billions of dollars Nigeria earns from its oil, little has been done to improve the living conditions of the people living in the oil-producing regions, some of whom are the poorest in Nigeria. These people have demonstrated, often violently, against the oil companies about the environmental degradation of their land, and have demanded a greater share of Nigeria's oil revenue. More than 4,000 oil spills have been recorded in Nigeria's Niger Delta over the past four decades. Since 2000, oil installations have been frequently attacked, causing costly disruption to production.

Nigeria has a major foreign debt problem, a large chunk being interest and payment arrears. Any long-term debt relief will require strong and sustained economic reforms by Nigeria over a number of years. Nigeria faces a choice between privatisation and greater reliance on the private sector, or remaining dependent on the public sector, namely oil. Nigeria is also keen to attract foreign investment and needs foreign capital to reinvigorate the economy and reduce the foreign debt payments. But this is hindered by security concerns as well as by a shaky infrastructure. Nigeria's economy also could gain substantially if the government is able to persuade Nigerians with funds abroad to return home to boost investment. Since 1993, Nigerian capital flight has been estimated at around US$2 billion a year. To get the economy back on track, and starting with oil, one of the major priorities is to build more oil refineries. Whilst Nigeria exports some two million barrels of crude oil a day, it then imports the refined product at a far higher price. Exporting refined oil would earn far greater revenues and end the chronic fuel shortages that routinely plague Nigeria. The other priority is for the Nigerian government to lessen this unhealthy dependence on crude oil and perhaps develop the long-neglected agricultural sector.

One huge boost for the economy is the development of the natural gas industry – Nigeria is believed to have an estimated 3.5 trillion cubic metres of proven natural gas reserves, making it the world's ninth-largest source. But the infrastructure is poor and Nigeria currently flares 75% of the gas it produces – the World Bank estimates that Nigeria accounts for 12.5% of the world's total gas flare. (Unused gas is 'flared' or burnt off, which in turn causes major health and environmental problems such as respiratory disease and acid rain.) In 1997, the US$569 million Escravos Gas Project became Nigeria's first gas exporter. Then, in

1999, the US$4 billion Nigeria Liquefied Natural Gas Scheme, Africa's single-biggest engineering project, started producing liquefied natural gas from its plant at Bonny Island. The facility is capable of processing 77 billion cubic metres of natural gas annually. Homes in Lagos have already been connected up to domestic gas and a proposed US$580 million pipeline will supply gas to central and northern Nigeria.

Despite this diversification attempt, however, Nigeria's economy stands to remain dependent on fossil fuels, and in the future will no doubt be hit hard once again when the global community begins to substitute renewable energy sources for fossil fuels.

## Infrastructure

Nigeria's transportation infrastructure is a major constraint to economic development – it's quite simply a mess. Of the 200,000km of roads, only 60,000km are officially paved, but many are in very bad shape and have been decaying for years. Throughout the country are thousands of police and army roadblocks that hamper travel, and through which most Nigerians have to pay a bribe, locally known as dash (whether personally or within the price of a bus ticket) to get through. The principal ports at Lagos, Port Harcourt and Calabar charge docking fees for freighters that are amongst the highest in the world, and the inspection procedure for imported goods is riddled with corruption. Nigeria has four international airports at Lagos, Kano, Port Harcourt and Abuja, which are some of the busiest in the world (the London–Port Harcourt route is one of Virgin Atlantic's most profitable routes), but the government-owned airline, Nigerian Airways, collapsed in 2003 due to mismanagement, high debt and an old and vastly shrunken fleet. Trains on the railways have stopped moving. After years of neglect, the state-run National Electric Power Authority (NEPA) now produces below half its generating capacity of nearly 6,000 megawatts and power cuts are part of daily life. In Nigeria, NEPA is commonly referred to as 'Never Expect Power Again' and for good reason. Faulty and ageing facilities are in desperate need of repair, and currently only 10% of rural households and approximately 40% of Nigeria's total population have access to electricity – and then only sporadically so. Access to water is another daily problem; in the cities it rarely flows from any tap and households have resorted to buying plastic water tanks to store water, and which are filled when it does miraculously appear from a tap, or from water sellers – all over Nigeria you will see men pushing handcarts with jerry cans of water for sale and crowds of people around public taps and wells.

## Daily life

To summarise, the biggest tragedy has been Nigeria's failure to reach its economic potential. Despite its abundance of natural and human resources, Nigeria remains desperately poor. At the top end of the scale, some 1–2% of the population are filthy rich; namely government officials and industry heads who have acquired great wealth from the rich pickings of corruption. Stories abound of how obscenely rich these people are: I heard one about a government minister sending a private plane to the UK to buy a certain brand of orange juice that his young son favoured and wasn't available in Nigeria. Elsewhere in the country, 7% of all Nigerian children don't live until the age of one, 18% don't see their fifth birthday, and those that do survive childhood can only expect to live until the age of 51. Most die because of appalling living conditions and inadequate healthcare, or from malnutrition or routine diseases such as malaria or diarrhoea that could be treated if resources were available. Nigeria's government-provided public healthcare facilities are few and far between, are of a very poor standard, and are subject to shortages of doctors and nurses, drugs, equipment and electricity. Because of the lack of fundamental healthcare, many Nigerians resort to traditional doctors and medicine that could further endanger their health. Over 40% of the colossal population of nearly 140 million is under the age of 14, and although education is mandatory for all, finding school fees and places in schools and universities is difficult for the average Nigerian family, and many children are taught in rudimentary privately run schools, often in the back street of a city or outdoors in a village. For a Third-World country where the majority of people are living on a few naira a day, food prices are high, because of the lack of agriculture and the reliance on imported goods. The average Nigerian consumes only between 85% and 90% of the calories needed to live a healthy life, and only 38% have access to safe drinking water. There are few jobs in the public sector, save for the largely ineffective civil service where scores of people are employed as paper pushers; there is hardly any industry, no agricultural sector to speak of, and very few factories or large-scale employers; only a small section of the population works in formal employment. Most people eke out a living as traders on the streets and markets, as transport drivers and conductors, or as local service providers. And Nigeria has to cope with an increasing population rate of monstrous proportions, one that at current rates could see 300 million people living in the country by the middle of the 21st century – roughly half of the population of the whole of Africa. This enormous population pressure will almost inevitably doom Nigerians to become even poorer.

## THE ENVIRONMENT
### Geography
Nigeria has 800km of unbroken sandy beaches that are routinely pounded by the relentless Atlantic swells. Travelling inland from south to north, away from the coast, you first encounter the tropical coastal plain, an area that receives more rain annually than the rest of the country. The plain extends inland for about 75km before rising to an elevation of 40–50m at its northern boundary. The eastern and western sections are separated by the mangrove swamps of the Niger Delta that extends over an area of about 10,000km$^2$; it's characterised by soggy, mosquito-infested swamplands separated by numerous islands that hold Nigeria's most precious commodity, oil. Away from the coast, in the southeast, are forests full of oil palms, and away from the coast on the western side, are tracts of ebony and mahogany forests. The forest belt leads to higher savanna grasslands in the central regions where the Niger and Benue rivers converge, whilst further north, the landscape is hot semi-arid bush that borders the Sahara Desert in neighbouring Niger. This is known as the Sahel region and consists purely of scrubby and sandy terrain. Some of the country's higher points are the Bauchi and Jos plateaus at 600–1,200m in the centre, and the Adamawa Massif (which continues into Cameroon) in the east, where Nigeria's highest mountain range, the Chapal Wadi, reaches heights of over 2,000m, with the Gangarwal Peak being Nigeria's tallest at 2,419m. In the far northwest, and in the northeast where the Chad Basin is located, elevation falls again to below 300m.

The Niger is West Africa's greatest river and the country's main geographical feature, together with its principal tributary the Benue. The Niger boasts an extraordinary course, rising little more than 300km from the sea in Sierra Leone, flowing northeastwards to brush the Sahara at Timbuktu, before completing its great bend across Nigeria's savanna and forest to the labyrinthine creeks and mangrove swamps of its long, mysterious delta. The Delta extends inland for more than 200km and along the coast for 100km, eventually reaching the sea at the Bight of Benin. The Niger River traverses four countries – though the whole basin covers nine – that together represent a kaleidoscope of cultures and landscapes. The upper reaches of these rivers form narrow valleys with falls and rapids, though most of the lower parts are rapid-free, with extensive floodplains and numerous channels. The Benue rises in Cameroon, flows from the northeast, and joins the Niger at the confluence town of Lokoja. These two rivers form a great 'Y' in the southern part of the country and essentially divide Nigeria's three dominant ethnic groups; the Igbo in the southeast, the Hausa in the north, and the Yoruba in the southwest.

Whilst Nigeria has extraordinary biological diversity, it faces many environmental problems brought on by ever-increasing population numbers, poverty and industrial damage. These include frequent oil spills in the Delta region and rampant deforestation (in West Africa, only Ivory Coast cuts down more trees than Nigeria). A century ago there were five million ha of trees and in 1897 two-thirds of Nigeria was covered by rich tropical rainforest. Today only 4% of this original rainforest remains, with most of the deforestation having happened since the 1980s – between 1981 and 1994 Nigeria lost 3.7 million ha of rainforest through logging and bush burning. Causes include fuel wood gathering, conversion of natural forest to commercial tree plantations, oil exploration, mining, and urbanisation. And of what's left, over 3% is lost annually, and only a third is in protected areas, either under the protection of the forestry department or in national parks. Hundreds of plant species are threatened with extinction, as is some of the wildlife that is unique to Nigeria, such as the white-throated monkey, Sclater's guenon, Niger Delta red colobus monkey, and the Niger Delta pygmy hippo.

## Climate

Although Nigeria is wholly within the tropics, its climate varies from tropical at the coast, to sub-tropical further inland, to arid in the north. It experiences two distinct climates – dry and wet. The length of each season varies around the country depending on elevation and latitude but generally the dry season is November–March and the rainy season April–August, with shorter rains in September and October. However, on the coast the rainy season kicks in during February or March when a moist Atlantic air mass, known as the southwest monsoon, routinely batters the coast. The coast, and predominantly the Niger Delta, receives more rain annually than the rest of the country – up to 4,000mm per year, approximately five times that of London. In contrast, the semi-arid Sahel in the northernmost part of the country receives the least rainfall – about 500mm annually. The peak of the rainy season here is in August, when air from the Atlantic covers the entire country. However, Nigeria has suffered from a number of droughts over recent years, particularly in the Sahel, and the 20th century is considered among the driest periods of the last several centuries, with well-publicised droughts during the 1970s–80s. These drought periods indicate the great variability of climate across tropical Africa.

Nigeria's temperature is high year round, and is frequently accompanied by high humidity in low-lying and coastal areas where temperatures average around 32°C. In the north, temperatures generally average 37°C, with extreme northern desert regions averaging 45°C during the day and 6°C at night. Temperatures are highest from February to April in the south and from March to June in the north and lowest from October to January over most of the country. The dry season brings both cooler temperatures and chaotic dry

## WHAT A WASTE...

Nigeria has got the most alarming rubbish problem I have ever seen and the main culprit is non-biodegradable plastic and the Nigerians' terrible attitude towards litter – they simply throw it on the ground. Throughout the country there are unsightly heaps of rubbish everywhere – mountains of garbage are dumped on pavements, central reservations, under bridges and flyovers, in drains and canals, and just about on any available piece of land. The majority of it is plastic and the curse of the rubbish problem is the small half-litre water packets of what is known as *pure water*, which everyone relies on for drinking water, that simply get dropped on the ground as soon as they are finished. In markets vendors believe in good presentation and almost all street food is presented in little plastic bags and even the cheapest market products are wrapped in plastic. Of the almost 140 million people, if each of these drops say, two pieces of plastic litter per day, you can imagine the immensity of the problem. Although there are some public dumps at the edge of the cities (the one on the road into Lagos from Ibadan is overwhelmingly vast and several metres deep), Nigeria has not got any kind of system or service to dispose of its rubbish. Everywhere are ad hoc rubbish dumps, where pigs and cows forage, and where humans openly go to the toilet, that when set alight emit dangerous toxic fumes and terrible odours. They produce a number of health hazards and are breeding grounds for flies, cockroaches, rats and mosquitoes, and when it rains the water mixes with the rubbish to create a toxic slush that contaminates water sources, causing typhoid and diarrhoea. In particular, vagrants and scavengers in the rubbish dumps are subjected to high health risks. Unfortunately you will have to do the same, and drop your rubbish on the ground. What's the alternative? Carrying rubbish with you until you get to a hotel room and throw it in the bin? These bins are then emptied by simply throwing their contents over the nearest wall. It's tragic. If you are a visitor or are living in Nigeria, try and keep the rubbish you accrue to a bare minimum – buy cold drinks and beer in recyclable bottles, not cans; refill plastic water bottles with clean treated water; and re-use processed food containers and plastic bags.

northeast winds, referred to locally as the Harmattan, that carry fine sand from the Sahara across the country. The dust-filled air during this time can be irritating and uncomfortable and appears as a dense fog. The Harmattan is more common in the north but affects the entire country, except for a narrow strip along the southwest coast. However, an occasional strong Harmattan can sweep as far south as Lagos, pushing clouds of dust out to sea and providing relief from high humidity in the capital.

## National parks

Despite rapid deforestation in Nigeria, there are still a number of reserves dotted around the country, and Nigeria currently has eight national parks. In 1979, the first Obasanjo administration established Lake Kainji National Park as Nigeria's first national park and since then seven others have been created, mostly carved out of former forest or game reserves. They cover about 3% or 24,000km² of the country, though only two of these are well known, or even visited – these are Lake Kainji

National Park and Yankari National Park. The others are Cross River, Gashaka-Gumpti, Okomu, Kamuka, Old Oyo and Chad Basin national parks. They are run by the Federal National Parks Service (FNPS) which receives funding direct from the federal government, but they suffer from serious underfunding, poor protection and weak management, and poaching is a serious problem in all the parks. Evidently, a few years ago there were some moves to create facilities at the parks (Lake Kainji and Yankari today being the only ones with functioning visitors' camps), and building was started at some to construct accommodation chalets and restaurants etc. Even today the limited tourist brochures available on the parks (some printed at least a decade ago) promise fully furnished rooms and services, from food and drink to game drives. Don't believe them! Due to a complete lack of visitors (Gashaka-Gumpti National Park apparently received 12 visitors in 2003) these facilities, if they were ever built at all, have fallen into disrepair and are rarely staffed. I spoke to an overland tour leader that came through Nigeria in 2004 and she told me that they took their truck and passengers to one of the two sections of Cross River National Park where she had heard that there was a campsite and some basic facilities. They found a locked gate, and it then took half a day to find the man with the key; there was no-one there to take any entry fees; they ripped the exhaust off the truck on the non-maintained track into the park; and at the 'camp' there was nothing more than a bunch of unmanned derelict buildings.

Added to this is the complete lack of knowledge of what and how many animals are in each park. Even the park rangers have no idea! And again, despite what the Federal National Parks Service says, their figures are likely to be seriously over-inflated, given that there hasn't been a game census in Yankari since 1991, and that in some of the other parks there hasn't been a game count ever. In reality, there is sadly every chance that there are very few animals left at all. In 2000 Obasanjo presented the prime minister of Norway with a pair of carved ivory tusks – a perfect example of Nigeria's appalling attitude towards its wildlife.

On a more promising note, however, Nigeria has 904 documented species of birds thanks to a survey by Birdlife International in 2002, so figures for birds, unlike animals, should be fairly accurate. Of these, 436 species are breeding residents, while the rest are migrants, many of them from Europe, that come to northern Nigeria during the winter months – the wetlands of the Chad Basin National Park have been declared a Ramsar site, so called after the 1971 Convention of Wetlands, held in Ramsar, Iran. And in recent years, gorillas (once thought to have left the area long ago), were discovered in the forests of Cross River National Park and reclassified from a lowland gorilla to a Cross River gorilla (thought to be a new sub-species of gorilla – see box on page 233).

There has been some progress in the management of the parks, and the National Park Decree of 1999 gives the park staff special powers and regulations to fine and capture anyone poaching in the parks. Poachers caught in the environs of the park can be tried and punished under national park laws and not in the local courts, because the national parks are federal land. We saw evidence of this being successful at Lake Kainji National Park. Also, several NGOs (Non-Governmental Organisations) devoted to environmental protection in Nigeria have been formed, some of which are very active. This has been accompanied by a gradual increase in environmental awareness throughout Nigeria, including in the government, which is starting to adopt conservation strategies, and Nigerians are becoming more conscious of their natural heritage. Let's hope that in the future, through better management and by more Nigerians wanting to actually visit the parks, Nigeria's parks will be rejuvenated and the senseless plundering of natural resources and their ever-decreasing stocks of wildlife will stop.

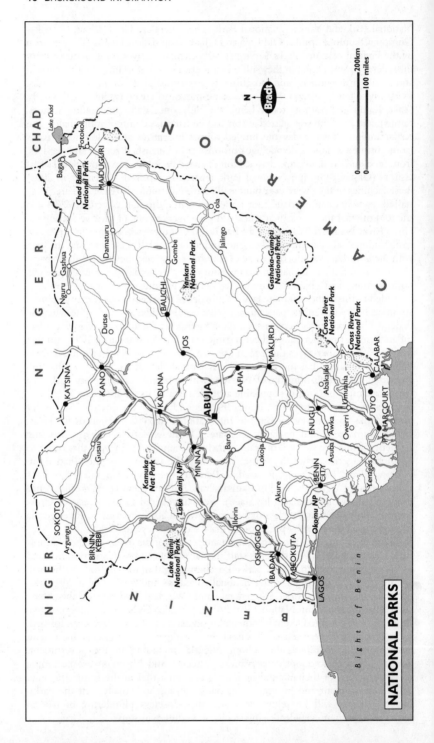

For now, you can still feasibly visit the parks, but except for Yankari and Lake Kainji, you will need your own vehicle, preferably a 4WD, and possibly a GPS, and if you want to stay overnight be fully self-contained and self-sufficient, and be prepared to camp.

## Wildlife

The first animal you will see in Nigeria is the comical and colourful agama lizard; they are everywhere, so you'll have to get used to lizards scurrying around your feet and up walls. The much brighter males have bright orange heads and brilliant blue bodies and can reach lengths of 20cm, whilst the plainer and smaller females are brown. Given my comments above about the national parks, you are very unlikely to spot much wildlife in Nigeria so there's little point in producing an extensive list of what might or might not be there. You are sadly more likely to see wildlife dead rather than alive, for sale as bushmeat at the side of the road, fashioned into so-called curios in the markets, or as black magic ingredients on a *juju* doctor's stall. The animals I have listed here are all very seriously endangered in Nigeria and it is imperative that they are protected immediately before they completely disappear from Nigeria's forests. For that reason alone I am going to group them together here to highlight this fact, despite the fact that you are unlikely to see them. There used to be several species of big game in Nigeria, as attested to by the skins and pelts hanging up in museums and curio and *juju* markets, cheetah and leopard being prime examples, but it's very unlikely that they still exist in the wild, though there may still be lion in Yankari. Giraffe used to stalk the savanna areas in the north, but they are now extinct in Nigeria thanks to hunting. The last giraffe on record appears to have been a lone animal that strayed into a village in the then Gongola State (where it was killed) in 1987. There may perhaps still be a small population of African hunting dog in the Gashaka-Gumpti National Park, but again there's no way of knowing for sure. Of all the parks Gashaka-Gumpti holds the most hope of still having relatively large populations of animals, and researchers have discovered a healthy-sized community of chimpanzees here. It's very remote and inaccessible, so the problem of poaching hasn't been so intense here.

### Endangered species

There are some 30 sites around Nigeria that meet the criteria of Birdlife International for important bird areas, and birds endemic to Nigeria are the **Anambra waxbill**, the **Jos Plateau indigobird**, the **rock fire-finch** and the **Ibadan malimbe**. Nigeria is home to one of the most endangered birds in Africa, the **grey-neck picathartes**, of which there may be as few as 2,500 individuals in the forests of Cross River State. **Secretary birds**, *Sagittarius serpentarius*, are occasionally seen in Yankari and Lake Kainji national parks. This tall bird with a raptor's beak, long legs and a stalking gait has black and grey plumage and is largely terrestrial. They feed on snakes that they pound to death with their strong feet. The **African grey parrot**, *Psittacus erithacus*, is an unmistakable grey parrot with a scarlet tail. It draws attention to itself by flying directly between roosting and feeding grounds screeching loudly, and it grips the branches of trees whilst climbing. It is seriously threatened by trapping, deforestation and the international pet trade. In Nigeria you are most likely to see them in inadequately sized cages hanging outside people's houses. **Ostriches**, *Struthio camelus*, can only be found in small groups in northeastern Nigeria around the Chad Basin, and are seriously threatened by egg collection. They are distinguished by their great size; males have black plumage and a long pink neck, whilst the plainer females have grey feathers and are smaller. The **giant forest hog**, *Hylochoerus meinertzhageni*, is a huge pig, heavily built with a rump higher than its shoulders and relatively long legs and a long head with tusks. Its coat is coarse and entirely jet black, and it could possibly still exist in Gashaka-Gumpti.

Antelopes are seriously endangered in Nigeria, as antelope meat is considered a delicacy, and, in the poorer rural areas, a source of free food. The **sitatunga**, *Tragelaphus spekei*, is a large antelope with hindquarters higher than its forequarters, giving the animal a peculiar hunched appearance. The coat is fairly long and shabby, and the males have long and twisted horns. It is a very shy and timid animal that spends its time hidden amongst thick vegetation along river banks, and it only ventures from its watery refuge at night to feed on drier ground. As soon as it senses danger it slips into the water and swims away, and can remain submerged with only its muzzle above the surface of the water. It was once common around the swamps of Lake Chad, but is now very rare. The **roan antelope**, *Hippotragus equinus*, is one of the largest of the antelopes and resembles a horse in terms of its proportions. It has contrasting black and white face markings, very long pointed ears with tufts on their tips, and moderately long horns that curve backwards. It is particularly susceptible to drought and is only present in Lake Kainji, Yankari and Gashaka-Gumpti national parks. The **bohor reed buck**, *Redunca redunca*, is a medium-sized graceful antelope with a thick coat and short tail, with a fawn colour on its back and a bright white underbelly seen clearly when the tail is held erect. Only males have horns, which are curved backwards and then sharply forward forming hooks on their tips. They are very seriously threatened in Nigeria, but may possibly still exist in the remote northern savanna regions.

The **pygmy hippopotamus**, *Choeropsis liberiensis*, is much smaller and lighter than a regular hippo and usually reaches a weight of about half a ton. It spends the greater part of the day submerged in a lake or river, and comes out at night to feed on the swampy borders of forest streams, and unlike a regular hippo it is largely solitary. Again there are very few left in Nigeria and populations are restricted to pockets of the Niger Delta. The **lion**, *Panthera leo*, is a large powerful cat that used to stalk most of West Africa. In Nigeria there are small populations of lion in Yankari, Lake Kainji, and Gashaka-Gumpti National Parks but visitors are very unlikely to see them, and the park authorities have no idea how many remain. They are very sociable and are rarely seen alone and the female is more lightly built than the male, and doesn't have a mane. It's females that hunt in a combined operation by stalking or ambushing their prey, such as antelope and buffalo, before killing them by strangulation. The problem for the survival of lion in Nigeria is the lack of prey.

The **African elephant** is the largest terrestrial animal and adults weigh up to 6,000kg. It uses its trunk for feeding, drinking, grooming and fighting, whilst its third upper incisors grow tusks which grow throughout its life. There is a marked difference between the African savanna elephant, *Loxodonta Africana*, and the forest elephant, *Loxodonta Africana cyclotis*. The latter has straighter tusks and more rounded ears and is considerably smaller. Despite their size elephants can run very quickly over a short distance and can live to be up to 70 years old. There may perhaps still be forest elephants in Okumu, Omo and Cross River national parks and there's a fairly big herd of savanna elephant in Yankari National Park (and we count ourselves very privileged and lucky to have seen a herd about 70 strong). They used to be found in Lake Kainji but this population has all migrated to Benin due to hunting pressures. There is also a sad pair of elephants in a ridiculously inadequate enclosure at Jos Zoo.

All primates are seriously endangered in Nigeria, not because they are necessarily eaten (though that does sometimes happen), but because of deforestation and the popularity of using monkeys for *juju*. **Sclater's guenon**, *Cercopithecus sclateri*, is Africa's rarest and least-known monkey. Rather frighteningly it is only found in Nigeria, in a few isolated patches of forest between the Niger and Cross rivers in the southeast. The characteristic features of the species are its white ears, white nose, and red and grey tail. The monkey is a sacred animal in two Igbo villages, but it is still seriously threatened with extinction due to hunting, habitat loss and the erosion of traditions. The **white-throated monkey**, *Cercopithecus erythrogaster*, is another seriously threatened species of monkey endemic to Nigeria, though it has recently been spotted in the Benin Republic. This unique primate has a beautiful gold crown and striking white throat. In Nigeria its last hope for survival is in the Okomu National Park, although there are a few in some zoos. **Preuss's guenon**, *Cercopithecus preussi*, is only found in forests higher than 1,000m and is restricted to southeast Nigeria, around the Obudu Plateau, and southwest Cameroon. It has dark smoky fur with a ruff of white under its chin. The **red colobus monkey**, *Procolobus badius waldroni*, was only discovered in Nigeria in recent years and is a red, long-furred and limbed forest monkey. It lives in forest pockets of the Niger Delta and could be endemic to Nigeria in West Africa, after becoming extinct in other countries such as Ghana.

The **chimpanzee**, *Pan troglodytes*, can easily be distinguished from the gorilla by its large characteristic turned-out ears, big eyes and long arms. It is regarded as the most man-like of all the apes, not only because of its anatomy, but because of certain behaviours, such as community defence and the use of tools. One of their daily rituals is to build a nest five metres or so above the ground in the canopy of the forest for the group to sleep in at night. They were once found in all of Nigeria's southern forests, but have been poached and hunted for bushmeat or for the illegal trade in pets or zoo animals. There is, however, a fairly healthy population in the remote and unexplored forests of Gashaka-Gumpti National Park, and visitors can visit rescued chimps at the Afi Drill Ranch.

The **gorilla**, *Gorilla gorilla*, is the strongest and largest of all the primates. It has a big head, protruding brow, large nostrils and arms longer than its legs. Dominant adult males have a band of silver hairs on their back, hence the term silverback. As with the chimpanzee, the group builds nests to sleep in at night some five metres up in the canopy of the forest and they seldom spend two successive nights in the same place. Thought to be extinct in Nigeria for many years, a few individuals have been discovered in small pockets of forest in Cross River State and across the border in Cameroon. They have recently been re-classified as the Cross Border gorilla and it's believed there are around 150–200 gorillas in the Nigeria–Cameroon (Cross River) area, making them the most critically endangered gorillas on earth. (Also see box on page 223.)

Finally, another primate that is critically endangered is the **drill monkey**, *Mandrillus leucophaeus,* which is a short-tailed rainforest monkey restricted to the forested parts of the southeast of Nigeria, parts of Cameroon, and on Bioko Island, Equatorial Guinea. The males are much like a baboon in shape, with a big head, a bright pink scrotum, and a black face surrounded by a ring of brilliant white fur. They are seriously threatened by habitat loss and hunting, especially by dogs. When confronted by a dog, a drill will instinctively stand and fight rather than flee in confusion. This usually gives the hunter ample opportunity to shoot and slaughter a whole troop in a matter of seconds. It's not known for sure how many drills remain in the wild, but the population is generally believed to be fewer than 10,000, and possibly as low as only 3,000. (Also see box on page 227.)

# CULTURE
## Family life

Family structures in Nigeria are shaped by religion and vary from one ethnic group to another, but almost all are male dominated. The practice of polygamy is not uncommon as it is allowed under Islamic law and in traditional culture; a Muslim male can have up to four wives with the consent of the others and the law requires him to provide for each wife equally. The status of Muslim women in Nigeria is similar to that in other Islamic countries. Most non-Muslim women enjoy more of a degree of freedom and influence family decisions, and work outside of the family home, and generally non-Muslim women have made more gains in Nigeria than other African countries. Marriage customs vary, but the payment of a bridal dowry is common throughout the country and the groom is expected to give money or property to the bride's family. Western-style dating is not common in rural areas, where arranged marriages are still sometimes practised, but is increasingly common amongst young people in the cities. Women usually marry by the time they are 20, men in their mid-20s, though living together before marriage is common, as many couples simply find a wedding to be too expensive. Names given to children at birth are usually based on events surrounding their birth – for example, we met lots of people called Sunday. Whilst over the last few decades there has been a great migration from rural areas to the cities, most Nigerians keep kinship alive and frequently visit their 'village', which is either their place of birth or where they might still have relatives living. This explains the massive amount of travelling people do all over Nigeria. I imagine that once upon a time, when Nigeria was largely rural, they were indeed visiting mostly villages. This is not always the case today – I met one lady and her husband who lived in Kaduna who were on their way home from visiting their 'village'. It turned out that their village was Bauchi – only a village of a couple of million people then?

## Art

In the north, because Islam frowns on the representation of people and animals, art forms such as ceremonial carvings are virtually absent, whilst in the south indigenous people had produced their own art long before the Europeans arrived. Nigerian crafts are grouped into textiles, pottery and ceramics; bronze, brass and iron works; woodworks, calabash decorations and leather works; and jewellery. Nigeria has over 2,000 years of art history, going back to the Iron-Age Nok culture that existed between 500BC and AD200. This era is represented by sophisticated terracotta sculptures found in present-day Kaduna State that depict the early life and spirituality of the Nok people. Here clay figures ranging in size from about 10cm–120cm, with detailed patterns of elaborate hairstyles, jewellery and clothing, were unearthed in the first few decades of the 20th century. Some of the sculptures can be seen in Nigeria's museums, but many were lost during the colonial period when they were taken overseas. Besides the Nok terracotta figures, Benin City is famous for its wax bronze casting, which decorated the palace of Benin for centuries before the British burnt and looted it at the end of the 19th century, though today there has been some revival of the art, and bronze casters again practise their unique tradition in Benin. The Yoruba are famous for their art and craftwork, and everything in this society was traditionally carved, from doors and drums to ritual masks. Doors were often covered with carved panels of scenes of everyday life, history, or mythology. Even the hinge posts were carved with figures. Their masks are simple facial carvings that represent different types of Yoruba religious people like the trader, the servant and the seducer, as well as the many Yoruba gods.

Cloth plays an important role in Nigerian society for use in traditional dress, and has been used as an item of trade for centuries. Although these days much of it is manufactured, traditional homemade weaving and dyeing techniques are still used by some women. These include Yoruba batik, which uses wax and natural dyes (such as the distinctive indigo) to depict traditional themes and motifs. *Adire* is the traditional Yoruba hand-painted cloth on which patterns are made by tying and stitching with raffia or cotton thread, or by using chicken feathers to paint cassava paste on the cloth which then acts as a resist dye, much like the wax method used on the batiks. *Asa-oke* is hand woven on horizontal looms and is sold in strips which are then sewed together to make material for men's gowns and women's scarves. Again, for centuries beads have been used as trade goods in Nigeria and indeed throughout all of West Africa. The earliest beads found so far date back to about the 9th century, and would have been traded via the long-established Sahara route. Even today they are worn by many Nigerians – men and women, young and old, and even babies. You'll see the most impressive beads around the necks of the chiefs and other dignitaries. Bead types and styles can symbolise wealth and status or they can be used to ward off evil. Apart from the old stuff, Nigeria has many good contemporary artists. See the *Oshogbo* section for more details – this town is undoubtedly the country's art capital.

## Festivals

Nigeria's cultural heritage is woven from threads of history, legend and conquest, and is rich in oral traditions, philosophy, rites and rituals, which are traditionally expressed through festivals. Nigeria has many local festivals that cover an enormous range of events, from harvest festivals, betrothal festivals and festivals marking events in traditional religions, to the investing of a new chief and funerals. It seems odd to Western ways of thinking to see a funeral as something to be celebrated, but for many of Nigeria's ethnic groups, death means joining the ancestors, and the deceased must get a good send-off. Many festivals feature dance, acrobatics, music and masquerades, though in modern Nigeria they have in recent years started to fall out of fashion and young Nigerians seem less intent to carry these traditions on (as is the case with traditional art). One that still seems to occur from time to time in the south is the Osun Festival at the Oshogbo Sacred Forest, generally held at the end of the rainy season (August to September), which pays homage to Osun, the Yoruba goddess of fertility and the river. The Iriji-Mmanwu (masquerade) Festival is sometimes staged in Enugu around August, with a colourful parade of masquerades from different parts of Igboland, considered in Igbo tradition to be a reincarnation of the dead with supernatural powers. The Benin Festival takes place at the end of the rainy season in Benin State, after the harvest has been gathered. Partly a kind of harvest festival, it's also an opportunity for eligible young men and women to take part in the matchmaking ceremony. The festival only occurs once every four years, and only the very wealthy can afford to have their children put on display, although everyone joins in the festival atmosphere. The people living in the Niger Delta hold the Ikwerre, Kalabari and Okrika festivals, to celebrate the water spirits of their region. The masqueraders wear carved headdresses that imitate the heads of fish or water birds. Many communities, including those in the north, have a version of the harvest festival. In the south, this is often a new yam festival, celebrated when the first of the season's yams are ready to eat, between August and October. This is also when the Maidens Coming of Age Festival is, when traditionally girls go into rooms to learn how to be good wives and mothers, and during this time they are allowed to eat the best of foods to emerge robust and radiant – the rooms are dubbed fattening rooms.

In the predominantly Muslim north, festivals are associated with Islam rather than the older traditional beliefs, and the Muslim year revolves around the three major festivals, Eid-el-Fitir, Eid-el-Kabir and Id Al Maulud. The main event in the Islamic calendar is Ramadan, a month-long observation of fasting. During the hours of sunlight no-one must eat or drink; some very religious people will not even swallow. Each evening at dusk there is a celebration of sorts, as the family prepares to break the fast. In towns people do so by going out to one of the markets, where stallholders will be prepared for the hungry people. At the end of Ramadan there is a celebration, which varies in style among the different Muslim groups. Also featured in northern communities are durbars, long lines of horsemen led by a band, the horses in quilted armour with the riders wearing quilted coats and wielding ceremonial swords. Usually celebrated to mark the annual Eid-el-Fitir and Eid-el-Kabir festivals in major cities of northern Nigeria, the durbar is a colourful parade of gaily dressed riders on horses and camels displaying their riding skills, battle readiness, and loyalty to the traditional institutions. Drumming, dancing and singing accompany the parade. Also in the north, the Argungu Fishing Festival occasion takes place in Argungu, in Sokoto State, during February or March. The festival involves traditional methods of fishing and dates back to the 16th century. During the festival, hundreds of local men and boys enter the water armed with large fishnet scoops, and the competition is to catch the biggest fish.

## Dress

One of the distinctive features of Nigeria, as in other countries in West Africa, is the brightly coloured and elaborate dress. Nigerian fabrics are known for their vivid colours and unique patterns, and there's a wide range of traditional dress distinctive to each ethnic group. Outside of the cities traditional dress is worn on an everyday basis. Traditional Nigerian dress for men is loose and comfortable and they usually wear caps when in their full regalia. *Buba* and *sokoto* is top and trousers, whilst *agbada,* mostly by worn by men in the north, is similar to *buba* and *sokoto* but has extra widths of material in the top which is then folded back across the shoulders in layers. A long man's dress without trousers is a *kaftan.* Some men in the north wear elaborate and heavy turbans, particularly those with some rank in the community, and the emirs, palace guards, chiefs and local dignitaries are always the best dressed, with grand flowing gowns and elaborate head gear. An *akede* is a woman's scarf, which most women use to make intricately folded and glamorous headdresses. On Sundays and special occasions they become bigger and shinier, and married women wear the largest and most complicated ones. An *oshoke* is a matching two-piece scarf set, one for the head and one draped around shoulders or tied around the waist. In the north Muslim women wear traditional headscarves, though not veils like in other strict Islamic countries, and their flowing dresses are even more colourful than in the south, with lots of bright patterns worn together. Most women in the south wear the traditional *iro* and *buba,* a long, wraparound skirt and short-sleeved top. Both men and women select fabric in the market and discuss with their tailors (who are all men) what sort of design they want for their outfits. On Sundays in the south you will see a glittering display of traditional clothing when everyone dresses up for church.

For women, despite frequently covering up their hair in headdresses, their hair is also an important aspect of their appearance and there are some wonderful plaited and weaved styles, some with extensions or with wire woven into it, and there are hairdressers everywhere, or more informally, ladies 'do' each other's hair whilst they tend to their stalls in the markets. For many ethnic groups facial scarring is also a method of decoration. If you can picture the singer Seal (who is Nigerian) you'll know what I mean. Faces are cut in slices around the corner of the mouth or nose or sliced in lines across the cheeks and sometimes neck.

## Music

Traditional Nigerian music is played on a number of instruments from an obo (a stringed zither), used during masquerade festivals in the villages of the Niger Delta, to trumpets heralding the arrival of an emir in the north, to the Yoruba 'talking' drum used to accompany a story teller of oral traditions – though you won't hear much traditional music in Nigeria these days, except at festivals or important ceremonies, and the average Nigerian listens to tapes of either church or pop music.

From independence to the late 1980s (when the last international record company packed up and left the country) Nigeria was a hotbed for African popular music and there was something of a renaissance in African music during this period thanks to some notable musicians that acquired worldwide fame and success. These include the world-renowned King Sunny Ade and Fela Kuti, and a number of types of music emerged from this era including juju, Afro-beat, highlife and makossa. These days the Nigerian live music scene is somewhat overrated. In recent years many of the more popular musicians have moved overseas – you're just as likely to hear a Nigerian band in London as in Lagos. At one concert we went to see at the Jazz Hole Bookshop, most of the musicians had airline tags on their instrument cases, and had flown in from overseas especially for the occasion, though the good people of Jazz Hole are attempting to revive Lagos's music scene, and at the time of writing they were planning a series of concerts over an annual calendar at a variety of venues.

One of the most phenomenal success stories in African music as a whole was the release of Prince Nico Mbarga's 1976 mega-hit 'Sweet Mother'. This heartfelt tribute of a son's affection and gratitude sold an amazing 13 million copies, and its mix of Nigerian highlife, Cameroonian ashiko, and Zairean rumba managed to please just about everyone on the entire continent of Africa. Prince Nico, the son of a Cameroonian father and a Nigerian mother, sang in Pidgin English.

Highlife is considered the first of Nigeria's contemporary music styles, with its origins in the 1930s in Ghana, and in Nigeria in the 1950s. It's like an early African jazz using wind and brass instruments, and is very easy to dance to. The first major Nigerian highlife star was Bobby Benson, who formed his first band in Lagos in 1947 and created such classic songs as 'Taxi Driver'. He was elected the first president of the Nigerian Musicians Union, formed in the independence year of 1960, and continued to be active in music until his death in 1983. Victor Olaiya and Rex Lawson are the other highlife greats.

Juju music is hugely popular all over West Africa and beyond. It was originally traditional Yoruba music before the guitar and other western instruments were introduced. It's essentially infectious dance music with upbeat tempo and rhythms, and the word is thought to be a corruption of the Yoruba word *jo jo*, meaning dance. In the early 1960s, Chief Commander Ebenezer Obey cut his first record in 1963, and was followed shortly by his main rival, King Sunny Ade, who released his first album in 1967. For decades these two battled it out over the juju throne, and Ade gained ascendancy when he was signed to Island Records in 1982. Following the success of reggae singer Bob Marley, Island was open to incorporating other world artists and in the early 1980s Nigerian music, and especially King Sunny Ade, enjoyed unprecedented international limelight. However, this was short-lived, and Island dropped the King after three albums. In

Nigeria, he occasionally still performs at the MUSON Centre as well as internationally.

Fuji music is traditional Yoruba Muslim music blended with the more contemporary juju sound. Ayinde Barnster and Wasiu Ayinde Marshall are famous Nigerian fuji artistes. Makossa is pop music imported from Cameroon, a mixture of highlife and soul; its rhythms are purely dance music. Afro-beat is a fusion of African music with jazz and soul played on non-African instruments such as guitars and saxophones. Its creator was the Nigerian Fela Kuti who studied music in London and who went on to discover James Brown and black politics in the US in the 1960s. When he returned to Nigeria, he created the lively Afro-beat music, sung in Pidgin English and mostly with a strong protest element. Songs such as 'Expensive Shit', 'Zombie', 'Sorrow, Tears and Blood', and 'ITT' (International Thief Thief), which attacked such targets as corrupt politicians, hypocritical businessmen, and societal suffering, earned him the enmity of the authorities. Fela's complete rejection of governmental authority through the establishment of his 'Kalakuta Republic' in the Surulere suburb of Lagos and his flagrant marijuana use were other challenges to the establishment, and the government unleashed a series of attacks on Fela, his family and property. Fela died of AIDS in 1997, but his son, Femi Kuti continues the musical tradition and regularly plays in Lagos and overseas. Another Nigerian Afro-beat and jazz musician popular today is Funsho Ogundipe, a pianist and a barrister living in the UK where he has a band which also returns to Lagos on occasion for concerts. Lagbaja! occasionally plays in Lagos at his own venue on the mainland, Motherlan'. He is a skilful saxophone player but also sings and tells stories about life in Lagos and is usually accompanied by a female vocalist. His fans haven't seen his face for many years as he always performs wearing a traditional Yoruba masquerade mask. In Yoruba, Lagbaja! means variously: somebody, anybody, everybody or nobody. It refers to those without identity, and Lagbaja! sings on behalf of the faceless masses.

Younger Nigerians tend to listen to the same chart-topping music as their contemporaries all over the world, and FM music radio stations are popular in the south. Especially popular are US rap bands, with the likes of Sean Paul occasionally performing in stadiums in Lagos. Up-and-coming Nigerian bands are following suit and aggressive rap is perhaps giving the more soulful and jazzy melodies of the music coined in the 1960s–70s a run for its money amongst Nigerian record labels.

## Sport

Nigerian sport only appeared on the international scene in the 1950s, with Nigeria's first appearance in the 1952 Olympic Games at Helsinki. Nigeria was awarded its first international medal in 1954, when Emmanuel Ifeanjuna won the gold in the high jump at the Commonwealth Games in Cardiff. Nigeria emerged on the international football scene in 1960 when it first entered the World Cup, but failed to qualify for the finals. It eventually qualified for the 1970 World Cup in Mexico, and the Nigerian National Football League was established in 1972. Since then Nigeria has consistently fared well internationally in the fields of football and athletics. Nigeria hosted the 2003 All Africa Games in Abuja, for which a new 60,000-seat National Stadium was built.

Football is hugely popular amongst millions of Nigerian men, and is played and watched throughout the country. *Everywhere*, whether it is a cleared spot in a city rubbish dump, a dusty pitch in the middle of a village, or even a pitch on an unfinished road, people play and watch football. If people don't have their own TVs showing local and European league games, they can watch football even in the smallest village or side street where a satellite TV will be set up for an important match. There is a small fee of, say, N10 to watch, and even in the remotest possible places we saw blackboards and scribbled posters proclaiming '*UK Premier Division; Liverpool v Blackburn; tonite; 19.30*', or '*Real Madrid qualifying match; here 18.00; with suya*' (barbecued meat). Football shirts are also hugely popular, and I saw hundreds of Michael Owens and perhaps thousands of David Beckhams! The Nigeria Football Association introduced the Professional League in 1990. Now the Nigerian Premier League, it is sponsored by one of the large telecommunications companies, Globacom, with 18 teams from throughout the country. Other football clubs feature in division two or three or in the amateur leagues. Nigeria has produced seasoned soccer players, both male and female, and the national Super Eagles team, who usually make it to the football World Cup, was until recently regarded as the best in Africa and one of the world's top football teams. The Super Eagles won the gold medal for football at the 1996 Olympics in Atlanta (when Nigeria also won long jump gold) and routinely do well in African competitions such as the FIFA Africa Cup of Nations. Nigeria last won this in 1994, but lost out to Cameroon on penalties in the final in 2000 when it was played in Nigeria. Nigeria's national female team won the African Women's League Championship in 1998. Nigeria made a bid for the first FIFA World Cup to be held on African soil in 2010, but lost out to South Africa.

In other sports, Nigerian athletes do well in the Olympics and have won a number of medals in track and field events. In professional boxing, Nigeria has produced three world champions – Hogan 'Kid' Bassey (featherweight, 1957–59); Dick Tiger (middleweight, 1962–63); and US resident Bash Ali (cruiserweight, 1987). Dozens of Nigerians are today professional athletes in Europe and in the US, and at the end of the 1990s, a Nigerian based in the US, Hakeem Olajuwon, was considered to be the best basketball player in the world. John Fashanu, the British footballer who used to play for Wimbledon and Aston Villa in the late 1980s–90s, Nwankwo Kanu, who used to play for Arsenal up until 2004, and currently plays for West Bromwich Albion, and Augustine 'Jay Jay' Okocha, who once played for the French club, Paris St Germain and at the time of writing was playing for Bolton Wanderers, are all Nigerian.

56

Bradt Travel Guides is a partner to the 'know before you go' campaign, masterminded by the UK Foreign and Commonwealth Office to promote the importance of finding out about a destination before you travel. By combining the up-to-date advice of the FCO with the in-depth knowledge of Bradt authors, you'll ensure that your trip will be as trouble-free as possible.

**www.fco.gov.uk/knowbeforeyougo**

**THE ULTIMATE TRAVEL MAGAZINE**

Launched in 1993, *Wanderlust* is an inspirational magazine dedicated to free-spirited travel. It has become the essential companion for independent-minded travellers of all ages and interests, with readers in over 100 countries.

A one-year, 6-issue subscription carries a money-back guarantee – for further details:

**Tel.+44 (0)1753 620426**
**Fax. +44 (0)1753 620474**

or check the *Wanderlust* website, which has

details of the latest issue, and where

you can subscribe on-line:

**www.wanderlust.co.uk**

# Planning and Preparation

2

## WHEN TO GO

Nigeria is consistently hot all year round with very little change in temperature, and in the south there is a constant uncomfortable humidity. Temperatures are highest from February to April in the south and from March to June in the north, and lowest from October to January over most of the country. This is the dry season which brings cooler temperatures but chaotic dry northeast winds, referred to locally as the Harmattan, that carry fine sand across the country from the Sahara. The dust–filled air during this time can be irritating and uncomfortable and appears as a dense fog. The Harmattan is more common in the north but affects the entire country except for a narrow strip along the southwest coast. However, the dry season is still the best time to go, as heavy rains during the rainy season (April–August) severely hamper travel when roads are flooded, motor parks become quagmires, and Lagos's streets turn into rivers of rubbish. On the coast, the rainy season kicks in earlier than in the rest of the country and starts in February or March through until August. It's best to avoid travel in the south during this time – the sky is continually overcast, it's hot, humid and wet, and if travelling by public transport, you'll need gum boots to wade through the mud in the motor parks.

## HIGHLIGHTS

If the truth be known, there is very little in the way of conventional sightseeing in Nigeria and the real joy of travelling here is meeting its culturally diverse peoples. Of the historic sights that do exist, they are very dilapidated, badly maintained or ignored, and Nigerians generally have little interest in their historical heritage. (The **Kano Wall** is a fine example – a thousand-year-old wall is today a sorry mound of earth that is covered in rubbish. People routinely dig out chunks of it and cart it home in wheelbarrows to be used as house bricks.) Nigeria also has an awful attitude to its natural heritage, as the several pitiful zoos and eight largely empty national parks attest to (as do all the bi-products made from dead animals found in the curio and *juju* markets). And there obviously has never been a tourism industry to support such things as old architecture or Nigerian animals.

There are other places in more remote spots of the extreme east of Nigeria along the border with Cameroon that few people have ever seen, and that are impossible to get to unless you are completely self-sufficient with your own 4WD vehicle: the **UNESCO World Heritage Site** at **Sukur** is a prime example, as are some of the national parks such as the **Gashaka-Gumpti National Park**, though for adventurous overlanders they are worth the effort of getting there and you are likely to be among the very first visitors to such attractions. Then there are other 'sights' that are perfectly accessible by public transport but are really not worth the effort of getting there – **Zuma Rock** near Abuja being our favourite 'why did we bother?'. The real reason for going to Nigeria is to immerse yourself in the cultures of millions of people, and to see how they live in a place where hardly anything works; to talk to people who have so much personality and rhythm in their souls; and to enjoy and embrace the unexpected, the bizarre, the enchanting, the appalling, the funny, and the downright obscure aspects of everyday life in Nigeria.

The Nigerian character can be enjoyed in all the main cities, and **Lagos** is without doubt West Africa's wildest and most vibrant metropolis, and despite the chaos, is the place where you can experience a few Western comforts. If Lagos becomes too overwhelming then leave the city and visit the other Yoruba towns in the cluttered southwest of the country. **Abeokuta** is famous for its sacred **Olumo Rock**, whilst **Ife**, as the centre of the Yoruba culture, has palaces and a museum, and **Oshogbo** has its eerie collection of weirdly shaped shrines in the **sacred forest**. If you are interested in the Yoruba culture then the better museums in this region are the **National Museum** in Lagos and the **Ibadan Museum**. Further to the east is **Benin City**, once the capital of a powerful and wealthy kingdom, where you can see examples of the traditional art of **bronze wax casting** in the museum and in the workshops along Igun Street. To the southeast of Nigeria where the River Niger spills into the creeks and watery channels of the **Niger Delta**, there are some nondescript towns that support the massive oil industry in the Delta. Because of ongoing disputes between the communities that live around the oil fields, not all of these are especially safe to visit (Warri was off limits when we were there). **Port Harcourt** to the extreme south is an industrial giant heaving with people, and far more interesting is the colonial town of **Calabar**, easily one of Nigeria's most relaxed and even relatively clean cities, with an excellent museum and a couple of conservation projects for Nigeria's endangered wildlife that are well worth a visit. To the north of Calabar are the dense tropical rainforests of Cross River State, some of which have been cordoned off into the newly established **Cross River National Park**. There are no facilities as yet for visitors, but it is possible to appreciate the forests at the **Afi Drill Ranch**, a sanctuary for the endangered drill monkeys and chimpanzees, easily one of the highlights of Nigeria.

Central Nigeria has a higher terrain of grassy plains dotted with outcrops of giant rocks. In the new capital of **Abuja** there is little to see, though people crossing Nigeria overland may need to stop here to obtain onward visas. Despite being less than 20 years old, the city is already of considerable size and has some Western trappings associated with governments and embassies such as large hotels and conference centres. To the east of Abuja is the pleasantly located city of **Jos** on a high plateau with nice countryside, which has an interesting line of museums. To the east of Jos is Nigeria's best-known national park, **Yankari National Park**, which still contains some wildlife, including a fairly healthy population of elephant. Here are the **Wikki Warm Springs**, a stunning swathe of mildly warm crystal-clear water in a forested valley.

The north of the country is dominated by the Hausa-Fulani walled cities that for over a thousand years have been powerful centres founded on trade and Islam. In these you will meet the more interesting of Nigeria's peoples, for whom traditional dress, language and deeply devout religion are an important part of everyday life. Some of the mosques here fill with thousands of worshippers for Friday prayers, and the **durbar festivals** at the end of Ramadan are among the most colourful and spectacular events in West Africa. In **Kano** are the famous **dye pits** that produce some of the traditional cloths of Nigeria, and the ancient and claustrophobic **Kurmi Market,** where for centuries trans-Sahara camel caravans exchanged a wealth of goods with the Hausa traders. In **Zaria** is a fine example of an emir's palace. To the extreme northeast are the shrinking watery channels of **Lake Chad**, once one of Africa's superlakes that has now largely disappeared, but if you make it this far you will be rewarded with the sight of the ancient Kanuri people, who still trade with people in Chad by canoe, and who could plausibly be one of the least-visited peoples of the world.

## RED TAPE

A **passport** (valid for at least six months and preferably with several blank pages) and a Nigerian **visa** are required for entry into the country. Visa exemptions are granted only to citizens of some of Nigeria's neighbouring West African countries. Nigerian embassies or consulates are located in the capitals of most European, North American and African countries together with Hong Kong, Tokyo and Canberra. Some countries may have several visa offices (for example Washington, New York and San Francisco in the United States). British consulates often represent Nigerian overseas missions if there is no Nigerian Embassy in the country. The two visas readers of this book are likely to apply for are the short-term visitors' visa, valid for a stay of not more than one month (though they are generally extendible in-country), or, for those going to work, the temporary work permit, issued to expatriate 'experts' to work on specific projects, which is initially valid for three months but which is extendible up to a maximum of six months (if the expat stays long-term it can be changed into a long-term residency visa). When applying for your visa, you need to produce (along with your passport) your return airline ticket, and maybe evidence of funds that you will spend in Nigeria, four passport pictures, and the non-refundable fee; at the time of writing this was £45 in the UK and US$100 in the US. If you are going to Nigeria to work, you will also need to produce a supporting letter from your employer stating the nature of your business and guaranteeing sufficient financial support for the visit. Generally, visa turnaround is three to seven days.

Once you have your visa, ensure that you make a photocopy of it and the passport page with your photograph on it. Some travellers choose to scan them in and store them at their email address so you can always access your documentation and print it out. For security reasons, it is advisable to detail all your important information on one document, photocopy it, leave a copy with family or friends at home and distribute copies through your luggage. Details might include things like passport and visa number, travel insurance policy details and 24-hour emergency contact number, and details of relatives or friends to be contacted in case of an emergency. However, whilst other guidebooks recommend that you also put credit card details and travellers' cheque numbers on this document, this is *not* the case for Nigeria, not because you aren't going to be able use either travellers' cheques or credit cards anyway, but because of the big prevalence of fraud.

If you are going to Nigeria to work or are staying a considerable time, it might be an idea to register with your embassy or high commission on arrival. They can advise you of travel warnings, keep records of next of kin, provide passport services, absentee voting arrangements etc. They will also put you on what is referred to as the Warden System, which enables them to contact you in case of an emergency in Nigeria. For UK citizens in Lagos this is not done actually at the embassy but at the Kingfisher Club in Ikoyi (see page 134 in the *Lagos* chapter, page 134, for details), the social club for the high commission, where there are forms to fill out.

Should there be any possibility that you will want to drive in Nigeria, obtain an **international driving licence** (available at post offices in the UK, and from www.nationalautoclub.com in the US, for a nominal fee). Whilst most expats have drivers, there are occasions at night and the weekends that they drive themselves. Overlanders will need additional paperwork for their vehicle such as a **carnet de passage**, registration document, and third-party insurance.

## Nigerian embassies and high commissions

The following countries have embassies unless otherwise stated. A complete list of Nigerian embassies and high commissions worldwide can be found at www.nigerianembassy.org.

**Australia** (High Commission) 7 Terrigal Crescent, O'Malley ACT 26, Canberra; tel: +61 6 286 5332

**Canada** (High Commission), 295 Metcalfe St, Ottawa, Ontario K2P 1R9; tel: +1 613 236 0521–3; 236 0527

**France** 173 Av Victor Hugo, 75116 Paris; tel: +33 1 47 04 68 65–6

**Germany** (Consulate-General) Platanen Strasse 98A, 13156 Berlin; tel: +49 30 477 2555; www.nigeria-online.de

**Ireland** 56 Leeson Park, Dublin; tel: +353 1 660 4366

**Italy** Via Orazio 14/18, 00193 Rome, tel: +39 6 6896231; www.nigerian.it

**Netherlands** Wagenaarweg 5, 2597 LL, The Hague; tel: +31 70 355 1110

**UK** (High Commission) 9 Northumberland Av, London WC2N 5BX; tel: 020 7839 1244; www.nigeriahc.org.uk

**USA** 3519 International Court, Washington DC 20008; tel: +1 020 986 8400; www.nigeriaembassyusa.org

If you are travelling overland from Europe, you will most probably need to get a Nigerian visa en route. Below are some of the embassies in countries north of Nigeria. By all accounts, and speaking to experienced overlanders, the Nigerian High Commission in Accra is the best bet.

**Algeria** BP 629, Alger Gare, Algiers; tel: +213 2 693278/693726

**Côte D'Ivoire** Embassy of Nigeria, 35 Bd de la République, 01-BP 1906, Abidjan; tel: +225 1 222658/212291

**Ghana** (High Commission) Josif Broz Tito Av, Accra; tel: +233 21 776158/776159/777280

**Morocco** 70 Av Umar Ibn El Khattab Agdat, Rabat; tel: +212 7 78325/770367

## GETTING THERE
## By air

Nigeria's international airports are Murtala Mohammed International Airport, Lagos, Aminu Kano International Airport, Kano, Port Harcourt International Airport, and Nnamdi Azikiwe International Airport, Abuja. Many international airlines operate to and from Nigeria and there are a huge number of flights – not, unfortunately, because lots of tourists are visiting the country, but because many millions of Nigerians want to live anywhere else in the world but Nigeria. Established airlines serving Nigeria include Air France, British Airways, Egypt Air, Ethiopian Airlines, Ghana Airways, Kenya Airways, KLM, Lufthansa, Emirates, South African Airways, Swiss (formerly Swissair) and Virgin, variously offering good connections with London, Paris and Dubai, and a number of Dutch and German cities, as well as with Addis Ababa, Nairobi and Johannesburg in east and southern Africa. Since the demise of the national airline, Nigeria Airways, in 2003, there have been no direct flights to/from the US, so US travellers must at present pass through Europe. By the time you read this, though, Continental Airlines may have begun a service between New York and Lagos, currently announced for end 2005. This will be the only scheduled non-stop trans-Atlantic service to Nigeria. In September 2004, the Nigerian government signed an agreement with Virgin for the establishment of a new airline, Virgin Nigeria (www.virginnigeria.com), to be based at Murtala Mohammed International Airport in Lagos. Plans are yet to be finalised, but it is envisaged that the company will operate both on international routes to destinations in the Middle East, the USA and Europe, and on regional and domestic routes.

From Lagos to London, it's a six-hour flight. Virgin's first baby was born on a London–Lagos flight in March 2004 to Nigerian parents, and the plane had to be diverted back to Lagos. Most airlines fly to Lagos, but KLM fly between Amsterdam and Abuja and Kano, Virgin between London and Port Harcourt, and Air France between Paris and Port Harcourt. Note that Air France accepts Thomas Cook travellers' cheques in all their Nigerian offices.

With all these airlines serving Nigeria you should be able to get a competitively priced ticket from Europe, but be warned the flights are very popular and fill up quickly. The Emirates and Kenya Airways (via Nairobi) flights from Lagos to Dubai are extremely popular with wealthy Nigerians on shopping trips, and the London–Port Harcourt flight is one of Virgin's most profitable routes. London especially has dozens of travel agents specialising in cheap flights to Africa, many of which can be combined for onward travel. Remember, it is essential that you have a return or onward ticket to get a visa for Nigeria. For a starter you can try these, most of which have several branches around the UK and some of which have outlets in Australia, New Zealand and the US: **Bridge the World**, www.b-t-w.co.uk; **Flight Centre**, www.flightcentre.com; **STA Travel**, www.sta-travel.com; and **Trailfinders**, www.trailfinders.com.

## By sea
You can actually get to Nigeria by boat from Cameroon, but this is not for the faint-hearted and I have heard stories about motor boats packed full of people simply disappearing. Boats arrive and depart from Orun in Cross River State and this is dealt with under the Calabar section.

## Overland
The major overland route from Europe through West Africa roughly runs through Morocco, Mauritania, Senegal, Mali, Burkina Faso, Ghana, Togo, Benin, Nigeria and Cameroon. From Cameroon it's sometimes possible to cross into East Africa via Chad and Sudan but this route is routinely closed due to unrest in these countries. You can do all or part of this epic journey with an overland company (see below) or in your own vehicle, though of course you will have to be fully kitted out and self-sufficient, with a 4WD and all the gear. For inspiration to start your own overland, visit www.africa-overland.net, which is the website for the Africa Overland Network and which has lots of useful information and links to over 200 websites of people's individual trips by landie, bicycle and motorbike.

You can enter Nigeria by road from Benin, Cameroon and Niger. The easiest and quickest route is from Zinder in Niger through to Kano, then west to Maiduguri, and into Cameroon at Mora. But it's much more interesting to continue south to Jos and then on down to Calabar via perhaps Yankari National Park. The alternative overland route is from Benin along Nigeria's coastal highway, the fastest route between Lagos and Cameroon. When crossing into Nigeria get rid of all money from the previous country as it's hard to change once across the border. Also fill up with diesel, as diesel is not always available everywhere in Nigeria. Once in Nigeria fill jerry cans or water tanks whenever you can, as water is also hard to get (for a small fee you can fill up from public taps). Finally, if you're not in your own vehicle, public transport links the closest cities in the neighbouring countries with the closest cities in Nigeria, so feasibly backpackers can move about from country to country.

### Via Benin

The principal link and the busiest border crossing is at Kraké on the Benin side of the Badagry–Lagos Expressway. Roads on both sides are tar-sealed and in reasonably good condition, but the traffic's heavy and the border is notoriously slow. You can get public transport from Cotonou direct to Lagos. Alternatively get yourself to Porto Novo on the Benin side and cross into Nigeria at the Idi-oroko border post some 30km to the north of Kraké. From here the road goes to Ikeja in northern mainland Lagos, and public transport from Porto Novo arrives at the Oshodi Motor Park from where you could feasibly get transport for onward travel without going into Lagos proper if you didn't want to. Recommended to me by one of the overland companies is the crossing at Kétou, on the Benin side, which is approximately 120km north of Porto Novo via Pobé. Andi from *Oasis Overland* says the following: 'Customs is in Kétou town; 17km further on is Benin immigration, and then you need to go to the Nigerian immigration which is very easy to miss as it's not on the road at all. Ask lots of people for directions. Meko is the first town on the Nigerian side 10km further on. You can change money with the border guys. This is a good border and really quiet. After Meko for 5-10km the road is dirt and is really bad, with huge potholes, then it's tar-seal to Abeokuta.'

### Via Cameroon and Chad

There are two principal borders between Nigeria and Cameroon, one in the south near Ikom north of Calabar and one in the north near Maiduguri. Mfun border is 30km to the east of Ikom where the road is tar-seal to the border. Here there is a rather grand suspension bridge over the Cross River, which forms part of the border. From Ekok, the first town on the Cameroon side, you simply walk down the hill to the Cameroon customs and immigration sheds before crossing the bridge to complete the Nigerian formalities on the other side. There are hotels and money changers in Ekok if you get stuck here. In Cameroon there are bush taxis from Mamfé to the border on a horrendous road, and there are regular vehicles on the Nigerian side to Ikom. There is another road directly from Calabar to this border but it's not tar-sealed and I hear it's in very bad shape. It may be better to go the long way round via Ikom if coming from Calabar. Andi from Oasis Overland says of this border: 'The Nigerian side was very easy and only took an hour; we just had to fill out a few forms. The dirt road on the other side was terrible, with huge. deep ruts. It took us five hours to go 20km once we were in Cameroon and we had to keep stopping to build the ditches up as the bottom lockers of the truck were scraping the ground and we had to remove the exhaust. Avoid this road if it's wet.'

The main crossing in the north is from Mora in Cameroon to Maiduguri. This is an infrequently used border and relatively simple to negotiate; again the road on the Cameroon side is nothing more than a rough track, though the Nigerian side is tar-sealed. From Mora it is possible to get a vehicle to the border and change there on to one to Maiduguri; vehicles are fairly frequent, and money changers hang out on both sides of the border. If you are in your own vehicle this is the most sensible crossing if you want to go to Waze National Park in Cameroon. If you want to go to Chad (despite sharing a border with Chad, Nigeria and Chad do not have a road crossing), the best border to cross is the Ngala border, in the extreme northeast of the country about 140km east of Maiduguri, that crosses to Fotokol on the Cameroon side, where the road leads directly across a 100km bottleneck of Cameroon to Kousséri. Here a bridge over the confluence of the Chari and Logone rivers links Kousséri with the capital of Chad, Ndjamena, on the other side. From Maiduguri, get a vehicle to Ngala, and another to cover the short distance to the border, and then a bush taxi on the Cameroon side to take you to Kousséri. The total journey is roughly 250km and can be managed in a day. You'll need a visa for Chad but if you are only crossing this small section of Cameroon and not going elsewhere in the country, transit visas are issued at the border at each end.

## Via Niger

There are several tar-sealed roads between Niger and Nigeria that many Hausa traders use frequently. The most common crossing and the closest to the Niger capital of Niamey, is from Birnin-Nkonni in Niger to Ilela in Nigeria, 85km north of Sokoto. The other main crossings are Maradi in Niger to Katsina, 45km from the border; and Zinder in Niger to Kano, which is roughly 140km from the border. All crossings are reasonably straightforward and roads are tar-sealed, though they do have a few potholes. In Niger, there are buses from Niamey to the borders at Birnin-Nkonni and Maradi, and another service to Zinder, from all of which you can get public transport to the borders themselves, though the best bet is Birnin-Nkonni, which is right on the border itself. Here you can find a bush taxi going directly to Sokoto. In Maradi, you can get a bush taxi to the border town of Dan-Issa and change vehicles there for onward travel to Katsina in Nigeria, and in Zinder you can again get a bush taxi to the border, where you can change on to another one heading towards Kano.

## Tour operators

The only operators to go through Nigeria are the overland operators. The ones listed below are reputable companies with decades of experience in the overland game, running trans-Africa overland tours through West Africa at least once or twice a year. Generally, the trucks spend two to three weeks in Nigeria crossing from the Benin border through Abuja, and then out of Nigeria to Cameroon in the southeast. Few trucks now go through Lagos, as visas for onward countries are now obtainable in Abuja, but there's no reason why you can't jump truck for a few days if you want to visit Lagos or elsewhere.

**Oasis Overland** Tel: 01963 363400; email: info@oasisoverland.co.uk; www.oasisoverland.co.uk. Oasis run a yearly trip departing from the UK in November and finishing in Cape Town in June, and if there is space you can also jump on or off at Accra in Ghana or at Nairobi in Kenya.
**African Trails** Tel: 020 7706 7384; email: sales@africantrails.co.uk; www.africantrails.co.uk. African Trails operates in much the same way as Oasis and they have two departures a year from the UK in March and November, arriving in Cape Town in September and June respectively.
**Dragoman** and **Encounter** Tel: 01728 861133; email: info@dragoman.co.uk; www.dragoman.com. Encounter run one overland a year from the UK to Cape Town departing in August, and one in reverse departing from Cape Town in November that takes between 34 and 35 weeks, but again you can jump on and off in Accra, Nairobi or Livingstone in Zambia. Dragoman has two departures per year between the UK and Cape Town in each direction that take 30 weeks; they leave from both in August and September, but these long trips are broken into much shorter sections – the one that covers Nigeria is the 4½-week Accra–Douala tour.

# WHAT TO TAKE

It is necessary to put some thought into what to take to Nigeria. This is because of the fact that you need to dress for the constant heat and humidity and, at certain times of the year, the rain, because both men and women should adhere to a certain dress code in the Muslim north, and because medical supplies and other basic necessities are inadequate or are simply not available. The initial choice is to take everything that you may possibly need, but at the same time, it's important not to carry too much. You need to strike a balance, something that probably depends on personal experience more than anything else.

## Carrying luggage

Unless you are only ever going to see Nigeria from the compound of the Sheraton Hotel, Nigeria is not a place where you want to lug several suitcases around, or even leave them free-standing for any length of time. Keep luggage small and light enough to keep on you at all times while you travel until you can safely deposit it in a hotel room. If you are travelling by public transport, space for luggage in vehicles is extremely limited, and you will often have to put your luggage on your knees. You need to take strong luggage that will survive bouncy potholed roads, sudden breaking by manic drivers, and the brute force of vehicle conductors, who fill every conceivable space in a vehicle with luggage and people. And rather uniquely to Nigeria, because of the traffic (and human) congestion, you cannot always rely on taxis in the form of cars to take you from A to B – for example, often a motor park will be on the edge of town, and the only way to get into town and to a hotel is to cover the distance by *okada* (motorbike taxi), as inner-city public transport has even less room for luggage than inter-city transport.

This is what we went with and we did OK: I had a 20-litre daypack and a small canvas bag worn across the chest; Darren had a 50-litre backpack and a camera bag worn across the chest. Between us we could fit in everything we needed and more, including extensive camera equipment, and we managed to travel on hundreds of *okadas* reasonably comfortably. We found that having two different-sized backpacks appeased many of the drivers and conductors – they only had to find space for the bigger one, whilst the smaller one and the camera bag could be kept on our knees if necessary. We also had the option of carrying just the daypack between us during excursions. Extra items we carried between us were a camera tripod and an 'Effie' – a plastic Thermos lunch bucket we had to buy in Nigeria to carry and keep cool camera film (specifically near hot car engines) and named after a very nice driver called Effiong we met in Lagos who ate his lunch out of a similar bucket.

Avoid taking a backpack with several pockets on the outside and if possible lock the zips with padlocks. There is the danger of wandering hands making their way inside unlocked pockets not just in hotels or on public transport but also by baggage handlers at the airports (and not just in Nigeria). If you can, get one with one of those extra flaps that cover the straps on a backpack as this helps to avoid damage when the pack is shoved into small spaces in vehicles. The only other problem we encountered with packs and public transport was the dirt and sometimes oil on the floor of the vehicles, which of course leaves nasty stains on your clothes once you put your pack on your back – insist that your luggage goes in the back of the vehicle at all times if possible.

## Clothes

Nigerians are generally snappy dressers and the various dresses, robes and head gear they wear are quite spectacular and colourful. It always amazed me how neat and unruffled Nigerians looked in their elaborate clothing, while we managed to attract all the dirt and melted in the heat. Women travellers to Nigeria should **dress modestly**, and respect local customs regarding dress, especially in the Muslim north, where it is inadvisable for women to even wear trousers. But a word of advice for the ladies – if wearing a long skirt, ensure that it is quite full; I had a few problems sitting astride an *okada* in a too-tight long skirt that showed too much leg. As hard as it is not to wear typical summer clothes in such heat it is important to cover up. Both men and women should avoid revealing shoulders and legs, and women should avoid tight-fitting clothing, bare midriffs, cleavage etc. A staunch Muslim emir in northern Nigeria will not want to see your belly ring. If you are on business in Nigeria, a lightweight suit and tie may be necessary for men for formal meetings, and a jacket in some upmarket restaurants. If it's the rainy season, you'll need a light raincoat, and you may want to throw in swimwear and shorts (only to be worn at the beach). You are very unlikely to need anything warm to wear anywhere except at the top of Obudu Plateau.

Take **light cotton clothes**, not heavy material like denim or even T-shirt material (heavy, hot, and takes forever to dry), but thin (not transparent) cotton pants, skirts and loose-fitting shirts. Ideally, you want fabrics that you can rinse out each night when there is water available; hang them up over the back of a chair, and with the help of a little air conditioning, they will be dry by morning. Remember that Nigeria is hot and humid all year round – you will sweat a lot walking around the streets in the humidity and crowded public transport, so expect to have to wash your clothes at the end of each day when possible. Small packets of washing powder are available to buy for next to nothing, so if you have clothes that can be easily washed and dried, than you will have to take very little with you. Once in Nigeria, manufactured clothes are available in all the markets but they are not especially cheap. Fabric is also available everywhere and most Nigerians who wear traditional clothing choose a fabric and then get a tailor to make up a dress or robe.

**Shoes** are a personal choice, given that you'll be trudging around a fair number of rubbish-filled streets: boots or trainers are unbearably hot but offer greater protection from the filth, whilst thongs or sandals are cooler but less protective. Careful choice of open shoes is needed to give better protection. We found that the only time closed shoes were essential was in the national parks and forests in the east of Nigeria where the insects and ants were a constant problem. Finally, my own personal recommendation for both men and women, and an item I never go travelling without, is a **sarong**, or a more masculine East African version, a *kikoi*. They have a multitude of uses and take up very little room. The obvious use is as a wrap-around long skirt for women and men (this is very acceptable all over Africa), or if you suddenly have to cover up, say when leaving the beach. They can be used for shade, as a towel (as they are quick drying and much lighter than a fluffy version), or as a woman's headscarf. If it's unbearably hot at night or you have a temperature, you can lie underneath a sarong soaked in cold water. And finally, you can even use your sarong to tie up your laundry.

## Other useful items

Most budget travellers carry the obligatory **sleeping bag**. This is not necessary in Nigeria, where it never cools down enough for you to want to climb into it. Unless you are in an overland vehicle you won't be camping anywhere and most hotels provide adequate bedding. All you really need is a **sheet sleeping bag**, something you can easily make yourself, to use in places where the sheets look somewhat dubious. Very few hotels provide a **towel** so take a small hand towel, a travel towel or a sarong. Other **basics** include medical kit (discussed in chapter four) sunglasses, torch and spare batteries, alarm clock, sun protection cream, and a Swiss army knife or Leatherman. Also essential is a **money belt** that's not too big and that has an elastic waistband, as this will make it far more comfortable when you're scrunched up in a minibus. **Toiletries** should be kept to a minimum and basics like soap, toilet paper and toothbrushes and toothpaste are readily available in Nigerian markets (in motor parks just look out for the toothbrush man with everything you need for oral hygiene perched on his head), though items that Nigerians are less likely to use, such as razors, shampoo and conditioner, and deodorant, are only available in the few upmarket supermarkets dealing in imported goods, and are very expensive. Also, beware of buying toiletries such as moisturisers and face cream in Nigeria – their shelf life is dubious and counterfeit products abound. Items that are not easily found once there include contact lens solution, sanitary products, mosquito repellent and medical supplies, so bring enough with you to cover the length of your stay. Quite frankly I would suggest leaving **contact lenses** at home and reverting to glasses. Darren, who has had his eyes zapped by lasers, claimed that there was no way he could have coped with wearing lenses in Nigeria. The tremendous dust, pollution, the fact that you are constantly going in and out of air conditioning, and the fact that your hands may never be entirely clean when putting them in and taking them out, leads to all sorts of irritations and possible infection. Other items you may want to consider taking are a **cell phone** and charger (plus adaptor if your charger doesn't have a three-pin British-style plug). If your phone is on international roaming, you can get cell phone reception just about all over Nigeria, and whilst you may not have much luck getting through to any Nigerian telephone numbers, it's good to carry one in the event of an emergency. A **calculator** is useful to work out exchange rates, and I never go anywhere without one of those **electrical elements** and a Thermos cup to make tea first thing in the morning. There will be the opportunity to read **books**, on long journeys and perhaps by torchlight when the power and the TV go off. Rather than lugging expensive novels around, buy cheap, locally produced books in Nigeria at the various bookshops – Nigeria is well known for its writers and this is a good opportunity to delve into some Nigerian literature. Finally, something that I didn't think about taking but wished I had, was a **plug**. All washbasins and baths in Nigerian hotels are plugless, so to wash with a limited amount of water or to wash your clothes, you may want to consider bringing a universal plastic plug, usually found in travel-gear shops.

# In Nigeria

For a glossary of Nigerian phrases, see *Appendix 2*, page 332.

## INFORMATION

Nigeria has a network of tourism offices, but you'll be hard pushed to actually get any tourist information out of them. Most come under the wing of the **Nigerian Tourism Development Council** (NTDC) which has its central offices in Abuja. The NTDC has a few regional offices and they are well staffed (though what these people do all day is beyond me), but if you were to go into any of these offices and present yourself as a tourist and ask for some information, the above-mentioned staff are likely to fall off their chairs. Other than a few dusty leaflets that were printed circa 1975, they usually haven't got anything to give out or any information to tell you. It's not that they are unfriendly or unhelpful, just that they have *no* tourist information. In addition to branches of the NTDC there are some **state tourist offices** which are just as ineffectual, and where you will be required to make an appointment. All of these offices are nothing more than government or state civil service departments employing people to sit at empty desks (in one I went in to someone was sleeping at his desk). I also found that most of the staff simply did not understand our need for tourist information and I had to go through a whole rigmarole of making appointments with the local director, who invariably had nothing to offer and who politely wanted to know what I was doing wasting his time. I even found this at the head office of the Nigerian Tourism Development Council in Abuja, where we struggled to talk to anyone. In short, *there is no tourist information,* so don't bother trying to find these offices. If you are in Nigeria long-term, it might be worth contacting the **Nigerian Field Society**, which is run by a bunch of expats, as they occasionally organise field trips out of Lagos, particularly to the durbar festivals in the northern cities. You'll find up-to-date telephone numbers if you ask around expat circles or visit www.nigerianfield.org.

## Maps

There are three country-specific maps of Nigeria available: The *Spectrum Road Map, Nigeria* (1:1,500 000) was last published in 2002 by Spectrum Books in Nigeria, and is available there at many of the bookshops; *Nigeria* (1:1,900,000) from International Travel Maps, Vancouver, Canada (ISBN 1553413512), www.itmb.com; and *Nigeria Road Map* (1:1,500 000) from Freytag & Berndt, Wein, Germany. All are perfectly functional, though they're a little outdated and as such do not show some of the new roads and the new names for the national parks that were created out of old game reserves. Of the three, the one from International Travel Maps, on which the regional maps in this book are based, is the most detailed as well as the most lightweight. The *West Africa* Michelin map is very detailed for Nigeria, with fairly accurate kilometre markings, and is essential if travelling through West Africa overland.

## PUBLIC HOLIDAYS

| | | | |
|---|---|---|---|
| January 1 | New Year's Day | May 1 | Labour Day |
| October 1 | National Day | | |

In addition, both Christian and Muslim holy days are celebrated throughout the entire country. Muslim holidays vary according to the lunar calendar and include *Maulid an-Nabi,* which is Mohammed's birthday, usually celebrated in September or October; *Idul Fitr,* a three-day feast that ends the month-long fast of Ramadan; and *Idul Adha,* a feast that commemorates the faith and obedience of the prophet Ibrahim (Abraham) in his preparedness to sacrifice his own son, usually held in June or July. Christian holidays include Easter (Friday to Monday), Christmas Day (December 25), and Boxing Day (December 26).

## MONEY

Nigeria's unit of currency is the naira (pronounced *nieera*), which is written as an 'N' preceding numbers. 1 naira (N) = 100 kobo (k). Notes are in denominations of N500, 200, 100, 50, 20, 10 and 5. Coins are in denominations of 10k, 25k, 50k and N1, though you will rarely come across any coins as these are hardly used in everyday transactions, even if they are still legal tender. The following figures are included as a guide to the movements of the Nigerian naira against the pound sterling and the US dollar in recent years:

| | 2001 | 2002 | 2003 | 2004★ | 2005 (April) |
|---|---|---|---|---|---|
| US$1 | N115 | N118 | N127 | N138 | N133 |
| GB£1 | N165 | N170 | N200 | N243 | N256 |

★ used in researching this guide

### Foreign exchange

Changing foreign currency into naira is not easy to do, despite there being banks *everywhere*. In Lagos alone there are over 90 bank companies (with many branches) but **they don't change money!** Very oddly, the banks give out US$ cash but don't take it in. Many are affiliated with Western Union, and offer a service of supplying US$ cash. I can only presume this is because of the large amount of Nigerians that travel abroad. The best currency to take to Nigeria is the good old greenback (US$) – you'll have a great deal of difficulty changing anything else. In fact you'll have a great deal of difficulty changing anything. There is an active and tolerated black market in Nigeria referred to as the 'parallel market', which offers slightly higher exchange rates than the official bank rate (not that any bank actually changes money) published in the newspapers alongside the black market rate. You are very likely to have to resort to changing money with black marketeers on the street. The most daunting time will be on arrival at the airport in Lagos (and the other international airports) where your only option is to change money outside the airport terminal with the money changers in the car park. If you don't want to do this, the only suggestion I can give here is to try and negotiate a taxi ride from the airport to your chosen hotel in US$ (apart from in a couple of the most exclusive hotels, this is perhaps the only time in Nigeria that you can pay for something in US$ in the place of naira). Once at your hotel, ask the hotel reception where the nearest place is to change money. You will inevitably need naira to check in and pay the deposit. When changing money on the street (this is actually deemed acceptable in Nigeria) try and go to the money changer's office or shop if possible, and count out the naira carefully before handing over your US$. If you feel hurried or distracted, abort the transaction immediately. You'll find that you'll get a lower exchange rate for small denomination US$ notes than for bigger ones, so in Nigeria small notes are not much use. Most Nigerian money changers are sharp businessmen with whom you may have to haggle over the exchange rate, but most are also pretty straightforward and honest, and you'll experience few problems.

In this guide, I have listed the very few places where you can change money, and as there are only a handful around the country, read ahead and make sure that there is somewhere to change money to avoid being caught short. Basically, my advice is to change money when you can. One piece of advice is to approach other foreigners – expats or Lebanese businessmen. Many expats get some of their salary paid in naira and may be happy to change it over into hard currency. Then there are a few Lebanese shops and restaurants where the Lebanese owners may also be happy to change money given that they import much of their produce. There are a clutch of bureaux de change, which I have listed, but many of them are attached to more upmarket hotels, and will sometimes insist that they only offer a foreign exchange service to hotel guests. If you get stuck it is still worthwhile asking at these, even if you're not staying at the hotel. If you get *really* stuck, you might want to approach an actual bank and talk very nicely to the manager, who may grudgingly exchange a small amount of money, say US$100, at a very poor rate, but don't rely on this.

Travellers' cheques or credit cards are not recommended. There is a very real risk of credit card fraud, and the only place I heard of that would perhaps be willing to change Thomas Cook travellers' cheques in Lagos, if not the whole of Nigeria, was the Thomas Cook/Travelex office at 23 Marina Street, Lagos Island. It's on the 13th floor of the Maman Kotangoro building and you need to ask for Stella. Don't hold your breath.

If you are travelling overland and arrive in Nigeria on a land border, it's usually possible to exchange both US$ cash and East and West CFAs (Communauté Financiére de l'Afrique) used in the West Africa Francophile countries, with money changers at the border, though you are going to get a poorer rate than elsewhere. When I spoke to people who came through on overland trucks from the Republic of Benin, their advice was to fill up the truck with diesel in Benin (diesel is only found sporadically in Nigeria, though petrol is not such a problem) and to change enough money at the border to cover the journey to Abuja (where money changers near the Sheraton offer a much better exchange rate – see page 248). All overlanders will inevitably end up in Abuja as this is where they obtain onward visas. Note, the Western CFA is used in certain countries to the west of Nigeria: Benin, Togo, Burkina Faso, Ivory Coast, Mali, Senegal, Guinea-Bissau, and Niger to the north of Nigeria. The Eastern CFA is used in countries to the east of Nigeria: Cameroon, Chad, Central African Republic, Gabon, Equatorial Guinea, and the Republic of Congo. The two types of CFA are not interchangeable, so if you are crossing Nigeria overland you need to get rid of either excess Western or Eastern CFAs (depending in which direction you are travelling in) at the border.

Finally, it's important to remember that the climate in Nigeria will make you sweat. On more than a couple of occasions I fished out some rather damp US$100 notes from my money belt to exchange with a Lebanese shop owner who was not impressed! Keep your money in a plastic bag.

## Small change

You'll need to keep a lot of your naira in small change – preferably N20 notes, which are the most useful. It is my theory that Nigeria prints more of these than any other note, as this is seemingly the cost for any vehicle to get through a road block, and inexplicably there are many newer N20 notes than any other notes. N10 and N5 notes are very old and rarely seen, and are not of much use, except perhaps for buying packets of *pure water* or a small snack such as peanuts. N20s are very useful for short bus fares, *okada* trips and soft drinks, and if the vendor or driver can't give you change from a N20 then it's not going to really matter. Most notes are pretty dirty and have changed hands thousands of times. People *hold* money all the time – just look out for the conductors in the motor parks or market traders and you will see them constantly counting the wedge of cash in their hands.

## Prices

Nigeria is not the cheapest of African countries, even for Nigerians. As budget travellers we got around on roughly US$50–60 a day for two people and quite frankly I don't think we could have done it for much less. This amount did however cover accommodation, local food, extensive long-distance travel by public transport, frequent short-distance transport around the cities, and the odd entry fee and dash (see *Dashing*, page 90) for a guide. Prices for food and accommodation are fixed, though the cost of inter-city or intra-city transport varies depending on distance, type of vehicle and the haggling power of the individual, and you may spend an average of about US$10 a day if moving around by bush taxis, minibuses and *okadas*. We paid on average about US$15 for a double room and perhaps about US$8 each on food and the odd beer. Expect to spend more in Lagos; the cost of accommodation and restaurant meals, and even *okada* rides, is much more here than it is in the rest of the country (see the *Lagos* chapter for some idea of prices). A business traveller who stays and eats in the best hotel in any city and pays for what is generally known as car hire (comes with a driver) may spend upwards of US$200–300 a day. Lagos expats who have some experience of costs and facilities in Nigeria can feasibly move around Nigeria with their own vehicles and stay at mid-range hotels for around US$50 for two, and eat at the few upmarket restaurants for roughly US$25 for a meal for two with drinks.

I have usually kept prices in the guide in naira; partly because of the confusing deposit system used in Nigerian hotels, where prices are neatly rounded up in naira (this would look a bit odd in US$), and partly because prices in Nigeria have been consistent for a long time and are likely to remain so. In addition, you will have to pay for everything in naira so it's more useful to know exactly how many N1,000s you'll need. The naira has been pretty steady against the US dollar in recent years and when talking in dollars I have used N138=US$1 and N243=£1 as the exchange rates. To help you digest the prices, work in N1,000s – N1,000 is just over US$7 or £4.10.

## GETTING AROUND
### By air

There are 20 regional airports in Nigeria and many of Nigeria's state capitals have their own airports so in theory it is feasible to travel around by air. Some 7.26 million Nigerians took domestic flights in 2003 and there are about 30 different airlines. At the bigger airports such as Lagos and Abuja, you just pitch up for a ticket at the airport, though in the smaller cities some of the airlines have desks in local hotels where you can purchase a ticket. On a flight from Lagos to Abuja with Bellview, we had Dulux paint charts in our seat pockets! Given that nobody paints anything in Nigeria, this was one of our 'obscure moments of the day'.

Domestic airfares are reasonably cheap, though they vary slightly by N1,000–2,000 between the various airlines. Expect to pay roughly the following: Lagos–Abuja, N9,000; Lagos–Jos, N9,000–10,000; Lagos–Kaduna, N10,000; Lagos–Port Harcourt, N9,000–10,000; Lagos–Warri, N8,000; Lagos–Maiduguri,

N22,000; Lagos–Benin City, N6,000–7,000; Lagos–Calabar, N10,000–11,000; Lagos–Kano, N10,000; Lagos–Sokoto, N11,000; Lagos–Yola, N20,000; Lagos–Enugu, N9,000. There are scores of additional fares from Abuja to these destinations and between the other cities, but you can get an idea of price versus distance from the above. Schedules are frequently changed without notice. Below are some of the flights on offer; the airlines are too numerous to mention in full (see also the *Getting there and away* sections of destination chapters); **Sosoliso Airlines** flies between Lagos and Enugu three times a day, and Lagos and Port Harcourt twice a day, on Monday, Tuesday, Wednesday and Thursday. **Bellview Airlines** operates five flights a day between Lagos and Abuja, three flights a day between Lagos and Port Harcourt, and one flight a day between Lagos and Kano (this departs Lagos at 06.50 and returns from Kano at 11.30). **Aero Contractors** has one daily flight to Abuja, two to Port Harcourt and two to Warri that all return on the same day, with one less flight at the weekends. Very, very usefully, all domestic airline schedules and prices can be found online at www.enigeria.org. Some of the more popular airlines include:

**Aero Contractors** Tel: 01 774 9723
**ADC Airlines** Tel: 01 496 5750
**Bellview Airlines** Tel: 01 493 1731/5, 497 0061, 497 7715; email:
reservation@flybellview.com; www.bellviewair.com. Bellview is the only airline to fly out of Nigeria, and at the time of writing it had services to Abidjan, Accra, Banjul, Conakry, Doula, Dakar, Freetown and Monrovia.
**Sosoliso Airlines** Tel: 01 496 1962; www.sosolisoairline.com
**Chanchangi Airlines** Tel: 01 493 9744/55.

## Car rental and driving

The national road system links all the main centres, and traffic drives on the right. However, roads in Nigeria are generally very poor, causing damage to vehicles and contributing to hazardous driving conditions. Of Nigeria's 200,000km of roads, only about 60,000km are paved, but many of these are in very bad shape and have been decaying for years. Excessive speed, unpredictable driving habits, and the lack of basic maintenance on many vehicles are additional hazards (as burnt-out wrecks and mangled vehicles along the road will attest). The rainy season from May to October is especially dangerous because of flooded roads. The worst roads are in the southeast of the country. There are few traffic lights or stop signs, and drivers seldom yield the right-of-way or give consideration to pedestrians and cyclists. Gridlock is common in urban areas, especially in Lagos, which is known for its 'go-slow', and outside of the cities traffic is made worse by trucks and buses having to make up for the inadequate rail system. Chronic fuel shortages have led to long lines at service stations, which can disrupt or even block traffic. Night driving should be avoided as the streets are very poorly lit and many vehicles are missing one or both headlights. (Also see *Road accidents* in the *Health and Safety* chapter, page 107.)

Road travel in Africa is generally erratic, but in Nigeria you will have to also get used to the whole ethos of 'me first' – each motorist has absolute power and authority over the road, regardless of whether a pedestrian is walking in front of his vehicle, whether he is on the wrong side of the road and a truck is heading down a hill towards him, or whether he wants to get from point A to point B via an embankment, a pavement, or a central reservation. There is a good reason why hire cars only come with a driver in Nigeria, and why the more comfortable front seats of a go-when-full minibus are often the last to fill – the views through the eyes of the driver can be very unnerving!

# DISTANCES BETWEEN MAJOR CITIES

*Approximate distances in kilometres between major cities by road*

| | Abeokuta | Abuja | Bauchi | Benin City | Calabar | Enugu | Ibadan | Ilorin | Jos | Kaduna | Kano | Katsina | Lagos | Lokoja | Maiduguri | Makurdi | Port Harcourt | Sokoto |
|---|---|---|---|---|---|---|---|---|---|---|---|---|---|---|---|---|---|---|
| Abeokuta | — | | | | | | | | | | | | | | | | | |
| Abuja | 740 | — | | | | | | | | | | | | | | | | |
| Bauchi | 1,072 | 445 | — | | | | | | | | | | | | | | | |
| Benin City | 329 | 450 | 893 | — | | | | | | | | | | | | | | |
| Calabar | 765 | 857 | 998 | 436 | — | | | | | | | | | | | | | |
| Enugu | 577 | 400 | 741 | 248 | 283 | — | | | | | | | | | | | | |
| Ibadan | 77 | 659 | 1,069 | 291 | 530 | 539 | — | | | | | | | | | | | |
| Ilorin | 236 | 500 | 913 | 362 | 826 | 649 | 159 | — | | | | | | | | | | |
| Jos | 995 | 313 | 132 | 761 | 866 | 609 | 863 | 781 | — | | | | | | | | | |
| Kaduna | 836 | 180 | 412 | 791 | 1,015 | 765 | 759 | 600 | 280 | — | | | | | | | | |
| Kano | 1,086 | 410 | 321 | 1,057 | 1,283 | 1,074 | 1,009 | 850 | 421 | 242 | — | | | | | | | |
| Katsina | 1,169 | 563 | 494 | 1,230 | 1,425 | 1,095 | 1,052 | 893 | 575 | 398 | 173 | — | | | | | | |
| Lagos | 81 | 800 | 1,199 | 328 | 766 | 526 | 147 | 306 | 986 | 906 | 1,156 | 1,199 | — | | | | | |
| Lokoja | 489 | 173 | 603 | 290 | 610 | 382 | 580 | 310 | 471 | 505 | 767 | 899 | 539 | — | | | | |
| Maiduguri | 1,536 | 908 | 464 | 1,357 | 1,462 | 1,179 | 1,520 | 1,377 | 596 | 876 | 614 | 776 | 1,660 | 1,067 | — | | | |
| Makurdi | 950 | 323 | 471 | 492 | 529 | 270 | 871 | 824 | 339 | 502 | 760 | 851 | 820 | 319 | 935 | — | | |
| Port Harcourt | 693 | 700 | 996 | 364 | 184 | 255 | 625 | 799 | 864 | 987 | 1,230 | 1,370 | 662 | 557 | 1,460 | 525 | — | |
| Sokoto | 969 | 793 | 778 | 1,095 | 1,498 | 1,249 | 892 | 732 | 646 | 487 | 583 | 428 | 1,050 | 938 | 1,183 | 985 | 1,214 | — |

When you are on the road, signposts are sporadic, but do look out for the white marker stones next to the road featuring the first three letters of the next and previous towns and the distances to each in kilometres. Petrol and diesel costs N40–42 a litre, though the price routinely changes depending on fluctuations in Nigeria's oil-based economy. Price hikes often cause strikes and riots. Of the two, diesel is harder to find, and overland trucks need to fill up whenever they can. All the petrol stations have rather comical signs outside saying 'Yes petrol, Yes diesel, Yes paraffin'. If they don't have one of these products they simply scrub out the 'Yes' bit! Cheating at petrol stations is quite common (ie: pumps are either tampered with or the displays on them don't work at all). Another scam is to fit extra-long nozzles on pumps that traps an accurate measure of fuel going into a tank whereby the tank reader gives a misreading of how full the tank is, or to fail to zero the pump before starting to fill a tank. As from 2003 it has been a law for Nigerian drivers and front-seat passengers to wear seat belts, although what they do if their vehicle doesn't have them is beyond me. This law is taken quite seriously, particularly in Lagos, where most taxi drivers buckle up and ask you to do the same.

Very few foreigners actually drive in Nigeria because of high accident rates, hectic traffic, and confusing or non-existent traffic rules – expats usually have their own chauffeur-driven cars and car hire always includes a driver. There is effectively no such thing as traditional car hire, and the division between taking a taxi and hiring a car is somewhat blurred. You cannot hire a car without a driver and it's the driver that pays for the petrol, so in essence you're just taking a taxi. It's not difficult to hire a car in Lagos and Abuja, but it is best to go through one of the major hotels. Expect to haggle over rates, and remember that deals can be done for periods of more than a day. In the Sheraton, for example, reasonable cars with a driver cost N12,000 a day, with cheaper rates for three days or more, while elsewhere a beat-up old Peugeot with a driver costs in the region of N5,000 a day. There really is no such thing as taking a car and driver from city to city – to do this you will have to negotiate with a driver, which basically is the same as taking a bush taxi (see below) as a drop, meaning you have got the vehicle for your exclusive use and that you will therefore have to pay the same as if it was full of passengers.

## Rail
Nigeria has over 3,500km of railways, but you won't see a moving train. The two main railways are from Lagos to Kano (via Ibadan–Oyo–Ogbombosho–Kaduna–Zaria); and from Port Harcourt to Maiduguri (via Aba–Enugu–Makurdi–Jos). There is also a branch line from Zaria to Gusau. In theory, a daily passenger service runs on both main routes. However, years of neglect of both the rolling stock and tracks have seriously reduced the capacity and utility of the railways and rail services have been largely suspended because of sabotage and a lack of maintenance.

## Minibuses and bush taxis
Except for the smallest of villages, every settlement in Nigeria has a motor park, and some of the larger cities have several. All public transport goes from these and you will inevitably spend a great deal of time hanging around them waiting for vehicles to go-when-full. Sometimes you may be lucky and arrive at a motor park and find a vehicle with only a couple of seats left and depart almost immediately, whilst at other times you may be the first to arrive and have to hang around for another 16 or so people that want to go in the same direction as you. This could plausibly take a few hours and we found Sundays especially quiet. Whilst they seem completely chaotic at first, motor parks are fairly organised and someone will point you in the right direction of the vehicle you want. Always look out for the men in the green

## ROADBLOCKS

Police roadblocks are frequent (we counted 22 roadblocks on a 100km stretch of road between Lagos and Abeokuta). These are manned variously by men in black police uniforms, men wearing army fatigues or armoured vests, and men in nothing more than baseball caps, T-shirts with the sleeves ripped off, and mirrored sunglasses. Whatever the attire, no-one argues with the AK47s or pistols that these men invariably carry. These roadblocks can also be extra intimidating at night. If you are on public transport you have nothing to worry about, as it is the driver who has to deal with the situation and not the passengers. Only very occasionally will the passengers be asked to get out so that the vehicle can be searched. When setting off in a bush taxi or minibus, you will notice the driver roll up a pile of N20 notes and stick them in a row above the driver's door. These are for what I like to call the '40km/h handshake'. The driver slows down at a roadblock, takes one of the rolled-up N20 notes, and neatly deposits it in the policeman's hand as he drives past. Nigerians seem to have two differing opinions about roadblocks. In some of the vehicles we were travelling in, everybody groaned and tutted in disapproval when the driver handed over a dash or if we got delayed. In one, someone even complained to the driver that he shouldn't have dashed the policeman as he was only carrying a stick and not a gun. Then, by contrast, there were many other people who wholly approved of the roadblocks: it was explained to us that they did catch armed robbers, and were doing a good job in keeping the roads safe, and that it was only right that they should be dashed as a thank you. One passenger commented that the police had a very hard job standing on the road in the hot sun all day, and that it was only fair to give them N20 for a Coke.

Foreigners in their own vehicle are usually just waved through. If you are

and white uniform of the National Union of Road Transport Workers (NURTW), who patrol the motor parks and take the fee paid by the drivers for the use of the motor park. He will take you straight to the right bus. There are queues of vehicles and the one that is filling up first will have a wooden pyramid sign on top with the first three letters of the town or city it's going to. When the vehicle departs, this is simply plonked on to the top of the next one. In nearly all of the motor parks you can hire a wheelbarrow and driver to carry your luggage.

No vehicle moves until the required amount of people are in place. In a minibus this means when two people are in the front plus the driver, five are on the back seat, four are across the middle seats (with another couple of additional people squashed on to the engine cover at the back of the front seat), and the conductor is sat right in the doorway. In a bush taxi (any kind of car), it's when two people are on the front seat plus the driver and four are on the back seat, and in the case of Peugeot 504s, when another three are on the second back seat. Expect to be completely squashed and uncomfortable. There is not enough space for everyone to sit back on their seats so you will have to get used to frequently 'shifting' as the Nigerians like to call it – as in 'shift up', 'shift back' etc. This means everyone in the vehicle takes random turns at sitting to the front of the seats whilst other passengers sit back, and arms and legs are routinely shifted to accommodate everyone else's limbs. In a minibus, if you are sitting opposite someone sitting on the engine cover behind the driver you'll also have to weave your knees with theirs, and on the middle seat at the front and in the passenger seat of a car (that takes two people) expect to sit astride the gear stick (with the driver negotiating gear changes stopped it's likely that the police are just curious and want to have a chat; as long as you are not breaking the law (by not having your licence with you, or not wearing a seatbelt, for example), there is nothing to be nervous about. If you have your own driver, they are in the best position to answer police questions. The police may attempt to try and 'fine' you if the steering wheel is on the wrong side, for a number plate that is not big enough for their liking, or for advertising (ie: displaying an overland-company logo on the side of the vehicle). There are also incidents of so-called 'tax collectors', often wearing yellow work vests and setting themselves up on roads leading into and out of towns. They have been known to throw down a piece of wood spiked with nails in front of your car and to demand a 'tax' that entitles you to free access to the town/city. This is nothing short of extortion; if you are stopped in this manner try to deal with it with a sense of humour and patience, and try and talk your way out of it. Try to avoid stopping for anyone who is not in a uniform. If you are stopped, ask for ID and say that you want to go to the police.

Reports suggest that things have improved greatly over recent years, which is good news if you are travelling overland through Nigeria. Many of my overland truck-driver friends tell me that a decade ago it cost several hundred dollars in bribes to police and army checkpoints simply to drive from one side of Nigeria to the other. However, they now tell me how refreshing it is not to be asked for dash, and that when they are stopped, it is often only so the police can have a look at their trucks or talk to their passengers. One proudly told me that when he crossed in 2004 all he paid in dash was one can of peaches! And another driver told me that in an emergency, when one of his passengers was ill, a policeman at a roadblock offered his mobile phone so the driver could call the passenger's travel insurance company in Australia!

from between your legs!). If you are doing a lot of travelling in these vehicles it might be a good idea to try out all the positions in the vehicle to find the most comfortable seat so that you know which to bag first at a motor park. Also, always eye up the other passengers; you most certainly don't want to be pinned up against a six-foot hulking man on the front seat of an impossibly small car like a Golf.

You'll pay a few hundred naira more for a bush taxi than a minibus. The reason for this is that bush taxis fill up and go quicker. If it looks like you may be waiting around for a long time for a minibus to fill up, hold off paying your fare to give you the option of switching to a bush taxi if you get fed up waiting. Occasionally you'll hear that a minibus is 'taking three across'. This means that one less person is put on each seat and that the vehicle is actually comfortably full, with more or less the amount of people it was designed to carry. For this though, you'll pay considerably more. Quite bizarrely, on some of the longer routes you will be required to fill out a form with your contact details for insurance purposes in case of an accident, and N50 or so of your fare will go towards an insurance policy. All fares are set and everyone pays the same. Occasionally, if a vehicle is taking a long time to fill up the passengers will club together and pay for the extra seat so the vehicle can get going. In a minibus expect to pay roughly N250 for a journey of about 100km or two hours, rising to N900 for a journey of 500km and several hours, and add on approximately 30% to this for a bush taxi. As a foreigner, you will inevitably be asked at every motor park if you want a drop – meaning that you can take the vehicle for your exclusive use but will have to pay the same as if the vehicle was full of the correct amount of people. This is easy enough to work out:

## MOTOR PARKS

Motor parks are chaotic, crowded and usually filthy, stuffed to the gills with vehicles and market stalls, and are frequented by hawkers, food-is-ready stands, and conductors and touts shouting out destinations and arguing over passengers. They are full of life and great places to observe daily Nigerian street life. Once everyone has got over the shock of the arrival of an *oyibo* and you have located and decided on what vehicle you are going to take, you'll receive no hassles and it's a fabulous opportunity to see everyone at work and chat to the people around you. Motor parks are frantic places where everyone wants to sell you something; the hawkers do their rounds with loaves of bread, peanuts, sticks of *suya*, soft drinks, *pure water*, and various other street food, boxes of imitation watches, underwear, and handkerchiefs (a very useful item in a sweaty bus). Then there are the hawkers offering services such as the shoe doctor or mobile tailor (amazingly these men walk around with old black Singer sewing machines on their heads), and my absolute favourite, *International Finger Cutter* men. These are manicurists who wander around the motor parks clacking their scissors and administering what look like rather harsh manicures and pedicures to any man who desires to have his nails buffed (presumably women conduct this grooming procedure at home). Then there are the beggars; the blind, crippled, and maimed who throw their hands through minibus windows and rattle their enamel plates. And there are also the lay preachers, who come to each vehicle and pray to God for all the passengers to have a safe journey. This often turns into a bit of impromptu hymn-singing, after which the passengers are expected to pay the preacher some dash. We were often 'sprinkled with the blood of Jesus' for safe travelling. Quite often a passenger in the vehicle will say another prayer before departing. Finally there are the traditional doctors, who roam the motor parks proclaiming through loudspeakers that they have the medicine, the book, and the power to cure all the ailments of the world, which on one occasion included 'unfriendly body odour' and a 'weeping penis'! This same gentleman advised putting undiluted petrol on a tooth three times a week to cure toothache, washing your hair in urine to cure dandruff, and using an onion (?) to cure premature ejaculation. The man I was sitting next to on the bus, who was a real doctor, told me irritably that the traditional doctor was 'confusing the common man'. It was a priceless moment.

if a small car takes six at, say, N500 per person, it will cost N3,000 for you to have the car to yourself. The longest journey you can take on a minibus or bush taxi is around six or seven hours (more than long enough to be stuck in a squashed and sweaty vehicle). I think our longest ride was from Maiduguri to Kano, which was roughly seven hours. For longer distances you will have to break your journey and swap vehicles in a motor park.

Finally, when the vehicle is ready to depart, luggage is strapped on the roof, is squashed under seats, goes in the boot, and sometimes has to sit on your knees, and the conductors use brute force to fit everything in. When all that's done and the door is shut someone goes off to find the driver. When he eventually turns up and gets in, what follows is an obligatory argument with the National Union of Road Transport Workers man about how much the driver should pay to use the motor park.

## 'Luxury' buses

Inter-city, or 'luxury' buses as they are known (basically big coaches), are more comfortable than minibuses or bush taxis, but that isn't saying much except that you will have more leg room and your own seat all to yourself. These buses cover longer distances than the smaller vehicles but are also not in great condition, and they nearly always travel at night so are not generally recommended, even by Nigerians. The 'luxury' buses connect all the main cities, and there are some 75 different companies, many with delightful names: Young Shall Grow Motors, Fruit of Labour Motors, God's Will Transport, Vote for Jesus Motors, or Glory is My Shepard Motors. Each bus company has its own bus stand which is often not at the motor parks, so finding them isn't always easy. Often the buses are too big to fit inside the motor parks proper and collect on a vacant side of the road that's big enough to accommodate them. And locations change depending on the use of that particular piece of land. This is extremely awkward, as unlike minibuses that go when full, you actually have to pre-book a seat on a 'luxury' bus earlier in the day that you want to travel. This means you have to find the bus, book and pay for a ticket, and then return again at the departure time later in the day. Finally, and even more awkwardly, if they fill up they leave earlier than the scheduled time of departure. Fares vary between the companies, but expect to pay N2,500 for a 1,000km overnight trip from Lagos to Kano, for example.

## *Okadas* and city transport

There must be hundreds of thousands, if not millions, of motorcycle taxis in Nigeria. In the south they are generally called *okadas* (after a defunct airline), whilst in the north they are known as *achabas*. If you get stuck, just simply say bike. You'll see the odd meaty Suzuki, but the majority of Nigerian *okadas* are Jinchengs imported from China, and I have been reliably told that a new one costs around N70,000. Millions of young men make a living as *okada* drivers, and if they are successful, as they get older and when they can afford to buy a car, they become taxi drivers. They usually carry one person on the back but it's not uncommon to see two or more people plus an assortment of luggage. (I saw one where the passenger had a double mattress on his head.) In the cities they are faster than regular taxis but are not for the faint-hearted, though you can always tell your driver to slow down. You will always have to negotiate a ride, which will be as little as N30 for a short hop outside of Lagos, and N50 in Lagos, whilst a journey of a kilometre or two will cost upwards of N100. Given that you won't have a crash helmet, it's not a good idea to take these on busy expressways where the traffic is moving fast. But as long as you don't have too much luggage, it's easy enough to arrive at a city motor park and hop on the back of an *okada* to get to your hotel. Taxis are available everywhere (though less so at night), and whilst some are painted in specific colours, nearly all cars serve as taxis for the right price. Agree on the fare before getting in and remember that a drop is when you specifically want the vehicle to yourself. Expect to pay about three times more for a drop in a car than you would pay for an *okada*, but remember if there are a few of you then a drop will work out cheaper than you all taking individual *okadas*. Minibuses and shared taxis operate along specific routes that you simply hail down on the side of the street in the general direction you want to go. The price for both is usually set at about N20–40 depending on the distance you travel in them. Pay the correct fare, and pay it only once, no matter how many times the conductor or driver goes around collecting.

## Boats and ferries

There are some local ferry services which are dealt with in the relative chapters.

## SLEEPING, EATING AND DRINKING
### Accommodation

Apart from Lagos and Abuja, which have a couple of international-standard hotels (there is no star grading system in Nigeria), Nigerian hotels are generally run down, dilapidated, poorly maintained, have limited services, are often not wholly clean, and have not seen a lick of paint for perhaps 20 or 30 years. That said, as long as you know what to expect, then you will find adequate and comfortable accommodation just about everywhere.

In 2001, there was some decree that all foreigners must pay for hotels in foreign currency. This never happened and you'll struggle to find anywhere to accept your US$ except at the very top end of the market – unless otherwise stated all rooms must be paid for in naira. Also, hotels are supposed to use a two-tiered price system for residents and non-residents – this never happens either, except at a handful of hotels. You'll always be asked to pay up front and to pay a sizeable deposit, and in the more expensive hotels a 5% VAT levy and a 10% service charge will be added to the bill (see below). If you are prepared to pay over US$200 for a room, you'll get good standards, but at the very bottom end of the scale, where hotel rooms go for as little as US$15, you'll get ancient and scuffed furnishings, dirty carpets, frequent power and water cuts, rattling or defunct air-conditioning units, leaking fridges, and bad smells. Budget travellers will really want to be checking if there are clean sheets and that there is water available, even if it's in a bucket. Even for a little more, roughly US$40–50, you'll get the same in the so-called State hotels – these were obviously built during the 1970s–80s oil boom, and whilst they are huge, with vast public areas, cavernous empty restaurants and often defunct shops, no maintenance work or improvements have been done on them since they were built, and everything is very faded and old fashioned. For what you do or do not get, accommodation in Nigeria is not especially good value (and Lagos hotels are particularly expensive), though on the upside even the cheapest establishments have en-suite rooms with air conditioning and TV. Finally, it's almost impossible to pre-book a hotel in Nigeria, not only because of the inefficient phone and email services (I haven't even bothered listing fax numbers here as sending a fax is nigh on impossible), but because the only way to reserve a room is by paying the deposit upfront, and as you are strongly urged not to use a credit card, this is almost impossible to do unless you are already there. However, you will rarely find that a hotel is full, unless there is a large conference on.

Camping is not really an option in Nigeria and there are no formal campsites with ablution blocks. Though self-sufficient overlanders manage to cross Nigeria and bush camp in quarries, timber yards, and down dirt tracks on the side of the road without any problems, there are no facilities. Be wary of camping near towns and cities or any congested areas as you are bound to attract unwanted attention, and news of your impromptu bush camp will spread like wildfire. Many of the hotels have large compounds and car parks (essential if you are driving) and at these places there's no reason why you can't ask if you can put a tent up, though you'll have to negotiate a price for camping. This is really only suitable for large groups as they will be expected to take at least one room for use of the shower and toilet. In the southeast of the country ignore the signs that say 'camp ground' – these are not campsites at all but venues for large religious gatherings that frequently take place on Sundays and go on all night.

### Glossary of accommodation terms – read this first!

**Tariff**  The tariff is a list of room rates which is almost always available at the hotel reception. There is often a mind-boggling array of rates and types of room from

## LONG-TERM ACCOMMODATION

If you have gone to Nigeria to work then rented accommodation is the obvious option. Most companies provide accommodation for their employees, and in Lagos there are many large expat communities on Victoria Island and Ikoyi living in apartment blocks, company compounds or private houses. There may sometimes be waiting lists for accommodation and it's not uncommon for new expats to spend the first few months of their stay in a hotel. Bear in mind rents can be upwards of a whopping US$50,000 a year for a two-bedroomed apartment in a compound, plus an annual service charge of US$10,000 or more, though it's the companies that usually meet these expenses. Most of the apartment blocks have their own boreholes and generators for uninterrupted water and power supplies, and extras such as a swimming pool and tennis court, and service charges cover all maintenance. In houses however, which tend to rely on the public water supply, the tenant is responsible for services and maintenance, and it's essential that you get a generator rigged up and consider some sort of security. There is the added hassle of organising things to be fixed in your house. Many expats employ a steward or maid who live in separate staff quarters. If you need to employ your own staff, it's essential that you talk to other expats for recommendations; reference letters are easily forged and previous employers may be hard to contact once they have left Nigeria. Potential expats and their wives are usually invited to Nigeria for a few days by their sponsoring company on what is termed in expat language as a 'look-see', before they decide to commit to a contract. They are usually put up in a very nice hotel, making the prospect of living in Lagos seem slightly brighter, and are often shown around by another expat or his wife. Work contracts tend to be long (at least two or three years), and it's essential that you go on a 'look-see', and talk to lots of other expats, before committing to a lengthy stay in Nigeria.

'standard' or 'classic' rooms, to all different types of suites, family rooms, and specific rooms for diplomats, presidents, and even monarchs. Except in the most expensive hotels such as the Sheraton and the Hilton, the difference is usually that the more expensive rooms are bigger and/or have bigger beds (Nigerian beds reach mammoth proportions). Always ask the difference between each room rate, and *always* look at one or more rooms before you decide. Note that the 15% and the deposit (see below) are also outlined on the tariff, so it's imperative that you study it before filling out the registration form and paying for a hotel room.

**The 15%** In addition to the quoted fee, hotels and many restaurants are supposed to charge an additional 5% VAT and a 10% service charge. In the bigger cities such as Lagos and Abuja they certainly do, making a room or a meal significantly more expensive here than elsewhere, and you have to remember to include this in your budget. In the cheaper establishments, it's either included in the rate or they don't bother with it at all. In the hotel listings in this book, I have indicated whether the 15% is included in the room rate.

**Deposit** A deposit is required for even the cheapest hotel room. Deposits vary between 125% and 200% of the room rate. When you are checking into a hotel you pay the deposit price, which is considerably higher than the room rate, but when checking out you get the balance back, minus any additional expenses such as minibar, meals, telephone calls etc. A room at the Sheraton Hotel in Lagos, for example, costs US$305 but the deposit is US$400. When you check in you must pay the US$400 deposit price. This system is the same at just about all hotels in Nigeria whether it costs N1,000 or US$1,000 a night. Always take the deposit price into consideration when budgeting because this is the amount of ready cash you'll need to stay anywhere for the night, though invariably you'll get a portion of this back. Also, always keep all your receipts for any piddly amount of deposit money you expect back, as what with Nigerians being rather officious about their paperwork (a legacy from the British I expect), you may not get the remainder of your deposit back without it.

**NEPA** The Nigeria Electric Power Authority in theory supplies Nigeria with electricity. Locally it's dubbed Never Expect Power Again – and for good reason. The power routinely goes off several times a day; often it's not even on during daylight hours, and when it comes on at dusk there is such a power surge, it fails within minutes. 'No NEPA' is a familiar term throughout the country. Despite fuelling lights, air-conditioning units and fans, NEPA also powers pumps to get water from water tanks to the taps in hotel rooms.

**Gen** Gen is short for generator (electricity provider run on diesel). In any hotel always make sure there is a generator – I found even the cheapest fleapit had one. The generator kicks in (assuming that there is diesel available) as soon as NEPA goes off. There is generally a few moments' overlap as NEPA dies, and someone runs to crank up the gen, and the noise of the gen roaring into action becomes quite familiar. The generator systems in some hotels are very elaborate and resemble small electricity sub-stations, particularly if they have to power hundreds of rooms, whilst at the smaller and cheaper places it's often just a single unit. In these cases the gen is often switched off between 23.00–07.00 to conserve diesel – an important consideration if it's stinking hot and you are relying on air conditioning to ward off mosquitoes, or if you happen to be midway through a good movie on TV. Candles and a torch are essential. Remember the terms 'on' and 'off' as verbs when enquiring about hotel accommodation, as in 'what time do you off the generator?'

**Bucket showers** Almost all hotel rooms are en suite with either a bath or shower or both. Whilst these facilities in themselves may be perfectly functional, running water through the shower head or taps is not. Even in the more expensive Nigerian hotels buckets and scoops are provided. You'll need to keep the bucket constantly filled from the tap when there is water, as you'll need it to flush the loo as well as for washing when there isn't any water. If there is never any water in the taps then ask for someone to fill the bucket for you from the hotel's main water tank.

**Bed size** There is no such thing as a single bed in a Nigerian hotel. A standard room advertised on the tariff is often presumed by the hotel staff to be for one person, but it has generally got a normal sized (for Europeans) double bed in it. Hotel receptionists in Nigeria will find it difficult to comprehend that two people might want to spend the night in a bed that size. A double is usually a room with a queen- or king-sized bed, whilst a so-called suite or executive room contains a bed so vast that it is wider than it is long. Room rates on the tariff often vary because of the size of the bed, so it's up to you how much you pay for sleeping space. Room rates are per room and not per person. Most hotels supply a top and bottom sheet, though where there is no top sheet and where the sheets do not look especially clean, I would advise you to use your own sleeping sheet (see page 65).

**Fridge** Many hotels have (usually empty and ancient) fridges in the rooms. This could be a throwback to a few decades ago when perhaps someone entertained the idea of offering a minibar service. They are of course NEPA dependent, but we did find them quite useful to keep water and camera film cool.

**Suite** A suite (sometimes spelt *suit* on the tariff) is quite simply a hotel room with more than a bedroom and bathroom. The extra room(s) will perhaps have a sofa, a table and chairs (often plastic), an additional TV, or an old desk (in which case it's confusingly very similar to an 'executive' room). In every sense it's a suite of rooms, but very far from the expectations of a suite in the real world of hotels.

**Conference facility** If a hotel advertises a conference facility, this usually means that they have anything from a shed at the back of the cheapest hotels, to a vast range of halls in the plusher hotels, that can be hired out, occasionally for conferences, but usually for weddings, funerals, memorials, church services and similar events that draw hundreds of people, especially at the weekend. These can get noisy and you have the additional concern that there are hundreds of non-hotel guests wandering around, so give the hotel a miss if there's a large 'conference' on.

**Toilet roll and soap** Rather amusingly, when checking into a hotel you will be presented with a toilet roll and a small bar of soap stuffed down the middle of the cardboard tube at reception – if you run out they will not be replaced automatically but if you ask, you'll get more. Towels are only provided in the upmarket hotels.

**Tea-bread-and-eggs** Inexplicably, breakfast is sometimes included in the price of a hotel room for *one* person. This is always tea-bread-and-eggs, the standard Nigerian breakfast – Lipton tea with powdered milk and sugar, a hunk of bread and a pale-looking fried and greasy omelette. Rather confusingly, if you ask for just tea (as in a cup of tea) it will also come with bread, so you must always stipulate if you only want the tea (something that is not always got across very easily). If breakfast is not included in the room rate, tea-bread-and-eggs is generally available for around N200–300.

**Breakfast items** In some of the more expensive hotels, they will have a menu of breakfast items. These usually cost around N100–200 per item and you make up your own breakfast from tea, coffee, bread, toast, eggs, baked beans, chips, yam chips, sometimes Vienna sausage, and very occasionally bacon.

**Luxury** This word is frequently used on hotel tariffs describing the most expensive rooms. It doesn't mean luxury in the normal sense at all, and the 'luxury' rooms are usually the biggest suites with the biggest beds. An 'executive' room usually means that it has got a desk. *Always* look at a room before deciding.

**AC** AC is of course a universal acronym for air conditioning, though if you said air conditioning and not AC to the average Nigerian hotel receptionist, he or she would have no idea what you were talking about. Surprisingly, even the cheapest of hotels almost always has AC, but whether it works or not (no NEPA) is another thing. In many hotels the AC units are as old as the ark; be wary of touching the control knobs or power points if they look especially hazardous. All rooms listed in this book have AC unless otherwise stated.

**Catering services** If a hotel offers a catering service, it means it does food. Not all hotels have restaurants, but those that don't may offer the option of cooking you a plate of food and bringing it to your room, and sometimes they have beers and soft drinks as well. When checking in ask what sort of food they have that day as all the items shown on a menu will not necessarily be available.

**TV** Even the cheapest of hotel rooms normally have a working TV (when of course there is power), but there are three different kinds of reception. **Local TV** is the national station which is run by the state television corporation, and all you'll usually get is the local news broadcast between 18.00 and 20.00, read by ladies in enormous shiny headdresses in bare television studios. **DSTV** (Digital Satellite Television) is South African satellite TV, with several channels. These include Supersport, a sports channel with a South African slant popular because of its coverage of football; CNN; US news channel; MNET movie channel, reasonably current Hollywood movies; MNET Open Time, South African soaps between 17.00 and 19.00; and MNET Africa, a clever business move by DSTV as this channel shows only Nigerian 'Nollywood' movies and is specifically broadcast in Nigeria. 'Nollywood' movies are hugely popular low-budget dramas usually filmed on hand-held video cameras, and it is estimated some 70 a week of these movies are released on to the video market in Nigeria. You have to watch one – they are hilariously badly made with the most bizarre story lines. In the top hotels you'll also get BBC News, BBC Prime, the History Channel, Discovery and the like. If the TV in your room has got DSTV then you will be able to choose what you watch – unlike **Saudi Arabian Satellite TV.** This is a unique concept. Some hotels will offer one station of satellite TV but it inexplicably comes from Saudi Arabia (all the adverts are in Arabic and whilst most of the programmes are in English, they have Arabic sub-titles). Like DSTV there are a number of TV channels, but as the satellite receiver can only pick up one channel at a time, whoever is sitting at the reception desk of the hotel gets to choose what to watch. For example, you could be midway through watching a movie and the man at reception gets tired of watching it himself and flicks channels to watch the football and suddenly you are watching David Beckham instead of Brad Pitt and there is nothing you can do about it!

**Check-out time** In just about all of Nigeria's hotels check-out time is at 12.00 and check-in time is at 14.00. These are much later and earlier than in, say, European hotels, when check-out time is usually 10.00. The advantage of this is that you can leave your luggage in the room undisturbed until 12.00, giving you time in the morning to explore somewhere without lugging everything around. I also found that most hotels will happily store your gear safely at the reception desk after this time and you do not have to worry about theft. On just about all the tariffs it says that check out after 12.00 will incur an additional charge that's 50% of the room rate, and full room rate is charged after 18.00.

## Drinks

Starting with the obvious, international branded soft drinks such as Coca-Cola, Fanta, Sprite and Schweppes lemon are available everywhere, from roadside stalls to buckets on top of people's heads, and in all the country's restaurants and bars. They're not always cold so check first before handing over the N30 or so it costs for a 350ml bottle – you give the bottle back as soon as you have finished. Occasionally you'll see disposable cans but these are quadruple the price of a bottle. There are a variety of brands of locally produced and hugely popular malt drinks

## NATIONAL FOOD AND DRUGS ADMINISTRATIVE CONTROL (NAFDAC)

NAFDAC is the Nigerian government agency that is in charge of the regulation and control of processed food and drugs. In Nigeria all locally produced food is supposed to go through checks with NAFDAC that ensure that it is fit for consumption. You'll see the NAFDAC logo on packets of *pure water* for example. It's quite a powerful organisation and when we were in Nigeria NAFDAC closed down the *Indomie* (instant two-minute noodles) factory when someone died after eating *Indomie* noodles. They conducted a thorough investigation into possible contaminated noodles before allowing the factory to reopen. The noodles are popular throughout the country and are often taken to school by children to eat for lunch. Since *Indomie* first began producing the noodles in Nigeria a decade ago, they have sold one billion (I'll repeat that), *one billion* packets of noodles. The man had actually died from a severe diarrhoea attack, but his last meal had been the noodles, and *Indomie* made a statement in the press about how NAFDAC could not necessarily lay the blame for the death on the company. Nevertheless the incident caused countrywide panic.

At the time of writing, the head of NAFDAC, a woman called Dora Akunyili, was embarking on a campaign to root out fake, sub-standard and adulterated drugs, and to ensure that items imported into Nigeria and made in Nigeria met the required standards. There are enthusiastic campaigns on Nigerian TV showing mounds of 'unwholesome' products being burned, that appeal to the public to report 'perpetrators' of counterfeit food and drugs manufacture to their local NAFDAC office – on the TV ad, one such perpetrator is shown (dramatic music and all) being led away in handcuffs for ultimate effect. In Lagos, NAFDAC has offices at the Federal Secretariat buildings on Ikoyi. The buildings are about 15 stories high and one section of one of the blocks has been completely burnt out. The fire happened in early 2004 and was started deliberately by a group of criminals dealing in counterfeit drugs. Supposedly Akunyili kept much of her paperwork at the Federal Secretariat, which the arsonists managed to destroy, as all the floors of NAFDAC were burnt out, and a similar inferno razed its Kaduna office a few hours later, which destroyed state-of-the-art laboratory equipment used for testing drugs. Within two weeks of this incident there were two attempts on Akunyili's life. Quite clearly the illegal production of fake drugs is big business in Nigeria – sugar or aspirin, for example, are often substituted for the real ingredient of any given drug, though sometimes more sinister ingredients such as arsenic have been used.

in brown bottles; one such drink is brewed by Guinness, and is served very cold. It tastes like a thick, non-alcoholic Guinness. They're advertised as being very good for you and it's common to see a couple in a bar with the man drinking a beer and a woman drinking a malt drink. A drink called Chapmans is hard to find except in the more upmarket restaurants, and is expensive at about N250 for a glass, but as far as I am aware it is unique to Nigeria and very refreshing; it's a deep red berry colour and tastes a bit like a non-alcoholic Pimms, and is served with a slice of lemon and cucumber (the only time, I think, that I actually saw cucumber being used anywhere in Nigeria). At most motor parks you'll see men trundling around on bicycles selling chilled flavoured yoghurt drinks. These taste nice, but I'd give them a wide berth as despite being served out of cooler boxes, you have no idea how many times they've warmed up in the sun. You're better off buying these from a supermarket.

As a Great British Tea Drinker, I am happy to report that Lipton tea-bags are readily available, as are small tins of condensed milk, small packets of milk powder, and small tins of Nescafé. When ordering tea and coffee in a restaurant, this is what you'll get, and it invariably comes with bread. If like me, you are unable to speak to anyone in the morning before a caffeine fix, I suggest you bring one of those electric elements you heat water with and a plastic or Thermos mug, as all the ingredients are available in Nigeria. In a hotel, you may wait for an hour before a simple cup of tea emerges from the hotel kitchen. All over Nigeria in the mornings, on the side of the road and in the motor parks, you'll see tea-and-bread sellers who serve huge plastic mugs of tea and a hunk of bread for N50, but as they boil the sugar in the water, the tea is exceptionally sweet.

Bottled water is available, though sporadically so, so try and buy it when you see it. Expect to pay around N70 for a half-litre bottle. Much more common and sold literally everywhere are half-litre plastic packets of what is known as *pure water*. Not everyone trusts the purity of pure water and it's generally believed to be tap water, neatly packaged by pure water packaging machines that are freely advertised in the newspapers for anyone to buy and set up their own pure water business. (One Lebanese businessman I spoke to told me that this is exactly what happens.) Always presume that you are drinking ordinary tap water and not any kind of special mineral water. For this reason I would probably avoid them in Lagos and the bigger cities, where tap water is more likely to be contaminated. One pure water brand we saw in Sokoto was called *Acceptable Water*, which says it all really.

Except in the northern cities, you won't have a problem finding alcohol, and there are many excellent brands of locally brewed beer, which are sold in big half-litre re-usable bottles for about N120–150. The most popular are Star and Gulder; of the two, Star has the lighter taste. Big bottles of dark Guinness are hugely popular, but it's not served in quite the same way as it is in the emerald isle; you'll get it very cold and, quite bizarrely, it usually comes with a straw, which of course speeds up the effect of the alcohol. You'll need to ask for a glass. As Nigerian Breweries is under license to the Heineken label, you'll sometimes see cans of Heineken, but as it comes in cans and not re-usable bottles, they are more expensive at around N300–400. Local drinks include *emu*, or palm wine, the favourite drink in southern Nigeria, which is a natural sweet, frothy juice with a foul smell. It has to be drunk fresh and is potently alcoholic, and gets more so as the day wears on; administer with care. The distilled version of palm wine is *ogogoro*, a strong local gin, but it's very discreetly sold. You'll sometimes see Gordon's Spark, which is a Nigerian version of an alcopop made with gin. Imported spirits and wines are obviously expensive and can only be found in the upmarket restaurants and hotels, and the few supermarkets dealing in imported goods, and are very rarely seen outside of Lagos or Abuja.

## Food

Although typical of what is found throughout West Africa, traditional Nigerian food is more diverse because of the number of ethnic groups in the country. It differs between the south and north depending on what food products are available. The two main terms for food are **chop** and **food-is-ready**. Chop simply means food or a meal, and restaurants are generally referred to as a chop house, while a snack is a small chop. Food-is-ready needs little explanation; it simply means that there is food ready to eat instantly which doesn't have to be cooked after it's ordered. In a restaurant, despite the fact that there are often extensive menus, you'll get used to asking 'what food-is-ready?' Alternatively, if you choose something from a menu that isn't already prepared, you'll be told that the 'food-isn't-ready' and that you will have to wait.

As a general rule of thumb, Nigerians are fond of some kind of starchy staple accompanied by an (often spicy) soup – this is actually more like a sauce or relish and is not runny like a soup. They use a lot of palm oil, a reddish coloured oil made from ground palm kernels, and a lot of chillies ground into a red powder (known in Nigeria as simply pepper). The starches include *pounded yam,* which is boiled yams literally pounded in a giant pestle and mortar until the consistency is light and fluffy; it looks a bit like mashed potato. Others are *eba* or *garri,* porridges made from pounded cassava; *amala,* ground yam peels that are boiled into a stiff paste and have a darker brown colour; and *semovita,* made from maize flour, another mashed potato-looking concoction and similar to *mealie meal* or *pap* eaten all over East and southern Africa. Most of these starch-based staples have little taste and are very bland, and some have a fairly slimy texture, but they are cheap and filling and soak

## WET AND DRY

Nigerians in the south are great beer and Guinness drinkers, but of course in the Muslim north Sharia law prevents the consumption of alcohol. This doesn't mean alcohol cannot be found at all though. Whilst the northern cities are predominantly Muslim there are also considerable populations of Christians living there. Sabon Gari is Hausa for 'foreigners' town' (often meaning the Yoruba or Igbo, and sometimes Christian quarter) and in some (not all) of the northern cities bars can be found in these areas. Beer is also sold in a few hotels, given that they are catering for visitors from other parts of the country and not local Muslims. And then there is the case of government-owned, or federal land, that doesn't come under the local state's law. These areas include military land, where soldiers are permitted to drink alcohol, and regions of interest to the visitor, such as the national parks. Both Yankari and Lake Kainji national parks lie within Sharia states, but as they are federal property both have bars selling beer. At the time of writing the driest cities were Katsina, Sokoto and Maiduguri, where we never saw beer for sale. Also at the time of research, in Kano in 2004, a bill had been passed through the Kano State government banning all sales and consumption of alcohol within the state for both Muslims *and* non-Muslims. The punishments bandied about in the newspapers at the time for getting caught with alcohol were put at 80 lashes for a Muslim and a N50,000 fine or a year in prison, or both, for non-Muslims. This has yet to come into force, and if it does, it will certainly modify my listings under Kano, and will, I imagine, cause considerable tension between the two communities. Still on the wet/dry subject, swimming pools at the hotels in the Sharia states are generally empty. Sharia does not permit public swimming. At one that did have water in its pool, I asked if we (male and female) could swim at the same time, and the confused receptionist answered that it was 'a very difficult question to answer'. I presume that because so few foreigners visit she was not sure how Sharia deals with this predicament. We came away from Nigeria none the wiser, so if there is water in your hotel pool, my only advice is to speak to the manager about actually swimming in it.

up the flavour of the sauce that comes with them. Alternatively you can opt for rice, which is served plain or cooked with peppers and palm oil; the latter is called *jollof rice*, which is bright orange, fairly hot and very tasty.

Most of the soups are made with lots of palm oil and some meat-based stock, and a few pieces of your chosen meat are plonked on top. Nigeria is renowned for its fiery *obe ata* (pepper soup), which effectively is the country's national dish; it's a thick sauce made by boiling tomatoes, ground pepper, meat or fish broth, onions, palm oil and other spices. A Nigerian must-do is to try dried fish, beef, or chicken *pepper soup* with your choice of starch and be prepared for your eyeballs to melt and your nose to explode, though you may choose to pass on the hugely popular *isiewu* (goat's head pepper soup) – every part of the goat's head is swimming around in it. Other soups include the tasty *egusi soup,* made from ground melon seeds and bitter leaf (a sort of spinach); *okra soup,* made from okra, also known as ladies' fingers; *draw soup,* made from palm nuts, which is horribly slimy and viciously hot and is so called because the spices are 'drawn' out; *groundnut soup,* which is made from peanuts and lends a slight satay flavour to the sauce; and *efo,* a vegetable soup (but vegetarians need to remember that even the vegetable soups have a meat-based gravy). You can add additional meat to these meals, which usually consists of a few pieces of very tough beef or goat, cooked dried fish with its head still intact, or a piece of chicken; the latter ranges from delicious KFC-styled fried chicken to a piece of bone with hardly any flesh on that has been boiled dry. It's worth remembering that you'll get very good or very bad versions of these meals; there is often no way of telling which it's going to be. Nevertheless, if you're lucky you'll get a big plate of steaming starch, tasty soup and tender meat. If there's also *dodo* on the menu add this – it's a delicious dish of fried plantains.

Because of the prevalence of tsetse fly, cattle are scarce in the coastal regions, so consequently more fish is eaten in the south, whilst meat is more popular in the north. Look out for *suya,* which is delicious barbecued beef on sticks, though you can also get offal and goat *suya,* and *kilishi,* spiced dried meat that is very thinly sliced and dried outside in the sun. You'll often see bushmeat on the menu, which is considered a delicacy. Sometimes it's antelope that's unfortunately been poached out of the countryside, but more often than not it's *grasscutters* (cane rats) or giant rubbery snails called *igbin.* In the southeastern regions where meat is rare, beans are used to supplement protein in soups, and *moin-moin,* or bean cakes with a slightly gelatinous texture about them, are served as snacks wrapped up in banana leaves. Vegetables such as onions, tomatoes, bitter leaf and yam are plentiful throughout Nigeria, though more exotic vegetables can be found in Lagos and the markets of the bigger cities. Outside of Lagos we only really saw potatoes (and chips) on the menu in the north. Strangely given the dry climate, we also found more salads in the north, and they were surprisingly delicious, with lettuce, onions and tomatoes, a spattering of tinned baked beans, hard-boiled eggs, and a big dollop of mayonnaise. Fruit is plentiful and bananas, mangos and slices of fresh pineapple, or even coconut, are often seen on the side of the road, as are imported apples and sometimes pears from South Africa. Dairy products are scarce and you are unlikely to see cheese outside of the posh restaurants on Victoria Island, though tinned condensed milk, milk powder and canned margarine are available.

Lagos has by far the best restaurants in the country for international fare – elsewhere you will struggle to find a non-Nigerian meal, though you'll sometimes find basic items such as omelette or chicken and chips and a rare stab at something continental, even if it's not always terribly authentic – on one menu I saw 'marshed potatoes' and 'spaghetti boneless'. But the imported ingredients and accompanying wine and other imported alcoholic drinks on Lagos menus and at the few outlying

**33029100030832**  ARNHOLDT

... teen novels *The Thing About*
... *s It Happens*, *One Night That*
... *Two-way Street*, *Right of Way*,
... is also the author of the middle
... *cret Identity of Devon Delaney*,
... *ould Totally Know Better*, *Four*
... *ules for Secret Keeping*, *Fake*
... *e Girl Meets Ghost* series. She
... *ssachusetts*. Visit her online at
... *t.com*.

**LAUREN BARNHOLDT ON**

... nformation on your favorite
... authors and artists, visit www.authortracker.com.

Also available as an ebook.

...graduation,
I promise to... *learn to trust.*

Lyla McAfee can't wait for her senior trip to Florida. Nothing but sun, sand, and time alone with her boyfriend, Derrick.

Too bad nothing goes as planned.

Lyla's forced to hitch a ride to the airport with Beckett, the school player. Of course that leads to a nasty fight with Derrick. And to top it all off, she's sharing a hotel room with her two ex–best friends, Aven and Quinn.

And then there's that email. The one she wrote to herself as a freshman and scheduled to be delivered right before graduation—an email promising that she'd learn to trust by the end of senior year. Which is ironic since she came up with the idea to message her future self with Aven and Quinn . . . right before they betrayed her.

But now that she's gotten the email she can't ignore the promise she made to herself. Even if Derrick is acting strangely. Even if Beckett keeps showing up out of the blue. And, hardest of all, even if trusting her heart might get it broken.

## Look for Quinn's and Aven's stories!

FIND US ON
WWW.EPICREADS.COM

**HARPER TEEN**
*An Imprint of HarperCollinsPublishers*

Cover art © 2015 by
Oriana Layendecker/ImageBrief.com

Cover design by
Annemieke Beemster Leverenz

US $9.99 / $12.50 CAN
ISBN 978-0-06-232139-8

5 0 9 9 9

9 780062 321398

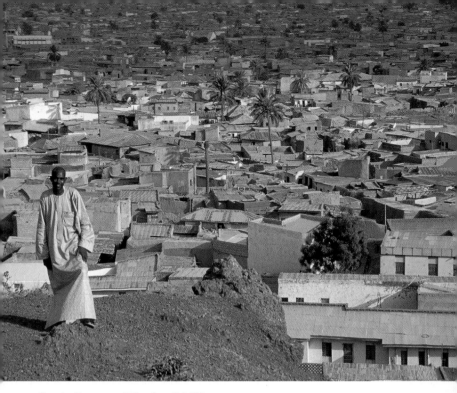

*Above* Looking across old Kano from Dala Hill

*Below* The view from Obudu Plateau towards Cameroon

*Above* In the south, Christians dress up in their finest clothes for church on Sundays
*Above right* Portrait of a Nigerian man; there are over 250 ethnic groups in Nigeria
*Below* Palace guard, Zaria; one of hundreds who would accompany an emir at all times
*Below right* Scars on the face and neck are a common form of decoration for many of Nigeria's ethnic groups

## STREET FOOD

As Nigeria is one big market, where even in the smallest settlements you'll find street stalls and hawkers with trays balanced on their heads, street food is available just about anywhere. If you are travelling around by public transport and spend considerable time in the motor parks, then occasionally this will be your only option for eating during the day. Every time a vehicle stops at a petrol station or in a traffic jam, you will inevitably be offered a host of snack items through the window. Bread is everywhere; sold in small or big packets, the sliced stuff is usually older and tougher, and the yellow bread (also usually sliced) is a somewhat acquired taste as it is made from maize flour. Look out for the small unsliced loaves, as these are the nicest and the freshest and can be eaten immediately with perhaps a cooked egg (make sure the eggs *are* cooked – we made this mistake!). Peanuts are sold in little plastic bags and are nutritious and filling and easy to eat in a packed vehicle, but a word of warning: shelled peanuts can carry hepatitis. You may see prepared slices of fresh coconut or pineapple, mangos if they are in season, and imported apples and pears from South Africa. Oranges are sold with the peel scuffed in a way that extracts the juice without taking the whole peel off. Plantain chips are a Yoruba local snack prepared with unripened plantain sliced the full length and then fried and sold in plastic bags. Boys carry around wooden boxes of meat pastries and dough balls, and men carry huge enamel pots on their heads of *suya* meat and onions and tomatoes, which they slice and wrap up in portions in newspaper. Other street food includes *moin-moin* (bean cakes wrapped in banana leaves), packets of biscuits, and bags of washed carrots. None of these items costs more than N10–20.

continental restaurants in the rest of the country come at a price. In a Nigerian restaurant outside of Lagos you can expect to pay around N300–600 for a Nigerian dish and perhaps N150 at the most for a local beer. In a Lagos restaurant serving 'western' food, a main dish alone averages N1,000–1,500, and that's without extras such as drinks and the 15% VAT and service charge, which nearly all Lagos eateries add on (unlike restaurants in the rest of the country). Even a not very special meal for two with drinks in Lagos can cost around US$50 and much more in the better restaurants. Those with a bit more cash can splurge at the various Lebanese, Indian or Chinese restaurants found in the larger cities. Also worth a mention are the fast-food chains Tantalizers and Mr Biggs – these are relatively new chains that are found in practically all of the big cities serving eat-in or take-away Nigerian fast food in a clean AC environment not too dissimilar to any other Westernised fast-food chain (I recommend the toilets). Food here has been standardised throughout the branches – box of chicken *jollof* rice, beefburger, *moin-moin*, Scotch egg, meat pies, doughnuts etc. Darren loved it (easy food in AC) while I hated it (everything is deep fried), so make up your own mind.

# MEETING THE PEOPLE
## Business hours

Most shops and offices are generally open from 08.00–17.00, Monday to Friday and sometimes for a few hours on Saturday morning. Local markets are open Monday to Saturday 08.00–19.00, though some districts have night markets which stay open until midnight, and food stalls are usually the last to close. Government offices usually close by 15.00 each day. In the south, Sunday is mostly observed as a day of rest, while in the north it's Friday, reflecting the Christian/Muslim divide, though in the north you'll find that all Christian-run businesses will stay open on Friday and vice versa on a Sunday in the south. Note that Sanitation Day is the last Saturday in the month, when between 07.00 and 10.30 traffic is not allowed on the streets, and in theory people are supposed to clean up around them. This does actually happen, although a little half-heartedly, in Lagos.

## Shopping and bargaining

Nigeria is one big market and the country's economic and social character is founded on trade. Everyone is a buyer or seller and there are markets simply everywhere. As in many other African countries, shopping from a vehicle from streetside vendors is common, especially in Lagos where traffic is almost at a standstill anyway. You'll see hundreds of people hawking their wares on any city street, and you can buy the most unbelievable items, from cold drinks, *pure water*, towels, belts and net curtains, to blow-up Santa Clauses and god-awful oil paintings of God. There are a few upmarket supermarkets in Nigeria dealing in imported goods which tend to sell everything from food to household goods and clothes. These are generally frequented by the expat community or the Nigerian elite, who can afford to buy at over-inflated prices, whilst the man and woman on the street shops right there on the street.

Prices in shops are fixed, but in the markets everything is negotiable. The Yoruba and the Hausa have their own accepted ways of bargaining. A Hausa trader uses the standard African method. It is expected that you offer about one third of the asking price and go from there until a mutually agreed price is reached. However, a Yoruba trader bargains completely differently. They will give you a price and you immediately reduce it by N50, and if he/she agrees you reduce it again by N50, and this goes on until the trader stops agreeing and that is the price you will pay. For both methods, if you still think the price is too high, walk away, and if you are not called back to continue the negotiations again, it means that the price is probably about right.

For the visitor to Nigeria, there are a number of curios and souvenirs to pick up and specific markets and shops are listed in the relevant chapters. Of these, cloth is the most prolific and is for sale in all the markets, and Nigeria is renowned for the rich variety of designs, colours, materials and production techniques of its textile craftsmen (see under *Art*, page 50). There is also a fair amount of pottery, leatherwork, wood carvings, beads, jewellery, basketry, drums and masks on offer, and designs vary greatly, with many cities having their own distinctive style. Crocodile products, cowrie shells and ivory can be bought in Nigeria, but it may be illegal to import them into your own country. I think (and hope) that much of the ivory seen in the curio markets is plastic – there is just too much of it for it to be real given the lack of elephants in West Africa. Very unfortunately, the leopard, cheetah, caracal, civet cat, and black and white colobus monkey skins, the elephant feet, the handbag I saw made from lion fur, and the various dried monkey heads, snakes and amphibians in the *juju* markets, are very real and would explain why these animals are now so rare in Nigeria's national parks. If you are buying antiquities (remember a trader can make something look old even if it isn't) then you are required to get a permit from the National Commission for Museum and Monuments to export it from Nigeria. In theory export permits can be obtained at any of the National Museums in the country, but your best bet is to go to the museum in Lagos.

## Women travellers

Nigerian women all over the country travel on their own, be it on long journeys by bus or for a short hop on the back of an *okada*. Every time I jumped on the back of an *okada*, however, everyone stopped and stared incredulously. But the attention you get stops there, and you will soon get used to being stared at. Darren got stared at for his long hair, and people shouted out 'Italian?' or 'Brazilian?' This confused us greatly as he is Australian, and it was a few weeks before we realised that these jibes were because of football on TV – it seems many European and South American footballers have long hair! While we travelled together, we did go off on our own on occasion, and I didn't feel threatened in any way, though I had a million pairs of eyes on me (as did Darren). The most prevalent attitude you are going to meet is complete bemusement. Nigerian society is conducted on the street and Nigerians are by character great socialisers and talkers, and they'll often approach you for a chat. Almost all of the time it is just out of inquisitiveness and simply just to say 'welcome'. Not once did I receive any rude or suggestive comments, and (only!) once was I approached in a bar environment to ask if I wanted company – as happens anywhere in the world. The guy in question left very politely when I declined.

One word of advice for women travellers (at least for anyone over the age of 21!) is to say that you are married even if you're not. This is not for any practical reason; you certainly won't be asked if you are married to get a hotel room, even in the Muslim north. But if you are over 21 and not married, Nigerians, male and female, *will not get it*, and you'll be embroiled in a lengthy and analytical conversation about *why you're not married*. Believe me, it's just easier to say you are. Whilst there have been occasions in Nigerian history where rape and sexual assault have been an issue, they have only really occurred during war times when the army has used rape as a weapon against women. Other than that, sexual crime is almost unheard of in Nigerian society. Hopefully this is because it doesn't happen rather than because it's not being reported. The most important thing for a woman to consider is to dress modestly, especially in the Muslim north, though despite the strict Sharia code, Western women are not expected to cover their hair. This is because many Christians live in the northern cities and wear what they like, though as a visitor it's always sensible to respect the local customs. There are other Islamic considerations to take into account: women are generally not welcome at mosques, particularly at prayer times, and as prayers often happen outside of mosques or in open prayer compounds at the side of the road or in markets, it's a good idea not to get too close, and under no circumstances should you stop and stare. In the northern cities, Darren went to the main Friday prayers to see several thousand men praying in and around the main mosque. It wasn't appropriate for me to go and he says that all the women in the area simply melted away during prayer time.

## Greetings

Greetings are highly valued in Nigeria and neglecting to greet another person is a sign of disrespect. Shaking hands with everyone is customary on meeting and departing. Because of the diversity of cultures, customs and dialects in Nigeria, English is widely used throughout the country for exchanging greetings even if the conversation continues in another language. Before *any* conversation, even if it's a quick request to ask directions or if you are buying something in a shop or at a stall, you will be expected to go through a whole range of greetings, first starting with 'hello' and 'how are you?' and responding politely to the answers. Everywhere you'll go you'll hear 'you are welcome'; a phrase which is used to simply say 'hello', shouted at you from the street. And more formally, 'good afternoon madam' – in fact, rather wonderfully you'll get 'good morning', 'good afternoon' and 'good evening' from the same person if you see them at various occasions during the day. We also got *oyibo* or *batauri* (both meaning white person in the south and north respectively) yelled out to us in the street, but unlike in East Africa where people yell out *mzungu* (white person) repeatedly and aggressively when they are usually asking for things, in Nigeria *oyibo* and *batauri* fall out of people's mouths as yelps of surprise. Rather amusingly, we also got Mr and Mrs White!

It is respectable to address Nigerians by their surnames until you know them very well, and titles are important. There are many chiefs, high chiefs, doctors, professors, madams, princes, emirs, and honorable so-and-sos, and Nigerians love to have lengthy names. Children generally address their elders with a title, ie: Mr or Miss before someone's name, even if they are using the Christian name. Nigerians often wink at their children if they want them to leave the room. Gestures differ from one ethnic group to another. In Yorubaland it is a sign of respect for women to curtsey when meeting someone (we got 'bobbed' at a lot), and to enquire after relations. You'll have to adapt slightly to avoid further questions; 'yes my grandmother is very well' (dead for 20 years), or 'my husband's business is going very well' (not married). Visiting family and friends is an important part in maintaining ties, and unexpected guests are welcome, simply because planning ahead is not always possible in areas where there are no phones.

## Dashing

Dash = bribe, tip, donation (verb and noun). Despite Nigeria's huge reputation as one of the most corrupt countries in the world (which it is at business and government level), as a simple tourist you are unlikely to experience many instances of being asked for a bribe. The notable exception is at the roadblocks (see box pages 74–5), and even then you'll only be asked if you are driving your own vehicle. The only time we paid dash was when we extended our visas at the government immigration department. It is, however, a different story if you are working in Nigeria, when bribery is very much part of getting things done on a business level. One story I heard was from an expat who was working for a telecommunications company installing reception towers for a cell phone company. The dash needed to pay landowners for the proposed sites was included in his official company budget. In the event that someone performs a 'kind' act for you, such as carrying your luggage to your room, then of course you should offer them a small tip. Then there are the odd occasions when (quite rightly) you need to pay dash for a museum guide or to people who very kindly agree to be photographed. Generally Nigerians do not tip, and in the more upmarket restaurants and hotels, 10% service charge is added on to your bill. And even in the cheapest of hotels, if someone brings food or drink to your room, a small fee for 'room service' is added to your bill. It's up to you if you want to leave any extra tip: it will be greatly appreciated, but certainly not expected.

The only other times you'll be asked for a dash is from beggars. They are quite prevalent all over Nigeria and unfortunately some are seriously handicapped. One lady in the south asked me why we wanted to travel to the north: 'There, people only have one leg or arm,' she declared. Whatever southerners think, this is obviously not true, but there are certainly more beggars in the poorer regions. There will be countless occasions on the streets and in the motor parks where someone will shove a plate in front of you, but not once did we find beggars irritating or intrusive – I live in South Africa and the beggars there are far more aggressive. And very refreshingly, nowhere in Nigeria did we hear '(Please) give me…', a phrase uttered all over Africa in any country that is used to seeing tourists. In Nigeria there simply are no tourists and the people there have no idea about the concept of asking and being readily handed something by a Westerner who doesn't know any better. Nigerians themselves tend to respond to beggars, especially better-off Muslims who frequently dash poor people who collect around mosques. In vehicles in motor parks, after people have paid for their seat, they'll often hand over the small change to a beggar through the window, and if at the end of the day a chop or food-is-ready stall has left-over food, the ladies running the stalls will often feed the street children and beggars.

## Public toilets

What public toilets? The only communal toilets you will find are in a few hotels and restaurants, and none of them are that flash. As an *oyibo* you will get away with asking if you can use them, regardless of whether or not you are utilising that establishment. Everyone, especially men, goes to the toilet in public. Oddly, the Muslim men in the north squat and urinate beneath their long cloths, whereas men in the south just get their tackle out. Whilst you will see ladies crouching down in their skirts at the side of the road and behind walls, it's not as common a sight as it is for men.

If you get caught short the problem is where to go – there are people everywhere and there's very little privacy. If travelling by public transport sometimes someone will stop the driver if there is some urgency to go to the toilet. If this happens go then, as once at your urban destination there may not be anywhere to go until you get inside your hotel room. My advice generally is to go to the loo when you can and squeeze it out. Ask in restaurants and hotels, though remember that the more basic chop houses or food-is-ready stalls are not going to have any facilities. If you are absolutely desperate, ask a local of the same gender and perhaps she or he can recommend somewhere. Most Nigerians are not going to know the terms bathroom, restroom, take a leak or a piss, or even the words dump or shit; in one restaurant I asked a waiter where the toilet was and he replied by asking if I wanted 'to easy myself'? Even if you have found a toilet, the chances are there will be no water, the toilets themselves won't flush, and you won't be able to wash your hands. You may want to consider carrying wet-wipes with you, and you'll most certainly need to have a roll of toilet paper handy.

All over Nigeria you will see the rudimentary signs painted on walls that say 'do not urinate here'. On a wall in Ibadan I saw the words 'do not urinate here (again)' and in Calabar 'do not urinate here by order of a native doctor' accompanied by the skull and crossbones sign! In one motor park in Lagos we actually saw a few modern 'port-a-loos' with signs saying 'Pay as you shit' and an advertisement for the company saying 'Our business is shit business'. Fabulous!

Here is Darren's description of what happened when he went to watch Friday prayers in Zaria: 'I was, of course, the object of much visual curiosity, which although, I dare say, may have had something to do with me being a scruffy, long-haired '*batauri*' (northern slang for the southern equivalent of '*oyibo*'), may also have had something to do with the fact that I was standing smack-bang in the middle of the communal ablutions area! It was only when everyone went quiet and started their prayer rituals that I looked around to see I was surrounded by hundreds of tiny, and not-so-tiny, dollops of human residue scattered around the patch of earth that I had considered to be the prime-viewing site. I nonchalantly stepped ten paces to my left to what I hoped was a turd-free zone.'

# MEDIA AND COMMUNICATIONS

Nigeria has all the modern communication systems any country in the developing world could wish for – landline telephones, cellular networks, internet service providers, and satellite television. But with a massive demand for communication tools and an infrastructure that is perilously overloaded, and with unreliable power sources and high maintenance demands, communication is far from reliable and interruptions in services are the norm. Go there expecting nothing to work, and when it does be gratefully delighted.

## Telephone

Nigeria's landline telephone system is totally inadequate and poorly maintained, and phone lines are often out of order. You will notice from our listings that we often give more than one telephone number for businesses and organisations, because many companies have installed multiple phone lines due to the fact that one or more of their lines may be down. This is attested to by the thousands of tangled telephone wires between all the telephone poles. And take note of phone numbers in this book and elsewhere – whilst apparently it does exist, the Nigerian telephone directory is a rare creature indeed. You may see fairly new-looking public telephone boxes around Lagos and Abuja, but there are no phones inside!

The national phone company is called **NITEL**, but for the life of me I couldn't find out what the letters stand for. There are public NITEL offices in the main cities from where you can make both local and international calls. You need to buy a **phonecard** from the attendant who usually has a list of call charges so you can work out what price to pay for a card depending on how long you think you may want to talk. A N300 card will give you around two minutes to Europe. There are only usually one or two phones that you can phone internationally from and you'll need a specific international card. A scam here is that touts buy up all the international cards from the NITEL office and then sell them outside for more than they are worth. For some unfathomable reason it is sometimes easier to get an international line out of Nigeria than to make a local phone call around the corner, and if you do get through anywhere expect to be cut off at any time. To get a line out of Nigeria first dial 009 followed by the country code. Dialling into Nigeria, the international code is 234. To make a reverse-charge (collect) call, phone the international operator on 191. Note that the fax machine has become almost obsolete in Nigeria and fax numbers rarely work. International calls can be made directly from a few of the more upmarket hotels, with the usual premium rate attached, and some internet cafés double up as call centres.

The era of the **cell phone** (commonly referred to as GSM in Nigeria: Global System for Mobile Communications) has taken off and cell network providers have boomed in Nigeria in recent years. But the course of the telecommunications boom has not run smoothly and the cell phone network is just as chaotic as the landline system, with frequent interruptions. The networks are confusingly not all connected to each other – it may be the case that one cell phone company doesn't let you connect to numbers of another company or doesn't allow you to phone a landline, and landlines cannot reach many of the cell phone providers. This is worth considering when choosing between making a call on a cell phone or from a landline depending on whom you are calling. **NB** If your own cell phone has got international roaming it may well work in Nigeria (on mine I could text but not phone).

The most common way that Nigerians make local phone calls is from the **phone stalls** on the street, which offer both landline phones (brought out from the nearest building on a very long extension cord) and GSM or cell phones. Many thousands of people have their own business of a phone stall that usually consists of one plastic table, two plastic chairs (one for the attendant with a working wrist watch, and one for the caller), one yellow umbrella usually sponsored by the cellular company such as MTN, and one phone. You give the attendant the telephone number, he or she dials it (sometimes repeatedly) until someone answers and then hands the phone to you. It's marvellously simple. Throughout the country costs are around N30–40 per minute nationally, and slightly less for a local call. Very occasionally you'll see phones that can call internationally and they cost around N60 per minute.

Major city codes are as follows:

| | | | | | |
|---|---|---|---|---|---|
| Abeokuta | 039 | Abuja | 09 | Bauchi | 077 |
| Benin City | 052 | Calabar | 087 | Enugu | 042 |
| Ibadan | 02 | Jos | 073 | Kaduna | 062 |
| Kano | 064 | Katsina | 065 | Lagos | 01 |
| Maiduguri | 076 | Makurdi | 044 | Oshogbo | 035 |
| Port Harcourt | 084 | Zaria | 069 | | |

## Post

There are differing opinions about the reliability of the Nigerian postal service. To put this to the test we sent a couple of letters home from Nigeria. They haven't turned up yet! Stamps are in denominations of N20, N30, N40 and N50, and it costs about N80 to send a letter to Europe. Post offices are generally open Monday to Friday 08.00–17.00 and Saturday 09.00–13.00. Some offer services for EMS Speedpost and some, like nearly all of the banks, are agents for Western Union. If you are sending anything home of sentimental or other value, I suggest using a courier company (see under *Listings* in the *Lagos* chapter).

## Electric devices

Electricity is 220 volts at 50Hz. If appliances do not fall within this specification then an adapter or voltage converter is needed. Three-pin British-style 13 amp plugs and sockets are the norm in Nigeria but don't assume all sockets have been earthed. In most buildings the electricity supply is precariously overloaded and in parts broken – there are wires hanging all over the place and a Nigerian fuse box would take pride of place in an electricity museum if such a place existed. Be very wary of touching any electrical socket or appliance that looks especially dodgy. Power cuts are common all day every day, particularly during the dry season when there is not enough hydro-electric power to feed the national grid. A torch and spare batteries are essential, though the major hotels do have backup generators. In the unlikely event that you are travelling with a laptop, remember power surges can be especially damaging (and if you're visiting from the US, you may need to bring a voltage regulator).

## Radio and television

The government grants licences to about 30 private stations which are generally all local stations run by each state. Programmes are broadcast in English as well as Yoruba, Hausa and Igbo. You are not going to watch much on these except the local news between 18.00 and 20.00, although they occasionally show CNN during the day. The South African media corporation, MTN, has set up multi-channel subscription television under its offshoot company called DSTV (Digital Satellite Television). An increasing number of hotels, even some of the cheaper ones, as well as bars and restaurants, subscribe to DSTV and although the packages vary, the service generally includes M-Net (South Africa's best-quality channel with up-to-date movies, documentaries and serials), Movie Magic (mostly one- to two-year-old movies), BBC World, CNN and Supersport (South Africa's 24-hour sports channel). More and more individual Nigerians are subscribing to the service if nothing more to watch the football (including the Manchester United FC TV satellite channel, whose existence I didn't even know about before going to Nigeria) and MNETAfrica (a channel that only shows Nigerian 'Nollywood' movies). Even in the cheapest chop house you may find all the occupants glued to an especially gripping 'Nollywood' movie on the TV in the corner. (See *TV* on page 82 earlier in this chapter for more details.)

Nigeria has well over 100 radio stations, so the best way to find out what is available is to hit the search button on your radio. Consequently, radio is hugely competitive and a number of FM stations have emerged, with Ray Power (100.5 FM), Cool FM (96.9 FM) and Rhythm (93.7 FM) being the most popular. Travellers with short-wave radios can pick up Voice of America, the World Service and Radio France Internationale. However, these do not broadcast 24 hours a day and their frequencies and times change throughout the year. It is worth checking their websites for schedules and programming.

## Internet and email

Internet cafés are open everywhere for easy and affordable internet access, though speed and availability of the web varies depending on whether the café uses an international service provider via satellite or the inferior and unreliable NITEL. Remember never to use internet banking in a Nigerian internet café. Servers are painfully slow compared to those in Europe or the US, though on occasion you'll find one that is super-quick. Often, as you do for photocopying, you pay slightly more for an hour's internet time 'during gen' than 'during NEPA' (see page 332 for an explanation of these terms). Expect to pay in the region of N150 per hour. Finally, when I asked a security guard at one office block if there was an 'internet café' there he said no very definitely, but when I asked him if there was a 'cyber café', he said 'Oh yes madam, it's upstairs'.

## Newspapers and magazines

In Lagos, thanks to the frequency of arrivals by international airlines, you can buy up-to-date international newspapers and magazines at vastly inflated prices from the bookshops of the major hotels. These include one- or two-day-old newspapers including *The Telegraph, The Times, The European, Le Monde, USA Today* and *The International Herald Tribune*, and magazines as far ranging as *PC World* to *Hello!* The Nigerian press is privately owned and thus fairly open and opinionated (and sometimes downright funny) and local English-language newspapers include *The Guardian, The Comet, This Day* (the paper whose articles caused controversy during the 2002 Miss World competition), *Daily Times, Daily News, Vanguard* and several others, though few feature much international news. There are also scores of weekly news magazines that in presentation at least have copied the style of the US *Times* and *Newsweek* (also available).

## Film processing

The quality of film processing is not consistent, but there are modern film-processing shops all over Nigeria, mostly Agfa shops. To have a film processed you must pay up front.

# Health and Safety

Nigeria's poor infrastructure, colossal population, poverty, terrible roads and high crime rate combine to create what can only be described as not a very healthy or safe place to visit. Travelling in tropical Africa exposes us to diseases caused by parasites, bacteria and viruses, some so bizarre we may never have heard of them before. Illnesses are passed around in food and water, or by insects and bugs, and can even be contracted from passing an infected person on the street. Added to this is the high crime rate and manic, highly publicised congestion on the roads. If you are still in some doubt about going to Nigeria then this is the chapter that is likely to scare you off for good. However, remember that with the right precautions and a sensible attitude, the following events or illnesses are unlikely to happen to you. Getting fully acquainted with them in the first place, and knowing what to do if something goes wrong when you get there, can minimise all Nigeria's health and safety risks. Prevention is the best way to stay healthy and safe. For this reason it's important to digest the information in this chapter right through to the end, which will help you to prepare for your trip effectively. To put things in perspective, after malaria, which can be prevented by taking the right precautions, the biggest danger for a traveller in Nigeria is being involved in a road accident.

## HEALTH
*with Dr Jane Wilson-Howarth and Dr Felicity Nicholson*

It's important to mention right from the start that Nigeria's healthcare system is seriously inadequate. Do not even consider going if you have an existing medical condition that needs regular attention or if you think you might be pregnant, though on the flipside, if you are a traveller with adequate medical insurance or an expat with healthcare sponsored by your company, then the chances are that top-class facilities will be made available to you in the case of an emergency, and people who contract serious injury or illness will be evacuated to their country of origin. Obviously there are under-developed areas, urban as well as rural; Lagos is one of the unhealthiest places on earth, with poor sanitation, dire healthcare facilities, and waste and rubbish problems. These are places where infectious diseases thrive, but for the tourist or business traveller who pays attention to hygiene and to what they are eating and drinking, and who stays in an adequate hotel, they won't pose too much of a threat.

## Before you go
### Preparation
Ideally you should visit your GP or travel clinic at least eight weeks before your departure to discuss your health generally and to organise the relevant immunisations and malaria medication. If you don't already know it, this is the time to find out what blood group you are. Visit your dentist if you are going to be away for some time, and if you have a serious allergy or long-term condition such

as diabetes or epilepsy make sure someone knows about it or get a Medic Alert bracelet. Nigeria has a serious problem with fake drugs – some of which can be lethal – and imported medical products, if they are genuine in the first place, are very expensive. Ensure that you bring any necessary prescription or over-the-counter medication with you, and if you have to buy drugs in Nigeria only go to a reputable recommended pharmacist.

## Travel insurance
Don't leave home without it. Comprehensive medical insurance is essential and the cover must include repatriation to your home country by air in case of an emergency. Remember to carry the details and phone number of the insurance company with you.

## Immunisations
Immunisation against **yellow fever** is essential and proof may be required on entry, and always if you are coming from another yellow fever infected area. There is a real risk of contracting yellow fever, particularly in the bigger cities. **Cholera** is a serious risk in high-density urban areas, so if you have time then consider having the oral cholera vaccine (Dukoral) now available in the UK. This palatable berry-flavoured drink is said to offer about 75% protection against the more common strains of cholera. For adults and children six years and over, two doses are needed, taken at least one week but no more than six weeks apart. Ideally the second dose should be taken at least one week before entering an infected area. Two doses of vaccine will provide cover for two years. For children aged two to five, three doses are needed for the same efficacy, but protection lasts only for six months. Despite World Health Organisation guidelines issued in 1973, stating that a cholera vaccination certificate is not a condition of entry to Nigeria, there have been instances of certain nationals being asked to produce proof of vaccination on entry. If you don't have time to take the vaccine or are going for just a short visit (less than three–four weeks) then the easiest way round this is to get your doctor to stamp your vaccination card with a 'cholera exempt' stamp. **Typhoid** and **hepatitis A** and **B** are present in Nigeria and immunisations are highly recommended. **Meningitis** and **rabies** immunisations should also be seriously considered. Routine immunisations, such as **tetanus**, **diphtheria** and **polio**, should be reviewed and updated. If you do decide to have an armful of jabs, start organising them at least six weeks before departure, and remember that a yellow fever certificate becomes valid only ten days after you've had the vaccination.

## Children
If you are travelling with children, especially if you are an expat who intends to take your family with you to Nigeria, they should in addition be properly protected against whooping cough, haemophilus influenzae, mumps, measles and rubella (German measles). An invaluable book is *Your Child Abroad: A travel health guide* by Dr Jane Wilson-Howarth and Dr Matthew Ellis (Bradt Tavel Guides, 2005).

## Malaria
Malaria exists *all* year round *all* over Nigeria, including in urban areas, and is the biggest health threat to Nigerians. It's essential to take sensible malaria preventative steps. The obvious advice is to avoid getting bitten in the first place. Wear long trousers and sleeves in the evening and use insect repellents, and choose a hotel room that is as mossie proof as possible. (See under *Insects and bugs*, page 103, for further advice on how to avoid mosquito bites.)

Malaria kills an estimated one million Africans annually, and is the biggest health threat to travellers in tropical Africa. There are four types of malaria, but only one, the falciparum strain, can lead to death if not treated promptly. In Nigeria 90–95% of all malaria is caused by the potentially deadly falciparum strain. As someone who has had malaria more times than she would care to remember, I cannot stress here strongly enough how important it is to prepare yourself against catching malaria *before* going to Nigeria. All malaria is dangerous but the falciparum strain of malaria has been known to kill in less than 24 hours.

Malaria is caused by a parasite carried in the saliva of the female *Anopheles* mosquito, which flies between dusk and dawn, generally near to the ground. The parasite is transmitted into the bloodstream through a mosquito bite, where it will multiply and infect the blood, liver and eventually the brain. It starts out as something resembling severe flu, with symptoms such as headaches, fever, lethargy, and aching limbs, and sometimes vomiting and diarrhoea. Soon after the sufferer will experience extreme fevers that come in waves, inducing excessive sweating and shivering, a rapid rise in body temperature, and fluid loss. If the disease is allowed to develop further, what follows are fits, delirium, coma, organ failure, and eventually death.

It's important to remember that malarial symptoms can subside for up to 48 hours before returning, so just because you may start to feel better it doesn't mean you don't have malaria – still get treated. The disease has an incubation period of between a few days and several weeks so you can fall ill some time after an infected mosquito has bitten you. If you are pregnant or have very small children, it would be wise to consider *not* travelling to such a high-risk malarial area; such travellers are likely to succumb rapidly to the disease.

## Prophylactic drugs

Despite valiant efforts there is still no vaccine against malaria, so the only sensible option is to take prophylactic drugs and use insect repellents. Prophylactic drugs greatly reduce the chances of getting the disease and if you still contract malaria whilst taking the drugs, you are likely to get a milder bout. Travellers to Africa are unable to build up any resistance to malaria and those that don't take prophylactic drugs will be risking their lives. The falciparum strain has been reported to be resistant to chloroquine. So, the combination prophylactic of chloroquine and Proguanil/Paludrine is only used as a last resort when no other tablet is suitable to take. At the time of writing, the prophylactics advised are mefloquine (Lariam), doxycycline, or atovaquone (Malarone). Because no malaria drug is 100% effective, seek immediate medical attention for any fever or flu-like symptoms occurring within three months of your return home, and be sure to tell your doctor your travel history.

Lariam or mefloquine (250mg tablet once a week) is effective but doesn't suit everyone; 20–30% of users suffer from significant side effects and have to discontinue use and change to an alternative prophylactic. Psychological effects such as paranoia and psychosis have been reported in some cases and it is not advised for anyone with a history of psychiatric problems or epilepsy. It should only be taken on a doctor's recommendation and if you have never used it before then you should start at least two-and-a-half weeks before departure to check that it suits you. If you have used Lariam before then you can start one week before, and either way the drug should be continued for four weeks after leaving the last malarial area. Doxycycline (100mg daily), a broad-based antibiotic, is a good alternative prophylactic if you can't take Lariam, and you only need to start taking it one day before arriving and again four weeks after being in a malarial area. Doxy is not advised for pregnant women or children under 12. There are few side effects, but women on the pill should use alternative forms of contraception for the first four weeks, and between 1% and 3% of people taking it suffer from sun sensitivity on their skin. If this happens then you must stop taking the doxycycline as it is an allergic reaction which may get worse. Malarone is a newer and very effective drug that is started one to two days before arriving and that needs to be taken for only seven days after visiting a malarial area. Reports so far record that it is as effective as Lariam and both are probably slightly more effective than doxycycline. It is expensive but it has the advantage of having fewer side effects.

If you are going to Nigeria to work on a long contract, it's perhaps not advisable to continually take anti-malarial drugs for what feasibly could be a number of years. Discuss this with your doctor. Some expats I spoke to took nothing and never got malaria, though they often rarely left their air-conditioned homes, offices and cars, whilst another I spoke to had been taking Lariam for six years and when he stopped he got malaria! However, this practice is not to be recommended as Lariam should not be continued for more than two years.

### Diagnosis and treatment

Self-test kits for malaria are now available from some pharmacists and you may want to consider carrying one with you. However, they are far from 100% accurate, and if you've never had malaria before I would strongly advise against using them. For someone like me who has had malaria before and instantly recognises the symptoms that are unique to my body, they are useful to carry. But for someone who has contracted the disease for the first time, doesn't know what is happening to his or her body, and is probably too ill to do the test correctly enough to make the right diagnosis, it is dangerous to rely on self-test kits. If you think you may have symptoms, and have a very high suspicion of all symptoms however vague they may be, get a full malarial blood test done by a doctor as soon as possible. Local doctors in Nigeria are more than familiar with the disease and any clinic or hospital will be able to give you a malaria test. The most common form of treatment is quinine and Fansidar, because it is cheap. However, it is not considered to be the most effective any more, so you may wish to take more up-to-date treatment with you. Consult a specialist before you go to get the most appropriate medication. Newer and more effective treatments include Malarone and Riamet. Halfan – a previously popular treatment – is no longer recommended for anyone. Note that the Royal Homeopathic Hospital in the UK does not advocate any homeopathic options for malaria prevention or treatment.

### Travel clinics and health information

A full list of current travel clinic websites worldwide is available from the International Society of Travel Medicine on www.istm.org. For other journey preparation information, consult www.tripprep.com. Information about various medications may be found on www.emedicine.com.

### UK

**Berkeley Travel Clinic** 32 Berkeley St, London W1J 8EL (near Green Park tube station); tel: 020 7629 6233

**British Airways Travel Clinic and Immunisation Service** There are two BA clinics in London, both on tel: 0845 600 2236; www.ba.com/travelclinics. Appointments only Mon–Fri 9.00–16.30 at 101 Cheapside, London EC2V 6DT; or walk-in service Mon–Fri 09.30–17.30, Sat 10.00–16.00 at 213 Piccadilly, London W1J 9HQ. Apart from providing inoculations and malaria prevention, they sell a variety of health-related goods.

**Edinburgh Travel Clinic** Regional Infectious Diseases Unit, Ward 41 OPD, Western General Hospital, Crewe Rd South, Edinburgh EH4 2UX; tel: 0131 537 2822; www.link.med.ed.ac.uk/ridu. Travel helpline (0906 589 0380) open 09.00–12.00 weekdays. Provides inoculations and anti-malarial prophylaxis and advises on travel-related health risks.

**Fleet Street Travel Clinic** 29 Fleet St, London EC4Y 1AA; tel: 020 7353 5678; www.fleetstreetclinic.com. Vaccinations, travel products and latest advice.

**Hospital for Tropical Diseases Travel Clinic** Mortimer Market Building, Capper St (off Tottenham Ct Rd), London WC1E 6AU; tel: 020 7388 9600; www.thehtd.org. Offers consultations and advice, and is able to provide all necessary drugs and vaccines for travellers. Runs a healthline (09061 337733) for country-specific information and health hazards. Also stocks nets, water purification equipment and personal protection measures.

**Interhealth Worldwide** Partnership House, 157 Waterloo Rd, London SE1 8US; tel: 020 7902 9000; www.interhealth.org.uk. Competitively priced, one-stop travel health service. All profits go to their affiliated company, InterHealth, which provides health care for overseas workers on Christian projects.

**MASTA** (Medical Advisory Service for Travellers Abroad) London School of Hygiene and Tropical Medicine, Keppel St, London WC1 7HT; tel: 09065 501402; www.masta.org. Individually tailored health briefs available for a fee, with up-to-date information on how to stay healthy, inoculations and what to bring. There are currently 30 MASTA pre-travel clinics in Britain. Call 0870 241 6843 or check online for the nearest. Clinics also sell malaria prophylaxis memory cards, treatment kits, bednets, net treatment kits.

**NHS travel website** www.fitfortravel.scot.nhs.uk, provides country-by-country advice on immunisation and malaria, plus details of recent developments, and a list of relevant health organisations.

**Nomad Travel Store/Clinic** 3–4 Wellington Terrace, Turnpike Lane, London N8 0PX; tel: 020 8889 7014; travel-health line (office hours only) 09068 633414; email: sales@nomadtravel.co.uk; www.nomadtravel.co.uk. Also at 40 Bernard St, London WC1N 1LJ; tel: 020 7833 4114; 52 Grosvenor Gardens, London SW1W 0AG; 020 7823 5823; and 43 Queens Rd, Bristol BS8 1QH; tel: 0117 922 6567. For health advice, equipment such as mosquito nets and other anti-bug devices, and an excellent range of adventure travel gear.

**Trailfinders Travel Clinic** 194 Kensington High St, London W8 7RG; tel: 020 7938 3999; www.trailfinders.com/clinic.htm

**Cambridge Travel Clinic** 48a Mill Rd, Cambridge CB1 2AS; tel: 01223 367362; email: enquiries@cambridgetravelclinic.co.uk; www.cambridgetravelclinic.co.uk. Open 12.00–19.00 Tue–Fri, 10.00–16.00 Sat.

**Travelpharm** The Travelpharm website, www.travelpharm.com, offers up-to-date guidance on travel-related health and has a range of medications available through their online mini-pharmacy.

## Irish Republic
**Tropical Medical Bureau** Grafton Street Medical Centre, Grafton Buildings, 34 Grafton St, Dublin 2; tel: 1 671 9200; www.tmb.ie. A useful website specific to tropical destinations. Also check website for other bureau locations throughout Ireland.

## USA
**Centers for Disease Control** 1600 Clifton Rd, Atlanta, GA 30333; tel: 800 311 3435; travellers' health hotline 888 232 3299; www.cdc.gov/travel. The central source of travel information in the USA. Maps and outbreak alerts, and general travel health advice. The invaluable Health Information for International Travel, published annually, is available online or from the Division of Quarantine at this address.

**Connaught Laboratories** PO Box 187, Swiftwater, PA 18370; tel: 800 822 2463. They will send a free list of specialist tropical-medicine physicians in your state.
**IAMAT** (International Association for Medical Assistance to Travelers) 1623 Military Rd, 279, Niagara Falls, NY14304-1745; tel: 716 754 4883; email: info@iamat.org; www.iamat.org. A non-profit organisation that provides lists of English-speaking doctors abroad.
**International Medicine Center** 920 Frostwood Drive, Suite 670, Houston, TX 77024; tel: 713 550 2000; www.traveldoc.com

## Canada
**IAMAT** Suite 1, 1287 St Clair Av W, Toronto, Ontario M6E 1B8; tel: 416 652 0137; www.iamat.org
**TMVC** (Travel Doctors Group) Sulphur Springs Rd, Ancaster, Ontario; tel: 905 648 1112; www.tmvc-group.com

## Australia, New Zealand, Singapore
**TMVC** Tel: 1300 65 88 44; www.tmvc.com.au. Twenty-three clinics in Australia, New Zealand and Singapore including:
*Auckland* Canterbury Arcade, 170 Queen St, Auckland; tel: 9 373 3531
*Brisbane* 6th floor, 247 Adelaide St, Brisbane, QLD 4000; tel: 7 3221 9066
*Melbourne* 393 Little Bourke St, 2nd floor, Melbourne, VIC 3000; tel: 3 9602 5788
*Sydney* Dymocks Building, 7th Floor, 428 George St, Sydney, NSW 2000; tel: 2 9221 7133
**IAMAT** PO Box 5049, Christchurch 5, New Zealand; www.iamat.org

## South Africa
**SAA-Netcare Travel Clinics** Private Bag X34, Benmore 2010; www.travelclinic.co.za. Clinics throughout South Africa.
**TMVC** 113 DF Malan Drive, Roosevelt Park, Johannesburg; tel: 011 888 7488; www.tmvc.com.au. Consult the website for details of eight other clinics in South Africa.

## Switzerland
**IAMAT** 57 Chemin des Voirets, 1212 Grand Lancy, Geneva; www.iamat.org

## Medical kit
A comprehensive medical kit is an important part of your luggage when going to Nigeria, especially if you are staying long-term to, say, work. Whilst nobody wants to lumber themselves up with too heavy a medical kit when travelling, it is important to remember that Nigeria has an appalling reputation for supplying fake and out-of-date drugs, so it is best to go well prepared. None of the items listed here are readily available in Nigeria so take sufficient amounts with you. Your medical kit should contain malaria prophylactics, malaria treatment (only to be used if prescribed for you by a doctor), soluble aspirin or paracetamol (good for gargling for mouth and throat infections and to reduce fever and aches and pains), iodine (for sterilising water and cleaning wounds), antiseptic cream or powder, antihistamine cream or tablets (for irritated mossie bites), Imodium (a standby for when diarrhoea occurs at an awkward time), oral rehydration sachets (to replace lost salts during diarrhoea), and a broad-based antibiotic such as doxycycline or Ciproxin (Ciprofloxacin) or Flagyl or tinidazole (for problem diarrhoea). Also, take bandages, plasters and tweezers. Other items not to forget include sunblock, mosquito repellent, condoms, contact-lens cleaning solution, and sanitary wear (all rarely found in Nigeria).

For a range of books related to health issues, see *Further Reading*, page 337.

# In Nigeria
## Medical facilities
Nigeria's government-provided public healthcare facilities are of a poor standard and are subject to shortages of doctors and nurses, drugs, equipment, and even electricity. You would be ill advised to seek treatment in a public hospital and it is essential that you take a sufficient supply of drugs or medication to meet personal needs. There are some adequate private facilities in Lagos where the standards approach those of Europe, but facilities are expensive and doctors and hospitals often expect immediate cash payment up front for health services. Medical insurance is essential. In this book we list medical facilities recommended to us by Nigeria's expat community, but if you are in any doubt consult your embassy in Nigeria for their recommendation of a clinic or hospital used by diplomats.

## Health hazards
### Bilharzia
Bilharzia or *schistosomiasis* is a tiny parasite carried by freshwater snails and is prevalent in Nigeria's rivers and dams. The parasite burrows into human skin and multiplies in the bloodstream, eventually working its way up to the bladder and intestine, where it lay its eggs. Symptoms vary but can include blood in the urine or faeces, fever and flu-like symptoms, lethargy, and swelling of the liver or spleen. The disease is much harder to treat when advanced, though it doesn't cause too much discomfort if caught early enough and it's just a matter of taking a one-off treatment of the drug praziquantel. Avoid swimming and paddling in fresh water and if there is any chance you may have contracted bilharzia have a blood test as soon as you get home. Swimming pools that are well maintained and chlorinated are safe.

### Cholera
Cholera is caused by bacteria carried in polluted water or contaminated vegetables, and infects the lining of the intestine. Symptoms include abdominal cramps, diarrhoea, vomiting and rapid dehydration. Diarrhoea can be so severe that several litres of fluids can be lost from the body in a single day, and it is especially dangerous in small children who dehydrate very quickly. Treatment consists of fluid replacement and antibiotics, but as it tends to break out only in overcrowded areas with poor sanitation, it poses little threat to the well-nourished traveller. For those at higher risk, for example if you have a chronic and potentially debilitating disease such as diabetes, or if you are living and working in areas of poor sanitation, then consider taking the newer oral cholera vaccine (Dukoral).

### Food and drink
Quite a few diseases, including hepatitis A and typhoid, are transmitted by unsanitary food handling and contaminated water. *All* tap water in Nigeria should be regarded as being potentially contaminated – especially city water such as that in Lagos, which is most definitely not suitable for drinking, or anything else for that matter save flushing the toilet. Water used for drinking, brushing teeth or making ice throughout the country should have first been boiled or sterilised; otherwise stick to bottled water. Beware of salads washed in water and ice in restaurants and hotels – as painful as it may seem, order drinks without ice (not that you'll see it very often) or order hot drinks such as tea and coffee. Also, be aware when buying bottled water, especially on the side of the road where bottles may have been filled up from the tap – check the seal is intact. Bottled water is not always easy to find so buy it when you see it. Most water in Nigeria is sold in half-

litre plastic bags generally called 'pure water', which are sold everywhere and are usually cold – the plastic bags are the scourge of Nigeria's rubbish problem. They are, however, far from pure, and are presumably filled from a tap. My advice is to avoid them like the plague in Lagos and perhaps the other bigger cities, but in the outlying regions they should be OK. We certainly didn't get sick from drinking 'pure water', but the problem is you can never be sure where the water has come from. Like other African countries, water in Nigeria does not contain fluoride supplements so those who are staying long term may want to consider fluoride treatments from their dentists before and after leaving home.

Milk is not pasteurised and should be boiled. Powdered or tinned milk is available and is the better bet, but make sure it is reconstituted with clean water. Avoid dairy products that are likely to have been made from unboiled milk, and only buy dairy products from one of the supermarkets specialising in imported goods. Many expats first freeze dairy products before using them just to be on the safe side and rinse their fruit and vegetables with a sterilising solution such as Milton before use.

## Heat and humidity

Nigeria is hot and humid pretty much all year round and sensible sun protection is essential. Tanning causes wrinkles and over-exposure to the sun is directly related to skin cancer. Use sunscreen with a high (15+) SPF and wear a broad-brimmed hat. Bring sunscreen with you, as it's not readily available in Nigeria. If you are coming from a cooler climate get used to the sun gradually or you will get burnt. On your first day start by only exposing your skin for a 20-minute period and increase this slowly to a maximum of two hours per day, avoiding the sun altogether in the middle of the day. Don't be lulled into complacency on cloudy days, as this is when UV levels can be especially high. Short-term over-exposure leads to burning, headaches and nausea, and in the extreme can lead to heatstroke and dehydration. If on your return home you notice any changes to moles on your body get them checked out. Melanomas can be removed if caught early enough, but malignant melanomas cause skin cancer if ignored.

In humid weather, we sweat more than normal, which can lead to dehydration, and Nigeria is a very sweaty place. As soon as you leave the confines of an air-conditioned room you will begin to sweat. It is important to remember to replace lost fluids and salt by drinking plenty of liquids and adding more salt to your food. There isn't much salt in Nigerian food, and outside of Lagos you are very unlikely to see a salt shaker on a restaurant table, so I strongly suggest that salt is something you should think about travelling around with.

Prickly heat, a fine pimply rash caused by sweat trapped under the skin, is common and harmless, but can be uncomfortable and itchy. Dab with cold water or soothe with a cooling lotion such as aloe vera. Humidity can also promote fungal infections, particularly on the scalp, feet and groin, so wear loose-fitting, preferably cotton clothing and pay attention to personal hygiene. If you notice an itchy and flaky rash between your toes or in the groin area this is likely to be a fungal infection and will need treating with Canesten (clotrimazole) cream.

## Hepatitis

Hepatitis is an infection of the liver which can be caused by one of several viruses spread by contact with blood, saliva and nasal mucus. It can also spread through contaminated food or foodstuff that has come from polluted water such as raw shellfish, and in the case of hepatitis B, through unprotected sexual intercourse. Symptoms include jaundice (yellowing of the skin and eyes), weakness, loss of appetite, abdominal pain, pale-coloured stools, and dark yellow urine. The severity of the illness varies considerably, and depending on which virus is involved some people may experience liver problems in later life. Some people may also show no symptoms but will still act as unwitting carriers. There is a growing list of types labelled from A through to E, with A and B being the most common. Both diseases are prevalent in Nigeria so immunisation against both of these is highly recommended. However, if you have not received these vaccines and suspect that you have been in contact with either disease then seek medical help at once. Immunisation, if given quickly after exposure, can be highly effective in preventing the disease.

## HIV/AIDS and sexually transmitted diseases

Nigeria has yet to hit the explosive rates of infection and death seen in eastern and southern Africa, but unless significant steps are taken, HIV/AIDS will truly take its toll in Nigeria if the present trends are not reversed, and any exposure to contaminated blood or body fluids may put an individual at risk. The estimated 3.5 million Nigerians living with HIV/AIDS is a figure larger than entire populations of other African nations. As with most African countries, the transmission of HIV/AIDS in Nigeria is through heterosexual activity, and the danger of catching the virus through unprotected sex is very real. There is widespread prostitution, and a high proportion of this population is likely to be HIV positive. Gonorrhoea and syphilis are also rampant in Nigeria and many strains are resistant to antibiotics. Abstinence from sex is the only 100% effective prevention, but using condoms or femidoms reduces the risk considerably. Catching the AIDS virus does not necessarily produce an illness in itself, though if you notice any genital warts or discharge seek prompt medical attention. The only way to feel sure if you have been put at risk is to have a blood test for HIV antibodies when you get home. Unfortunately, Nigeria has one of Africa's most inadequate HIV/AIDS educational programmes, and one of the highest rates of unsafe blood transfusions in the world. For peace of mind, pack a few needles and hypodermic syringes in your medical kit in the unlikely event that you have to have a blood transfusion in a public or remote hospital.

## Insects and bugs

Apart from malaria (see page 96), Nigeria's mosquitoes, flies, fleas, bugs and worms transmit a variety of diseases, or can simply just use your body as a temporary home. Personal protective measures are extremely important since insects are almost impossible to avoid. Most insects, including mosquitoes, are attracted to light. In hotel rooms, be aware that the longer you leave a light on, the more bugs you are likely to attract as bedmates. Even the cheapest Nigerian hotels have air conditioning or fans, which help combat the bug problem, but remember that the AC goes off when there's no NEPA or when the generator is switched off for a few hours in the middle of the night. Electric mosquito-zappers that you fit with a pad each night are reasonably effective, but again require electricity. It's also worthwhile blasting your room with a fly spray a couple of hours before going to bed. When choosing a hotel room check that the mosquito netting on the windows is intact; often it can be full of holes.

Wear long trousers, long sleeves, and socks from dusk onwards, and cover exposed parts of your body with an insect repellent, preferably a DEET (Diethyltoluamide) based product. Apply every few hours, and more often if you sweat heavily. If you prefer not to use a DEET product in case of allergy or reaction, then use a validated non-DEET product; Non-DEET, Mosiguard, and non-DEET

Autan have all been tested by the London School of Tropical Medicine and Hygiene. When walking through bush and forest areas through the day, it's also a good idea to use a repellent and to cover yourself to protect against irritating midges.

**Dengue fever** is contracted from the *Aedes* mosquito, which has a particular passion for shallow pools of water and freshly watered flowerpots and gardens where they like to breed. Also, these mosquitoes fly during daylight hours so make sure you apply repellents at all times. It's another severe flu-like illness; symptoms include fever, lethargy, a rash, and aching muscles. The disease follows a rather rollercoaster type of cycle, usually lasting around a week, though it can last much longer. It kicks in suddenly for about two to three days, and then appears to get better for a couple of days, before attacking again for another two to three days. There is no specific treatment save for rest, rehydration and recuperation.

**Hookworms** are parasitic worms that live in the soil in areas of poor sanitation or in the sand on beaches contaminated by dog faeces. They enter the bloodstream through the soles of your feet so avoid walking barefoot. They move around under the skin causing an unpleasant skin reaction of slowly moving itchy red lines, but can be effectively treated with antibiotics.

**Jiggers** or **sandfleas** latch on to your feet if you walk barefoot in contaminated places, such as damp soil and sand, or wet grass. They burrow under the skin of the foot, especially in the soft places between the toes where they cause a painful, hard, boil-like swelling. To get them out you need to carefully break the surface and draw out the worm by winding it around something like a pencil. It is repulsive, and as your feet are not easy to reach, it's best to let a local expert do it. If the jigger bursts on eviction, douse the hole with spirit alcohol to prevent further infestation.

**River blindness** or *onchocerciasis* is present in many West African countries and is spread by small black flies that breed near fast-flowing rivers and rapids. An egg is laid beneath the skin that in turn hatches into a worm, which will live in, and feed off, your bloodstream. Symptoms vary and as the worm can live inside your body for a considerable time (up to 18 years), it's difficult to diagnose. The most common symptom is irritable skin rashes caused by the worms moving around under the skin. In extreme cases, the worm will pass through the eyes causing damage, hence the term river blindness. The only prevention is to wear long sleeves and trousers to help keep them at bay. Citronella repellents don't work against them. Treatment is by an 150mg oral dosage of Ivermectin every 6–12 months. This doesn't kill the parasites, but prevents the disease progressing under the skin.

**Tick bites** can cause several unpleasant illnesses in Africa, the most common being tick-bite fever, which produces swollen glands, severe aching of the bones, backache and fever. There is no specific treatment; you just have to let it run its course for three to four days. The good news is that ticks you may find on yourself will not inevitably give you some disease, and you are unlikely to catch anything if you get the tick off quickly and completely. Grasp the tick as close to your body as possible and pull out cleanly at a right angle. Make sure you pull out the head as well as the body – it's not painful. Douse the wound with iodine or alcohol and if redness appears indicating an infection, you may need antibiotics.

**Tsetse** flies administer a sharp painful bite, which while irritating is on the whole harmless. Bigger than houseflies, they are prevalent in much of Nigeria and are much more of a threat to cattle, which explains the lack of dairy and beef products throughout the country. Tsetse flies are found in outlying rural areas, bite in daylight and are attracted to the colours blue and green. They can carry sleeping sickness but the disease is very limited to the tsetse fly's range and is of minimal threat to travellers.

**Tumbu** or **putsi** flies lay their eggs in wet clothing, bedding, or in damp soil. Expats living in Nigeria complain about them in the cushions of their garden furniture and most do not dry their washing outside. The eggs hatch in the fabric and can penetrate your skin to lay yet more eggs. After a day or two, the larvae develop into worms and an inflamed boil-like infection will appear on the skin that can sometimes be quite severe. After about eight days, they will emerge from the skin by themselves, but applying Vaseline to the lesion can speed up the process. This starves the worm of oxygen and brings it to the surface quicker, where it can be extracted with tweezers. Always dry clothes on an airy clothesline in direct sunlight until they are crisp, or iron with a hot iron afterwards – the heat kills the eggs.

## Meningitis

Meningitis is an inflammation of the meninges, the membranous coverings of the brain and spinal cord, and can be caused by one of several bacteria or viruses. The seriousness of the disease depends on the causative organism, which can spread through the air through coughing and sneezing. Infection can spread from something as simple as an ear or sinus infection to other parts of the body via the bloodstream. Symptoms include respiratory illness, fever, headaches, skin rashes, and sometimes vomiting. If you show symptoms, go to a doctor immediately, as prompt treatment with antibiotics is required. Immunisation against the most severe form of bacterial meningitis is available (meningitis ACWY vaccine) and is recommended for Nigeria.

## Rabies

Rabies, also known as hydrophobia, is a potentially fatal disease spread through blood or saliva. The most common way to get it is to be bitten by an infected animal but it can also be transmitted by a scratch, or a lick of an open wound. It's prevalent in African dogs and monkeys but can be carried by all mammals. The virus travels from the wound to the spinal cord and brain, and the incubation period can be as long as twelve months. Symptoms include fever, restlessness and depression, proceeding to more dramatic symptoms such as salivation, muscle spasms and a fear of drinking water (hence it being called hydrophobia). If you are bitten you must always assume that the animal is rabid and seek medical help as soon as possible. In the meantime, wash the wound with clean water and soap and then apply an iodine or alcohol solution, which will help stop the rabies virus entering the bloodstream and prevent other infections such as tetanus. Effective treatment is in the form of a vaccine, and remember to tell the doctor if you have already had a pre-exposure vaccine. If you haven't you will also need an injection of something called immunoglobulin, which is expensive and in short supply. For those who are specifically working with animals or will be away from medical help for prolonged periods, pre-exposure vaccination is advised. Ideally, three vaccines should be taken over a minimum period of 21 days for maximum protection.

## Tetanus

Tetanus, or lockjaw, is caused by bacteria living in soil or animal faeces and is transmitted through deep dirty wounds, such as those caused by a rusty nail or an animal bite. Ensure wounds are kept thoroughly cleaned and be sensible about first aid. The bacterium produces a poison that attacks the spinal cord nerves controlling muscle spasm. This leads to stiffness, especially in the jaw, difficulty in swallowing, restlessness and fever. A tetanus vaccination gives good cover for a ten-year period so make sure your immunisation is up to date or get a tetanus booster before you leave home. If you are involved in a serious accident or get bitten badly by, say, a dog, it's also wise to seek treatment.

## Travellers' diarrhoea

Most travellers to tropical Africa will suffer from a bout of diarrhoea, and the newer you are to tropical travel the more likely you are to get it. Indeed, one study showed that up to 70% of *all* travellers anywhere may suffer during their trip, so be fully prepared for a stomach bug in Nigeria. Nigerians refer to it quite aptly as a 'running stomach'; it needs no more description than that!

Diarrhoea is caused by bacteria spread through unhygienic food handling, and to a lesser extent, contaminated water. (See under *Food and drink* above for precautions you can take when eating and drinking.)

Dehydration or excess fluid loss is the reason diarrhoea makes you feel so awful, so the best cure is to rest and drink lots of clean water to flush the bacteria out of your system. The loss of salts cause stomach cramps and oral rehydration sachets such as Electrolade are a good idea. If these are not available, then make your own by adding a spoonful of salt and sugar to a glass of water topped with a tot of lemon or orange juice to improve the taste. If no safe drinking water is available than you can do the same with a glass of, preferably flat, Coke or similar carbonated drinks. Stick to plain starchy food such as dry biscuits, boiled rice and potatoes, and drink as much fluid as you can, especially if you have lost your appetite.

Avoid jumping for drugs immediately. Instead, let the diarrhoea run its course for at least the first 36–48 hours, which in most cases is long enough for it to clear up on its own. Blockers such as Imodium or Lomotil not only block the diarrhoea but the bacteria that caused it in the first place and don't cure anything, though you may need to resort to these temporarily if you are in an awkward location, such as when travelling on a bus, and do not have easy access to the toilet. If the diarrhoea persists for over 36 hours without improvement or is accompanied by other, unusual symptoms then see a doctor. Ciproxin (ciprofloxacin) is the antibiotic usually administered for severe diarrhoea with blood and/or slime in the stools and/or a fever. A single 500mg dose repeated 6–12 hours later usually does the trick if it is going to work at all. Ideally no medication should be taken until you have seen a doctor, but this may not always be possible.

Giardiasis is also a common form of gut illness which produces greasy, bulky stools, stomach cramps and characteristic 'eggy' burps. If you are suffering from these symptoms seek medical help as soon as possible. More experienced travellers may wish to carry tinidazole – an effective treatment for giardia. At the first sign of infection take four 500mg tablets in one go and if symptoms persist repeat the dose three to seven days later. Again it is always best to seek a doctor's advice before doing this.

## Typhoid

Typhoid is a bacteria spread through contaminated food and water or through direct contact with an infected person's faeces. Flies carrying the bacteria from faeces to food may also spread the disease. Symptoms include loss of appetite, aching muscles, vomiting, fever, abdominal pain and headaches. Some people get the infection without any symptoms, but can still pass it on to others and act as carriers for the disease. Symptoms are similar to malaria so in the event of testing negative for malaria ask your doctor to test for typhoid. Treatment is with antibiotics. A typhoid vaccine is extremely effective and recommended for Nigeria. Also, pay particular attention to sanitary food handling and drinking clean water.

## Tuberculosis

Tuberculosis (TB) is common in all developing countries, but Nigeria has a prevalence of over 100 cases per 100,000, putting it in the highest World Health Organisation risk category. TB is a highly contagious bacterial infection spread via respiratory secretions such as coughing and sneezing. Eating or drinking unpasteurised dairy products can also lead to pelvic TB that can cause infertility and intestinal blockage. Respiratory symptoms include coughing blood, night sweats, weight loss, and shortness of breath, and developed TB can spread to other organs causing a variety of serious symptoms. Treatment is a long course of antibiotics over at least six months. There have been cases of Nigerian expats contracting the disease from long-term exposure to infected household help. Although it's almost impossible to do, particularly in downtown Lagos, the only practical advice is to avoid people coughing in your face in crowded public places. Travellers planning to stay more than three months who have not received a BCG vaccination before should consult with a doctor at least six weeks before travelling, in case vaccination is recommended. If you have an unexplained illness on your return home, ask your doctor to consider TB.

# SAFETY
## Road accidents

Bugs, bowel movements and tropical diseases aside, your safety during any trip to Nigeria is most likely to be endangered by getting around by road. Traffic everywhere, and most famously in Lagos, is one big aggressive snarl-up. The city roads are choked and congested beyond belief, whilst the highways and expressways between the cities are poorly maintained, and they are utilised by manic drivers who have no respect for oncoming traffic. Road accidents are common, as attested to by the millions of battered-up vehicles in the country, and the thousands of mangled buses and cars on the sides of the road. If you are travelling around in a chauffeur-driven car, by overland vehicle, or by overcrowded public transport, always exercise caution on the roads.

Always be aware of your driver's road sense as soon as you get in a vehicle – which you should be able to judge pretty quickly. If you are very uncomfortable with his method of driving than stop and get out of the vehicle and find an alternative one.

Always avoid driving, or being driven, after dark. There are very few street lights, many vehicles do not have headlights, and there's the added problem of pedestrians and domestic animals on the road. If you are taking public transport over quite some distance, set off early in the day as you will inevitably have to wait for some time in the motor park for a vehicle that goes-when-full, and you will want to ensure that you reach your destination before dark. I would also not advise you to travel on the so-called 'luxury' buses (dealt with in the *Getting around* section) simply because they nearly always travel at night.

## Marine dangers

Nigeria's coastline has extremely strong undercurrents, whirlpools and frequent riptides, particularly in windy or rainy weather. Steep drop-offs and heavy surf mean the water can be deceptively deep. A few steps further out from being in knee-deep water can result in finding yourself totally out of your depth. Moreover, the surf is very powerful and can quickly drain one's energy. When the volume of water backed up against a steep beach becomes greater than the incoming surf, it will find the point of least resistance and funnel out to sea in a riptide. These currents can reach a speed of eight to ten knots, much faster than any swimmer, and it's not unheard of for a rip to sweep a swimmer out to sea for a kilometre or so. Be very wary when swimming

## THIS HOUSE IS NOT FOR SALE

All over Nigeria you will see 'this house is not for sale' painted on walls and gateways of houses. Sometimes the signs are more specific with 'this shop is not for sale', 'this block of flats is not for sale' or even 'this estate is not for sale'. I even saw 'this petrol station is not for sale' and 'this land is not for sale by order of Jesus'. Often scribbled next to this is 'Beware 419' – 419 being the common term used for all fraud. There's a scam going on that a so-called owner of a house will find a willing buyer of his or her property and take them to show them the house. If the buyer wants it, he pays the seller a considerable deposit or even all of the money for the house or property. The seller is of course not the owner of the property at all, and breaks into a property that is either standing empty or where the real owner is away, and sells it. In Nigeria I also saw in a cheap magazine an article entitled: 'What to do if your wife sells your house while you are at work'!

off the beaches and never swim alone or without someone knowing that you have gone into the water. If you are a weak swimmer, it's probably best to stick to paddling. If you do get caught in a riptide don't panic or try to fight it; it's a dangerous waste of valuable energy. Instead, swim or float on your back parallel to the shore until you reach the end of the rip, and only then try to get back to land. On the beach itself, always wear shoes, as there are man-of-war jellyfish in Nigerian waters that can inflict a nasty sting both in and out of the water. It goes without saying that you should never turn your back on a child playing in the surf – some expat parents insist on their children wearing life jackets when on the beach in Nigeria.

## Fraud

Financial fraud is very common in Nigeria. Keep all personal financial documents safe and don't let anyone know your home bank account details. The fraudsters are so sophisticated they can trace financial information to your home country. Avoid sending bank account details by post, phone, fax or email to and from Nigeria or checking internet bank accounts. Above all **do not** use a credit card in Nigeria – the number on your card can easily be used again and again once it's in the system. We spoke to one expat in Lagos who had specifically instructed her UK bank not to send her bank statement through the post to her address in Lagos. The bank ignored her request, the statement never arrived and her UK bank account was cleaned out.

Advance Fee Fraud (AFF) is known internationally as '419' fraud after the section of the Nigerian penal code which addresses fraud schemes. Indeed the term '419' is used so often in Nigeria, it's now used to describe all fraud, including the 'this house is not for sale' scam (see box). AFF simply means the demand for and payment of an advance fee in the form of a tax or loan under the pretence to close a business deal or transaction. It's particularly prevalent on the internet and your email account may have been targeted by these fraudsters before – an email about how you could receive millions of US dollars for simply offering the use of your foreign bank account. I know mine has on countless occasions. Some of these emails look extremely official, supported by a Nigerian government agency or law firm, or impersonating persons of social distinction, giving themselves bogus prefixes such as Doctor, Prince, Engineer, Chief, His Royal Highness etc. The usual story is that the sender is the owner of spectacular wealth in or out of Nigeria and for some reason or other needs to move the cash so he can gain access to it. To enable him to do this he needs to use a foreigner's bank account. In exchange, the holder of the bank account will receive a huge cash payment for providing this service, often running into millions of dollars. It is of course a blatant way of getting hold of your bank

## 419 LETTER

I am mrs.marriam Abacha, the wife to the late Head of State, of the federal Republic of Nigeria from 1993 –1998 – General Sani Abacha.

My late husband made a lot of money as the Head of state of Nigeria for 5years. He has different accounts in many banks of the world. He has not left any stone unturned in accruing riches for his family.

The present democratic government of Nigeria led by President (Gen.) (Rtd)Olusegun Obasanjo has not find favour with myfamily since their inception. This may be as a result of his hatred for my late husband who kept him in jail for over two years for a coup attempt, before the death of my father. He was released immediately my husband died and he was later made the present President.

He has confiscated and frozen all my family account in Nigeria and some other American, Europe and Asian continents, It has been in both the local and international news.Presently my son mohammed Abacha has been languishing in different prison centers in Nigeria for a case against his father which he knows nothing about.

Now, my purpose of all these introduction and proposal is just seeking for your candid assistance in saving this sum 0f $30.8.000,000.00 USD THIRTY.EIGHT MILLION.DOLLARS] which my late husband had hidden from the Nigerian govt.during his regime. and which is presently somewhere in a financial and security company outside the entire Nigeria and West African region.

This is a huge sum of money, I cannot trust much on most saboteur friends of my family in Nigeria who could not be trusted. I got your contact through our trade mission . I deemed it necessary to contact you for this trustworthy transaction.

All whom I needed is a sincere, honest, trustworthy andGod-fearing individuals whom my mind will absolve to help me in this deal.If you have feelings about my situation, don't hesitate to stand for me. If my proposal is sudden to you, all I need now is for you to stand as the Beneficiary of this money to claim it and save for me.

There is no difficulty, I will send your name as the recipient as well as the beneficiary of the money.On your identification and confirmation from me, the fund will be handle to you.

all i need is your confirmention of willingness and i will give you the full details. You will be compensated with 25% of the total fund for all your efforts in this transaction,provided this fund is save for me for your account in your country.

Please this is a very serious matter, it is a save my soul request from you and I will be delighted too much to receive a positive response from you in order to move into action. I will give you details on request from you.
THANKS
YOURS FAITHFULLY
MRS M ABACHA.

account details, and there have been countless incidents of people's accounts being cleaned out. These emails and letters will appear ridiculous to most, but unfortunately a large number of victims are enticed into believing they have been singled out from the masses to share in a multi-million dollar windfall for doing absolutely nothing, and Nigerian 419 fraud is believed to gross hundreds of millions of dollars a year. Do not respond to these emails.

Overleaf is an example of an email, spelling mistakes and all, which wormed its way into my yahoo account from (supposedly) Mrs Abacha.

## Crime and corruption

Nigeria has a reputation for crime and corruption and has more than its fair share of challenges to safety and security, and it is advisable to be security conscious always. Things do happen – armed robberies and carjackings are prevalent in Lagos and there is a threat of mugging. More disturbing are the huge numbers of guns in private possession and in the police and armed forces; both are susceptible to bribery and corruption, and thus could provide arms to civilians at the right price. There have also been incidents when the police themselves have been the perpetrators of crime. Some of the more outlandish crime that occurs in Nigeria is piracy, or armed robbery on ships anchored in Nigerian waters, or the illegal 'bunkering' of oil on to ships belonging to other nationalities. It's also not uncommon for gangs to hijack oilrigs off the coast to extort money from the oil companies. Also be aware that there have been incidents of hostage-taking for ransom, particularly in the Niger Delta, because of local community problems with the oil companies – people working in Nigeria for these companies should be especially vigilant and follow their employer's security guidelines.

Although it doesn't produce any drugs of its own, Nigeria is known as a major drug-trafficking country for Asian heroin smuggled to Europe and the US and for South American cocaine trafficked to Europe. Nigerian drug organisations are also heavily involved in other criminal activities such as document fabrication, illegal immigration and financial fraud. But Nigerians in Nigeria are generally not drug users. I live in Cape Town and at the end of my road is a large Nigerian community (a reported one million Nigerians live in South Africa, and three million in the US, with other large communities in Europe and elsewhere in the world). Some of Cape Town's Nigerian community, as well as many Capetonians, sell drugs on the street for a living. We never once got offered drugs on the street by a Nigerian in Nigeria.

Many Nigerians complain that the illegal activities of the offending minority have damaged the whole nation's image. It was also explained to me by the Publicity Director of the Nigeria Tourism Development Board that most of Nigeria's criminals were not in Nigeria at all, and made up the huge populations of Nigerians living overseas. He said these were the people who were capable of forging, stealing or bribing to get passports and visas, and, as illegal immigrants in other countries, resorting to criminal activity to make a living. Despite all this, Nigeria's awful reputation for crime is largely exaggerated, especially outside of Lagos where you will rarely feel threatened or be a victim of crime. Even in Lagos, long-term visitors may never see an Area Boy or someone out of uniform carrying a gun. But always remember that there is a criminal element in Nigeria and keep up your guard.

Finally, on a lighter note we once saw a man in Lagos selling those boxes of airplane food, complete with the little plastic bags of plastic cutlery and salt and pepper from the back of his car – 'fell off the back of a plane' perhaps? And in one Lagos market, we found six-packs of Fosters lager – 'fell off the back of an Australian diplomatic bag' perhaps?

## KANO RIOTS – OUR STORY

On Tuesday May 11 2004, we were in Kano researching the Kano chapter of this book when we witnessed the start of riots. It was mid-morning and I was in the Sabon Gari district to the north of the city looking for a hotel, whilst Darren was in the old city photographing part of the city wall. Suddenly, and without warning, everyone started running. On the street that I was on thousands of Muslims were running towards something, whilst Darren witnessed thousands of Christians running away from something. People just jumped out of cars and off motorbikes and ran, and at a school next to me the gates were opened and hundreds of teenage boys wearing identical white uniforms rushed out and joined the throng. The atmosphere was electric and it was quickly apparent that something was very wrong. Momentarily I was stunned and I stopped abruptly. One man ran past and yelled at me 'Go home, madam!' and I asked what was going on. He replied that it was a 'religious problem' and again implored me to go home. I didn't want to go in the same direction as the mob, but neither did I want to go against all the running people, so I briskly followed them for a few metres until I found the next turn off. I couldn't find an *okada* anywhere as all the drivers were jumping off their bikes and following the mob. Eventually a lady who was hurriedly packing up her roadside stall came to my aid and jumped out in front of an *okada* going in the opposite direction to the riot. My *okada* driver told me that he was a Christian and that after dropping me off at my hotel he was going straight home to keep his family safe. That day's riots led to 30 people being killed by knives or being burnt to death.

The riots were provoked by a massacre that had occurred in a village three weeks before, in neighbouring Plateau State, when Muslims were killed by Tarok (Christian) youths, though news on the ground was pretty patchy. The police said 67 people died, though the Red Cross said as many as 600 Muslims had been hacked to death. A prominent Imam in Kano made a speech at Friday prayers in the week before the Kano riots that was broadcast on the local radio, saying that the attacks on Muslims in Plateau State were part of a pre-planned annihilation of Muslims, a plan he further alleged was hatched by the West and was being executed by the Plateau State Governor Chief Joshua Dariye. What followed were the Tuesday riots, which started with a march by thousands of Muslims from one of Kano's leading mosques to the Kano Government House. First there were special prayers at the mosque for the downfall of all the enemies of Islam, which included the president of the United States and the prime minister of Israel as well as the governor of Plateau State. A short time later effigies of these three were burnt outside the Government House along with their respective flags. This march soon turned into a bloody riot and people were chased, clubbed to death or set on fire. One lady lost her whole family of nine when her house was set on fire (she had been selling soft drinks in another part of the city). Throughout the day the emir of Kano broadcast messages on TV and radio to stop the mayhem, and by 18.00 that evening a curfew had been clamped on the city. Some 30,000 displaced Christians slept that night in makeshift refugee camps before order was restored the following day. By 16.00 that afternoon we were in a minibus leaving Kano and were in Katsina that night.

## Petty theft

The culture of cheating is alive and kicking in Nigeria and you are more likely to be cheated out of something than having it simply stolen off you. Quite frankly this was one of the biggest surprises I had in Nigeria. As a seasoned traveller in East and southern Africa, where you guard your bags and possessions fiercely, I didn't feel the need to do this quite so attentively in Nigeria. Not once did we have anything stolen out of a hotel room, and after the first few outings on public transport when we crouched over our bags jealously, we would quite willingly throw them into the open back of a vehicle surrounded by hundreds of people and go for a wander around a motor park whilst waiting for the vehicle to go-when-full. Now I realise that this was our personal experience and we could have just been lucky, but there was definitely a general feeling that people don't openly steal from one another. They might scam, swindle, demand bribes or dupe you, but I really don't think they literally pick up something that does not belong to them and keep it. This could be due to the strong religious sentiment, both Christian and Muslim, of thou shall not steal, preached in churches and mosques daily throughout the country. I spoke to an expat in Jos, who one night went out, got horribly drunk, and left his wallet on the back seat of a taxi on the way home – the following morning the taxi driver found out where the expat was working and dropped off his wallet untouched at his place of work. If anyone has any less positive experiences I would be happy to hear their stories. Nevertheless, there will always be opportunist thieves wherever you travel, so don't put temptation in their path. Keep your valuables hidden, never flash your wealth, and leave anything of financial or sentimental value at home.

## Political risks

There is no doubt that political and religious tensions in Nigeria are high, and there has been a category of riots and violent incidents since Nigeria gained independence in 1960. There is no real science of assessing political risk, though it's a good idea to check your nationality's foreign office advice before you leave home and keep a close eye on Nigerian news. Outbreaks of localised civil unrest and violence can occur all over Nigeria without warning. If something does occur whilst you are in Nigeria, it is unlikely that a traveller will be targeted or involved, and most violent eruptions are based on local ethnic or religious spats. Potential trouble spots are in the northern cities (see box), and in the Niger Delta where the local communities resent the presence of the multi-national oil companies – here is the one place where foreigners could be specifically targeted if they are identified (mistakenly or not) as oil employees. It's worth being prepared for a threat to personal safety, so look out for the following: traffic suddenly becomes very light and the streets mysteriously clear of pedestrians (extremely unlikely in Lagos even if World War III breaks out); armoured vehicles or truckloads of armed police or soldiers; the noise of shooting or explosions, however distant; the disruption of TV and radio broadcasts; or streets thronged with chanting or stone-throwing groups. If unrest does occur, it is wise for a foreigner to be discreet and not join in on the action. Stay in your hotel and listen to the advice of the hotel manager who knows the area and situation much better than you do. Because the cities are so populated and everyone talks to each other, news of events going on elsewhere quickly does the rounds. If events get really bad, phone your embassy so that they are aware of your whereabouts, and listen carefully to the advice of embassy officials.

# Part Two

## The Guide

114

## KEY TO STANDARD SYMBOLS — Bradt

|  |  |
|---|---|
| —·—·— | International boundary |
| ------ | District boundary |
| ⊁⊀ | Border Post |
| National park |
| ✈ | Airport (international) |
| ✈ | Airport (other) |
| ✚ | Airstrip |
| Car ferry |
| Passenger ferry |
| Railway |
| Expressway/freeway |
| Main road |
| Other road |
| Minor road |
| ====== | Track (4 x 4 etc) |
| ☐ | Railway station |
| Bus station etc |
| ⓘ | Tourist information |
| Hotel, inn etc |
| Å | Campsite |
| ♀ | Bar, pub |
| ✗ | Restaurant, café |
| ⊠ | Post office |
| ⓔ | Internet access |
| Hospital, clinic, health centre |
| ✚ | Pharmacy |
| Museum |
| $ | Bank |
| Market |
| ☆ | Nightclub |

|  |  |
|---|---|
| Statue or monument |
| † | Cathedral or church |
| Mosque |
| • | Other place of interest |
| Archaeological or historic site |
| Historic building |
| Castle/fortress |
| Zoological garden |
| Ⓔ | Embassy |
| Petrol station |
| ℗ | Car park |
| City wall |
| Stadium |
| TV, Radio mast, antenna |
| • | Operator's office/consulate |
| Golf course |
| ▲ | Summit (height in metres) |
| ❋ | Scenic viewpoint |
| Botanical site |
| Bridge |
| Telephone |
| Urban park (town plans) |
| Main urban sprawl |
| ■ | Capital city |
| ● | Main town or city |
| ○ | Small town or village |
| ○ | Hot spring |
| Waterfall |
| Marsh |
| Beach |

*Other map symbols may be shown and explained in key boxes on individual maps.*

# Lagos

# 5

Although Nigeria's capital city is Abuja, with a population of roughly two million, it took over from Lagos as the country's official capital only in 1991, and Lagos remains Nigeria's largest and most overwhelmingly principal city. The city of Lagos is the capital of Lagos State, lying in the southwestern corner of the country. Rather ironically, it's the smallest state in the federation, and occupies an area of just 3,577km², 22% (or 787km²) of which consist of lagoons and creeks. This is not much bigger than a British county, but with a vastly higher population density. It shares its boundaries with Ogun State in both the north and east, the Republic of Benin to the west and a 180km of Atlantic coastline to the south. The Nigerian name for Lagos is Eko, and it wasn't until the 17th century that the Portuguese renamed it Lagos, meaning, quite simply, 'lagoons'.

Lagos is situated in one of the few gaps in the 200km-long sandbar that stretches from Benin to the eastern side of Lagos State. It lies in a swampy mangrove zone and is entirely flat, with no natural point being any higher than a metre or so above sea level. The metropolitan area covers approximately 300km² of land on three main islands and an ever-increasing section of the mainland spreading out in all directions. The waters of Lagos's lagoons stretch from a few hundred metres to 15km across, and in recent years landfills in the lagoons have been utilised for urbanisation. The city is basically a collection of islands that are connected together and to the mainland by long bridges – similar to Manhattan in New York City, though the comparison stops there. Now the largest city in Africa, the official population of greater Lagos is put at somewhere around 13 million, though there hasn't been a population census here since 1991. The government of Lagos State has more recently said it could be around 16 million, whilst the United Nations has said that by 2015 it could reach as high as 25 million. This enormous population represents every socio-economic level – evident from the sprawling, overcrowded shanty towns that are home to a mass of humanity, to the spacious leafy mansions on Victoria Island housing the wealthy and privileged.

The mere mention of its name evokes strong reactions from visitors and Nigerians alike. Most people either passionately love or virulently hate Lagos, but no visit to Nigeria is complete without experiencing this overpowering and mind-boggling city. It is stimulating and vibrant, and dirty and dangerous, all at the same time. Those that love it do so because of its diversity, and the majority of Lagosians proudly confess that they can't see themselves living anywhere else in Nigeria. Those who hate it find it a volatile place, with perhaps one of the world's worst reputations for congestion, crime, poverty and chaos. Whether you love it or hate it, you will undoubtedly find Lagos mind-blowing! That's the only word that even vaguely captures the essence of Lagos, where super-rich meets mega-destitute, cacophony meets peace and quiet, searing heat and humidity meet icy air conditioning, life meets death, hi-tech meets ancient, filth and squalor meet hygiene, and natural beauty jars head on with pollution.

## BRIEF HISTORY

Early settlements of hunters and fishermen, protected by the lagoon swamps and mangrove forest, marked the beginning of Lagos. It is believed that the first settlers on Lagos Island were the Olofin people in the 14th century. Their chief first settled on the Iddo Peninsula and divided the land on Lagos Island between his ten sons. One son, Aromire, used his land to grow vegetables, including peppers, and built his farm on the site that is today the location of the King's (Oba's) Palace, otherwise known as the *Iga Idunganran* or Pepper Palace. The town of Lagos then steadily grew as the fertile grounds attracted a number of farmers, and the sea attracted fishermen. Then, in the early 1400s, a quarrel broke out between the Olofin people and a wealthy woman named Aina, who they had falsely accused of being a witch. Aina sent for help from the king of Benin, who sent an army that defeated the Olofins, and Lagos became the southern outpost of the Benin Empire. They called it Eko, which was the Benin name for war camp. A Benin warrior called Ashipa was made king of the town and was given a royal drum, or *gbedu*, by the king of Benin. Since then, all of Lagos's kings have been descendants of that first king, Ashipa. His son, King Ado, built the Oba's Palace on Lagos Island, and Ado's successor, King Gabaro, went on to move the seat of government from Iddo to the Oba's Palace in the late 15th century. Whilst still under the jurisdiction of the Benin Empire, Gabaro was more lenient towards the Olofins than his predecessors and gave them land and chiefdoms. The descendants of these Olofin chiefs are today Lagos's chiefs or *idejos*, which means 'landowners'.

### Slave trade

The first Europeans to arrive in Lagos were the Portuguese, who landed on the coast in 1472, and who for the next four centuries traded with the kings and people of Lagos. They named the settlement Lago de Curamo, and finally Lagos, after the port in Portugal of the same name. In 1730, Gabaro's brother Akinshemoyin became king and invited Portuguese slave traders to Lagos. The Portuguese had already established trade links with the Kingdom of Benin and by the mid-18th century the empires on the coast were flourishing with wealth generated by the slave trade. Most of the slaves passed through the Lagos Slave Market en route to Europe and America, and Lagos continued to grow over the next hundred years. Although the British government outlawed slavery in all her territories in 1833, in Lagos the slave trade continued to operate well into the middle of the 19th century. In 1845, Kosoko wrenched the throne from his uncle Akitoye, who was not the rightful heir to the kingdom. Akitoye went to the British Consul John Beecroft and appealed to the British to help him get the throne back, in return for which he promised to stop the prohibited slave trade once and for all, and to strengthen trade links with Britain. Queen Victoria sent a message to Kosoko requesting that he end the slave trade and insisting that Lagos must sign an official treaty with Britain. Kosoko refused and the British retaliated in 1851 by attacking Lagos Island with five battleships and defeating Kosoko's army. On January 1 1852, Beecroft reinstated Akitoye as king of Lagos and the treaty with the British was signed, stating that the slave trade was to be abolished. Then, later in 1852, Akitoye died suddenly and was succeeded by his son Dosunmu, who over the next five years also failed to close down Lagos's slave markets. His failure resulted in the complete annexation of Lagos by the British and finally, in August 1861, Dosunmu signed the declaration of cessation and Lagos became a British colony. Dosunmu retained his role as oba and received an annual salary from the British – 1,200 bags of cowries that was worth about £1,000 – but overall his authority over Lagos was reduced to a minimum. Allegedly, the British took occupancy of Lagos 'not without some reluctance', but they had succeeded in finally stamping out the slave trade for good.

## Lagos under the British

Over the next few decades, Lagos was administered under a British governor and a small legislative council of British officials, and it became the main base for British imperial activities and penetration into the hinterland. As the colony strengthened economically, the British influence spread into Yorubaland and beyond, and trade links were established between other regions of the interior. Whilst Lagos retained its title as the British Colony of Lagos, these new areas inland were amalgamated and became known as the British Protectorate of Nigeria. People living in the colony of Lagos passed for British subjects, whilst those living in the protectorate were referred to as British protected persons. Finally, in January 1914 the British officially joined the two regions together as the Federation of Nigeria with Lagos as its capital, though effectively they were administered separately until 1946. After Nigeria gained independence from Britain in 1960, Lagos became the capital of the Federal Republic of Nigeria. This position was ceded to Abuja in 1991, since the latter occupies a more central location in the country, a move that is hoped will take the pressure off the already exhausted infrastructure of Lagos as the centre of both commerce and industry, and the seat of government. Today Lagos remains the capital city of Lagos State, with its administrative centre in Ikeja on the mainland.

## Growth of the city

While the city's growth and structure were influenced by its status as a colonial capital, there were never a large number of British settlers as such, and the social life and the culture remained largely Nigerian. As a formal capital city, Lagos grew phenomenally quickly from the end of the 19th century. In 1885, schools were built, by 1886 the railway had arrived and telephone links with Britain were established, and by 1898 the streets were lit with electric lights. People streamed in from all over Nigeria and other parts of West Africa, including repatriated slaves and their descendants. Returnee slaves, known as Creoles, returned to Lagos from Brazil, the West Indies and Freetown in Sierra Leone, swelling the population of the city. They had been introduced to Christianity and had the privilege of a Western education, and made remarkable contributions to education and the rapid modernisation of Lagos. They returned with knowledge of the wider world and the European way of life, and many of them had received training as doctors, architects or lawyers. Others were skilled workers: carpenters, bakers, mariners, or tailors. Brazilian returnees brought with them the skills they had acquired in Brazil. Most were master-builders and masons, and gave the distinct characteristics of Brazilian architecture to their residential buildings (some dilapidated examples can still be seen today on Lagos Island). For all practical purposes their arrival marked an era of modernisation in Lagos and Nigeria as a whole. With their educational, professional, and technical qualifications, many got employment in the colonial civil service and from Lagos were transferred to other parts of the country that were under British control. The Creole families of Lagos formed the nucleus of African colonial staff in the early decades of British administration.

From the 1920s, they also pioneered modern political activity in the country and agitated African participation in government – one of the leading nationalist movement's players, Herbert Macaulay, was a member of one of the Lagos Creole families, and the grandson of the legendary Bishop Samuel Crowther. Lagos became the centre of the anti-colonial struggle and was the headquarters of Macaulay 's Nigerian Democratic Party, the Nigerian Youth Movement, and the National Council for Nigeria and the Cameroon, as well as home to the anti-colonial press that helped get the message across to the common man to cast off the yoke of imperialism and alien rule. The city was also the centre of the trade union movement, which began to challenge British rule and fight for the rights of the working classes through a series of protest marches and strikes – a 45-day general strike in 1945 seriously disabled the whole country. From 1967, the two-and-a-half year Biafran War caused a further massive migration to the city. This, coupled with a huge wave of refugees and migrants from other African countries fleeing famine and drought, produced a population boom, with hundreds of thousands of people streaming into the city looking for jobs as an alternative to rural poverty. The growth of light industry in post-independence Lagos and the petroleum-related industry that dominated the 1970s both directly affected the rapid growth of Lagos.

## Lagos today

Lagos has grown too big too fast. On the eve of independence in 1960, the population was put at a little less than half a million. There hasn't been a census in Nigeria since 1991, but today the population of Lagos is thought to be around 13 million though it could plausibly be nearer 20 million. It's ranked the biggest city in Africa ahead of Cairo and the second-largest city in the world after Mexico City. But this phenomenal growth is at the expense of decent social services and infrastructure, which are stretched to breaking point, and which have failed to keep up with the population growth. Energy and water access, sewage, transportation and housing have all been adversely affected by the haphazard development of a geographically disjointed city. Lagos consumes 45% of the energy of the whole country, but suffers frequent power cuts and fuel shortages. There is a worsening water supply and due to inadequate sewage, much of the city's human waste is carried through rainwater drains and ditches to end up on the city's tidal flats.

Nigeria's failure to dispose of its rubbish is at its most acute here, and everywhere there are piles of garbage. Everything seemingly appears broken, disused or seriously dilapidated, and waste and discard are the order of the chaotic Lagos day. The streets are littered with abandoned yellow vehicles driven until they die, there are half-finished, derelict or burnt-out buildings, dysfunctional telephone and electricity wires are wrapped around broken poles, and yes, sometimes even dead bodies can be seen decomposing in the gutters. I've even seen a photograph of someone walking down a Lagos street with two muzzled and chained hyenas! Then there is the push-and-shove traffic and the thousands of yellow buses, minibuses and taxis, covered in scratches and dinks, with doors hanging off and rusting undercarriages, battered beyond recognition. And many more thousands of motorbikes, their handlebars shortened so they can squeeze through the traffic better, their toot-toot horns replaced with truck horns, which can be driven so recklessly I hear stories of the rider's legs being taken off. Snarl-ups and go-slows are a constant daily problem – it takes an average of two to three hours to travel 10–20km. And finally, despite there being pockets of adequate housing, for the majority of Lagos's many millions, home is in appalling slums that stretch as far as the eye can see, where people's aspirations for a decent lifestyle seem doomed to flounder in the filth and decay.

In her book, *Four Guineas*, the writer Elspeth Huxley describes Lagos so:

> Lagos assaults you with its squalor and vitality. The narrow streets, the
> houses – hovels, mainly – made of mud or old tin and packed as close as
> playing cards, the stinking open drains, the noise, the traffic, the jostling
> throngs…it's feeling that sheer naked human life, mere existence, bubbles
> and pullulates with the frightening fecundity of bacteria.

Not much has changed since her visit in 1954 then.

Despite all this, on a visit to Lagos you'll discover a city far more welcoming than the ferocious Lagos of modern myth. And whilst there are limited sights to see as such, all of the above is what Lagos is all about and that's what its major pull is. It's a Third-World megalopolis all right, and no-one would ever use words like 'pleasant' or 'relaxing' in reference to the commercial capital of West Africa, but Lagos is a lively, noisy, chaotic and fast-moving city. It has its own dynamic, if perhaps sometimes unappealing, personality, but go with confidence and get into its vibrant rhythm and don't be surprised if you leave Nigeria with a certain fondness and respect for Lagos. It will not fail to surprise.

# GETTING THERE AND AWAY
## By air
**Lagos (LOS) Murtala Mohammed International Airport** is 22km, or roughly one hour's drive (depending on the traffic), north of the islands that are the centre of Lagos proper. This airport used to have a notorious reputation for corrupt officials, con artists, bogus taxi drivers and pickpockets, but today security has been tightened up and by and large it resembles any other busy international airport. But it is still necessary to keep on your guard at all times, and to keep valuables close to you and your passport hidden. Do not hand over your passport to anyone other than the immigration authorities, and under no circumstances offer to pay dash. Procedures for immigration, customs and baggage collection are all straightforward and you will experience few problems. One word of advice, though, is that if you are arriving on a 30-day visa, providing you can show that you have an airline ticket with a date of departure on it, it is worth asking here on arrival if you can get a 90-day entry stamp. They may or may not oblige, but if they do this saves the hassle of extending your visa once in Lagos. You can hire a porter and a trolley for about US$1 (and can use US$ cash so bring some small notes with you). When you leave the baggage hall an official will inspect your airline tickets against the tag on your luggage to make sure you've got your bag and no-one else's – he will perhaps also discreetly ask for a dash for doing so, but you should politely ignore this.

Only a certain number of taxis are allowed to trade at the airport and prices are generally fixed at about N3,000 from the airport to the islands, though going from the islands to the airport you'll be able to negotiate a cheaper ride for about N2,000 with any taxi. The big hotels and some of the travel agents can arrange a meet-and-greet service at the airport, and all expats will be picked up by drivers from their respective companies. It's not really necessary, and a bit of a nightmare, to pre-arrange this, as catching a taxi is straightforward enough – just ensure that the driver knows the way to your destination. Once you're through the baggage hall and customs there is a tourist information desk, but you are very unlikely to find anyone there and there's certainly nothing to pick up in the way of tourist literature. Outside the building there is a throng of people behind a makeshift fence and gate across from the main concourse – only people with valid airline tickets are allowed beyond the fence so any drivers meeting you will be on the other side of this fence, and this is where you'll find taxis and a horde of money changers. There is no bank in the airport and you will have to change money in the car park! Don't be too alarmed by this, but ensure that you have the right amount of US$ cash ready to change – you certainly do not want to be dipping into your money belt or wallet in such a public area.

On departure, your luggage will inevitably be searched on a big table at the check-in desk, and as a foreigner you will be asked if you are carrying any antiquities. If you have bought souvenirs declare them, but unless they are really old pieces of Nigerian art for which a licence is required, you shouldn't have any problems (see page 88). Also on departure you may be asked by immigration how much naira you have. This is not a request for a bribe; it is illegal to take more than a small amount of Nigerian currency out of the country.

If you are departing from Lagos on a domestic flight note that the **domestic terminal** is in a separate building off Agege Motor Road. Look out for the old Nigeria Airways jumbo jets parked rather forlornly in a hangar next to the car park – like abandoned vehicles dumped all over Nigeria, since the demise of the national airline in 2003 the planes have just been left to grow rusty and be covered in the city's grime. Taxis to and from here cost roughly the same as to and from the international terminal. It is almost impossible to pre-book a ticket for a domestic flight, and to fly from Lagos to anywhere else in Nigeria you just have to pitch up at the domestic terminal. One reason for this is that the flights are relatively cheap and popular, and the domestic airlines do not pay commission to local travel agents, so it's simply not worth their while to sell and ticket domestic flights. The domestic departure hall is a tad chaotic, but once you get your bearings you'll find it is organised, in a manic sort of way. There are some 15 check-in desks for the different airlines, and above each desk are signs showing when the next plane is going where. Here is where you buy your ticket (which is hand written) and then point out your luggage to the luggage attendant who will take it (in theory) to the right plane. You won't get a boarding pass and the seat number is written on the front of the ticket. Once through into the frantically busy and noisy domestic departure hall, you'll find some small snack bars and a bookshop, and two public phones that actually appear to work, next to a kiosk where you can buy a phonecard.

To Abuja there are some 15 flights on a weekday and 11 at the weekends, so it's just a case of turning up at the airport and getting on the next flight. Once in Abuja you can connect to the other cities. There are also several direct flights a day to Port Harcourt, but to the other destinations they run less frequently and you may find yourself sitting at the airport for a few hours. (See the *Getting there and away* sections of the relevant destination chapters and the main *Getting around* section for details of fares and timetables.)

## By road

There are several motor parks on mainland Lagos that serve other destinations in Nigeria. The most useful are **Mile Two** for vehicles to the east of Lagos and to the border of the Benin Republic; and the **Ojota** old and new motor parks serving just about everywhere else. There are direct minibuses from these to the **Obalende** motor park between Lagos Island and Ikoyi. Except for those vehicles coming into Mile Two from the east, if you are arriving in Lagos on public transport from any other direction, vehicles could end their journey in motor parks at Oju Elegba, Iddo, Yaba, Ebute Eru or Oshodi (the latter being well known for its Area Boys, where you'll be knee-deep in mud if it's raining). But nearly all first stop at Ojota, so if you are catching a vehicle from an outlying city ask if it is going to Ojota and get the driver or conductor to tell you when to get off. The Ojota Motor Park is roughly spread around Ikorodu Road, that joins the Lagos–Ibadan Expressway, with the New Ojota Motor Park being about 300m or an N30 hop on an *okada*, to the south – it's a filthy and chaotic area where every last space is filled with rubbish and thousands of vehicles. You'll have to ask around for a vehicle going in your direction and expect to get hopelessly lost, but most people will helpfully assist you. Sometimes there are the wooden pyramid signs that sit on top of the vehicle with the destination written on, which are simply plonked on the next vehicle when the first one is full and ready to depart. Look out for a National Union Road Transport Workers (NURTW) man (they patrol the motor parks and take the fee off the drivers for the use of the motor park), who usually wears a green and white shirt and cap, and he will show you which vehicle to get on. On a personal note, we experienced no problems walking around Lagos's motor parks even with our luggage, but nevertheless always exercise caution.

There are scores of 'luxury' bus companies that operate out of Lagos, though as mentioned in the general *Getting around* section, my advice is not to use these as they nearly always travel at night. Most 'luxury' bus stands are located near the main motor parks. It might be the case that you get to a motor park, find out where the buses go from and then make another journey to the 'luxury' bus stand. Major bus stands for buses heading north and east are on Western Avenue in Surulere near the National Stadium, and near Ojota and Oshodi motor parks, and for buses also heading north as well as west to the Benin Republic, on the Badagry Expressway near the Mile Two Motor Park. One of the most established 'luxury' bus companies is Ekene Dili Chukwu Transport Company, tel: 01 774 1596, that runs services from its stand near Ojota to Abuja, Port Harcourt, Aba, Kaduna, Kano and Maiduguri.

## By rail

The Lagos train station is just north of Lagos Island across the Carter Bridge, but you won't see a moving train. In the event that the railway starts running again, the station is on Murtala Muhammed Way, not far from the Iddo Motor Park.

## ORIENTATION

The Lagos metropolitan area covers a whopping 300km² and spreads over much of Lagos State on four principal islands and adjacent parts of the Nigerian mainland. Most visitors will spend the majority of their time on the islands, which are the real heart of the city, whilst the mainland is made up of a myriad mostly poverty-stricken neighbourhoods and suburbs stretching as far as the eye can see. The principal islands are **Lagos Island**, which is the site of the original settlement and today the predominant commercial district of the city; **Ikoyi**, which is now merged with Lagos Island by landfill and is an area of leafy suburbs and big houses that was once the Government Reserved Area (GRA) during the colonial days, and is also the location of some federal buildings; between the two is the working-class district of **Obalende** where the Obalende Motor Park serves as the link for public transport between the islands and the rest of Lagos; **Victoria Island,** to the south of Ikoyi, is the business district where banks, embassies, hotels and most of the restaurants can be found; and the **Lekki Peninsula**, to the east, is now joined to Victoria Island by another landfill that is today being hurriedly covered up by new development and middle-class housing estates. Ikoyi and Victoria Island are separated by the **Five Cowrie Creek**, so called because it used to cost five cowries to cross it by ferry long before any bridges were built.

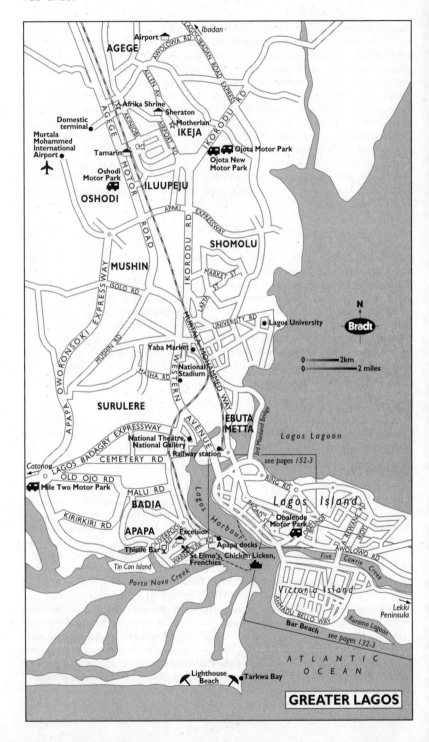

GREATER LAGOS

Lagos Island is joined to the northwestern tip of Victoria Island by **Independence Bridge**, whilst Ikoyi connects with Victoria Island by what must be one of the busiest roads in the city, the **Falomo Bridge**. Three bridges connect Lagos Island with the mainland: the oldest is **Carter Bridge**, built in 1900 and repeatedly bolstered by new concrete (when we were there it was discovered that some of the bridge supports had eroded away); the **Eko Bridge**; and the **Third Mainland Bridge** which stretches several kilometres across the Lagos Lagoon to join the Lagos–Ibadan Highway (look out for the hectic shanty town built on stilts between the bridge and the mainland). Whether you come to Lagos by road or air, your point of entry will be on the mainland. The airport is near the district of **Ikeja**, the mainland's most upmarket suburb, where there are a few hotels serving the airport. The main **motor parks** for long-distance road transport are scattered around the mainland in various working-class suburbs, from which you can feasibly get to the islands by public transport.

Initially it is a bit confusing finding your way around the islands as landfills have merged existing islands and street names have changed several times over the years, to appease certain government characters, and are often referred to by more than one name. Kingsway in Ikoyi that leads to the Falomo Bridge is a prime example: it is now Alfred Rewane Road, though everyone still refers to it by its old name. If you can get hold of a street map (see *Maps and publications* in *Listings*, page 147) it helps a lot. I found that a good landmark to get my bearings and about as central to the islands as you're going to get, was the **1004 apartments** to the left of Falomo Bridge on Victoria Island. A massive sprawl of run-down concrete blocks that used to house government ministers and officials when Lagos was the capital city, it now houses civil servants (there's a sign on the entrance saying 'this estate is not for sale'!)

## GETTING AROUND

Public transport in Lagos is absolutely chaotic, but it is perhaps the rusting and overcrowded *molues* (big yellow buses), the swarm of yellow Peugeot 504 taxis, the thousands of battered *danfos* (minibuses), and the hundreds of thousands of customised *okadas* (motorbikes), that give Lagos some of its frantic charm. The city suffers from chronic traffic congestion, which makes it impossible for buses and taxis to operate efficiently, especially during the rush hours. All of Lagos's vehicles are scratched, dented, and smashed up beyond belief – the sides have thousands of scratches on them where they have jostled with each other in the chaotic motor parks, and the vehicles are so ancient there are rust holes in the bodywork, doors have fallen off, and tail lights hang off rusted bumpers. They are simply driven until they die, and all over Lagos you will see abandoned wrecked yellow vehicles on the side of the road, sometimes with chickens living inside, where they were just left when they finally stopped working. Most of the minibuses, buses and taxis in Lagos are yellow, and they are an ubiquitous part of the city. The exceptions are those on Victoria Island and the adjoining Lekki Peninsula, which are green and white. The story goes (whether it's true or not I don't know) that the one-time Minister of Transport did some deal with a paint company (from which he got a huge dash) to lay down a decree that all the vehicles on Victoria Island must be painted with a particular colour of green that was only available from this particular paint company.

If you are beginning a journey at a motor park, vehicles go-when-full - nothing moves until the required amount of people are in place. In a motor park you'll have to ask around for a vehicle going in the direction you want to go, and some of them have the name of their destination (usually another motor park in a different part of the city) painted in small letters on the side of the vehicle towards the back. Also look out for a National Union Road Transport Workers man, and he will show you which vehicle to get on. On the streets, vehicles do not run to any timetables – you just hail one down in the general direction that you want to go and they'll stop if they have a space. Around Victoria Island are bus stops denoted by either a square green sign or a round blue sign with a picture of a bus on them, where all public transport is supposed to stop (though they stop anywhere if they are not already in a 'go-slow').

Minibuses and buses are not negotiable; taxis and *okadas* are always negotiable, and you'll have to bargain harder in Lagos than in any other part of the country. Minibuses within the islands cost N30–50 for a short hop; taxis or 'drops', meaning you have a car to yourself, cost in the region of N200 for a short journey, and N300–400 for a longer journey across the islands; *okadas* cost N50 for a short journey (roughly under a kilometre), whilst to go from one island to another, for example for a ride across the Falomo Bridge (never walk across here), expect to pay N100–150. Expect to pay about three times more for a drop in a car than you would pay for an *okada*, but remember if there are a few of you than a drop will work out cheaper than you all taking individual *okadas*. The latter are, however, infinitely quicker – it's not uncommon for an expat with a car and driver to jump out of the car if it's stuck in traffic and to hop on an *okada* to get to a meeting. Because of the problem of Area Boys in some parts of Lagos Island, especially around the streets under the Independence Bridge leading to Victoria Island, you may find that *okada* drivers from Victoria Island will not be willing to take you across the bridge to Lagos Island and vice versa. This is one of the few regions that the Area Boys operate on the islands but they are quite common in other parts of the mainland.

## AREA BOYS

'Area Boys' are local hoodlums and thieves that have been prevalent in Lagos since the 1960s. They basically use physical intimidation to get what they want and simply stop people and demand money or property whilst threatening them with belts, whips, sticks or worse, guns. It's basically mugging – and in broad daylight and in front of thousands of other people. They also get aggressive towards drivers of vehicles who they will not let pass until they've received their dash, often snatching the keys out of a vehicle, and they think nothing of throwing a punch at an *okada* or minibus driver. If a brave victim objects, there is also the further threat of calling in more Area Boys to deal with him. They typically hang around the bus stops and motor parks, and under flyover bridges or major road junctions, mostly in mainland Lagos. Notable spots on the islands are Bar Beach on Victoria Island, and under the flyovers and bridges on Lagos Island. Someone told us to go to Oshodi, a particularly notorious motor park on the mainland, 'early, as the Area Boys don't wake up until late morning'. He also added that this spot was known locally as the 'Area Boys' University'. That said, you are very unlikely to be a victim of an Area Boy; quite frankly an attack on someone who is an obvious visitor to Nigeria, and I have to say it, a white person, would draw too much attention. Only very rarely will foreigners be stopped in their cars and the driver asked for a dash. Nevertheless keep your wits about you at all times. Area Boys are relatively unique to Lagos and are not found on a grand scale in other Nigerian cities.

**BAD DRIVERS HAVE THEIR HEADS EXAMINED**
I found the following article on the front page of South Africa's *Sunday Times* newspaper in July 2003. 'Lagos residents caught driving against oncoming traffic are being forced to submit themselves for mental-health evaluation. They have to deliver blood and urine samples, then sit IQ tests. The process takes five days to complete and drivers' cars are impounded until the tests are complete. Traffic jams, known as 'go-slows', are notorious in this huge city of 13 million people. Locals resort to desperate measures to try and beat the traffic, including driving in the wrong lane in the opposite direction of the traffic. Yemi Odubela, chief executive of the city's traffic agency, told *The Sunday Times* that mandatory psychiatric evaluation was intended to act as a deterrent to anarchic driving in the city. He said that tough measures became necessary because traffic jams were so bad that motorists spent the night in their cars, unable to reach their homes. *Festus Eriye, Lagos.*

Getting around the islands doesn't present too many problems and it's easy enough to flag down an *okada* or taxi, both of which hang out at street corners, outside shops and restaurants, and in hotel car parks. Minibuses run along all the main arteries but there is no way of telling what destination they are going to. But it's simple enough to jump on one in the direction you want to go, and if it turns off towards somewhere else get off, and jump on another that is going towards your destination. There are several motor parks in mainland Lagos where vehicles depart to other destinations outside of Lagos (dealt with under *Getting there and away*). To get to any of these from the islands, you need to go to Obalende Motor Park between Ikoyi and Lagos Island. This massive motor park with its queues of yellow vehicles snaking their way down all the access roads is under a tangle of flyovers that eventually lead to the mainland via the Carter or Third Mainland bridges. Here you will find vehicles that go-when-full going directly to Ojota, Mile Two, and Oshodi, the main motor parks for long-distance vehicles, and the journey from the islands across the city in a minibus should cost around N50.

There's a ferry service between Lagos Island and Apapa. Three boats that are big old hulking things and that are routinely overcrowded run back and forth intermittently during daylight hours between a midway point on Apongbon Street on Lagos Island and the Apapa port for N50. In the residential area of southeast Ikoyi, on Oyinkan Abayomi Drive, is another ferry service by motorboat across Five Cowrie Creek to a point midway between Victoria Island and Lekki that is very useful and that avoids a drive through the traffic on Falomo Bridge. On the Ikoyi side there's a small makeshift jetty where the boats generally go-when-full. Most Ikoyi *okada* drivers will know where it is and many hang out there waiting for passengers coming off the boat. The ride across takes less than a minute and costs N30. You'll see the Tarzan jetty and double-storey Tarzan bar on the opposite side of the creek, which is where boats also go to the beach at Tarkwa Bay (see page 165 for details).

# WHERE TO STAY

In a city the size of Lagos, there are many hotels catering for the large expat community and for local business people – very, very few can say that they've actually received a tourist as a guest. Most are scattered over Victoria Island and Ikoyi, or in the upmarket suburb of Ikeja near the airport. Despite there being a competitive range of hotels, given that their customers are nearly always business orientated none of them are especially cheap and there really aren't many budget options. There are cheap local hotels in more dubious parts of mainland Lagos, but you'd be ill-advised to spend the night in these areas. For the most part you are looking at spending not less than US$60 a night for two people in a double room, rising to US$300–400, which is considerably more than in the rest of Nigeria. And as outlined in the *In Nigeria* chapter under *Accommodation*, don't expect the same sort of quality that you would get for these prices as you would back home. Re-read the *Accommodation terms – read this first!* section on page 78 and modify your expectations accordingly. In any hotel, always ask to see a room first, and remember, just because a hotel advertises facilities and services such as a business centre or even a tennis court, it does not necessarily mean that they are functioning. Nevertheless, Lagos does have some of the nicest hotels in Nigeria, and there are a couple of establishments that could qualify for international-class standards. Many are used by visiting Nigerian government officials from Abuja, or to house new expats whilst they wait for long-term accommodation to become available, and upper-crust hotels are used by companies to host potential expats on their look-sees.

Here, I have grouped hotels under three categories based on the price of the cheapest double room. This is because of the whole 'suite' scenario, when a hotel could have a whole selection of rooms of different sizes and with bigger beds resulting in some instances of room rates ranging from US$60 to US$800 in one establishment. Unless otherwise stated all rooms have en-suite bathrooms and AC, and all hotels have their own generators so power is pretty consistent.

## Upmarket: US$200 and above

**Eko Hotel** Adetokunbo Ademola St, Victoria Island; tel: 01 262 4600/19; email: reservation@ekohotels.com. This is a largely business travellers' hotel set in a central spot on Victoria Island on a huge wedge of land with nice gardens backing on to the Kuramo Lagoon. The open and airy reception area is contemporarily decorated with plants, African prints and objets d'art, and with wooden walkways leading through to the swimming pool, where there are sun loungers and a great outside bar overlooking the lagoon. The 492 rooms have phone, minibar and DSTV, and there's a gym, sauna, tennis and volleyball courts, and several top-class restaurants and bars listed individually in the *Where to eat and drink* section. Room rates are US$300 (US$400 deposit) for a double, US$340 (US$450 deposit) for a sea view, and US$475 (US$600 deposit) for a suite. Cheaper accommodation is available in the adjacent Kuramo Lodge, where a much better value standard single/double starts from US$120 (US$200 deposit). Add 15% to all rates. The Eko is one of Lagos's nicest hotels, but the open lobby is not especially secure, and there have been security issues here in the past.
**The Moorhouse** 1 Bankole Oki Rd, Ikoyi; tel: 01 267 0231/40; email: mhsofitel@hyperia.com; www.sofitel.com. This intimate and professional guesthouse has excellent service and friendly staff and is part of the international Sofitel chain. It's Lagos's finest boutique hotel, located in a quiet corner of Ikoyi and well signposted off Alfred Rewane Road (formerly Kingsway). It's also consistently full as this is the place expats stay when they come to Lagos for a 'look-see' and the companies want to impress them. The 44 rooms and eight suites with DSTV and minibar are modern and immaculate, and some have an additional balcony and lounge area. There is fine dining to be had in the L'Aquarelle (French for watercolour) restaurant (guests only), where breakfast is US$18 and a main course at dinner US$20–25, and there's a separate bar, reliable business centre, swimming pool, and gym. Rates for a double are a cool US$340 (US$440 deposit; note that payment is only taken in US$), plus the 15% on accommodation and food, and they have been known to take credit cards but check first. Try booking through the website.

**Sheraton Lagos Hotel and Towers** 30 Mobolaji Bank Anthony Way, Ikeja; tel: 01 497 8660/9; www.starwood.com/sheraton. For a Sheraton the décor is a bit dated – very 1980s – and somewhat scuffed, but it's conveniently located near the airport and the hotel runs a shuttle service (airline crews stay here). There are 341 spacious rooms with DSTV and minibar; the more expensive rooms and suites in the Towers section are on the sixth floor with a separate check-in desk, lounge and café, and other extras, such as someone to turn down your bed. Facilities include a business centre, ballroom, tennis courts, mosque, swimming pool, various conference halls and several top-notch restaurants dealt with under *Where to eat and drink*. The expensive hotel shop sells books and curios and international magazines and newspapers. In the lobby are desks for Virgin Atlantic and British Airways, and a desk for Planet Car Hire. Rates are US$305 (US$400 deposit) for a classic room, and for larger rooms and suites in the towers section rates range from US$350–950 (add roughly US$100 more to these rates for the deposit); single occupancy is a few dollars less but only slightly. Unusually rates include breakfast, but not of course the 15%.

**Protea Hotel Victoria Island** Violet Yough Close, Victoria Island; tel: 01 320 4717/27/37; www.proteahotels.com. You can also make a reservation through the South African office which you may want to consider doing if you want to use a credit card over the phone – you must never do this in Nigeria. Tel/fax: +21 (21) 430 5330. This is a new and quality hotel on a prime site on Victoria Island managed by the South African Protea chain, and is about the nearest to international standards as you are going to get in Lagos, with a rim-flow swimming pool, modern restaurants and hi-tech bar, conference and business facilities, and a gym with equipment air-freighted in from South Africa. The 42 rooms have all the (working) mod cons with imported hotel furniture and good views of the city. Airport transfers can be arranged for US$75 each way. There are three standards of room here starting from US$280 (US$320 deposit), US$300 (US$340 deposit), and US$385 (US$425 deposit), plus the 15% (rates may be paid only in US$).

**Federal Palace Hotel** Ahmadu Bello Way, Victoria Island; tel: 01 262 3116/25, 262 6180/199; email: reservation@federalpalacehotel.com; www.federalpalacehotel.com. The Federal Palace is a landmark on VI – a tall concrete tower with a big circular orange symbol on the side standing to the east of Victoria Island overlooking Lagos Harbour. The standards here are not on the same level as Lagos's other big hotels in the same price range although a new, more modern wing is presently under construction. The Executive Floor on the 14th floor of the existing block has already been refurbished, and has 18 rooms with much nicer furniture than elsewhere in the hotel and wooden floors, with a private check-in desk, international newspapers and magazines, business centre, and a lounge with complimentary tea and coffee where you can also take breakfast or eat meals sent up from the restaurant. The other 600-odd rooms and 80 suites are spacious, with one or two enormous double beds, but they smell terribly musty and have old-fashioned furniture. All rooms, however, have a balcony, DSTV and minibar, and face the harbour. Facilities include the completely overhauled swimming pool and terrace with wooden sun loungers which have a great view of the broken ships in the harbour, a curio market out in the car park, a conference venue built out on a concrete island in the water, useful desks in the lobby for courier services and car hire, and restaurants (covered under *Where to eat and drink*). Deposits are fairly hefty here and room rates inclusive of the 15% start from US$240 (US$300 deposit) for a standard double, and US$340 (US$500 deposit) for a business suite. The far nicer rooms on the Executive Floor are US$280 (US$350 deposit) for a standard double, and US$425 (US$600 deposit) for a business suite. If you're in this league it's definitely worth spending the extra for these rooms, which are much nicer and which have the best views at the top of the hotel.

## Mid-range: between US$100 and US$200
**The Elion House** 7–8 Agbeken Rotinwa St, off Hannat Balogun St, Dolphin Estate, Ikoyi; tel: 01 461 4191/95. This is a brand new two-storey boutique hotel tucked away in a quiet

suburb of Ikoyi. There's stringent security to get through the gate and even into the housing estate where it's located. To find it you need to be on the expressway that goes from the Third Mainland Bridge across the top of Ikoyi and then take the turn off (past a huge pile of rubbish and a resident family of pigs) signposted to the Federal Secretariat – three high-rise buildings (one of them a burnt-out shell) to the northwest of Ikoyi. This road comes to what is effectively a dead end just before the Federal Secretariat, but the Elion House is on the last road to the right (there is a signpost). You can't get here by road from Alfred Rewane Rd (formerly Kingsway Rd) in the middle of Ikoyi – you have to go via the expressway. Once at the hotel, look out for the clocks above the reception desk that show times in Lagos, London, and Beirut – the Lebanese management imports paint from Lebanon each month to maintain the place! There are sweeping staircases, marble floors, fine art on the walls and antiques everywhere, and the 24 enormous rooms are individually decorated, with DSTV, minibar, safe, and some have corner baths. There's 24-hour room service, a secure car park, a water-treatment plant, gym, and an immaculate swimming pool. Fine wines and Italian and Lebanese food are served in the Olive Garden restaurant (guests only), and the Classico bar and lounge serves cocktails whilst someone plays the piano. Rates are surprisingly low for this quality and include breakfast but not the 15% that goes on everything: US$180 for a double, US$265 for a suite, US$325 for an executive suite. There are plans to extend, and prices may go up once it has established a reputation. At the time of writing they also didn't require a deposit, but again that may change.

**Logisitics Guesthouse** 836 Adetokunbo Ademola St, opposite the Villa Medici restaurant, Victoria Island; tel: 01 804 3537, 261 9696, 261 2462; email: logistics@cyberspace.net.ng. A mid-range hotel used by oil companies and the like to put up their employees until they find something more permanent. The 18 rooms have DSTV, minibar, phone, fat velour armchairs and enormous beds. The basic restaurant serves Nigerian and some continental meals plus beers and soft drinks, though there is easy access to nearby restaurants. Room rates, paid in naira, are equivalent to US$138 (US$200 deposit), which includes the 15% and a full continental breakfast.

**Michael's Lodge** Plot 1411 Adetokunbo Ademola St, Victoria Island; tel: 01 261 0191/2, 261 0188; email: michael@hyperia.com. This is a fairly new small guesthouse with only ten rooms, though there are plans for extensions, in a good location close to Bar Beach on Victoria Island and the much more expensive Eko and Protea hotels. The décor and furnishings are still quite fresh, and there's a small, bright blue sparkling pool. The good restaurant here is also open to non-guests and is dealt with under *Where to eat and drink*, and there's plenty of secure parking within the compound. Rooms have DSTV, fridges, and minuscule bathrooms with a shower, but are modern and spotlessly clean. Rates exclusive of the 15%, but including laundry and breakfast for one person, are N12,000–16,000 (with huge deposits of N25,000–35,000) depending on the size of the room.

**The Camelot Rest House** Plot 1425b Amodu Tijani Close, Victoria Island; tel: 01 261 2103, 262 5797; email: camelot@mwebafrica.com. A brand spanking new hotel with enthusiastic staff (the chef will greet you personally) in a central location on Victoria Island at the end of a quiet cul-de-sac. It features all new furniture and appliances, including a state-of-the-art reservations system and hairdryers in the rooms, and a huge car park with security guards where there are plans to build a swimming pool. The medieval theme continues in the Dragon's Den Bush Bar on the roof ,which is open 24 hours, with good views of the city, the downstairs Merlin's Bar and Coffee Shoppe that serves snacks and sandwiches, and the King Arthur restaurant that serves a range of Oriental, Lebanese and continental dishes and Italian wines. Breakfast costs N1,700 for continental and N2,200 for full English, while a main course at dinner is about N2,500. The 32 rooms have enormous beds, minibar, DSTV, and at the time of writing telephones that actually worked; the bigger suites have balconies and fat sofas. Rates are only payable in US$ and start from US$150 (US$200 deposit) for a standard room, rising to US$300 (US$380 deposit) for the biggest suite, exclusive of the 15%.

**B-Jay's Hotel** 24 Samuel Manuwa St, Victoria Island; tel: 01 262 2902, 262 3706/8, 268 0429, 774 6900/1; email: bjays@alpha.inkserve.com, bjayshotel24@yahoo.com. A reasonably small hotel with friendly staff on the outer rim of Victoria Island overlooking Five Cowrie Creek, with 34 clean rooms with DSTV, small fridge and phone. Ask about weekend specials – sometimes three nights for the price of two. The L-shaped Cowrie bar and restaurant has recently had a refit and is stunning; it's definitely worthwhile coming to eat or drink here even if you're not staying (see under *Where to eat and drink*). You can hire cars from a stand across the street. The room rates are confusing and vary depending on who you are. There are different rates for Nigerian residents, diplomats, United Nations agencies, and visitors with no residency permits. A foreigner can expect to pay in the region of US$140 (US$220 deposit) for a standard room, and US$160 (US$250 deposit) for an executive room. These rates are inclusive of the 15% and include tea or coffee and toast in the morning. I especially loved the ripped-up pages of the DSTV television guide in the loos in the event that the toilet paper runs out – how very thoughtful!

## Moderate: under US$100

**Airport Hotel** 111 Obafemi Awolowo Way, Ikeja; tel: 01 497 8670/9; email: laph@rcl.nig.com. This is a huge complex close to the roundabout that joins Obafemi Awolowo Way and Allen Avenue in Ikeja, a few kilometres north of the Sheraton in the Ikeja GRA. It's in amongst the heaving mass of markets and vehicles that is the centre of Ikeja proper. It's a terribly tired-looking old hotel, the bulk of it having been built in 1961, and with seemingly not much being done to it since. It started life as the Grand Hotel, Lagos in 1942 with just five rooms. The present 1960s monstrosity has 277 rooms spread over three L-shaped blocks. All the rooms have fridge and local TV, but the décor is hideous, with beaten-up and old-fashioned dressing tables and garish flowery curtains and sheets. There are three car parks, four bars, one Nigerian and one Chinese restaurant, an Olympic-sized swimming pool, and six vast conference halls which are often overrun with conference delegates or noisy weddings, funerals, church services and the like. Facilities include car hire (beat-up Peugeots in the car park for roughly N4,000 for half a day), an airport shuttle bus, and a bookshop stuffed from floor to ceiling with books and pamphlets – we picked up some ancient guides to Lagos here, but you need to tell them what you are looking for. In the shopping arcade outside are some bureaux de changes and travel agents. With four giant generators and three boreholes, the power and water supply is fairly consistent, and the staff are generally good, as many of them have worked there for years. Their brochure was clearly printed many years ago, but it amused me greatly – 'Tired or bored? Spooky or dingy? Make a way to any of our bars and wash off a little'. Room rates start at US$60–70 (US$80–90 deposit) for a double, US$100–140 (US$120–160 deposit) for a suite, plus the 15%. Again rooms are paid in naira.

**Excelsior Hotel** 3–15 Ede St, Apapa; tel: 01 587 6095; email: excelsior@infoweb.abs.net. This is located in the suburb of Apapa near the port area on the mainland. It's a popular but very rundown hotel, with dusty nicotine-coloured walls throughout, but nevertheless it is one of the cheapest places to stay. Facilities include a bright red Chinese restaurant called the Double O, a very faded hotel dining room for basic Nigerian meals, and a dodgy bar for hard-core drinking (I encountered some rather unpleasant expat men here who looked like they'd got lost in Lagos about 20 years ago). The 130-odd rooms on three floors have local TV, fridge, scratched furniture and dusty armchairs, and dilapidated bathrooms with buckets, though they are clean enough to use. Rates including the 15% are N6,900 for a double, and you may or may not be asked for N1,000–2,000 more for the deposit. Outside the hotel are a few curio sellers and some Hausa money changers, and a few blocks south of here, on Warehouse Road, are a couple of fast-food joints.

**Victoria Lodge** 5 Ologun Agbaje St, Victoria Island; tel: 01 262 0885, 261 7177. This establishment is very plain and old, but functional, with friendly staff in a central area of

Victoria Island. There's a large bar and lobby area serving beer and soft drinks, and a basic restaurant offering snacks throughout the day such as burgers, Spanish omelettes and Nigerian stews. The 13 clean and enormous rooms have very dated décor, but all have local TV, fridge, extra sofas, and a hot water cylinder above the bath. Room rates are N9,000 (N12,000 deposit) for a single, and N10,000 (N15,000 deposit) for a double.

**Hotel Victoria Palace** 1623 Saka Jojo St, Victoria Island; tel: 01 262 5901/8; email: hotelvp@alpha.linkserve.com. This is one of Victoria Island's cheapest hotels, with 30 rooms on three floors in a surprisingly quiet street and exceptionally friendly staff. The rooms are basic but adequate, with fridge, DSTV and big old beds, and the bathrooms have seen a lick of paint in recent years; shame they couldn't have replaced the ancient bathroom fittings at the same time. The back rooms look out on to the noisy launderette, so ask to see a few rooms before you decide. The Bombay Palace restaurant is (supposedly) open 24 hours, for Indian, Nigerian and continental dishes, but this is rather dependent on what ingredients they've got, and there's a pool table and dart board in the guest lounge. Remarkably there is a gym here with a mirrored wall, stereo, plus one weight machine, one bike, two treadmills, and a set of bathroom scales! And the *best* thing about this hotel is the row of clocks in reception – you know, time in London, time in New York etc. They have one for the time in Timisora (apparently it's in Romania). Room rates are inclusive of the 15% and breakfast; N8,250 (N13,000 deposit) for a single, N11,000 (N16,000 deposit) for a double, and N15,000 (N20,000 deposit) for a suite.

**Tamarin Hotel** 158 Adekunle Fajuyi Way, GRA, Ikeja; tel: 01 497 9160/9; email: tamarin@linkserve.com. This is an affordable and well-run hotel in the relatively peaceful Ikeja GRA not too far from the airport (the domestic terminal is only about a 10min drive). To get here, either make use of the hotel's shuttle service (though you will struggle to pre-arrange this before arriving), or get a taxi straight from the airport, as most drivers will know the way. Adekunle Fajiuyi runs parallel to Agege Motor Rd with the railway line separating the two streets so you can see the hotel from Agege Motor Rd as well. There's a restaurant and bar serving mainly Nigerian food, a swimming pool and a gym with one weight machine, one treadmill, one bike, and one dart board (?). The range of comfortable rooms and suites are spread over several wings, and are spacious with DSTV, fridge, enormous beds and old furniture. The best value rooms are the Olive Chalets at US$75 (US$100 deposit) for two people, but out of a total of 103 rooms there are only nine of these. The standard double, of which there are 60, goes for US$100 (US$150 deposit). Rates are inclusive of the 15%. Prices are quoted in dollars but paid in naira.

**YMCA** 77 Awolowo Rd, Ikoyi; tel: 01 773 3599. This is strictly men only, so for blokes on a budget this is the cheapest place to stay in Lagos, though it's pretty grim and I cannot be sure how secure it is. A block back from Awolowo Road, though well signposted behind the BG Mart shop (look up for the sign), the 'Y' has several rooms around a cool courtyard in a concrete block. The bare dorms (N350) have two double bunks in each with a separate bathroom with little more than a loo, tap and bucket, whilst the rooms (N1,500) have an additional shower, a fan and a chair. It's very basic and not wholly clean, there's no AC or reliable gen, and you'll need your own bedding. On the plus side the doors lock and there is intact mossie screening on the windows. The maximum stay is seven days and you'll need to be a member (about N300 to join) – many of the guests are from other West African countries and may be quite staunchly religious. There is a YWCA in Lagos but it's on Lagos Island and as there is absolutely no way that I am going to encourage even the most hard-nosed single female traveller to stay there, I am not going to even tell you where it is.

## WHERE TO EAT AND DRINK

Lagos has by far the best restaurants in the country for international fare – elsewhere you will struggle to find a non-Nigerian meal – but the imported ingredients and accompanying wine and other imported alcoholic drinks on the menus come at a price. In a Lagos restaurant serving international or 'Western' food, a main dish alone averages N1,000–1,500, and that's without extras such as drinks and the 15% VAT and service charge, which nearly all Lagos eateries add on, so even a not very special meal for two with drinks can cost around N7,000 and much more in the better restaurants. Nevertheless, Lagos has an excellent variety of international restaurants and plenty of people prepared to pay, from the expat community and upper elite of Lagos society. European, Lebanese, and Oriental food are readily available, and most menus feature both international dishes and Nigerian food, of which the latter is always cheaper. However, one of the biggest problems in Lagos restaurants is the inconsistency of the food and service, and not all the dishes are terribly authentic (in one I had beef stroganoff, which despite being a very tasty beef and vegetable stew, resembled nothing like a creamy stroganoff). You might have a great meal there one day, and a truly awful one the next – it all rather depends on what chef or waiter is on duty.

For very cheap Nigerian food, as is the case everywhere in Nigeria, there are the street food hawkers and the food-is-ready stalls. While they are plentiful in the market areas of Lagos Island and the mainland, they are not found readily in the more upmarket Ikoyi and Victoria Island, though cheap chop can be found around the Obalende Motor Park on Ikoyi and along Bar Beach on Victoria Island. These islands do, however, have a smattering of fairly modern fast-food joints for those on a budget. In Ikoyi, most moderately priced restaurants are clustered along or around Awolowo Road, which is without doubt the restaurant strip of Lagos, whilst the more expensive options are dotted around Victoria Island or in the upmarket hotels.

Finally, for those living in Lagos, many restaurants on the islands have a home/office delivery service (if of course you can get through by phone to make an order!), and home delivery is effectively easy thanks to the *okada* culture. Expect to pay in the region of N100–200 delivery charge on top of the price of your food within the environs of Victoria Island and Ikoyi. I have included telephone numbers where it may be advisable to make a reservation at a restaurant or where a home delivery service is on offer.

## Ikoyi

The majority of restaurants in Ikoyi are grouped around Awolowo Road, which is where many of Lagos's better shops are also located, so it's feasible enough to walk up and down during the day and find what interests you. During the evening, unless they are within a few metres of each other, always get a taxi between places.

Starting at the top end of Awolowo Road where it joins Alfred Rewane Road (formerly Kingsway) and the Falomo Bridge to Victoria Island, and on the tenth floor of the Golden Plaza shopping centre, is the **Golden Plaza** Chinese restaurant (open daily for lunch 12.00–16.00), which has a standard and affordable Chinese menu and a good dim sum special lunchtime menu; the restaurant is shut in the evenings when it's used for church services! A few metres along Awolowo Road to the west, and past the Falomo Shopping Centre and the Goodies Supermarket on the left-hand side of the road, is the **Dolce Vita**, 184 Awolowo Road; tel: 01 269 3763/4 (open daily 11.00–23.00). On offer is an extensive range of medium-priced Italian dishes cooked by an authentic Italian chef, in a neat setting with faded pictures of Italy on the walls. There are antipasto, risotto, pizza, chicken and meat dishes on the menu, but I am sure mamma back in Naples never makes *Italian goat*, or *pollo al peper oncino* – chicken with pepper sauce! Pastas go from N1,200, while prawns, lobster and fish start from N2,000, and there's a good selection of Italian wines.

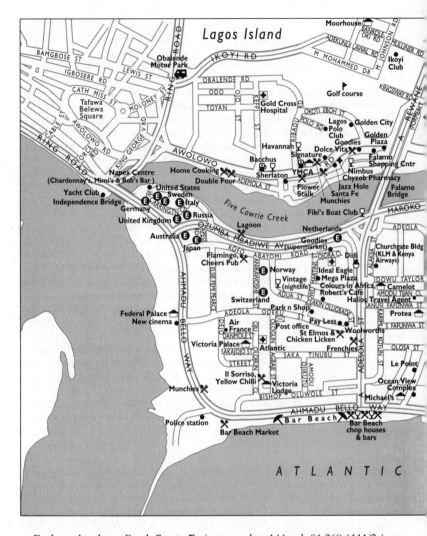

Back on Awolowo Road, **Santa Fe** is at number 144; tel: 01 269 6111/2 (open daily, lunch 12.00–17.00; dinner 18.00–23.00). This place receives consistently good reports for its food and service and is all set in a mock-up Wild West saloon decorated with Stetsons, reward notices, paraffin lamps, and saddles. There's a huge range of imported drinks available, the menu (in the shape of a cowboy hat of course) offers hearty portions of tex mex favourites, such as fajitas or blackened fish, and there's a huge range of world food to choose from, including Thai and Chinese. It's not cheap, with starters averaging around N700 and mains from N1,800 but there's a great atmosphere and a live band plays most nights. Across the street is a branch of **Munchies**, a fast-food joint serving take-away or sit-down pies, burgers, spicy fried chicken, *jollof* rice, potato wedges and onion rings. A meal with a coke costs about N500. Avoid the ice-cream – Munchies, like other fast-food chains in Nigeria, makes ice-cream in one of those machines using milk, water and pre-mixed powder, a combination that is bound to make you sick.

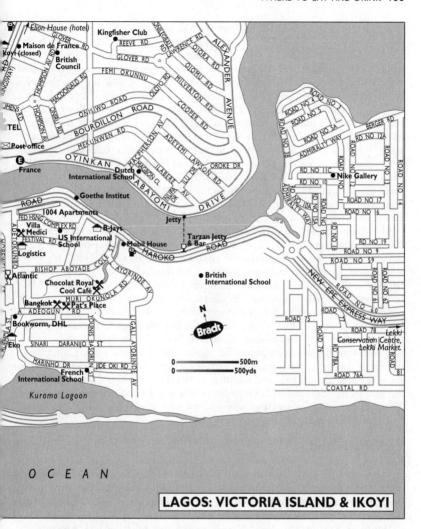

LAGOS: VICTORIA ISLAND & IKOYI

A few doors along and above a bank (look up) is **Flowerstalk**, 114 Awolowo Road; tel: 01 269 2660 (open daily 10.00–18.00), a brand new upmarket florist with an attached tearoom serving gourmet salads, fresh juice and occasional treats such as foie gras. The shop sells trendy plants, vases and some stunning flowers, and it's a lovely place to sit surrounded by all the greenery. A few doors along, the **Sherlaton**, 108 Awolowo Road; tel: 01 269 1275, 269 1282 (open daily for lunch 12.00–15.00; on Sunday last orders for lunch 17.00; dinner 19.00–23.30), serves great and very authentic Indian food for reasonable prices. There's vegetarian, chicken, fish and mutton but no pork or beef – vegetarians will be in chick pea, lentil, spinach and cottage cheese heaven. There are also some unusual desserts on offer, such as saffron-flavoured Indian ice-cream with pistachios and almonds, and *gajar halwa* – grated carrot cooked in milk and sugar. To drink, try a cold lassi with either salt or sugar. Main dishes go for as little as N600, which is good value for Lagos.

A few blocks along is **Double Four**, 44 Awolowo Road; tel: 01 269 3012, 269 3524 (open daily 11.00–23.00), which is predominantly Lebanese but which also has burgers, pizzas and ice-cream, with some 150 dishes on the menu – more western ones include beef stroganoff, chicken Kiev, and prawn curry for around N800. The atmosphere is noisy with blaring television, but it's popular with business people at lunchtime for the good food, and there's a bar area with a real espresso machine. The general manager, Awni, is quite a character and we managed to have quite an animated conversation with him about the state of Middle East politics (on which he has a lot of opinions). A bunch of Lebanese men at the table next to the door appear to do the same all day over coffee and cigarettes. A few doors along on the same side of the road is **Home Cooking**, tel: 01 473 5320 (open Monday–Saturday 10.00–22.00), a good Nigerian restaurant specialising in cheap and tasty food from the Effik/Calabar region, including goat's head, cow's leg, bushmeat, or oxtail pepper soup, plus dried fish, snails, and a variety of starches and soups. Friendly atmosphere but slow service.

Elsewhere on Ikoyi, the **Golden Gate** restaurant is on Alfred Rewane Road (formerly Kingsway Road); tel: 01 269 5337/9 (open daily for lunch 12.00–16.00; dinner 19.00–22.00), a few metres north of the now-defunct Ikoyi Hotel. It's a very formal and upmarket Oriental restaurant serving good but pricey Chinese, Japanese and Thai food in different restaurant areas; you can request that no MSG be put in your food. The terrace on the roof has great views of the city and is a popular venue for company/embassy receptions. To the east of the old Kingsway Road in a residential district of the island is the **British High Commission Club** (also known as the **Kingfisher Club**), 4 Reeve Road; tel: 01 461 5661/2. Wednesday nights are open nights for guests outside of the High Commission (though if you go regularly you will be expected to pay a fee to join), when you can get very cheap British beer and traditional fish and chips. You must first apply at the gate of the club for an ID card for which you'll need two passport photos. There's also a range of sporting facilities here such as netball, tennis, and squash courts, and the expat gatherings are very social.

## Victoria Island

Restaurants and bars are dotted all over Victoria Island, some of them in large residential streets some distance apart from one another, so for ease I am simply going to list them alphabetically and you can pinpoint them on the map. In any event, the venues here are far from a pub crawl circuit, and you will have to get transport or drive between each one.

**Bangkok Restaurant**, 244a Muri Okunola Street; tel: 01 461 9124 (open daily 11.00–23.00), serves excellent Thai and other Asian dishes flavoured with traditional lemon grass and coconut, great authentic green and red curries and pad Thai noodles, in an informal setting with efficient service and friendly owners. Prices are not too steep with a good sized main course costing N1,000–1,500 and take-aways are also available. There is parking and security guards outside to watch your car. The menu here is delightfully misspelt – try the *spaer ribs* or the *sring rools*! There's another branch of the Bangkok in Cape Town, South Africa, that also has an excellent reputation. **Chicken Licken** and **St Elmo's Pizzeria** are opposite Woolworth's at 80 Adeola Odeku Street (open daily 09.00–22.00), and are both part of South African chains that are popping up all over Africa. Chicken Licken is a bit like KFC, serving fried chicken, fries and coleslaw, whilst St Elmo's serves excellent pizzas and some pasta dishes.

**Chardonnay's**, 3 Louis Farrakan Crescent, Napex Complex on Walter Carrington Crescent; tel: 01 614113, 611046 (open daily 12.00 until the last person

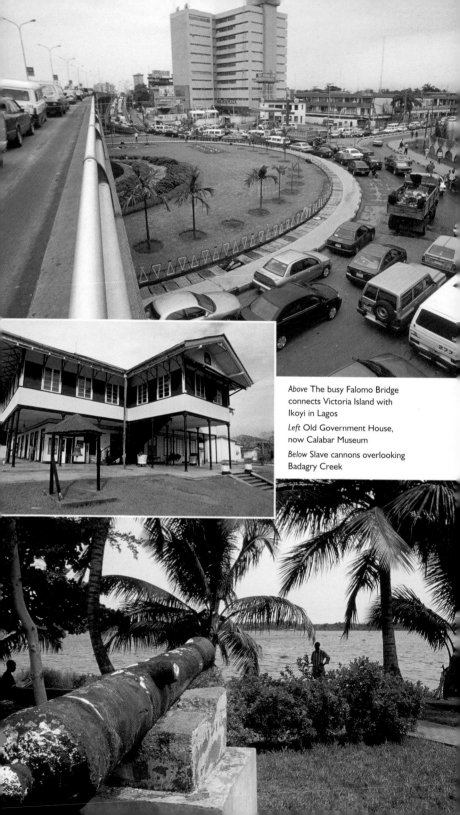

*Above* The busy Falomo Bridge
connects Victoria Island with
Ikoyi in Lagos

*Left* Old Government House,
now Calabar Museum

*Below* Slave cannons overlooking
Badagry Creek

*Above* The art of bronze casting has been revived in Benin City

*Above right* In the Kano dye pits, cloth is traditionally dyed in indigo and ironed with mahogany pounds

*Below* Decoration of hands, feet and faces with henna is popular among many northern ethnic groups

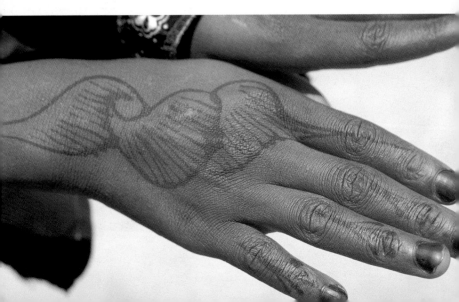

leaves), is definitely one of Lagos's best-kept secrets; you would never imagine this place would be in the tip-of-a-place, run down, Napex Complex. To find it go to the back left-hand corner of the complex, where there is space for parking outside with a security guard. It's a popular haunt for embassy people from the nearby Walter Carrington Crescent. There's great moody blues music such as Aretha Franklin, a wooden floor and luxurious drapes at the windows, fresh flowers, super trendy furniture, a small bar with fat sofas, and a cosy atmosphere. The food is gourmet cuisine from the south of France, accompanied by fine French and South African wines and cigars. Start with scrambled eggs and prawns or delicate spare ribs for around N700, followed by lamb with couscous or red snapper for about N2,000. Recommended for a treat and there's dinner dancing on Wednesday and Saturday, and live jazz on Friday. **China Town**, 3rd Floor, Mega Plaza, 14 Idowu Martins Street; tel: 01 774 4477, 613341 (open daily 11.00–23.00), offers sit-down, take-away or home delivery Chinese and Thai, with quick and reliable service in a large air-conditioned dining area with a big-screen TV showing sport. Authentic dishes including excellent coconut-based soups, though you may want to pass on the beef with HP sauce. Main dishes cost N1,200–1,600, and there are take-away and home-delivery specials.

**Chocolat Royal**, AIM Plaza, next to the Cool FM radio building, Etim Inyang Crescent; tel: 01 262 3055/6 (open daily 07.00–22.00), is a glitzy French-style patisserie serving the best pastries and fresh cream cakes in Lagos, and *the* place to be seen for besuited executives with cell phones attached to their ears at lunchtime – from the outside tables note the line of BMWs and Land Cruisers with waiting drivers. Serves sweet and savoury snacks, huge salads with all the trimmings, ice-cream, muffins, divine handmade chocolates, cappuccino and freshly ground coffee. It's packed to the gills, the waiters glide around in crisp white uniforms, and there's a buzzy atmosphere. It's pricey but fabulous and great for a treat. Across the street and a few metres up, opposite Cool FM, is the **Cool Café**, which hadn't opened yet when we visited but which was almost ready, with brand new, very trendy tables and chairs and all the kitchen equipment in place, and a poster promising a 24-hour internet café.

The **Cowrie Restaurant and Bar** in B-Jay's Hotel, 24 Samuel Manuwa Street; tel: 01 774 6900/1, 262 2902 (open daily 10.00–22.30), is in an L-shaped room with one arm as the bar and the other as the restaurant. It's a very stylish place with good service, relaxing music, sociable atmosphere and recently refurbished earthy décor – lose yourself in the enormous leather sofas. There's also an outside terrace, but unfortunately it's right next to the traffic. The cuisine is continental and Nigerian; there's a full buffet on Wednesday and Sunday with live music, low-calorie specials on a Thursday, and a happy hour 19.00–20.00 on a Friday. The bar has a broad selection of wine and imported spirits. Quite bizarrely, the menu not only lists the dishes and the prices, but also the time it takes to make the food. So, cream of tomato soup is N500/25 min; sweet and sour prawns, N1,900/50 min; Cordon Bleu steak, N1,300/40 min; which takes the same time as an egg sandwich, N600/40 min! There are occasional jazz nights here which are worth asking about. **The Flamingo Restaurant and Cheers Pub**, 10 Kofo Abayomi Street; tel: 01 262 2225, 261 0387 (open daily 12.00–23.30), has a huge range of Chinese, Indian and continental dishes, of which the Indian food is the best: good nan bread, vindaloo, tikka and sizzling tandoori dishes. It's great for vegetarians, with several dishes just for them, including veggie curries and cutlets, and Chinese soups they will cook without the meat. Home delivery available. **Foods of the Sun** in the Eko Hotel, Adetokunbo Ademola Street; tel: 01 262 4600/19 (open Monday–Saturday 19.00–22.30), is the best French restaurant in Lagos with a small but exquisite menu, with daily chef's specials and the finest of French wines. The décor, though, is very ordinary, in quite a plain-looking hotel dining room, and there's not much atmosphere. The food, however, is to be relished, and at N1,500 for a starter of goose liver pate with caramelised apples, followed by a main course of veal, lamb or crocodile for N3,000–5,000, it needs to be. Don't forget the 15% which adds considerably to a bill here.

**Frenchies**, 29 Akin Adesola Street; tel: 01 261 0096, 261 0186 (open daily 07.00–20.30), has a ground-floor café with a bakery selling pies, cakes and pizza, and a first-floor licensed restaurant serving grills and kebabs with an outside terrace overlooking the traffic. Excellent affordable sandwiches thanks to the great freshly baked white bread. There's another branch in Lekki Market. **Il Sorriso**, 27a Oju Olobun Close; tel: 01 261 0153, 774 9382 (open daily 11.00–23.00), is the best traditional Italian restaurant and pizzeria in Lagos run by an authentic and friendly Italian family – even the menu is in Italian. Popular with the expat community and deservedly so, and as it's small and intimate, reservations are essential. Pasta and risotto dishes start from N1,600, though expect to pay more for truffles, prawns and salmon. Good range of Italian wines, and home delivery pizzas (order 5 get 1 free). Just in front of the entrance in a small building is the **Yellow Chilli** that serves good and cheap Nigerian food-is-ready. The **Kuramo Sports Café** in the Eko Hotel, Adetokunbo Ademola Street; tel: 01 262 4600/19, is a cavern of a place decorated, as the name suggests, with all things sporty, including giant TV screens showing the South African sports channel Supersport. There are continental and Nigerian all-you-can-eat buffets for breakfast (06.00–10.30), lunch (12.00–16.00) and dinner (20.00–01.00), costing between N2,000 and N2,500, which is not bad value for a big hotel if you're very hungry. The Nigerian dishes include bushmeat stew and chicken pepper soup. The bar serves local and imported beers, spirits and wines. A good place to be if you want to stuff yourself silly in front of a big match. The hotel's **Poolside Terrace** (open daily 12.00–22.00), has a snack menu and it's a perfect venue for an afternoon drink overlooking Kuramo Lagoon.

**The Lagoon**, 1c Ozumba Mbadiwe Av; tel: 01 261 1616, 261 6888 (open daily 11.00–23.00), has a formal dining room overlooking Five Cowrie Creek serving continental, Chinese, some Indian, and West African dishes washed down with French wine. Upmarket and good quality but with extremely slow service. Main meat courses start from N1,800; double this for seafood. There's a huge and secure car park here, and cheaper take-aways such as burgers and pizzas are available from a kiosk outside on the terrace. The **Lighthouse Restaurant** in the Federal Palace Hotel, Ahmadu Bello Way; tel: 01 262 3116/25, 262 6180/199 (open daily 06.00–22.00), is a relaxing restaurant with buffets for breakfast, lunch and dinner, with a variety of continental, Chinese and Nigerian food on offer. There are also à la carte items like fish and chips and spaghetti, and main dishes cost about N1,800. Enjoy a drink or a cocktail in the hotel bar first for a fine view of the shipwrecks in Lagos Harbour. You can also get snacks at the hotel's **Poolside Café** (open daily 10.00–19.00) The **Mega Plaza Coffee Bar** on the 2nd floor of the Mega Plaza, 14 Idowu Martins St (open daily 11.00–21.30), had good coffee, fresh juice, salads and sandwiches, beer and wine and a few cane tables and chairs amongst the shops of the Mega Plaza.

**Michael's Restaurant**, Plot 1411, Adetokunbo Ademola Street; tel: 01 261 0191/2, 261 0188, in the lodge of the same name (open Tuesday–Sunday 10.00–23.00). Good food in large portions, and nice décor and atmosphere. A wide selection of soups, salads, pastas, standard steak, chicken and fish; you'll need to ask if you want anything other than chips with your meal. There's sometimes live music on Saturday evenings, and as it's part of a lodge there's plenty of secure parking in the compound. There's another branch of **Munchies** on Ahmadu Bello Road not far from the western end of Bar Beach. Look out for the 'M' sign, which is a bit of a take on McDonald's. At the **Oceanview Complex** on Adetokunbo Ademola Street, opposite Michael's (above), is the **Coral Snack Bar** (open daily 11.00–23.00) with its cool air conditioning and modern long marble bar where you can sample a glass of freshly made Chapmans. The menu consists of burgers, pizzas, salads and wraps, and it's good food, though a tad on the expensive side for the size of the portions; around N1,200 for a main dish. Next door is the **Ocean Pearl Chinese Restaurant** (open daily 11.00–23.00), a very ordinary Chinese with a big menu that's popular for business lunches.

**Robert's Café**, 5a Akin Olugbade Street; tel: 01 270 2606, is in the Colours in Africa shop (see under *Shopping*), just around the corner from both the Mega Plaza and Park 'n' Shop, so it's the perfect venue for expat ladies to take tea whilst they are out shopping (open Monday–Friday 09.00–18.00; Saturday 10.00–19.00). This is one of Lagos's most elegant and expensive coffee-and-cake cafés, with bright white tablecloths, stylish furniture, intimate music and personalised service. Drink freshly brewed coffee or tea from china cups and indulge in rich chocolate cake, black forest gateaux, or cheesecake for around N600 a slice. There's also a menu of authentic cocktails such as margaritas and bloody Marys. Very nice!

**Villa Medici**, 1 Alhaji Babatunde Jose Road (formerly Festival Road); tel: 01 262 1717, 261 0484 (open for lunch Monday–Friday 12.00–14.30; dinner Monday–Saturday 19.00–22.30), is pricey but serves excellent French and Italian food and wine in a lovely atmosphere with elegant dressed-up tables with black tablecloths, sparkling silverware and crystal glasses, arranged around an indoor pond with its own footbridge. Starters are N1,500–2,000 and main courses are N2,500–4,000, and for these prices expect the likes of beef fillet medallions and lobster – don't forget to add on the 15%. The service is superb and you'll need to dress up. Recommended for a special night out. Security guards outside watch your car.

**Wraps** is in the **Mega Plaza Food Court** next to the main entrance of the Mega Plaza, 14 Idowu Martins Street; tel: 01 776 6677. Serves fancy wraps, subs, burgers, chips and salads, and also does home delivery – order four or more items and they'll let you off the delivery charge. Unusual (for Nigeria) items on the menu include bacon and mushrooms, but prices reflect the imported ingredients (presumably bought from the supermarket upstairs in the food court) with a burger and chips costing around N1,000. Personally, I would be wary of the milkshakes. There are a variety of other cheaper stalls in the Mega Plaza Food Court selling snacks such as *shawarmas*, hot dogs and spring rolls – though you may choose to stay clear of the liver, gizzards and snails – as well as cold soft drinks and beer. Snacks cost as little as N50, while chicken and chips is around N250. There are outside tables in the centre in the baking sun, and as most of the food at the stalls is fried, this is stinking hot during the day – it's better to come in the early evening when you can fill up with good, cheap food and a cold beer.

## Lagos Island

**La Scala**, MUSON Centre, 8–9 Marina (entrance opposite the National Museum on Awolowo Road); tel: 01 264 6885, 264 6391 (open for lunch Monday–Friday 12.00–14.30; dinner Monday–Saturday 19.00–22.30, though it's sometimes closed for private upscale functions) is consistently known as the best restaurant in Lagos with quality continental cuisine, silver service, luxurious décor with wooden floors and ceilings, crisp tablecloths, fine china and silverware, and an intimate bar. Starters such as steamed asparagus go for about N1,000, while main dishes such as grilled sole with prawns wrapped in bacon, or fillet steak with brandy and Madeira sauce, are around N3,000. There's an extensive selection of fine wines from France, Italy and South Africa starting at about N6,000 a bottle, while a bottle of Moet is N12,000. Don't forget the 15% which adds considerably to the bill here. There is secure parking in the MUSON Centre's car park. Unbeatable atmosphere and very elegant; reservations are essential and you need to dress up.

## The mainland
### Apapa
At 20 Warehouse Road in Apapa is another branch of **Chicken Licken**, and **St Elmo's** (both open daily 09.00–22.00), and there's also another branch of **Frenchies** a few doors along at 14b Warehouse Road (open Monday–Saturday 08.00–20.00). The **Thistle Bar** at 36 New Marine Road is almost worth a special trip out to Apapa in itself (open Sunday–Thursday 09.00–midnight; Friday–Saturday 09.00–03.00). There's an odd mixture of things here but it's a fun and lively venue and the food is excellent. There's an outside thatched bar with fans (single ladies are not permitted) – happy hour is on Monday and Wednesday 17.30–19.30, and on Wednesday, Friday and Saturday there's live music. The menu is called the *Investment Schedule;* starters are called *Opening Accounts;* and Nigerian dishes, *African Development Banks.* There's a wide range of good and affordable food from pizzas and pastas for around N800, prawns and fish for N1,200, and authentic western dishes such as chilli con carne and beef stroganoff, plus daily specials. In the main building at the back is a much smaller bar frequented by a mostly German expat clientele and at the entrance is a stall selling a surprisingly large variety of international magazines and newspapers from UK *Marie Claire* to German *Stern* and just about every German newspaper there is. Finally, upstairs to the back of the outside bar there is a gym! (open daily 09.00–11.00 and 17.00–20.30) which costs N300 per hour and has a few weight machines, bikes and treadmills.

### Ikeja
The best place to eat in Ikeja is in the restaurants at the **Sheraton**. The hotel's best gourmet restaurant is the **Pili Pili** (open Monday–Saturday 18.30–22.30), which offers chef's specials such as scallops, tiger prawns, or crusted fillet of beef for N2,500–3,500, followed by fine cognacs and cigars. The **Crockpot** (open 24 hours) has breakfast, lunch and dinner buffets for N1,500/2,500/3,000 on the go all day and night, with speciality buffets on some evenings. The **Pool Bar** does the same, with an American night on a Wednesday, an Arabian night on a Saturday and the like, for around N2,200 for a buffet. The **Italian Restaurant** serves pizzas and pastas for around N2,000 using authentic ingredients. All the restaurants have good wine lists and plenty of options for vegetarians. Finally, the informal British-style pub **Goodies** provides live music on most nights and satellite television, and stays open until 03.00.

## NIGHTLIFE
For the adventurous, Lagos has a vibrant and pumping nightlife scene that often doesn't even begin to get going until well after 23.00 – if you show up before then you'll be helping the bartender polish the glasses – with bars, discos, and live-music clubs carrying on until dawn. Some daytime restaurants mentioned above have dance floors and crank it up after 21.00 when they attract cover charges, particularly at the weekends. Safety on the streets after dark in Lagos is a major concern, so exercise caution and preferably go clubbing accompanied by a local – essential if you are going to the clubs on the mainland. As with any major city, Lagos has its fair share of prostitutes, locally known as 'nightriders'.

The **Havannah Bar** on Ribadu Road in Ikoyi is a good late-night drinking option after eating in one of the restaurants on Awolowo Road, with a huge menu of imported alcoholic drinks, shooters and cocktails. It's small and smokey, with a good pub-like atmosphere, and the giant bouncers at the door who will also help you find a taxi to get home. Also in Ikoyi is **Bacchus** at 57 Awolowo Road (open daily from 18.00 until the last person leaves; N1,000 cover charge), a Lebanese and Nigerian restaurant in the early evening, and then a late-night disco with thumping western music and nightriders. It's hugely popular with Lagos's younger Lebanese community. If you are out and about on Awolowo Road at night, Bacchus is a good central location to find a taxi home as there are bouncers at the door and loads of cars and people outside. Just be wary of the beggars in wheelchairs and on skate boards that target the wealthy Lebanese as they go in and out.

**Nimbus** at 10–12 Maitama Sule Street, Ikoyi; a comfortable, relaxed bar and restaurant for drinking and conversation and *the* place to meet Lagos's expat press corps (the Associated Press building is near here). Standard but filling chicken and chips and other westernised basics cost around N1,000, and there's a stage in the garden that features anything from a lone guitarist during the week to a full jazz or highlife band at the weekend (Friday and Saturday 19.00; cover charge N2,000–2,500). Try and catch Yinka Davies and the Five and Six Band who occasionally play here – she has a tremendous soulful voice.

On Victoria Island there are a couple of dark and dingy bars in the Napex Centre on Walter Carrington Crescent, **Mimi's** and **Bob's Bar**, where football fans watch Supersport until 21.00 (when the TV is switched over to the music channels). They're pretty rough and ready, but stay open for hard-core drinking until 06.00. At the **Tarzan** jetty on Maroko Road between Victoria island and Lekki is a 24-hour bar on two stories overlooking Five Cowrie Creek with lots of cold beer and Guinness, comfortable cane furniture, pool table, and a stage where a makossa band plays from 17.00–23.00 on a Sunday, which attracts a huge crowd, in front of which is a gravel space for dancing. The **Fiki Boat Club** on Ozumba Mbadiwe Road, almost under the Falomo Bridge on the Victoria Island side, also has a 24-hour bar, with a terrace and plastic chairs next to Five Cowrie Creek. Fish, chicken, chips and rice are on offer and the Star and Heineken beer is always cold. There is a live makossa and highlife band on Wednesday, Friday and Sunday nights.

**Vintage** at Plot 138, Musa Yar'adua Street, Victoria Island; tel: 01 320 0576 (open 12.00–23.00 on weekdays, and 12.00–02.00 at weekends), is an upscale bar and restaurant in a house set back from the road behind a gate, with half a football field of lawn to cross and with ample parking in the grounds. The ultra-modern bar upstairs has a full range of imported drinks, western pop tunes, a bar snack menu, and a good vibey atmosphere. The impressive menu in the downstairs restaurant has mixed cuisine with plenty of good-quality steaks and beef dishes from N1,500 and some vegetarian options.

**Pat's Place**, Plot 292C Ajose Adeogun Street, Victoria Island; tel: 01 320 0424/5; email: patsonvi@yahoo.com (opens at 10.00 and closes when the last person leaves), is a Lagos expat institution run by the larger-than-life Pat Roberts, the congenial host and ex-rugby player (he played for Zambia and England) who has lived in Lagos for over 25 years. There are four bars and several rooms decorated with dart boards and framed rugby shirts, and oddly, a US combat jacket. Very attentive waitresses serve up huge portions of English-style pub grub such as steak and kidney pie and chicken and chips for N1,200–1,800. Major sports are shown on a big DSTV screen, and Pat boasts that he has the largest selection of single malt whiskies in West Africa. It's a fun atmosphere, especially when there's a crucial rugby match on. On Thursday from 20.00 there's live music from two female singers who belt out jazz and blues, and there's a disco on Saturday night when the place is heaving. Parking is on the street, but there are security guards.

At **'A' (Atlantic) Bar**, 14 B Adeola Hopewell Street, Victoria Island (open daily 12.00 until the early hours), you'll find a younger, well-heeled Nigerian crowd in a sophisticated setting, with very good music from enormous speakers with makossa on a Wednesday night and DJs and live music from 23.00 at the weekends. Bar snacks are N300 for buffalo wings or spring rolls, and main continental dishes go from N1,000, including chicken everything – creole, kebab, fried, grilled, sweet and sour, and Mexican. Nigerian dishes go for around N700 with a full range of soups and starch.

There are two very popular and well-known clubs on the mainland but you really should only go accompanied by a Lagosian. The **Afrika Shrine** is on Pepple Street, Ikeja (open Thursday–Sunday 20.00–dawn; N250 cover charge) which sometimes features live performances by renowned saxophonist and Grammy award nominee Femi Kuti (the son of the late Fela Kuti) when he is in Lagos. He's famous for his own personalised form of Afro-beat. There's a haze of dope in the air here. The **Motherlan'** at 64 Opebi Road, Ikeja (open midnight–dawn; N1,000 cover charge) is an enormous outdoor amphitheatre on the edge of a canal in Ikeja with a hi-tech sound system, and it has live performances by Lagbaja! (another saxophonist) and The Colours Band, usually on the last Friday of every month. This is the guy that plays in a mask (see page 54).

## CHANGING MONEY

As explained in the *In Nigeria* chapter (see page 68), there are thousands of banks all over Lagos where you will *not* be able to change money. There are hundreds on Victoria Island alone, many of which are agents for Western Union, where you can take out US$ cash but not exchange US$ cash or other currencies for naira. Of the very few bureaux de changes that are scattered around town, try the ones at the Napex Complex at the end of Walter Carrington Crescent on Victoria Island or outside the defunct Ikoyi Hotel. Black market money changers hang out at various locations – on Broad Street on Lagos Island, outside the Excelsior Hotel in Apapa, outside the (closed) Ikoyi Hotel in Ikoyi, and outside the Eko and Federal Palace hotels on Victoria Island (at the Federal Palace you can make transactions in the car park without even getting out of your car). Personally, I would first change enough for a taxi and your first day or two with the money changers on arrival at the airport, and then once in the city, attempt to change money at the reception desks inside the big hotels, where they advertise a foreign exchange service for their guests only; failing that, try the money changers outside. Changing money on the black market is tolerated – they print the black market rate along with the bank rate in the newspapers, so you shouldn't have too many problems. Just ensure that you count all the naira first before handing over US$ cash. If you feel uncomfortable with this than try the Mega Plaza on Victoria Island – the Lebanese management here gave us good US$ and GBP rates. You'll find them in the cash desk behind all the TVs. Finally, if you know of an expat that may want to change money this is the best bet. Many get a certain part of their wage in naira and are more than willing to swap it over for hard currency. If you are travelling to other parts of Nigeria read those chapters carefully, as there are few other options to change money outside of Lagos and you may need to do the bulk of money changing here. The only place I heard of that would perhaps be willing to change Thomas Cook travellers' cheques in Lagos, if not the whole of Nigeria, was the Thomas Cook/Travelex office at 23 Marina Street, Lagos Island. It's the Travelex head office on the 13th floor of the Maman Kotangoro building, but don't hold your breath.

# SHOPPING
## Books and music

**Bookworm** Unit 6, Eko Hotel Shopping Complex (not to be confused with the bookshop in the Eko Hotel – this shopping centre is outside and to the north of the hotel complex where there is also a branch of DHL), Ajose Adeogun St, Victoria Island; tel: 01 614560, 320 0606, email: bookworm@nova.net.ng (open Mon–Fri 09.00–19.00; Sat 10.00–17.00). By far the best bookshop in Nigeria, with a range of imported books from the UK; hardbacks, new novels, some CD ROMs, children's books, board games such as Monopoly and Scrabble, and some classical music CDs. The staff here are knowledgeable and friendly, and can order just about anything you want from their UK suppliers. Not that you cannot do this directly from Amazon and the like over the internet, but if you are wary about sending credit card details through the web from Nigeria then this is a good alternative option.

**CMS Book Shop** 50–52 Broad St, Lagos Island (open Mon–Fri 08.30–17.30; Sat 09.00–15.00). This sells a huge range of text and school books and some paperbacks (I found *Harry Potter* here).

**Glendora** Shop 4, Falomo Shopping Centre, Awolowo Rd, Ikoyi: tel: 01 269 2762, 686870; email: sales@glendorabooks.com; www.glendorabooks.com (open Mon–Sat 08.00–18.30), with other branches at the Jazz Hole and Eko Hotel (see below) and a well-stocked kiosk in the departure hall of the airport (open daily 06.30–22.00). It's an old-fashioned and somewhat dusty shop with floor-to-ceiling shelves of new and secondhand novels, text and school books, literature and classics, children's books, and some of Nigeria's (limited) selection of maps. They publish the quarterly *Glendora Review,* which is a fat magazine on West African art and music available at all their outlets.

**Jazz Hole** 168 Awolowo Rd, Ikoyi; tel: 01 480 5222; www.jazzholerecords.com. Open Mon–Sat 10.00–19.30. A wonderful, cavernous shop stuffed with interesting things; you could spend hours browsing in here and the music is great. Sells art and photography books, magazines and newspapers, intelligent novels, all the famous Nigerian writers, social, political and philosophy journals, coffee-table books, plays, sheet music, and an excellent variety of African and world music CDs, from West African chant reggae to Latino American blues. The helpful staff will let you listen before you buy. If you email them you can get a regular listing of what's on at the shop. They have their own record label and produce great compilations in unique 'Jazz Hole' covers, and they host regular concerts (often free) to plug their CDs.

The **Glendora Eko Hotel Book Shop** in the far corner past the main reception area; tel: 01 624600, ext: 6217 (open Mon–Fri 08.00–21.00; Sat 08.00–19.00), has an excellent range of foreign publications including up-to-date French and English newspapers and magazines, and the likes of *Time* and *Newsweek*. This is also one of the best places to pick up a street guide to Lagos and Abuja and it has a similar, though much smaller, range of books to the other Glendora branches above.

**Quintessence** Falomo Shopping Centre, Awolowo Rd, Ikoyi; tel: 01 269 4680; email: qltd@infoweb.abs.net; www.quintessenceltd.com (open Mon–Sat 09.00–18.00). One of the best and most upmarket book and craft shops in Lagos, with hefty price tags to match. Here you'll find trendy clothes, coffee-table books on Africa, batiks and Nigerian fabrics, stylish jewellery, international magazines, and high-calibre souvenirs. It's also a good place to pick up leaflets and flyers on what's on around the city, and they sell tickets for concerts, plays and events at the MUSON Centre on Lagos Island.

## Crafts and curios

There are several craft markets in Lagos, though the cheapest and the best is in Lekki Market which is dealt with under *What to see and do* (see page 164). Nigerian crafts include wood carvings, masks, drums, decorated calabashes, leather goods, gold, bronzeware, silver, bead jewellery, pottery, batiks and other colourful fabrics. Outside the **Eko Hotel** is a market in a cabana to the left of the main entrance of the hotel as you enter the driveway. It's stuffed to the gills with arts and crafts, though I would hope that the vast amounts of ivory on offer are not real even though the traders insist it is. Very unfortunately the leopard and cheetah skins hanging on the walls are very real. Do not purchase these items – you will be encouraging an illegal trade and the chances of you getting them into your home country are zero. When bargaining, which you'll have to do very hard, make out that you live in Lagos even if you don't. This usually gives you a bit of an edge as the trader will think you have had experience of bargaining on a daily basis. The target is usually about a third of the asking price. There's another similar market outside of the **Federal Palace Hotel** to the right of the car park just before the entrance of the circular elevated driveway, and another one outside of the **Ikoyi Hotel**, which is still here despite the hotel being closed. All these curio markets are open daily 08.00–20.00. Finally, there's a whole range of craft and curio shops in the international departure lounge of the **Murtala Mohammed Airport**, but prices here are obviously more expensive, though still negotiable.

**Signature** 107 Awolowo Rd, Ikoyi; tel: 01 776 0900, www.soleilgallery.com. If you are at all interested in Nigerian art, check out their website or visit their outlet at 156 Portobello Road in London. Here is a wonderful collection of objets d'art from all over West Africa, and a few pieces from East and southern Africa; oil, watercolour and charcoal paintings, sculpture, exquisite furniture, antiques, fabric, mirrors, vases, and wood carvings. Downstairs is the main shop, whilst upstairs is a gallery with changing exhibits of local artists. All the pieces are of very high quality with prices to match. Paintings go from US$400 while a small drum is US$150. They can arrange to air-freight items worldwide. They also sell imported art materials such as oil, watercolour and acrylic paints, paint brushes, canvasses and paper, and have a picture-framing service.

**Earthworks** 3rd Floor, Mega Plaza, Idowu Martins St, Victoria Island. This is a curio and art shop on the top floor of the Mega Plaza selling a similar range of goods as Signature above, but not nearly as nicely presented and the staff are not as knowledgeable. Again they can also arrange shipping here. Look out for some unique clay sculptures by artist Reuben Ugbine (sold here, at Signature, and in Colours in Africa below). They are of Nigerian people in a variety of poses, from old bent men, young muscled boys or women pounding yam, to people chatting or individuals pondering with heads in hands. They are quite remarkable, unique to Lagos, and there's a lot of warmth and life in the figures.

**Colours in Africa and Robert's Café** 5a Akin Olugbade St, Victoria Island; tel: 01 270 1346 (open Mon–Fri 09.00–18.00; Sat 10.00–19.00). This is a very stylish shop on two floors with the trendy Robert's Café out front (see under *Where to eat and drink*). It's stuffed with high-quality curios from all over Africa, including baskets from Swaziland, pots from Kenya, wood carvings from Zimbabwe, and wire sculptures from South Africa. I especially liked the brightly painted Nigerian trucks and buses on the wall, made from shiny metal in the character of the beat-up vehicles decorated with stickers and slogans. There's also furniture, screens, jewellery, crockery, some batik clothing and handmade leather shoes. Well worth a browse followed by tea and cake in the café.

## Food and general goods

If you are living in Lagos than you will no doubt depend on the few shops specialising in imported food. **Le Point** Adetokunbo Ademola Street, 200m south of the Eko Hotel (open Monday–Saturday 09.00–18.00) is a quality delicatessen for imported goods such as Belgian chocolates, fine wines and champagnes, with a deli counter selling cured hams, a broad selection of cheese, and excellent cuts of fresh meat including pork and lamb, which are usually hard to find – according to some expats this is the best meat in town. At 192 Awolowo Road in Ikoyi is **Goodies**, an upmarket supermarket selling expensive goods that are hard to find elsewhere. There's a good selection of toiletries, and wine and spirits, a deli counter, and a fruit and veg stall in the car park outside. There's another branch on Ojora Close on Victoria Island. Also on Victoria Island, on Adeola Odeku Street, is **Woolworth's**, an upmarket South African chain very similar to Marks & Spencer in the UK that sells clothes imported from South Africa, but no food. Near here is also **Payless** and **Park 'n' Shop**, for imported food and household goods.

At 14 Idowu Martins Street is the **Mega Plaza**; tel: 01 262 4624/6. Here you'll find probably the best selection of imported goods in the country, but it's expensive – I saw a flat-screen TV here for N1.9 million! In the basement is office equipment, generators and white goods; on the ground floor stereos, DVD and video players, rental and sales of DVDs and videos, luggage, sports equipment and cameras; on the first floor is a counter selling imported booze and the **Mega Plaza Coffee Shop**; and on the second floor is a defunct internet café, the **Earthworks** curio shop (see opposite), and the **China Town** restaurant (dealt with under *Where to eat and drink*). For those visitors who don't necessarily need to buy a washing machine, the Mega Plaza is handy for hard-to-find items such as camera film, disposable cameras, batteries, toiletries and razors, and the air-conditioned coffee shop is good for a cup of tea or coffee and a sit down. There's a secure car park across the road for a few naira, and outside and to the left of the main entrance is a food court with a variety of stalls selling cheap snacks. Up some steps from the food court is a supermarket selling imported food items, booze, and frozen meat. The whole complex is open daily from 10.00–22.00.

## THE WORLDWIDE WEB

There are hundreds of internet cafés all over Lagos and I could easily fill a few pages listing them, but I am not going to bother. The reason for this is whilst within the last couple of years there must have been an internet boom, many of these establishments are today non-functioning, not just because of the inconsistent NEPA, but because the service providers, like cell phone networks, come and go rapidly or fail miserably to maintain their connections. Don't get me wrong, you will find internet access, but you may have to do some leg work to find a place that actually is working. There's no shortage of places to try and just about every street on Victoria Island has a few spots. At the **Westside Cyber Café** on Adetokunbo Ademola St, just south of the Eko Hotel, where there are several very new (and very blank) hi-tech terminals, brand new office furniture and refreshing air conditioning, I asked the girl who worked there what hours the cyber café was open. She told me in great detail and I got prices and the full address and telephone number from her. She then added that 'the internet was down'. I asked how long it had been down, and she answered that she didn't know as she had only been working there for $2^1/_2$ months. The café stays open, employs someone who switches on the air conditioning, and the internet has been down for over $2^1/_2$ months! There's another swish cyber café on the top floor of the Mega Plaza on Idowu Martins St on Victoria Island; again all the computers are covered in dust, with an attendant sitting there with a price list in front of him, and where the internet has 'been down' for the last year.

## SAFETY

Lagos is often dubbed the most dangerous city in the world, and as with any impoverished city in the Third World, it does have its problems of crime brought on by the millions of people trying to eke out a living in a confined space. But remember crime statistics are high because of the colossal population, and they have actually decreased in recent years. The islands are considered lower risk than the mainland. As a foreigner it will be assumed that you have relative wealth, and muggings, carjackings, and armed robberies do occur. If you talk to Lagos's expats, stories abound, and most of this excessively paranoid community live in highly secure compounds and travel around with drivers, some of them armed. Shortly before my visit to Lagos, there was in incident at the Eko Hotel on Victoria Island when a party of Chinese businessmen arranged a transfer to another part of the city by coach. The coach pulled up in front of the hotel where they all piled in, and they were then driven off to a remote spot and robbed at gunpoint. A few moments after they had departed, the 'real' coach pulled up outside the hotel. The Eko Hotel now advises guests not to believe early-morning phone calls telling guests that their pick-up time has changed. Other incidents that happened whilst I was in Nigeria included an airline flight crew being robbed at gunpoint whilst eating in a restaurant close to the Sheraton Hotel in Ikeja, and an armed robbery at a bar on Victoria Island popular with expat oil employees. It seems likely that high-powered business people are generally the target for robbers and fraudsters, and our personal experience as budget travellers was that we had no problems whatsoever, and even negotiated the motor parks on the mainland unscathed, which are notoriously known as stomping grounds for Area Boys (see box on page 124). Nevertheless, it's obviously essential that you take note of your surroundings at all times and develop a sense of street savvy. Most people get through their stay in Lagos safely, and are surprised to find the city a friendly rather than dangerous place. Finally, when you are on the streets beware of the traffic, which is possibly the biggest threat to your safety in Lagos. Pedestrians most definitely do not have the right of way; it's survival of the biggest and the heaviest, and Lagos drivers are renowned for their aggressive tactics.

## LISTINGS
### Airlines

**ADC Airlines** Airport desk; tel: 01 496 5750

**Aero Contractors** Airport desk; tel: 01 774 9723

**Air France** ICON House, Plot 999F Idejo/Danmole St, off Adeola Odeku, Victoria Island; tel: 01 461 0461; email: los@airfrance.fr

**Bellview Airlines** Airport desk; tel: 01 791 9215; plot 270, Ozumba Mbadiwe Av, Victoria Island; tel: 01 262 1373; email: reservation@flybellview.com; www.bellviewair.com. Bellview is the only domestic airline to fly out of Nigeria and at the time of writing also had services to Abidjan, Accra, Banjul, Conakry, Doula, Dakar, Freetown and Monrovia.

**British Airways** 1st floor, C & C Towers, plot 1684 Sanusi Fafunwa St, Victoria Island; tel: 01 261 1225/8 – there is also a desk at the Sheraton Hotel in Ikeja; email: contact.1.nigeria@britishairways.com; www.britishairways.com/nigeria

**Cameroon Airlines** Plot 16 Oko-Awo Close, Victoria Island; tel: 01 261 1172, 261 6270, 774 5129

**Chanchangi Airlines** Airport desk; tel: 01 493 9744/55; Eko Hotel; tel: 01 262 4600

**Egypt Air** 22b Idowu Taylor St, Victoria Island; tel: 01 619 2332, 262 0081

**Ethiopian Air** 3 Idowu Taylor St, Victoria Island; tel: 01 263 7655, 263 2690

**Ghana Airways** 128 Awolowo Rd, Ikoyi; tel: 01 269 2363, 269 1397, 269 5379

**KLM and Kenya Airways** Churchgate Tower, 30 Afribank St, Victoria Island; tel: 01 461 2501, 461 2574/7

**Lufthansa** 150 Broad St, Lagos; tel: 01 266 4430, 266 4173, 266 4883
**Middle East Airlines** Plot 1682 Sanusi Fafunwa St, Victoria Island; tel: 01 261 5106, 261 5380
**Sosoliso Airlines** Airport desk; tel: 01 496 1962; www.sosolisoairline.com
**South African Airlines** 28c Adetokunbo Ademola St, Victoria Island; tel: 01 262 0607/9, 262 5783
**Virgin Atlantic** Sheraton Hotel; tel: 01 461 2747, 320 2747

## Car hire

As explained in the *In Nigeria* chapter, there is effectively no such thing as car hire and the division between taking a taxi and hiring a car is somewhat blurred. You cannot hire a car without a driver and it's the driver who pays for the petrol, so in all essence you're taking a taxi. You can find cars and drivers outside all the major hotels – ask the hotel reception staff to recommend a particular driver. There is a bunch of cars in the car park at the Eko Hotel near the curio market, at the (closed) Ikoyi Hotel in the car park, and in the lobbies of the Federal Palace and Sheraton hotels are desks for **Planet Rentals**, Sheraton Hotel; tel: 01 497 8660/9, ext: 8049; Federal Palace Hotel; tel: 01 497 8660/29, ext: 8049. Planet charges about US$90 for a reasonably good car and driver for the day, with rates coming down if you take a car for more than three days. Elsewhere, you might get more battered cars for cheaper – we paid N5,000 for a day's car hire with driver between 09.00 and 17.00 and a further N600 per hour after that. Alternatively, if you come across a taxi driver you like and trust, make him an offer and expect to bargain hard.

## Cinemas

Whilst Nigeria has a vibrant home-grown film and video industry dubbed Nollywood, there are no cinemas in Lagos screening Hollywood or European releases. However, expat organisations and the foreign cultural centres occasionally show films, and at the time of writing a new cinema had just opened to the south of the Federal Palace Hotel, that will show Hollywood movies.

## Courier services

**DHL** has various offices around Lagos, which include express offices at the Eko Hotel Shopping Complex at the roundabout just north of the hotel itself on Ademola Street, Victoria Island, and another at the top end of Isaac John Street near the Sheraton in Ikeja. Other courier companies include **United Parcel Service** (UPS), at 11 Idowu Taylor Street, Victoria Island, and **TNT** at 94 Awolowo Road, Ikoyi.

## Cultural centres

**Alliance Française (French Cultural Centre)** at La Maison de France, opposite the closed Ikoyi Hotel, Alfred Rewane Rd (formerly Kingsway Rd); tel: 01 269 2365, 269 2035. This is one of Lagos's top venues for music concerts, which they hold almost every night, from classical to fairly well-known Nigerian musicians, plus art exhibitions, and an internet café. French films are shown once a week, usually on Monday nights, and there's an excellent café, La Source, where you can enjoy some real French coffee and bistro-style snacks. There are French newspapers and magazines and a library with over 800 mostly French books. The library is open to all daily between 10.00 and 19.00 and for a small fee and deposit members can borrow books, DVDs, videos and CDs. If you are living in Lagos, you can learn to speak French here with four- to six-week courses starting each month. These courses come highly recommended. The centre produces a useful leaflet of what's-on each month that you can pick up at La Maison de France itself, or at Quintessence, the upmarket gift shop on Awolowo

Road. If you are living in Lagos make sure you get a copy each month, as there are many worthwhile events to go to even if you can't speak French, especially the Nigerian music concerts.

**The British Council** 20 Thompson Av, Ikoyi; tel: 01 269 2188/2192; www.britishcouncil.org/nigeria (open Mon–Thu 07.30–16.00; Fri, 07.30–12.30. The library is open Mon–Fri 09.00–18.00, and Sat 09.30–12.30). Here there is a lounge area with English newspapers and magazines, an internet café with over 20 reliable terminals, a library with a good selection of books and videos, and a good café. Anyone is allowed inside to browse but to borrow items from the library there is an annual membership of about US$35, which includes unlimited use of the internet.

**Goethe-Institut (German Cultural Centre)** 10 Ozumba Mbadiwe Av (on Five Cowrie Creek, not far from B-Jay's Hotel and opposite the 1004 apartment complex), Victoria Island; tel: 01 261 0717, 774 6888; email: gilagosb@infoweb.abs.net; www.goethe.de/lagos. The library, with an extensive range of German books and newspapers, is open daily 10.00–13.00, 15.00–17.00, and until 19.00 on Tuesday and Thursday. You can browse for free but to borrow there's a very small annual fee of N500. The centre is set in big grounds and the gardens and an inside gallery (sponsored by Lufthansa) hold regular exhibitions of contemporary art. It's well worth checking out what's showing, and the centre also has information on other cultural events in Lagos.

## Embassies and high commissions

**Australia** 2 Ozumba Mbadiwe St, Victoria Island; tel: 01 261 8875
**Austria** Fabac Centre, 3b Ligali Ayorinde Av, Victoria Island; tel: 01 261 6081
**Belgium** 1A Murtala Muhammed Drive, Ikoyi; tel: 01 269 1507/11
**Benin** 4 Abuou Smith St, Victoria Island; tel: 01 261 4411
**Cameroon** 5 Elsie Femi Pearse St, Victoria Island; tel: 01 261 2226
**Canada** 4 Idowu Taylor St, Victoria Island; tel: 01 262 2516/8
**Denmark** 4 Walter Carrington Crescent, Victoria Island; tel: 01 261 0660, 261 0537
**Finland** Plot 13, Walter Carrington Crescent, Victoria Island; tel: 01 261 0916, 261 0524
**France** 1 Oyinkan Abayomi Drive, Ikoyi; tel: 01 269 3427/30
**Gabon** 8 Norman Williams St, Ikoyi; tel: 01 268 4566, 268 4673
**Germany** 15 Walter Carrington Crescent, Victoria Island; tel: 01 261 1011, 261 1082
**Ghana** 21/23 Island Club Rd, Onikan, Lagos Island; tel: 01 263 0015, 263 0934
**Italy** 12 Walter Carrington Crescent, Victoria Island; tel: 01 261 9881, 261 4066
**Japan** 24/25 Apese St, off Kofo Abayomi St, Victoria Island; tel: 01 261 4929, 261 3797
**Mauritania** 31 Gafa Animashaun St, Victoria Island; tel: 01 261 8966
**Netherlands** 24 Ozumba Mbadiwe Av, Victoria Island; tel: 01 261 3653, 261 0705
**Niger** 15 Adeola Odeku St, Victoria Island; tel: 01 261 2300, 261 2330
**Norway** 3 Anifowoshe St, Victoria Island; tel: 01 261 8467/8
**Senegal** 12/14 Kofo Abayomi St, Victoria Island; tel: 01 261 1722
**South Africa** 4 Maduke St, off Raymond Njoku St, Ikoyi; tel: 01 269 2174, 269 2709
**Sudan** 2b Kofo Abayomi St, Victoria Island; tel: 01 261 5889
**Sweden** 17 Walter Carrington Crescent, Victoria Island; tel: 01 261 0240, 261 8743
**Switzerland** 5 Anifowoshe St, off Kofo Abayomi St, Victoria Island; tel: 01 261 3918
**Togo** Plot 976, Oju-Olobun Close, Victoria Island; tel: 01 261 7449
**United Kingdom** 11 Walter Carrington Crescent, Victoria Island; tel: 01 261 9541, 261 9537; visa & consular services; tel: 262 5930/37
**United States** 2 Walter Carrington Crescent, Victoria Island; tel: 01 261 0150, 261 0139

## Hospitals

The following hospitals have been recommended to me and all have 24-hour emergency units, but in the event that you do have to go to hospital, if you possibly can, contact your embassy or high commission first and ask them which hospital they are currently recommending in Lagos.

**Atlantic Medical Centre** 7 Oju Olobun Close, Victoria Island; tel: 01 261 4465. This is one of the best private hospitals in Lagos and is on a retainer with many US companies.
**Gold Cross Hospital** top of Keffi St, Obalende, Ikoyi; tel: 01 269 5670
**Ideal Eagle Hospital** Plot 247, Ojora Close (near to Goodies supermarket), Victoria Island; tel: 01 262 0953
**Radmed Diagnostics** 3b Ligali Ayorinde St, Victoria Island; tel: 01 261 0959, 261 9774
**St Nicholas Hospital** 57 Campbell St, Lagos Island; tel: 01 260 0070. This is currently the preferred hospital for many of the foreign companies operating in Lagos for emergency treatments, including malaria cases.

## Information for visitors
Whilst there is an office of the **Nigeria Tourism Development Board** in Lagos, the staff here are likely to fall off their chairs if you walk in and ask for some tourist information – they haven't got anything to give out, so don't bother. It's not that they are unfriendly or unhelpful, it's just that they have *no* tourist information. If you insist on visiting, the office is on the mainland on the second floor of the Hanaco Plaza, 113 Ikorodu Road, close to the Fadeyi bus stop; tel: 01 493 0220, 497 8150. This is the main Ibadan Highway and the office is located on a slip road to the east.

## Maps and publications
The indispensable **Lagos Street Map** (West African Book Publishers Ltd) can be found at most of the bookshops for around N1,000; I found the branch of Glendora Books at the Eko Hotel was the best place for maps, and if you are also going to Abuja, pick up a map here as well as they are not readily available in Abuja itself. The Lagos Street Map is clear and concise and as close to an A to Z as you are going to find for Lagos. It's published as both a book and a fold-out version. A small booklet, **Lagos: the City Arts Guide**, is published occasionally (supposedly quarterly) and can be found at the Jazz Hole and the other bookshops on Awolowo Road in Ikoyi for N500. If there is no recent one you might be able to at least pick up an old copy, but some are a couple of years old and so are not terribly accurate. It lists galleries, restaurants, nightclubs, and cultural events and has a couple of basic maps at the front. I'm not too sure about some of the listings though – for one market on the mainland it says, 'it sells virtually everything except marijuana and human parts' and for one bar it says 'the hunting ground for free ladies looking for expatriates'. Oh, I see.

The weighty **Lagos Easy Access** is the expat Bible and deservedly so. It's in its second edition now and quite rare, but try the bookshop at the airport, or Quintessence and the other bookshops on Awolowo Road. It costs in the region of N2,500. Some expats in Lagos say that they prefer the first edition as the maps are better, and as such these copies are even more revered and are passed on amongst expats as they come and go. It is published by the American Women's Club (the first edition came out in 1998) and it tries to fill the vast gap between what an expat has heard about Lagos from his or her home country and what it is actually like – as I hope to do in this book. There is a wealth of information in the book about coming to Lagos, domestic staff, shops and markets, social clubs, housing, buying furniture, shipping things to and from Nigeria, and a full directory of shops and services in Lagos.

*Lagos: The Miracle City* by John Olu Faoseke, was published in 2002 and is now a little dated, but you should be able to find it in most of the bookshops. It's a cheaply made, A4-sized pamphlet that includes a little bit of history on Lagos, some photographs, and some useful street maps. In fact the author covers a bit of a mish-mash of subjects, and expresses a lot of his own (fairly high-powered) opinions, which makes for delightful reading. In his acknowledgements, he says: 'Above all, I thank the Heavenly Father for blessing me with the gift of Divine Intelligence which I humbly used as inspirational guide in this memoir for the benefit of mankind.' And: 'You must serve yourself a juicy recipe for more successes with copies of all other books by this author.' There are chapters entitled '419: How to Avoid Devil Business', 'Driving Culture of Motorists', and 'Thoughts on Good Manners'. He also issues a dire warning to Lagos motorists: 'To drive on the road with aggression, impatience, recklessness and ill-temperament does not portray you as a good driver and responsible citizen before international tourists and visitors to Nigeria.' And finally, he says: 'If New York is America's Big Apple, than Lagos is Nigeria's Big Mongo.' I have no idea what this means – does he mean mango perhaps?

## Newspapers and magazines

One- or two-day-old international newspapers including the *The Daily Telegraph, The Times, The European, Le Monde, USA Today,* and the *International Herald Tribune* are available at the bookshops in the major hotels such as the Eko Hotel on Victoria Island and the Sheraton Hotel in Ikeja. Also at the Eko, in the grounds at the back of the curio market, is a useful shop selling a broad range of international newspapers and magazines, where you'll be able to pick up new and old copies of anything from *Time* and *Newsweek* to *Cosmo*.

## Pharmacies

There are pharmacies all over Lagos but because of the prevalence of fake drugs, it's a good idea to check out locally what places are being recommended if you're staying in Lagos for some time. These have been recommended:

**Chyzob Pharmacy** 168 Awolowo Rd, Ikoyi (next to the Jazz Hole bookshop); tel: 01 269 4545 (open Mon–Sat 08.00–20.00). They import drugs from the UK and US.

**Medicines Plus** in the Mega Plaza, 14 Idowu Martins St, Victoria Island (open Mon–Sat 10.00–21.00; Sun 13.00–21.00). Again, they import drugs and you can order specific items from abroad.

**Day Spring** 9a Adeola Odeku St, Victoria Island (next to the Wrangler shop). This could possibly be the only place in Nigeria that sells contact lens solution.

## Post

The main post offices are located at Adeola Odeku Street, Victoria Island (which is also an agent for Western Union and EMS Speed Post); about 200m east of where Alfred Rewane Road (formerly Kingsway) joins Awolowo Road on Bourdillon Road near the Falomo Bridge in Ikoyi; 33 Marina, Lagos Island; and the corner of Mobolaji Bank Anthony and Medical Road, Ikeja, close to the domestic airport. All are generally open Monday–Friday 08.00–17.00; and Saturday 10.00–15.00.

## Sports

**British High Commission Club (also known as the Kingfisher Club)** 4 Reeve Rd, Ikoyi; tel: 01 461 5661/2. You must first apply at the gate of the club for an ID card, for which you'll need two passport photos. There's a range of sporting facilities here such as netball, tennis, and squash courts, and the expat gatherings are very social.

**Hash House Harriers** Contact Pat Roberts at his bar, Pat's Place, Plot 292C, Ajose Adeogun St, Victoria Island; tel: 01 320 0424/5; email: patsonvi@yahoo.com. Pat has all the details about the local Hash club, which runs around three times a week.

**Ikoyi Club** Ikoyi Club Rd, Ikoyi; tel: 01 269 3485, 269 2879, 269 5133. Here is the only 18-hole golf course in Lagos and there's a full range of other sports on offer such as badminton, squash, gym, fitness classes and tennis. Again the atmosphere is very sociable, with a club bar suitable for long-term visitors, and there is an annual membership fee.

**Lagos Yacht Club** Tel: 01 496 3511, 496 6742. Just south of the museum and Tafawa Balewa Square on Lagos Island; the entrance is down an alley off the ring road just a few metres before it goes across the bridge to Victoria Island. Established in 1932, the yacht club is a hugely popular members-only expat haunt, and if you are new in Lagos it's a great place to meet people. There's a club house with bar and restaurant and a nice outdoor terrace right on the very tip of Lagos Island almost under the bridge itself. If you are living in Lagos for a while you may want to consider joining (about US$600 per annum) and even buying a boat or hobie-cat. The yacht club can help with this – boats tend to change ownership amongst expats as they come and go. Despite being highly sociable the members of the yacht club take their sailing seriously and it's not just a venue for a few beers, so you do obviously have to know how to sail as membership is dependent on a certain amount of sailing experience – you will be expected to sail about eight times a year. If you don't have your own boat, it's possible to hook up as a crew member with another member who does. There are races in the harbour every Saturday afternoon, and on Sunday there are often sails out to one of the private beach resorts up the creek or out to sea, and every year there's a race to Badagry. They also organise various functions, parties and balls. The barman here has been serving expat sailors for over 20 years. Newcomer's night is the first Tuesday of every month at 19.30.

## Swimming

Unless you are staying in one of the very few hotels with a pool, choices for swimming are limited to the Eko and the Federal Palace hotels, both of which have very nice pools. But these are not much good for short-term visitors as the Eko charges an annual fee to use the pool, gym, tennis courts and sauna, whilst the Federal Palace charges an annual, quarterly or monthly fee to use the pool. Swimming off Bar Beach on Victoria Island is not encouraged; this is not the sort of beach to sit and sunbathe on or where you would want to frolic in the waves: the water is filthy and covered in a sheen of oil. The best place to go in Lagos is Tarkwa Beach (see page 165) where the sea is cleaner and the environment safer.

## Telephone

For international phone calls, try the big hotels, though the cost of calls will be at a premium. There are **NITEL** offices on Cable Street on Lagos Island and just to the east of the roundabout at the northern end of Falomo Bridge in Ikoyi, at 3 Alfred Rewane Road (formerly Kingsway Road); the entrance is through the Mammy's market (open 24 hours), where you can buy a phonecard for an international call and try your luck at actually getting through. For local calls, there are **MTN cell phone stands** all over the place, especially on Victoria Island – just look for the distinctive yellow umbrellas – and some **landline stands**. Expect to pay around N30–40 per minute. You may come across the odd public phone box, but there are no phones inside.

## Theatre

Lagos is not renowned for its theatre and the only venues of note are the Eko Hotel, which has an auditorium popular for beauty pageants and fashion shows, and the **MUSON (Musical Society of Nigeria) Centre** opposite the museum on Awolowo Road on Lagos Island; tel: 01 264 6670, 264 6665. Here is a relatively modern theatre that holds regular concerts, recitals, operas and plays (*Joseph and his Technicolour Dreamcoat* was showing when we visited). Often, concerts are accompanied by dinner; the acclaimed Nigerian musician Sunny Ade sometimes plays here with dinner for N5,000. To find out what's on, ask at the box office, or visit the Goethe-Institut (German Cultural Centre) on Victoria Island (page 146 or Quintessence, the book and craft shop in the Falomo Shopping Centre on Awolowo Road in Ikoyi (page 141). Both have full programmes of events at the centre and Quintessence also sells tickets.

## Travel agents
Again there are hundreds of travel agents all over Lagos, mostly dealing with flights out of Nigeria, and very few are used to dealing with inbound travellers. I found the following travel agents particularly helpful:

**Dolphin Travels and Tours** on the first floor of the Federal Palace Hotel, Ahmadu Bello Way, Victoria Island; tel: 01 261 4927, 262 6112; email: firstdolphin@hyperia.com. Flights and IATA ticketing, and can organise meet-and-greet services at the airport.
**Soltan Travel and Tours** Glitter House, 214c Eti-Osa Way, Dolphin Estate, Ikoyi; tel: 01 269 3358; email: soltan@hyperia.com; www.soltantravel.com. Ask for the charming Victoria Soluade, who is the lady in charge and who is extremely friendly and helpful. There is another branch in Abuja. The office is a bit out of the way but it's one of the few companies that looks after inbound visitors to Nigeria – on their website they actually offer services within the country.
**Halios Travel Agencies** 9 Amodu Tijani Close, Victoria Island; tel: 01 774 4000, 774 3302, 320 0531; email: waltsteinheimer@aol.com. Run by a German expat, this is an established travel agent offering flight ticketing, airport meet-and-greets, and home or hotel delivery of airline tickets.

## Visas
If you need to extend your visa once you have arrived in Nigeria you need to go to the **immigration office** on Alagbon Close in Ikoyi (this street is not marked on any map I can find). To get there, take a taxi or *okada* to the Federal Secretariat in Ikoyi – the three big high-rise blocks, one of which is burnt out. Alagbon Close is a small road with a busy little market running down the west side of the compound of buildings (if you are facing the Federal Secretariat it is on the left). Walk down and on the right-hand side is a jumble of low-rise tatty buildings that are the immigration offices. There is a sign for the Alien's Immigration Office. You need to have a huge amount of patience and you may be asked for certain paperwork such as your invitation letter. Above all be very friendly as the immigration officers have a somewhat boring job, so if you can brighten their day, you may get somewhere. You are also very likely to be asked for a dash. Our experience was that we paid N3,500 each to extend our visas and there was no way of knowing if this was the fee or an outright bribe. I am assuming the latter as the starting price was much higher, and I was involved in a bit of negotiation about the price without either the immigration official or myself admitting that he was offering to extend our visas for a bribe. This, I might add, was the only time I paid dash during our whole time in Nigeria. If you don't feel comfortable with this, you can alternatively, for a fee, go through **Quartum Resources Limited**, 22 Child Avenue, Apapa; tel: 01 545 1010; cell: 0803 717 6616; fax: + 1 928 222 1639 (this is a US e-fax number); email: quartum@nigol.net.ng; contact Hugh Thorley or

Jide Omotola. Hugh is an expat who runs a service in Lagos for advice and anything to do with Nigerian visas, quotas, work permits etc. If you give him your passport, he will extend your visa at Alagbon Close on your behalf. This is a reliable company that many of the foreign organisations use to sort out paperwork for expats.

## WHAT TO SEE AND DO

Like the rest of Nigeria, Lagos doesn't have a great deal in the way of architecture or old buildings, or museums and galleries, and what there is in the city is generally so dilapidated it's in danger of collapse. But Lagos has atmosphere, and it's definitely well worth exploring some of it by foot. Given that the expat community is ferried around in chauffeur-driven cars, an *oyibo* walking or riding an *okada* around any part of Lagos attracts some attention. Very few white people do this and you can spend a whole week on the streets of Lagos without encountering another white face. But whilst people will be surprised to see you, you'll be most welcome wherever you go and receive very little hassle.

Don't be afraid to walk around the islands of Lagos during the day – sometimes it's much quicker to walk than to travel by car because of the hectic traffic. Just try and avoid carrying anything valuable. It's another story on the mainland and anywhere at night, however. As there is very little to do or see on the mainland there's little reason to venture there. Taxis are easy to catch after dark on the islands, so this shouldn't present any problems.

## THE ISLANDS
### Lagos Island
**NB** Whilst it is reasonably safe to walk around the central lanes and streets of Lagos Island during the day, stay well clear of walking under the flyovers and major road intersections on the outer rim of the island, as these are territories of the notorious Area Boys (see box on page 124). And I stress, *never* go on to the island after dark.

Lagos Island is home to the row of high-rise concrete blocks that dominate the skyline of Lagos, and it's the site of the first settlement and the oldest part of the city. Today it's no longer an island marooned in the lagoon, but has instead been joined by a landfill with the more upmarket district of Ikoyi, the working-class district of Obalende serving as a buffer zone between the two very different suburbs. Despite being a somewhat daunting experience, a wander through the people-packed narrow lanes and heaving markets of Lagos Island will reward you with a real insight into what is the heart of the city – one of the most frantic and densely packed areas of Africa, if not the world. It is a fascinating area to explore. At first glance the streets appear to be one massive market, but a surprisingly organised one at that, with each section selling one kind of product. The limited sights in the area include the Oba's Palace, the National Museum and a few examples of Brazilian architecture, built by freed slaves repatriated from Brazil to Nigeria when slavery was finally abolished that today struggle to survive against the onslaught of time and indifferent attitudes towards both modern practical maintenance and historical pride. The highlight here is to immerse yourself into the street life – to drink in the chaos, breathe in the electric atmosphere, and inhale the sights, smells and sounds of millions of African people going about their daily lives.

Driving is all but impossible in downtown Lagos Island; the streets are too crowded and narrow, there are many dead ends and one-way systems, and the traffic is choked to a virtual standstill. Here, I have put together a walking tour starting at the National Museum at Onikan. This is a good start/finish point simply

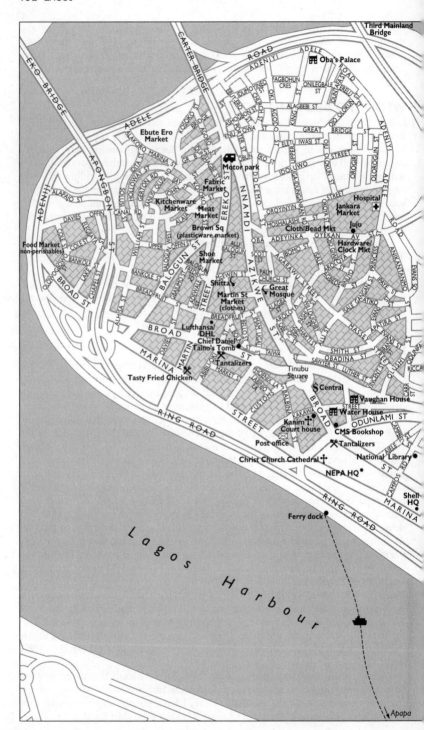

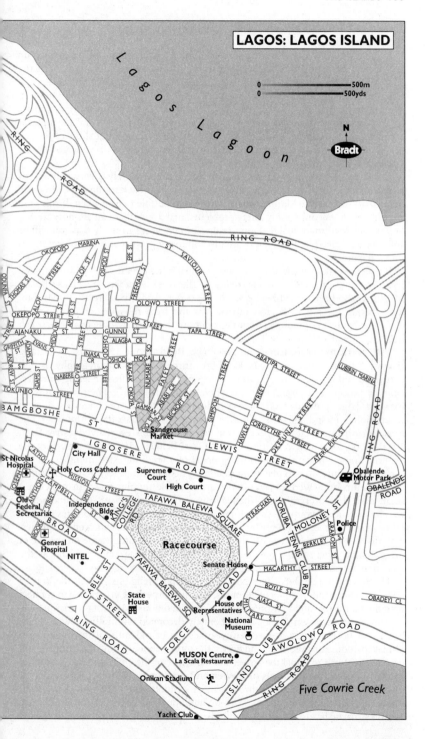

LAGOS: LAGOS ISLAND

because as a landmark, it's reasonably straightforward to get to by public transport, and because there's safe parking available if you have your own car. There is an *okada* park opposite the museum, so you shouldn't have any problems picking up a drop taxi here, and there is secure parking in the museum grounds or at the MUSON Centre on the opposite side of Awolowo Road. Give yourself a few hours to complete the tour, which includes a couple of hours in the museum itself, and enough time before dark to get back to your car, or by public transport, to get back to where you are staying off Lagos Island. Whilst there are a couple of accommodation options on Lagos Island itself, they are nothing short of flea-pit hotels, and because of the prevalence of Area Boys and crime in general, you are strongly advised not to be here at night.

Once in the throng of streets, if you get completely overwhelmed or claustrophobic, or if you simply get lost, grab an *okada* back to the museum or an outer road such as the Marina, where you should be able to find a taxi. Whilst you are unlikely to encounter any safety problems, make sure that you are not carrying or wearing anything valuable. Don't bring a camera as it's unlikely that you will be able to freely take pictures – there are just too many people who will object if you start 'snapping'.

It's also worth considering dressing reasonably conservatively; as a traditional area for commerce and markets, many of the market traders are Hausa-Fulani Muslims who have settled here over the centuries. And if you are a non-Muslim, it's a good idea not to be too intrusive at the local mosques or the open-air designated prayer compounds found throughout the markets – the people here can be a little hostile to non-worshippers.

The **National Museum** is on Awolowo Road, about 150m east of Tafawa Balewa Square (open daily 09.00–17.00; entry N100 – photography is not permitted and if you do have a camera, you will be asked to leave it at the entrance, another reason not to bring your camera on to Lagos Island). The museum is set back in large grounds and houses numerous exhibits of Nigeria's ancient civilisations, including some famous bronze and terracotta sculptures. The museum organises cultural lectures in its board room every Wednesday from 10.00–11.00, for which a contribution of at least N300 is expected at the end of the lecture. These survive thanks to the support of a few interested members of the expat community, so you may want to consider combining a lecture with a visit to the museum on a Wednesday. Guides are available for the museum itself for a small dash, but everything is labelled reasonably clearly so it's easy enough to wander around by yourself, though rather infuriatingly there are no dates marked on anything, so there is no way of telling how old things are, and even the guides, who do little more than read off the labels anyway, are a little vague on the age of the exhibits. There are a few dusty old books and magazines for sale in the reception area but nothing of great interest.

The museum's exhibits cover Nigeria's traditional religions such as the Yoruba gods and deities and masquerade festivals, which many ethnic groups use to connect with their ancestors and to express their cultural traditions. Many of the masquerade costumes and masks on display are elaborately decorated with raffia, cowrie shells, beads and horns. There is an extensive selection of old musical instruments on display including drums, flutes and horns, the most elaborate being the trumpets still used in the north to signal the arrival and departure of the emir at Friday prayers or special events. In the **Symbols of Power and Authority Gallery**, is a selection of royal paraphernalia, including thrones and footstools that once graced the royal palaces, and clothing and crowns worn by traditional rulers (rather comically worn by papier maché heads and arms), Yoruba beaded crowns, Igbo felt crowns decorated with plumes, and Hausa-Fulani turban crowns. Old jewellery on display includes giant brass, iron and ivory bracelets, and manacles and anklets that were also used as currency during the slave trade. There are some scary-looking war dresses and shields, presumably used in the Yoruba wars of the 19th century. Some are made from chain mail – reminiscent of *orc* costumes from *Lord of the Rings* – and all are designed to instil fear into the enemy, and are prepared by witchdoctors who laid spells on the outfits and attached fetishes and charms. Other exhibits include decorated household calabashes and pottery used to store water and grain.

One of the most important displays is of the Benin bronze plaques in the **Benin Gallery** that once adorned the royal palace at Benin City. Benin brass casters only worked for the Benin royal household and the unique and delicate figurines and plaques showing traditional ceremonies or royal scenes were used to decorate altars and walls within the palace. When the British conquered the Benin Empire in 1897, they looted the Oba's Palace of many thousands of these artworks, many of which are now on display in the British Museum and other European museums. There is also a rumour that the few on display in the Lagos museum are fake – stolen during the various military regimes and replaced with wax castings. When looking at them it's hard to tell if they are the real thing or not, as it is looking at the hoard of carved ivory tusks that also used to adorn the Oba's Palace at Benin.

In the museum's courtyard, there are some interesting photographs on body painting, women's hairstyles and scarring – many of Nigeria's ethnic groups still use facial scarring as a form of decoration. (The UK singer Seal is Nigerian by birth and has deep facial scars from the side of his nose to the corners of his mouth.)

Outside of the main museum block, a separate building houses a display entitled **The Government of Yesterday and Today**. Here there are some early drawings and faded photographs of some pre-colonial traditional rulers, colonial governors, and some photographs of Queen Elizabeth II's visits to Nigeria – of her watching the durbar in Kaduna in 1956, and her overseeing independence proceedings in 1960. There's also a chronological line of photographs of Nigeria's presidents, governors and military generals from independence through to 1993 and General Abacha. (The exhibit hasn't been updated since then, and quite frankly it doesn't look like the room has been cleaned since then either.) The most interesting exhibit is the car of Murtala Mohammed, one of Nigeria's more popular leaders, a black Mercedes limousine in which he was assassinated in February 1976. There are three bullet holes through the windscreen directly over the front passenger seat leaving spidery cracks through the windscreen, more bullet holes in the side, and several in the back seat of the car where presumably he was sitting. When he was shot dead (by disgruntled members of the military), his car was stuck in a traffic jam between a mosque where he had just been to Friday prayers and Lagos Airport where he was heading – the airport was subsequently named the Murtala Mohammed Airport in his memory.

At the back of the museum are a couple of craft huts and the **Museum Kitchen** (closed at weekends when it's often hired out for functions). This outdoor boma serves plates of cheap Nigerian staples such as *jollof* rice, *eba* or *semovita*, with some sort of soup or stew and cold soft drinks.

Opposite the museum on Awolowo Road is the **MUSON (Musical Society of Nigeria) Centre** (tel: 01 264 6670, 264 6665), a tall modern office block in well-kept gardens that contains the country's only branch of Barclays Bank (used by expats as a secure way of transferring their wages from Nigeria back to the UK) and the relatively modern theatre, the Glover Memorial Hall, and other smaller venues. One of the finest restaurants in Lagos, La Scala, is also at the MUSON Centre (see under *Where to eat*, page 137).

## EYO MASQUERADE

The *Eyo* Masquerade is a Yoruba festival unique to Lagos Island, and it is widely believed to be the forerunner of the modern-day Rio Carnival, thanks to slaves from Nigeria ending up in Brazil. On *Eyo* Day, the main highway in the heart of Lagos Island, Nnamdi Azikiwe Street, is closed to traffic from the end of Carter Bridge to Tinubu Square to allow for a procession. The participants pay homage to the oba of Lagos and it takes place whenever occasion and tradition demand, but is usually held as the final burial rites at the death of a Lagos oba. The first performance in Lagos was in 1854 in memory of Oba Akintoye, and since then it has been performed over 70 times, the last being at the funeral of Oba Adeyinka Oyekan, who died in 2003. The procession is led by *Eyo* dressed in masquerade costume, an elegant white-clad and veiled figure with a European-looking hat who carries a tall staff and various charms and fetishes under his cloak. He leads the procession and there is much dancing and chanting to oversee the oba's spirit joining his ancestors. You can see statues of *Eyo* at the entrance of Tafawa Balewa Square.

From the MUSON Centre it's a few metres' walk to **Tafawa Balewa Square** – though it's actually not a square at all, but a huge oval stadium and race course (though no horse races have been held here since the colonial years). When the British arrived in the early 1900s, they built barracks and partly prefabricated houses on the site. The story goes that accompanying each set of structures that were shipped from England was a team of British craftsmen; two bricklayers, two joiners, one plasterer and three coffins – early expats clearly suffered serious health problems in Lagos. In later years, the British built a race course, and at independence in 1960, the shift of power was officially handed over to the new Nigerian government at the race course when temporary grandstands were built for the occasion. The present grandstand and shopping complex was built in 1975 and named after the first president of the federation. The venue is still used for major political events and inaugural ceremonies for new ministers, governors etc. The main entrance to the south is flanked by four larger-than-life statues of men dressed in Yoruba masquerade costumes with pointed hats and masks, and four concrete horses rearing up, behind a chaotic motor park full of battered yellow buses and taxis.

A few metres southwest of the square on Cable Street is the **NITEL building** (open daily 24 hours) for local and international telephone calls. It's an ugly concrete tower, but is reputedly the tallest building in Nigeria. It was renovated in the 1980s after a large fire. Look out for sculptures of traditional musicians and praise singers around the main entrance door. From Cable Street, two of Lagos Island's main thoroughfares run roughly northwest and parallel with each other; **Broad Street** and **Marina Street**. The latter is simply referred to as Marina, and as its name suggests, it was once next to the water and was the location of the docks, before the area was filled in to build the ring road that circles Lagos Island in the 1970s. Apparently it was once lined with tall almond and palm trees, with benches where people could sit and admire the views of Lagos Harbour. There also used to be buildings here for the customs and port authorities, and booking offices and waiting rooms for passengers awaiting a berth on a steam ship to Europe. Little remains of this era today, and the area is now dominated by concrete high rises – mostly bank or oil buildings – and Marina lies 200m or so back from the water beyond the ground level and elevated sections of the ring road. The only building of note in this area of Marina is **State House**, which was the residence of the governor during colonial times. At independence in 1960, it became the residence of the president, including that of the first military ruler Major General Ironsi after the first coup of 1966. But when General Gowon became head of state after the second coup of 1966, he chose to live in the perhaps more secure Dodon Barracks in Ikoyi. You can still make out some of the colonial-style architecture on the State House, such as the vertical columns on the outside and its imposing entrance, but you'll have to look really hard as the building was modified almost beyond recognition in the 1970s.

**Lagos Harbour** is the biggest and busiest in Africa, and hundreds of ships and tankers line up out to sea waiting to unload their cargos or be pumped full of oil at the Apapa Docks to the south of Lagos Island. In the harbour itself are rusting ships that, just like other vehicles all over Nigeria, have simply been abandoned.

Back at Tafawa Balewa Square and Cable Street, the walk continues along Broad Street, which increasingly gets busier and busier as you head north. Broad Street was once widened by the British colonial government to create a fire break through Lagos at a time when most buildings had thatched roofs. On your left between Broad Street and Marina is the very dilapidated and non-functioning **General Hospital** that dates from the 1930s, on the site of the original hospital built in 1895, when it was called the African Hospital. Apparently, at one time coffin sellers strategically set up their wares at the entrance of the hospital's morgue around the corner on Brooke Street.

From Broad Street, at the junction with Bank Anthony Way turn right and continue across the intersection with Campbell Street to the next intersection where the **Holy Cross Roman Catholic Cathedral** is on the right. The history of this cathedral begins with a priest who came from Dahomey in 1863 but who left again two years later after failing to convert anyone in early Lagos to Christianity. A second group of missionaries arrived in 1869 and built the first church on the spot from bamboo, after a group of Brazilian slave repatriates known as *Agudas,* who had been Roman Catholic in Brazil, were brought into the church and successfully converted local people to Christianity by combining Catholicism with the worship of Yoruba gods. The present cathedral was built in 1934 under the supervision of Father Aime Simon, a French priest who based it on 18th-century European church architecture, with Gothic columns, vaulted arches, side altars and buttresses. Some of the materials were imported from France. If the door is open you can go inside, and it's a welcome relief from the frenetic streets – look out for the French *fleur-de-lis* motifs in the mouldings in the side chapels.

Back along Broad Street are the decaying buildings of what used to be the **Old Secretariat** during the colonial times. Built in 1906, there is little evidence of the colonial architecture today, as over the decades the exteriors have been added to and plastered with concrete, and today they are simply falling down. Until the New Federal Secretariat complex opened on Ikoyi in the 1970s, these offices were home to the government ministries – there is still a sign on the corner of one proclaiming it as the home of the Federal Ministry of Transport and Aviation.

Continuing along Broad Street and just after Joseph Street is the **Shell headquarters** tower block on the left. A few metres up and also on the left is the **NEPA building,** with a bronze statue outside of Shango, the Yoruba god of thunder holding up his staff of power. Beyond here, at 50–52 Broad Street on the northeastern corner of the junction with Odunlami Street, is Bookshop House, with the modern **CMS Bookshop**, which sells a huge range of text and school books and some paperbacks. If you take Odunlami Street right, past Bookshop

House, there are street vendors around King Street selling more textbooks. Diagonally across the junction from Bookshop House is the old and now defunct CMS Bookshop – you can still see the sign on the front of the two-storey building, which during the colonial times also had its own printing press. On this corner is also **Tantalisers** fast-food restaurant, with its filthy plastic tables and dodgy fried chicken, which is a good stop for a whoosh of air conditioning and a cold drink and to use the OK toilets. (Don't be fooled by the pretty pictures of the food – it's pretty grim – and stay well clear of the ice-cream.)

It's in this area that the markets of Lagos Island start proper, and a range of meat is for sale at this junction, including pungent dried fish and goats' heads. And more of the distinctive yellow buses and taxis converge at what is known as the CMS Motor Park. You'll find black marketeers on the corner outside of Bookshop House and you're likely to be asked by several if you want to change money. (More money changers hang out to the west of Lagos Island on Breadfruit Street.) It's probably reasonably safe to do so and they offer competitive exchange rates, but you certainly do not want to be carrying wads of cash on a walk around Lagos Island.

Just to the south of the Broad and Odunlami street junction, and back on Marina, is the **Christ Church Anglican Cathedral**. There has been a church on the site since 1867, but construction of the present cathedral began in 1925 and was finally finished in 1947. It's easily one of the largest churches in the city, and it's a fine white (though traffic-stained) building with a commanding square steeple and a cavernous interior. The design is classic neo-Gothic, with arched stained-glass windows and a wooden pulpit, but with additional Brazilian decorative single-flower motifs in the plasterwork. Again, if you can get inside, it offers a relatively peaceful moment away from the busy streets. Just up Marina, on the northwestern side of Odunlami Street, is Lagos's main **post office.**

Continue from Odunlami Road along Broad Street for a couple of hundred metres to Kakawa Street. On the left-hand corner is the old colonial magistrates' **Court House**, built in 1925 – note the inscription to King George V on the façade. Next door is the **Trinity Methodist Church** built in 1966, on the site where Methodist missionaries built their first church out of bamboo in 1861. Turn right into Kakawa Street, which was once a fashionable street of Brazilian architecture, but which today is little more than a run-down alley, and look for the **Water House** on the right at number 12, and the **Vaughan House** on the left at number 29 – though you will have to look very hard, as they are seriously falling down and masked by busy shops. The Water House was built in 1885 by the Da Rocha family, some of the first people to lead repatriated slaves from Brazil, and the house was named after the water the family used to sell from the well in their back yard. At the time, Lagos's drinking water was brought by canoe down the Oyan River from Abeokuta, so the family's well was in great demand. The Vaughan House was built in 1900 by the Vaughan family, who were freed American slaves.

From here, Broad Street opens up into **Tinubu Square**, but what with the rapid increase of market activity you will hardly be aware that you are in a square at all. It's named after Efunroye Tinubu, a successful female trader and an anti-colonial activist. The Central Bank of Nigeria building dominates the southern corner, where there is another busy motor park. In the middle of the square, amongst all the stalls, is the now-defunct Independence Fountain – a gift to the city made in 1960 by the Lebanese community during independence celebrations. Whichever direction you follow from Tinubu Square into the heart of Lagos's commercial area, you will inevitably get lost, but these streets are well worth a wander to soak up the atmosphere. You'll lose sight of any street names, but if you can, roughly follow Nnamdi Azikiwe Street. Along this street is the **Central**

## AN ODE TO LAGOS

Here are a few lines from a poem called *The Search*, written by Nigerian Helon Habila (see page 335). He has won numerous prizes for his poetry, his first novel *Waiting for an Angel* was voted one of the five best debut novels of 2002 by the UK *Observer*, and he spent much of 2002–03 as writer in residence at the East Anglia University in Norwich in the UK.

**Bus stops**
The hawkers are a blur in motion
Needle weaving through metal fabric
Yellow buses that come and go, their anaemic limbs
Joined each to each by rust, 69 seated, 99 standing.
Prehensile bus conductors monkey on and off running boards
Calling bus stops, places…

**Broad Street**
On Broad Street there are no people
Only streams of intentions; sellers, buyers, opportunity addicts
Sidling to you, flashing wristwatches, jewellery, and drugs
The money-changer waits by the kerb
Catching your eye, beckoning in pounds and dollars
Floating from Tinubu Square to Marina…
You soon discover
Here are all predators, and you the only prey…

**Mosque**, which was rebuilt in the 1980s to replace an older one, with its large central dome and ornate minarets, serving Muslims in an area that has traditionally been occupied by Hausa-Fulani immigrants to the city for centuries. The stalls outside of the mosque sell items of an Islamic nature, such as copies of the Koran or scripture boards. Another notable mosque in the area is the **Shitta Mosque**, a few blocks south of the Central Mosque on Martin Street, built by Shitta Bey, a repatriated slave from Sierra Leone who returned to Lagos as a wealthy merchant and a Muslim, and who built his own mosque in 1892. It was officially opened by the then British governor of Lagos, Governor Carter, in 1894. Just to the south of here on Broad Street is another branch of **Tantalisers** and a similar set-up can be found around the corner at **Tasty Fried Chicken** on Martin Street. A few metres across from Tantalisers is **Chief Daniel Taiwo's tomb**, an ornate white statue in a fenced-off square, and a memorial to the chief who died in 1901, reputedly at the grand old age of 120.

If at this point you have not felt you were in the commercial centre of Lagos, then you will now. From here on the markets are heaving, and every inch of space on these streets teems with stalls, where you will wade through crowds of thousands of people and crawling traffic. From Tinubu Square, to the north and east the buildings and streets of Lagos Island disappear under one massive blanket of a market.

Unlike the skyscrapers around Marina and the southern end of Broad Street, most of the buildings in this district of Lagos Island are only a couple of storeys high and were built as part of a central renovation project in the 1950s. Over the years, each family has developed their commercial activity, and now each house and structure burgeons with trade at the front whilst many trading families still reside above or behind their overflowing shops. You can find almost anything for sale in these streets. Stalls are frequently grouped together depending on what they sell. For example, all the stalls in one alley may only sell clocks, another hardware, or manufactured clothes, shoes, batteries, car parts, plastic piping, beds, meat etc; even the smallest items such as padlocks or pens are all sold from a hundred stalls next to each other. Rather amusingly, and so very traditionally, you may find (as we did) that in the areas that sold cloth, meat or vegetables, females are approached by the vendors as the 'madam', whilst in the hardware, car parts or trouser districts, it's the males or 'master' who receives all the attention. Amongst all of the permanent stalls are the informal traders who wander around all the districts selling their wares – sour milk sold in little plastic packets out of buckets, dead cane rats hanging off a string, packets of dried fish bones and plastic water bags balanced on heads, shiny imitation gold watches and jewellery in a presentation glass box, fresh chicken thighs on an enamel platter, or giant yams stacked up in a wheel barrow.

One worthwhile detour is to the **Jankara Market**, which sells locally dyed cotton and hand-woven cloth, leather goods, musical instruments, beads, and one sight that you have to see – *juju* (black magic) items. To get there head west from Nnamdi Azikiwe Street along Oba Adeyinka Oyekan Avenue (also known by its old name of Idumagbo Avenue) for about 200m. After the junction with Okoya Street, Jankara is a low-rise section of stalls on your left. Keep walking past the market until you reach the end at Princess Street and then enter; the *juju* section is in this southeastern corner of the market. Here is where you'll find piles of dried monkeys' heads, animal skins and fur, bizarre collections of twigs and sticks, dried frogs, chameleons and insects, bottles and jars of ointments and potent poisons, and a whole host of other weird and wacky things used by the 'doctors' that run the stalls as charms, fetishes and for traditional medicine. (Here I was asked by one giggling lady if I wanted something to 'make my man grow bigger'!) It's fascinating, absorbing and appalling all at the same time.

For fabrics and beads, head up Okoya Street to the northwestern corner of the market before heading in. Once inside the market, a word of warning – watch where you're stepping; there are myriad open drains, rough ground and the inevitable rubbish. Like the stalls outside on the streets, Jankara and other similar designated markets sell just about anything. The only difference is that these were originally built as markets with narrow walkways between the stalls rather than stalls lining the traffic-choked streets.

The other (not very good) distraction in the northern part of Lagos Island is the **Oba's Palace**, the site of the official residence of Lagos's kings since 1670, though today's building is only perhaps a few decades old. Follow Adeniji Adele Road from Jankara around the top of the island and beneath the shadow of the Third Mainland Bridge. The unremarkable Oba's Palace is a few metres down Upper King Street, but there's nothing really to see. The squat building has a couple of old cannons outside, a few fat goats wandering up and down the steps, and judging by the amount of Mercedes parked outside, probably a few fat-cat councillors inside. From either the Oba's Palace or Jankara Market you can head back to Nnamdi Azikiwe Street and to the junction with Martin Street, just to the south of Carter Bridge that crosses to the mainland. At this junction is another chaotic motor park where every inch of available space is taken up by the ubiquitous decrepit yellow vehicles hemmed in by yet more market stalls. From here it's possible to catch a vehicle back in the direction you've come from to the southwest of Lagos Island, somewhere near the museum. Try asking for a vehicle going to the motor park at the front of Tafawa Balewa Square and you'll more or less be back at where you started. But given that the traffic hardly moves on Lagos Island, you'd be better off walking or catching an *okada*. Notice that towards the end of the day another layer of markets on the already-congested narrow lanes appears – of traders selling dried fish, chicken pieces, chillies and tomatoes for shoppers heading home to make dinner.

# Ikoyi

When the first European settlers arrived on Lagos Island in 1852, they were rapidly being killed off by bad sanitation and malaria from the mosquito-infested swamps, and sought refuge on neighbouring Ikoyi Island. Palatial European-style houses were built on the island in the late 1800s and early 1900s, and a sprawling leafy suburb was created as a Government Reserved Area (GRA); reserved, that is, for Europeans. Very little of this architecture survives today and the space is slowly being given over to high-rise apartment blocks, though it is still the location of some of the biggest houses in Lagos, and there are many expat compounds here. Ikoyi was once separated from Lagos Island by the MacGregor Canal, but this has been long since filled in, and there is no discernible border between the two islands except for a tangle of flyovers. There is little to see as such, and Ikoyi lacks the frantic atmosphere and teeming streets of Lagos Island, though there are some worthwhile shops and restaurants in the area, and there's a very convenient motor park at **Obalende**, the district where Ikoyi ends and Lagos Island begins, where you can get minibuses out to all the outlying motor parks on the mainland, from where public transport goes out of Lagos to other areas of the country.

Ikoyi is bisected neatly by Alfred Rewane Road, which was formerly, and often still is, called Kingsway Road. One major landmark is the defunct **Ikoyi Hotel** at 43 Alfred Rewane Road, which is one of the oldest hotels in Lagos, but it's currently closed (supposedly) for refurbishment. Time will tell if it will ever reopen. However, it is still worth a mention as there is a thriving curio market outside in the car park where you can also change money with the Hausa traders, and there are more permanent bureaux de change. The main shopping district of Ikoyi is on **Awolowo Road** in southwest Ikoyi, where some of the most expensive and exclusive shops are located, as well as the Polo Club. It's worthwhile going for a stroll along Awolowo Road, though it is of course ubiquitously filled with choking traffic, but there is an excellent selection of restaurants here as well as some good bookshops. It's also recently been upgraded with smooth tar and level concrete pavements (and even pedestrian underpasses) so it's easy enough to walk along and even cross the road. Starting from Alfred Rewane Road, Awolowo Road heads east to Lagos Island via Obalende. It's the first few hundred metres or so at the Ikoyi end that has the most interesting of distractions. At this junction, the **Falomo Bridge** rises over Five Cowrie Creek as it takes a constant stream of traffic over to Victoria Island. The bridge is littered with hawkers selling anything and everything, and beggars making the most of the go-slow. To ride an *okada* over the bridge is far from being the most sensible thing to do in Lagos, but it's an exhilarating experience.

At the Awolowo Road end of the bridge is a giant roundabout with a surprising patch of garden on top of it. Just to the east of the roundabout is a **NITEL** office for international phone calls, and there's a **post office** on Bourdillion Road. To the southwest of the roundabout and behind a petrol station is the **Golden Plaza,** with nine floors of shops and a Chinese restaurant on the tenth floor (dealt with under *Where to eat and drink*). Here are mainly fairly upmarket Chinese and Indian shops selling imported items such as clothes and shoes, furniture, electronics and household goods. On the ground floor is a small café called the Cafeteria where you can get a cappuccino or espresso in icy air conditioning with a spring roll or samosa and watch (though not necessarily understand) Chinese CNN on the TV in the corner.

Once on Awolowo Road, the **Falomo Shopping Centre** is on the left behind a fence, where there is an excellent CD shop **Urbanground**, the good **Glendora** bookshop, and the upmarket souvenir shop **Quintessence** (all dealt with under *Listings*) that are well worth a browse. At the back of Falomo Shopping Centre, down Raymond Njoku Street, is the small **Falomo Market**, with a few stalls selling clothes made from traditional Nigerian fabrics and some batiks. The first right turn off Awolowo Road is Omo Osagie Street, and a few metres up on the left-hand side you'll find the red-brick **Golden City** complex with its pagoda-style entrance gate. It's a collection of Chinese-run shops around a central car park/courtyard selling everything imaginable made in China, from steering wheel covers, cheap clothes and plastic shoes to playing cards and garish framed pictures of God. There is a warren of stalls at the back where larger ladies rummage around in boxes of enormous nylon bras and giant knickers. It's a vibrant place to wander around and it's full of people, including many Chinese who speak to their shop staff in Yoruba. I had a great conversation with a shop girl here who patiently demonstrated how to 'on' and 'off' a rechargeable plastic torch. Back on Awolowo Road on the other side of the street, you can peek through the gates of the **Polo Club**, where the elegant polo horses graze on the field. Remarkably these horses are often taken through the hectic traffic of Lagos and even over Falomo Bridge to be exercised along Bar Beach on the south side of Victoria Island.

## Victoria Island

Locally dubbed VI, Victoria Island is reached by crossing the Falomo Bridge from Ikoyi, though the island is no longer an island as landfill has now joined it with the Lekki Peninsula. It started out as a residential area divided up into thousands of plots, but today it is the location of many hotels, banks, offices, embassies, and very few sights per se, though there are some useful shops, and the best of Lagos's restaurants are on VI. Unlike Lagos Island or Awolowo Road, there's little sense in walking around here as everything is spread out.

The **Didi Museum** at 175 Akin Adesola Street, the main road that runs south from Falomo Bridge; tel: 01 262 9281, 461 6968 (open Monday–Friday 09.00–17.00; free entry), is a privately owned gallery of truly uninspiring Nigerian art next to the owner's house. There are only about half a dozen paintings here of different styles, none of which especially stand out, but if you are trawling around the hot and noisy streets of Victoria Island you can take a breather and sit down in the peaceful garden outside the gallery.

The **Napex Complex** is to the northeast of the island at the end of Walter Carrington Crescent (also referred to by its old name of Eleke Crescent) after all the embassies. It's a huge and filthy sort of yard lined with makeshift shops and stalls and one large (nigh-on empty) supermarket. Most of the stalls deal with embassy-related matters such as passport pictures or photocopying, especially for the queue of people continuously lined up outside the nearby US Embassy (across the street from the embassy are rows of seats that people can rent, and there are even people you can hire to stand in the queue on your behalf!). There is little to see at the Napex Complex but it is the rather incongruous location of the excellent **Chardonnay's** restaurant, a rough and ready bar called **Mimi's**, where hard-core football fans watch games in the darkened interior, a few scattered chop stalls, and most usefully, several bureaux de change offering good rates.

**Bar Beach**, also known as Victoria Beach, is very popular though not especially attractive or clean, and is the main beach that runs along the south of Victoria

## NIKE DAVIES-OKUNDAYE

Born to a family of craftsmen, Nike was brought up by her great grandmother, who was a cloth weaver, adire maker, indigo dyer and head of the village women. She had an extremely tough early life, with her problems beginning at age six when her mother died and she was sent out to make a living selling banana leaves. At the age of 16 she ran away from her father and an arranged marriage to join a travelling theatre group, and later wed a well-known contemporary artist who was a graduate of the Oshogbo art workshops during the 1960s. As one of 15 wives, she spent 16 years in a violent, abusive and deprived polygamist marriage. Throughout her life she has been determined to inspire other women to expand their horizons, and her principles have been to empower other Nigerian women through art. She opened the Oshogbo Nike Centre for Art and Culture (see page 189) in 1983 and took on some 150 students, some from overseas. Art mediums included adire, batik, wood carving, painting, beadwork, mosaics, drum making and dancing. One of her own most famous pieces is a batik called *Breastless Blind Woman,* which tells the story of a woman born blind and without breasts, and of her will and determination to overcome her handicaps in a society where the handicapped are normally kept behind closed doors. She has done much to keep the traditional Yoruba art forms alive, and aside from her Lagos and Oshogbo galleries, she has a representative and gallery in New York run by Stanley Ledermann at Apartment 3D, 200 East End Avenue, NY 10128; tel: 01 212 427 1253. There's a book about her life, *The Woman of the Artistic Brush (A lifestyle of a Yoruba Batik Artist – Nike Davies)* by Kim Marie Vaz, and she has produced her own video, *Adire amongst the Yoruba,* on the traditional Nigerian method of adire and indigo dyeing.

Island parallel to Ahmadu Bello Way. It's not safe for swimming and the water is truly filthy and covered with a sheen of oil. The sand routinely gets washed away by the sea and occasionally a batch of new sand is dumped here. There's a small market at the western end selling a few shells and batiks, but mostly fruit and veg. You can walk along Bar Beach reasonably safely during the day, though there are a few Area Boys asking for a 'fee' to get on to the beach. At night it's a different story – then it's frequented by drug pushers, prostitutes and people smoking dope on the sand, and – quite by contrast – makeshift churches, though if you take sensible precautions you can visit the line of bars and chop houses at the eastern end that sell a good range of cheap food and plenty of beer. It's certainly a lively enough place and the area attracts up to about 3,000 people a night, and there's often live music. Just don't go too far away from the bright lights and don't go on to any isolated stretch of sand in the dark. Note that some expats visit here with armed guards.

## LEKKI PENINSULA

The Lekki Peninsula is to the east of Victoria Island. To get there take a minibus along Maroko Road for about 2km. After B-Jay's Hotel you'll pass the Mobil House Building and then the British International School on the right-hand side, then you'll get to a series of roundabouts on the Lekki–Epe Expressway that is Lekki proper. There is currently a huge building project going on here and a large housing estate of big homes is going up, one of which is the house and gallery of the famous batik artist, **Chief (Mrs) Nike Davies-Okundaye**. Her house is at 4 Augustine Anozie Street (formerly 11c Lekki Housing Estate), off Admiralty Way, off the Lekki–Epe Expressway. This address is confusing because plots were given numbers before they were built on and then renamed when the houses went up; tel: 01 270 5965, 555 5552; email: ronike@21ctl.com; www.nikeart.com (open daily 10.00–20.00). To get there take a minibus to the first roundabout in Lekki. From here take an *okada* or walk about 700m along the road to the left, which is Admiralty Way, and follow it around a big bend and turn right on to Wole Ariyo Road. Nike's house is down the third road to your right. Some of the minibuses that go along Makola Road have 'Lekki estate' marked on the side – these turn left at the roundabout on to Admiralty Way into Lekki housing estate, and will take you much closer to Nike's House. Pick up one of these from outside B-Jay's Hotel. If you want to stay with her, Nike has two rooms for visitors – contact her to discuss rates. Her house on three floors is full to the brim of exquisite Nigerian art of excellent quality and this is easily the best display of art in the country. The gallery exhibits her own work as well as that of other Nigerian artists, and there are several rooms of paintings, batiks, sculptures, and the unique indigo dresses that she favours herself. There are also samples of all of the most popular Nigerian cloths, so you can order whatever you want to be made up. Nike is charming and a clever businesswoman. Along with her husband, who is from Ghana and quite a character, and her very smiley sister, she makes you feel very welcome in their home even if you don't buy anything. In the book *Lagos Easy Access,* it says that '*one of life's pleasures in Lagos is meeting Nike and visiting her gallery'.*

Further along the Lekki–Epe Expressway and about nine kilometres from the centre of Victoria Island is the Ilasan Market, confusingly also known as the Ola Elegushi Market, or simply just as **Lekki Market**. Get off the minibus at the roundabout near Heroes furniture shop (the bus drivers and conductors should know where the market is if you ask). If you see the Chevron building from the bus it means you have gone too far. Once off the minibus, follow the road south from the roundabout, by foot or *okada*, for about 50m and then turn left for another 200m or so, and you'll find the sprawling market on your right. It is full of fruit and vegetables and all sorts of mundane household items, but if you walk through to the back, you'll find the excellent curio section which sells arts and crafts from all over West Africa. The market traders are known for their aggressive tactics, but if you bargain hard, this can be the cheapest place to buy such items in Lagos. It's actually best to go on a weekday, as prices are higher at the weekends. If you're feeling peckish, look out for the branch of Frenchies (also on Victoria Island and Apapa) at shop number G1 in the market. There is no point trying to describe where this is, but someone will point you in the right direction once in the market.

Another kilometre or so along the expressway is a dirt road that leads down roughly two kilometres to **Lekki Beach**. This is an attractive beach with shelters made of palm fronds and umbrellas available for rent and some local chop stalls, though the surf can be dangerous for swimming. Occasionally live bands play here, and Lekki Beach hosts Nigeria's answer to Jamaica's famous musical Sunsplash Festival each year on Boxing Day, though be very cautious here as we had a run-in with some Area Boys who guard the entrance of the beach with a selection of sticks, belts and whips and no-one will get past them without paying a dash.

The **Lekki Conservation Centre** is at Km19 on the Lekki–Epe Expressway, which is also the location of the Nigerian Conservation Foundation (NCF) office; tel: 01 264 2498; email: ncf@hyperia.com (open Monday–Friday 08.00–19.00; Saturday–Sunday 12.00–18.00). To get here you can catch a minibus along the Lekki–Epe Expressway, and the entrance to the conservation centre is opposite the

Chevron Complex, so ask to get off here. This is a small 78ha nature reserve enclosed by a concrete wall. Entry is N50 and there's a whole range of ridiculous fees for cameras; N700 for a fixed lens camera; N1,000 for a zoom lens; N1,000 for a SLR with telephoto lens; N2,000 for a digital camera; and N5,000 for a video camera. It's a rectangular-shaped piece of swampy marshland between the Lagos Lagoon and the Atlantic Ocean. The vegetation consists of grassland and flooded mangrove forest that can have a water depth of around a metre during rainy season. There is a figure-of-eight path through the reserve, some of which follows elevated wooden walkways, that's around a kilometre long and it's a fairly pleasant walk through a patch of forest, though you are unlikely to see any of the few animals. These include mona monkeys, monitor lizards, cane rats (grass cutters), small crocodiles, giant forest squirrels, giant rats, pangolins, bush buck and Maxwell's duikers. It also attracts a number of birds, such as kingfishers, herons, hornbills, kites, wagtails, egrets and cuckoos, and some 118 bird species have been recorded in the reserve. And, as you can imagine, there are plenty of lizards and amphibians. The centre was established in 1990 to preserve a piece of the Lekki Peninsula not earmarked for development, and as an education centre for awareness for natural resources, particularly for Lagos school children. At the entrance there's a rondavel with an exhibition of photographs of some of the animals in Nigeria's national parks that was put up for the benefit of Prince Philip who visited here in 2003. (Where and how the photographer found these animals in Nigeria is beyond me! Nevertheless it's an excellent display of wildlife photography.) There's also a small library of wildlife publications (open daily 09.00–16.00), and the staff canteen here doubles up as a café for visitors offering big plates of cheap Nigerian fare such as fiery *jollof* rice and meat, soft drinks and tea. The centre is practically deserted during the week but it's popular at weekends. Unfortunately, despite being surrounded by a wall, the reserve is not free from the scourge of poaching, and *Tunde,* a tame sitatunga that was donated to the reserve by the people that run the Drill Ranch in Calabar, was killed by poachers for bushmeat in 2002.

## TARKWA BAY

There are a number of beaches in the Lagos area, but the sea can be unpredictable (see *Marine Dangers* in the *Health and Safety* chapter, page 107). The major problem is the amount of rubbish on the beaches and the oil in the water – oil tankers flush out their tanks before filling up with oil again at Lagos Harbour and the sea is covered with slimy film. Up the Porto Novo Creek, or up-the-creek as it's generally known, on the sand bar between the ocean and the creek that goes all the way to the border with Benin, are a number of private beaches and beach houses lined with mangroves and palms, but you have to have your own boat (or know someone that does) to get there, as there are no roads. The water is much cleaner up here and once past the environs of Lagos there's much less rubbish.

The best public beach closest to the city is Tarkwa Bay, which is a reasonably sheltered beach located on the sand bar between the city and the ocean, and next to the main entrance of Lagos Harbour – you'll get one hell of a shock when an oil tanker passes by seemingly only metres away! It's only accessible by boat, from Maroko Road or from under the Falomo Bridge on Victoria Island (see below). It's a popular spot as a daytrip from Lagos, with safe swimming conditions, even for small children, as there's no surf. The beach is about 800m long and is mostly kept clean and there's a long line of deck chairs for which you will have to negotiate a price with one of the beach touts. Behind the deck chairs and sun shades are a few makeshift stalls selling *suya* and food-is-ready, as well as cold beers and soft drinks. Beach vendors casually walk up and down selling beads, baskets, carved calabashes and pieces of sarong-sized cloth, as well as watches and belts. You'll have to be firm with them to leave you alone.

If you walk to the south end of the beach, sandy paths lead up to an old jetty built out of a line of boulders and then on, 500m or so, to the adjacent **Lighthouse Beach** on the other side. Lighthouse Beach is on the Atlantic Coast proper, whilst Tarkwa Bay is in the lip of the harbour and Lagos Lagoon. Unlike Tarkwa, Lighthouse Beach is pounded by the Atlantic waves and is not safe for swimming. Also unlike Tarkwa, there has been no effort to keep it clean and what would normally be a majestic swathe of white sand is full to the brim with countless discarded items of plastic rubbish that have been swept here by the ocean from Lagos – it's a tragic sight. In the far distance, you can see a shipwreck of an oil tanker leaning into the waves as they break over the beach and this is a great, if isolated walk (walk on the shoreline where the waves break as there's less rubbish). Lighthouse Beach also has the best view of the hundreds (literally) of oil tankers and other ships queuing up in the sea to get into Lagos Harbour. It's quite a staggering sight, and there are ships moored way out into the ocean as far as the eye can see.

If you are here on a Sunday, you may see a church service on the beach, with the worshippers dressed in flowing white robes and fervently throwing themselves down in the sand in prayer. Between the two beaches are some ad hoc stables where you can negotiate a horse ride along either beach. Try not to ride in the middle of the day when the heat is at its most intense – while you may be able to manage this, it's not good for the poorly looked-after horses.

## Getting there and away

You can catch a boat to Tarkwa daily from the **Tarzan** jetty on Victoria Island on Maroko Road as it heads towards the Lekki Peninsula. From the Falomo Bridge, you'll need to catch a minibus or *okada* along Maroko Road, past Mobil House, and get off roughly when you see the British International School. Tarzan is to the north of here through a jumbled boat yard. From here there are also speed boats that go directly to Ikoyi on the opposite side of Five Cowrie Creek every few minutes for N30. This is a very useful service and saves a long journey from Ikoyi to Victoria Island through the traffic. Throughout the morning and early afternoon, the small speed boats to Tarkwa go-when-full and carry about half a dozen people. They take about 20min and as no life jackets are provided you'll need to hang on tight! The cost is N800 return, and you pay the full price up front and get a ticket that covers the return journey. A boat returns from Tarkwa at 14.00, 15.00, 16.00, 17.00, and 18.00, and you must stipulate which boat you want to come back on when you buy your ticket so the boatman has some idea of how many people he is picking up. On the way out to Tarkwa, look out for the two massive oil pipelines in the harbour that stretch out to sea where the oil tankers dock to fill up with oil. One of them is abandoned and full of holes, whilst the other is the newer one in use today. Once at the beach, the boats dock on the south side where you will have to jump out and wade in. Just hang around in the same area to catch the boat back and someone will point you to the Tarzan boat. The Tarzan jetty is not a bad place to hang around, despite being surrounded by abandoned boats and a rubbish-strewn beach. There's a 24-hour bar here (see under *Where to eat and drink*, page 139) where a band plays on a Sunday evening. Plan to come back from Tarkwa on a later boat and enjoy a few sundowners at Tarzan. At the weekends other boats for the same sort of price and arrangement go to Tarkwa from the **Fiki Boat Club** on Ozumba Mbadiwe Road, almost under the Falomo Bridge, on the Victoria Island side. Like Tarzan there's also a 24-hour bar here.

## THE MAINLAND
### National Theatre and Gallery

The **National Theatre and Gallery** rises out of a cluster of ring roads and flyovers just north of Lagos Island across the Eko Bridge in the Ebute-Metta suburb of the mainland. Its distinctive white concave roof is a notable landmark on the skyline of the mainland. Because of the confusing road system, the only way to get here is to take a drop taxi from the islands. The building was built in the 1970s for the 1977 FESTAC festival that featured a number of international performers, including Stevie Wonder, but today it's very run-down and poorly maintained. The entrance to the National Gallery, with its exhibition of contemporary art including sculpture and pottery, is at Entrance B of the theatre (open daily 09.00–17.00; entry fee N100, plus a dash for the guide; no photography is permitted and you have to leave any bags at the entrance). In the **Portrait Gallery** are huge oil paintings and some sculptures of Nigeria's leading statesmen, such as past premiers Abello and Azikiwe. There is an interesting range of portraits of famous characters from Nigeria's history painted in 1976 by a certain Mr Emokpae, including prominent obas, war lords, chiefs, emirs and missionaries – there's also one of Samuel Crowther, the first African bishop and a repatriated slave, and Herbert Macaulay, founder of the Nigerian Nationalism Movement. There are also portraits of modern writers and academics such as Wole Soyinka and Chinua Achebe. In the **Contemporary Hall** are abstract works and modern art, and some pottery and batiks. Look out for the excellent pieces by celebrated Nigerian artist Bruce Onabrakpeya, who worked in the 1970s; they are unusual and lively plaster-cast paintings of busy market scenes and abstract people.

After visiting the gallery, you can get a drink or snack at the small bar at the main theatre entrance. The theatre itself is huge, but since the FESTAC event it has only really been used for seminars or conferences and is not much more than a big, run-down white elephant of a place. A couple of years ago there were rumours that it was going to be sold off and turned into a casino. More recently the theatre has been used to show Nigerian 'Nollywood' movies on a Sunday afternoon (known as **The Theatre on a Sunday)** which has proved a popular move. So much so, in fact, that often stars and producers of the movies pitch up to meet their fans! Shows start at '12-to', and '3-to' – ie: 12.00 and 15.00. To the northwest of the theatre complex is a line of drinks and snack stalls which literally heave at the weekends, when people come to socialise and picnic on the lawns.

## AROUND LAGOS STATE
### Badagry

Badagry is 45km from Lagos and makes for a reasonably interesting day out, and is a popular day trip for Lagos school children and Lagos people at the weekends. It's a small town pleasantly located on the Porto Novo Creek, called here the Badagry Lagoon, which extends from Lagos to the border with the Republic of Benin, cutting off the long sand bar that lies between the mainland proper and the Atlantic Ocean. It has an interesting if sombre history, as Badagry was a major slave port and a key entry point for many of Nigeria's missionaries. A slave market was established here in 1502, and on the sand bar across the lagoon is the 'point of no return'. Slaves left the mainland of Africa by rowing boat to this strip of land between the creek and the ocean, where they were herded along a sand path for a few metres to the waiting ships in the sea on the other side. 'The point of no return' was probably the last they saw of their African homeland. Slavery was finally abolished in Badagry in 1886. Badagry is also the site of the first two-storey building in Nigeria, built in 1845 and still standing on its original site. The townspeople are exceptionally friendly and will often offer to act as your guide. In 2001 and 2002 an annual Black Heritage Festival was held here, but this hasn't happened for a couple of years. Also, the town has been visited in the past by black Americans keen to discover their slave 'roots'. About 20–30km beyond Badagry, towards the border with Benin, are some stretches of attractive beaches lined with coconut palms, but you'll need a car to get to them.

## Getting there and away

Badagry is about an hour and a quarter's drive west of Lagos on the Badagry Expressway, towards the Republic of Benin. Minibuses and bush taxis go from the Mile Two Motor Park in Apapa for around N150. If you are coming from the Lagos islands, catch a vehicle from Obalende to Mile Two first. Badagry can also be reached by boat along the Porto Novo Creek, though there are no commercial boats. At Badagry, the motor park is on the Expressway, and from here you will need to catch an *okada* into the town proper, which lies a kilometre or so to the south on the creek. Tell the driver you want to go to Chief Mobee's house, as this is on the waterfront and as good as place as any to start exploring.

## Where to stay and eat

**Soketta Hotel** on Hospital Road is a short walk around the corner and north from the Heritage Museum near the cemetery; tel: 01 723 4318 (the telephone code in Badagry is the same as in Lagos). Rather astonishingly, part of the ground floor is taken up by an internet café with (when I visited) 35 terminals, all in use and powered by a 24-hour gen. The 14 double rooms and two suites are dark and grim but have giant beds, local TV and fridge. There are a few chairs outside in the pleasant garden area under a thatched hut, but it's very noisy here if the gen is on. Nigerian meals are available, plus occasional continental dishes, such as not-so-fiery chicken curry and rice for around N400 a plate, and breakfast items go for N100. Rates are N2,100 for a double and N2,900 for a larger suite, plus approximately N600 extra on each for the deposit.

## What to see and do

The best place to start exploring Badagry's slave relics is to begin at the **chief's house** on the Marina, which is the road running along the creek to the south of town. Here you can pick up a guide (for a small dash) who will take you to all the places of interest along the Marina and in the back streets a short walk from here. The present chief is Chief Menu-Toyon II, also referred to as the Mobee of Badagry, and his house is at 127 Marina, on the corner of Mobee Street, just around the corner from the Mobee Museum. He is part of a long line of chiefs whose family line has been in Badagry since the 15th century. The story goes that Mobee means 'take koala nuts', presumably an offering from the local chief when the Europeans first pitched up, who thought that was his name and it stuck. The present chief spends his days in the front room of his house, attending to chiefdom matters, such as consulting on his neighbours' disputes and problems. Here is his throne, and the room is adorned with photos of his coronation, and he will happily show you his scrap books and photo albums or let you take photos. In front of the throne is a pot where you will be expected to make some sort of offering (dash). Next to the chief's house is another house where the family sell cold Cokes and Fantas, or, if you're really lucky, the chief's wife might offer you a Nescafé.

Like most southern regions of Nigeria, Badagry is split into a number of quarters, each under the jurisdiction of a different chief, who then reports to the oba (king) of the town or region. Their powers are limited as far as governing the town is concerned, and their roles are largely ceremonial these days, but they are consulted on local matters and are held in high regard as upright and wise members of the community. To be chosen as a chief, an application (usually from the same family line as the existing or previous chief) is sent to first the local government and oba's office, and then on to the state government for consideration. If there is no objection, then the proposed chief goes through a three-month period of isolation and contemplation in his quarters to prepare himself for his coronation. Coronation festivities go on for nine days, before he is finally crowned by the oba on his new throne.

The **Slave Relic Museum**, on Mobee Street (open daily; entry N50) is in Chief Mobee's compound and is maintained by the Mobee family. The museum consists of a single room at the back of his house with a row of slave chains on the wall, some supposedly from the 1600s, and one of the giant water pots that slaves were made to drink out of crouched down like dogs. There's also a horrific iron 'lip-lock' which was used to stop the slaves eating sugarcane when they were on the plantations of the New World, and a leg shackle with a spike through it that went through the slave's foot to immobilise him. Also in the room is the headstone and grave of a previous Chief Mobee who died in 1893, and who was involved in selling slaves to the European slave traders at the Badagry slave market (black Africans were also part of the slave trade).

A few metres along the Marina to the east is Nigeria's **first two-storey building**, built in 1845 by a Reverend C A Gollmer of the Church Missionary Society as the first parsonage in Nigeria. This is also where Bishop Samuel Crowther, a freed slave and Nigeria's first black bishop, translated the Bible from English to Yoruba in 1846. The house has shuttered windows, a rusty tin roof and an outside staircase leading up to the second floor. The house next door has much grander architecture – though it's on the verge of falling down – with arches and a balcony, and a sweeping staircase up to the second level. Built in 1919 this is where Lord Lugard once stayed.

The **Heritage Museum** around the next corner (open daily 09.00–17.00; entry N100) is an excellent museum, and here we had a superbly informative guide who was very easy to understand – though it's a little gloomy inside if there's no NEPA. The two-storey, pale blue building has been restored in recent years, although it was first built in 1853 as the district officer's office. Allow at least an hour or two here as there's an excellent display of exhibits all about the slave trade, from old photographs, slave chains and a mock-up plywood model of a slave ship demonstrating how many thousands of slaves were crammed inside, to pictures and drawings of slaves working on plantations in the New World. There are also a few local masquerade costumes, and the guide will explain how masquerades were used to warn off unwelcome European slave traders on the coast centuries before any police force was established. A few streets back from the Heritage Museum on Old Post Office Road is the **missionary cemetery**, which has the tombs of the first missionaries that arrived on the coast, and the tomb of George Fremingo, also known as Huntokomu, the first Portuguese slave merchant to arrive in Badagry, who was killed when he got there in 1620.

A few streets back from the Marina (you will need a guide to find all these things) is the site of the first Christian church and the **Agla Tree Monument** on Market Street. It was supposedly under this tree that Christianity was first preached in Nigeria by Thomas Birch Freeman, a Methodist missionary, and Henry Townsend, an Anglican missionary, who both arrived in Badagry in 1842, though there are other spots in Nigeria that have staked this auspicious claim. The tree survived another century or so before being blown down in a storm in 1959.

Today there is a simple cross and a concrete monument and a little lizard-filled garden enclosed by a fence marking the spot, but there's not much to see. Not far from here is the Badagry **Slave Market**, which was established in 1502. Inside the simple compound is a yard of deep sand surrounded by concrete walls, and to the left of the gate is a small shrine that, judging by the chicken feathers scattered around, is still in use today. The well here is also still used by the townsfolk and the water is supposed to have magical properties. This is presumably the last place the slaves got to drink, from the big communal pots seen in the museums, before being carted off to the slave ships.

Back on the Marina and opposite the chief's house is the **Slave Port** (entry N50) that was in use between the 15th and 18th centuries. The slaves were taken from the slave market to here and then transported across the lagoon to 'the point of no return', and then on to the slave ships waiting in the sea at the other side of the sand bar. There's a garden here and a stone wall and gate leading on to a short jetty, and a couple of rusty cannons that were used against the slave traders during the abolition of slavery in 1886. Across the street and next to the chief's house is the **Brazilian Baracoon**, built in the 1840s; it's a low squat and crumbling brown building with a tin roof that used to hold up to 40 slaves at a time as they were being ferried from the slave market to the jetty. You can arrange a **boat ride** across to the 'point of no return' with the man that takes the entry fee for the Slave Port for about N600 per person, though less if there's more than two people in the boat. You can get out on the sand bar and walk though the 'point of no return' and imagine what it was like for the slaves in their last moment on African soil, before strolling along the beach for a bit whilst the boat waits for you to take you back to Badagry.

# Southwestern Nigeria

Aside from Lagos, the southwest of Nigeria is easily the most densely populated part of the country. This is Yorubaland, and there are many cities here steeped in history and the mythical origins of the key players in the traditional Yoruba religion. These towns are still governed to some extent by obas (ostensibly kings, though they come under an array of other names too), who sit regally in old palaces and wield a certain degree of political clout. Whilst their positions in the communities are largely ceremonial these days, their stature and spiritual role are still important and all can trace their origins back to the founders of the powerful Yoruba empires, many of whom were (supposedly) the Yoruba gods themselves. Throughout the region are testaments to the Yoruba religion, such as shrines where sacrifices are still made, which at times may seem strange and complicated, but are without doubt a compelling sight. In recent years much of traditional religion has been lost under the cloak of Christianity that chokes much of the southwest, but it's worth exploring the Sacred Forest at Oshogbo, the Olumo Rock at Abeokuta, and the mythical city of Ife, the spiritual home of all Yorubas, for an insight into the Yoruba religion, and to hear the stories and oral traditions that have been passed down through the centuries. Finally, there is Benin City, which has its own unique history, and which is near enough to Lagos to be lumped in with this chapter. Between the heavily populated urban areas the countryside is a rich and tropical expanse of dense green palms dotted with busy villages, and travelling between the major centres is not difficult. It's easy enough to hop from one motor park to the next, and all of the places mentioned in this chapter can be feasibly be visited on a day trip from Lagos. The southwest of Nigeria is also renowned for its art, especially in Oshogbo, which underwent an art renaissance in the 1960s, and where there are still some good galleries to purchase some unique pieces of art. It's also a region that is highly educated and industrialised, and is home to a number of educational institutions such as Nigeria's premier university, the University of Ibadan, established in 1948 during colonial times, and the Obafemi Awolowo University at Ife.

## ABEOKUTA

Abeokuta is the capital of Ogun State and is around 100km north of Lagos on the old Ibadan road. It's a historical town for the Yoruba people and its most famous landmark, the Olumo Rock, is considered sacred. Abeokuta was founded in the 1830s by the Egba clan of the Yoruba, who were seeking refuge from the **Yoruba** civil wars. Traditionally, they had lived in scattered villages, but with the threat of war with more powerful neighbours, they sought strength and protection in unity, and giving themselves a king they gathered together on the defensive western side

171

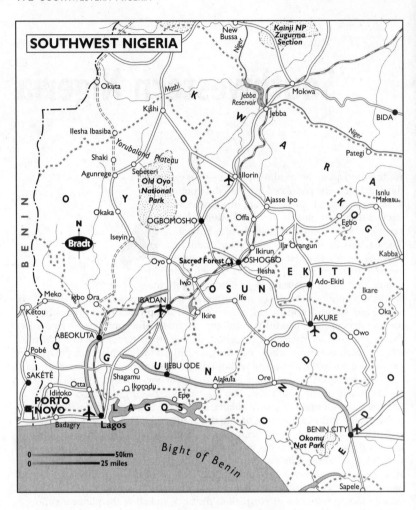

SOUTHWEST NIGERIA

of Olumo Rock. Abeokuta means literally 'under the rock'. The Egba were essentially middlemen in the slave trade, providing slaves from the interior to the slave markets on the coast, and with European guns obtained in exchange for slaves, they managed to protect their newly formed kingdom during the Yoruba wars. By the 1840s, and towards the end of the slave trade, some 500 returnee slaves, or *Creoles* as they were known, settled in Abeokuta and were the early nucleus of the Christian community. Among them was Samuel Crowther, a Yoruba by birth, who had been rescued as a boy from a slave ship by a British warship and taken and educated in Sierra Leone. He returned to Yorubaland and was the first West African to be ordained an Anglican bishop. He ran a prestigious Christian mission in the town, and word of his good works got sent back to Queen Victoria in England who sent two Bibles – in English and Arabic – to the Alake (king) of Abeokuta. When Crowther later went to England, he was granted an audience with the queen, when he recited the Lord's Prayer in Yoruba. She reputedly described it as 'soft and melodious'. The town is not only famous for its easily climbable rock, but there's a good selection of traditional adire and batik cloth on offer in the market, and it's also the birth place of the famous Nigerian writer Wole Soyinka, and President Obasanjo.

## Getting there and away

Abeokuta is roughly two hours' drive northeast of Lagos; pick up a vehicle in Ojota Motor Park in Lagos for around N150 and it will drop you at Kuto Motor Park in Abeokuta, which is just to the south of the main roundabout at the top end of town near the Gateway Hotel. Vehicles from Ibadan, roughly the same distance away as Lagos, but to the north, also drop off at Kuto Motor Park, where you can pick up taxis and *okadas* to get around town. The road to Ibadan has a few potholes.

## Where to stay and eat

The **Gateway Hotel,** just off Ibrahim Babangida (IBB) Boulevard and clearly signposted from the roundabout; tel: 039 241904, 243904, 242642; email: ghabk@infoweb.abs.net, is the town's principal state hotel and is a vast property on extensive grounds. The place is cavernous. with tall corridors, a vast lobby and enormous conference halls making you feel a bit like a shrunken Alice in Wonderland. The Wonderland comparison stops there though, as it was obviously built during the 1970–80 oil boom by the government, when no expense was spared, but it now looks very tired and frumpy. The restaurant serves basic dishes of Nigerian food for around N1,000 and occasionally there are evening buffets of continental dishes. There's a dark bar with a TV showing constant football, and a rather specifically priced menu of alcoholic tots from N34 to N306.67! The 200 rooms are old-fashioned but adequate, and there's a 24-hour gen, swimming pool and tennis court. Double rooms start from N6,000 (N10,000 deposit) and suites are from N20,000 (N25,000 deposit) and upwards; plus the 15%.

By far the nicest hotel in town is the **Dusmar Presidential Hotel** at 1 IBB Boulevard, just around the corner from the Kuto Motor Park; tel: 039 245179, 245218; email: dusmarhotels@hyperia.com. It has 41 rooms in a tidy three-storey block with secure car park next to the MKO Abiola Stadium, with a very neat restaurant with crisp white tablecloths, silver cutlery and glasses, muted music and a well-stocked bar with satellite TV. It's relatively new and the rooms have good furnishings with a fridge and a desk. A double room with DSTV is N4,600 (N6,000 deposit), with suites starting from N6,000 (N10,000 deposit); plus the 15%.

The much cheaper but pretty dire **Gateway Hotel Annex**, on Ademola Road; tel: 039 240004, is a few streets away. Head towards the tall white OPIC building

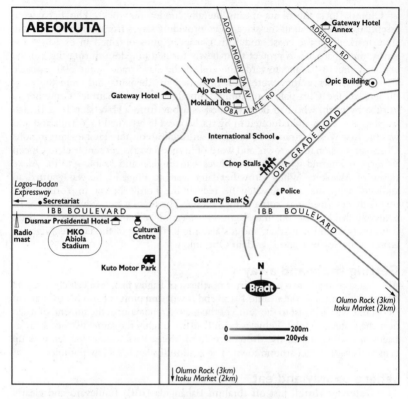

and at this roundabout turn left on to Ademola Road. The Gateway Annex is on the right through a red gate opposite Oba Alake Road. There are just a few basic huts here, spread around unkempt gardens that appear to be seldom used and it doesn't look terribly secure. The reception desk is in the white building at the back of the complex where there is also a restaurant, but again that doesn't look like it has been used for a long time. A very basic double with a bucket and loo costs N2,875 (N3,000 deposit) but the rooms are pretty filthy.

There are better options on Oba Alake Road opposite here, which is in the quieter and nicer GRA part of town called the Ibara Housing Estate. The friendly and much better value **Ajol Castle** at 4 Aduke Ayorinda Avenue; tel: 039 242220, 241712, has clean and neat rooms with fridge and DSTV, and the bigger rooms have two king-sized beds next to each other, which equates to about 3m of bed space. There are cold beers in the fridge in reception, and the small restaurant serves Nigerian food and the odd continental dish like chicken and chips. It seems quite popular and deservedly so, so try and phone the owner Mr Johnson first. A double goes for N2,750 (N3,000 deposit) plus the 15%, and there's a good range of rooms and a car park. Next door, **Ayo Inn** at 6 Aduke Ayorinda Avenue; tel: 039 241735, is very rough and ready, with seven dark and gloomy rooms with stained walls and battered AC units. Tea-eggs-and-bread breakfast is N300 and they can rustle up a plain rice dish for dinner on request, and there's beer for sale at reception. The cheaper rooms at the back have a shared bathroom and go for N2,000 whilst the en-suite rooms are N2,750 (no deposit).

The **Mokland Inn** around the corner at 7 Oba Alake Road; tel: 039 240060, 242054, has a big range of rooms spread through a row of four houses behind big gates where there is plenty of parking. You can get cold beers and soft drinks at reception and there's a fairly wide choice of food on the menu, such as spaghetti and some sort of meat and chips for around N300, which they can bring to your room. The rooms are spacious, with local TV and new fans, and water actually comes out of the big shower heads. Doubles start from N2,300 (N2,800 deposit) and there's a row of slightly cheaper but smaller rooms at the back of one of the buildings.

## What to see and do

You can climb the **Olumo Rock** for an impressive view of the city (entry N50; parking N25; camera N150; video camera N250; plus dash for the guide). The rock is 3km through town beyond the markets, and a taxi from the Koto Motor Park will cost about N100 (less for an *okada*). Taxis in Abeokuta are green with a horizontal yellow stripe. Olumo is an impressive outcrop of large granite boulders and the founding site of Abeokuta, and the highest point of the main rock is 137m. It's quite a steep walk from the car park up 52 steps with a railing to the base of the main boulder. The first thing you'll see here in a cave under a lip of the rock is the main Olumo Shrine with bits of fur and feathers stuck to the door and stoop – if a recent sacrifice has been made then you may also see decomposed pigeons, cow parts, kola nuts and snails. People still come regularly to pop money in the door to appease the Yoruba gods, and to ask for wealth, and barren women pray to become pregnant. At one time, and reputedly within the last hundred years, human beings were sacrificed here. The Olumo Festival takes place on August 5 each year, when thousands of people come at midnight to make sacrifices, and a priest will pray over each one. Traditionally a new oba of Abeokuta will spend four days in solitary confinement in the cave behind the locked door of the shrine, followed by three months of solitary contemplation in a room in his palace before his coronation.

Further around the base of the rock is a bigger cave several metres wide, but only a metre or so high. Inside the cave are remains of some low walls, with bowls carved into the floor and light niches into the walls where the Yoruba leaders hid out during the Yoruba wars between 1820 and 1830. Around the corner from the cave are a few huts where some women and children live as guardians of the Orisa Igun (God of thunder) Shrine decorated with sticks that represent iron and thunder. Next to the shrine is a tree where the oba takes a leaf to put on his forehead during his coronation, known as the Akoko leaf. There is another shrine to the god of smallpox, and another to the devil, where people pray and make sacrifices to ask the devil to stop doing whatever he is doing wrong. You are expected to pay a small dash to the keepers of the shrines. The guide will also point out some faces etched out in the stone of Yoruba warriors decorated in cowries. To get to the very top of the rock there's a steep set of iron steps up a cleft in the boulder, and the last few metres involve a bit of daredevil scrambling on the smooth granite surface. There are great views over the brown rusted tin roofs of town, from where you can hear the drifting music from the cassette sellers in the markets. President Obasanjo was born and went to high school in Abeokuta, and the guide will point out the big white school next to a radio tower on the top of a neighbouring hill. Quite bizarrely, on our tour we were accompanied by four policemen in black shirts with tear-gas canisters strapped to their belts. They took off their black shoes and socks and came with us to the summit of the rock. Apparently Olumo Rock also serves as a police post, as they can see far and wide over the town. They were also fascinated with the stories our guide was telling us about Yoruba history, and added their own bits and pieces as well.

Abeokuta is also famous as a centre for cloth, especially *adire*, the tie-dyed indigo cloth. The **Itoku Market** is located in the centre of town near the white pyramid obelisk that sits on a roundabout, from where the market spreads out in all directions; you can catch any vehicle from Kuto Motor Park and ask for the market. There are huge amounts of cloth here stacked up in bales in hundreds of stalls, and all the women are beautifully dressed in colourful fabrics. The market also has a large *juju* section where you'll see live chameleons in tiny cages, dried frogs and insects, more of the appalling dried monkey's heads, crocodile and snake skins, bits of twigs and dried leaves used to make magical potions, and tails, paws and heads, or beaks of various small animals and birds used as fetishes and charms. The market is fine to walk around and have a look at the weird and wonderful bits and pieces, but if you are female expect to get a bit of friendly hassle from the ladies who sell the cloth. There are also a few money changers hanging about who may approach you and ask if you want to change money.

# IBADAN

Ibadan is spread over acres of hills and valleys and is the capital of Oyo State, and was until recently the second-largest city in Nigeria, with a population of somewhere between five and eight million (it's generally believed that Kano has now superceded it). During the first half of the 20th century and before Nigerian independence, Ibadan was reputedly the largest city in sub-Saharan Africa. It started life as a military camp in the 1830s, and the phenomenal growth in size is derived largely from the Yoruba wars, when hundreds of thousands of retreating and displaced refugees gathered in one place. In 1840, Ibadan forces defeated Fulani invaders from the north at the battle of Oshogbo, thus protecting south Yorubaland from further attack and stopping the advance of the jihad through Yorubaland towards the sea. Easy access to fertile land encouraged people to settle there, and even today the region is the most important agricultural area in Nigeria – it essentially feeds Lagos. The city came under British protection in 1893, and was later the capital of Nigeria's former Western Region. The introduction of the cash-crop, cocoa, by the British brought increasing prosperity and Ibadan became the centre of Nigeria's cocoa belt, which for decades assured the prosperity of the Yoruba. Little cocoa is grown today in the region, but the 25-storey Cocoa House is one of the only high-rise buildings on Ibadan's skyline and serves as a good landmark.

There's not a great deal to see or do here; Ibadan is most famous for its university and its market (one of the biggest in Nigeria) and very unfortunately a god-awful zoo, though it is a convenient base for trips to the other, more traditional, old towns of Oyo State. It's a sprawling metropolis that goes on seemingly to all points on the horizon, over several hills dotted with granite boulders affording good views of the rusty corrugated iron rooftops of yellow stucco-walled houses. The University of Ibadan (founded as a college of the University of London in 1948, and as an autonomous university in 1962) was Nigeria's first university, and several libraries and research institutes are located in the city. The city is very religious for both Muslims and Christians, and there are scores of churches and mosques, and on Sundays whole streets close to traffic for open-air church services. In the evening look out for the thousands of kites that fly over Ibadan at sunset – it's quite a remarkable sight.

## Getting there and away

Ibadan is two hours' drive north of Lagos (N200) and one hour 45 minutes from Abeokuta (N180), and there are regular vehicles throughout the day. From these destinations you are likely to be dropped off at the Dugbe Market around Oyo

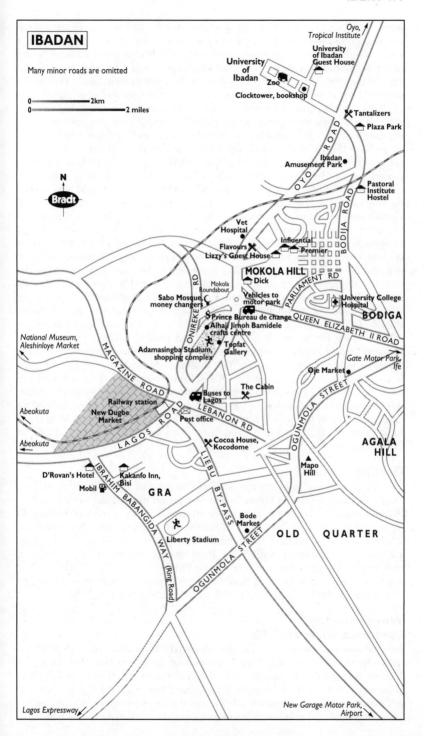

IBADAN

Many minor roads are omitted

0 ————— 2km
0 ————— 2 miles

N

Bradt

Oyo,
Tropical Institute

University of Ibadan Guest House

University of Ibadan

Zoo

Clocktower, bookshop

Tantalizers

Plaza Park

Ibadan Amusement Park

Pastoral Institute Hostel

OYO ROAD

BODIJA ROAD

Vet Hospital

Flavours
Lizzy's Guest House

Influential Premier

MOKOLA HILL

Dick

PARLIAMENT RD

Mokola Roundabout

Sabo Mosque, money changers

Vehicles to motor park

University College Hospital

BODIGA

ONIREKE RD

Prince Bureau de change

Alhaji Jimoh Bamidele crafts centre

QUEEN ELIZABETH II ROAD

National Museum, Aleshinloye Market

Adamasingba Stadium, shopping complex

Topfat Gallery

Oje Market

Gate Motor Park, Ife

MAGAZINE ROAD

Buses to Lagos

The Cabin

OGUNMOLA STREET

Abeokuta

Railway station
New Dugbe Market

LAGOS ROAD

LEBANON RD

Post office

AGALA HILL

Abeokuta

Cocoa House, Kocodome

LIEBU BY-PASS

Mapo Hill

D'Rovan's Hotel

IBRAHIM BABANGIDA WAY (Ring Road)

Kakanfo Inn, Bisi

Mobil

GRA

Bode Market

OLD    QUARTER

Liberty Stadium

OGUNMOLA STREET

Lagos Expressway

New Garage Motor Park, Airport

Road (confusingly here also called Dugbe Road) which is a pretty central destination, and where there are plenty of okadas and taxis to take you to a hotel. If you are coming from elsewhere or if you are leaving Ibadan you need to get to one of the bigger motor parks listed below, which are several kilometres away on the edge of the city. To get to any of these go to the Mokola roundabout 1km to the north of Dugbe, and here you will find lines of shared taxis and minibuses that go to all the motor parks. It's a very spread-out city and the traffic is bad, so give yourself at least an hour to get out to an outlying motor park. For destinations to the southeast such as Benin City, Warri and Onitsha, and for Lagos, you'll need to go to New Garage to the southeast of the city, though there are some vehicles going directly to Lagos from near the Dugbe Market on Oyo Road. To get to New Garage you first have to get a vehicle from the Mokola roundabout to somewhere called Challenge (it's very vaguely beyond Cocoa House and the GRA, and around the ring road of Ibadan). Once at Challenge (a suburban motor park surrounding a petrol station) you need to swap on to another vehicle going to New Garage. For buses to the north and northeast (with the exception of Oyo – see below), vehicles go from Agodi Gate Motor Park in the east, simply referred to as just 'Gate'. To get here take a vehicle directly from the Mokola roundabout. Everyone will help you find the right bus and it shouldn't cost much more than N20 to get from the centre of Ibadan to the motor parks. To get to and from Oyo, only 52km directly north of Ibadan, buses go from a motor park in a sprawling market roughly three kilometres north of the university on Oyo Road. To get there take any city bus or shared taxi heading north up Oyo Road. Ibadan is a central transit point for vehicles going further north, so you may find yourself changing vehicles here between Lagos and other points north, which may involve a trip from one motor park to another by city transport. The dysfunctional train station is on Dugbe Road, which is an extension of Oyo Road. Ibadan's airport is 12km southeast of town, but given its proximity to Lagos there are very few flights. Overland Airways (no phone, but there's a desk at the airport, or get information from their Abuja office; tel: 09 810 0223) flies between Ibadan and Abuja (one hour) Monday to Friday at 08.30, 11.30, and 17.30; and from Abuja to Ibadan Monday to Friday at 07.00, 10.00, and 16.00.

## Getting around

The commercial centre of the city is effectively the area around the train station, Dugbe Market and Cocoa House, where you'll find most of the market activity. Ibadan's cloth market, supposedly every 16 days, is at the corner of Ogunmola Street and Bodija Road, and you will have to ask in the area when it's next on. There are bread sellers here all the time. Opposite the entrance to the university are book and stationery stalls. Oyo Road bisects the city neatly, though it confusingly changes name; it is referred to as Dugbe Road near the Dugbe Market, and to the very south it's Lagos Road. There is a stream of minibuses and shared taxis going up and down this main road and a short hop will cost N20–30.

## Where to stay
### Upmarket: above US$100

**International Institute of Tropical Agriculture (IITA)** Oyo Rd, 5km north of the university; tel: 02 241 2626 and ask for the International House; email: hotel@cgiar.org. The best place to stay in Ibadan, but you have to make a reservation. This is a private guest house set in a 600-acre tropical estate, with pool, tennis, badminton and squash, a nine-hole golf course and fishing in a large lake. It's also a great place for hiking and birdwatching. There are several cafés and restaurants with excellent food, and accommodation is in singles and doubles and one- to two-bedroomed flats with fully equipped kitchens. Expect to pay in the region of N15,000 for a double.

**Kakanfo Inn** 1 Nihinlola St, off Ibrahim Babangida Way, which is also referred to as Mobil Petrol Station Ring Road; tel: 02 231 1471/3, 231 8600/1; email: kakanfoinn@ibadan.skannet.com.ng; www.kakanfoinn.com. This is very professionally run and is one of the nicest hotels in Ibadan, opened in 1989 and tucked away in a quiet area of the GRA. The 70 rooms and 12 suites all have balconies, with slightly dated but comfortable furnishings with fridge and DSTV, 24-hour power and running hot and cold water. There's a good restaurant serving Indian and Nigerian food, an L-shaped swimming pool and relaxing poolside terrace, a curio shop in the lobby, and a small gym with some weight machines. Unusually you are quite likely to be charged the non-resident rate on the tariff here, though of course pay the actual bill in naira. Try and negotiate with the receptionist to pay the lower resident's rate. Non-residents rates are US$90 (US$130 deposit) for a double, and US$110–220 (US$150–300 deposit) for a range of different-sized executive rooms and suites, plus the 15%. Discounts are available at the weekend.

## Mid-range: US$25–50

**Premier Hotel** Mokola Hill; tel: 02 241 1234, 241 4122, 241 4245. This is the state hotel perched on top of Mokola Hill, and it is easily seen from any approach to the city. Built in 1966 and six storeys high, it's now quite shabby, but reasonably comfortable, with 80 double rooms and 6 suites with DSTV, and the best views in the city. In the huge car park you can arrange car hire, and there are a few batiks and wood carvings for sale. The hotel has its own boreholes and giant gens, tennis court, gym, another vast lobby, bakery, mosque, bureau de change (guests only), bookshop, dark but comfy bar with TV showing CNN, and Olympic-size pool, which is clean but set in scruffy grounds, with the odd broken sun-lounger or plastic chair. You can swim here for a small fee even if you're not staying. Finally there is a Chinese restaurant covered under *Eating*. Doubles start from N6,500 (N8,600 deposit), and twins from N7.500 (N11,000 deposit), plus the 15%. Rates are discounted by 25% at the weekends.

**D'Rovans Hotel** Chief Francis Aiyegbeni Close, Ring Rd; tel: 02 231 2908, 231 3617/8. email: drovans@skannet.com.ng. Rooms here are tiny but not too tired-looking, with reasonably modern furniture, and there's a reasonably consistent power supply, too. There's a great bar next to the swimming pool with comfy seats and fans and sometimes live juju or highlife bands. Other facilities include a small gym, a restaurant serving unremarkable meals, conference facilities and plenty of parking. Rates are N6,325 (N7,000 deposit) for a single, N7,475 (N8,000 deposit) for a double, and N8,625–17,250 (N9,500–18,000 deposit) for the bigger suites.

**Hotel Influential** Mokola Hill, a few metres to the south of the main entrance to the car park of the Hotel Presidential on M. Fadahunsi Onilegogoro Street; tel: 02 241 4894, 415039. This is a nice and neat, reasonably new, business hotel, also at the top of Mokola Hill, with a smart lounge and dining room, modern cool tiles, fat sofas, a cosy bar area, plants, friendly staff and welcoming Spanish flamenco music. The spotless rooms have giant beds and there are a few spaces for cars in the compound and a 24-hour gen. Breakfast items go from N100–200, and a dinner of beans and dodo, meat and a variety of soups is about N600, while continental dishes of chicken and fried rice go from N1,000. A double room is N5,520 (N7,000 deposit), and larger suites are N11,000 (N14,000 deposit), plus the 15%.

**University of Ibadan Guest House** Tel: 02 810 0041, 810 2143, 810 2297. This is located on the campus of the university – to get here follow the road from the entrance of the campus for 300m or so to the main buildings, and specifically the large bookshop, and turn right; the guesthouse is a few metres along this road on the right-hand side. There are just over 100 rooms here in three two-storey wings of faded brown paint. The corridors and stairwells are grimy and the staff surly, but the rooms themselves are actually quite clean and spacious, with local TV and fridge, and, in my opinion, a slightly odd smell. There is a huge car park, reasonable gardens, a hotel dining room serving food-is-ready, and at the back a small internet place for students and a tatty bar with old sofas, and again a very funny smell, with crates of beer stacked everywhere and a blaring TV. Rates are N4,600 (N6,500 deposit) for a room with a queen-size bed, and around another N1,000 for a room with two double beds.

### Budget: below US$25
**Plaza Park Hotel** Bodija Rd; tel: 02 810 2221, 810 3569, 810 3370. Also near the university, there's a clean bar and restaurant in a brick shed serving Nigerian staples and a new wall around the compound provides secure parking. It's all very concretey though, and the rooms with local TV are very plain, though they have been scrubbed up and painted in recent years. Rates include the 15%; singles are N3,500 and doubles N4,000.

**Lizzy Guest House** 844 Adenle Av, off Easy Life Rd, Mokola Hill; tel: 02 241 3350. This is an excellent and friendly budget option with good views from the first-floor balcony over the busy street and into people's busy houses and over Ibadan's rooftops. It's well signposted from Oyo Road and most *okada* drivers seem to know where it is – look out for the tattered Nigerian flag on top. There's parking in the street only, and the street is routinely closed for church services. It boasts 14 small and clean rooms and friendly staff; check that the rusty AC is working or ask for a room with a fan. Water comes out of the shower in a single cold line and there's a gen – when there's no NEPA this is the only house on the street with power. Out the back is a small room where a lady wearing an immaculate chef's uniform will make tea-bread-and-eggs but nothing else. All rooms are N2,500.

**Pastoral Institution Hostel** Bodija Rd; tel: 02 810 3928. This is a well looked-after, pale blue building set in very peaceful grounds not far from the university. It's nice and it's cheap, but it is very much a God-fearing place, with a strict curfew from 22.30, and you have to be well behaved. The sister in charge usually lets guests stay on a weekly basis, but if you are very polite and it's not already full, she may let you stay for one night. There's a whole list of house rules here about being courteous and not deceiving God and there is a church service in the main hall downstairs each morning at 06.15, more on Sundays, plus a Christian bookshop. Basic meals can be arranged in advance at the canteen and of course there is no booze. Rooms are sparse but spotlessly clean and the showers work and there's mossie netting at the windows. A single is N1,500, and a double is N1,800, which includes breakfast; pay N800 extra for AC.

## Where to eat and drink
**Kocodome** in the car park at Cocoa House (open daily 09.00–23.00) serves Lebanese and continental food and is hugely popular. It boasts all sorts of treats, including a swimming pool open until 19.00, and frequent live music. Downstairs is a bar serving Chapmans, tea and coffee, and plenty of beer and Guinness, whilst upstairs is a more formal restaurant. In both there is the same extensive and excellent-value menu of Nigerian dishes from N600, plus toasted sandwiches and Lebanese *shawarmas*, grills and kebabs, and a good mezze selection for N500 per plate. Next door is a thumping nightclub which is open from 23.00–dawn on Friday and Saturday; if you eat at the restaurant first there is no charge at the door. **Bisi**, at the upmarket Kakanfo Inn (see above, open daily 11.00–21.30), is a great albeit expensive Indian restaurant serving authentic biriyani, masala and jalfresi dishes in nice surroundings, and it has several vegetarian choices. The **Golden Dragon**, at the Premier Hotel (open 12.00–15.00; 19.00–22.30; closed Monday lunch), serves fairly authentic Chinese food, though again it's not especially cheap; we paid N4,000 for two with beer, but Chinese people do actually eat here and the food is delicious. If you are not staying at the Premier, this is within walking

distance of the Influential Hotel and Lizzy Guest House, but beware of bumping into goats on the way home in the dark! **Flavours,** just off Oyo Road at 3 Okommade Street, opposite the vet hospital and just north of the Makola roundabout (open Monday–Saturday 08.00–22.00; Sunday 12.00–22.00), is a brand new café serving good Nigerian food, with a new internet café next door. Both are in a small compound with a garden and there is a big signpost off Oyo Road. Eat at the outside tables or inside in the cool AC at bright white plastic tables and chairs. It's spotlessly clean and modern and there's a good variety of Nigerian food and beers on offer. Dishes start from as little as N150 through to N480 for the goat's head pepper soup, and there's snails and bushmeat on the menu. For the timid I recommend the fried chicken, which was one of the best I had in Nigeria.

**Dick Hotel,** Alhaji Bagvdv Waziri Street, off Oyo Road, Mokola. Despite this being called a hotel, you certainly do not want to stay in the awful rooms upstairs, but this is a good, if rough and ready, music venue that serves up cheap beers in the space out front, where there is a stage and a bank of giant speakers, and juju and fuji bands play most nights. The **Cabin,** at 10 Awolowo Avenue, east of Oyo Road, used to be a bar with pool tables and western food, but when we visited it was being rebuilt. It might be worth checking out when it reopens, as they seem to be spending a fair amount of money on the refurbishments. Opposite the entrance to the university on Oyo Road is a branch of **Tantalizers**, for cheap Nigerian fast food in AC.

## Communications and changing money

On Oyo road are a number of internet cafés, some open 24 hours if there is NEPA; there's a particularly dense crop of them about 100m north of the Mokola roundabout, along with some pharmacies and a branch of **DHL** at number 51. Look out for the **Goset Cybercafé** (open 24 hours; N50 for 30 minutes and special deals for night surfing after 21.00). You can also sometimes make international phone calls from here. The chaotic **post office** is on Dugbe/Oyo Road, more or less opposite the train station (open Monday–Friday 08.00–17.00; Saturday 09.00–13.00). To **change money**, ignore all the banks and head for the area around the Sabo Mosque, where you will find plenty of Hausa money changers, some with their own offices. From the Mokola Roundabout take the road left or to the east (I could not find the name of this street) for about 100m and just before the Sabo mosque, which is on the right-hand side, you'll find money changers on either side of the road. Look out for Prince Bureau de Change, a small office with mirrored glass doors, on the left.

## What to see and do

The **University of Ibadan** is Nigeria's premier university, and was established in 1948 as a college of the University of London, and as an autonomous university in 1962. It's on an enormous campus with lots of mosques and churches, and the main buildings are 300m from the entrance on Oyo road; there are plenty of minibuses and *okadas* if you don't want to walk. The University **Bookshop** is worth a look and has a wide selection of Nigerian-published books. From the main entrance of the university go straight down towards the clocktower and the bookshop is on the right (open Monday–Friday 08.00–16.30). You may be able to pick up some Nigerian maps here (though none of Ibadan), and we found some old copies of *National Geographic*. There's a vast selection of text books and a comprehensive section on Nigerian writers, plus Christian books and dog-eared romantic novels. At the back of the University Guest House, a few metres north of the bookshop, are a few stalls selling batiks and clothes, but the traders are quite aggressive. The university also has a **zoo**, with a large collection of monkeys and large primates. It's along the road to the left of the bookshop and clocktower; just follow it around and someone will direct you or get an *okada* – having said that, however, I implore you not to go there, pay the piddly N100 gate fee, and encourage the existence of this zoo anyway! It is thoroughly depressing and archaic, and has been neglected for decades. Just through the entrance is a juvenile chimp in an inadequately small cage where people were throwing peanuts at it through the chicken wire. The ducks and the 'selection of water birds' had a bigger cage than the chimp. Next up were several porcupines in a bird cage – whilst the cage was very tall the animals had no space whatsoever on the floor. The saddest inhabitant was an old, lonely female gorilla in a patch of grass about 7m by 10m surrounded by a moat, with only about half a metre of shade. When we visited she was sitting forlornly against the bars, wanting to get inside her night cage, with absolute despair on her face and sighing heavily. A keeper was trying to get her to stand up for a bunch of uninterested school children by throwing mangos at her. Many of the monkeys are housed next to the kids' playground, where many of the same uninterested school kids were yelling and screaming, which completely unnerved all the primates, most of which were totally mad – this is, after all, the country that dries monkey heads for *juju*. The lions, including some new-born cubs, were kept in dark concrete cages all day. In the grounds is the Department of Psychology Experimental Animal Laboratory Unit, with mice in cages and ominous-looking concrete slabs. I could go on, I won't; don't go there, it's terribly sad.

On a lighter note **Ibadan Amusement Park**, just south of the university, is a very bizarre place (entry N50). It's a bleak spot of open ground, but it seems popular with families for its ancient and rusty amusement rides, most of them now defunct, though the Ferris wheel and dodgems are still working. Consider carefully the state of all machinery in Nigeria, and the fact that the power goes off and on all the time, before hopping on a ride. You can get a soft drink and a snack at the shops. The most worthwhile of Ibadan's limited sights is the **National Museum**; tel: 02 241 2797 (open daily 09.00–17.00, N60 entry; plus dash for the excellent guides. No photography is permitted and you may be asked to leave your camera at the entrance). It's off Dick Road near Aleshinloye Market, and whilst *okada* drivers probably won't know where the museum is, they will know where the market is, and it's easy enough to find the museum from here. It's located in a little park where there is a museum kitchen popular for weddings and functions and where you might sometimes be able to get a cold drink. This is a fairly new museum (it only opened in 2001), and is one of the best I saw in Nigeria. Consequently it's not too dusty and the exhibits are presented in three bright halls with everything clearly labelled. One hall is packed to the gills with drums, including a pair of very tall Badagry drums that you have to jump up and down to play. Ayan is the Yoruba goddess of drums, so Ayan is added to all the individual names of the drums in the museum. There is a selection of masquerade masks and costumes; the one from Cross River is covered in raffia and bells and looks particularly scary. Also look out for the beautiful oba's coat, which is covered with hundreds of thousands of brightly coloured beads. Another hall is full of over 300 pots; some were used as incense burners, some for storage, and some as stoves, and there are the ritual pots that were once presented to widows and new brides, or used for sacrifices or to bury the placenta of a new-born baby. There are also displays on the traditional art of ironmongery, tie-dyeing indigo cloth, weaving Aso Oke cloth, and wood carving.

For more art that you can buy, Ibadan has a couple of good shops. The artist Tope Fatunmlsi has his **Topfat Gallery** at Shop 156 Adamasingba Shopping

Complex; this shop faces Oyo Road. Tope is a very good local artist for Nigerian landscapes, portraits and excellent abstracts with prices from N25,000–55,000. The **Alhaji Jimoh Bamidele Crafts Centre** is at 75 Lekan Salami Shopping Complex, at the back of the stadium (you need to walk to the opposite side of the stadium from the Topfat Gallery). Here are two shops next to each other filled with traditional carvings from all over the country, though it's mostly Yoruba artwork, plus antiques and furniture. For views of Ibadan, you can climb up **Mapo Hill** in the oldest quarter of the city, where Mapo Hall was built in a commanding position on the summit by the British in the 1920s. This is a good spot for taking photos of Ibadan's densely packed houses with their rusting brown roofs; go later in the day when the light enhances them better.

## IFE

Ife is a southwestern city with perhaps around 500,000 inhabitants The Obafemi Awolowo University sprawls over expansive land, and a wide spectrum of disciplines and the presence of many thousands of students in Ife brings some life to an otherwise unremarkable town. Like Ibadan it used to be another important centre on Nigeria's cocoa belt. Look out for the single-storey 1940s colonial houses scattered around that were built during the height of the cocoa trade. Some are still standing in a reasonably good, if rather faded, state of repair, showing perhaps that things were built of a higher standard back then.

Ife has special significance for all Yorubas, as they regard it as their first city, and Ile-Ife, the ancient name meaning 'old Ife', is the cradle of Yoruba culture and religion. All Yoruba chiefs and obas trace their descent from Oduduwa, the first mythical ruler of Ife and the founder of the Yorubas, and they regard the reigning oba (here called Oni) of Ife as their ritual superior. Archaeological excavations have put Ife's origins in the 9th century, and from the 12th to the 17th centuries it was the most powerful Yoruba kingdom. There are two theories of where Oduduwa came from. One is that the supreme god, Olodumare, threw down an iron ladder from the heavens to the world, which then was only a mass of water, and ordered his son Oduduwa and his lieutenants down it to create earth and the human race. He gave him a ball of sand, a palm nut and a chicken. The ladder landed in Ife where he accomplished his task. He threw sand on the water and created land, on which he let the chicken loose to scratch around to spread the land and planted the palm oil tree. The other theory is that Oduduwa and his people migrated to Ife from Egypt after a political crisis over the rise of Islam. Terracotta sculptures made in the area as early as the 12th century, some of which are displayed in the Ife Museum, vaguely resemble artefacts found in Nubia in Egypt, a fact which lends itself to the migration theory. Once he established his own kingdom at Ile-Ife, he gave his children crowns and sent

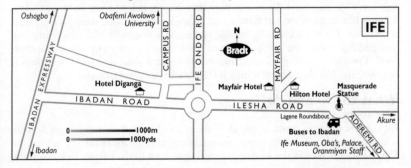

them off to establish the other Yoruba towns. The newer town of Ife was built on the spot of Ile-Ife in 1882.

## Getting there and away

Ife is 86km from Ibadan, where you'll have to change vehicles if coming from Lagos. Vehicles to and from Ibadan drop off outside the university gate first, and then in town itself, around the Lagare roundabout. From here you can also get vehicles to some of the other southern towns including Oshogbo and Benin City. Within Ife, plenty of shared taxis and minibuses ply the main routes for about N20–40.

## Where to stay and eat

**Hotel Diganga** 1 Ife-Ibadan Road, near the entrance to the university; tel: 036 231791, 233200. Here, presumably because of its location near the university and visiting students, you have to sign a 'lodging regulations' slip stating that 'This hotel does not under any circumstances allow lodgers to turn their hotel room into a disco night meeting or any form of gathering. This has been done by some people under the disguise of ordinary being a lodger...' Despite the no disco rules, this is the best option in town and not badly priced. The rooms are perfectly presentable, with clean bathrooms, DSTV and phones that actually work, and you can order room service. The only downside is there is no gen, and you will be woken up by chickens in the morning, as there is a chicken coop right against the back wall of the hotel. There's secure parking behind a security-manned boom gate. The comfy bar has fat velour sofas and fish tanks, and there's a good restaurant, though inexplicably they had emu on the menu (Darren, who is Australian, was dumbfounded). The staff are very friendly and the girl who cooked our breakfast was *so* excited to serve us she couldn't stop giggling, and practically dragged us out of bed! Breakfast items go from N150 whilst a plate of chicken and rice will cost N500. Rooms cost N2,750 for a double (N3,000 deposit) including the 15%. There are rooms within the university campus itself at the **Obafemi Awolowo University Guest House**; tel: 036 230809, in an ugly concrete block, and everything is very dated, but the 69 rooms are passable, with clean carpet, satellite TV, big beds, and large sunny windows with balconies overlooking other bits of concrete and a nice patch of forest in the distance. The large restaurant serves daily Nigerian specials and snacks such as pies and doughnuts, and buffet breakfasts. It is some distance from the main university buildings, so you'll need to catch an *okada* to the east of the campus. Doubles are from N2,700–3,500 (add another N1,000 for the deposit) inclusive of the 15%. The **Hilton Hotel** on Mayfair Road, just down the hill from Ife/Ilesa Road; tel: 036 232819, is another good option – the 20 rooms have AC and a fan, one or two giant beds, brand new fridges and satellite TVs, nice tiled floors and they have seen a lick of paint in recent years. There's hot water in the bathrooms, and, new shower curtains, an item rarely seen in Nigeria. There's a bar with outside tables and a few umbrellas in a courtyard, and parking within the compound, and the restaurant serves up cheap Nigerian food. The cheapest doubles start from N1,450 with a small deposit. The Hilton is opposite the **Mayfair Hotel** which is truly awful, so avoid that one.

## What to see and do
### The town

Of the few sights in town, nearly all of them are clustered around Enuwa Square, a kilometre or so from the Lagere roundabout; jump on an *okada* and ask for the Oba's Palace. Once in the square and with your back to the palace, look down the street and you'll see two imposing towers, both about six stories high, opposite each other. The one on the left is a modern red building with windows all the way up and is part of a mosque, whilst the older one on the right is white and square with a cone on top and slit windows. The latter is a memorial to Oduduwa and is surrounded by gardens that are well looked after, with lawns and flower beds, but unfortunately it's locked. This is the **Oduduwa Afewonro Park**, where there is also a statue of Oduduwa draped in robes and jewellery holding up a staff and chicken, with another chicken at his feet. At the **Oba's Palace** one of the palace guards at the gate will show you around the grounds for a small dash. There's a big hall used for ceremonial occasions, with a carved door and elephant tusk above it, a statue of Oduduwa in Egyptian dress (giving the theory that he came from Egypt some credence), and in the middle of the compound a large statue of Moremi wrapped in beads and holding a staff. This was the woman who was supposedly the earliest leader of Ife, with whom Oduduwa had to battle for power when he arrived in Ife. Also in the compound is the local criminal court, with two basic steps for the criminals to stand or sit on and a line of chairs where the oba and chiefs decide their fate. To one side is the shrine of Ogun (the god of war and iron) – it's a rectangular piece of earth surrounded by a low concrete wall decorated with shells, where people come regularly to pray and make sacrifices, and there are several mounds of earth covered in feathers, dollops of pounded yam and snail shells.

Next door to the palace is the **Ife Museum** (open daily 08.00–18.00; N20 entry fee plus dash for the guide), which has many fine bronze and terracotta sculptures dating back to the 13th century, a collection of brass heads that were unearthed in the town in 1938, and that are thought to be from the 11th–12th centuries, a rock thought to be a piece of 11th-century Ife pavement, and a terracotta royal footstool that is one of the largest pieces of terracotta found in Africa. Also on display are some *juju* (black magic) items – *juju* was described to us by the museum guide as 'modern-day Africa's remote control' though I am struggling to put a meaning to this! There's quite a good display of fading drawings of obas, farmers, chiefs and prominent community members in their traditional dress, much of which is still worn today. Everything is displayed around a lovely and serene courtyard with a garden of shrubs and aged farming implements, and the building itself is an old circular colonial building built in 1948 – look out for the original wooden louvered windows and parquet floor.

The **Opa Oranmiyan** is an engraved monolith 5.18m high that is popularly believed to be the walking stick (opa means staff) of the giant Oranmiyan, who was the warrior son of either Oduduwa or the god Ogun. According to legend Oranmiyan was the powerful first oba of Oyo, and after his death the obelisk was erected supposedly on the spot where he was buried, though there's no grave. There is however, a more mythical story. Oranmiyan the warrior left Ife and marched south conquering all that got in his way, but he promised his people back home that if he was ever needed by them he would return. Ife was under threat and all the people got together and shouted out his name in a plea for Oranmiyan to help them in their hour of need. Oranmiyan heard and came striding back to Ife, still slaying anyone that got in his way. When he looked down at one warrior he had killed, he recognised him as a friend and realised he was again amongst his own people. So distressed was he that he'd killed someone from Ife, he plunged his staff into the ground, where it petrified and became the monolith, and strode off into the forest never to be seen again. On one side of the staff are some faded carvings, and inexplicably there are some nails driven into it. The meaning of these is unknown. The staff is just to the south of the palace off Ikyekere Street and to get to it you'll need to jump on an *okada*, but it's just a very straight, rather phallic-looking piece of granite in a small unkempt garden, and it really isn't worth the trek when you can see pictures and learn the story at the museum.

## The university

Ife's Obafemi Awolowo University, on the Ibadan road, a few kilometres to the west of town, is Nigeria's biggest university with some 20,000 students and a number of faculties. Once at the main gate you'll have to catch another minibus for N20 to the university campus, which is another 1.3km, though from town there are direct 'campus' minibuses that drop you in the heart of things. The main buildings of the university are a bunch of hideous concrete blocks built in the 1960s, and some evidently were never finished, as there are a few derelict blocks. Nevertheless, there are some attractive squares and gardens, the campus is relatively rubbish free, and it's teeming with students, lecturers and staff, all of whom will 'welcome' you. There's another excellent university **bookshop** here (open Monday–Friday 08.00–16.45) with a good range of Nigerian literature and factual books on the economy and politics, many autobiographies of Nigeria's past politicians and leaders (all of whom seem to find it necessary to write a book as soon as they have retired from office), books on African history, and specifically on Yoruba and Hausa history. There's a post office next to the bookshop and you can check email at the nearby **C@ fé Net et Cetera**. Across from the bookshop is the **Forks n Fingers** canteen where you can get a cold drink and eat a big plate of stew and rice with the chatty students. Outside and to the right of the restaurant is a 'photocopy' market – rows and rows of photocopiers and attendants. On the 4th floor of the Archaeological Faculty (I can't explain where this is in the jumble of concrete, but someone will show you the way) is the **Museum of Natural History** (open Monday–Friday 08.30–16.30; free entry). Here you will find a well-labelled and well-lit geology section, a few stuffed animals in glass cages, a collection of insects and bugs, and, rather oddly, skeletons of a giant anteater, a one-humped camel, and a llama. One exhibit of interest is the skull of a now-extinct marine crocodile dug up near Sokoto in 1971. The label explains that Nigeria was once linked to the Mediterranean by sea before the plates of earth shifted. At the entrance of the museum (the *natural history* museum, I might add) is a sign with a quote from one Walter Rodney (whoever he may be) that says: 'Wealth has to be produced out of nature, from tilling the land or mining minerals, or felling trees, or turning raw materials into finished products for human consumption.' For me, this completely highlighted the total lack of conservation concern Nigeria has. This was compounded by a visit to the thoroughly depressing zoo in the university grounds, where we were told that the lions had been shot and stuffed to be put on display in the museum. At the zoo are only a handful of animals left in dreadful, dilapidated bare concrete enclosures; and it looks like it will be closed down soon. It's awful; don't go there. On a lighter note, when we paid our N5 entry fee into the zoo, we were given a receipt for a fine for an overdue library book.

# OSHOGBO

Oshogbo is about 80km to the northeast of Ibadan and is the capital of Osun State, which is dubbed the 'State of the Living Spring' (on car number plates) because of the Osun River that runs through Oshogbo. The Yoruba city was thought to have been founded in the 17th century, and in 1839 it was the site of a decisive battle between the Yoruba from Ibadan and the Fulani from **Ilorin**, but the Fulani did not succeed in taking Oshogbo and it remained an important town in the Yoruba culture. An influx of refugees after the battle swelled Oshogbo's population, which is currently at about 500,000 (a small town by Nigerian standards).

## YORUBA GODS

*Olodumare* is the divine spirit who sent his son *Oduduwa* to Ife to create the Yoruba. Of the other important Yoruba gods, *Shango*, who had four wives each personified by a major Nigerian river, is the god that creates the weather. He does this by casting down to earth 'thunderstones' that create thunder and lightning. *Ogun* is the god of war, of the hunt, and rather curiously, of ironmongery, and is patron god to blacksmiths, warriors, and all who use metal in their occupations. He also presides over deals and contracts, and in traditional Yoruba courts, witnesses swear to tell the truth in the name of *Ogun*. The Yoruba consider *Ogun* fearsome and terrible in his revenge, and if someone breaks a pact made in his name, swift retribution will follow. He added yet another feather to his formidable cap when, according to legend, he built Africa's first road, as he was the only god who had the right implements to carve through the dense jungle. *Eshu* is the god of *Ifa*, a form of writing using a complex system of nuts, signs and squares that the Yoruba use to predict the future. Today many Yoruba do not make a major life decision without consulting it. He is also the divine trickster and is responsible for many of the world's ill doings, and needs regular attention to maintain harmony in the community. *Shokpona* is the god of smallpox – he became a high-ranking god because of the smallpox plagues spread by various inter-ethnic wars over the centuries. Priests of *Shokpona* wielded immense power and it was believed that they could give smallpox to their enemies. They reputedly made potions from the skin of those who died from smallpox, which they would pour in an enemy's house or village to spread the disease. *Osun* is the goddess of the river that flows through Oshogbo, and is the bringer of fertility in women. *Lyamapo* is the goddess of all women's crafts, including childbirth, and is held responsible for *Aje*, the destructive or malevolent aspects of womanhood.

It's primarily a farming and commercial city, with cotton gins, a steel-rolling mill, and a cigarette factory, but it's best known as being the centre of Nigerian art. Oshogbo is the founding centre of the internationally renowned School of Oshogbo, that in the 1960s produced a collection of artists that went on to become successful and wealthy on an international scale. Historically the town has always been an art centre for the Yoruba, but it underwent a renaissance in the late 1950s when three European àrtists, the Austrian sculptress Susanne Wenger, the writer Ulli Beier (who used to be married to Susanne Wenger), and the artist Georgina Beier, started a series of art schools that rejuvenated Nigeria's art world and produced some excellent local contemporary artists. These include Jimoh Buraimoh, Twins Seven Seven ('the Art Man'), Nike Davies-Okundaye (who now lives in Lagos but who has a gallery in Oshogbo and who used to be married to Twins Seven Seven) and many others. Oshogbo remains the centre of Nigerian art and there are some good galleries to visit. It's also home to the shrines and grove of Osun, the Yoruba goddess of fertility, in the Oshogbo Sacred Forest, where the Osun Festival takes place in August each year.

Despite being the state capital, Oshogbo is a particularly scruffy town. It's well worth coming here for a few hours to visit the galleries and the Sacred Forest, but most of Oshogbo's accommodation is especially appalling, so I'd advise you to think about visiting Oshogbo on the way to somewhere else.

## Getting there and away

From Ibadan, a minibus will cost around N200 on a potholed road (where we saw giant snails and a dead civet cat for sale on the side of the road). Oshogbo's motor park is spread haphazardly around Okefia Road and the two roundabouts near Dugbe Market. From here you can find vehicles to Lagos, Ilorin, Oyo, Ife, Benin City and Ibadan. Just walk around and someone will show you which area you need to be in for a vehicle going in your direction. The train station is on Alhaji Sonmonu Hassan Road in the event a train ever pulls into Oshogbo again.

## Practicalities

All Oshogbo **taxis** are painted the same colour – blue with a yellow stripe over the top and middle. Most city transport is by way of *okada*s, or shared taxis that go up and down the major streets, and a short ride will cost N30 on either. The **post office** is at the north end of Station Road, whilst **NITEL** is to the south, towards King's Market (just look for the tower).

## Where to stay and eat

By far the nicest place to stay in Oshogbo, and a very peaceful retreat, is the **Nike Ambassador Guest House**. It's roughly 6km to the west of the gallery, almost in the countryside, at Ido Osun Junction on the Ede Road (go the Nike Gallery; tel: 035 242254, first, to tell them of your arrival and the staff will direct you). This is one of Nike Davies-Okundaye's houses and you must pre-arrange a visit here at her gallery in Lagos (see page 163). It's a big house in lovely gardens in a quiet suburb and ambassadors have stayed here, hence the name. There are over a dozen rooms in two bright white blocks, with several living and dining rooms all decorated with art from Nike's shops, and extras include slippers and dressing gowns in the rooms. Only two of the rooms are en suite, but there are several palatial bathrooms. Meals are served on a balcony or on the grassy lawns where ducks, peacocks, antelope and turkeys wander around. Nike can also organise a cultural troupe to entertain at the guesthouse with singing and dancing. Rates start from N15,000 per room and N750 per meal, and there's coffee, tea and beer available.

One of the better choices for budget travellers is the **Hotel Heritage International** on Gbongan/Ife Road (behind the Coca-Cola bottling plant, and well signposted off the main road); tel: 035 241881, 240228. Rooms are in three big blocks painted brightly outside, but they are very dark once inside, with old furniture, but nevertheless clean and good value. The better and newer rooms are in the blocks in the car park, but they fill up quickly – arrive early to get one of these. It's a great spot if you are in a party mood, as there's a big and lively bar with comfy old red velvet booths, loads of cold beer and a brand new, large-screen satellite TV showing football, and quite remarkably a disco at the weekends that goes on until 08.00! You can get food here, but you'll wait at least an hour. When I asked what they had I got 'rice and plantain, rice, fried rice, egg and rice, and bread and rice' – you'll get to love those carbohydrates! There's also a chop house in the car park for suya. Rates are a good value N1,265 (N2,000 deposit) for a standard double with a fan and a bucket and N1,955 (N3,000 deposit) for a room with AC and a shower; all rooms have local TV and a fridge, and are inclusive of the 15%. A suite with an extra living room is N3,000 plus. This hotel is owned by the artist Jimoh Buraimoh (see below) who sometimes pops in for a beer in the evening.

If you ask around town for a hotel you will be directed to the Osun **Presidential Hotel** on Old Ikirun Road, as it's the state hotel, but it's terribly run

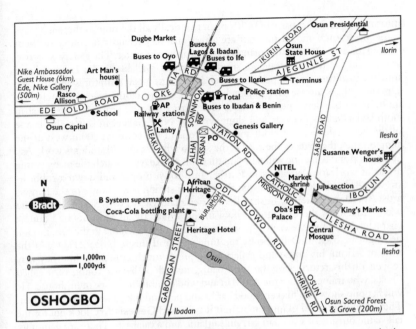

down. Even worse is the **Terminus Hotel** on Ajegunle Street – someone sits in reception and hands out keys, but it's nigh-on derelict. Avoid. The **Osun Capital Hotel** (Ede Road; tel: 035 240396) is newly painted outside, but pretty seedy inside, with dusty halls and peeling paint. There are 20 basic rooms with buckets, the water supply is very hit and miss, and there's no parking, but it's cheap and the sheets and tiles in the bathroom are clean. The restaurant serves Nigerian starch and there's a busy bar that keeps going well into the night. A single is N850, a double N1,600, or N2,100 for AC and a TV. Add another N200 for the deposit. The **Rasco Allison Hotel** (Ede Road; tel: 035 240705) has 16 rooms in a big concrete block in a compound with limited parking. It's grimy but the rooms are big, with new fans and satellite TV. There's a communal living room and you can get Nigerian meals sent to your room. A double is N1,500 (N2,500 deposit) and a single is N1,000 (N1,500 deposit). The **Lanby Restaurant** (3 Alekuwolo Street) is a clean, single-storey detached building with a big sign where you can get cheap and filling food-is-ready and soft drinks for less than N500. Oshogbo's biggest surprise is the **B System Supermarket** on Gbongan Road, which has a very exciting variety of things for sale, and it's open quite late if you get stuck for something to eat in the evening. You'll find things like Mars bars, Twix and other chocolate bars, Pringles, peanut butter and loads of booze, from scotch and gin to Baileys and Amarula (South Africa's version of Baileys). I never saw these for sale anywhere else in Nigeria. More useful items include batteries and razor blades.

## What to see and do
### Art galleries
Oshogbo is renowned for its art and other than the galleries, you may be approached in the street by hopeful artists who offer their cards and invite you to their studios or homes to look at their work. To the east of Oshogbo on Old Ede Road (tel: 035 242254) is the **Nike Gallery**, a studio and shop of one of Nigeria's most celebrated artists, Nike Davies-Okundaye (see the *Lagos* chapter for more

information on Nike, page 163). It's open practically all the time as there is always someone around, and all the staff are artists and very friendly (a couple of them danced for us!). Dotun is the manager and an abstract painter. The gallery is on two stories and the items on sale are similar to what's available in the Lagos gallery; unusual furniture, batiks, paintings, wood carvings, metal sculptures and baskets. Upstairs (the staircase is completely carved) is the cloth; readymade clothes, quilting, embroidery, antique Hausa cloth that's over 80 years old, *aso-eke* strip cloth and *adire* indigo cloth, and along with the Nike Gallery in Lagos, this is one of the best collections of cloth and art there is in the country; 500m west of the shop on the other side of the road is the studio where some 70 students work. Ask at the shop and someone will take you there on weekdays to watch the many young artists at work for a small dash. Further into town proper and down a rubbish-strewn alley off Ede Road near the Boras petrol station is the house of the famous artist **Art Man** (Nike's ex-husband), otherwise known as Twins Seven Seven, who was a student of the Oshogbo School in the 1960s. By all accounts he's quite a character, but when we visited he was lecturing in Philadelphia in the US, though he might be back in Oshogbo by the time you read this; tel: 035 233349. At the time of writing his house and gallery were pretty much closed up, but they may reopen on his return. For the time being, next door lives a young man called Osaka, who trained under the Art Man and who exhibits his work in his house. He will happily show you his very good batiks and pen and ink paintings on rice paper. There's another good gallery on Station Road called **Genesis Art**; look out for the tall statue outside of a woman carrying a flame and a calabash. There are paintings, wood carvings and metal sculptures. At the **Africa Heritage Gallery**, in a big house just off Odi Olowo Road at 1 Buraimoh Street (tel: 035 241864; www.buraimoh.com) is a wonderful display of vividly coloured abstract paintings made from tiny beads and oil paint by artist Jimoh Buraimoh (so famous they named the street after him). If he is at home (he frequently exhibits in the US) you will meet him, and he's a charming man. Some of his work is sold through galleries in London and New York, and he has four paintings on display in the National Gallery in Lagos. He's the first painter to be known to use tiny glittering beads in his art; the same method is used to decorate Yoruba traditional royal cloaks and crowns, and each painting takes two to three weeks to make. His work is expensive but stunning, and if you want to buy, he can ship paintings abroad and accepts payment into his US bank account. You can visit his house and gallery any day before 17.00. He's also the main organiser of the Osun Festival (see below).

## The town

There's a cluster of sights around the crossroads of Catholic Mission Street and Osun Shrine Road. The **central mosque** is on the southeastern corner and is a large domed building with an 'Islamic' market outside selling worry beads, Korans and stickers of Allah and, oddly, of Jesus. There are few mosques in the southern regions and Muslims often have to resort to open prayer compounds – indeed, many of the southern states forbid the building of mosques. Opposite the mosque is the **King's Market** where you might want to gawp at the teeming *juju* section, where we saw python skins and domestic cat's heads. It's in the north of the market on the Sabo Road side. Behind the market, follow Ibokun Street for a couple of hundred metres and you'll get to **Susanne Wenger's house** (Adunni is her Yoruba name), with its large keyhole-shaped door. It's a weird-looking house behind a huge flowering tree on four stories, and is quite broken down, with lots of kids and chickens running around outside. There is a line of chairs where we met her doctor (who was having his nails done by International Finger Cutter Man at the time!) who allowed us to look in the first floor of the house, where there are some of her sculptures and statues similar to those found in the Sacred Forest (see below). Her art is very surreal and she uses a lot of symbolism, and the room is quite spooky and eerie. Susanne Wenger still lives here and it's possible to visit her (she lives on the second floor), but she's quite frail and almost 90 now, and by all accounts quite kooky; when she got to Oshogbo in the 1950s she became a born-again Yoruba and later a high priestess.

Opposite the market is the **Market Shrine**, a low building made from brown earth with a rusted roof that is so dilapidated it leans to one side and has a tree growing in part of it. This was the original Oba's Palace, and could feasibly be quite old. If you look through the door edged with carved wooden door posts, you'll see a line of broken thrones. Also at this crossroads is the dilapidated **Oba's Palace** – the entrance is opposite the Market Shrine, but there's nothing really to see except another line of old thrones under a balcony. Once through the various buildings you'll find (with difficulty) the **Oba's Shrine** in a squat building painted red and black, where you might be invited inside – but don't bother. There's nothing to see inside. There's also a small museum but it was firmly shut when we visited and it looked like it had been for some time. Along Catholic Mission Street to the northwest are a number of two-storey buildings characterised by **Brazilian architecture** (see page 117).

## The Sacred Forest

The Osun Sacred Groves and Forest (open daily 10.00–18.00) are Oshogbo's main attraction, if not one of the biggest attractions in Nigeria (all the signs for them say 'Sacred Grooves' – this kept us giggling for a long time). In the traditional Yoruba religion groves are sacred places reserved for rituals or shrines. The forest is a 75ha patch of delightful, butterfly-filled greenery that was once inhabited by the early settlers and founders of Oshogbo some 400 years ago (see box). Despite being completely surrounded by Oshogbo, the forest supports a remarkable diversity of monkeys, birds, snakes, forest antelopes and other fauna. The sacred nature of the forest means that it is protected, and none of the animals are hunted because they are regarded as physical manifestations of the goddess Osun. This is a rare example of protected rainforest in Nigeria, and an example of conservation as a local initiative, where indigenous people have endeavoured to protect their culture and their environment. Many of the animals in the groves, particularly the monkeys, are fairly tame and easy to see as they jump around overhead in the trees. The artist Susanne Wenger has done much to revive the cult of Osun in recent decades, and together with Yoruba artists, she restored the site from the 1950s and created many strange and interesting sculptures and shrines, which you can wander around with a guide on a forest trail that winds throughout the forest.

To get there it's a N50 hop on an *okada* or N100 for a drop taxi from town, but you can easily walk the 700–800m from the King's Market down Osun Shrine Road, and the chances are you will have to walk back as there is no transport around the groves. On the road leading up to the entrance are clay walls with abstract figures on them, and on the main gate are elaborate abstract metal sculptures of elephants, mermaids, soldiers and farmers. Why these particular figures have been grouped together is beyond me. Entry is N100, plus dash for the guide; N500 for a camera; N2,500 for a video camera; and a staggering N20,000 if you want to take commercial photos (it's on the price list!). There's a thatched reception area with a few curios for sale, and as there are no refreshments, bring water, as it's a hot walk around the forest.

In the grove there are sculptures and artistic impressions representing various gods and goddesses. Each one is essentially a reflection of the activities, life and

## THE OSUN FESTIVAL

The Osun (sometimes spelt Oshun) Festival usually takes place on the second Friday in August, and is popular enough to be shown live on state TV. If you are in Nigeria at that time foreigners are allowed to attend, but you must get permission from the Osun priests first. Osun is the Yoruba word meaning 'water of life' and is given to the river goddess who is the spiritual mother of Oshogbo and an important deity in the Yoruba religion. Legend has it that she was the youngest of the three wives of Shango, the god of thunder, who was at one time also alafin (king) of Oyo. Oba and Oya were his other wives but Osun was his favourite. This resulted in Oya and Osun having a fight and Osun left Oyo and went on to marry Larooye, who created Oshogbo (loosely translated as the place of wizards) some half a millennium ago. Larooye and his migrant people were cutting down a tree to build huts for a new settlement when the tree fell into the river and the forest, in a loud and furious voice, shouted 'pele o, Osogbo ikoko aro mi le ti fo tan' – meaning 'in the forest, all my dye pots have been broken by you.' In appeasement Larooye and his people offered a sacrifice to the gods of the forest and the river. In response the gods instructed Larooye to move his settlement to higher ground away from the river's floodplains and pledged abundant blessing and protection of the people. The banks of the river became Osun's centre of activities and the sacred waters were renamed the Osun River. She became learned in medicine and the water of the river was said to have the healing power to cure infertility. When the river burst its bank, Osun was said to have made offerings to it to appease its anger, as people still do today during the Osun festival. Osun became a Yoruba goddess and was also credited for playing a part in protecting Oshogbo during the Fulani jihad in the early 19th century, when she disguised herself as a food seller and sold poisoned bean soup to the Fulani enemies and caused a fatal epidemic in their war camp. The Osun Festival is regarded as a celebration of the founding of Oshogbo, commemorating the pact or marriage of Larooye and Osun. The 16-day Osun festival still asks the gods for protection, and during rituals the priests lay down their offerings and sacrifices to the statue of Osun standing next to the river with her arms open, indicating she is the goddess of care, protection, cure and mother to all. On the last day a maid of Osun carries a symbolic calabash at the head of a procession of worshippers, chiefs and priests, through the Oshogbo Sacred Forest, to present to Osun, and to ask for blessing and protection for all the people of Oshogbo.

preoccupations of the gods whilst they established Oshogbo. Some of these are the first market, the first palace and courtyard, shrine and temple. The sculptures are scattered through the forest on either side of the approach road, but from the main entrance you are led firstly to Oya Grove, which reaches a tranquil spot on the Osun River, where there is the statue of Osun built beneath giant sycamore trees. The river is full of tangled vines and surrounded by ferns and you have to look carefully amongst the rocks and tree roots to see some of the smaller statues and figurines, as they are overgrown and covered in moss. Other shrines and statues depict the various gods, and one very tall structure is called *Aiye Dakun Yipada*, literally meaning 'the world, I beg you to reconsider your ways'. Obatala, the white god, who is responsible for giving people human form, is represented in a statue where he sits with hands stretched towards heaven on the top of an elephant, and surrounding the base of the elephant are lions, his messengers. Another statue of three elderly men holding hands represents compromise. Over the river is an old suspension bridge that has nothing to do with the shrines – it was built in 1936 by a Welsh colonial officer. It's just about falling down now, but there are nice views from it of the meandering river. Away from the river and further into the forest are other statues, some several metres high, including two alien-looking creatures with giant teeth, a massive chameleon, and one of Lyamaro, the messenger of Osun, which has a big eye, tentacle-like legs and several pointing arms, that has to be over 12m tall. Another is of Obaluaye, another messenger of Osun, which has a fly-like head and a mix of spidery legs and arms beneath which people are begging. Ela, another messenger, is a very straight sculpture over 20m high with hands outstretched to the sky. Another imposing statue is that of Lyamapo, the god of all women's craft, including childbirth. She is represented on her back with her children at her feet and with three pairs of arms which gesture advice, blessing, and regrets. The meaning of this is that if you take positive advice you will be blessed and if you don't you will regret it. She also has wings to represent her supernatural power of flight. They all must have looked very surreal when they were first made in the 1950s. The first-ever market in Oshogbo is said to be the Oja Ontotoo – a market for supernatural and subterranean beings represented by a fantastic market scene of heavenly and earthly characters riding to market on flying tortoises, pigs, elephants, and giant snakes.

At the end of the tour you will be expected to give a small dash to the Osun priest who sits at reception, as well as to the guide. Recently some work has been done to restore a few of the statues and the receptionist told us that they had tried using different mixes of concrete and sand and were waiting a year to see which mix lasted better. This is a weird and wonderful place and the sculptures are completely unique and mysterious, but after 50 years they are somewhat weather-beaten; all the more reason, then, why their preservation is imperative.

# OYO

Oyo, 52km north of Ibadan, is a bustling town of perhaps 250,000 people, but there isn't really anything to see or do, though you are quite likely to pass through it on the way to somewhere else. If that is the case, then it's worth jumping off a bus or pulling over to visit the drum shops (see below). It has some old Portuguese-style houses with rusting brown roofs similar to those in Ibadan, and is best known as the capital of the old Oyo Empire, established by the Yoruba, which controlled a wide area between the Niger and the Volta rivers in present-day Ghana in the mid-17th century, and which was the biggest of the Yoruba kingdoms. According to legend, Ile (old) Oyo was established by Oduduwa's son, Oranmiyan (of the Ife staff fame – above), some time around the 12th century on a site north of modern Oyo in what is today Old Oyo National Park. Because of frequent spats with neighbouring communities in the 16th century, the Kingdom of Oyo established an army of 1,000 foot soldiers and 1,000 horses; the area was relatively free of tsetse fly so horses could be used for war and transport in the region. From then until the early 18th century the Oyo army was highly developed and went about conquering neighbouring lands, and was the largest political unit in Yorubaland, if not West Africa, during the mid-17th century, and remained so until the Yoruba wars in the 1820s–30s, when the Oyo Empire all but collapsed when they lost against the invading jihadists from the north. Ile-Oyo was abandoned and many Oyo refugees either fled to Ibadan or further south, where they founded the city of Oyo in its present location. Oyo is still referred to as 'the city of warriors'. The British bombarded the capital in 1895 with shells, and burnt down the *alafin*'s palace, though the alafin was permitted to stay in Oyo under the British system of indirect rule.

## Getting there and away

Minibuses and bush taxis pick up and drop off at the motor park opposite the Mobil petrol station, a few metres south of the Agip petrol station on the Ilorin–Ibadan road as it goes through the district of Owode in the centre of town. There are frequent vehicles between here and Ibadan and to Ilorin to the north, 109km away via Ogbomoso. In Ilorin you'll need to change vehicles to get anywhere north, whilst in Ibadan you'll need to change to get to Lagos and the south, or any point east. All the roads in any direction from Oyo are full of potholes.

## Where to stay and eat

If you need to stay overnight in Oyo, then the **La Bamba** (tel: 038 240443, 240444), roughly 1km south of Owode on the Ibadan road, is the best hotel in town. There are 50 well-kept chalets (pronounced by the staff as it is spelt – take the French accent off the word to make *shalett*) in unusually expansive grounds full of flame and neem trees. The complex is set a few hundred metres back from the road, though the first thing you'll see is the open-air chop stall and bar just within the gate, which according to my *okada* driver sells the best *suya* in town. You order meals from reception and beers and soft drinks from the fridge behind the reception desk, and everything will be delivered to your room. Choice depends on what is available in the kitchen, so expect a plate of *jollof* rice and chicken and the like for around N600 plus 15%. Built in 1979 the décor in the rooms hasn't changed much, but there's running water and DSTV. From outside the hotel gate you can flag down a minibus to Ibadan. Room rates start at N2,875 for a standard double (N3,500 deposit). Overlanders could try and negotiate camping here as there's loads of grass and space for vehicles. Budget travellers might want to try the **Oyo Merry Guest House** (tel: 038 230344), located conveniently on the main Agip roundabout in Owode, and close to the drum shops. Here there are a few spartan rooms above a grey and white building and a large room full of plastic chairs used as the New Covenant Church. Ask nicely and they might let you stay, but on Sundays and most weekends the room is packed to the gills with fervent worshippers. A double is approximately N1,200 but there's no food available. Around the corner on Oyo Road, opposite the AP petrol station, is the **'D' Bar**, serving beers, malt drinks and soft drinks, and next to it is **Tasty Bites**, that probably serves cheap chop, though it didn't look particularly functional when I visited. Other than that, you will have to rely on *suya* stalls around the market, where you may also be able to find palm wine.

## What to see and do

Yoruba drums and calabashes are for sale on Oyo Road in Owede. There are two shops next to each other that are well worth a visit – the first selling predominantly drums, and the second selling carved calabashes – about 100m north of the Agip roundabout on the left-hand side. If you are in your own car there is reasonable space to pull up and park directly outside. The drum shop is the Owode Co-operative. A big drum is called an *iya ilu*, a small drum a *kanango,* and there are also the famous Yoruba talking drums called *dundun*. Also for sale is a selection of leather bags, poufs and fans, plus some wood carvings, and the traders are happy to let you 'look for free' without too much hassle. Most of the items have prices on, but you could try a spot of bargaining with the good-natured traders. Prices vary from N6,000–10,000 for a large free-standing drum to N600 for a hand-held drum – considerably cheaper than in Lagos's markets. Perhaps unique to this shop (I certainly didn't see them anywhere else) are the hand drums called *sakara,* which are made by stretching a piece of skin over a clay ring and which are beaten with a bamboo stick decorated with scraps of material called a *congo.* All of the drums have stickers on them with the name of the person who made them. In the second shop next door are carved and painted calabashes. There's another drum and craft shop just a few minutes' walk away to the south of the Mobil petrol station, more or less opposite the motor park, and more calabashes can be found in the main market where you might see them being worked on. The main market is called Akesan Market, and Akesan Market Road goes west from the main Agip roundabout. Catch a minibus for about a kilometre and ask to be dropped off at the post office; the myriad streets to the market are opposite the post office. Just ask around and someone will point out the calabash stall, which is only a few metres in amongst the piles of yams and buckets of bright red palm oil used to make the fiery *jollof* rice.

## Around Oyo

Heading north from Oyo along the A1, the main road that neatly bisects the west of Nigeria all the way to Sokoto in the far north, you'll pass though some of the other Yoruba towns, but there's little reason to stop. There are frequent vehicles going up and down the A1 from centre to centre, and you're most likely to be travelling along this road if you're heading towards Lake Kainji National Park (see page 267). It's worth noting that this road is a blackspot for accidents, as attested to by the mangled wrecks on the side of the road, and it's horrendously busy. From Ibadan through to Ilorin it's potholed and fairly hilly, and drivers of big trucks think nothing of overtaking when going up hills. Between Ilorin and Mokwa, where it crosses the River Niger, there's a new and broad highway that hasn't been opened yet, and traffic still uses the old road alongside. Work on this road started and then stopped goodness knows when (I heard a rumour that the government was in huge debt to the foreign-owned road-building companies) so when this will be finished and opened is anyone's guess. For now people graze their cows on the grass that has grown on the new embankments and kids play football on the unfinished gravel surface.

You'll quite likely pass through unremarkable **Ogbomosho**, 53km north of Oyo, that was thought to have been established by the Yoruba in the 17th century. It resisted **Fulani** invasions in the early 19th century and grew rapidly by absorbing refugees from other towns destroyed by the Fulani. Today it is a sprawling industrial centre and there's nothing to see. The same can be said of **Ilorin**, 66km further north along the A1, though you are likely to swap vehicles in Ilorin's sprawling motor park if heading further north or east. It's a large market city for livestock and vegetables, and as part of the Fulani Empire in the 19th century it has a strong Muslim influence, and at just over 300km northeast of Lagos, is considered to be the gateway of the south–north, Christian–Muslim religious divide. Ilorin was the capital of a **Yoruba** kingdom that, with the assistance of the **Fulani**, successfully rebelled against the **Oyo** Empire in 1817. Then, in the 1820s, it became a Muslim emirate associated with the Fulani caliphate of **Sokoto**, and increased its territory through wars against Oyo and **Ibadan** in the late 19th century. In 1897, it was conquered by troops of the British-chartered Royal Niger Company, led by Sir George **Goldie**. If you get stuck here, try the **Kwara State Hotel** (Ahmadu Bello Avenue; tel: 031 221490). It's another white elephant of a state hotel and not brilliant, and the Chinese restaurant here is about the only place to eat non-Nigerian food.

## OLD OYO NATIONAL PARK

Old Oyo National Park covers an area of 2,512km² and was established in 1991, when it was carved out of the Upper Ogun Game Reserve that was first established in 1936. It's located in the northern part of Oyo State, roughly two hours' drive from Oyo on rough roads, and you'll only get there in your own vehicle. Very few people visit the park and it's only open in the dry season between December and April, so you'll need to be completely self-sufficient, and whilst there are four very basic chalets at Ibuya within the park, don't expect them to be functional or open. The park entrance is at the village of Sepeteri (on arrival ask around for the gateman, who will perhaps have a vague idea of how much it is to get in). From Oyo it's approximately 160km to Sepeteri, on a back road through Kwara State via Iseyin, a large Yoruba agricultural town. There is very little reliable information on what species exist in the park, and for years it has suffered from mismanagement and neglect. Park rangers know little about the interior of the park, and hunting, cattle grazing, logging and bush-burning have gone on undeterred. Villages surround the park boundaries, and the species that do still exist are restricted to small, remote areas of the park. The terrain is savanna scrub with patches of tropical rainforest along the rivers, and whilst it was once home to lion and elephant, the chances of these still being present in the park are virtually zero, though it may still be home to a few species of antelope, baboons, black and white colobus monkeys, and possibly a few hardy buffalo. The national park also contains the ruins of the ancient Yoruba city of Ile-Oyo, the historical capital of the Oyo Empire (see above), but nothing has been done to protect them and very few people even know where they are. The Old Oyo National Park office is on the outskirts of Oyo on Iseyin Road (tel: 038 240125, 240690). There is a signpost at the Agip petrol station at the roundabout in the centre of town from where you follow Akesan Market Road, but with the headquarters being located so far away from the park itself, the management effectively do not run the park, and quite frankly this is just another fine example of civil servants in a government institution being employed to do and know nothing.

## BENIN CITY

The capital of Edo State is Benin City, which is famous for its unique bronze, brass and ivory works of art. Modern Benin City is a rapidly developing metropolis and the centre of Nigeria's rubber industry, but there are a few reminders of its long and turbulent history. The old city's moat and wall survive in places, and the National Museum houses an interesting collection of Benin royal art. Benin is to the west of Igboland, and it's mainly populated by the Edo and Bini people, hence its name.

An early traveller, a Mr Cyril Punch, wrote of Benin before it was destroyed in 1897:

> Benin has an extraordinary fascination for me which I cannot explain. All the rest of West Africa that I know is squalid. Benin in the old days was more than squalid, it was gruesome…No-one who went there came away without being impressed.

Benin served as the capital of the Benin Kingdom, which ruled much of the Yoruba, Igbo, Ijo, and Itsekiri peoples, and was probably founded in the 13th century. According to legend the warrior Oranmiyan stalked south from Ife and married a local woman. Their son Eweka became the first oba of Benin and the palace was thought to have been built during his reign. The kingdom flourished from the 14th–17th centuries, when it was ruled under the dynamic leadership of a chain of warrior kings and traditional obas. Benin City was the first inland settlement to be visited by the Europeans, despite not being near the sea or having a river port, but the reputation of the Benin civilisation motivated the Portuguese in the 15th century to seek it out. By the early 16th century, Benin Kingdom had sent an ambassador to Lisbon, and in return, the king of Portugal had sent missionaries to Benin. Portuguese was to remain the foreign language for the Benin aristocracy for centuries, and elements of the language have continued to survive in palace circles even today. Early trade items included cowries, ivory, pepper, and palm products. Although some slaves were exchanged for goods, Benin was not a slave-dealing nation, preferring to use its manpower and prisoners of war as construction workers, to build and maintain the royal palace, the expansive residencies of the aristocracy, and the city walls, moats, and ditches that surrounded the city. At the height of the Benin Kingdom, great walls were built between 1450 and 1550, and the city was split up into the Oba's Palace and 40 wards, and the network of walls stretched from the city and enclosed the surrounding villages in a radius of over 100km. There could have perhaps been over 5,000km of wall. These walls enclosed over 500 compounds and were 9m tall at their highest. Then the palace is said to have been flanked by an enormous gate of two towers, each surmounted by a bronze python some 15m long. The walls were made of red mud but the inside was thought to be very ornate and full of ivory, brass, and iron figures and bronze busts. In each of the city's wards were communities of artisans who made items to decorate the palace. Benin is known predominantly for its 15th-century wax bronzes, which are considered to be some of the finest African ancient art.

The Benin Kingdom declined after 1700, and not much is known of what went on in the city before the British arrived. The conquest of Benin in 1897 was sparked by the massacre of the British consul and his party, who were on their way to investigate reports of ritual human sacrifice. Human sacrifice was going on, but it was assumed that this was a last-ditch effort by the oba at the time to appease the gods and stop the encroachment of the British, and in the only way he knew. Here is a chilling account from a member of the British party that attacked Benin, a Captain Alan Boisragon, who wrote in *The Benin Massacre* in 1898:

> As we neared Benin City we passed several human sacrifices, live woman slaves gagged and pegged on their backs to the ground, the abdominal wall being cut in the form of a cross, and the uninjured gut hanging out. Men slaves, with their hands tied at the back and feet lashed together, also gagged, were lying about. As we neared the city, sacrificed human beings were laying in the path and bush – even in the king's compound the sight and stench of them was awful. Dead and mutilated bodies were everywhere – by God! May I never see such sights again! In the King's compound, on a raised platform or altar, beautiful idols were found. All of them were caked over in human blood. Lying about were big bronze heads, dozens in a row, with holes in the top, in which immense carved ivory tusks were fixed. The whole place reeked of blood. Fresh blood was dripping off the figures and altars.

On discovering these atrocities, the British promptly ransacked the palace of its artwork, massacred most of the heathen people, and torched the city. That was the end of the Benin Kingdom. Boisragon went on to say:

> ...fire, smoke and charcoal seemed to have removed all the smell, and the city became sweet and pure again.

The British took an estimated 5,000 pieces of artwork, and only the few that escaped their notice remain in the Benin Museum and Lagos Museum. Much of it was sold off in Europe (some of it is in the British Museum), but most has never been recovered. The reigning oba was exiled to Calabar where he died in 1913, and a new palace was built by his son; it was said to be about a tenth of the size of the old one.

## Getting there and away

There are several daily flights between Benin City and Lagos (40 minutes) with Associated Aviation and Capital Airlines, both of which have desks at the Motel Benin Plaza, but as the airport is only 2km from the centre to the south west, it's just as easy to go straight there. Discoop Buses runs a service to Lagos directly from its terminal at 8 Dawson Road, which is very centrally located, and Lagos is about a four-hour journey. In Lagos, vehicles to and from Benin City generally drop off at the Ojota Motor Park, and it costs roughly N500 for this journey. There are several other motor parks also close to the centre of town, and you should find a bus going in any direction from up and down Urubi Street, where vehicles are clumped together in little groups close to the petrol stations. Alternatively, Delta Lines depart from the Edo Delta Hotel. From here you'll be able to get to any of the southwestern towns, as well as Onitsha and Warri (dealt with in the *Southeastern Nigeria* chapter; see page 205).

## Practicalities

**City transport** is mostly in the shape of red and yellow and shared taxis, and minibuses go up and down the main roads. Expect to pay around N20 per ride. *Okada*s are reasonably cheap and you can get just about anywhere for N50. Benin City is fairly easy to navigate around, with most things of interest being centred around King's Square, which is not a square at all but an enormous roundabout with the **museum** in the middle of it. There are a number of **internet** places opposite the Total and Mobil petrol stations on Akpakpava Road. Try Presok Cyber Café at number 128, which was the cheapest internet access I think I found in Nigeria, at N70 per hour and N250 for night surfing after 21.00, or the Sy Cyber Café at number 90, which charges N100 per hour; both are open 24 hours. If you need to **change money** there is a line of bureaux de change between about 40 and 50 Sakpoba Road.

## Where to stay and eat
### Mid-range: above US$25

**Motel Benin Plaza** 1 Reservation Rd, GRA; tel: 052 254779; www.motelbeninplaza.com. The highlight here is the great bar around a small swimming pool under fans with big sofas, a big range of spirits and a live band most nights. There's also a *suya* spot here, and it's a fun place when there's football on the strategically placed TVs. The lovely restaurant has white tablecloths, good service, some wine, and continental dishes for around N1,200. Alternatively, try mud fish or cow intestine pepper soup in the bar! The comfortable rooms are in chalets with motel-style parking. Rates start at N5,175 (N9,000 deposit) for a single, N5,750 (N10,000 deposit) for a double, and suites start at N8,050 (N13,000 deposit), plus the 15%.

**Saidi Centre** 271 Murtala Muhammed Way (between Sapele and Sakpoba roads); tel: 052 250460, 252125, 255632. This is a totally kitsch place, with all sorts of different décor, and it looks a bit like a castle complete with turrets and all. There are psychedelic murals, curved staircases and gilt mirrors, and the restaurant has very Arabic décor, with lots of gold and padded booths, and is in an old disco equipped with a glittering DJ's podium. The main courses start from N1,000, and the chef will have a stab at continental food, such as chicken chasseur or 'mixed drill'. You might be better off sticking to the oriental dishes, given that the chef is Chinese. The fabulous pool has deep blue tiles and crystal clear water, and the pool bar is a big meeting place for expats working in Warri, and it serves up *suya* and *shawarmas*. Rooms have balconies or patios, and rates are N5,500–N8,000 for a double, and for suites or apartments with two bedrooms and a lounge area, N11,000 plus the 15%.

**Hotel Felona** 6 Dawson Rd; tel: 052 251194. A good option and fairly new, the four-storey block only opened in 2002, so consequently everything is quite fresh, and this a good-value, mid-range hotel with reliable power and water. The large restaurant and comfortable bar is wood-panelled, with a good atmosphere and proper tablecloths and napkins, and there's lots of chicken on the menu and some attempt at western dishes. There's good security with parking behind a manned boom gate. A double goes for N4,025 (N6,000 deposit) inclusive of the 15%.

## Budget: below US$25

**Lixborr Hotel** 4 Sakpoba Rd; tel: 052 256699. This is in a big compound with a snack bar in the car park selling meat pies and drinks, and there are larger-than-life statues of a drummer and mother and child at the front door. It's the best-value hotel in town, with 40 rooms on three stories, and it's in a great location, right opposite the bronze casters on Igun Street. There's a very comfortable modern bar and restaurant, with reasonable Nigerian and some continental dishes for around N700, and it's deservedly popular, so you may need to try and get through by phone to make a reservation. The rooms have working showers in tiled bathrooms, new AC units and fans, and DSTV, and a double goes for N2,800 (N3,500 deposit) inclusive of the 15%.

**Central Hotel** 90 Akpakpava Rd; tel: 052 250536. Rooms here are gloomy but functional, with buckets in the bathroom, grumbling old AC units and big beds. There's limited space for parking, but it's centrally located, with a restaurant and bar on the first floor serving basic Nigerian food-is-ready. A double with a fan and DSTV is N2,000. although it's worth paying N500 more for AC.

**Edo-Delta Hotel** 128–134 Akpakpava St; tel: 052 252722. There is a rabbit warren of rooms here. in chalets and in a two-storey building, behind which is a makeshift church that is hugely noisy on a Sunday morning thanks to the very loud PA system and a very enthusiastic preacher. There's a good bar with cheap food and very friendly staff and there's a kiosk for snacks (and bottles of gin) in the car park. The rooms are basic but there's water in the showers and satellite TVs (in cages) showing BBC World. The smallest rooms with fans are N1,700 and the larger ones with AC start from N2,500.

Around the corner from the Edo-Delta on Lagos Road is the **Unique Kitchen** (look out for the bright blue plastic chairs) which is an illicit palm-wine-drinking joint. To the south of here, **Suzzy restaurant**, at 2 Hudson Lane off Akpakpava Road (open daily 08.00–20.00), is a cheap canteen serving hot and tasty food-is-ready, and a variety of soups and starch, but no booze. It's a yellow building up the lane behind the Mobil petrol station. In other parts of town, there's a branch of **Mr Biggs** at 43 Sapele Road, and the **Rima Restaurant** at 226 Murtala Muhammed Way in the Imaro House (open daily 09.00–22.00) has a snack bar and bakery to the left selling meat pies and sandwiches, and a more formal dining area behind a curtain to the right serving steak and chips with pepper sauce, and some spaghetti dishes for around N900, and a cheaper full Nigerian menu.

## What to see and do

The **National Museum** (open Monday–Friday 09.00–18.00; Saturday–Sunday 10.00–16.00; N20 entry fee) is in the middle of the central roundabout at King's Square. The trouble here is trying to get across the road to it, given that there are several lanes of traffic. Just before the museum is a statue on a tall pillar of the Tomb of the Unknown Soldier, commemorating both world wars. The museum is in a circular building and there are three floors of exhibits, including some of Benin's famous bronze plaques, but unfortunately some of the glass cases are empty, and rather infuriatingly nothing is dated. Most of the plaques are of the obas in traditional or supernatural forms, and they are very detailed, with the tiny obas carrying swords and shields. Some plaques show Portuguese traders holding manilas (used as currency), and one plaque is of the messenger of Ogiuwu, the chief of all executioners – if past inhabitants of the Kingdom of Benin got presented with this, it reputedly sentenced them to death. Also on display is an executioner's sword. Upstairs are masquerade costumes, a replica of a pair of wooden stools sent from Benin to the king of Portugal, with a coiled snake around the stand and monkey heads and snakes at the base, and a big map of what Benin City used to look like, with its wards and walls. On the third floor is an ad hoc display of some Yoruba art and carvings, drums, masks, weapons, musical instruments and old fishing tackle from the Niger Delta.

To the northwest of the roundabout on Oba Market Street is the **Oba's Market**, a big grey concrete block on two levels, which is easy to navigate. Downstairs is fresh food whilst upstairs are manufactured clothes and shoes and lots of impromptu hairdressers on the stairs in between. Nearby, on Mission Road, is a bunch of bookshops; look out for **Jomos Bookshop** at number 3, which has a lot of secondhand novels, and which sells the Spectrum map of Nigeria. The **Central Market** further up Akpakpava Road sells fresh produce, material and everything plastic. It's sort of covered but has big holes in the corrugated roof.

Back at the roundabout and to the southwest is the **Oba's Palace**, in a huge compound with unassuming low wooden buildings, a vast car park and a basketball court! At the gate on Monday–Friday between 08.00 and 16.00 you can ask if there is someone to show you around the grounds for a small dash, but not at the weekends or if there is some function on. Unfortunately there was a function on when I visited, so I am afraid I cannot disclose any details of this tour, though from what I could gather your guide will tell you a bit about the present oba and his role in the city. But instead, I did get to see semi-naked chiefs dressed in beads and white skirts and with oddly shaved heads being led to the Oba's Palace by their teams of little helpers to make an annual thank you to the oba for bestowing them their chiefdoms. Following them was a crowd dressed in their very best clothes and biggest headdresses and hats, shaking calabashes covered in plastic beads (a sort of maraca). It was very colourful, so if you're lucky you might see something similar.

If you follow Sakpoba Road to the east of the roundabout for a few metres, you'll find Igun Street opposite the Lixborr Hotel. This is the home of Benin's **bronze casters**, on a bricked street with an arched entrance that was done up a few years ago from money donated by UNESCO. To the left as you walk up the street is a small café for beer, soft drinks, meat pies and pepper soup. Since old Benin was destroyed the art of bronze casting had been extinct for many decades, until the UNESCO project turned Igun Street into a series of shops and workshops where many young artists turned their attention to bronze casting. There are about 20 stalls here, with the craftsmen working outside each on the street, and hundreds of pieces on display, and despite the fact the traders get very few visitors they don't hassle you too much. The casting technique is as follows: firstly, the bronze caster makes a rudimentary mould out of clay, which he covers in wax and moulds into shape using thin strips of wax to make the relief details. He then covers the statue with more clay and the wax is melted out by holding it over hot charcoal. Then the hot bronze is poured into the space left by the wax and

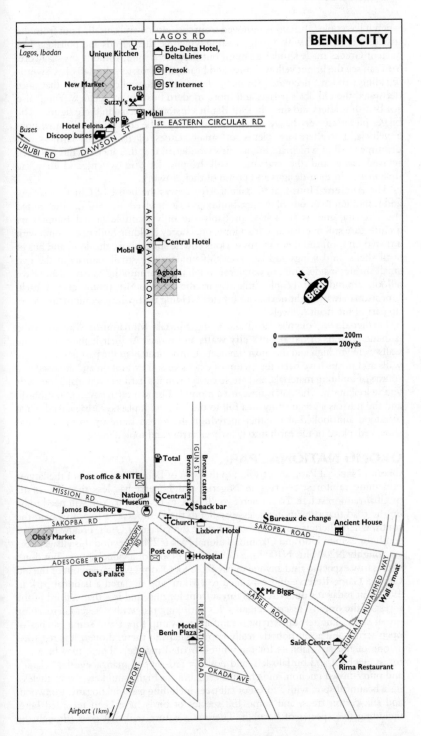

**BENIN CITY**

LAGOS RD

Lagos, Ibadan

Unique Kitchen

New Market

Total

Suzzy's

Agip

Mobil

Hotel Felona

Discoop buses

Buses

URUBI RD

DAWSON ST

AKPAKPAVA ROAD

Edo-Delta Hotel, Delta Lines

Presok

SY Internet

1st EASTERN CIRCULAR RD

Mobil

Central Hotel

Agbada Market

N

Bradt

0 ——— 200m
0 ——— 200yds

Total

IGUN ST

Bronze casters

Bronze casters

BRONZE ST

Post office & NITEL

MISSION RD

Jomos Bookshop

SAKOPBA RD

Oba's Market

National Museum

Central

Snack bar

Church

Lixborr Hotel

Bureaux de change

Ancient House

SAKOPBA ROAD

URMOKOPTA RD

ADESOGBE RD

Oba's Palace

Post office

Hospital

SAFELE ROAD

Mr Biggs

MURTALA MUHAMMED WAY

Wall & moat

RESERVATION ROAD

Motel Benin Plaza

OKADA AVE

Saidi Centre

Rima Restaurant

AIRPORT RD

Airport (1km)

when it has cooled the clay is removed from the outside and chiselled out from the inside, and he is left with a rough casting which he then grinds and polishes. The ancient Greeks made similar castings, but they were solid, without any clay core. You can see the bright yellow figures and heads of elaborately dressed obas, sword-wielding maidens, decorated (bronze) elephant tusks, replicas of items that once decorated the old oba's palace, and more modern busts of local chiefs. You'll also see British soldiers and the whole of Benin's history reflected in these figures. The bigger pieces are very heavy and you are unlikely to be able to shift them without a vehicle, but there are plenty of small statues of fisherman, farmers and drummers, all of which are unique. It's wonderful that this ancient craft has been revived again and the craftsmen will happily let you watch, and they are imaginative in their designs and proud of their artwork.

The **Ancient House**, at 97 Sakpoba Road, was the house of Chief Ogiamen, and is thought to be one of the few buildings that survived the 1897 fire that gutted the old city, and as such it is probably the only example of old Benin City architecture still in existence. It's a long, one-storey building built of red mud with a rusted tin roof, and there are mysterious cowrie shells above the door, and bits of snail shells, bird wings and jaw bones of unidentified small animals in the two small shrines inside. You can wander through the door into the courtyard and have a look around, but people still live in the corridor of rooms at the back. Unfortunately it's right next to an outside welding stall, whose equipment covers up part of the front.

Further down Sakpoba Road and along Murtala Muhammed Way are some pathetic remains of old Benin's **city walls** and moats. At their highest point, the walls were 9m high and the moat 9m deep. Unfortunately in the past few years, the walls and moats have been the victim of extensive soil excavation and are used as a source of building materials, and are so overgrown it's hard to even make out what you're looking at. The wall is now just a mound of brown earth covered in rubbish, and the moat is a green slimy area full to the brim with plastic garbage. And while we stood and looked at it rather incredulously, a man came up to the wall and shovelled a load of the earth into his wheelbarrow and took it away.

## OKOMU NATIONAL PARK

Okomu National Park, about 40km to the west of Benin City, is one of the largest remaining rainforest reserves in Nigeria, and Nigeria has less than 5% of its original rainforest left. To get here, you'll have to be in a car. You will need to be on the road that runs more or less parallel to the Benin–Lagos Expressway to the south, where there is a sign to the park near the village of Orah. Follow this road south for 2km to Udo and Okomu National Park is 20km beyond this village. Fees are roughly N200 plus N100 for a camera and N500 for a video camera, but don't necessarily expect to find anyone to pay these to. Okomu was carved out of the old Ologbo Game Reserve and expanded to 181km$^2$ and declared a national park in 1999. But today it's under serious threat from logging, and less than a third of the forest of the original reserve remains. It's shrinking fast, with villages encroaching on all sides. The terrain is typical rainforest, swamp forest and some patches of open scrub, and again nobody really knows what's in there, though it is regarded as one of the last habitats for the white-throated monkey. There may be a few forest elephant and buffalo left, and possibly red-capped mangabey, the Sclater's and putty-nosed guenon, and chimpanzees, but it's highly unlikely. Nevertheless, it's a beautiful spot, with a forest of tall trees including giant mahogany, ironwood, and silk-cotton trees, and some 150 species of birds have been recorded here, including five species of hornbill. There is a nature trail that goes through the forest, and a ladder up to a viewing platform 50m high in a lofty silk-cotton tree which provides a fantastic panoramic view of the forest. You'll also see many butterflies and birds. If the Arakbuan Stream is full it's possible to swim, and as this stream is also worshipped by the local community you might see bits of snails and chickens left as sacrifices.

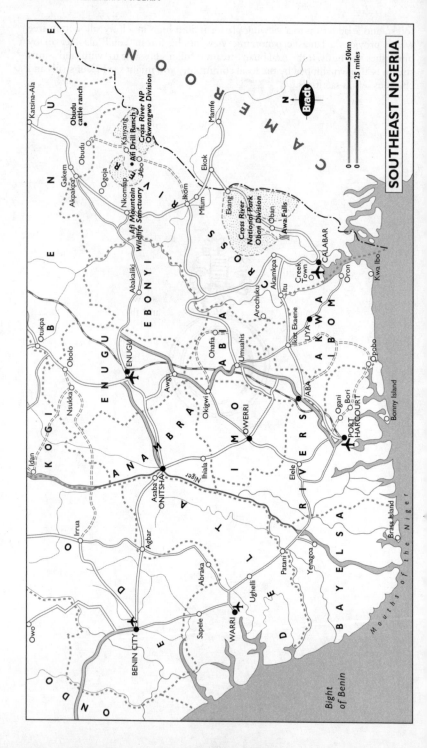

SOUTHEAST NIGERIA

# Southeastern Nigeria

The southeast of Nigeria is crowded with industrial and commercial towns, but away from the urban centres, the region is perhaps the most scenic corner of the country, thanks to the forests of Cross River State and the watery channels of the Niger Delta. This is Igboland, though there are numerous other ethnic groups, and some of those living in the delta still retain traditions that are centuries old. This was the region that proclaimed itself as a Republic in 1967, a move which started the Biafran War, when many of the cities were ravaged by heavy military bombardment, and the Igbo people shifted around the region as the Nigerian army beat and starved them into submission. Going further back in time it was also one of the first regions to be visited by Europeans, firstly during the slave trade and then by early missionaries and colonial officers, whose legacies can still be seen in Old Calabar's 19th-century architecture. You may also see the odd gentleman or chief in this region still dressed in buttoned-up striped shirts and bowler hats carrying umbrellas or walking sticks, as they did at the turn of the 20th century. Calabar is definitely worth heading for, as it's the location of the country's best museum, two excellent primate sanctuaries, and it's a convenient base from which to explore the area around the Cross River National Park, an ancient but fragile patch of beautiful rainforest of enormous trees and craggy peaks. With the exception of Calabar, none of the towns and cities have a great deal to see or do, but you will inevitably find yourself jumping from one to the next even if you don't venture out of the motor parks. This is also the area of Nigeria where the River Niger fans out in endless meandering lagoons and creeks to form the Niger Delta. Here are beautifully forested islands of mangroves and ancient fishing communities, but unfortunately the additional presence of oil has damaged the environment greatly, and damaged the peaceful existence of the delta people, and it's not an especially safe place to venture to.

## ENUGU

The capital of Enugu State is sprawled at the foot of the Udi Hills and is the gateway city to the southeast of Nigeria, and effectively the capital of Igboland. It's a fairly prosperous city with many manufacturing plants around its outskirts, including a vast 7-up bottling plant, a Nigerian Breweries brewery, and a Mercedes assembly plant, and when we visited there was some major road-building going on. It doesn't have a long history, as the Igbo people generally never gathered in cities as the Yoruba did, preferring their village life amongst the watery channels of the Niger Delta. In 1909, a British expedition set out to the Udi Hills to explore for silver but instead located a seam of coal below the village of Enugu Ngwo (*enu ugwu* means top of the hill in Igbo). This was the beginning of Enugu on its present site, referred to as the coal city, and a colliery was opened in 1914 by Lord Lugard, who initially called it Enugu Coal Camp to distinguish it from Enugu Ngwo. The railroad to Port Harcourt was completed in 1912, from where the coal was shipped to Lagos. Coal workers here took part in the general strike of 1945, and again went on strike in 1949 when 21 miners were shot by the British, an incident that fuelled the nationalist movement. Today the coal mines are still here, but the need for coal has fallen away since the railways switched to diesel and then stopped working altogether, though the local cement factory still uses Enugu coal for fuel. Enugu was also the capital of the secessionist state of Biafra (1967–70) and managed to survive the Biafran War pretty much intact.

There is very little to see or do in Enugu, though the **National Stadium** in Enugu hosted the FIFA World Youth Football Championships in 1999. But if you are travelling by public transport there's a good chance that you will change vehicles at Enugu's motor park to get to any point to the southeast from anywhere else in the country. If you do need to spend the night here en route to somewhere else then there are a couple of excellent accommodation options at each end of the budget scale. Finally, there is a **National Museum**, and it's quite good as it is one of a number of museums that opened in the country in 2001. But it's a pig of a place to find, being three kilometres north of the city on Abakaliki Road, and receives so few visitors it is locked most of the time. You'll see the usual display of masquerade costumes, musical instruments, and pots.

## Getting there and away

The **railway station** is on Ogui Street next to the unmissable National Stadium, and the crazy **Ogbete Motor Park** is clustered around Market Road where it joins Okpapra Avenue right in the heart of the city. There are so many vehicles here that the roads are hugely congested and the frantic market along Market Road means that even walking is difficult amongst the throngs of people, animals and cars. However, despite the chaos, the motor park is surprisingly well organised, though you'll have to ask around to find the area for vehicles going to your destination (don't forget the National Union of Road Transport Workers men in the green and white uniforms). There are vehicles to all destinations in the southeast, as well as to Makurdi, Onitsha and Benin City, and overnight 'luxury' buses to Abuja and Lagos. To Abuja, some of these also go during the day. Enugu Airport is roughly 10km north of the city and Sosoliso Airlines; tel: 042 553500, airport desk; tel: 042 557000, desk at Nike Holiday Resort; www.sosolisoairline.com, is presently the only airline serving Enugu, with daily **flights** to and from Lagos and Abuja. To Lagos these go at 07.30, 11.15 and 15.00 on weekdays, and slightly later at the weekends, and flights depart Lagos for Enugu at 09.30, 13.00 and 16.30 on weekdays, on Saturday at 09.30 and 12.00, and on Sunday at 10.15, 13.45 and 17.15. To Abuja flights depart from Enugu at 08.00 and 10.40 on weekdays, 08.00 on Saturday, and 09.00 on Sunday. To Enugu, they depart Abuja at 09.30 and 16.30 during the week, 09.30 on Saturday, and 10.30 on Sunday.

## Where to stay and eat

**Nike Holiday Resort** Nike Lake Rd, Abekpa-Nike Village; tel: 042 557000, 557679; now managed by the South African Protea group; www.proteahotels.com. You can also make a reservation through the South African office, which you may want to consider doing if you want to use a credit card over the phone; tel/fax: +21 (21) 430 5330. This relaxing resort is 7–8km from Enugu. To get there follow the airport road out of town and turn off on to the Onitsha/Abakpa road and follow the signs. The resort is set on the Nike Lake that has rowing boats and short walking trails through the bird-filled surrounding forest. Completely refurbished by Protea, the hotel has 216 luxury rooms and suites with DSTV, minibar, and balconies. There is a mini-golf course, tennis courts, a brand new gym and a large pool. There are also several houses that are rented out to expats working on local projects. There's a hi-tech business centre, a few shops in the lobby, and a big modern restaurant serving buffet meals; lunch is N2,000 and dinner is N2,800. If you want to come here for the weekend from Lagos, for around N1,300 you can make use of the shuttle service between the resort and either the town or the airport. A double is N15,000 (N20,000 deposit); suites start from N24,000 (N32,000 deposit), both including a buffet breakfast but not the 15%.

**Placia Guest House** 25 Edinburgh Rd; tel: 042 251565, 255851. This is a good budget option not far from the motor park, though far enough to get an *okada*. Follow Market Rd south across the railway line and turn right into Zik Av. Edinburgh Rd is opposite the post office. This is a good-value spot with refreshing tiled floors, good bathrooms, high ceilings and DSTV. There is no restaurant or bar, but (very good) Nigerian food and beers are brought to your room and the staff are friendly. Rates for a double start at N2,500 and include tea-bread-and-eggs that is brought to your room in the morning at an allocated time. Across the street from the main gate are a couple of palm wine-drinking joints, and the street vendors sell *suya*, and prepared slices of pineapple and paw paw, and finally there's an internet café on the second floor of the building opposite.

# ONITSHA

Onitsha is a port on the eastern bank of the Niger River just over 100km to the west of Enugu. The growth of Onitsha over the centuries probably derives from its strategic location on the river, and it's believed immigrants from Benin probably established the city in the 16th century. Long before the British arrived it was a centre for trade and a meeting place for a variety of the region's tribes. Despite

## ONITSHA MARKET LITERATURE

In 1857, a British trading station and a Christian mission were established in Onitsha, and most of the earliest missionary and educational institutes in the southeast of Nigeria were established in the city, including Anglican grammar schools and Roman Catholic cathedrals and training colleges. Today the city has perhaps one of the highest concentrations of schools outside of Lagos. In her 1954 book *Four Guineas*, Elspeth Huxley describes a conversation she had in Onitsha about what the rich traders and lawyers in the town spent their money on:

'I asked what they spent their money on, apart from cars and houses. "Educating children – their own and other people's," said the District Officer. "I get at least two applications a week for youngsters to go to the UK to train in every imaginable subject, from electrical engineering to confectionery. Their sponsors pay all the expenses." Onitsha is education mad, and possesses no less than 16 secondary schools.'

Perhaps this history of learning explains the popularity of what is known locally in Nigeria as Onitsha market literature – small, cheaply produced novels, pamphlets and brochures of varying quality written by amateur writers, students, traders, and fledgling journalists, for sale all over Nigeria in the markets or hawked around the motor parks. They are about 50 pages long and printed on hand presses, and are on just about any given subject from money-making schemes and how-to books, to sex and religion. A young girl sitting next to me on a bus was reading *How to Choose a Husband from your Church*.

being in Igboland it has historically been inhabited by people from other parts of the country, and even today there is a large Hausa-Fulani community. Onitsha was hit harder than most during the Biafran War, and was almost completely destroyed by shelling. Today's concrete monstrosities are from the 1970s rebuilding era, and it's a rather ugly, commercial town, with no reason to stay, though you may pass through it and cross Onitsha's rather impressive road bridge over the Niger that was built in 1965 that is a vital link between eastern and western Nigeria. The river is very wide here, perhaps well over a kilometre.

## UMUAHIA

Umuahia straddles the main Enugu–Port Harcourt Expressway roughly 120km south of Enugu. Today, it is an unremarkable town, but it's best known as being the central military headquarters during the Biafran War, though things are very peaceful now. The only reason to stop here is to visit the **National War Museum** which is a worthwhile detour off the expressway. If you are coming from the Enugu direction, get off the vehicle at the roundabout that has a big unmissable sign and statue that says 'Welcome to Abia; God's Own State'. Vehicles stop on the top right-hand corner of this roundabout if you have Enugu behind you, where there is a mini motor park with plenty of bush taxis and minibuses to and from Enugu, Aba and Port Harcourt. To get to the museum you need to take the left-hand road from the roundabout called Mission Hill, that goes east through town proper; the museum is roughly three kilometres on the other side. You will of course need to find a taxi or an *okada* driver that knows where it is but we managed all right. Expect to pay around N200 on an *okada* or N400 in a drop taxi for the journey out there. A couple of hundred metres down this road from the roundabout is the **Novotel International Hotel** at 62 Mission Hill; tel: 088 220440/1, a neat and tidy two-storey hotel with a restaurant and bar and adequate rooms from N2,500 if you get stuck in Umuahia and need to stay the night. But there's no reason why you can't visit the museum on the way to somewhere else.

**The National War Museum** (open daily 10.00–18.00, N20 entry fee). As you can imagine the war museum displays relics of the Nigerian civil war and it is a largely outdoor display of armoured vehicles, artillery and planes, spread about in a field amongst some mango trees. The first thing you'll see on approaching the museum is the 1966 NS *Bonny*, and it comes as quite a shock to see a warship in the middle of a field miles away from the sea. The museum opened in 1985 and is largely a collection of military supplies used by both sides in the Biafran War. The differences between the homemade Biafran items and those made in proper international arms factories are more than evident, and many of the exhibits are usefully displayed next to each other to highlight the differences. An informative guide will show you around for a small dash and he will start at a shed housing the Biafrans' rudimentary 'red devil' armoured cars. These are displayed in chronological order from the first ones built, that are nothing more than simple box-like metal cars, through to the ones later in the war, whose shape had been modified, rocket launchers added, the wheels removed and replaced by tank tracks. They are still not a patch on the meaty Nigerian Russian-built tanks standing next to them, however. Also on display is a homemade, box-like assault boat with an anti-submarine gun and some torpedoes that was used in the sea off Port Harcourt before the Nigerians recaptured the city, and then in the Niger Delta.

Not all the military hardware was hand-made, however; the Biafrans also resorted to using ancient World War II items, including Russian-built heavy artillery guns and anti-tank guns that they had to fix up and make useable again. The

## THE BIAFRAN WAR

Lieutenant Colonel Odemugwu Ojukwu declared the Eastern Region as the Republic of Biafra on May 30 1967, citing the predominant cause for his action as the Nigerian government's inability to safeguard the lives of the Igbo people. The federal military government of Nigeria declared war against the new republic and a brutal and disastrous civil war raged over the next three years and left an estimated 1–3 million dead through fighting and starvation. The Biafran army was an ill-equipped, undermanned, and under-trained rebel force up against a Nigerian army 250,000 strong. Some of Biafra's military supplies came with unofficial assistance from France and its former West African colonies, but it wasn't enough. Meanwhile, the federal government of Nigeria got its artillery, fighter planes and gunboats from the international arms market, with official support from Britain and the Soviet Union. The United States remained neutral. Without international help, the Biafrans resorted to making their own artillery and vehicles, and at the beginning of the war set up a group of engineers, railway workers from Enugu, and university professors to design and assemble fabricated weapons. These people had no experience of making guns or armoured cars and they literally had to invent them from scratch, and the resulting artillery was a lot less sophisticated than that on the Nigerian side. Nevertheless they worked, and Biafra had some successes during the war, and they even made their own landmines and called them *ogbinigwe* meaning 'muscular'. But Biafra's homemade anti-aircraft guns, tanks, and rocket launchers were constantly beaten down by Nigeria's superior firepower. Throughout the war the fighting was confusing and vicious, and many of the major cities such as Port Harcourt, Enugu, Aba, Calabar and Umuahia kept changing hands and were routinely attacked by air and at the coast by gunboats. The Nigerians eventually retook the coast and when the Nigerians captured Port Harcourt they found that the Biafrans were distilling their own petrol from crude oil in makeshift refineries to fuel their war vehicles. The Biafran army was eventually reduced to an enclave in the Niger Delta around Owerri. On January 12 1970, after 31 months of civil war, the Biafran forces surrendered and by the end of the war, Biafra was no more than 60km wide and just a few kilometres deep, crowded with some three million Igbo refugees.

ones on display date from 1943 but were used again in 1969–70. There are several Nigerian fighter planes, including one MiG, all imported from Russia, including the Ilyushin, nicknamed 'Genocide', a four-crew bomber capable of carrying 1,000kg of explosives that was brought into Nigeria by an Egyptian pilot for the Biafrans but was actually used on both sides of the war as it was subsequently captured by the Nigerians. This plane completely dwarfs the 'Biafran Baby', an impossibly small two-seater sports plane that was donated to the Biafran side by one Count Von Rosen, who flew it from Sweden. It could carry 12 rockets and as it could fly low, went undetected by radar and quite remarkably in 1969, managed to bomb and destroy many much more superior Nigerian planes and MiGs when they were sitting on the tarmac in Port Harcourt after Nigeria had taken that city.

The NS *Bonny* was built by the British in 1966 and used by the Nigerian side to bomb and capture Calabar and Bonny. You'll be relieved to know it came to the museum in parts and was reassembled. You can clamber over the boat and wind the anti-aircraft gun up and down. It's now rather charmingly a restaurant, though it's stinking hot below deck, but there are plastic chairs and tables on the outside deck and you can get a cold drink and food-is-ready. The site of the museum was chosen as it was here that the Voice of Biafra was transmitted on the radio from the former Eastern Nigeria Television Station. This was the method the leaders of the ill-fated republic communicated with their people throughout the war. At one stage the radio station was moved to a bunker, which is still there today. You can ask to go inside, though if there is no NEPA it's pitch black. There's also an indoor display of old uniforms and photographs, but again if there is no NEPA it will be shut.

## ABA

Further south on the Enugu–Port Harcourt Expressway, approximately 60km south of Umuahia, and one hour's drive from Port Harcourt, is Aba, a large town in Imo State on the Aba River. Inexplicably, it's also known as Enyimba City (Enyi is Igbo for elephant). It is an important regional market town, attracting people from all around because of its strategic position in the fertile belt of the Niger Delta, and is a manufacturing centre for cement, textiles, pharmaceuticals, tyres, plastics, soap, and the proverbial two opposites, beer and mineral water. Originally a village, Aba was developed by the British as an administrative centre in the early 20th century. It is famous for the 1929 Aba Women's Riots involving Igbo, Ibibio, and Opobo women who rioted against Britain's arbitrary use of indigenous persons as rulers, and also in protest at the local chiefs of the time including women in their head count and making them pay taxes. There was a series of mass protests, and women burnt buildings and attacked the local chiefs. Colonial troops were sent in and opened fire, and some 50 women were killed at Aba and another 50 or so in the surrounding region. After the incident the British set up an inquiry and the event was a leading milestone in the history of Nigerian nationalism.

Aba is the filthiest town I think we saw in Nigeria, with its massive Ariara Market spilling out on the Port Harcourt Expressway. The edges of all the roads are stacked high with plastic rubbish, broken-down and abandoned oil tankers and tractor units, the central reservations are full of derelict cars, and there is so much rubbish people had resorted to selling yams from on top of it. Aba's only sight per se is the **Museum of Colonial History** (open daily 09.00–17.00, N20 entry fee), which is within walking distance of the main motor park on Ikot Ekpene Road as it heads out to the east of town. (Vehicles running between Port Harcourt and Calabar drive straight past it so you could feasibly break your journey here.) The museum is housed in a freshly painted, bright yellow colonial consulate building and was opened in 1995. Exhibits include old photographs of colonial times recalling the early growth of Aba, and portraits of Nigeria's shakers and movers during the build up to and after independence, but you'll struggle to see anything if there's no NEPA. You can grab a cold drink from the stalls in the garden. If you have to stay in Aba, though there's little need to, then the best option in town is the **Crystal Park Hotel and Flamingo Restaurant** (Crystal Park Avenue off Port Harcourt Road; tel: 082 221588, 221742), which has good rooms for N7,000 and Indian and Chinese food in the restaurant. Everything else is pretty rough, so budget travellers may as well move on.

## PORT HARCOURT

The approach to Port Harcourt, the capital of Rivers State, is from the Aba Expressway that just gets busier and busier, until you eventually join the go-slow on the Aba Road in the city proper. The pollution is palpable here and you'll immediately see the oil flares to the south of town emitting big black clouds of smoke. This is the centre of Nigeria's oil industry. Port Harcourt, the capital of Rivers State, has long been an important merchant port, and is an industrial giant in a region producing steel and aluminium products, pressed concrete, tyres, and motor vehicles. But predominantly Port Harcourt is the collection point for all the oil pumped out of the wells of the Niger Delta. Pipelines carry oil from the delta directly to Port Harcourt's wharfs and on to Bonny Island to be pumped into the tankers for export.

Port Harcourt is a relatively young city and was founded by the British in 1912 as southeastern Nigeria's railhead and sea port for the shipment of coal mined from the new Enugu coal fields. The spot was chosen because of a natural deep-water harbour on the Bonny River and was named after Viscount Lewis Harcourt, secretary of state for the colonies (1910–15). In addition to its physical advantages, the area had the advantage of being sparsely inhabited by fishing folk and was not under the jurisdiction of any meddlesome traditional leaders. Like Jos, Kaduna and Enugu, Port Harcourt became one of the colonial new towns. Its port grew quickly, and after Lagos it's now the second-busiest and biggest in the country, taking away business from the pre-colonial ports of Calabar, Brass and Bonny islands. As a new town it attracted people from other regions and other countries, including Lagosians and Creoles (returned slaves), and a fair amount of British traders. Asian entrepreneurs from Lebanon, India, and Syria formed the bulk of the middlemen between the big European firms and the African traders. (There are still Lebanese supermarkets on Azikiwe Road.) Pidgin English has its roots in Port Harcourt as a general language for people of varying tongues to use during the city's formative years. The original one square mile town was designed by orderly British town planners, with plenty of open spaces, parks, and playing fields – few of these serve their purpose today, but nevertheless it earned the city the title of Nigeria's 'Garden City'.

Since the discovery of oil in the delta, Port Harcourt has been primarily an oil city and the first shipment of Nigerian crude oil left here in 1958. The Nigerian National Petroleum Corporation, the federal government's agency for oil, has its headquarters here, and there are two oil refineries and a petrochemical complex near Okirika, about 20km southeast of Port Harcourt. There is a large expat community in Port Harcourt working in the oil industry. Today the city is huge and choked with traffic on almost the same scale as Lagos, and its population could plausibly be several million.

## Getting there and away
### By air
Port Harcourt International Airport is 40km or about 45 minutes' drive (depending on the traffic) from Port Harcourt, north on Owerri Road. A drop taxi is your only option and should cost in the region of N2,000. Air France and Virgin are the only airlines that have **international flights** to Port Harcourt directly from Europe. Presently there are two flights a week between Port Harcourt and Paris in each direction on Air France, and two with Virgin between here and London's Gatwick twice a week in each direction. This is reputedly one of Virgin's most profitable routes. There are **domestic flights** between Port Harcourt and Lagos, Abuja, Kano, Kaduna and Calabar. Chanchangi Airlines has flights from Port Harcourt to Lagos (one hour) at 08.00, 11.30 and 15.30 daily. To Port Harcourt flights depart from Lagos at 09.30, 13.30 and 16.45 during the week and at 10.00, 12.00 and 15.00 at the weekends. Bellview has three flights a day to Lagos at 09.00, 14.45 and 18.00, and slightly later at the weekends. Sosoliso flies to Abuja

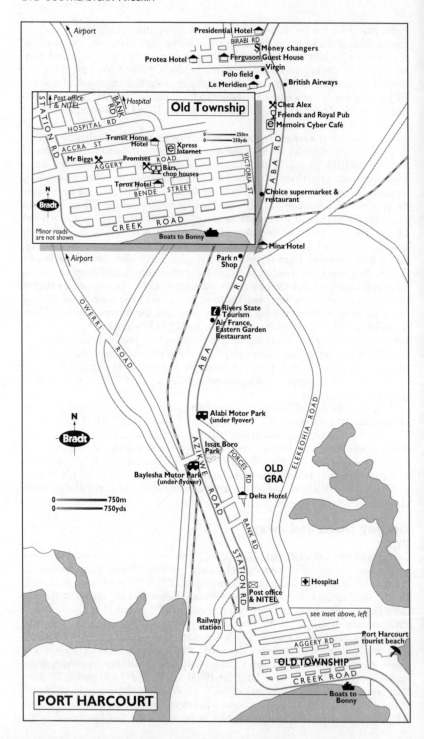

three times a day Monday to Fridays at 07.45, 12.00 and 15.30, Saturday at 08.30, and Sunday at 10.45 and 14.30, and from Abuja at 09.50, 13.45 and 17.00 on weekdays, and at 10.30 on Saturday and 12.45 and 16.30 on Sunday.

### Airlines

**British Airways** In the Broadbank building, 180 Aba Rd; tel: 084 238351, 233011
**Chanchangi Airlines** Airport desk; tel: 084 231920; desk at the Presidential Hotel; tel: 084 234937
**KLM** and **Kenya Airways**; tel: 084 231645, 235468; **Air France**; 084 486901/2; email: phc@airfrance.fr; and **Bellview**; tel: 084 230518/9; are all upstairs in the shopping plaza at 47 Aba Road, above the Eastern Garden Chinese Restaurant.
**Lufthansa** Has an office at the Hotel Presidential; tel: 084 232014; www.lufthansa.com.ng
**Sosoliso Airlines** Airport desk; tel: 084 231908; desk at the Presidential Hotel; tel: 084 571946; www.sosolisoairline.com
**Virgin** 175 Aba Road (above the Zenith Bank); tel: 084 467000/6

### By road

The sprawling Alabi Motor Park is on Aba Road and you can look down at the chaotic compound stuffed to the gills with vehicles from the flyover that takes Aba Road into the city proper, where it turns into Azikiwe Road. Just to the south of here and under the flyover is the Baylesha Motor Park, opposite the gate to the Issac Boro Park, which is far less frantic and is where the slightly more expensive private companies such as Crosslines or Delta Transport go from, offering a 'three-across' service (fewer people). Vehicles in each of the motor parks go to all the cities in the southeast and as far as Benin City, where you'll need to change for Lagos, and Enugu, and also for points north. There's also the overnight 'luxury' buses to Lagos, Kano and Abuja. Non-trainspotters should head for the train station at the end of Azikiwe Road.

## Getting around

Port Harcourt is bisected neatly by the Aba Road that goes over a series of flyovers and starts life as the Aba Expressway 64km north in Aba, turns into **Aba Road** as it enters the city, and then **Azikiwe Road** as it heads towards the Old Township and the wharfs to the south of the city. This is literally the end of the road in southeastern Nigeria, and any point south of here in the Niger Delta is reached by boat. This road is routinely choked with traffic to the point that a pedestrian will be unable to cross the road, thanks partly to a big concrete buffer thing in the middle of it. Street vendors hound vehicles in their droves. *Okadas* are useful here. The city is roughly divided into five suburbs – **Old GRA, GRA 1, GRA 2, GRA 3, and Old Township**. The latter is a bustling (though not necessarily safe) area of frantic commerce and congested streets, and the further south you get towards the wharfs on Creek Road and Bonny Street, the less likely you are going to be able to navigate this area by car. **Shared taxis** and **minibuses** in Port Harcourt can be any colour, but the majority are blue with a white stripe on the side, and they run up and down the major arteries.

## Where to stay

Accommodation in Port Harcourt is reasonably good and there are a couple of upmarket spots that clearly cater for the international oil company executives. There are a number of compounds around Port Harcourt for employees of the big oil corporations such as Shell, Africa Oilfield Services, and Intel. If you are working, you may find yourself living at one of these.

## Upmarket: US$100 and above

**Le Meridien Ogeyi Place** 45 Tombia St, GRA 2; tel: 084 231064, 236952; email: reservation@lemeridienphc.com; www.lemeridien.com. Reservations can be made directly through the website or from the UK, through Le Meridien's toll-free number; tel: 0870 400 8440. This is without doubt the best hotel in Nigeria and is the only one that hits the five-star mark by international standards – it is stunning. It's a brand new luxury hotel overlooking the Port Harcourt Polo Club, with 84 modern rooms, six penthouses, a health club, business centre, and swimming pool. The Ororo Restaurant and bar faces the polo field and overlooks the pool terrace. Rooms have all the trimmings you would expect of an international five-star hotel and are super luxurious, and the suites have extras such as flat screen TV, kidney-shaped bath tubs and walk-in showers. There are certainly no power or water problems here and it's probably the best you're going to get in the whole of West Africa. Rates for single or double occupancy are US$320 for a room and US$510 for a suite overlooking the city, and US$340/US$530 for a room/suite overlooking the polo field. The Presidential Suite is a cool US$1,260. Deposits are 25% more than the room rates.

**Protea Hotel Port Harcourt** 3 Isaiah Odulu St, GRA 1; tel: 084 231557; www.proteahotels.com. You can also make a reservation through the South African office which you may want to consider if you want to use a credit card over the phone; tel/fax: +21 (21) 430 5330. These are luxurious apartments, but each of the several rooms in the eight apartments can be let out separately from between US$140 and US$185 per room inclusive of full English breakfast and the 15%. This is an odd, almost Gothic-looking slate-coloured building, but it's very modern and all the uncluttered bedrooms and communal areas are decorated with polished wood, sumptuous brown leather sofas and gleaming white tiles and mirrors. It opened in 2003, and each apartment is spread over seven floors of living rooms, bedrooms, studies and bathrooms. The apartments can also be taken for long stays for a cool US$70,000 a year and are fully serviced with DSTV, AC, and balconies. There's a small restaurant and bar serving continental food exclusively for the guests, and a small pool and tiled barbecue area. Of interest to long-term guests, Nigerian Breweries is next door, where you can buy slabs of Heineken from the side of the road.

**Presidential Hotel** at the northern end of Aba Road before it turns into Aba Expressway, GRA 1; tel: 084 575802/4, 236260. This has been the city's principal hotel for decades, and there are lots of useful services here, but it's quite shabby and old fashioned these days. There are several bars and restaurants, a swimming pool with terrace where you can play table tennis, a welcome desk for Shell (as many expat oil workers arrive and start their term of service here), and a coffee shop in the lobby. In the row of shops are domestic airline desks, and a bookshop where you can pick up a map of Port Harcourt that quite frankly makes no sense whatsoever. There are no fewer than 12 types of accommodation in 307 rooms, all with myriad names. The cheapest is the Upper Room at N14,550 (N25,000 deposit), followed by the Garden Room at N18,520 (N28,000 deposit), and then a whole bunch of suites from N21,000–45,000 (the deposits are roughly a steep N10,000 more than the rates), plus the 15%.

## Moderate: below US$100

The **Mina Hotel** 23 Igbodo St, Old GRA; tel: 084 236356, 236357; email: minahotel@yahoo.com. Fairly new, with enthusiastic staff, and is in a good location just off Aba Road. The décor is still in very good condition and things work reasonably well. The 41 rooms have DSTV and fridge, and are newly painted and modern with new carpets and tiles in the bathrooms. The restaurant and bar serve Nigerian and continental food, there's a Sosoliso Airlines desk and you can arrange car hire. Two giant gens provide 24-hour power and this place even has its own water-treatment plant to treat the tap water. Standard rooms (with a normal double bed) are N6,900 (N10,000 deposit), doubles N9,200 (N12,000 deposit), and suites range upward of N11,500, all inclusive of the 15%. There are discounts at the weekend and for long-staying guests.

**Transit Home Hotel** 27 Accra St, Old Township; tel: 084 232653. Overpriced for what you get, with rooms stuffed with old furniture, DSTV and fridge, for N4,600–6,000, but there's a very good restaurant and comfy bar here serving excellent chicken and chips and a brand new gen outside.

**Ferguson Guest House** 1b Elelenwo St, GRA 2; tel: 083 230505. A small establishment with 16 rooms in a compound, with parking and a tiny restaurant with three tables and a range of Nigerian soups and starch on the menu. The 16 rooms are freshly painted, with fridge, satellite TV, big beds, plastic armchairs, new shower heads and hot-water tanks, and a single (but with a double bed) costs N3,400, and a double, N4,900.

**Delta Hotel** 1–3 Harley St, Old GRA; tel: 084 236650. A great budget option in a quiet area set in nice tree-filled grounds where there is plenty of parking and friendly and attentive service (they will spray your room with fly spray to attack the mossies before you retire). There's an old-fashioned but comfy bar, and the good restaurant serves some continental dishes such as chicken, coleslaw and chips for about N800. The only drawback is that the gen goes off at 22.30. Rooms have new AC units and fridges, lots of furniture and satellite TV, and go from N2,500–5,000.

**Torox Hotel** 29 Bende St, Old Township; tel: 084 233102. It's in a seedy area but it's very smart, with modern tiled bathrooms with great showers, but there's no space to swing a cat or a backpack in the rooms and no restaurant or bar, so at N2,800 for a small double it's not especially good value.

## Where to eat and drink

Most places are along Aba Road, and going from north to south, starting with the Presidential Hotel where there are several restaurants and bars. These include the **Why Not** Lebanese restaurant and **4-5-6** Chinese restaurant, that both serve authentic food, though I was a bit puzzled by the sign on the door about the dress code that says 'no dressing gowns'. The **Rivers restaurant** on the second floor is a plain hotel dining room serving over-priced buffets of Nigerian and continental food for N2,400. Back on Aba Road and further south **Chez Alex** (143 Aba Road; tel: 084 232358, 235200; open daily 12.00–15.00 for lunch; 19.00–22.30 for dinner) is a charming restaurant run by a very extended Lebanese family, with nice décor, a long bar, and candlelit tables. There's an enormous menu (though you may want to skip the brains, tongue and gizzards), with mezze items from N400, main dishes of seafood paella, lobster, or fried prawns from N2,500, and oriental dishes and pizza from N1,000. Wines are Italian and French. A few doors down on the same side of the road is **Friends** and **Royal Pub** at 131 Aba Road. It's cheap and seedy, with prostitutes galore, but it's an atmospheric bar and disco serving Nigerian snacks and is open from 17.00 to dawn and has an enormous dance floor. There's a small cover charge later in the evening. To the east of Aba Road, the **Ororo Restaurant** in the lobby of the Le Meridien Hotel is superb but at a price. A bottle of Moet will set you back N10,000, a tot of Remy Martin N3,500, and a bottle of French wine N8,000. The themed buffets, Sunday lunch, and main dishes off the à la carte menu cost N3,500. Even if you just pop in for coffee you need to be dressed very smart. Watch the well-groomed polo horses trotting around the polo field, and if there is a match on you'll get a bird's-eye view from the pool terrace. **Choice** (107 Aba Road; tel: 084 230425, 239405) is another Lebanese supermarket with a restaurant next door, and you may be able to change money here. There's a full deli with cheese and hams and smoked salmon, and a full range of imported food, and the plain restaurant next door has a menu of Lebanese food from N1,600 for a main course of mixed grills and all things meaty. The **Eastern Garden** is a Chinese restaurant in the Air France building at 47 Aba Road, to the side of a flyover, with big tall pillars and a packed car park. This is a very stylish restaurant on two floors with an enormous 16-page menu of every imaginable Chinese dish. Meat main dishes go from N1,200 and seafood from N2,500, and there are good options for vegetarians. Next door is a small bakery selling cakes, sandwiches and cold drinks throughout the day. **Park n Shop** on Aba Road to the west of a flyover is a huge supermarket dealing in imported goods and is similar to the branch in Lagos. There's a good bakery here for meat and cheese pies. In the Old Township, on Victoria Road, are lots of bars (and brothels) serving plates of hot pepper soup, and there are good *suya* stands on the corner. Exercise caution in this area and stay within the confines of the brightly lit bars, but if you do go for a drink down here you'll certainly see some sights. There is a branch of **Mr Biggs** on Aggery Street for boxed fast food and **Promises**, a similar concept to Mr Biggs.

## Communications and practicalities

If you need to **change money**, then try and approach the management of the Lebanese Choice Supermarket (see below) or the Hausa money changers who hang out on the street to the south of the Presidential Hotel just off Aba Road. There's also an official bureau de change at 90 Aba Road. For **internet access** there are several spots in town, including Memoirs Cyber Café at 169 Aba Road next to the defunct Nigerian Airways office (there's also a DHL office here), or Xpress Internet on Aggery Road in the Old Township. This is a very flash modern cyber café and also an internet service provider, so email access is consistent and fast. Expect to pay N150 per hour and as it is open 24 hours, night surfing from 21.00 is N400. The **post office** is on Station Road and the **NITEL** office is directly behind it. The office for **Rivers State Tourism** is at 37 Aba Road, a couple of blocks to the north of the Air France building. There is a sign, but if you go down the filthy corridor and actually find the office, you will first have to wake up the receptionist at his desk and ask to see the director, who will be most surprised to see you and somewhat embarrassed that he hasn't got anything to give out (as was our experience). The **British Council** is at Plot 127, Olu Obasanjo Road, GRA 2; tel: 084 237173, 231776; www.britishcouncil.org/nigeria.

## What to see and do

Again there's not much to see, but if you happen to be walking up and down Aba Road the **Isaac Boro Park** (open 09.00–21.00; N20 entry), opposite a flyover and near the Abali Motor Park, may distract you. The 5.7ha patch of green grass was named after an army officer, and it's also the location of the cenotaph of the Unknown Soldier, where there are concrete models of a tank, war plane and war ship. It's a very ordinary park, but it's litter-free where people actually sit on the grass, though it's hardly peaceful being next to the flyover and the packed motor park. The **Port Harcourt Tourist Beach** (N100 entry) is to the extreme east of the Old Township and overlooks an area of harbour and creek, the rubbish-infested city shorelines, and a pile of shipwrecked boats. It's not a beach right next to the water as such, but a swath of clean sand in a park where there are plenty of tables and a couple of bars to have a beer or soft drink, and it is a popular spot for families and couples at the weekend. There is a small arts centre with the odd statue and animal skin (I would hazard a guess from the zoo – see below), and obligatory portraits of local chiefs, governors and of course the president, plus a couple of horses that children can take short rides on, and a dreadful zoo. We saw some terrible zoos in Nigeria but this was the worst. It was overgrown, full of rubbish, all the enclosures were falling down and all it contained were two dead-looking crocodiles, one insane baboon and one ostrich that constantly ran up and down in a concrete pen about one metre wide, that would have been insane except for the fact that ostriches have got very short-term memories. Shocking. Despite the zoo, which you can easily avoid as it's behind a wall, the tourist beach is not a bad place for a drink in the afternoon. Back on Aggery Road, look out for the Saros building, an imposing white block which was Ken Saro-Wiwa's publishing house where he spent much of his time.

# THE NIGER DELTA
## Bonny and Brass islands
To the south and east of Port Harcourt are the numerous islands separated by the ever-expansive creeks and waterways of the Niger Delta. The most accessible are Bonny and Brass, with the latter being the nicer of the two. In the 18th and 19th centuries these were powerful sites for slave exportation from West Africa, and from 1885 to 1894 Bonny was the administrative centre of the British Oil Rivers Protectorate. On both there are still some old colonial buildings and cemeteries featuring headstones of past missionaries and colonial officers. Bonny declined in the 20th century but was revived after 1961, when its port was modernised as the export point for oil, and today it is the principal port for the Niger Delta. Bonny was off limits during our visit due to a kidnapping incident of two US oil employees in Warri to the west of Port Harcourt. Be aware that it will be assumed that all foreigners are oil employees in this region. If it's considered safe to go, then direct ferries to Bonny go from Creek Road in the Old Township of Port Harcourt. This port area is not renowned for its safety and there are a few unsavoury characters hanging around. This is one of the very few places in the whole of Nigeria that we found unnerving, though nothing happened, but we did get a few warnings from other Nigerians to be careful. Just watch yourself down here. It's a heaving area of trade in large goods such as timber, steel, and aluminium sheets.

Before the kidnapping incident, we did make it to the village of Brass however, which is located at the very tip of the delta to the southwest of Port Harcourt. The village is on the northern creek side of an island whilst the sea is on the other side. It's populated by the Nembe people and was named Brass because when the British arrived a colonial officer grabbed a woman by the arm and asked a little too eagerly 'Where are we?' The woman replied 'Barasi' and the name stuck. (Barasi means 'leave me alone' in the Nembe language.) Around the jetty there are a couple of old colonial buildings, presumably built in the 1900s as they have the same architectural style as the Lugard houses found in Lokoja and elsewhere, built on stilts because of the reptiles and flooding. But today they are hopelessly falling down. To the east of the jetty a track leads to the older fishing village, which is much more primitive than the main section of Brass that has seen some modern building in recent years. You may see the odd Italian expat here, as Brass is home to a big Agip oil installation that is Italian owned. Sadly, even for such a little place it's again full of rubbish, which is piled up in the creek that runs through the village and on the beach. But everyone is very friendly here and you can wander around the village alongside very large cows with enormous horns, and chat to the people. Brass's enormous church is a very smart affair built in 2003 with a shiny aluminium roof, which is full to the brim with shiny headdresses on a Sunday. Opposite is the village's football pitch, where you can watch future Nwankwo Kanus battle it out on a Saturday afternoon, in full football strip but with no shoes.

### Getting there and away
Getting to Brass is half the fun. First you need to get yourself to Yenagoa, the capital of neighbouring Baylesa State, approximately 120km to the west of Port Harcourt and halfway to Warri. You can get a minibus from Port Harcourt for around N300

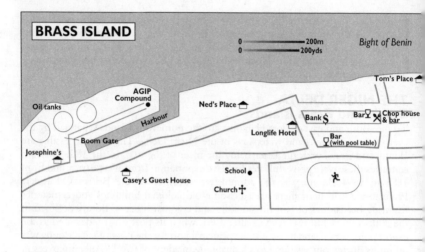

and the road goes west out of the city near the airport and past Port Harcourt University. Once at Yenagoa, a sprawling commercial town that is presently undergoing new road building (Yenagoa is a fairly new state capital), things start to get confusing. Yenagoa is on the Orashi River, a tributary of the Niger, that begins to spread its arms here and turn into a number of creeks that get wider and wider until they reach the sea. From the motor park in the centre of town you need to head to the boat office at the new market at Nembe. *Okadas* are the only vehicles that will get into the densely packed market and the boat office is right in the middle of it. It's so hectic you'll have to walk the last few metres and get the *okada* drivers to park their bikes and go with you because quite frankly you'll never find it by yourself. Our *okada* drivers were very helpful and it was quite an astonishing moment when we finally got to the anonymous shed surrounded by packed stalls next to the river. In the shed (bizarrely decorated in Christmas decorations in April) are rows of desks; look for the Brass Unit sign. A public boat that goes-when-full to Brass costs N1,220 each way. Other boats go to Abk and Silga, other villages in the Niger Delta. You pay for your boat ride and the man will write your name down on the list for the next boat, which usually takes about a dozen people. We waited two hours. The man at the desk will ring a hand bell when the boat is ready to depart. There a line of benches to sit on and wait; it's a great spot to watch the market activity and you can buy snacks and drinks from the ladies around you, or you can wander around the market (listening out for the bell).

The motor-boat ride to Brass takes about 1½ hours and the boat goes very fast, and once out in the wider creeks closer to the sea it's a very bumpy and painful ride, so you'll need to hang on as there are no life jackets, and it's also very squashed. If it rains the boat driver pulls a tarpaulin over the passengers. Believe me its not comfortable. However the views of the delta's forested creeks, khaki waters and fishing villages are tremendous. The watery channels are full of mangroves and storks and kingfishers, and people toing and froing in canoes with tiny sails, fishing or moving around between the tiny settlements. How the boat driver navigates the endless and intertwining creeks is beyond me. There are also larger, more colourful slower boats packed with people and cargo and crates of Coke and beer that wend from village to village, and you may see a tug or launch pulling a big piece of equipment needed at the oil installations and oil rigs, such as cranes. Also look out for the oil pipelines that carve tracks in the forests.

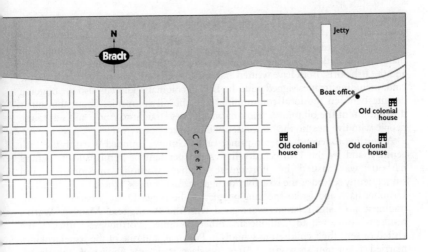

## Where to stay and eat

Most accommodation on the island is in ad hoc rooms in people's houses, but they don't serve food. The best place to stay is **Tom's Place** on the beach, which is a smart new building still surrounded by sand and bricks. There are several clean and neat rooms here, with new bathrooms and local TV, and a double with AC costs N2,500 and one with a fan N2,000, but there's no gen so it's NEPA dependent. At **Casey's Guest House** towards the Agip oil installation, you can get a plain double in a modern building for N1,000. The bare rooms have a bed and table, but the bathrooms are tiled, though you still have to use a bucket. The gen is switched on for a few hours at night when you can watch DSTV in the comfy communal lounge with Victoria and her family, who own the place. There are no signs, but *okada* drivers seem to know where it is. If you can't get rooms at the above you can also find cheap and basic accommodation at **Ned's Place** on the right towards Agip, the **Longlife Hotel**, a low yellow building just north of the school, or at **Josephine's** house just beyond the turnoff to Agip. Near the football pitch is a good bar with a pool table and there are others in the back streets. There are, however, very few places to eat. In the boat house where you book your space on the boat back to Port Harcourt is a small café serving tea-eggs-and-bread in the mornings and food-is-ready in the afternoons. Opposite the boat office at the jetty is a line of chop and drink stalls for snacks – look out for the skewers of deep-fried palm tree maggots (yuk!). I was told that they taste quite sweet, but no way was I going to try them. In the village, one of the bars does food-is-ready such as fish pepper soup, and there are a couple of plastic tables outside where you can eat, have a beer and watch a Nollywood movie on the TV and discuss with the madam of the house the goings-on of the characters in the story. But go early before the food runs out or ask her to save you something. There's also a canteen at the Agip complex, and if you ask nicely at the gate you may be allowed in to eat there.

## Warri

We were unable to visit Warri, 205km northwest of Port Harcourt in Delta State, during our research in Nigeria, because when we were in the delta region two US oil workers, and several Nigerian employees of a local oil company, were kidnapped and murdered there. Local advice was to stay away, which we duly followed. If you plan to visit Warri and anywhere else in this region, get up-to-the-minute advice on safety and security, especially if you are working for an oil company. This area has witnessed the worst of the delta violence, and many of the delta waterways and remote island settlements around Warri are controlled by ethnic militia groups. The main dispute is the ownership of the strip of land that is Warri between the Ijaws and the Itshekiris. Both have written and oral histories supporting their claim to the land, including treaties signed with the British colonials. There is also the ongoing dispute between the local communities and the oil companies about the unfair distribution of the oil money, most of which goes straight to Abuja and not to the people who live next to the oil wells, often in abject poverty.

According to legend, a Benin prince called Ginuwa founded Warri in the 15th century, and by the 17th century it was independent of Benin, and its natural harbour was visited by Portuguese Roman Catholic missionaries, and subsequently served as the base for Portuguese slave traders. Home to the Itshekiri, Urhobo, Ijaw, and Isoko-speaking peoples of the Niger Delta, it became a major trading centre and relations were good with the Portuguese. Many of Warri's residents converted to Catholicism, others assumed Portuguese names, some visited or sent their children to schools in Portugal, and one of the Itshekiri kings married a Portuguese woman. After the slave trade was abolished, the British replaced the Portuguese as trade partners, and by the 19th century it had become wealthy in the palm oil trade. Britain was determined to keep her claim on the Niger Delta, and after a peaceful treaty with local leaders failed, Britain resorted to using force when in 1894 they attacked the most powerful of the Itshekiri rulers, Chief Nana. This particular battle featured one of the earliest uses by the British of the newly invented automatic, self-firing guns that were later to become known as machine guns, against which the people of Warri didn't stand a chance. Chief Nana was captured and exiled, and Itshekiriland came under British administration with Warri as the regional capital. The subsequent British conquest of the city of Benin three years later opened up the western Niger Delta for British commerce in palm oil, timber, and rubber, and Warri port was developed to transport goods back to Europe. On return voyages, ships would bring back consumer and household goods from Europe. The people of Warri acted as middlemen and distributed these goods by canoe through the creeks and waterways before the British built roads between Warri and Sapele and Benin City.

Today Warri is still a major sea port and an oil and steel city. Oil and natural gas fields are prolific in the area, there's a refinery here, and Warri is also home to the headquarters of the Nigerian Petroleum Institute. Refined oil is transported via pipeline from here to northern Nigeria. There's also an enormous steel plant that sprawls across the Aladja district of Warri, and a major petrochemical complex producing plastics, pharmaceuticals, and paints. Aero Contractors (tel: 053 250713, 256279) has flights between Warri and Lagos and Port Harcourt. At Abraka, some 60km northeast of Warri on the Ethiope River, is a spring fed with crystal-clear water and a natural sandy beach. This used to be a popular spot with expat weekenders a few years ago, and I have an account from an overland driver who went through Nigeria a decade ago that this was once a beautiful forested spot, and that there used to be a resort here. Whether this is still the case I didn't manage to find out, so if anyone knows anything more, I'd be happy to hear from them.

# EAST OF PORT HARCOURT
## Calabar
The capital of Cross Rivers State, Calabar is a pleasant town in a beautiful setting high on a hill above a curve in the Cross River. It was originally called Old Calabar to distinguish it from another town called Kalabari. It has a long history of being

Nigeria's eastern port on an estuary of the Gulf of Guinea, and an estimated third of the slaves that left Nigeria were transported through Calabar. It is also the cultural centre for the Efik people who dabbled in the slave trade as middlemen. It's made up of the old Efik settlements of Creek Town (Obio Oko), Duke Town (Atakpa), Old Town (Obutong), and Henshaw Town (Nsidung). It's also well known as the home of the Scottish missionary Mary Slessor, who arrived in 1878 from the United Free Church of Scotland. It grew as an important Niger Delta trading state in the 19th century, thanks to the lucrative palm oil trade, and today rubber and timber pass through Calabar's port, and tyre manufacturer Dunlop has rubber plantations around Calabar. It's surrounded by saltwater swamps and dense tropical forest, and the markets are full of fish, pineapples, bananas, plantains, cassava and palm oil. For a short time (1893–1906) it was the capital of the British Protectorate of Southern Nigeria, before the capital was moved to Lagos, and was the region's principal port during the early colonial days before it was eclipsed by Port Harcourt. The older part of town along the Calabar River has some beautiful colonial buildings but they are in various stages of decay. These were shipped from Liverpool frame by frame, with the carpenters, and were not only used by the colonial offices; many of the local chiefs liked the British architecture so much that they ordered their own houses and period furniture from England and this architecture was the hallmark of Old Calabar. These chiefs even took British names: these were the Dukes, the Jameses, and the Henshaws. The best place to explore Calabar's history is in the excellent museum. By contrast, Calabar today is also home to two interesting conservation organisations that are doing something worthwhile to help Nigeria's primates in the nearby Cross River forests. Finally, on an environmental note, whilst not being totally rubbish free, Calabar is by far the cleanest city in Nigeria, and the state government is doing something to address the rubbish problem. Here I saw a rare creature to Nigeria indeed – a rubbish truck!

## Getting there and away

Calabar's Margaret Ekpo Airport is just to the east of Ndidem Nsang Iso Road, and very centrally located. ADC Airlines; tel: 087 234477 airport desk, has **flights** between Calabar and Lagos twice a day and once a day between Calabar and Port Harcourt. Minibuses and bush taxis arrive and depart from the **motor park** on Mary Slessor Avenue, for vehicles to Aba and Port Harcourt to the east and Ikom, Obudu and Ogoja to the north. I would probably suggest you arrive early, as we waited nearly two hours for a bush taxi to go-when-full from Calabar to Ikom, which is really not that far away. Coming into Calabar vehicles may also drop off at Watt Market. The private bus company Crosslines (that specialises in three-across) has its own terminal just north of the Metropolitan Hotel, and has a service to Port Harcourt. **Boats** go from the wharf near the independence statue on Marina Road to Creek Town and to Oron (for onward boats to Cameroon see below). These are mostly motorised canoes that go-when-full, and the boat yard here is very similar to a typical motor park surrounded by stalls and food-is-ready joints. Both services cost little more than N100 and you can actually request a life jacket here.

## Getting around

The original Old Calabar is split from the more modern areas by Calabar Road, on which Watt Market is at the centre of things. To the west of this road are the old townships and busy wharfs along the river, where it is quite congested, so this area is best explored by *okada* or by foot, though it's fairly hilly. Getting around Calabar

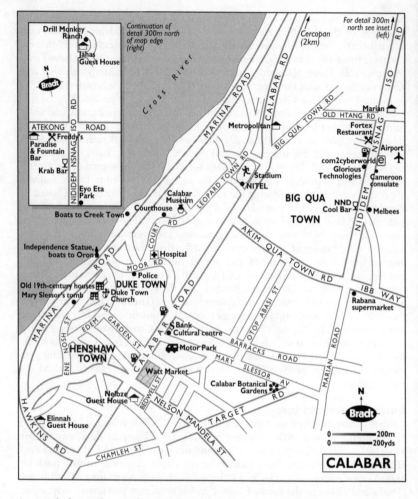

**CALABAR**

is straightforward enough, and **shared taxis** and **minibuses** run up and down Calabar Road and Ndidem Nsang Iso Road, on the modern side of town, which are the two main arteries of the city, for little more than N20. The latter turns into Marian Road further south.

## Where to stay

There is not a brilliant choice of accommodation in Calabar and unfortunately nothing stands out, so use your time to explore Calabar (and its nightlife) rather than your hotel. The **Metropolitan Hotel** (tel: 087 230911) is on Murtala Muhammed Way, the main road leading into town. This is the principal town hotel, but its very tired-looking, with a gloomy, narrow cocktail bar, a standard hotel dining room with a set continental and Nigerian meal at lunch and dinner for N1,000, and a pool (though there's a sign that says the pool is being treated and is out of use that looks like it's been there for a very long time). You should be able to organise car hire here as there's a bank of taxis outside. The 114 old-fashioned rooms start from N5,500 (N7,000 deposit). The **Marian Hotel Ltd** (125 Old Ikang Road; tel: 087 220233,

220234) has 37 rooms in a newly painted block, but it's dark and dusty inside. Again it has set three-course meals for N1,000. Nevertheless rooms are comfortable, with DSTV, and next door is a garden bar with plastic chairs and there's plenty of parking. A double is N4,600 (N5,000 deposit), and a suite N6,900 (N7,000 deposit). **Paradise City Hotel** (86–88 Atekong Drive; tel: 087 235726) has an ornate restaurant with chandeliers and fans, but ordinary Nigerian food and some Lebanese dishes, and outside there is a bar in the garden and a big car park. The 32 rooms in an old concrete block are on three floors, with nice Persian-style rugs on the floor, vast beds, some of the showers work, DSTV and fridge, and they are spacious and clean. Rates are N3,450 for the smallest bed (N5,000 deposit), which is an ordinary double, and then go up depending on the size of the bed.

    **Nelbee Guest House** (5 Dan Achibong Street, off Calabar Road; tel: 087 232684) is a good and friendly budget option close to the market, with parking in a compound, and a small restaurant serving up a dish of the day, and if you give them a bit of notice they will come up with something continental. It's Muslim-owned so there's no alcohol. The six rooms are neat and clean with new fridges, DSTV, running water in the showers, and are excellent value at N2,530 for a double. The appearance of the **Jahas Guest House** (107 Marian Road; no phone). is severely dilapidated, but the rooms inside are OK, with AC, local TV, leaky fridge, big bathrooms with buckets, and it's in a quiet area close to the Drill Monkey Ranch. There are only six rooms that go for N2,000–2,500 and don't bank on being able to get anything to eat here. **Elinnah Guest House** (25 Hawkins Road; tel: 087 233151, 235727) is a few rooms in a lady's house where (presumably) her sons sleep on the floor in the central living room. It's friendly enough though, and cheap, with nice views of the river; it's N1,500 a room and the rooms are clean, with AC and a bucket in the bathroom, but no food or drink, though there's a small chop house further up the street. **NB** *Okada* drivers didn't like this area after dark and said it was full of 'bandits'.

## Where to eat and drink
The **Rabana Supermarket** at 56 Marian Road sells some imported goods such as booze, tins and juice, plus useful items like razors and batteries. A little further up at number 10 is **Melbees**, where you might be able to get buns, pies and sausage rolls, but when we looked in there were only four cans of Coke in the fridge. Opposite is a food-is-ready shop called **NND Cool Bar**, but it's pretty grimy. Next up on Marian Road and on the opposite side of the road is the **Eyo Eta Park** run by the Calabar Lions Club, where there are a couple of thumping outdoor bars selling beer and good *suya*. There's the same sort of set-up further up on the left at the **Krab Bar and Car Wash**, a vast outdoor bar where you can conveniently get your car washed at the same time, and it's open until 02.00. This place is packed to the gills and is unmissable thanks to all the neon signs, and again you can get hot and spicy *suya* with your cold beer. For good and cheap Nigerian food in spotless surroundings try the **Fortex Restaurant** on Ioto Effiom Street just off Ndidem Nsang Iso Road. There are bright white plastic tables inside and on a small terrace, and it serves a selection of garri, pounded yam, soups, fried rice and snails for as little as N300 a dish, but no alcohol. **Freddy's Restaurant** (90 Atekong Drive; tel: 087 232821; open for lunch Monday–Saturday 11.30–15.00; dinner daily 18.30–23.00) is the best restaurant in town and an expat haunt, with nicely dressed tables, dart board, big, well-stocked bar, and DSTV. Lebanese mezze items start from N400, steaks are N1,300, *shawarmas* are N1,300 and a prawn kebab is N1,800, plus the 15%. A meal here for two with drinks will cost in the region of N5,000. It's got a good atmosphere and when we were there Whitney Houston was belting

out *I Have Nothing* from the TV (now there's a thing: Nigerians love Whitney Houston – we heard her everywhere!). Further along this street and next to and under the same Lebanese management as the Paradise City Hotel is the **Fountain Bar** (open Thursday–Saturday 21.00–04.00), which is a surreal place. It's vast, and centred around a defunct fountain of giant and grotesque-looking concrete fish, with loads of dance floors, tables with plastic tablecloths and flowers, plenty of beer and snacks such as chips, fried chicken, and meat pies. This place heats up after 21.00 and it boasts a fun if rather illicit atmosphere, and prostitutes abound, but we found it a reasonably comfortable place to visit.

## Practicalities

There are a couple of **internet** spots opposite each other near the Cameroon Consulate on Ndidan Usang Iso Road. At number 34 is Glorious Technologies, and at number 35 is Com2cyberworld, both open until about 21.00 and charging N150 per hour. The **post office** is on Calabar Road, whilst the **NITEL** office is at 2 Club Road near the stadium, a few metres to the south of the Metropolitan Hotel. For those travelling on in West Africa, the **Cameroon Consulate** is at 21 Ndidam Usang Iso Road (tel: 087 222782; open Monday–Friday, 09.00–15.30; pick up visas, 15.50–17.00). You need to write a letter to apply for the application form saying what you are doing and where you are going; the man at the gate will tell you what to write and will then hand the letter in, to be given to the consulate to read. Once the letter is approved, they give you two application forms, which you fill in and hand back with three passport photos; you'll need to buy a stamp for a few naira, and the fee is currently N8,000/US$55. If you are in a vehicle you need to present photocopies of the vehicle's paperwork such as the carnet etc. In theory visas should be processed in 48 hours, but it may be less if you go early and speak nicely to the officials. Be reasonably pushy (ie: if the right person isn't there, politely ask them to go and find the right person). Whilst there are plenty of banks, there are no obvious places to **change money** in Calabar, though I would suggest approaching any Lebanese businessman or ask at the Metropolitan Hotel.

## What to see and do
### The city

The **Calabar Museum** (open daily, 09.00–18.00; N20 entry fee) is housed in a beautifully restored old colonial building, built on top of a hill between Duke Town and Old Town, that was erected in 1884 for the British Council for the Bight of Benin and Biafra. Prefabricated and shipped from England, it is one of the finest examples of colonial architecture in the country, and is beyond doubt Nigeria's best museum. From 1884 it was the seat of the Oil Rivers and Niger Coast Protectorate, then from 1914 the Old Calabar Province, then in the 1950s it was used as a guesthouse. After the civil war it became the office of the new Southeastern State, and was fully renovated in 1986 to become the Calabar Museum. The building is painted a bright yellow and has wonderful wooden floors, shutters and original fittings. Unlike other Nigerian museums, which are often stuffed full of anything they can get hold of, here the items have been selected carefully for their relevance to the Calabar region, and there are some valuable items with weighty historical importance. There's also loads of knowledgeable staff and a surprising amount of Nigerian visitors. At the entrance is a craft and bookshop where you pay your entry fee. The library at the side of the museum is quite remarkable, and contains all the original paperwork, some of it in near-perfect condition, of the colonial office throughout the era that the British were here. These include the British Parliamentary Paper sent out yearly to

Calabar on the roles of the civil service and police, and announcing any new or amended laws that were to be used to govern the colony; a chronologically full set of All England Law Reports from 1951–70; and the Nigerian Gazette from 1926–55 that covered promotions, leave of absences, and new appointments in the colonial service. You can just pick these up and flick through them, when by rights they should be in the museum proper.

In the grounds is an old red British pillar box, and an old 1848 bell that was first used aboard ship and was rung to bring people together for instructions, before being erected at the site in Calabar where it was used to signify the start and finish of a working day in Old Calabar; many of the trading stations on the Calabar River had their own bells. The exhibits in the museum are excellently presented, but very unfortunately I missed seeing some of the upstairs rooms thanks to the lack of NEPA, as without power the interior rooms are plunged into darkness. The first thing you are likely to see is an early 20th-century motorbike (perhaps one of Nigeria's first *okadas*), which was generally used around Calabar by the missionaries. Downstairs there's a very good hall on the production of palm oil that was the 'red gold' of southern Nigeria for the first half of the 20th century; the most successful period was during World War II, when palm oil was used as industrial oil for the military machines. On display are pots used to carry the palm oil, which were inspected on the beach for quality before being sealed and taken to the waiting ships. Young boys collected the palm husks from 10m palms and they were boiled until the oil floated to the surface and could be scooped off. There's a selection of money on display that's been used in the region over the centuries, including cowrie shells, 17th-century manilas of copper and brass, flat iron bars used in the early 19th century (when you reputedly needed 36 of them to buy a slave), and a very rare Republic of Biafra one pound note. Other displays cover the slave trade, the arrival of the Portuguese, the British penetration of Nigeria, and trade on the Calabar River. There are some original documents and memoirs of the trade ship captains, some 19th-century furniture (including an 1885 organ), some pictures of the Queen's 1956 visit to Calabar when she visited Mary Slessor's grave, and a hall dedicated to the culture of the local Efik people. From the upstairs rooms are fabulous views of the old town and the river, and it's not difficult to imagine the colonial officers surveying the river full of boats carrying palm oil on to waiting ships. In the grounds is the Heritage Bar and Grill, which serves *suya* and fried plantain, and you can sit in the huts and watch football on TV surrounded by nice gardens and trimmed hedges, and even play chess! I never saw this anywhere else in Nigeria. Throughout the huts men and women were playing chess, and there seemed to be some league going on as there were lists of names pinned up on the wall. Most bizarre.

From the museum you can stroll to the river down Court Road, past the old brick courthouse, the hospital and the Governor's Lodge, a very elegant white building with a green roof surrounded by manicured gardens. Towards the bottom of Court Road look out for a restored colonial house that is now the headquarters for the Crosslines bus company, and next door, rather amusingly, is the Basic Detective School. On Marina Road next to the river are more old warehouses with shuttered windows, and an **independence memorial** with a lion on top. This is an atmospheric place to walk and everyone is busy on the wharfs hauling fish in or waiting for boats to cross the river, and there are few bars to sit at, distinguished by the Star and Maltina flags. From Marina Road you can climb the hill again at Edem Street, to the 1904 **Duke Town Church** established by Presbyterian missionaries, where you'll see its still-working clock on the steeple, and its bell across the street. On Boco Street, the next road back down the hill at number 19, is a dilapidated old

19th-century pre-fabricated British building; look out for the brass wind chime and weathercock on the top. Around the corner of Enendem Street is another similar building, again hopelessly falling down, which was once the home of Chief Ekpo Bassey, who ordered the building from England. At the top of Enendem Street is the **Mary Slessor Memorial Tomb,** in a nicely tended graveyard with tall palm trees overlooking the river, though you may find the gate locked. Mary Slessor was one of Nigeria's most influential missionaries in the 19th century. Her tombstone notes her Scottish roots and describes her as the heroine that ended the killing of twins and their mothers in the Calabar region, which once used to go on amongst the highly superstitious Efik people. **Mary Slessor's cottage** is in Ekenge across the river from Calabar, and it's a fine, double-storied house with an outside staircase and wooden doors and windows, and a roof made from corrugated iron sheets that has been reasonably well preserved. Apart from the outside of the house, there's nothing to see, but you can get there by catching a boat from the wharf on Marina Road.

The Old Calabar **Botanic Garden** was established in Nigeria by the Royal Botanic Gardens, Kew in 1893. The Cross River State Forestry Department converted the garden into a zoo in the 1970s for a brief spell, but the grounds have been derelict for the last 20 years. At the time of writing, the Iroko Foundation, a UK-based NGO, together with Cercopan (see below), had a new master-plan to reopen the gardens, and again the design for the gardens has come from Kew Gardens in London. (You can find more details on the website www.irokofoundation.org.) The new garden will incorporate a nature trail, medicinal plant nursery, primate rehabilitation facilities and an environmental education centre, and will educate Nigerians about the endangered African rainforests of Cross River State. The expected opening date is in late 2005 and it will be on the corner of Target Road and Mary Slessor Avenue.

## Calabar Drill Monkey Ranch

The Drill Monkey Ranch (open daily, 09.00–17.00; no fee but a donation is greatly appreciated) is a rehabilitation centre and captive-breeding programme to establish a viable captive population and re-introduce drill monkeys to the wild. It is run by Pandrillus, a Calabar-based organisation owned by Peter Jenkins and Liza Gadsby; tel: 087 234310; email: drill@hyperia.com. To get to the ranch turn off Ndidem Usang Iso Road at the Atekong Drive junction and follow the road behind the Jahas Guest House around to the left. This is the most successful primate captive-breeding programme in the world, and has won an award from the Primate Society of Great Britain, and the 1996 Whitley Conservation Award (www.whitley-award.org/Articles/projects/gold/LizaGadsby.html). The couple got to Nigeria in the 1980s during their own tour of West Africa by Land Rover, and after starting up Pandrillus in 1988, have lived in Cross River State for 16 years. Whilst doing field research, Peter and Liza saw captured infant drills whose mothers had been shot for bushmeat. They were an important conservation and genetic resource so they decided, with the co-operation of the Nigerian government, to rescue them from their solitary lives and bring them up in natural-sized social groups for captive breeding. They started with one female drill named Calabar who was found in a shoebox in a bush bar with a mangled finger that had been chewed by a rat, and who is now the mother of seven and grandmother of five, and is presently enjoying her retirement at the Calabar ranch. Today, the project has a total population of 171, which represents 70% of all the world's captive drills. The first drill was born at the ranch in 1994, and since then another 115 drills have been born to mothers that arrived as orphans. In 2002 a female delivered the first drill

## DRILL MONKEYS

Drill monkeys, *Mandrillus leucophaeus*, are short-tailed rainforest monkeys that survive only in Cross River State, Nigeria, in southwestern Cameroon, and on Bioko Island, Equatorial Guinea, and they are one of Africa's most endangered primates. Drills should not be confused with the more common mandrill, *Mandrillus sphinx*, found from southern Cameroon down to Gabon and the Congo Basin. Male mandrills have bright red and blue faces, whilst the male drill has a smooth black face, but otherwise they look fairly similar. Groups are led by an alpha male who is similar in size and shape to a large male baboon, and can reach over 40kg. Drills are impressive creatures, especially the males with their bright fuchsia and purple skin, beautiful grey fur and 7cm fangs, and defined white frame around their faces that is displayed when the males reach adulthood; similar to a dominant male gorilla becoming a silverback. Unlike most monkeys, drills are semi-terrestrial and spend much of their time on the ground searching for roots, insects and leaves, and they climb trees in search of fruit and to sleep at night. They are semi-nomadic, travelling long distances in the forest, perhaps following fruiting seasons of certain trees. They communicate with each other using facial and vocal expressions, and like most primates they live in highly social groups of 15–30 animals. On mainland Africa, their natural range is only about 40,000km², about the same size as Switzerland, an area that is frequently at the mercy of loggers, hunters, farmers and encroaching development. Hunting for bushmeat is the biggest threat to their survival, and as most of this trade is commercial (not just to feed a hunter's family but to provide bushmeat for cash at local markets) then hunters kill as many animals as they can. It's not known for sure how many drills remain in the wild, but the population is certainly fewer than 10,000 and possibly as low as only 3,000. On Bioko Island in Equatorial Guinea, numbers are put at only 500. In zoos in Europe and the US, drills number only about 60 and they have bred poorly. In the wild, female drills give birth to only one infant a year at most. It's against the law to hunt drills in both Nigeria and Cameroon, but laws are difficult to enforce, even in the protected areas of national parks. In reality, drills in these areas do not receive effective protection from being poached out of existence forever.

twins ever born in captivity. Most of the drills that turn up at the centre are donated by local people, and by park rangers who liberate them from hunters after their mothers have been shot. Two were recovered from Asia, where they had been taken by international smugglers. In 1996, the first drill group was taken by helicopter to their new home at Afi Mountain Drill Ranch on the edge of Cross River National Park, north of Calabar, and released into a solar-powered electric enclosure of naturally forested drill habitat (a visit to Afi is covered on page 234). Today, there are five such enclosures at Afi for five separate groups of drills, and one family lives at the Calabar ranch.

The Calabar Drill Ranch and the Afi Drill Ranch also provide a home to orphaned chimpanzees and have a total of 23 individuals. The 18 biggest and oldest (aged 5–24 years) live in their own spacious natural forest enclosure at Afi, whilst the younger ones are cared for in Calabar until they become old and self-sufficient enough to make the move to Afi. Chimpanzees are again highly threatened in Nigeria, and the project offers needy Nigerian chimps a chance to live with their own kind, but they are not allowed to breed. Unlike the drills, which are bred to simply save the species, chimpanzees, once partially habituated to humans, are more difficult to return completely to the wild and breeding chimps in captivity would fill limited space needed for wild-orphaned chimps. Two of the young chimps currently at the Calabar Drill Ranch were found in a box at Calabar Motor Park.

The forests of Afi Mountain are a natural home to drills, gorillas, and chimpanzees. Peter and Liza have been involved in conservation-orientated research and survey work in both Nigeria and Cameroon and initiated the gazetting by the Cross River State government of Afi Mountain Wildlife Sanctuary. The Pandrillus project has done much to educate local people at Afi and Calabar and has taught them that it is socially and environmentally not acceptable to kill primates, and it has worked with various levels of government to enforce existing laws which protect wildlife. The project is solely funded by donations, large and small. It has no regular income and non-Nigerian staff such as Liza and Peter work for free, gainfully employing 42 Nigerian staff on a salary. Long-term financial support for the project is seriously needed, and funding of any kind, and in-kind support like animal food, medicine, building materials etc, will go a long way to preserving part of Nigeria's unique natural heritage. Their next projects are to establish another 25ha enclosure at the Afi Drill Ranch for chimpanzees and to build a new walkway for visitors (including school children) in the canopy of the forest. The project accepts European volunteers on placements, but applicants must have proven skills that can help the project. The Pandrillus Foundation in Oregon in the US helps raise funds to support the projects in Africa. Contact them if you would like to make a donation; email: pandrillus@earthlink.net.

At the Calabar ranch there will always be someone around to show you the drills and chimpanzees, and you will undeniably have an informative and educational visit, and it is a project that is well worth supporting. If you want to stay at Afi Drill Ranch, you will also need to arrange this here.

## Cercopan

The other excellent primate sanctuary, Cercopan, is at 4 Ishie Lane off Murtala Muhammed Way, behind the All States Bank (tel: 087 234670; email: cercopan@compuserve.com; www.cercopan.org). Founded in 1994, Cercopan is a non-profit making NGO involved in primate protection, rainforest conservation, education and research. It offers sanctuary to orphaned monkeys that have been victims of habitat loss and the ever-increasing bushmeat trade. Whereas the drill ranch is home to drills and chimpanzees, Cercopan is home to guenons and mangabeys – both indigenous to the tropical forests of West Africa. The project currently has six species – Sclater's guenon, only found in Nigeria between the Cross and Niger rivers and highly endangered, mona guenon, Preuss's guenon, only found around the Obudu plateau in Nigeria, red-eared guenon, putty-nose guenon, and red-capped mangabey. Most are orphans whose mothers were shot for bushmeat or sold as pets, and were donated or have been confiscated by park rangers, though some of the animals were born here. Again, like the drill ranch, the animals are organised as troops in the enclosures and when the troop is established, often when a male becomes dominant, a family unit is moved from the Calabar site and released into a much larger enclosure in the Rhoko Forest, a 4,000ha area of protected forest in the Akamkpa Local Government Area near the village of Iko Esai, on the edge of Cross River

National Park to the north of Calabar. In 2003, Cercopan moved the first group of 18 red-capped mangabeys to the forest site. Leo, a mona guenon, was the first monkey of the project, and at the time of writing was ten years old, and the project now cares for 102 monkeys, of which about a quarter are at the forest site and the rest in Calabar. You can visit the centre (open daily, 09.00–17.00; no fee but a donation is appreciated) and someone will show you around and introduce you to the monkeys.

Jerry Akparawa is the local Nigerian education officer and he runs an excellent education project and goes out to over 40 schools around Calabar and sets up conservation clubs that meet at Cercopan on Saturdays. The centre gets around 12,000 visitors a year, mostly school children, and there's a similar project at the schools and churches around the Rhoko Forest. Jerry talks to the children about the plight of monkeys, and produces an activity booklet for kids explaining why monkeys should be with their families, and in simple terms why 'monkeys are finishing' – using language that Nigerian children can understand easily – 'Monkeys will finish if the number of monkeys killed is more than the number of monkeys born.'

The centre employs 28 Nigerians and is run by volunteers mainly from the UK, including vets and administrators, and if you are at all interested in a placement contact them. They also rely on donations and overseas grants to survive, so again if you have any interest in preserving Nigeria's natural heritage this is a worthwhile project to support. Future projects include moving more of the animals to big enclosures at Rhoko and building more accommodation and classrooms up in the trees, and Cercopan is also involved in a project with the UK-based Iroko Foundation to turn the old site of Calabar Zoo (which was thankfully shut down) into a botanical garden and to move some of the monkeys there.

## GIVING SOMETHING BACK

On two occasions in Nigeria we were offered primates to buy. The first occasion was in Katsina in the north when a man approached us and asked if we wanted to buy a patas monkey (he pointed up to the creature chained to a balcony on his house). The second and more shocking time was whilst talking to a director of one of Nigeria's (appalling) zoos; he candidly told me that he was on very good terms with the local hunters, could give them a specific order, and could get me (or anyone else for that matter) a chimpanzee for US$5,000. He added 'they are more expensive than other monkeys because they are quite rare you know', and 'we do not cheat the hunters over their prices, so they don't stop coming here.' This was the same zoo that was responsible for illegally sending two captive gorillas to a Malaysian zoo in 2002. Primates are critically endangered in Nigeria, and some, such as the Sclater's guenon, which are endemic to Nigeria, are so rare that no-one knows how many individuals remain in the Cross River forests. You are sadly more likely to see primates dead than alive in Nigeria, as black magic ingredients on a *juju* doctor's stall, and in the forests of southeastern Nigeria monkeys are still eaten. The chimpanzee incident shocked me to the core, and for this reason I would like to highlight and encourage support for both the Pandrillus and Cercopan projects detailed above. They are both excellent community-based charities working towards primate conservation and education and their work is imperative; without them many primate species will disappear from Nigeria's forests forever.

Rhoko Camp is used by researchers and students, but at the time of writing the project was close to establishing the same sort of arrangement as the Afi Drill Ranch, that the camp can receive visitors, and it should all be up and running by the time this book comes out. The set-up here is almost identical to that at Afi (see page 234), with three rustic, raffia-roofed sleeping huts that sleep four in each, a kitchen hut with a wood fire, an open shower and long-drop toilets. You'll need to bring all your provisions with you and Iko Esai is 3½ hours north of Calabar on the Ikom road, from where the Rhoko Camp is accessible by *okada* or 4WD. To arrange a visit, and possibly a transfer if any staff are going up there, you first need to go to the Calabar office and then they will radio through to the camp. To get there by public transport, take a vehicle towards Ikom and the Cercopan staff will tell you exactly where to get off. An overnight stay costs N1,000 per person, which includes a guided forest walk to see the monkeys, plus N500 extra for a fun tree climb and abseil and N100 for a community fee.

## Around Calabar
### Creek Town
A short relaxing trip up the river from Calabar is the small settlement of Creek Town. To get there **boats** go from the wharf near the independence statue on Marina Road at approximately 12.00 and return at 14.00, and depart again at 16.00 (but don't return). Note that there is no accommodation at Creek Town. It's a pleasant one-hour ride and you'll get to see the fishermen and villagers going about their business amongst the thick mangroves and dense palms on the banks of the Cross River. There's nothing really to see once at Creek Town, though look out for the church, a fine colonial building that is thought to be older than the Duke Town church in Old Calabar. You can also wander through the small market and chat to the locals, and maybe indulge in a gourdful of palm wine.

## ORON
Oron is a small town across the creek from Calabar and makes for an interesting excursion, and it's also the departure point for boats to Cameroon. **Boats** to and from Calabar go-when-full from the wharf, cost about N100 and take a little over 20 minutes. Pay for your ticket in the boat shed and one of the touts will show you to the right boat. You can also get boats here to Limbé and Doula in Cameroon a few hundred metres to the left of the Calabar boats (a short hop on an *okada* through the back streets). Again they are small motor boats that carry 20 people and go-when-full, at roughly 07.00 and 12.00 daily, and they cost N4,000. Unlike the ferries between Calabar, these boats carry two engines as a back up, though I hear dire stories about whole boats being lost at sea, as they are often perilously overloaded and in poor condition; you may want to consider taking a drop boat (ie: having the boat to yourselves), but this will cost considerably more and you'll have to negotiate hard over a price. There's an immigration shed near where the boats depart, where the boatman will take you to have your passport stamped out of Nigeria, and the police here will undoubtedly search your luggage, and on arrival in Cameroon (where you need a visa) you go through the same procedures. If you need to stay overnight in Oron, the perfectly acceptable **Bakibum Beach Hotel,** 1 Oron Road (no phone), and easily spotted, as it's the tallest building in town very close to the wharf, is quite a surprise with new windows, new doors, new AC units, stone floors, satellite TV, and hot water, and fabulous views of the river and all the activity in the streets below. It's on six stories, but has only 19 rooms, and at N2,500 per room it's excellent value. The chef will cook Nigerian food or chicken and chips on request, but give him plenty of notice. The **Oron Museum** (open

*Above* Palm-oil sellers at the market in Oyo

*Right* Pure-water seller in a Lagos motor park

*Below right* Chilli peppers are used in most Nigerian dishes

*Bottom right Isiewu*, goat's-head pepper soup, is arguably Nigeria's national dish

*Below* A popular scam throughout Nigeria is to sell a property whilst the real owner is away

THIS HOUSE IS NOT FOR SALE

BE WARNED

GOAT HEAD IS SOLD HERE

*Above* Zuma Rock, Suleja, considered to be the geographical centre of Nigeria

*Left* Oshun Sacred Forest, Oshogbo. The Austrian artist Suzanne Wenger created statues and shrines to honour the Yoruba deities

*Below* National Mosque, Abuja, erected opposite the unfinished National Church when the new capital was built

daily, 09.00–17.00; N20 entry fee) is also a worthy distraction whilst you're waiting for a boat, just a few metres to the right of the Calabar boats. The most important exhibit here is the Ekpo wood carvings, mostly heads, that were used to contact ancestors and pray for assistance. Ekpo is the local traditional religion and refers to souls and ghosts that haven't yet reached their resting place in the underworld. The museum opened in 1959 to preserve over 600 of these statues of deities, as the traditional religion had fallen away in the face of Christianity, but the museum was shelled during the Biafran War in 1967, and many of the statues were destroyed or lost, though around 100 remain here today. There are also some elaborate Ekpo masquerade costumes and masks made of wood and straw. Some of the masks are quite ugly and strange; some are skin masks, presumably made from animal hide, though they were once made from human skin and look spookily lifelike. There's an exhibit on the Ibibio puppet plays, that before the advent of Christianity used to be used as entertainment, but also to spread moral tales, and the plays featured subjects such as abortion, adultery, theft or greed (the male puppets on display have enormous genitals). There are ceremonial calabashes for drinking palm wine at special events such as weddings or funerals, and it was believed that if a witch or thief drank from a ceremonial pot they would die. In the grounds of the museum is a bunker from the Biafran War with a rather frightening-looking, life-size model of a soldier, and beyond here is a lovely patch of gardens right next to the riverbank called the **Prince Chris Abasieyu Garden**. It's a very tranquil spot with tables and chairs and an outdoor pool table popular with courting couples. From here you can watch the fishermen on the river and the jungle of palms on the other side, and sip on a malt drink, or occasionally palm wine, bought at the museum kitchen.

## KWA FALLS

The impressive Kwa Waterfalls are located at the southern edge of the Oban Division of Cross River National Park, about 40km north from Calabar at Aningeje, towards the town of Oban on a newly tarred road. You can drive right to the top of the falls, and they are in a deep valley with beautiful forest surroundings, and you can walk down the 150 or so steps to the river below and swim. When there's lots of water there is quite a torrent of white water flowing down the rocks. A signpost at the turn-off to the falls says 'Kwa Falls Police Station and Plantation'. From here, follow this road for two to three kilometres up a gravel track, go over a concrete bridge, and then turn right at a small junction and go to the end of this road down a dip and past a couple of buildings until you get to a white building on its own. If you are self-sufficient, you can negotiate with the local people to camp here, and they can also arrange to get beers and soft drinks from one of the local villages, or possibly even palm wine.

## CROSS RIVER NATIONAL PARK

The Cross River National Park is the largest area of undisturbed rainforest in the country, and has been described as the Amazon of Nigeria, that seemingly goes on forever, over into Cameroon. The park is spectacularly beautiful, with green, rainforest-cloaked mountains and enormous trees. The park is split into two parts; the Oban Division and the Okwangwo Division (that also includes parts of the Obudu Plateau), which are approximately 40km apart on either side of the Cross River to the north of Calabar. The park covers approximately 4,000km$^2$ of the Cross River State and the terrain is tough, with hilly escarpments and steep valleys, and with peaks that generally rise higher than the surrounding deep forest, some of which reach nearly 1,000m. These rainforests are some of the oldest and richest in the whole of Africa, and many reports written by biologists, going as far back as the

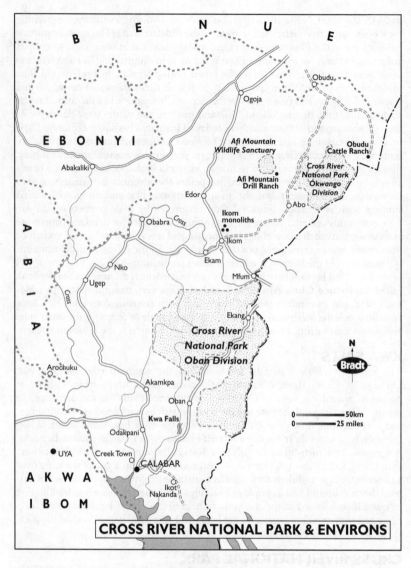

**CROSS RIVER NATIONAL PARK & ENVIRONS**

1920s, emphasise the extreme biological richness of the area, their relatively intact status and the increasing threat from uncontrolled farming, logging and hunting. The Oban division has an estimated 1,558 plant species, whilst the Okwangwo division has 1,545 species, 77 of which are endemic to Nigeria. The unique nature of Cross River State tropical forest is due in part to its high annual rainfall of over 4,000mm, and its relatively short dry season. Consequently, this forest, together with that immediately adjacent in southwest Cameroon, is classified as the only true evergreen rainforest in Africa. Over 60% of Nigeria's endangered plant and animal species are found only within these forests. These include 132 tree species listed by the World Conservation Monitoring Centre as globally threatened. As many as 200 species have been recorded from a single 0.05ha plot, a diversity matched only in exceptionally rich sites in South America. These trees also attract butterflies, and these forests are richer in butterflies than any other part of Africa.

The Okwangwo Division, home to about 80% of all wild primate species in Nigeria, is where Cross River gorillas share the same habitat with other primates, including chimpanzees and drills. Other rare species include possibly leopard, small antelope, a variety of monkeys, as well as buffalo and forest elephants. The gorilla, which had been declared extinct in Nigeria 40 years earlier, was rediscovered in 1987, and the huge amount of international publicity which this generated helped to persuade the government to gazette Cross River National Park in 1988. Nevertheless, as in Nigeria's other parks, mismanagement and neglect have taken their toll, and whilst the forests of the park are largely intact, they have been subjected to recent small-scale logging in some areas, and hunting continues to be practised throughout, endangering many species, notably the drill, chimpanzee, some of the monkeys such as Preuss's and Sclater's guenons, and the forest elephant.

## Getting there and away

From southern Nigeria, Calabar is the starting place to see the park. The Oban Division headquarters are located at Akampka, about one hour's drive north of Calabar. The Okwangwo Division is a six-hour drive north from Calabar via Ikom. From Ikom take the Obudu road and approximately 60km from Ikom is the Kanyang Field Station. However, you will find no facilities at either of these places, and the gates will probably be locked. About four years ago some half-hearted attempt was made to build visitors' camps, but any work has fallen derelict since then. If you are in your own vehicle and are completely self-sufficient for camping

### CROSS RIVER GORILLAS

In the late 1980s, news reached the outside world that gorilla populations still survived in the mountainous region on the Nigeria-Cameroon border, an area in which it was thought that gorillas might be extinct. Nigeria's gorillas are the most northerly and westerly in Africa. There are two distinct populations of gorillas in Cross River National Park. These populations were probably in contact in the past but are almost certainly isolated from each other today. One occurs at the northern end of the park in the forests of the former Boshi Extension Forest Reserve, originally established as a gorilla sanctuary in 1958. The other is found in the southwestern part of the former Okwangwo Forest Reserve, immediately adjacent to Cameroon's Takamanda Forest Reserve. There are some indications that the Boshi gorillas migrate seasonally across the Nigerian border into Takamanda Forest Reserve.

The Nigeria-Cameroon gorillas are recognised as a subspecies of the western lowland gorilla, and are dubbed the Cross River gorilla. It has been difficult to get accurate numbers, but it's generally believed there are around 150–200 gorillas in this region, and as such they are critically endangered, facing an extremely high risk of extinction in the wild in the immediate future. The chances of seeing these gorillas are minimal and they are not habituated to humans; if they were their lives would be under even more of a threat from hunters. One researcher we spoke to had spent two months in Cross River National Park, and whilst he had heard them and saw their night nests, he never saw the gorillas themselves.

and are willing to persevere, you may be able to find wardens, who may find keys, and a secretary who will perhaps take some sort of entrance fee, but be warned the roads into the forest are overgrown and badly maintained. The best way to appreciate the Cross River forests are from the Kwa Falls, at the Cercopan bush camp (dealt with under *Calabar*), or the Afi Drill Ranch (see below), all of which occupy good positions on the edge of Cross River National Park, as does the Obudu Cattle Ranch (below), which despite being on a beautiful high plateau is less forested than the other places.

## AFI DRILL RANCH

The Afi Mountain Wildlife Sanctuary was created in 2000 by the Cross River State Government and the dense forests, jutting pinnacles and sheer rock faces are one of the most scenic areas in the state. The region is a natural home to chimpanzees, drill monkeys and gorillas, and many other forest animals, including bush pig, several species of monkey, parrots, eagles, pangolin, civet cats, and mongooses. The Afi Drill Ranch is located on the edge of Afi Mountain Wildlife Sanctuary, from where there are tremendous views of the Afi massif towering above. The land is leased from the village of Buanchor, giving them an annual cash income as well as providing local people with jobs at the ranch and supporting local farmers by buying food for the ranch's animals. (For a complete background on Pandrillus, who operate both the Afi and Calabar ranches, see page 226 under the *Calabar* section.) In 1996, the first drill group was taken by helicopter to their new home at Afi, a solar-powered electric enclosure of naturally forested drill habitat. Today, there are five such enclosures at Afi and one for chimpanzees, and all told there are around 25ha of enclosed forest. In 2001, President Obasanjo visited the ranch, went for a walk to see the animals, and planted a tree. The path from the camp to the enclosures is now dubbed Obasanjo Way.

This is a stunning and remote spot, and the views from the camp of the giant tangled trees and brooding mountains are outstanding. The mist-filled air is full of bats and soaring raptors in the early mornings and evenings, and butterflies and twittering insects during the day. There are easy hikes and walks to the swimming holes and waterfalls on the Bano Stream, and one of the staff will go with you into sections of the Afi Mountain Wildlife Sanctuary. You can visit the demonstration tree nursery of native fruit and tree seedlings, and of course the drills and chimpanzees, in their vast and thoroughly natural enclosures. On our visit, the guide took us on a walk into one of the enclosures, where we watched a drill family frolic about around the alpha male, whilst the other males kept to their own areas, waiting for their chance one day – our guide called them Area Boys! At the chimpanzee enclosure is a raised platform from where you can get a chimpanzee's-eye view of the forest and the animals playing, eating or grooming each other, or simply lying back on the grass contemplating their surroundings. There are also other monkeys in the trees in and out of the enclosures, which are lighter than the chimps and drills and which can therefore move through the enclosures at treetop level.

The camp consists of a kitchen hut with a fire, fridge, and the manager's desk and radio; a few sleeping huts with double beds and mosquito nets; a long-drop toilet and open-air bush shower, with a water supply from a hand-filled tank (the staff will heat the water first over a fire, but this is not really necessary and time-consuming for them); and a viewing hut with a wooden balcony and chairs, which provides the perfect spot to look up at Afi Mountain and the forest canopy. You need to bring all your own food and the staff will make sure that there is a fire for you to cook on in the kitchen hut, and that there is always a kettle on the go. Water is available and is fine to drink, as it comes directly from one of the mountain streams (except during the dry season when you need to bring your own). There are a few plates and pots available to use, but we found it useful to have our own plastic bowls and spoons (bought very cheaply from any market) and big groups need their own equipment. Take things that are easy to cook – we took instant noodles, tins of baked beans, sweet corn, tuna, packet soup, bread, tea bags, powdered milk and the like. You'll need to get these items from one of the supermarkets in Port Harcourt or Calabar as they are not available locally. A torch is essential. Warm beers and soft drinks can be ordered from the local village, but you will need to pre-arrange delivery as the staff only go in and out of the ranch by truck once daily. The nearest petrol station and markets are in either Ikom or Obudu, so be sure to stock up. If you want a hut, it's essential that you arrange a visit with Liza and Peter in Calabar first and they can radio through to Afi to tell them when you are coming. Camping isn't a problem, and if you are fully equipped you can just pitch up. Huts are N2,000 per person per night, camping is N1,000, plus N500 per vehicle, and every visitor is required to pay an additional N200 per night that goes directly into the Buanchor Community Development Fund. The forest at Afi is full of insects, and closed shoes, socks, and long trousers are essential despite the heat, though take swimming gear, as during most times of the year you can swim at the waterfalls at Bano Stream.

## Getting there and away

If coming from Calabar, follow the road from Ikom towards Obudu. Drive for 56km north, towards Obudu, to a dirt track on the left (10km after Abo Ogbagante). If you get to Kanyang you've gone too far. Drive 6km west to the village of Katabang, crossing the Afi River, then turn right at the T-junction in Katabang and continue north for 6.5km to the marked turn into Drill Ranch. If coming from the north go south from Obudu on the Ikom road 60km (55km from the Obudu Cattle Ranch turn-off). The dirt track is on the right, 4km south of the village of Kanyang. The road into the ranch is windy and steep in parts, and you may need a 4WD vehicle with high clearance in the wet season. Overland groups are more than welcome, but Peter and Liza would rather the truck itself was left down in the village, as the road is only really suitable for smaller vehicles such as Land Rovers. And as they quite rightly say, if the road is negotiable for an overland truck, then it can also be used by the big vehicles of the logging companies. Trucks can park at the school at Katabang and the group can walk or find an *okada* in the village to take them the final 6.5km, but they will have to carry all their equipment if staying overnight, though it's easy enough to visit on a day trip. By public transport get a bush taxi at Ikom Motor Park to Obudu and asked to be dropped off at Kanyang. This is past the turn-off to Katabang if you are coming from the south, but you will have more of a chance of getting *okadas* here than in the Abo Ogbagante further back. We found it quite easily thanks to everyone else in the bush taxi telling us 'that is where the white people live'! Ask in the village for *okadas* and it shouldn't take long for them to miraculously appear. Negotiate with the drivers for the journey from the main road through the forest to the ranch, which is thrilling by bike and takes roughly an hour. If you are coming from the north and Obudu, get dropped off on the road at the village of Wula, which is only 30km or so south of Obudu, and arrange for an *okada* here to approach the ranch from the north via the village of Boki. There is another road between Ikom and Obudu via Ogoja; make sure you are on the right road and in the right bush taxi.

# OBUDU CATTLE RANCH

**Protea Hotel Ranch Resort** (tel: 087 238994/5, 238997/9; www.proteahotels.com; you can also make a reservation through the South African office, which you may want to consider doing if you want to use a credit card over the phone; tel/fax: +21 (21) 430 5330) is now run by the South African company Protea, and called the Ranch Resort; this used to be the Obudu Cattle Ranch and is somewhat of an institution from the colonial days. It's not far from the Cameroon border and is situated on a beautiful plateau 1,576m high on the Oshie Ridge at the base of the Sonkwala Mountains. The ranch has a long history and was of course originally a cattle ranch established in 1951 by Scottish farmers. The mountain range was first explored in 1949 by one Mr McCaughley, who camped on top of the mountain for a month, when he presumably decided that it would be the ideal spot for raising a few cattle. He returned a couple of years later with a Mr Jones and a Dr Crawford, who between them established a ranch on the rolling green plateau. Its heyday was in the 1950s–60s, when it was the retreat for the colonials and the wealthy, but for the couple of decades before Protea took over in 2002, it was a shadow of its former self and an extremely dilapidated place, where you couldn't even get anything to eat or drink. Protea fully refurbished it and it's now back up there as one of Nigeria's leading places to stay.

The malaria-free plateau is fabulously situated on a land area of about 10,000ha, with a semi-temperate climate; it rarely reaches over 20°C (you'll need warm clothes) and it makes a refreshing change from the rest of the sweaty south. The best time to visit is between October and March just before the rainy season. It's tremendously scenic and the resort has beautiful and captivating scenery of rolling grassland, deep wooded valleys and waterfalls. The region is frequently referred to as 'Land of the Clouds'. The highlight here is the great hikes that can be arranged from the resort from one to six hours; expect to pay roughly N300 per hour for a guide. These go to local waterfalls and various view points, including the misspelt 'intestine road view point'. I think they mean the intense road view point, referring to the scenic switch-back road that climbs up the mountain to the ranch. There are also stables where horse riding can be arranged for about N500 per hour, and the ranch can also organise visits to the Afi Drill Ranch if you don't have your own vehicle. Other facilities include two floodlit tennis courts, squash court, mini-golf, brand new mountain bikes for hire, and at the time of writing they were building a nine-hole golf course. You can swim in a natural rock pool about a ten-minute walk away (though you'd be mad in this weather), and there's a gym with very odd, purple plastic blow-up Turkish baths (I've never seen anything like them before).

Accommodation is in 54 double chalets, most of which have a log fire, and 20 suites, and whilst we were there, a house for President Obasanjo was being built. All the chalets have DSTV, fridge, heater and phone. NEPA hasn't reached this far at all, so all the power comes from the gens, which are not put on during the day, but which stay on consistently at night to fuel the room heaters. Up here in the clouds, this means that things are a little gloomy during the day and you can't watch TV etc, but it's a laudable way of saving fuel. The restaurant has a daily changing menu with a choice of soup or salad, two Nigerian and two continental dishes to choose from, and a dessert. Rates for a standard double are N7,000 (N10,000 deposit). A chalet with a fireplace and armchairs is N9,000 (N12,000 deposit) and suites with separate living rooms and some with kitchenettes are N12,000–20,000 (N15,000–25,000 deposit), plus the 15%. The resort is fast becoming one of Nigeria's leading convention centres, so always check first if there's space, as it's a long way to come and find out it is full.

## Getting there and away

Flight packages start and finish on Wednesday, Friday and Sunday (when there are flights to the Bebi Airstrip roughly 40km towards Obudu), so you can effectively arrange a two-, three-, four- or seven-night package. Packages include flights, accommodation in a standard double room, transfers to and from Bebi Airstrip, all meals, and free use of all the facilities, including a free baby-sitting service and complimentary guides for hiking. Flights go between Bebi Airstrip and Abuja, Port Harcourt and Calabar. From Lagos another flight to either of these places is added into the package price. A two-night package for two people from Abuja, Port Harcourt or Calabar costs N87,000, and from Lagos N119,000; three nights N103,000/135,000; four nights N119,000/150,000; five nights N133,000/167,000; and seven nights N162,000/194,000.

The highlight here is the getting there, thanks to a wonderfully scenic and exhilarating road that climbs 11km from the bottom to the top pf the plateau through 22 hairpin bends, the most dramatic being about half-way up (it is called the Devil's Elbow). The wooden gate at the bottom of the road has a wooden bull's head above it and an office where you are required to sign in. The road is stunning, and at each turn the view of rolling hills and intensely green pastures get wider, and the mountain air fresher and cooler. To get to the ranch by public transport you will need to arrange a drop by taxi for roughly N2,000 from the Obudu Motor Park 65km away.

## IKOM

Finally, there's nothing of note in Ikom, but if you are travelling by public transport in the southeast you may pass through the **motor park** here, which is big, square and less hectic than many of the other motor parks in Nigeria, with vehicles parked neatly in rows. You'll also need to be here to get transport to the **Cameroon border** 30km away, usually provided by Peugeot bush taxis with wooden signs on top saying 'border'. The town is on the small side, with a big aluminium plant, and it serves the local logging companies that are making their way into the Cross River forests; look out for the enormous logging depot just to the south of town if coming from Calabar. There's a decent hotel if you get stuck to the left of the main Calabar road as it comes into town, and it's unmissable as it's one of the town's few high-rise blocks. The **Heritage Hotel** (no phone) is fairly modern, with parking in a compound, satellite TV, and clean rooms with a bucket for N2,200. At Alok, 22km north of Ikom on the Ogoja Road, are some **stone monoliths** on the roadside, which are curiously carved and set in circles about half a metre high with abstract human figures on them. It is thought that they could date back as far as AD200, but nothing is known about them. You don't have to come this far to see them, however, as there is one in the grounds of the Calabar Museum, and another at the Oron Museum.

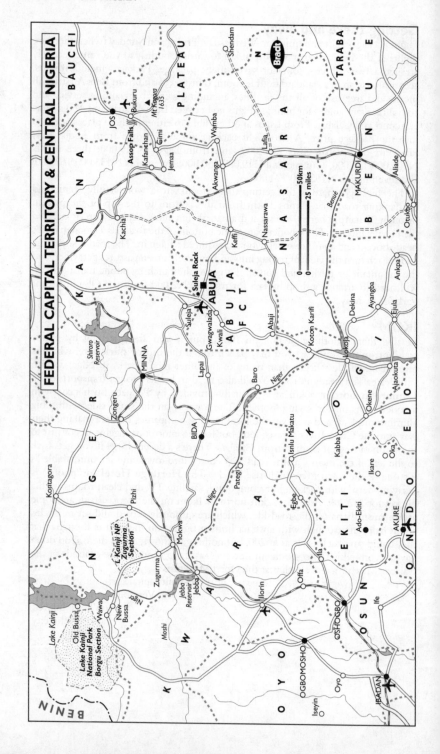

FEDERAL CAPITAL TERRITORY & CENTRAL NIGERIA

# Central Nigeria

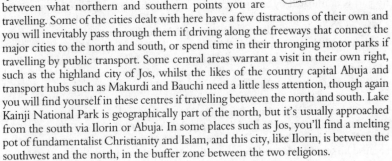

Central Nigeria is loosely the broad band that separates the distinctive southern and northern regions of Nigeria. I have lumped these areas together not for any chronological order of visiting, but simply because they do not fit into the northern or southern regions, and you'll have to dip into this Central Nigeria chapter sporadically depending on which direction, and between what northern and southern points you are travelling. Some of the cities dealt with here have a few distractions of their own and you will inevitably pass through them if driving along the freeways that connect the major cities to the north and south, or spend time in their thronging motor parks if travelling by public transport. Some central areas warrant a visit in their own right, such as the highland city of Jos, whilst the likes of the country capital Abuja and transport hubs such as Makurdi and Bauchi need a little less attention, though again you will find yourself in these centres if travelling between the north and south. Lake Kainji National Park is geographically part of the north, but it's usually approached from the south via Ilorin or Abuja. In some places such as Jos, you'll find a melting pot of fundamentalist Christianity and Islam, and this city, like Ilorin, is between the southwest and the north, in the buffer zone between the two religions.

## ABUJA

The site of Abuja, the new federal capital of Nigeria since 1991, was chosen for its strategic position at the centre of the country, its good climate, and for the fact that it was at the time of choosing sparsely populated by people who didn't have any particular religious or ethnic allegiance. The original inhabitants were mainly Gwari people who farmed the central savanna region. The Gwari women are known for carrying their loads on their shoulders and not their heads, as the Gwari people believe the head is the most sacred part of the body, which is already saddled with the burden of thinking for the whole body, and which therefore should not be over-burdened. Abuja is a purpose-built capital surrounded by large granite hills, and much of it is still under construction. Very oddly for a new city, there's also much demolition going on and throughout the city you'll see big red crosses marked on buildings earmarked to be pulled down. Allegedly, as the city grew many buildings went up without formal planning permission, and as it is all federal land, the government is pulling down those they don't want. As it's fairly new, Abuja consequently has the best infrastructure in Nigeria, with speedy expressways and traffic lights that actually work. But despite two new dams being built in the 1980s to supply the city, services such as water suffer the same fate as in the rest of the country, and Abuja is still on the national grid and is NEPA dependent. It's a moderately attractive place to live, with wide open spaces and parks, though given that construction started in the late 1970s, there's a fair amount of the ugly concrete so fashionable in that era, and it's already starting to look very dated. Abuja is sometimes criticised, even by Nigerians, for being sterile and without much colour or culture, but nevertheless those who have made the move from Lagos say that the general standard of living is better in Abuja. There's hardly anything to see or do and it's not a city for walking, as everything is very spread out along wide freeways, though like Lagos it has some of the trappings of Westernisation, thanks to the embassies and conference centres, and you'll find luxury hotels, good food and some decent shops. Also like Lagos, you'll find prices are much higher in Abuja than in the rest of the country.

## Brief history

By 1970 it was clear that Lagos, with its small islands, could no longer cope with the exploding population and inferior infrastructure needed for a country capital. General Murtala Mohammed set up a commission to decide on a central spot that was accessible from all parts of the country and that was ethnically neutral. Given that the civil war had just finished it was evident that Lagos, with its 75% Yoruba population, was not conducive to easing ethnic tensions. Abuja had neither a founder nor a settler, and even today it is populated by various ethnic migrants and no part is dominated by any particular group or religion, and there are no GRAs established by the British or townships for people from specific ethnic groups like in Nigeria's other cities, though areas are split by socio-economic divides. Plans to build the capital were approved in 1976, and a 7,770km² Federal Capital Territory was created near the old town of Abuja (renamed Suleja), and with immediate effect the ownership and control of that land became vested in the federal government. Given that this was the era of the oil boom, the government also had money to spend. The land was designated from parts of the Kwara Plateau and Niger States and is 2½ times larger than Lagos State. Abu Ja was an exiled king from Zaria who became king of the old settlement of Abuja (now Suleja) in 1825. His full name was Abubakar, but he was called Abu for short. Legend has it that because he was fair skinned, he was called Abu-ja (*ja* means red or fair in Hausa) or 'Abu-the-red-one'. The new name of Suleja came from keeping the *ja* bit but adding the *Sule*, which was the shortened name of the emir at the time of the name swap (whether that particular gentlemen was fair skinned or not I don't know!).

Construction of the city began during the late 1970s, and from its outset it was reckoned that it would take 15–20 years to build, but towards the end of that decade the oil money began to dry up, and what with corruption amongst the building contractors, construction slowed to a snail's pace and still continues today. It was decided that the land at the foot of Aso Rock would be the seat of government, and today this is where the main government buildings are located in the Three Arm Zone. The first administrator of the Federal Capital Territory Authority (FCTA) was Mobboolaji Ajose Adeogun – who has an awful lot of streets in Nigeria named after him – who embarked on a massive recruitment of town planners, architects, engineers and other professionals to work on creating the new city. The FCTA started out with an office in Lagos in 1976 before moving operations closer to the new territory in Kaduna a year later, and then again to Suleja town, where the offices were set-up in makeshift caravans as development began. For the next three years until 1980 these mobile caravan units oversaw the construction of the first roads and land clearing, and the first housing development, which was erected to accommodate the officials and eventually the construction workers. Then a Federal Secretariat was built at the village of Garki to move officialdom officially in. This has since been dwarfed by the building of the New Federal Secretariat near the State House, which was just about up and running at the time of writing. Meanwhile whole villages that fell under the FCT area were relocated from their original sites and transferred to land around Garki – these included Wuse, Maitama and Asokoro, which are now very much part and parcel of inner-city Abuja. The original villages were levelled by bulldozers and new districts created in their wake. Only Garki survived on the spot of the original village. The development attracted a huge influx of people in a sort of 'gold rush' manner for the good job opportunities and better standard of living because of the modern, new and efficient services and infrastructure. First were the road builders and construction contractors, followed by the workmen and labourers, followed by the service providers – people had to sleep and eat after all. The development of housing could not keep pace with the torrent of new arrivals, unleashing an acute housing problem that still exists today.

From its inception Abuja has been a pet project of Nigeria's incumbent presidents, who often visited Abuja to survey the building sites, and who used its flashy new hotels as a retreat to escape Lagos, and occasionally to receive foreign leaders. This tradition continued until the federal government officially moved here in 1991 during the presidency of General Babangida, when Aso Rock State House, the official residency of the head of state, was completed. In Lagos, Babangida signed the decree formally declaring Abuja as the new federal capital of the Federal Republic of Nigeria, before boarding the presidential plane and making the historic one-hour flight to Abuja in much pomp and circumstance. When he got there he was received at Abuja's concrete city gate that straddles the highway from the airport by all his ministers and top civil servants, before being whisked off to the new seat of government at the foot of Aso Rock. The subsequent migration of officialdom, business, and governmental departments has been painfully slow, however, and many were and are reluctant to leave Lagos. Even today, many people who work in Abuja fly home to their families in Lagos at the weekends, but Abuja is more or less the proper working capital of Nigeria. In the 1991 census, the same time as the capital was officially moved, the population was put at 378,671. Today it's roughly two million.

## Getting there and away
### By air
Nnamdi Azikiwe International Airport is the second-busiest airport in Nigeria after Lagos. The airport is about 40km west of the city centre along the Abuja–Lokoja Highway. As in Lagos you can just pitch up at the airport and book a flight to just about anywhere in the country on a first-come first-served basis, though here you can also go to the domestic airline desks at the Hilton and Sheraton hotels and book a ticket as well as an airport transfer. There are numerous flights to Lagos (one hour) throughout the day, as well as weekday flights to Port Harcourt, Kano, Maiduguri, Enugu and Makurdi. Airline offices are detailed under *Listings* below. Sosoliso Airlines (tel: 09 810 0122 airport desk; www.sosolisoairline.com) has three flights a day between Abuja and Port Harcourt from Monday–Friday, one on Saturday, and two on Sunday, and two flights a day between Abuja and Enugu Monday–Friday, and one on Saturday and Sunday. IRS Airlines has a flight from Abuja to Maiduguri at 11.00 on weekdays and 12.00 on Saturday that returns from Maiduguri to Abuja at 14.00 and 14.30 respectively. Overland Airways flies between Ibadan and Abuja (one hour) Monday–Friday at 08.30, 11.30, and 17.30; and from Abuja to Ibadan Monday–Friday at 07.00, 10.00, and 16.00. To get from the airport to Abuja taxis line up in the car park outside the terminal building, and a drop taxi is your only choice, as there are no minibuses,

and the 40km is an expensive ride; roughly N2,800. For budget travellers there is no reason why you can't ask around on the plane or at the airport if you can grab a lift with someone.

## By road

Zuba Motor Park, on the junction of Murtala Muhammed Expressway and the Kaduna–Lokaja Expressway, is the city's main motor park for buses and taxis going just about everywhere, including Lokoja, Jos, Kaduna and Makurdi; you'll need to change vehicles in these places to get to points beyond them. There are also overnight 'luxury' buses to Lagos and Benin City with companies such as *The Young Shall Grow, ABC* and *Chisco*. This was the only time we encountered Area Boys outside Lagos, but they paid no attention to us. To get to Zuba you can pick up minibuses around the Wuse Market in Wuse or at the stadium roundabout on the ring road at Garki, but it's easier to take a drop taxi directly there, depending on which part of the city you are in. Vehicles coming into Abuja may also drop off on Herbert Macaulay Way in Wuse.

## Orientation

Abuja has very much been built with drivers in mind, and there are long distances to walk between places. City transport is nowhere near as frequent as in Lagos or other cities, though if you're prepared to wait around a bit for minibuses and shared taxis you should be able to navigate the city all right. Vehicles run up and down the main roads, and you just need to flag one down going in your general direction; expect to pay N30–40 for a short hop. City buses and taxis are green with a white horizontal stripe, but just about any vehicle serves as a taxi. As usual *okada*s are everywhere, but I would advise you to avoid using these on the faster expressways and ring road with no crash helmet, and Abuja *okada* drivers, mostly young Hausa boys, are known to be rather reckless, so tell them to slow down if you're not comfortable. You'll also find very few speak English, as they have migrated here from the north.

If you look at the map, the **Central District** of the city is like a spine that runs through from the foot of Aso Rock and the Three Arms Zone to the southern base of the ring road, which completely circles the city, though there is some development starting to happen on the outer side. This district is the central business zone of the city, accommodating government and multi-national corporation head offices and embassies. The central district divides the city into southern and northern wings, with **Maitama**, the location of more embassies and the Hilton Hotel, and **Wuse**, for Wuse Market, to the north, and **Garki** and **Asokoro** to the south. Garki District is then subdivided into areas simply called Area 1, Area 2, etc, while Wuse is separated into zones; Zone 1, Zone 2 etc. The Central District has straight roads in a grid system.

## Where to stay

Because so many business people visit here from Lagos there must be at least a couple of hundred hotels in Abuja and more opening all the time. As the hotels are newer than elsewhere in the country, they are of a reasonably good standard, though as in Lagos, despite the competition, room rates in Abuja are fairly hefty and there is little choice when it comes to budget accommodation. Many hotels offer discounts of 20–50% on Fridays and Saturdays, and sometimes Sunday nights, so it's always worth asking, though Abuja is very quiet at the weekends, and if you are here to get visas for somewhere else the embassies will be shut. Abuja has some of the country's most upmarket hotels thanks to visiting presidents and the like, and the Le Meridien Hotel on Tafawa Balewa Way, directly behind the Abuja International Conference Centre, is likely to be the best hotel in the city, but it's not open yet. The Sheraton and the Hilton hotels are to the north of the Central District, whereas the cheaper hotels are to the south clustered around Garki. Here, I have grouped hotels under three categories based on the price of the cheapest double room.

## Upmarket: US$200 and above

**Nicon Hilton Hotel** Shehu Shagari Way, Maitama; tel: 09 413 1811–40 (29 lines); email: hilton.abuja@hilton.com; www.abuja.hilton.com. If you don't want to carry sacks of cash with you to Abuja to pay for the Hilton's mammoth deposit and room bill, book and pay through the Hilton website before arriving in Nigeria, or pay the deposit in the Lagos booking office on the 9th floor, Eleganza Biro Plaza, plot 634 Adeyemo Alakija St, Victoria Island; tel: 01 773 7934; email: sales.lagos@hilton.com. Built in 1987, the enormous Hilton is the biggest hotel in West Africa, with 442 rooms and 228 suites on ten floors, where you'll completely forget that you are in Nigeria. Nicon, by the way, stands for the National Insurance Corporation of Nigeria, which owns the building, but it's managed by Hilton International. Queen Elizabeth II, Bill Clinton, and more recently George Bush, have all stayed here. Facilities include everything you'd expect of a five-star hotel, such as pool, tennis and squash courts, gym, sauna, beauty salon, nightclub, several bars and restaurants (dealt with under *Where to eat and drink*), business centre and internet café. The Hilton's banqueting hall, that can take about 1,200 people, was the venue for boxing matches during the 2003 All African Games. The rooms and suites are elegantly decorated with DSTV and minibars and all the trimmings. If you just want to use the pool and sporting facilities, non-guests are charged a fee of N1,500 per day. On our visit the lobby was undergoing extensive renovations and they were building a new lounge bar, front desk and installing hi-tech computerised information screens throughout the hotel. There's also a full-on shopping mall, with a bureau de change, travel agencies, airline desks, a handicraft village, a bakery and extensive duty-free shops selling booze and perfume. The Hilton has so many generators banked together it resembles an electricity sub-station. Non-resident room rates are presented in US$, but you will have to pay in naira at the hotel's exchange rate, and rates vary hugely, with no fewer than 18 types of rooms. A standard double is US$230 (US$380 deposit), or US$310 (US$480 deposit) for one on the executive floor; suites start at US$590 (US$800 deposit); and for those with a kooky desire to sleep in the same bed as George Bush, the Presidential Suite comes in at a cool US$1,900 a night, and seemingly even presidents must pay a deposit, which is roughly US$2,500, plus of course the 15%.

**Sheraton Hotel & Towers** Ladi Kwali Way, Wuse Zone 3; tel: 09 523 0225/44 (19 lines); email: reservations.abuja@sheraton.com; www.starwood.com/sheraton. Another huge hotel with 611 rooms and suites, several bars and restaurants (see *Where to eat and drink*), nightclub, tennis and squash courts, gym with sauna, swimming pool and business centre. The art gallery in the lobby has some good paintings and there are a number of useful shops and travel agencies, including a good bookshop. The table tennis championships were held in the Sheraton during the All African Games. The Towers is the newly refurbished executive rooms on the eigth and ninth floors, with separate check in, complimentary breakfast, flat-screen TV and coffee maker. Rates are N17,000 (N27,000 deposit) for a single and N19,500 (N27,000) for a double in the main hotel, whilst in the Towers section singles go for N27,700 (N35,000 deposit) and doubles are N30,200 (N40,000 deposit). Don't forget the 15%.

## Mid-range: between US$100 and US$200

**Villa Hotel** Plot 1377, Borno St, Garki Area 10; tel: 09 234 2228/9, 234 7650; email: thevillahotel@hotmail.com. The very nice eight executive rooms here are above a branch

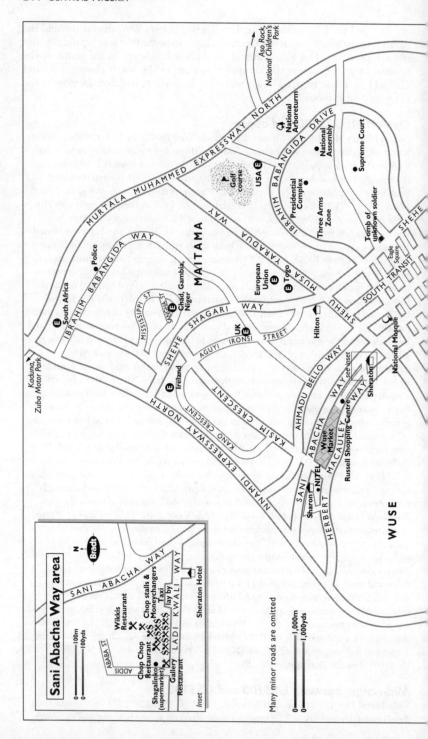

Aso Rock; National Children's Park

MURTALA MUHAMMED EXPRESSWAY NORTH

National Arboretum

IBRAHIM BABANGIDA DRIVE

National Assembly

Supreme Court

Golf course

USA Ⓔ

Presidential Complex

MAITAMA

MUSA YARADUA WAY

Three Arms Zone

Tomb of unknown soldier

IBRAHIM BABANGIDA WAY

Police

● South Africa

Ⓔ

MISSISSIPPI ST

SANTA ST

Ⓔ Chad, Gambia, Niger

SHEHE SHAGARI WAY

European Union Ⓔ

Ⓔ Togo

MUSA YARADUA WAY

SHEHE

SHEHU

SOUTH TRANSIT

Eagle Square

Ⓔ SHEHE

Ireland

AGUYI IRONSI STREET

UK Ⓔ

Hilton ▯

AHMADU BELLO WAY

National Mosque

KASIM CRESCENT

KANO CRESCENT

NNAMDI EXPRESSWAY NORTH

Kaduna, Zuba Motor Park

SANI ABACHA WAY

Wuse Market

MACAULEY WAY

Russell Shopping Centre

see inset

Sheraton ●

WUSE

HERBERT MACAULEY WAY

NITEL ●

Sharon ▯

LADI KWALI WAY

### Sani Abacha Way area

N ⬥ Bradt

0     100m
0     100yds

ABABA ST

ADDIS

Wikkis Restaurant ✕

✕S Chop stalls & Moneychangers

Taxi lay by

Chop Chop Restaurant ●

✕s✕s✕s

Shagalinko (supermarket) ●

✕s✕s✕s✕s

Gallery ● ✕ Restaurant

Sheraton Hotel ▯

SANI ABACHA WAY

0     1,000m
0     1,000yds

Many minor roads are omitted

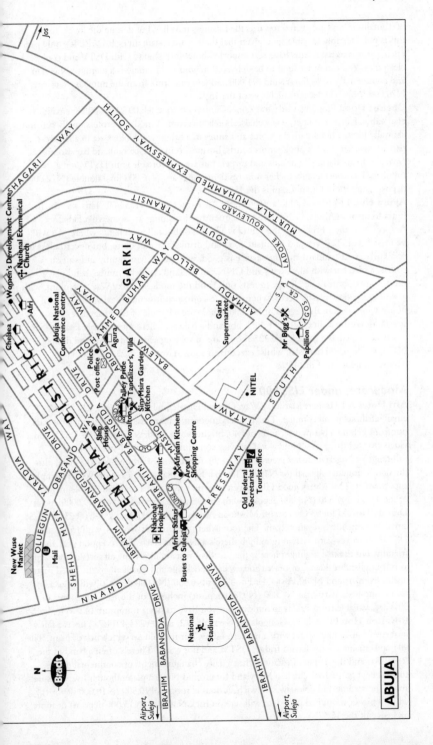

of Tantalisers, and are geared towards the business traveller, but despite the lovely rooms this is not a terribly sociable spot, given that there is no restaurant or bar area. It's only been open a year, and the rooms have real imported hotel furnishings, with DSTV and cool clean tiles. You can order food to be delivered to your room; there is a menu of Nigerian and continental dishes for around N1,000 and you can drink from the minibar. Rates are N20,000 (N29,000 deposit) inclusive of the 15%.

**Chelsea Hotel** Plot 389, Cadastral Zone, Central District; tel: 09 234 9080/98; email: chelseahotel@rosecom.net; www.chelseahotelabuja.com. A modern, professionally run and centrally located hotel with 75 rooms and suites in a bright white block set in a large car park and garden, with a pool, tennis courts, business centre, restaurant and bar. Rooms have got dreary dark red curtains and carpets but are comfortable with DSTV and a minibar. The considerably higher non-residents' rates are N16,000 for a double (N22,000 deposit), and more for suites, plus the 15%.

**Agura Hotel** Moshood Abiola Way, Garki Area 1; tel: 09 2341753/60. This was the first hotel to open in Abuja, in 1986, so consequently furnishings are somewhat faded. According to their brochure 'the Agura is a haven of boundless delights where you will be teased with Tee-Vee and exquisite food and drinks'. Er, not quite, but nevertheless it's of a fairly good standard and the service is good, with pool, gym, tennis and squash courts, a nice bar with Sky News and CNN on TV (and where a 'rumba' band plays most nights), bureau de change (guests only) and the modern Milky Way restaurant, with green-and-yellow plastic décor, where a three-course continental meal with a glass of house wine costs in the region of N2,500. There are a couple of travel agencies and several domestic airline desks in the lobby and a bakery, where inexplicably I saw a loaf of bread shaped as a turtle! The 135 rooms are of varying sizes and a standard double is N15,000 (N20,000 deposit), whilst executive rooms start from N23,000 (N28,000 deposit), inclusive of the 15%.

## Moderate: under US$100

**Afri Hotel** 281 Herbert Macaulay Way, Central District; tel: 09 234 3003, 234 9724/7; email: afrihotel@rosecom.net. This is a very modern, smart glass building with a car park out front behind a boom gate, and with 40, bright-white spotless rooms, with DSTV and a video channel that plays 'Nollywood' movies continually, and a well-stocked minibar. A full range of Nigerian dishes are available in the restaurant for around N400 a plate, plus the odd continental special for N1,400. The bar has so many bottles of drinks it resembles a supermarket. This is very good value given how nice it is, and a standard double inclusive of the 15% is N7,590 (N8,000 deposit) with suites starting from N8,000 (N9,000 deposit).

**Dannic Hotel** Plot 93 Oyo St, off Moshood Abiola Way, Garki Area 2; tel: 09 234 8183/5; email: adannichotels@yahoo.com. The rooms here are tiny but spotless, with fridge and DSTV, and a key-card system (good job there's a 24-hour gen). The reception staff are very friendly, but the real highlight here is the excellent restaurant serving all sorts of treats such as full English breakfasts, or prawn and avocado cocktails and excellent cream-based pasta dishes from around N700. A standard double is N6,530 (N8,000 deposit) with bigger rooms and beds starting at N7,800 (N9,000 deposit) inclusive of the 15%. Discounts of 50% are available from Friday to Sunday, but you have to stay a minimum of two nights.

**Royalton Hotel** Plot 1970, Gongola St, Garki Area 2; tel: 09 234 4914/7. This is a fairly neat tower up a quiet street with a modern lobby, but it could do with a lick of paint. The 90 good-quality rooms have a fridge, DSTV, and hot water. There's often a band in the Royal Bar and the Capital Restaurant has a daily changing menu of continental dishes such as beef goulash or chicken Maryland for around N900 a plate, though I wasn't sure about the sardine and coleslaw sandwich. A double room is N6,500 (N10,000 deposit), while a bigger room/bed or a suite will set you back N10,000 (N15,000 deposit) or more, inclusive of the 15%.

**Valley Pride Hotel** Plot 1373 Borno St, Garki Area 10; tel: 09 234 2401; email: valleypridehotel@hotmail.com. One of the best budget options in Abuja, with 20 plain but functional rooms with local TV. Rather oddly, there's a solicitor's office and a shop selling Guinness, pencils and greeting cards but little else in the lobby, and a restaurant offering western favourites such as spag bol and sweet and sour chicken for around N700. Rates are inclusive of the 15% and include one free breakfast of tea-bread-and-eggs per room, with the cheapest 'studio' room going for N4,500 (N6,000 deposit); a 'standard' is N6.900 (N8,000 deposit) and various suites go for N7,500–11,000 (N9,000–12,000 deposit). There is a 25% discount at weekends on all the rooms except for the 'studio' ones.

**Sharon International Hotel** Plot 220, Fort Lammy St, Wuse Zone 6; tel: 09 523 3444, 523 3445. There are 18 ordinary rooms in a fairly run-down block but everything works, with DSTV and fridge. It's in a useful location near to Wuse Market, in case you arrive late and get dropped there by bus. The small kitchen can rustle up Nigerian food and the odd Chinese dish for around N600, but there's no alcohol. A standard double is N3,500 (N4,500 deposit).

**Papillion Hotel** 449 Lagos Crescent, off Ladoke Atintola Bd, Garki Area 2; tel: 09 234 1613, 234 4835. Good budget option with clean doubles from N2,500 (N4,500 deposit) for a simple room with TV and bucket, and for extras such as a fridge and water heater expect to pay N4,000 (N6,000 deposit); all rooms have both AC and a fan. There's a communal lounge and dark restaurant serving basics, or eat at the chop houses and bars on lively Lagos Crescent.

**Africa Safari Hotel** Plot 11 Benue Crescent, Garki Area 1; tel: 09 234 7881, 234 1365. This is another good and friendly budget option in a housing estate within walking distance of the Area 1 Shopping Complex. The rooms with fridge and DSTV are old fashioned, but have new appliances, and there's a 24-hour gen. You can get Nigerian dishes and simple western items like egg and chips for under N500, and beers. Water is a problem here so keep your bucket full. Order it the night before and you'll be woken up with tea-bread-and-eggs in bed. Rooms are N2,500 (N3,000 deposit) with a 20% discount at weekends.

## Where to eat and drink

All the hotels have restaurants and most of them are fairly good. The area around Zone 4 Corner Shops (look for the sign on Ladi Kwali Way) and the adjoining Addis Ababa Crescent in Wuse District, close to the Sheraton, has over the years built up a reputation as the cuisine centre of Abuja, and it's busy from the afternoon until well after midnight. Here you'll find a line of chop and *suya* stalls lit by paraffin lamps after dark and it's quite an atmospheric spot. After eating around here you could duck into the Sheraton for an expensive nightcap. At the end of the lane behind the Corner Shops is **Wikkis**, in a prefabricated wooden building brilliantly lit by neon lights. This is an expat haunt with a great atmosphere, though the fabulous prawns and Indian curries are pricey, with main dishes starting from N1,800–2,500. There's lots of imported booze and eating and drinking is very sociable, with everyone sitting at long bench tables. The **Chop-Chop** restaurant, back on Ladi Kwali Way, has a huge selection of well-cooked and reasonably priced Nigerian food, again in a nice atmosphere, and this is Abuja's most upmarket chop house, with an outside bar and tables. The **Galaxy Restaurant** is on the corner of Addis Ababa Crescent, offering a broad menu of Lebanese appetisers, kebabs and grills, and a chicken or meat main dish will cost around N1,400, though there's not much for vegetarians except for the hummus. There's cold beer and a few wines, and plain décor, though the outside terrace is a good spot from which to watch all the action on the main road. The **Shagalinku Supermarket** around the corner at Addis Ababa Crescent is a Lebanese supermarket selling imported goods and it stays open late.

At the Sheraton itself is a range of restaurants (though none of them cheap) including the **Papillion Restaurant** (open daily 18.30–22.30) with a nightly buffet and theme nights such as Chinese or seafood, and **Luigi's** (open daily 18.00–23.00), that has authentic Italian food and décor with a small but good menu of antipasti and pizza and steaks on a Thursday. For a meat, veal or salmon dish expect to pay around N2,500. There's also an espresso machine. The **Boathouse** snack bar next to the pool serves snacks and beverages all day and there's a bakery in the lobby where you can get a trendy coffee and slice of cream cake for N700. The **Lobby Bar** has a live band in the evening, is open 24 hours, and happy hour is 18.00–19.00. Here you will meet many other Abuja expats. The **Aquarium Nightclub** (open Friday–Saturday 22.00–dawn) thumps at the weekends, but expect to pay a huge cover charge if you're not staying at the Sheraton. The **Elephant Bar** (open daily 18.00–22.00; closed Sunday) is an informal pub with nightly live music at the main entrance.

The Hilton too has a range of upmarket bars and restaurants. The **Zuma Grill** (open daily 19.00–23.30) has a nice patio for fine dining, with Mediterranean à la carte main courses from N2,000–3,500, whilst the **Bukka Restaurant** (open daily 19.00–23.30) has an extensive Nigerian and continental buffet for around N2,500. The **Oriental Restaurant** (open daily 19.00–22.30) serves Chinese, Thai and Mongolian (make up your own) stir-frys; the **Fulani Pool Restaurant and Bar** has BBQs and a Tandoori oven, with themed BBQ nights and all-you-can-eat buffets for N2,600; the **Lobby Bar** is open 24 hours and has live music in the evenings, as does the **Capital Bar** (open daily 19.00–midnight), which is like an English pub. Apparently, when Bill Clinton visited here in 2001, he had a good time listening to a James Brown impersonator! At the **Safari Nightclub** (open Friday–Saturday, midnight–dawn) there is a cover charge of N1,500 for non-guests of the hotel.

If you are staying in Garki, then head to the Area 1 Shopping Centre for cheap eating, where there are many chop and *suya* stalls – look out for *kilishi* (meat fried and dried in the sun with pepper and onions), and fruit stalls selling prepared slices of pineapple, coconut and mango. At the southwestern corner of the market, just off Moshood Abiola Way, is the **African Kitchen**, in a yard full of trees, where on outside tables you can get beer and plates of steaming food-is-ready plus snails and *suya* for around N400. There's a branch of **Tantalisers** further up Moshood Abiola Way in Garki Area 2 on Borno Street, just round the corner from the **Sim Msira Garden Kitchen**, back on Moshood Abiola Way. This is a lovely spot down some steps on a steep hill and it's a refreshing and unusual patch of manicured lawns and gardens, with shady palms and plastic chairs and tables scattered around the grass (and no rubbish). The outside thatched huts sell beers and soft drinks, *suya*, and food-is-ready, and it's open until 02.00 if the demand is there. More cheap eating can be found to the south of Garki on Lagos Crescent, just off Ahmadu Bello Way, where there is a long line of bars and chop houses distinguished by the plastic tables and Star and Gulder beer crates stacked outside. This is quite a lively area in the evening, when there's some serious drinking to be done. There's also a branch of **Mr Biggs** at 45 Lagos Crescent and a couple of cyber cafés that stay open late. Near here and back on Ahmadu Bello Way is **Garki Supermarket**, another Lebanese supermarket for expensive imported treats, at plot 465, next door to the Eddy Vic Hotel (the latter being truly awful and not recommended).

## Changing money

You can try the bureaux de change at the Sheraton and Hilton, which while they are supposed to only offer a service to guests may not ask if you're not staying there. Alternatively, head outside the gates of the Sheraton and go to the left-hand side and down the hill on the other side of the road to reach the area around Zone 4 Corner Shops. Here are a number of Hausa money changers, some of whom have shops and kiosks that offer good rates of exchange, and they are not difficult to find as they will probably approach *oyibo*s straight away. Money changers also hang out at the Area 1 Shopping Centre in Garki.

# Listings
## Airlines
**Aero Airlines** Airport desk; tel: 09 810 0197
**Air France** Plot 1267, Ahmadu Bello Way, Garki Area 2 (opposite Unity House); tel: 09 314 7419/20
**Bellview** Airport desk; tel: 09 810 0088–89; desk at the Sheraton; tel: 09 523 0225; desk at the Hilton; tel: 09 413 1811
**British Airways** Desk at the Hilton; tel: 09 413 9608, 413 9610; email: contact.1.nigeria@britishairways.com; www.britishairways.com/nigeria
**Chanchangi Airlines** Airport desk; tel: 09 810 0143; desk at the Sheraton; tel: 09 523 0011; the Hilton; tel: 09 413 4301
**KLM and Kenya Airways** Office at the Sheraton; tel: 09 523 9965, 523 9966
**Overland Airways** Airport desk; tel: 09 810 0223
**Sosoliso Airlines** Airport desk; tel: 09 810 0122

## Cultural centres
**British Council** Plot 2935 IBB Way (on the 'British Council Roundabout'); tel: 09 413 7870/7; www.britishcouncil.org/nigeria

## Embassies and high commissions
There are dozens of embassies and high commissions in Abuja. If you are travelling overland you might need to pick up a few visas in Abuja for onward travel, so here I have listed the most useful:

**Benin** Plot 2858 Danube St, off IBB Way, Maitama; tel: 09 523 8424
**Chad** 10 Mississippi St, Maitama; tel: 09 413 0751 (open Mon–Fri 08.00–16.30). You'll need roughly N3,000 and two passport photos, and there are two forms to fill out whilst in the office, and visas are usually ready the next day.
**European Union** Europe House, 63 Usuma St, Maitama; tel: 09 413 3146/8. The EU represents a number of European member countries including Bulgaria, Finland, France, Germany, Greece, Italy, Portugal, Spain, and Sweden.
**Gambia** Plot 25 Ontario Crescent, off Mississippi St, Maitama; tel: 09 413 0751
**Ghana** Plot 301 Olusegun Obasnjo Way, Garki Area 10; tel: 09 234 5192/3
**Ireland** Plot 415 Negro Crescent, Maitama; tel: 09 413 1751
**Mali** Plot 465 Nouakchott St, Wuse Zone 1; tel: 09 523 0494
**Niger** 7 Sangha St, off Mississippi St, Maitama; tel: 09 413 4434/6
**South Africa** Plot 676 Vaal St, off IBB Way, Maitama; tel: 09 413 3776
**Sudan** Plot 337 Mission Rd, Central District; tel: 09 234 6265 (open Mon–Fri 08.00–14.30). Recent reports from an overland company say visas cost roughly US$50 paid in naira (about N6,500) and you need three passport photos, a photocopy of the vehicle licence, carnet de passages, and a list of passenger names and passport details; on their last visit it took four hours to issue all visas for the group. I have heard that they do not issue visas to US citizens, though an overland truck going through in early 2003 managed to successfully get one issued for a US passenger.
**Togo** Plot 664 Usuma St, Maitama; tel: 09 413 9833

**United Kingdom** Dangote House, Aguyi Ironsi St, Maitama; tel: 09 413 2010/1, 413 2796
**United States** 9 Mambilla St, off Aso Dr, Maitama; tel: 09 523 0916/60

## Information for visitors

The head office of the **Nigeria Tourism Development Board** is at the Old Secretariat in Garki Area 1; tel: 09 234 2764; email: ntdc@metrong.com. They'll be most surprised to see visitors but if you do drop by, they will try and rustle up some (old) brochures to give you. The **National Parks Service** head office is on the Nnamdi Azikiwe Airport Expressway; tel: 09 234 5507, 234 5568. This office is roughly two kilometres out of town on the airport road, but there is absolutely no need to go there as it is the bureaucratic headquarters for the National Parks Service and they don't have any information to give out. Like the tourist offices, this is a largely dysfunctional organisation. Nigeria's most useful **tourist office** is in the arrivals hall of Abuja airport, which has a number of good books and a map of Abuja for sale, though the staff don't seem to know anything.

## Post and communications

The main **post office** is on Moshood Abiola Way in Garki Area 10 (open Monday–Friday 08.00–16.00). There's a branch office in the Area 1 Shopping Centre. There are a number of **internet** joints around, including flash internet cafés at the Sheraton and Hilton hotels, where you'll pay ridiculously expensive prices of about N250 for five minutes and N1,000 for 20 minutes. Cheaper places, where you'll pay a more standard N150 per hour, can be found in Garki at the Area 1 Shopping Centre, and on Lagos Crescent, where there are a few 24-hour cyber cafés. You can make (expensive) phone calls from any of the hotels, or from the public **NITEL** offices on Faskari Street off Tafawa Balewa Way in Garki, or on Herbert Macaulay Way near the market in Wuse. There are plenty of cell phone and landline **phone stalls** along the streets. The main branch of **DHL** is on Dambata Close, off Tafawa Balewa Way, Garki Area 7; tel: 09 234 6557/8, though there are other branches around the city.

## Travel agents

**Allstates Travel & Tours** At the Hilton Hotel; tel: 09 523 0404
**Air Transrapid Travel Agency** At the Agura Hotel; tel: 09 234 2671
**Habis Travel** At the Sheraton Hotel; tel: 09 523 2301
**Soltan Travel and Tours** Unit 2, Russell Shopping Centre, Mousterado St, Wuse Zone 2; tel: 09 524 0951; email: soltan@hyperia.com; www.soltantravel.com. Sister office to the Lagos branch.

## Shopping

**Wuse Market** is the largest market in Abuja, with over 500 stalls and many more hawkers selling everything imaginable. It's on Sir Kasim Ibrahim Road, but you can get to it from off Herbert Macaulay Way if you walk through the newer buildings. **Area 1 Shopping Centre** is another tightly packed market along Moshood Abiola Way in Garki, which sells all sorts of things, but you might be able to pick up traditional items such as carved calabashes, drums and beads. The **New Wuse Market** is located on a temporary site along Olusegun Obasanjo Way, and is referred to as the 'poor' market, where Friday is the main day. They moved the main Wuse market here when renovating it, and whilst many of the more formal traders went back, some of the more informal traders stayed at the site, working under colourful umbrellas rather than proper stalls, so presumably prices are cheaper if they do pay rent for stalls. For upmarket shopping there are curio shops at the big hotels, and **Signature**, at 65a Kano Crescent, Wuse Zone 2; tel: 09 523 3849; www.soleilgallery.com, is the sister shop to the Lagos branch, with a wonderful collection of objets d'art from all over West Africa, and a few pieces from East and southern Africa, including oil and watercolour paintings, sculpture, exquisite furniture, antiques, fabrics, mirrors, vases, and wood carvings. The famous batik artist, Nike Davies-Okundaye, also has a gallery at the **Nike Art Village**, Kilometre 8, Abuja Airport Road; tel: 080 231 31067 (GSM), though you'll need your own car or drop taxi to get out here as city transport doesn't go this far. There are art items on display and for sale similar to those in her other galleries in Lagos and Oshogbo.

## What to see and do
### The city
The problem with Abuja is that there is very little to see or do unless you are a fan of building sites and 1970s architecture. In fact, expats and Nigerians both generally find it a dull city, which explains why many fly back to Lagos at the weekend. When the city was being built, recreational facilities were not included in the grand scheme of things and as it's a new city there are no historic sights. There has been talk of building a National Museum in the city, but nothing has materialised yet, and when I trooped off to find the National Gallery of Art that was marked on one map I had, I discovered it had not been built!

The most interesting buildings are in the **Three Arms Zone** beneath the shadow of Aso Rock (*aso* means 'victory' or 'success'). The zone was fashioned after Capitol Hill in Washington DC, where the Congress, Supreme Court and the White House are within walking distance of each other. The Three Arms Zone derives its name from the three arms of the federal government structure, namely the executive, legislative and judicial arms. The zone is encircled by a ring road and includes the Presidential Villa, the Federal House of Assembly, the Supreme Court of Nigeria and the National Arboretum. The latter is 100ha of land, natural forest and other vegetation that could be feasibly described as the president's back garden. At the beginning of Shehu Shagari Road is the **Tomb of the Unknown Soldier**, where in the past visiting foreign heads have laid wreaths. But mere plebeians are not permitted to get close to any of these buildings or even the tomb, as armed soldiers patrol the area, and the arboretum is fenced and closed off to visitors. Opposite the tomb is the **Eagle Square**, an open space with some tiered bench seating used for formal ceremonies.

Two blocks further down are the **National Mosque** and **National Ecumenical Church** facing each other from opposite sides of Independence Avenue and dominating the skyline of Abuja, underlining the determination of the government to ensure the right of every Nigerian to worship as they like. The mosque is a fine building with a golden dome and tall minarets, but non-Muslims will not be allowed to get too close. Inexplicably, building work on the church has stopped, and despite the concrete frame being put in place, it's just an empty building site. When we were there Mrs Obasanjo, the wife of the president, was heading a campaign to raise funds to finish the church. Why does she just not ask her husband? Also in the Central District on Better Life Street is the **Women's Development Centre**, where in the entrance of the main auditorium is a hall of fame of portraits and sculptures of leading Nigerian women, overlooking some friendly ladies selling a few crafts and books, including the bright orange beads worn by brides on their wedding day. Other buildings of note include the new **Abuja International Conference Centre** on Herbert Macaulay Way in Garki, a vast glass building with a row of flags outside and with several meeting rooms and a main hall that can seat 2,000 people, which hosted the Commonwealth Heads of Government Meeting (CHOGM) in 2003; and **Ship House**, on Olusegun Obasanjo Way in the Central District and built in the shape of a ship, which is the headquarters of the Ministry of Defence. On the outskirts of the city, on the airport road, is the **National Stadium**, which was built at a staggering cost of US$330 million for the eighth All Africa Games that were held in Abuja in October 2003. It can seat 60,000 under cover, has an eight-lane running track, indoor sports hall, gym, Olympic-sized swimming pool, a 3,000-seater velodrome, a full-size football pitch and practice pitches, tennis courts and hockey fields. Whether these sporting facilities will ever be used again is anyone's guess. Look out for the enormous and deserted games village on the road from the airport that has nearly 700 flats where the athletes and coaches stayed during the games. Some 15,000 attended from 51 countries. It's now standing forlornly empty, though there are rumours that it will house government civil servants. Other than that there's an 18-hole **golf course**, probably the best in Nigeria, and the Ibrahim Badamasi Babangida Golf and Country Club is in Maitama.

## National Children's Park and Zoo

This is the newest and nicest zoo in Nigeria, located at the foot of Aso Rock in Asokoro (open Monday–Friday 10.00–18.00; Saturday–Sunday 10.00–18.30; N200 adults, N50 children). To get there you'll have to take an *okada* or a drop taxi, and you may need to ask them to come back in an hour or two as there's little public transport in the car park once you get out here. It's off the ring road, the Murtala Muhammed Expressway, to the east of the city. This was only built in 2002 so the design reflects a better attitude to caged animals than in Nigeria's other archaic concrete nightmare zoos built decades ago. It's a pretty tract of countryside that has been kept clean and rubbish free (there are rubbish bins everywhere!). The modern animal enclosures, with informative display boards, are spacious and thoughtfully designed with the welfare of the animals taken into consideration (though I did feel somewhat sorry for the cheetah whose enclosure was tantalisingly right next to the goats). It's essentially a children's activity park with many playgrounds, climbing frames, paths leading to rocks to climb, a football pitch, and other treats, but there's no reason why grown-up children cannot enjoy a wander around the pleasant gardens, and it's nice to see all the Nigerian school kids ooing and ahhing at the animals that they clearly have never seen before. Animals include wildebeest, various antelope, buffalo, giraffe, ostrich, zebra, lion and cheetah (presumably from other parts of Africa), a few monkeys and some domestic animals such as chickens, ducks, camels and donkeys. There's a very pretty lake right beneath Aso Rock where the **Lake Café** serves water and soft drinks. This is a good spot to admire the rock, which is the largest of the rocks in the immediate vicinity of Abuja City; look out for birds and (supposedly) crocodiles around the edges of the lake. A few metres before the gate of the park is the **Abuja Plant Nursery**, a botanical garden with many species of flowering and fruit trees and many other plants originally created to supply trees to landscape the new city.

## Zuma Rock and Suleja

The Zuma Rock is proclaimed as the gateway to Abuja, as the Federal Capital Territory (FCT) begins at the foot of the rook, where Niger State ends. It's also reputed to be the geographical centre of Nigeria. Located just outside of the town of Suleja, on the Abuja–Kaduna Expressway, 55km from Abuja, it's a huge rounded rock, 1km long and 300m high, with sheer cliffs on all sides and vertical lines carved on it by centuries of rainfall running down from the summit. Before the founding of the new federal capital, Suleja used to be called Abuja, and when the capital was being built many construction workers stayed in Suleja and commuted daily by taxi and lorry. There's nothing to see in the centre of town, though Suleja has a pretty active motor park, from where you can get vehicles to many destinations in the region. The road from Abuja goes directly to the base of the rock before curving off to the left towards Kaduna. On this road and opposite the rock is the Zuma Rock Tourist Village, but when we visited it was decidedly shut, and quite frankly looked like it had never been opened, which it was supposed to have done in 2001. There was a sign at the entrance saying the entry fee was N100 but there was not a soul around to collect it.

### Getting there and away
Direct buses to Suleja go from the stadium roundabout in Abuja for around N150. As you approach the rock and see it looming over the road in front of you, and as the bus turns left before it to get to Suleja proper, about another 5km away, then this is where you get off. There's a Total petrol station on this corner where you can buy a drink and pick up a vehicle to go back to Abuja. Zuma Rock is quite impressive, but not necessarily worth a special trip out to Suleja and it only takes a minute to look at. Rather, look out for it on a drive or bus journey between Abuja and Kaduna.

## SOUTH AND EAST OF ABUJA
### Lokoja
Roughly 140km south of Abuja on the A2, Lokoja is the capital of Kogi State, and is principally known as the location of the confluence of the Benue and Niger rivers. You can see the spot from the Confluence Hotel, where there's a nice view of the brown sludgy rivers drifting slowly alongside one another between separate sand banks until there are no more sand banks and the river is one. During the dry season Fulani herdsmen bring their cattle to the banks of the Niger–Benue confluence around Lokoja and you can spot solitary fishermen in tiny canoes. Now a busy, and not especially clean, market town, one of the first things you'll notice in Lokoja, apart from the piles of rubbish, are the very odd abstract statues on the roundabouts. One of them I can only describe as a giant concrete triangle with a fish.

Lokoja was also the first town in the hinterland to be settled by Europeans in what is now Nigeria in the British quest to control trade on the Niger. The African Association in London sent the likes of Mungo Park, Clapperton and the Lander brothers to trace the course of the Niger in the early 19th century, and they were followed by another multi-purpose expedition that set out by steamship in 1841 from the coast until it reached the confluence of the two rivers. Their quest was to open up the hinterland for trade, evangelism and Western civilisation, and it was on this journey that Bishop Samuel Crowther first preached the gospel along the banks of the Niger. At the confluence area the local chiefs ceded a plot of land 8x5km to the British expedition to build a model farm, from which Lokoja grew into a town under the leadership of Scottish explorer Doctor William Baikie. It was Baikie, in the course of sailing up and down the Niger, who discovered that white men could survive the scourge of malaria by using quinine, and he lived at Lokoja for over 30 years where he was dubbed 'King of Lokoja'. He nurtured trade links with the Hausa to the north and learnt their language, wrote a Hausa dictionary, and translated with the missionaries parts of the Bible into Hausa. The settlement of British traders continued to thrive and in 1879, under the leadership of British administrator George Goldie, all the British companies working along the Niger were amalgamated into the Royal Niger Company with headquarters in Lokoja, which had its own constabulary and gunboats on the river protecting the company's interests. The company negotiated trade treaties with Sokoto, Gwandu, and Nupe in the north. Meanwhile, the French were making progress in a southerly direction down the Niger from the French colonies in the northwest, and the company employed a Captain Frederick Lugard to form a military force to protect the northern states from possible invasion by the French. These military operations against a rival European colonial power soon proved too expensive for a private company and in 1897 the British government ended the charter, and by 1900 had taken control of the north, and Lugard became High Commissioner of the Protectorate of Northern Nigeria. His capital was Lokoja from 1900 to 1902, before it was moved to Kaduna. Lokoja remained an important centre on the river as a collection point for goods that were transported down the Niger to the port at Warri for export. These days trucks do that along the A2, and there is surprisingly little river traffic on West Africa's greatest river.

## Getting there and away

If you are coming from Abuja note that the road to Lokoja is another blackspot for accidents, and there are loads of wrecks on the side of the road. Lokoja's motor park is in the centre of town on Murtala Muhammed Way, which is the town's main street that more or less runs parallel to the River Niger where shared taxis run up and down for N30. At the motor park you can pick up buses on short hops to neighbouring towns and long-distance vehicles to Abuja, Kaduna, Kano, Zaria and Ilorin. For the south you need to get buses to Agauba or Ankpa and then change. Until recently the only way to get to the south on the other side of the Niger was by car ferry, but there's now a new road going directly south of Lokoja to Ajaokuta, roughly 30km, where there is an enormous steel-processing plant and a brand new and very long bridge over the Niger.

## Where to stay and eat

The principal state-owned hotel under the same management as the Federal Palace Hotel in Lagos is the aptly named **Confluence Beach Hotel** (tel: 058 221726, 221751/2; email: confluencebeachhotel@yahoo.com), literally on the beach overlooking the confluence of the two rivers. It's roughly 2km to the south of town on Ganaja Road. It's a huge and popular conference venue with a vast car park, and facilities include a small bar, a basic restaurant serving Nigerian staples, a swimming pool (empty), tennis, volley ball and basketball courts (overgrown), and a children's playground (rusting); it must have been quite grand in its day. Nevertheless, it's still the best spot in town, with a peaceful view of the two rivers gliding into one another, and the 156 rooms, spread around in low blocks, are comfortable and have AC, fridge and DSTV. Rates start from a not unreasonable N4,000–5,000 for a double room of varying sizes through to N10,000–15,000 for a suite, plus the 15%. Deposits here are double the room rate. The **Kogi Hotel** (1 Janet Ekundauyo Street in the GRA; tel: 058 221605, 220655) is also a good and friendly option in a quiet area. The 30 rooms, all with AC and fan, are either in the main block or in stand-alone stone buildings, but these are not terribly private. In the nice grounds there are palm trees, lots of parking, shady gardens with outside tables, and the restaurant and bar serves the odd continental dish. Room rates start from N3,000 for a standard double inclusive of the 15%. Expect to pay a small deposit.

Best of the cheap spots is the **Ava Hotel** (Aliyu Ibrahim Attah Road; tel: 058 220558). It's not brilliant, with a noisy gen and an outside bar in the car park where large groups of men come and watch football on TV. A chipped plate of

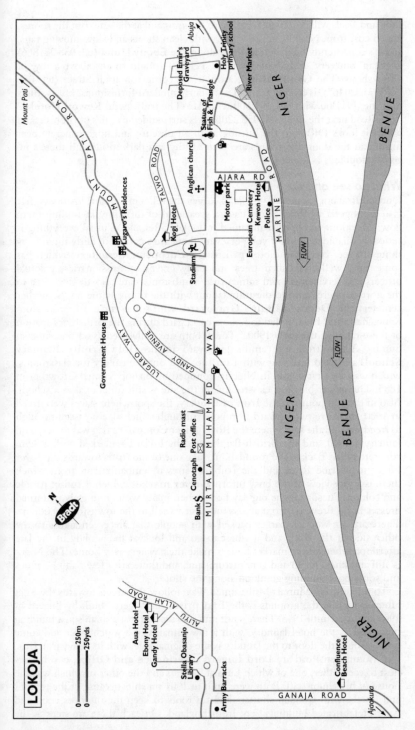

soup and *amala* will cost N400, and there's a *suya* stand at the gate. But the rooms, which cost from N1,450, are passable, with clean sheets and slow-moving fans, and it's consistently busy. A few doors along, the **Ebony Hotel** (tel: 058 221866) is cheap, but very seedy with badly lit, N1,000-a-night rooms above a row of noisy shops. The **Gandy Hotel**, around the corner on Inidi Street (tel: 058 220533, 220467), is freshly painted with fairly modern furnishings, but it stinks of urine; N1,300 with fan, N1,500 with AC. The truly awful **Kewon Hotel** (2 Ajara Road near the river; tel: 058 220633) is surrounded by piles of rubbish, and whilst it looks OK from the outside, with an obscure and huge concrete beer maiden at the door, the rooms are pretty filthy and dark inside and there's no gen. A double is N1,500.

### What to see and do

Queen Elizabeth II came to Lokoja to survey the relics of colonial history on her visit to Nigeria in 1956. She'd have a great deal of difficulty in finding them now, as nothing has been maintained or looked after and as usual everything is seriously dilapidated, but if you persevere there are a couple of fairly interesting things to see. Near the motor park is the **European Cemetery**, which has some fine, well-established trees and early graves of missionaries, colonial officers and servicemen, and some of the tombstones date back to 1867. Just to the north of here, beyond the roundabout with the funny statue on, is another cemetery, the **Deposed Emir's Graveyard**, with some graves of emirs from Kano, Zaria and Bida, exiled to Lokoja by Lugard during the British occupation of these cities in the early 1900s. Today both are sadly used as ad hoc rubbish dumps. Across from the emir's graveyard is the **Holy Trinity Primary School**, a broken building with a tin roof and outside gallery for classrooms, which was the first school in Nigeria, founded by Bishop Samuel Crowther in 1885. The newer block of classrooms on the site is still functional as a school. Also in the compound is the **Iron of Liberty**, the spot where slaves were freed in 1900; there are two upward iron poles through which slaves passed through to freedom, and the spot where the Royal Niger Company's flag was lowered on January 1 1900, and the British flag hoisted by Lugard – marked with a 2.5m concrete pillar. Back at the roundabout, take one of the roads towards the River Niger to Marine Road and the (rubbish-strewn) embankment, from which there is a nice view of the busy informal **river market**, which is full of people and colour. Tuesday is the big day here, when many women in gaily patterned dresses bring firewood from across the river to sell to the townsfolk of Lokoja. There are big wooden barges packed with people that are poled across to the other side of the river, and it's best to go and look at the activity in the late afternoon when all the market traders make their watery way home. The Niger is still and khaki green and very picturesque, and there are a few fishing canoes and some boat-building going on along the shore.

To the north of Murtala Muhammed Way, follow the streets towards the Kogi Hotel, where in the grounds is the **first prison** in Nigeria, built by Lugard in 1903 and used until 1945. There's not much to see: it's just a small squat building now used as the hotel laundry, with a few remains of a watchtower and some walls. Notice the door to the laundry is the original gate, with its heavy iron bars. On Mount Pati Road are **Lord Lugard's Residence and Office**, two houses next to each other, one of which Lugard lived in and the other of which was the house of his senior staff. Both were built in 1901 on stilts because of the reptiles and floods, with wooden shutters and tin roofs to keep the interiors cool, and were prefabricated buildings sent from England. On each there are steps at the front leading up to the main front door, whilst at the back is a ramp to the service entrance. You can go in both of them, and in Lugard's house on the left is the Kogi State Tourism Board, where you might be able to pick up a guide to show you around town for a small dash. The house on the right is a museum, though there is very little on display here, except a few faded photos of Lokoja, but someone there will tell you a little history if you make a donation. In the grounds are some old buoys that used to indicate the depth of the river, and an 1865 anchor. I was told that the museum has collected loads of Lugard's things, including many old photographs and original treaties he signed with the Africans, but unfortunately the well-meaning museum staff are still waiting for funds to make display cabinets and boards. A few metres to the west of these houses is **Government House**. It's a modern structure, but the front gate is the original, and was again built in 1901. Back on Murtala Muhammed Way, beyond the post office, is the **Cenotaph Monument**, a square concrete memorial behind a fence erected to commemorate the soldiers who died in both World Wars, with the names of the dead carved into it, and a few rusty cannons. Above the town is **Mount Pati** (a Nupe word meaning hill) and you can drive up it if you have a car for the great views. It's roughly 1,500m high, with a 2km radius at the summit, on which are a number of radio masts – reputedly Lugard used to go up here to watch the river with his telescope.

## MAKURDI

Makurdi, 323km to the southeast of Abuja, is the capital of Benue State, and is neatly bisected into north and south by the Benue River, which supports a boat-building industry that is supplied by the city's numerous sawmills. The combined road and rail bridge that spans the Benue here was built in 1932, opening up transport links between northeastern Nigeria and the southeast, and ultimately the sea. The newer, multi-laned expressway bridge is close to it. The city is one of the most important homelands for the Tiv ethnic group, and has some Islamic influence, with several Muslim organisations and mosques. The Tiv people are traditionally farmers and the region grows cassava, yams, groundnuts, grain and rice; for this reason, Benue State is dubbed 'Food Basket to the Nation' (on car number plates). In the run-up to independence the Tiv people resented being governed by the Northern Region and the capital of Kaduna, and formed the United Middle Belt Congress (UMBC) to campaign for regional self-government separate from the north. Although the leader of the congress, Joseph Tarka, was based in Jos, he was a Tiv. The movement peaked in 1960–61, with a series of riots and demonstrations demanding a separate region, during which hundreds of Tiv activists in Makurdi were arrested and imprisoned. After the military coup in the federal government staged by General Gowon in 1966, when Nigeria was split into 12 states, the creation of the Benue/Plateau State was generally regarded as a victory for the Tiv people. It was administered from Jos until 1976, when Benue State was restructured as its own, with Makurdi as the capital. There's nothing to see or do, but Makurdi is a transport hub for travel between the southeast and Abuja to the north, and the extreme west of Nigeria, and the chances are you may spend the night here.

Between Abuja and Makurdi you will pass through Lafia, a Hausa city and the capital of Nassarawa State, with an economy relying on the local coal mining industry. It was founded in the 1700s by the Hausas and developed into an important market town before being seized by the son of the sultan of Sokoto in the early 1900s and becoming part of the Fulani Empire. Nassarawa State is dubbed the 'Home of Solid Minerals' and is one of Nigeria's newest states, created by General Abacha in 1996.

## Getting there and away

Where you get dropped off in Makurdi by public transport rather depends on what direction you've come from. From the southeast you're likely to be dropped off on Gboko Road, the main road between the university and the town, from where you'll have to get an *okada* to the accommodation options another kilometre or so further on, again on or around Gboko Road in the Old GRA. Just before the university you'll find clutches of vehicles going south to Enugu and Katsina Ala (change here for Obudu and anywhere else south of Obudu). If coming from the north, you'll get dropped off at the Lafia Motor Park in the north of the city, on the main road that crosses the river on the new bridge. The motor park is roughly 500m north of the bridge, and it's not very obvious. It's opposite the Amajechris petrol station, concealed behind a row of trucks and grimy engine oil and tyre stalls. From this motor park, vehicles go to Jos, Abuja, and Suleja, to the north.

## Where to stay and eat

**Benue Hotel** 5/7 Ahmadu Bello Way; tel: 044 532228, 532178, 533719. This is within walking distance to the north of the Gboko Road roundabout; take Kashim Ibrahim Road and then turn right on to Ahmadu Bello Way. The faded state hotel, with 87 rooms, has seen better days, but it's still probably the best option in town, with a car park and 24-hour gen, restaurant and bar for excellent breakfasts; breakfast items start from N100 and dinner from N500. A comfortable double is N2,800 (N4,000 deposit), with larger rooms and two-roomed suites from N3,000–5,500 (N5,000–10,000 deposit) plus the 15%. According to the tariff it costs slightly more for a non-resident, but you are unlikely to be charged the extra.
**Father Moustache Hotel** 5 Kashim Ibrahim Rd; tel: 044 531072, 532073. Around the corner from the Benue is the delightfully named Father Moustache Hotel. It's a small house with a few cheap rooms (N1,500) in large grounds, where there is a popular outside bar and *suya* stand.
**Niima Hotel** 24 Gboko Rd, also near the roundabout; tel: 044 533731, is a Muslim spot, so there's no booze, although there is cheap but dire food that you can order to be sent to your room. Rooms are adequate, with satellite TV, big beds, and a bucket for N2,400 (N3,000 deposit).

On the roundabout itself is a branch of **Mr Biggs**.

# JOS

The region around Jos has its origins as far back as AD500, attested to by the discovery of the Nok terracotta on the Jos Plateau that's now on display in the Jos Museum. But Jos itself is a relatively new town, built by the British in the early 1900s as a tin-mining centre and developed rapidly following the completion of the railroad from Port Harcourt in 1914. Capital of Plateau State, Jos is located in central Nigeria on the Jos Plateau about 1,250m above sea level on the Delimi River. Although not part of the north, if you have travelled from anywhere in the south, this is the first place you'll notice the distinctive northern scenery of scrub plains and rocky plateaus, and sandy fields littered with mud-brick homesteads; it's all very different to the green and lush scenery in southern Nigeria. There are two theories on how Jos got its name. The first is that the original village at the foot of a hill where the present Jos Museum is located was called Gwosh and the early settlers mispronounced it; and the second is that the early Christian missionaries gave it its name as an acronym for 'Jesus our Saviour'. Around 1903, agents of the Niger Company discovered that local people were smelting tin and traced its origin to the traditional tin furnaces on what is now Jos Plateau, though Captain Clapperton reported that he had seen tin for sale in Kano Market in the 1820s. The exploitation of the tin ores began in earnest by the British from 1904, supported by an armed escort from the West African Frontier Force. Until the railway arrived, first the Zaria–Bukuru railway in 1914 and then the main railroad in 1927, the tin was carried by labour gangs of some 4,000 men to Loko, a port on the River Benue some 200km away, en route to the sea ports for export to Europe. The same gangs on their return journey brought back imported commodities to Jos. Barclays Bank and the Bank of British West Africa had opened their doors in the rapidly growing town by 1917, and encouraged more British, Indian, and Lebanese settlers to a town that had a fast-growing reputation as a place where you could grow rich overnight. Output grew to 10,000 tons a year during World War I thanks to the demand for tin, but production had all but died out in the 1930s because of a fall in prices. By the end of the 1950s, with investment chasing the smell of oil, production slowed even further, but tin is still mined around Jos today, and the industry attracts a number of expat workers.

With average monthly temperatures ranging between 21°C and 25°C, Jos is considerably cooler and more comfortable than other cities in Nigeria. During the colonial days, British officers were encouraged to spend some of their leave in Jos for the good of their health, and this requirement used to be written into the civil service code. The climate is also good for the growing of produce not found elsewhere in Nigeria, such as watermelons, lettuce and spinach. Today it's a city with a population of at least a couple of million, and curiously it's also home to lots of bread factories, and many subsidiaries of NASCO, a food-manufacturing company; you'll see the enormous NASCO biscuit factory on Murtala Muhammed Way. Also look out for the hill to the south of town covered in aerials and satellite dishes, and the enormous blue storage tanks of Swan Water, bottled water that is produced in the region. Like other Nigerian cities, Jos has its collection of weird-looking roundabout statues. Look out for the one on the roundabout near the market in the centre; it's of a 5m-tall woman in black concrete of almost cartoon-like appearance, with a child hanging on to her back and an enormous pot on her head. The Jos Ultra-Modern Market is not so ultra-modern any more, given that it burnt down in 2003 in a fire that thankfully started at 04.00 so no-one was hurt, though the 4,300 densely packed stalls reputedly burnt for many hours and it must have been quite an inferno. Today it remains in its burnt-out state, with rather sad-looking charred Milo and Indomie advertising hoardings, and the stalls have shifted to the sides of the roads instead, making this area very congested. One of the first impressions you'll get of Jos is the colourfully dressed people, many in bright fluorescent colours and lots of layers. There's also a big Muslim presence, with mosques and churches all over town, and you'll perhaps notice the numerous little parks scattered around the roads near the museum and on the road to the Hill Station Hotel. Some of these have benches and thatched seating areas, and are used for Muslim contemplation. Finally, be wary in the old town (around the Township Stadium) at night; this area is fairly rough and ready.

## Getting there and away

The **airport** is 29km to the south of the city, and the only option of getting to and from there is by drop taxi, which will cost in the region of N2,500. Slok Air has a desk at the Hill Station Hotel and there's a daily flight between Jos and Lagos. The office for KLM and Kenya Airways is located in the grounds of the Plateau Hotel; tel: 073 452185, 458249 (open Monday–Friday 08.00–17.00 and Saturday morning 08.00–12.00). The main motor park is Bauchi Motor Park to the north, 3km from the city centre on the Bauchi Road, for vehicles going to Makurdi, Abuja, Bauchi, Zaria, and Kaduna, though you may find yourself being dropped off at a number of smaller motor parks in the centre around Tafewa Balewa Street. 'Luxury' buses go overnight to Lagos and Port Harcourt from here and from the streets around the Township Stadium, but you'll have to ask around. Jos is located at the terminus of a spur (first built in 1915) of the railway from Port Harcourt to Maiduguri. The **railway station** is centrally located on Bauchi Road, just south of the market. It's still open and staffed, despite there being no trains.

Once in the city centre, most of the attractions are within walking distance of each other and it's easy enough to wander around. The hotels and some restaurants are however located further out, but there are plenty of *okada*s, and minibuses and shared taxis run up and down the long main road that runs north to south through the city. In the north it's called Bauchi Road, then turns into Murtala Muhammed Way in the middle of the city, before being renamed Yakuba Gowon Way to the south.

# Where to stay
## Moderate: US$25 and above
**County Home Hotel** NEPA Close; tel: 073 462479, 462865. This is a newly refurbished hotel and it's very nice, with lots of new, bright-green paint, and it's easily the best place to stay in Jos. Good breakfasts of fresh rolls and juice are available for N500 and non-Nigerian dishes for dinner start from N650. The 59 rooms have giant beds with new, crisp white sheets, hot water, new satellite TV, AC units and fridges, and are exceptionally comfortable. Doubles start from N4,830 (N6,800 deposit), though you'll pay slightly more for a fully fitted bathroom, plus the 15%.

**Hill Station Hotel** 10 Tundun Wada Rd; tel: 073 455300/2. Way past its prime but with faded charm, this is a bit of an institution in Jos, from the times when British colonial officers were instructed to spend their leave here for the good of their health. There's a functional swimming pool with a *suya* spot, established terraced gardens with jacaranda trees and good views over Jos and the hills beyond, and a few shops at the entrance selling curios, pottery and religious books. There's good uniformed service in the restaurant and bar with set menus of soup, a continental dish and a piece of fruit for around N1,200. In total, there are about ten different kinds of rooms and chalets ('shaletts') on the tariff, for varying prices, starting with a standard/single room (remember that these generally have a double bed) for N3,700 (N5,500 deposit) or N4,300 (N6,500 deposit) for a double, rising to around N14,000–17,000 (N22,000–25,000 deposit) for one of the suites. These are exclusive of the 15% and are residents' rates; whilst there are higher rates on the tariff for non-residents, you are unlikely to be charged them. It's possible to negotiate a 25% discount on Friday and Saturday nights.

## Budget: below US$25
**Plateau Hotel** Rest House Rd; tel: 073 455741. Located in a hilly and leafy suburb in pleasant grounds with plenty of parking, but it's deadly quiet and there's no water in the swimming pool. There's a comfortable lounge, a shop selling books and men's shirts, and the restaurant has a changing daily menu which includes continental dishes such as beef goulash or chicken casserole for around N800. As with all the other old state hotels, everything is seriously dilapidated, and the rooms are stuffed with ancient furniture, but they all have satellite TV and clean bathrooms, and at N2,500 (N5,000 deposit) plus the 15% for the cheapest double, they are good value and the service is good.

**Samora Hotel** 18 Pankshin St, opposite Jos Township Stadium; tel: 073 455516. This is a rough and ready spot with a few dubious characters stalking the corridors, though there is a security guard sitting at a desk at the top of the stairs at night. It's very friendly though, and has a good and cheap restaurant, serving the usual soups and starch, but also omelette and chips, chicken and fried rice and spaghetti for only N300, and there's a bar for watching and talking about football. It's N2,000 for a room with bucket, hot water, TV and fridge,

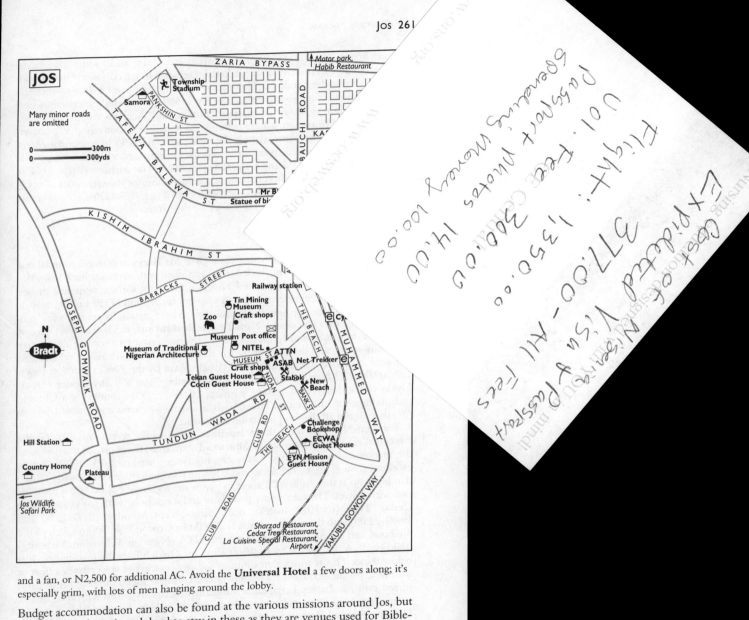

JOS

Many minor roads are omitted

0 — 300m
0 — 300yds

Bradt

ZARIA BYPASS

Motor park, Habib Restaurant

Township Stadium

Samora

PANKSHIN ST

TAFEWA BALEWA ST

BAUCHI ROAD

KA

Mr B
Statue of bi

KISHIM IBRAHIM ST

JOSEPH GOMWALK ROAD

BARRACKS STREET

Railway station

Tin Mining Museum

Craft shops

Zoo

Museum

Post office

NITEL

Museum of Traditional Nigerian Architecture

MUSEUM ST
Craft shops

ATTN

ASAB    Net Trekker

Stabok

Tekan Guest House
Cocin Guest House

New Beach

THE BEACH

MUHAMMED WAY

Cy

NOAD ST

WADA RD

BANK ST

TUNDUN

CLUB RD

Challenge Bookshop

THE BEACH

ECWA Guest House

EYN Mission Guest House

Hill Station

Country Home

Plateau

CLUB ROAD

YAKUBU GOWON WAY

Jos Wildlife Safari Park

Sharzad Restaurant,
Cedar Tree Restaurant,
La Cuisine Special Restaurant,
Airport

and a fan, or N2,500 for additional AC. Avoid the **Universal Hotel** a few doors along; it's especially grim, with lots of men hanging around the lobby.

Budget accommodation can also be found at the various missions around Jos, but you'll need to be quite subdued to stay in these as they are venues used for Bible-study classes and church services, and you may look somewhat out of place. Nevertheless, if you are well behaved they will let you stay and they are as cheap as chips! The **TEKAN Guest House** (6 Noad Street; tel: 073 453036) is a friendly mission which has a few rooms and which is conveniently located near the museum complex. The rooms (no couples allowed) are only twins and singles of monastic proportions, but they are clean, with a simple bed and a bucket in the bathrooms, and for N700 for a single and N1,000 for a twin they're dirt cheap. There's also a 22-bed dorm here, and for N300 you get a sheet and a blanket and use of a communal bathroom. Next door is another mission, **Cocin Guest House**

(5 Noad Street; tel: 073 452286). It's spartan but clean, and rooms have been freshly painted, with bed and desk, bucket and separate toilet, cool stone floors, and mossie netting in the windows. There's a restaurant that serves a dish-of-the-day in big pots, and a sitting room with a TV. For N500 per room it's great value, but it only admits single people or married couples, and there's a curfew of 22.00. **ECWA Guest House** on a road behind the Challenge Bookshop is another church mission with accommodation. There are several blocks in peaceful gardens centred around a large hall used for evangelist church services, where there is a canteen serving a basic dish, and a TV. Rates are N1,000 for a basic room and N450 for a dorm bed. You may also get basic accommodation for the same sort of price at the **EYN Mission Guest House** across the road (tel: 073 452056). As you can imagine, there are lots of Bibles for sale along this street.

## Where to eat and drink

Starting off with the obvious, there's a branch of **Mr Biggs** next to the roundabout near the market. **Stabok**, on Bank Street, is a plain restaurant set back from the street in a compound, with standard Nigerian food and some continental dishes such as chicken and chips, omelette and spag bol for around N350 a plate, though not everything on the menu is always available. There are also beers and a few tots of spirits in the bar. The nearby **New Beach Restaurant**, at 5 Bank Street (closed Sunday), is a popular and spotlessly clean Nigerian restaurant serving all manner of food-is-ready, and there's a lively bar next door. Good Nigerian food can also be found at **Habib Restaurant**, at 82 Bauchi Road by the Zololo junction (open daily 09.00–22.30), which has about a dozen tables and a flashy modern front. **Elysas** (open daily 12.00–15.00 for lunch, 19.00–22.00 for dinner) is a Chinese restaurant in the Hill Station Hotel, with an expansive menu and lots of tables in AC, though not all the food is terribly authentic.

For non-Nigerian food there are three worthwhile restaurants on Yakuba Gowon Way to the south of town. **Sharazad**, 2km from the centre of town around the market and on the left if you're coming from town; tel: 073 462281, serves excellent though pricey Lebanese and Chinese food in a huge venue, with a disco that heats up at the weekend. Expect to pay in the region of N4,000 for a meal for two with drinks. The mezzes are good here and it's popular with Jos's expats. The **Cedar Tree** (tel: 073 464890; open daily except Monday 12.00–15.00 and 19.00–22.00) is to the south of town at 17 Yakuba Gowon Way, 500m south of the Sharazad and a couple of doors from the NTA (Nigerian Television Authority) building; look out for the Swan Water tanks on a high hill, as the restaurant is just below these. This is some 5km south of the city centre, but is worth the effort of getting to for the good and reasonably priced Lebanese menu of hummus, kebabs, mixed grills, and spicy kofta, all accompanied by freshly baked flat bread. A few metres north of here and on the other side of Yakuba Gowon Way is the **La Cuisine Special Restaurant** (no phone; open daily 10.00–22.00), easily the best place to eat in Jos, with set tables with starched napkins and wine glasses. The fully continental menu includes lots of treats such as prawns, good steaks with sauces and sweet and sour chicken, and vegetarians will love the vegetarian lasagne or fried noodles with vegetables and nuts. Main dishes start from N700 and there's a full bar with some wines. Don't forget the 15%.

## Practicalities

If you need to **change money**, Asa Bureau de Change is on Museum Street opposite **NITEL**, which is very handily open daily 08.30–18.00, and changes GBP,

US$ and East and West CFAs (Communauté Financière de l'Afrique) used in the West Africa Francophile countries. You'll also find Hausa money changers at the entrance of the Hill Station Hotel. There's a manned **tourist office** at the Plateau Hotel (open Monday–Saturday 08.00–16.00), but the lady in question, who smiles a lot, has nothing to give out, though she does have a useful list of hotels in Jos. There's another tourist desk in the conference centre down the hill from the Hill Station Hotel, but when I looked in it wasn't manned. Reliable **internet access** can be found at the Cyberhut at 3 Murtala Muhammed Way, which has a satellite connection and a dozen or so terminals (open daily except Sunday 09.00–20.30, N160 per hour). Net Trekker is another internet joint at 38 Murtala Muhammed Way on the same side of the road, and the **post office** is on Ahmadu Bello Way.

## Shopping

The **Challenge Bookshop** on the Beach Road is a huge place stuffed to the gills with Christian books and Bibles, but you may be able to pick up a map of Jos here, and there is a small handicraft section. The **Alternative Trade Network of Nigeria** (ATNN) shop is at 1 Museum Street (tel: 073 450178; email: natn@hisen.org) opposite NITEL (open Monday–Friday 08.00–17.00; Saturday 10.00–18.00). It's a tiny but very well-meaning organisation that is part of the international NGO Fair Trade Network, and it is the smallest of the charity's outlets in West Africa. The Fair Trade Network supports small producers of craft items from all over the world, from disadvantaged or impoverished communities and developing economies, and mobilises and empowers them to continue their craft, as well as providing markets for what they produce. The Fair Trade principles include helping producers receive fair and appropriate value for their skills and labour, encouraging adequate working conditions and the positive use of working materials and traditional skills, and teaching local people the benefits of making a fair and equal business from their skills. In a nutshell, the Fair Trade movement supports grass-roots producers of mainly crafts and supports them by finding a market – for example, many craft items you find in Oxfam shops in the UK have originated from Fair Trade initiatives from all over the world. The small nucleus of staff in the shop are very keen to chat – one of them even told me his mother lives in Chalfont St Peter in the UK, the home of Bradt! The ATNN has a membership of 65 Nigerian co-operatives and individuals that make handicrafts that are sold in the shop. These include silver jewellery, baskets, pots, leather, paintings and well-made cotton indigo dresses. There are other craft stalls selling leather, carved calabashes and clothes; the latter you can get made up, on Museum Street and around the corner on Noad Avenue, and at more places in the museum complex.

## What to see and do
### Jos Museum Complex

The museum complex is best approached from Museum Road and it's a pleasant walk down the hill through lovely gardens full of gum and mango trees, and there are paths up to some rocky outcrops for local views. There are a number of attractions, and the UNESCO-sponsored School for Museum Technicians and the University of Jos Teaching Hospital are also located here. The **main museum** (open daily 08.00–17.30; N20 entry fee) is to the right as you reach the bottom of the hill, and is spread out on the light and airy downstairs floor and in the garden out back, so you can see just about everything if there is no NEPA. Exhibits include currencies, such as feathers, tobacco, manilas, kuntu cloth, and of course cowries, all of which have been used as money in West Africa over the centuries; in the 17th century a cupful of cowries equalled a wife or a slave. The museum also houses five pieces of the Nok terracotta sculptures (500BC) dug up in the Jos Plateau in 1943; they are all broken, but one head is more or less intact, and there's a 13th-century brass bust from Ife that's in very good condition. Another interesting item amongst the masquerade costumes and masks is an 18th-century brass royal throne with an elaborate python coiled around its feet. There's a selection of durbar horse attire, and the usual weapons and musical instruments. Outside, and leaning against a wall, is the original Kano city door, once erected at one of Kano's gates before the British knocked it down on their arrival in 1903. There's also a similar section of the original 1845 Bauchi town gate. At the back of the museum is a very peaceful garden full of birds and trees, and a delightful, bright green rectangular pool with tilapia fish in it, surrounded by hundreds of old pots for a variety of different uses.

The small **Tin Mining Museum** (open daily 08.00–17.30; N10 entry fee) is at the end of the lane that runs past the main museum, and as you can imagine is dedicated to the (not terribly) interesting industry of tin mining. Bizarrely, on my visit *Every Breath You Take* by the Police was playing on a cassette recorder! Outside of the building are some early railway engines and carriages on display. Near here is a fine line of craft and **curio stalls** where you can watch and have a friendly chat with the artists at work, including a wood-turner, a painter, and an indigo dyer. Also at the museum complex and opposite the main museum is a dreary **zoo** (N20 entry fee; N100 for cameras), which you can easily give a miss as it's quite depressing, though it does house a collection of highly endangered species. But they are trapped in cages that are old and way too small; this is especially true of the chimpanzees and monkeys, which are thrown unsuitable food and sweets by ignorant Nigerians.

Further down the hill, the **Museum of Traditional Nigerian Architecture** (free entry, but dash for a guide if you want one) holds a collection of full-size replicas representing different styles of Nigerian architecture, including Katsina Palace, Zaria Mosque, Illorin Mosque and the Kano Wall. The replicas are much more impressive than the real things, which have been largely destroyed or neglected, or have over time been altered. It contains various architectural designs of major Nigerian ethnic groups, and there are huts with carved wooden door posts. No-one could tell me when this site was opened, but evidently it was before 1982, as there is a monument at the entrance to the Polish professor who designed the museum, commemorating his death in 1982. They are built of mud and straw 'plugs' – round-shaped bricks – and the walls are then finished off with a smooth layer of the same mixture. This building material is fine for the drier climate in the north where the original buildings were once located, but in Jos's high climate the buildings get routinely battered by the rain, though very encouragingly they do get repaired and there was some major rebuilding going on at the time of writing. You can walk along the top of the Kano Wall, and go inside the Zaria Mosque, though evidently many other people have, as it seems to be the local toilet! Also at the entrance is the Bight of Benin restaurant in a replica of an old chief's house, with an ornamental snake above the door and a red tin roof. Inside is a bar and a courtyard with plenty of tree trunks to sit on, and the eaves are made from bamboo. It's quite dusty and tatty, but you can still get a steaming plate of stew here during the day, and a cold drink.

## Jos Wildlife Safari Park

The Jos Wildlife Park is situated to the west of the city and is signposted off Yakuba Gowon Way, but it can also be reached via back roads off the Zaria Bypass in the north of Jos. This is 7km² of grassy hills and streams, though most of the animals at the safari park are housed in a collection of cages near the entrance (open daily

10.00–18.00, N50 entry fee, N20 for a vehicle, N150 for a camera, N300 for a video camera). If you don't have transport an *okada* will take you here for around N100 from town, and it's an interesting ride though the back streets of the edge of the city, where Fulani cattle ranchers graze their cows on the patches of scrub. The Plateau State Tourism office is located near the entrance gate, and it's a reasonably well-meaning office, but again it doesn't have anything to give out. You can look at a few yellowed brochures and postcards that were produced by the Nigerian Tourism Development Board decades ago, but you can't take them away. Also at the entrance is the Wildlife Museum, which is full of badly stuffed animals and birds, and some snakes in jars. There's a buffalo head and two sets of buffalo feet, a shrunken elephant head with a droopy trunk and a sign saying 'of great potential because size attracts visitors' (?), and mangy lion and leopard heads – the taxidermy is so bad they look like corpses. Cages are set in a shady garden of mango, eucalyptus, jacaranda and pine trees, but despite the pretty location, the animals (and especially the lions) at the wildlife park are kept in cages that are too small and as such it's a depressing place to visit, though on a more positive note the two remaining elephants are free-ranging in a large space of land, where they live pretty normal and natural lives. Other animals on display include a variety of birds such as barn owls and parrots, and two enormous Marshall eagles, a big python in a pit, various monkeys, giant tortoises and a pygmy hippo. The café here is stuffed full of ornate velour lounge furniture and has some outside tables on a terrace above the lion cage with views over the surrounding countryside.

## Around Jos

If you have your own transport you can explore other areas on the Jos Plateau. The Shere Hills are good for hiking and are among the highest ranges of mountains in Nigeria; they're home to the Riyom Rock Formation, a dramatic valley of balancing rocks 25km from Jos along the Jos–Abuja road. If you are travelling by public transport you can see them from the road from a vehicle from Makurdi or Abuja. For anyone familiar with southern Africa, they are similar to the balancing rocks of Zimbabwe, where weather erosion has shaped the rock pinnacles in such a way that the once-solid structures are now a series of smooth boulders sitting on top of each other. On the same road and 64km south of Jos are the Assop Falls, a serene set of tumbling waterfalls where it is possible to swim in the pool at the bottom. If you are prepared to continue by infrequent bush taxi, you can break your journey between Jos and either Abuja or Makurdi here, but set out early as there is no accommodation outside of these centres. From the main road there is a Coca-Cola sign saying 'Assop Falls Tourist Resort' and there may be someone around to collect the N200 entry fee.

## WEST OF ABUJA
### Bida

Bida, a Hausa-Fulani town, dates back to around the 10th century, and has been traditionally Muslim, with several ancient mosques built by the Hausa kings. When the British visited Bida in the 1870s, they reported that the walls surrounding the city were 24km in circumference, but despite this considerable defence, the British still laid siege to Bida in 1897. Parts of the wall are still here, but they are mostly eroded. It was best known for its glass beads made from beer bottles and coloured glass jars, but the art of bead-making has largely fallen away and today there is only one shop now located in a residential area. It's almost impossible to find, and once there you are not going to be able to see inside the shop or watch the process without paying ridiculous amounts of dash. In the end we didn't bother and we advise you to do the same. You'll see many of the beads in other curio markets around the country.

Bida is about a four-hour drive, or roughly 230km, west of Abuja on a reasonably good road, and the only reason for being here is to perhaps change vehicles in the motor park or fill up with fuel on the way through. The main motor park, known as the Ilorin Garage, is on Ilorin Road in the heart of town. The accommodation options in Bida are so awful that I'm not even going to bother mentioning them. At one I looked at, I had to shoo away goats to get into a decrepit room. There is, however, a fairly good food-is-ready spot called the **Classey Restaurant**, 200m north of the Total petrol station on the main junction in the middle of town, and next door to a Texaco petrol station. There are some outside tables where you can get big plates of good and cheap chips, salad, fried eggs and Nigerian soups and starches; if you're driving through it's worth stopping for a meal here.

## New Bussa

New Bussa is an unremarkable and very sleepy town that's more like a big village, but it's exceptionally friendly and has one feature that's totally unique to Nigeria – constant, uninterrupted electricity! Thanks to the nearby Lake Kainji Hydro-electrical Dam, that supplies much of Nigeria's patchy electricity, New Bussa (as the nearest place to the dam and as the home to many NEPA employees) receives an unbroken supply of electricity. There's also a Nigerian air force base on the outskirts of New Bussa, where apparently German expats service the jets, though they remained elusive on our visit. To get here you need to turn off the main A1 108km north of Ilorin at Mokwa, and it's a further 100km to New Bussa along this road. There are direct bush taxis between New Bussa and Bida (220km, N400) and from Ilorin (208km, N700); otherwise, you may find yourself changing vehicles at the junction in Mokwa. New Bussa's motor park is located in the centre of the town – look for the Peugeots and other clapped-out cars parked under a small shelter. From here you can get buses the short distance to Wawa, 10km to the west and the nearest point to Lake Kainji National Park. The **NITEL** office and the **post office** are together, a few metres to the north of the motor park; as usual look out for the unmistakable NITEL tower. The Lake Kainji National Park office is 2km from New Bussa on the approach road (tel: 031 670315, 670424), though it's just as easy to go straight to the Kob Amusement Centre in Wawa, where you'll get more than adequate information about visiting the park (see below).

### Where to stay and eat
**Kainji Motel**, about 2km to the north of town on Niger Crescent at the end of Murtala Muhammed Way, in the GRA (tel: 031 670032), is NEPA-owned and is where many employees stay; it offers comfortable and clean accommodation with 24-hour power in peaceful and quiet gardens, with a car park behind a security boom gate. There's a restaurant for basic meals and the ladies will knock on your door in the morning and bring tea-bread-and-eggs for N300. Rates are N1,725 for a room with DSTV, fridge, and a big vat of water in the bathroom, and N1,225 without fridge and TV. Across the road is a huge football field, and if you ask nicely you can watch the kids from the nearby NEPA school in their smart blue uniforms play football. They are delightfully polite and you'll get lots of 'good afternoon madam/sir'. The **Imdro Hotel** (26 Wawa Road; tel: 031 670089) is less than a year old and very neat and tidy, with everything new and working, though it's quite conservative, with a mosque and ornate Arabic décor with bronze pillars and gilt mirrors. There's also a simple restaurant; ask in advance if they can rustle up something like an egg or chicken and chips or salad if you want something other than soup and starch. The 30 or so rooms

start at N2,100 (N2,500 deposit) inclusive of the 15% and you pay more for a bigger room and bed. Opposite the tiny motor park is a small **supermarket** selling a few surprising finds; we found chocolate, cornflakes, honey and jam.

# LAKE KAINJI NATIONAL PARK

The park is closely linked with the famous Lake Kainji hydro-electric complex, which supplies a greater part of Nigeria with electricity, and the Borgu Game Reserve, which was established in 1975 upon completion of the Kainji Dam, the largest dam in Nigeria. The 136km-long artificial lake behind the dam covers Old Bussa, where Mungo Park, the British explorer, was said to have been killed in 1805 when the local people mistook him and his party as Fulani jihadists. The Zugurma Forest section was added in 1991, when both Zugurma and Borgu were renamed the Lake Kainji National Park, covering in total 5,382km².

## The Borgu section

The park vegetation in the Borgu section, to the northwest of the tiny settlement of Wawa and stretching to the Benin border, is characterised by tall grassy savanna, patches of woodland and riverine vegetation. According to the National Parks Service, the 4,000km² Borgu sector has 241 species of birds, 63 mammals, 28 reptiles and amphibians, and 259 species of plants, but this is highly debatable and their statistics are likely to be very outdated. As in the other Nigerian national parks, an animal census hasn't been carried out for decades and most of the big game has probably been poached out, though there are possibly still some buffalo, roan antelope, kob, western hartebeest, warthog, aardvark and olive baboon, and perhaps even lion, as although the game rangers haven't seen any for ages, they do report hearing them and spotting footprints. There's also a fair number of hippo in the Oli River, though in the dry season the amount of water is fairly patchy, but there are enough pools of water to sustain some hippo pods. The hippo have been known to get out of the park and destroy local crops in villages around the edge of the park boundary, which puts them at risk of being shot. There used to be elephants here, and in the 1970s the population was put at around 1,000, but today these appear to have left the park and crossed the border into the Republic of Benin as a result of hunting pressure. Birdlife is abundant, especially at the Oli River near the camp inside the park, but animals are less often seen here than even in Yankari National Park. There's very basic but underused accommodation within the park (see below).

## The Zugurma section

The Zugurma section is nowhere near the Borgu section and lies some distance away on the road from Mokwa to New Bussa, approximately 25km on the left-hand side of the road if coming from Mokwa. As it is relatively new, there are few roads or trails within this section, and given the state of the parks in Nigeria today, it's unlikely that any development will happen in the park any time soon. However, it's a pretty patch of green forest, and if you're driving there's no reason why you couldn't stop at the well-signposted gate to see if there is anyone around, and ask if you can go inside. There could still be monkeys present, including baboon, red patus monkey, and black and white colobus monkey. Accommodation was built here a few years ago at the Ibbi Tourist Camp, but today it's all shut up simply due to lack of visitors. If there is any future demand, the National Parks Service may staff and reopen it, but for now you'll have to be completely self-sufficient for camping and negotiate with the local people to gain entrance.

## Kob Amusement Centre

The Kob Amusement Centre is in the village of Wawa, 10km west of New Bussa, and some 24km south of the main gate to the Lake Kainji National Park. You will be expected to visit here before entering the park to announce your arrival, and the staff and the many game rangers here will give you a brief introduction to the park and a tour of the wildlife museum. Quite frankly, they will also be completely bowled over and hugely delighted that any interested visitors have turned up. In the museum is a range of lion and antelope skins, various bones and skulls, including those of elephant, which are now extinct in the park; in fact, if you go by the animal skins decorating the walls of the museum, in Kainji there once resided leopard, cheetah, genet and civet cat, but whether these still exist within the park is impossible to determine, and whilst the rangers and the tourist blurb and ancient brochure insist that this is the case, it is highly likely they have all died or been poached out within the last couple of decades. There is a whole heap of dried out python skins, hedgehog and porcupine husks, and emancipated bird and monkey heads. It reminded me of a *juju* market! One of the more interesting features of the dusty museum is the collection of poacher's weapons collected by the rangers, which includes very rudimentary handmade rifles that use some sort of homemade gunpowder and that shoot poison darts and arrows. Hanging on the wall above the weapons is also a collection of charms, some containing *juju* powders, taken from the poachers when captured. The museum guide tells you that given that poachers will lose themselves in the forests for a number of days in pursuit of their prey, some of these charms are used to ward off sickness, to help with navigation when lost, to empower them with strength to run away from a dangerous animal, and, in the event that they can't find an animal, to give them the vision or luck to find their prey. It's an odd collection of bits of feather, leather, and strange and unexplainable *juju* animal charms, that is appalling and fascinating at the same time. On our visit, we were told that a group of 300 children on a school visit had been the week before and it was the museum's officer's role 'to teach the value of wildlife'. Yay! Kainji also employs a conservation education officer who goes to the local villages and talks to the traditional chief or leader, who then in turn talks to the local people about conservation. But also on our visit it was explained by the park staff that 'black men will always be after money' and that local people didn't always listen to the educational values the park staff spoke of.

### Getting there and away

The Kob Amusement Centre is in the small town of Wawa, 10km west of New Bussa. If you have made it to New Bussa by public transport, then it is a short N50 hop in a shared taxi on to Wawa, and when you arrive in Wawa you will almost immediately hit a T-junction – the main body of the town and the road into Lake Kainji National Park is to the right, whilst to the left you'll see the entrance of the Kob Amusement Centre a few metres along this road. Taxis and buses drop off and pick up at this junction. All visitors to the park should report to the Kob Amusement Centre first before driving into the park proper. Lake Kainji National Park is open from December to June, when the grass has died down and the animals have moved closer to the water. Whilst you can get as far as the Kob Amusement Centre by public transport, you need your own vehicle to enter the park, or take a chance on a lift from one of the park rangers. The park gate is a further 23km from Wawa, signposted off the road heading north out of town. Oli Camp within the park is 45km from the entrance, and in total 68km from Wawa. Entrance fees are paid at the gate but you must report to the Kob Amusement Centre first, from where they radio ahead and let staff at both the gate and Oli

## ANTI-POACHING AT KAINJI

Lake Kainji National Park, despite being nearly devoid of visitors and game, has today got to be one of the most protected national parks in Nigeria. There are continuing problems with poachers, and most of the big game has been poached out of the park since the 1970s, particularly antelope hunted for bushmeat, and especially waterbuck, of which large herds have been depleted. However, thanks to the conservation-aware game rangers at Kainji, the poachers get prosecuted if they are caught and the punishments are fairly severe. On our visit we were most impressed with the calibre and the enthusiasm of the park rangers, and when we asked rather flippantly, 'Have you caught any poachers recently?' we were surprised when one replied casually that he had, only three days previously, when he caught a man with a dead kob. 'We took his shirt off and beat him,' he replied. The culprit was then sent to jail and allegedly got a three-year term. When caught the poachers are under the jurisdiction of the national park rangers, with the assistance of the local police, as Lake Kainji National Park is federal land, and poachers are not accused, tried or sentenced under the local state laws, but under federal laws. We were also told that there was a 5km buffer zone around the park where the same sentences apply, and a culprit caught in this area was not necessarily entitled to a lawyer or trial in a local court. Poachers receive a variety of fines depending on the 'crime', from illegal entry and introducing domestic animals such as dogs or cows on to national park property, to carrying weapons within the park boundaries. If they are caught with a slain animal the fine can be as much as N50,000 or a term in jail. If a poacher is caught with a waterbuck – given that the stock of waterbuck has been severely depleted by poachers over the last few years – the sentence is more severe. A few years ago some of the park rangers underwent what they termed as paramilitary training. There was an initiative in 2000 when a British military expert came to Nigeria to train up a collection of national park employees in bush skills, such as following the poacher's footprints and bush signs in much the same way as a normal ranger would follow the tracks of animals. Today the rangers monitor the perimeter of the park in anti-poaching patrols in teams of five men. They also have, rather amazingly, a microlight for aerial patrols and a GPS. One of the ongoing problems the park rangers have had to face is being up against the Fulani cattle herders, who attempt to bring in their herds of cattle for fresh grazing. In recent years cows have been shot by park officials, and a park bulldozer was burned in retaliation.

Camp know that you are on your way. The road into Oli is rough but negotiable in a normal saloon car. Entry fees are N400; camera N1,000; video N2,000; (bizarrely) binoculars N200; car N400; truck N1,000. Despite there being daily game drives advertised, this is not the case: the park's bus was well and truly parked up at Wawa when we visited, so you will have to rely on your own vehicle for game driving. Once at Oli Camp you can hire a guide to accompany you in your own vehicle on a game drive for N300.

### Where to stay and eat

The Kob Amusement Centre is very friendly with excellent staff, and if you choose not to stay in the accommodation in New Bussa 10km away, at the centre is a lounge and restaurant/canteen with fat velour sofas, where beer is available (the national park is on federal land, whereas the surrounding towns are part of Kwara State, that falls within Sharia law), though you will have to order meals in advance so they have time to locate the ingredients. There's basic accommodation in a range of flatlets in a two-storey building, each with two bedrooms and a shared living room, a reasonable bathroom with bucket, a fridge and local TV, though none of the rooms have entertained visitors for a very long time, so expect to stay in a room that has been unused for years. Unlike New Bussa, NEPA is a far from guaranteed commodity here, despite its proximity to the Lake Kainji Dam. Rooms cost N1,550 inclusive of the 15% surcharges for either a single or double. At Oli Camp, within the park, there are 32 chalets – they're old and worn out of course, and you have to notify the staff there if you are going to turn up by way of (iffy) radio contact from the Kob Amusement Centre. A basic double chalet costs N2,000, or N3,000 for the so-called 'executive' version, and N4,000 for a larger suite, plus the 15%. The rooms are air conditioned but the generator is only used at night. At Oli Camp is a basic restaurant and bar serving beer, but again due to lack of visitors, arrange for a visit at the Kob Amusement Centre to ensure the camp staff are prepared for your arrival, and expect to be reasonably self-sufficient. If you are camping then there is no problem.

# East and Northeast Nigeria

The east and northeast of Nigeria are home to three of Nigeria's national parks. To the southeast of the region is the largely unexplored Gashaka-Gumpti National Park, so infrequently visited that very little is known about what's inside, but it supports a range of habitats, from densely forested valleys to Nigeria's highest mountain, and possibly some good populations of animals that have survived without the attention or accessibility of man. Nearer Abuja is the more accessible Yankari National Park and the fabulous Wikki Warm Spring, probably Nigeria's most famous highlight, though this park is not unscathed and sadly these days game has been largely decimated by poachers. The isolated northeast of Nigeria is probably the country's least-visited region, and few *batauris* have ever even made it to the extreme east on the Cameroon border or the extreme north on the border with Niger or Lake Chad. Again Lake Chad National Park has only ever been visited by a handful of people. Maiduguri is the major city of the northeast that you can easily reach from Kano or Gombe to the south. But away from the main roads, unless you want to spend days travelling in and waiting for the infrequent bush taxis that ply this remote region, the only option is to explore it in your own self-sufficient vehicle and be prepared to bush camp. To the north and northwest of Maiduguri is the Chad Basin that once contained Africa's superlake. Much of the region now is part of the Sahel, the southern reaches of the Sahara Desert and an arid flat area of palms, sun-baked earth, and ancient people that have adapted to the heat and the harsh living conditions. By contrast, the large Adamawa State that spreads southwards from Maiduguri along the Mandara Mountains on the Cameroon border to Taraba State, you will find the most haunting and spectacular mountain scenery, where traditions amongst its people haven't changed for thousands of years. Some of these regions are so remote that there are tales bandied around of tribes locked in the mountains that still don't wear clothes (or perhaps these are just stories to appease watchers of Nollywood movies and the Nigerian six o'clock news).

## EASTERN NIGERIA
### Bauchi

Bauchi is the capital of Bauchi State and is located on the northeastern edge of the Jos Plateau at just over 900m, and is 132km (or about one-and-a-half hour's drive) from Jos to the east. Despite its elevation it's a very dusty and searingly hot city. Bauchi is primarily an industrial city and home to an enormous truck and tractor assembly plant and large asbestos and cement factories. It's also the closest city to one of Nigeria's leading tourist attractions, the Yankari National Park, which is about 50km to the southeast, and as such you are quite likely to spend the night in

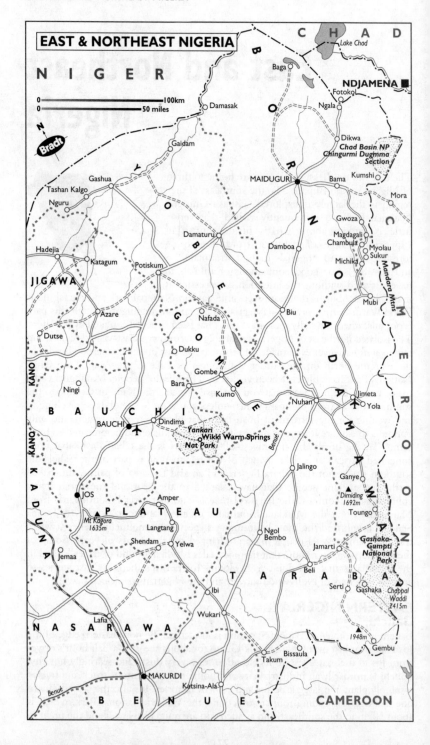

EAST & NORTHEAST NIGERIA

Bauchi before entering the park. Bauchi was established in 1809 as an emirate and slaving centre by Yakubu Germa, a commander appointed by Fulani chief and Islamic leader Usman dan Fodio during the jihad of the 19th century. The word bauchi means slave or pagan in the Hausa language. Many immigrants were attracted to the region for its good arable land and it soon blossomed with mosques, markets, wards and quarters. In 1902 the British occupied Bauchi, incorporating the emirate into northern Nigeria. Bauchi was to play a historic role during the de-colonisation of Nigeria thanks to it being the home of Abubakar Tafawa Balewa, a Bauchi teacher, who formed a social club in the town during the 1940s as a forum for discussing current affairs that went on to become the Northern People's Congress (NPC) – the political party that dominated the politics of the north in the run-up to independence. In 1960, Balewa became Nigeria's first prime minister, and he remained in office until his assassination in 1966. Balewa is buried in Bauchi in a tomb which is arguably the only interesting thing to see in the city.

## Getting there and away
The motor park is 1km north of the central market in Ran Road just off Murtala Muhammed Way, and there are direct vehicles to Abuja, Kaduna, Jalingo, Gombe, Makurdi and Jos. Bauchi is a stop on the railway from Port Harcourt to Maiduguri, and the train station is to the east of the city on the road to Gombe. You need an early start from Bauchi if heading towards Yankari (see below).

## Where to stay and eat
The Zaranda Hotel (Jos Road; tel: 077 543814/20) is approximately 3km to the east of the centre of town on the Jos Road. It's a bright white ten-storey building with an impressive row of flags outside, 184 rooms, giant gens for 24-hour power, and a water truck to keep the water tanks filled. If you are coming from Jos by public transport ask to be dropped off outside. In the vast car park are a couple of craft stalls selling carved calabashes and cloth. There are two very nice restaurants with flowers on the table, serving buffet meals or set Nigerian and continental menus for N1,000 and snacks such as toasted sandwiches or burgers from N500, and there's also a well-stocked cocktail bar. The swimming pool is half empty presumably because Bauchi is a Sharia state and public swimming is not permitted. A double is N5,810 (N7,000 deposit) and a suite N10,150 (N12,000 deposit) plus the usual 15%. In the lobby is the booking and information office for the Yankari National Park (open daily 08.00–20.00) where they astonishingly have Yankari caps, T-shirts and stickers of questionable age for sale (these are not available in the park itself). The helpful staff here will tell you how to get to Yankari (see below) so unless you want a T-shirt there's not much point coming here, as the park is so deserted there's no need to book. Across the road from the hotel is the abandoned Bauchi State Museum with a few outbuildings and dusty rocky enclosures – goodness knows what was once there.

The Obuna Royal Hotel (Murtala Muhammed Way; tel: 077 541941, 540011/21), is also a very good option and is a five-minute walk around the corner from the motor park or a quick hop by *okada*. Head towards the enormous football stadium on Murtala Muhammed Way and you'll see the hotel about 200m before the stadium. It's very friendly and comfortable and only a few years old and the 60 rooms on three stories have enormous beds, balconies, and spotless bathrooms where hot and cold water comes out of the taps. There's good food in the restaurant, such as chicken and coleslaw and yam chips and unusually, some vegetables such as carrots and beans, and there's a big bar with an outside courtyard. A double is N3,200 (N4,000 deposit). Across the road is the much grimier Monco Motel (no phone) which is clearly signposted from Murtala Muhammed Way and which has cheap rooms for N1,000 with fan, toilet, bucket and dubious sheets. If you were on a serious budget you could sleep here and use the restaurant and bar at the Obuna Royal Hotel.

## What to see and do

The tomb of Nigeria's first prime minister, Abubakar Tafawa Balewa, who was assassinated in Lagos in 1966, is 300m north of the central market roundabout on Ran Road (open daily 08.00–17.30; free entry but dash for the guide, which you can pick up at the office to the left of the gate). Opened in 1975 it's a square concrete block some 10m high and you can walk up a pitch-black concrete ramp and then down some stairs to the square outside the compound in the middle of it. The dark and light symbolise colonial repression and independence respectively. It's decorated with lots of different-coloured tiles that represent the different ethnic groups in Nigeria, and the square concrete stepping stones and the spaces in between on the floor symbolise the troubles of the Nigerian government, the coups, crises and civil disorder since Balewa was assassinated (the tomb was built in 1975). In the middle is a simple grave with a mound of stones, and the open top symbolises Balewa's open mindedness to all the people of Nigeria. Outside is a tall structure that was intended as a platform for a statue of Balewa, but his family never permitted a statue to be erected as Balewa was a Muslim and the Islamic faith prevents life representation in any form. In a room at the back of the complex is a display cabinet exhibiting a ceremonial sword presented to Balewa on a visit to Argentina, his watches, his radio, and a mini Sony TV presented to him by Queen Elizabeth II, and a small vial of oil, that is reputedly the first drop of oil to be extracted from the Niger Delta in the late 1950s and which was presented to Balewa in 1957 by Shell. Upstairs is a small library of his personal books, and if there is NEPA you can ask to watch a video of his speech at independence in 1960 – he was known as the Golden Voice of Africa for his good speaking voice. He was obviously good at other things too, as when he died Balewa left behind four wives and 19 children. On our visit we met a very old man there who thought he was about 85, and who was Balewa's house boy for 20 years. When Balewa died he accompanied the body from Lagos to Bauchi, and he has been the guardian of his tomb ever since.

## Yankari National Park

Yankari National Park and its Wikki Warm Spring is probably Nigeria's best-known reserve. It was upgraded to its present status as a national park by the government in 1991 and covers an area of 2,244km$^2$. Most of the park is made up of rolling hills of woodland savanna and is dominated by two rivers, the Gaji and the seasonal Yashi, that flow through the middle of the reserve, providing the main source of water for the wildlife. The park was established in 1950 after the then Minister of Animal and Forest Resources went to Sudan and visited the White Nile Game Reserve and saw herds of elephant, antelope and buffalo, and decided that game reserves should be created in Nigeria. On his return he gazetted Yankari, which was a region already rich in game. Between 1955 and 1962, local hunters and farmers were moved out of the area, jeep tracks were ploughed through the forest to allow visitors to go on game drives, and a base camp was built close to Wikki Warm Spring. But in the 1970s and '80s, wildlife populations declined dramatically due to a rinderpest epidemic and extensive and well-organised poaching by nomadic herdsmen. Marauding cattle were also sometimes killed by the lions leading to retaliation by the herdsmen.

Today Yankari is largely empty, though supposedly there are over 50 species of mammals present including leopard, antelope, lion, hyena and buffalo, though nobody knows how many of these are left in the park and they are rarely sighted. Several species of large mammal have become locally extinct since the area was first created as a game reserve, including African hunting dog, cheetah, giraffe, western kob, red-fronted gazelle and bohor reedbuck. But there are still approximately 500–600 elephant, a reasonably substantial herd of buffalo, baboons, roan antelope, waterbuck, various duikers, and perhaps even lion, as we think we *heard* one. The African rock python, the Nile crocodile and the Nile monitor lizard are fairly common and there's a pod of hippo in the Gaji River. Whilst most of the animals will remain elusive, Yankari is good for birdwatching, and more than 350 species of bird have been recorded in the park – of these 130 are residents, including saddlebill stork, grey-headed kingfisher, pied and giant kingfisher, hammercock, ibis, black magpie and cattle egret.

## Getting there and away
The gate to Yankari is about 120km to the southeast of Bauchi and the clearly signposted turn-off is 69km from Bauchi on the Gombe road, at the village of Dindima. From here follow the road for 52km to the village of Mainamaji and the gate, and then Wikki Camp is another 43km through the park from the gate. This road is tarred but full of potholes and gets slippery in the wet, but it is manageable in a normal car. All the other subsidiary roads are nothing short of sand tracks that are only suitable in a 4WD. You can get here by public transport but you will have to set off from Bauchi early in the day. From Bauchi there are direct vehicles to Mainamaji, though expect to wait for some time until one fills up. Once at the village's motor park the Yankari gate is 200m further on, and in the motor park you can negotiate a drop by taxi to take you to Wikki for around N2,500, or cheaper still take an *okada* the 43km (thanks to the lack of animals you're perfectly safe on the back of a bike) that should cost in the region of N700. Once at Wikki there is no transport, so your only option is to arrange with the driver to come and pick you up at a pre-arranged day and time, or hope that you can get a lift back to the gate with someone else, but remember Yankari only receives a handful of visitors at a time. When you fill in the register and pay the fees at the gate, it's a good idea to see if there is anyone else staying in the park that you could approach to ask for a lift out. Entrance fees to Yankari again include the ridiculous fees for cameras, which are often more than the fee per person to get in. They are as follows: park entry fee for a resident, N200 (expats will need to show copies of their residency permits to get this rate); for a non-resident, N300; car, N100; 'amateur' camera (which means without a zoom lens), N100; 'professional' camera (with a zoom lens), N500; digital camera, N1,000; and video camera, N1,500. Access to Wikki Warm Spring is another N200 for residents and N300 for non-residents, which is paid at reception when you pay for accommodation and is a one-off fee for your whole time there.

## Where to stay and eat
Wikki Camp (tel: 077 543674, 542174) is hopelessly dilapidated and very run down and of the 110 chalets only about 40 or so are functioning and (barely) habitable. Be very wary of touching the old AC units or even light sockets which sprout wires like old man's whiskers. Rates start from N800 (N1,200 deposit) for a very small and sparse double rondavel that is very old and damp. It's probably a good idea to pay a little more for a bigger 'luxury double' chalet with slightly newer tiles in the bathroom for N1,500 (N2,000 deposit). Bigger rooms with bigger beds go from

N2,000 (N3,000 deposit) whilst suites with an extra living room start from N3,000 (N5,000 deposit). It's just a case of finding a chalet that looks decent enough to sleep in. In the cheaper ones water is provided in a bucket and you can refill this from the water tanks outside in the grounds. The more expensive chalets have running water and AC that actually works when the gen is put on in the evening. Camping is N500 and there's plenty of grassy space, and again you can get water from the big water tanks, and there's a loo in the Activity Centre. Overland groups will be able to get one of the cheaper chalets for use of the bathroom. All these rates are exclusive of the 15% which is added on to accommodation and food.

The restaurant is quite cosy, with football on the TV and friendly service, and the food is good though choice is limited. Breakfast items go for N100, and set lunch and dinner each cost a reasonable N460. You'll get real soup to start, a main course of chicken casserole, macaroni, or omelette and chips, followed by a piece of fruit. The Activity Centre has a bar and DSTV where most of the staff watch movies all day, and two shops selling biscuits, chocolate, swimming costumes, rubber rings, batteries and camera film amongst other bits and pieces. Outside is a nice terrace with a good view over the savanna and a few odd plastic chairs, which is not a bad place to sit with a cold beer as a sundowner, but you won't see any animals except for the birds and baboons that occupy the giant mahogany trees and baobabs around the camp. There are abandoned tennis courts, but if you had your own rackets and balls you could probably still play.

## What to see and do
### Game viewing
Safaris go on a big green truck, which is an enormous and ancient beast of a thing that must have been in the park for decades, and which now has to be pushed down a hill to get it started. Expect to get stuck at some point on your game drive. You can also use your own vehicle and hire a guide, but you'll need to be in a 4WD. The morning game drive goes at 07.30 and the afternoon one at 15.30 and both last two hours and cost N200 for residents and N300 for non-residents, which is paid at the office near where the truck is parked just in front of reception. The dry season of November to March is the best period to visit the reserve as the dense vegetation has thinned and game gathers at the rivers. The tsetse flies are a problem in Yankari and administer a wicked bite. Just to give you an idea of the sort of game-watching experience you can expect in Yankari, whilst we were in the park we saw three baboons in the camp, one male waterbuck walked past our chalet during the night, we think we heard a lion, and on the game drive we saw one ground hornbill, one python in the river, and very, very luckily, a herd of about 40 elephant; these had previously not been spotted for four months.

### Wildlife Museum
The closest you are likely to get to most animals in Yankari is the Wildlife Museum at the reception block (open daily 08.00–12.00 and 15.30–17.00), which has a big board of rather amazing statistics about the visitors to the park. Apparently 20 Zimbabweans visited the park between 1989 and 2003, and in 1989 Yankari received 1,890 British visitors, compared to only 249 in 2003. Since it opened the park has received a total of 320,000 visitors, 250,000 of which were Nigerian. Other exhibits in the museum include bits of old stone and iron picked up in the park and the various remains of what used to be Yankari's inhabitants, such as lion, leopard and cheetah pelts, a few stuffed antelope, an elephant rib bone, an elephant pelvis, an elephant head, elephant feet, an elephant ear, an elephant eyebrow, and an elephant nipple! Oh, and a pair of hippo ears. There's also a whole bunch of

animal droppings on display. Judging by all the animal remains, Yankari was obviously once fairly packed with game, but poaching has sadly taken its toll, and in the museum is also a collection of weapons taken off poachers and the head of a dead ground hornbill that poachers have been known to wear as a disguise when they approach animals.

## Archaeological sites

The Dukke Wells were dug out about a century ago and were used as reservoirs to store water by the early settlers. There are 130 shallow wells at the site between 2.5–3.5m deep and around 50cm across that are interconnected below ground and hued out of red sandstone rock. These are roughly midway along the main access road into the park so you can stop and take a brief look. To get to the Marshall Caves you'll need your own 4WD and a guide from the camp. These are all about the same age and are man-made shelters that people used to live in up until the 1950s–60s when people were moved out of the region to create the park. They are roughly 1.5–4m in diameter and there are some 60 of them in the area around Borkono Gorge. They were named after a Mr P J Marshall, an ex-game ranger who found them in the 1980s. There are several old iron smelting sites in the park, crumbling conical clay furnaces that were once used to make farm implements and weapons, and several abandoned village sites from when the people that lived in the region were relocated when the park was gazetted in the 1950s.

## Wikki Warm Spring

The real reason to come to Yankari and one of Nigeria's highlights is the beautiful Wikki Warm Spring, a natural clear and pure swimming pool gushing out from under a cliff of red sandstone rock. Behind the camp restaurant a steep path takes you down to the spring in a lovely forested valley of dense greenery. Wikki has a constant temperature of 33°C and over 4,500,000 litres of water a day empty into the spring and are then carried to the Gaji River. The water is at least 2m deep, and the bathing area extends for about 200m to a large sandy beach, where you can take a soothing wallow in the warm shallows, which are about 9–10m wide. It's a lovely bright blue swathe of crystal-clear water with a sandy and mossy bottom surrounded by a thick forest of sausage and tamarind trees. Despite the ugly concrete platform built on the access side, it's an impossibly pretty spot and well worth the effort of getting to Yankari, even if you don't see any animals.

# Gombe

If you are heading east from Bauchi then the next city is Gombe, the capital of Gombe State – it is 187km due east of Bauchi past the turn-off to Yankari National Park. There's not much here and it's a sprawling city spread out in a wide valley with, unusually, a lot of road-building going on, but you are likely to swap vehicles here if you are heading to Maiduguri in the northeast or to Yola in the southeast. The motor park is close to a big central roundabout, and it's easy enough to swap vehicles without leaving the motor park, though if you get stuck late in the day try the Gombe State Hotel (GRA Road, Gombe; tel: 072 620230).

# Yola and Jimeta

Spacious and flat, this is a twin town situated south of the Benue River in the Benue Valley. Jimeta, 5km north of Yola, is the newer settlement and administrative centre, whilst Yola is the commercial hub and older Fulani town. Yola was founded in the mid-19th century from a war camp during the course of the jihad movement, when an emirate was established and trade links with the wealthier of the northern cities were established by way of the Benue and Niger rivers. By 1885 the valley had become a scene of European interest, with the British, German and French imperialists all trying to stake their claim. Eventually the British took the town by force in 1901, while the southern part of the emirate fell to the Germans (now in Cameroon). The British built the new town of Jimeta as the river port, to send hides, cotton and groundnuts down the Benue to Warri for export. Today the two towns are regarded as one community. There's nothing to see in the towns, but they are situated in some of the most scenic countryside in Nigeria, along the mountains of the Cameroon border. The motor park is in Jimeta on Galadima Aminu Way, where you will also find the acceptable Yola International Hotel (Kashim Ibrahim Road; tel: 075 624538), which opened in 1990 – although it's starting to fade, it is the best hotel in town, with good Nigerian and some attempt at Western food, and great views of the Benue River from the outside terrace where you can sit with a cold beer. The comfortable rooms have DSTV and a fridge, and a double will set you back around N4,500 (N6,000 deposit).

## Gashaka-Gumpti National Park

Located in the southeastern corner of Nigeria to the north of the Mambila Plateau and across Taraba and Adamawa states, Gashaka-Gumpti is an extension of the mountains of Cameroon, and at 6,600km² is one of the largest and least-explored territories in the whole of Africa. The largest park in Nigeria, it became a game reserve in 1972 and a national park in 1991 and is a vast expanse of wilderness. It comprises two sectors, each rich in its own unique flora and fauna species. The Gumpti sector is located in its northern fringe while the Gashaka is on the southern fringe. Very little is known about what's there, it's difficult to get to, and it receives only a handful of visitors each year. In 2003 visitor numbers were 12, mostly researchers on wildlife or plant research projects (WWF has conducted research here in recent years).

The park has a diverse range of habitats from guinea savanna, riverine forest and tropical rainforest, to steep mountains, deep jungle-filled gorges, and montane cloudforest, as well as montane meadows high up. The terrain supports hot springs, waterfalls and many networks of rivers and streams including the Taraba, a major tributary of the River Benue. Much of the park is mountainous, with steep hills rising 500–900m from their bases, and spectacular scenery. It is home to Nigeria's tallest mountain at 2,415m, Chappal Waddi, which simply means 'mountain of death'. The many different habitats of Gashaka-Gumpti support a great diversity of plant and animal species. Both savanna and forest animals are present, including buffalo, hartebeest, yellow-backed duiker, giant forest hog, warthog, lion, leopard, hyena, African hunting dogs, hippopotamus, chimpanzee, olive baboon, and colobus, patas and mona monkeys. The park is reputedly home to the best populations of primates in Nigeria, since the local people do not traditionally hunt these animals, though there are few statistics available and the park is largely untouched even by the game rangers employed by the National Parks Service. Some 366 bird species have been recorded here, including 13 species found only in this mountain chain along the Cameroon border, and the park is also a spawning ground for some fish species such as Nile perch, electric fish, and tilapia. It is, however, under threat for conversion to other forms of land use. Increased population pressure has led to encroachment of the park by farmers who cut the dense forest to farm; and, in the dry season, thousands of cattle are illegally put into the park to graze, causing serious destruction. Poaching pressure is also high, commercial bushmeat hunting is

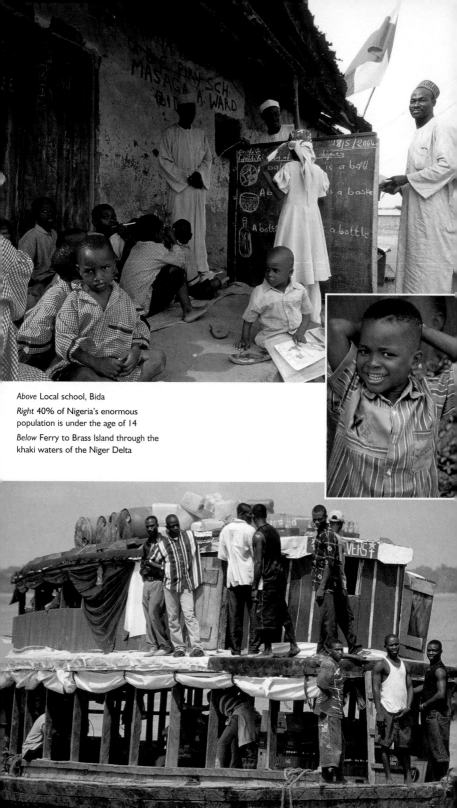

*Above* Local school, Bida

*Right* 40% of Nigeria's enormous population is under the age of 14

*Below* Ferry to Brass Island through the khaki waters of the Niger Delta

*Above* Wikki Warm Springs, Yankari National Park

*Right* The only game-viewing truck in Yankari National Park has to be pushed downhill to start

*Below* Drill Ranch, Calabar, an important refuge for drill monkeys and chimpanzees

## TREKKING IN GASHAKA-GUMPTI

*Hazel Chapman and Laura Sessions*

The nine of us, with ten porters, set out for our first ten-day trek through Gashaka-Gumpti. Many ethnic groups live in the enclaves of the park, but most settlers are Fulani pastoralists, who first arrived in the 18th century and settled here during the 1960s. The Gotel Mountains are the most remote area within the park, and we trekked north from the southern end of the mountains along the Nigerian/Cameroon border, and then looped southwest back to Gashaka village (the park headquarters). This is remote country, but with a local guide the paths are good. Our first survey was of Leinde Fadali forest, which kept up to its local reputation as 'chimp headquarters'. We spotted at least 20 chimpanzee nests and frequently heard their calls. Other wildlife included indirect evidence of bushbuck, duiker and buffalo, and sightings of warthog. Baboons were numerous and very bold, and we also saw colobus monkeys, and putty nose and vervet monkeys. But there has been a drastic reduction in wildlife since the 1970s; we saw evidence of hunters, and the wildlife round the forest was very shy. Despite being within Gashaka-Gumpti rangers rarely (if ever) visit this forest. Trekking on to the plateaus of Chappal Waddi and Gangirwal (Nigeria's highest mountain) we were awed by the beauty of the vistas and forest, but shocked by the number of cattle grazing the grassland. On Gangirwal we came across plant poachers on the upper slopes of the massif collecting edible tubers and lichen from rocks to sell for profit, some in Cameroon and some in Nigeria. This was in stark contrast to the 1970s, when people rarely ventured into the area. However, the montane forests were still very much as they had been in the 1970s. The main threats appeared to be cattle and fire encroaching into the valuable grassland-forest ecotone, and cattle grazing into the forest. Further along the Nigeria–Cameroon border, where few people trek, we were welcomed by the local Fulani headmen and their families.

*New Zealanders Hazel Chapman and Laura Sessions are authors of the field study 'The Forests of Taraba and Adamawa States, Nigeria', based on field work carried out by J D Chapman during the 1970s, and updated by Hazel and Laura on visits to Gashaka-Gumpti in 2003 and 2004.*

increasing on both sides of the border, and carnivores like lion and hyena are killed by cattle owners. Nevertheless, if you are prepared to spend time in the park and are confident about off-road driving (a GPS is essential here), this is the best place in Nigeria to look for its elusive wildlife, and the park is especially recommended for overlanders travelling through West Africa.

### Getting there and away

The reserve headquarters are in the Forest Rest Houses at Serti, on the main road between Bali and Gembu. These rest houses provide self-catering accommodation at a small fee, but don't bank on them being functional – there's no running water or electricity, though they have been used from time to time by researchers. Again the only option here is to come in a fully self-sufficient 4WD and be prepared to camp. The entrance to the park is about 15km south of Serti. In the dry season, it is possible to drive to the former headquarters at Gashaka village, some 30km from the entrance gate, where there is an office.

## What to see and do

There are a few rough jeep tracks within the park and it's essential that you take a guide with you in the vehicle as it's very easy to get hopelessly lost. It is also possible to go trekking on foot and go mountain climbing, and ranger escorts and porters can be arranged at the village of Serti, or at Gashaka village within the confines of the park, though nothing can be pre-organised before arrival, and expect to spend some time finding and negotiating for a guide. Everybody in these settlements is very helpful and the National Parks staff mostly speak some English. Visitors planning to climb Chappal Waddi should collect a ranger escort from Serti and then drive to Njawai in the northeastern corner of the park. Porters can be hired at Njawai and a two-day trek is then needed to reach the top of the mountain. If you are interested in this you might want to visit the National Parks office in Abuja first, as there are staff here who have done the climb and may be able to give advice. You may also want to consider visiting www.wwf-uk.org for reports on researchers' visits during the WWF initiative at Gashaka-Gumpti between 1998 and 2002.

# NORTHEAST NIGERIA
## Maiduguri

Maiduguri, the densely populated capital of Borno State, is in the extreme northeast of Nigeria on the edge of the Sahel, and is a blindingly hot and sandy city. It's surrounded by savanna scrubland and the encroaching sand belt of the Sahara, and camels, date palms and the indigenous Kanuri people, with their striking elaborate hair and colourful scarves, are a common sight. You may find yourself here if continuing into northern Cameroon, as Maiduguri is the closest Nigerian city to Cameroon, and there are two border posts within 140km to the east (see *Getting there* in the *Planning and Preparation* chapter for more details). It's also only 1½ hours' drive southwest of Lake Chad and again it's the nearest city to the country of Chad, and Ndjamena, the capital of Chad, is roughly 250km from Maiduguri and can be reached in a day via a short transit through Cameroon. Maiduguri was founded as a British military post in 1907, and like Kaduna and Jos, was a creation of Lord Lugard's empire building (see *History*, page 16). Maiduguri grew quickly and within 20 years of its establishment was home to 15,000 people, many of whom were from other parts of Nigeria. Whilst it is predominantly Muslim, the Sabon Gari concept never really took off here, and unlike in other northern cities, people live together without being warded off in their own sections of town. The population was boosted again after World War II when many returning servicemen settled here with their families, and it could today be plausibly over the million mark. Mosques are prolific throughout the city (each hotel has its own mosque) and hundreds of thousands of men pray several times a day. Remember to be sensitive around the mosque areas, which are often open prayer compounds on the side of the road.

From February to June this city is intolerably hot, with temperatures reaching well over 40°C, and the annual rainfall is a scanty 600mm. Any sightseeing should be done early, though there isn't much to see. The state government started an initiative telling people it was their duty to plant trees to provide shade, and there are some hardy neem trees lining the streets. Again this city is spattered with odd-looking roundabouts; the welcome roundabout is a green and white concrete circle and the west end roundabout has a curious giant fish on it. Borno State is a Sharia state, and you will not find alcohol anywhere in Maiduguri, though unlike in some of the other Sharia states, some of the hotel swimming pools have water in and foreigners may be permitted to swim. If you are here on a stinking-hot afternoon, you may feel every desire to do so.

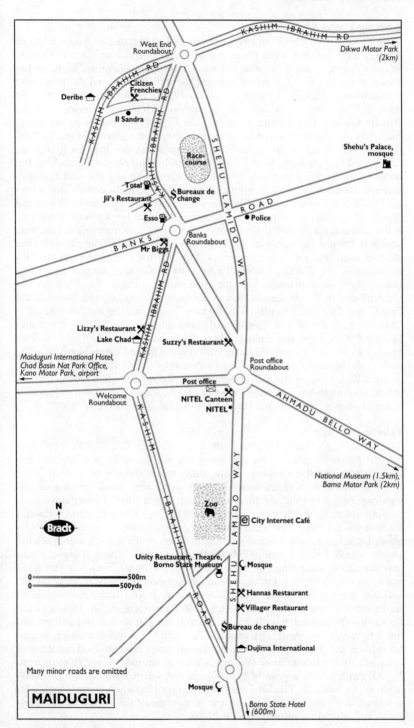

KASHIM IBRAHIM RD

West End Roundabout

Dikwa Motor Park (2km)

Citizen Frenchies

Deribe

Il Sandra

Race-course

SHEHU LAMIDO ROAD

Shehu's Palace, mosque

Total

Jil's Restaurant

Bureaux de change

Esso

Police

BANKS

Mr Biggs

Banks Roundabout

Lizzy's Restaurant

Lake Chad

Suzzy's Restaurant

Maiduguri International Hotel, Chad Basin Nat Park Office, Kano Motor Park, airport

Post office Roundabout

Post office

NITEL Canteen

NITEL

AHMADU BELLO WAY

Welcome Roundabout

KASHIM IBRAHIM RD

National Museum (1.5km), Bama Motor Park (2km)

Zoo

City Internet Café

SHEHU LAMIDO WAY

N

Bradt

Unity Restaurant, Theatre, Borno State Museum

Mosque

Hannas Restaurant

Villager Restaurant

0        500m
0        500yds

Bureau de change

Dujima International

Many minor roads are omitted

SHEHU LAMIDO ROAD

Mosque

**MAIDUGURI**

Borno State Hotel (600m)

## Getting there and away

To get to and from here from anywhere else by public transport, you need to set off very early. It's over seven hours in a bus to Kano and four hours to Gombe, where you swap to a vehicle going to Bauchi, which is another three hours, or Jos, which is another five. On arrival vehicles usefully drop around the post office roundabout, though for departure you'll need to get to the Kano Motor Park on Airport Road near the Maiduguri International Hotel for vehicles to Kano, Bauchi, Gashua, Gombe and Baga on Lake Chad. For vehicles to the south, including the Cameroon border near the Cameroon town of Mora, and the distant Yola, capital of Adamawa State (though along this road bush taxis are scarce), head for the Bama Motor Park on Bama Road off Ahmadu Bello Way. For transport to the most northerly border with Cameroon and the road that goes through a small section of Cameroon to reach Chad, go to the Dikwa Motor Park on Dikwa Road to the east of the city, where there are vehicles to Dikwa and Ngala, where you can swap on to another vehicle to the border itself. Maiduguri is the terminus for the terminally ill eastern branch railway from Jos, and the train station is 250m to the northeast of Sir Kashim Ibrahim Road. The airport is 6km west of town and the only option is a drop taxi for a reasonable N300. IRS Airlines; tel: 076 232028, has one flight a day between Maiduguri and Abuja (where there are connections with the same airline to Lagos, Port Harcourt and Calabar) that in theory departs from Maiduguri at 14.00 between Monday and Friday, and 14.30 on Saturday. The flight to Maiduguri departs from Abuja at 11.00 Monday–Friday and 12.00 Saturday and Sunday. The flight is sometimes cancelled if there are not enough takers. They also have some flights to Port Harcourt and Calabar, and you can get information at the Dujima Hotel, or at the desk at the International Hotel. Albarka Airways; tel: 076 230121, airport desk, also has flights once a day except Saturday between Maiduguri and Abuja with connections on to Lagos. (There's also a desk at the Lake Chad Hotel, and another at the Maiduguri International Hotel; tel: 076 235871/235102/235979.)

## Where to stay

The Borno State Hotel, 1 Talba Road, Old GRA; tel: 076 371008, 233919, at N5,750 (N8,000 deposit) plus the usual 15% for a double, is overpriced but nevertheless popular, and has seen some refurbishment in recent years. Accommodation is in different-sized chalets with new mossie netting on the windows, new doors and windows, and a fresh lick of paint. There's also a basic restaurant serving starch staples and soup. The Lake Chad Hotel, Sir Kashim Ibrahim Rd; tel: 076 232400, has 60–70 very worn rooms decorated with 1970s plastic bucket chairs and couches with plastic covers on them, but it's clean and the service is good. The very amicable chef in the kitchen will do his best to please, and may even cook something vegetarian; dishes go for N600. There's a very good stand here for international magazines and newspapers. A double room is N4,600 (N7,000 deposit) including the 15% surcharge. If you want to swim here, sometimes the pool has water and it costs N100 for non-guests. The Deribe Hotel, Sir Kashim Ibrahim Rd; tel: 076 231662, is easily the best place to stay in town and the 100 rooms are smart and clean, with satellite TV, reliable water, decent furnishings and cool tiled floors. The restaurant serves Nigerian food but the chef can rustle up something more Western if asked in advance. A double starts from N3,500 (with a hefty deposit of N7,000) and suites start from N6,000 (N10,000 deposit) plus the 15%. The fabulous swimming pool has a quiet terrace with seats and shade – it's not a bad place to come in the heat of the afternoon, and non-guests and non-Muslims can swim for N200.

The Dujima International Hotel, Shehu Lamido Way, Old GRA; tel: 076 232397, 233231, has tatty but comfortable rooms with satellite TV and fridge, big bathrooms with running water, and some with working showers, and there's lots of parking, though this is a busy place, so get there early to guarantee a room. The restaurant is pretty unreliable though. Doubles start from N3,200 (N4,500 deposit) inclusive of the 15%. Maiduguri International Hotel, Stadium Road; tel: 076 235102, 235871, 235979, is at least 3km out of town just past the Kano Motor Park. This vast state hotel was officially opened by General Abacha in 1997 and is something of a white elephant despite its modern appearance. It's also largely empty and only a few of the 300 rooms are used, hence the cheap rates. The rooms are fabulous and modern with great bathrooms, DSTV, and modern furnishings, but they are unbearably hot so if you can't get one with working AC I advise you not to stay here; even the walls are hot to touch! The lobby is ridiculously vast and there's a bright blue pool outside but no shade or chairs. The expensive restaurant serves not very authentic continental dishes for N850 a dish. A furnace of a double goes for N3,000 (N4,000 deposit) with one bed and rooms with two double beds go for N3,500 (N4,500 deposit).

## Where to eat

Not much happens in Maiduguri after dark and things tend to close quite early, and obviously there are no bars. Restaurants shut by about 21.00 at the latest and the later you go the less choice of food-is-ready there will be. It's a good idea to have a main meal during the day here. If you are not eating at the hotels, there are few non-Nigerian options. Citizens Frenchies Restaurant around the corner from the Deribe Hotel, stuffed full of tables and with ancient chandeliers hanging from the ceilings, serves chicken, fried and *jollof* rice, and spaghetti for about N600, but the food is not always ready and may take a while to materialise. Across the street is Il Sandra, which is open all day for substantial platefuls of food-is-ready, as is Jil's Restaurant on Leventis Road, further south after the Total petrol station. At the banks roundabout is a branch of the predictable Mr Biggs, the fast-food chain selling the standard Scotch eggs, chicken and *jollof* rice, pies and cakes. One of the most popular places to eat in town is Lizzy's Restaurant (open daily except Sunday 09.00–21.00) next door to the Lake Chad Hotel, an unmissable bright red and yellow building with a huge gen outside that's completely decked out in red and white Coca-Cola posters, flags, tables and fridges. It's consistently packed to the gills with guests and there's a huge menu offering semovita, rice, pounded yam, garri, and a variety of soups and fabulous salads with additional hard-boiled eggs and baked beans. Prices start from N300 an item. Suzzy's restaurant is a similar set-up on Shehu Lamido Way, just to the north of the post office roundabout. There's another branch of Lizzy's called Unity Restaurant just off Shehu Lamido Way at the entrance to the museum and theatre. Opposite the zoo, also on Shehu Lamido Way, are a couple of grimy chop houses next door to each other, Hannas and Villager, which serve basic chop and rice and sometimes spaghetti, and a few doors to the south is a *suya* spot and curio shop selling leather bags and carvings. Finally, at the post office roundabout, next door to the NITEL office in a smashed-up building, is the NITEL canteen, which is decidedly grubby and full of flies but which serves good food-is-ready, enormous salads with lots of vegetables, eggs and a dollop of mayonnaise, and cheap tea and coffee, doughnuts and pies during the day, so fill up here at lunchtime.

## Practicalities

Getting around is easy enough by *achaba* (motorbike), or shared taxis and minibuses up and down the main roads, and will cost little more than N20.

Walking would be a good option if it wasn't so hot. The City Internet Café on Shehu Lamido Way opposite the zoo (open daily 09.00–21.00) has reliable internet access (thanks to its big gen) for N120 per hour. There is a whole bunch of banks around banks roundabout, but to change money try the bureau de change further back, opposite the Esso petrol station in a row of wooden shops with a clear signpost above it. It's open from 08.00–18.00 but closed on Fridays and Sundays and will change US$ and CFAs. There's another bureau de change on Shehu Lamido Way near the Dujima Hotel, but again it's closed on Fridays. The post office and the NITEL office are on the corner of post office roundabout and there are landline and GSM phone stalls on the streets around them.

### What to see and do
Kyani Park on Shehu Lamido Way (open daily 09.00–17.00, entry N20), is a 42-acre dilapidated and neglected zoo. It is fairly spacious, though, and thanks to the neem trees it attracts a number of wild birds. But despite some of the enclosures being quite large, they only have the odd antelope in them, spread out as individuals rather than living together in a natural social group. And the first things you will see are the chimps locked up in tiny cages, and two elephants in a ridiculous pit full of their own shit. All the animals are a long way from their natural homes and look so dreadfully hot. Don't go there.

There are two museums in Maiduguri: the Borno State Museum is just off Shehu Lamido Way next to an open-air and rarely used theatre to the south of the zoo, and the National Museum is on Bama Road, to the north of Ahmadu Bello Way (both open Monday–Thursday 09.00–16.00; Friday 09.00–12.00; N20 entry fee). They house the usual collection of musical instruments, weapons, masquerade outfits and pots, but nothing of any special value, except for a replica of the Dufuna Canoe in the National Museum, reputedly the oldest boat ever found in Africa, which dates from perhaps 6000BC and which was unearthed near Damaturu in Yobe State. Nigeria's Commission for Museums and Monuments still has the original locked up somewhere. The only other mildly interesting sight is the Shehu of Borno's Palace at the end of Banks Road, a colonial building with a clock on top, and a huge mosque next to it, though you can't go inside. You might want to call into the Chad Basin National Parks office next to the Maiduguri International Hotel; tel: 076 342184, if you are heading to that region, though whilst they are friendly, they can't really tell you very much about the facilities of the park, though they can usefully give you directions to the different sections (dealt with under *Chad Basin National Park*, below).

## Around Maiduguri
### Baga and Lake Chad
In the extreme northeast of Nigeria lies Lake Chad, a small body of water which it shares with Niger, Chad and Cameroon. Lake Chad was once one of Africa's largest freshwater lakes, but it has dramatically decreased in size due to climate change and human demand for water. According to one study working with NASA's Earth Observing System, the lake is now 1/20th of the size it was 35 years ago. In the 1960s it had an area of more than 26,000km$^2$, but by 2000 this had fallen to less than 1,500km$^2$ – a puddle by comparison. The rapid shrinkage has been due to reduced rainfall combined with greatly increased amounts of irrigation water being drawn from the lake and the rivers which feed it. Droughts are quite common within the Chad basin, and by the end of each dry season evaporation occurs, and because it is very shallow, only 7m at its deepest, it always shows seasonal fluctuations in size. Whilst the shrinking of Lake Chad is widely regarded

as an environmental tragedy, it has provided benefits in some ways, especially in northern Nigeria. The water loss has uncovered more farmland, which is periodically moistened as the lake expands during the rainy season, and when the water contracts again at the onset of the dry season, valuable agricultural land is exposed, along with fish manure, which makes it even more fertile. And most importantly it's got soil moisture which can sustain agricultural crops another three months into the dry season. While other parts of Africa's Sahel are parched and prone to famine at times, the Lake Chad Basin remains agriculturally productive for an expanding population, and there haven't been any major famines there at all.

The most common species of vegetation currently found in the Lake Chad region are acacia, baobab tree, desert date, palm, African myrrh, and Indian jujube. In terms of aquatic plants, the most common species are papyrus, ambatch, water lilies, and reeds. Before the turn of the 20th century, those visiting the medieval Kingdom of Kanem reported an abundance of wildlife throughout the Lake Chad region. However, within the past hundred years there has been a dramatic decrease in the number of wildlife still living in the region. The main causes of this decrease are habitat loss, hunting, and of course competition from livestock. Reptiles and amphibians have fared somewhat better, however, and monitor lizards, crocodiles, rock pythons, and spitting cobras are all still quite common in the Lake Chad region. The migration of birds to Lake Chad each year is phenomenal. There are hundreds of species of bird that migrate to or live in the Lake Chad region. Some of the most abundant terrestrial birds of the region are the ostrich, secretary bird, Nubian bustard, and ground hornbill. There are also many different types of water and shore birds such as the garganey, marabou stork, shoveler, fulvous tree duck, Egyptian goose, pink-backed pelican, glossy ibis, and African spoonbill. The lake is also known for its excellent fishing resources – there are over 40 species of fish that are caught and sold by local fishermen. Accompanying all of these relatively commonplace animals are some ancient species which are native to Lake Chad. Both the lungfish and sailfin are and have been unique to this region for hundreds if not thousands of years.

You can visit Lake Chad from Baga (see below) but don't expect an endless vista of water. Today it's made up of watery channels that cover and create seasonal islands and it's similar in ecological character to the Okavango Delta in Botswana. Whilst there's not much to see in the way of lake scenery, a trip to one of Lake Chad's channels is a great way to see and meet the people of the lake, who are just as interesting as the lake itself, and it's a huge adventure just getting there. The best time to go is between December and February when the water is at its highest. Be warned, it can get very hot here and summer temperatures reach 45°C.

## Getting there and away

Expect to pay in the region of N500 for a bush taxi and a little less for a minibus from Maiduguri to Baga. Note there is no accommodation in Baga, and whilst there was once a hotel called the Baga State Hotel, it's presently being used as military accommodation, so you'll have to visit here on a day trip from Maiduguri. It takes just over two hours and is a little less than 200km. The taxi ride takes you into the Sahel proper, a vast wasteland of sand and scrub where you may see camels and more of the Kanuri people, with their olive skins, plaited hair and layers of patterned clothes. You may also see open trucks or land cruisers carrying sacks of maize, and perched on top you'll see hundreds of fantastically dressed men in flowing robes and brilliantly coloured turbans, wrapped so tightly around their faces because of the sand and wind that only their eyes are showing. The Sahel villages are made up of huts with pointed conical thatched roofs, with chickens and toddlers scratching around in the sand outside. The scenery is quite stark but eerily beautiful – this is one of the remotest corners of Nigeria. Baga itself is a sprawling town, much larger than the small settlements you pass through on the way here. Once at Baga Motor Park (that also serves as an enormous open-air mosque, where you will see many hundreds of men praying at the allotted times), negotiate with an *achaba* driver to take you to Lake Chad. Very few speak any English, though some understand French, and you may have to enlist the help of a local trader to explain that 'you want to see Lake Chad'. In any event your arrival in Baga will draw quite a crowd, but don't be intimidated as everyone will be delighted to see you and will be completely curious about how and why *batauris* have made it this far. We went to a place called Fish Dam, but there are several other tributaries of Lake Chad within 10km of Baga. If you have your own 4WD, just get someone to point you in the general direction and you can simply go exploring in the sand. A good tip is to follow the other well-worn tracks to the north of Baga, as they will inevitably lead to the edge of the lake.

You are doubtless going to have your own experience here depending on what you arrange when you get to Baga, but our experience went like this. We managed to negotiate a couple of *achabas* for N500 each for the round trip and waiting time – these were gutsy, fiery Suzuki's I might add, bikes much more suitable for the sandy terrain here than the normal Jincheng's, the Chinese bikes seen in the cities. The drivers took us through the back streets of Baga, where everyone we passed stopped and stared, and then out into the desert on a track of deep sand for about 6–7km. It was an exciting ride. When we got to Fish Dam, a busy little port area with a few shacks, our drivers deposited us at the immigration post where we duly sat down for a chat under a thatched shade, produced our passports for inspection, and asked very nicely if we could 'see Lake Chad'. I am presuming there are more of these at the other tributaries around Baga. They let us continue to the edge of the water, where we spent an hour or so observing what was going on, chatting to the people, and admiring the rippling channel surrounded by reeds. Here was a remarkably simple port on an ancient lake, of traditional lake people: men hauled sacks on and off wooden canoes, robed and turbaned traders sat on their haunches and discussed deals in numerous languages, fishermen hauled in their nets on the little beach, gaily dressed women sorted fish into baskets on their heads, numerous trucks and vehicles rumbled up with various boxes and sacks and were unloaded and loaded up again by the muscular porters, sacks of grain and maize arrived by canoe from other shores of the lake, regal-looking men in the most elaborate robes sat beneath thatched shelters and counted out wads of naira, deals were done, payments were made, and the atmosphere was that of such rich tradition, they might as well have been counting in cowries. It was a magical experience.

## Chad Basin National Park

At 2,258km², Chad Basin National Park is dotted across Borno and Yobe states in three independent sectors. The Chingurmi-Duguma sector is in Borno State on the Cameroon border south of Lake Chad. The Bade-Nguru Wetlands and the Bulatura Oasis are both located in Yobe State, some 400–500km to the northwest of the Chingurmi-Duguma sector. The park is generally described as the conventional basin of the famous but rapidly shrinking Lake Chad, though none of the sections are near to the shores of present-day Lake Chad itself. Prince Philip visited the Lake Chad Basin when he was president of WWF in 1989 and parts of the park were visited by Charles and Diana in 1990, but since then the park has received only a handful of visitors and can only be visited if you are in a self-sufficient 4WD vehicle. You may want to stop at the Chad Basin National Park office in Maiduguri (see above) to get some information, but the management know very little about the areas of the park themselves, and they don't even know what the park entrance fees are or if accommodation is available! It's not. Like Nigeria's other national parks, accommodation was built some time ago, but at Dagona and Gulumba base camps, at Bade-Nguru and Chingurmi-Duguma respectively, accommodation has simply fallen into disuse, there's no-one around to collect any park entrance fees and your only option is to bush camp. To gain access to any of the regions below you'll simply have to drive off road into the bush and hope for the best. Alternatively you could perhaps hire a guide from the office in Maiduguri.

Chingurmi-Duguma, the largest of the three areas, covering 1,228km² of Borno State, was first proclaimed a forest reserve in 1975, and is dominated by savanna dotted with acacia woodland, elephant grass, and swampy areas, and it effectively joins the Waze National Park on the other side of the border in Cameroon and shares a similar eco-system. Wildlife is seriously limited and whilst there used to be giraffe here, they are long gone, though there may still be a few ostrich and hardy spotted hyena, and antelopes including the western hartebeest and red-fronted gazelle, and many birds such as marabou storks, secretary birds and bateleur and tawny eagles. There is a possibility of there still being elephant in the region that migrate over the border from Cameroon from time to time.

Both the Bade-Nguru Wetlands and the Bulatura Oasis are found within an area known as the Hadejia-Nguru Wetlands, one of West Africa's most important stopover points for birds migrating from Europe; it has been proclaimed a Ramsar site (an important wetland habitat for birds under the 1971 Convention of Wetlands, and today supported by Birdlife International). During the dry season, many thousands of European birds seeking sanctuary in Africa during the harsh European winter come to these serene wetlands next to a vast desert terrain – a sudden belt of greenery on the edge of the Sahel. The birds' watering ground also serves a large human population of thousands who depend on the annually flooded wetlands for their agriculture, grazing and fishing. Floods in the wet season play a critical role in recharging groundwater, upon which Nguru town and the string of settlements along the channel and lake are dependent. Bade-Nguru covers 938km² and the wetlands are centred around a more permanent ox-bow lake, fed by the Jama'are River that rises in the Jos Plateau, and by the Hadejia that rises in the hills around Kano. Over winter a total of 377 species of birds have been recorded here, and birds that have nested in Europe and Asia begin to migrate to Africa from August and some stay as late as the following May. Roughly a quarter of a million birds make the Sahel zone of Nigeria their wintering range and families include ducks, geese, herons, storks, cattle egrets, ibises, pelicans, long-tailed cormorants, spotted redshanks, wood sandpipers, spur-winged plovers, and ruffs (waders) in their thousands.

The Bulatura Oasis is an area to the north of Bade-Nguru on the border with Niger, and it's a highly scenic chain of sand dunes some 10–30m high and 300–400m wide in the Sahel. The area is 92km², made up of both sand and swampy palm-filled valleys, hence its name. The water in the area attracts some antelope, and sometimes Fulani cattle herders and camels, but the tracks these make through the sand soon disappear after winds. This is the only spot where flamingoes have been recorded in Nigeria. The drive up here along sand tracks leading north of the Nguru–Gashua road will take you past nomadic Fulani settlements, easily some of the remotest in Nigeria.

## Getting there and away

To visit these areas, you will need to have your own vehicle and to be completely self-sufficient. The Bulatura Oasis and the Bade-Nguru Wetlands are best visited from Nguru. The Bade-Nguru Wetlands are located 15km from Nguru in the direction of Gashua. The route goes through a village midway along the Nguru–Gashua road called Tashan Kalgo, where there is a sign for the wetlands (though for its old name of Dagona Waterfowl Sanctuary), which is roughly 5km further on down this turning. It is advisable to ask in the village for permission to visit the sanctuary and request a guide to take you there. Someone will find the right person for you. To get to the Bulatura Oasis a guide is essential. Chingurmi-Duguma is accessible only during the dry season and is located approximately 140km, or a two-hour drive, to the southeast of Maiduguri, near the village of Kumshe.

## Sukur

To the southeast of Maiduguri, a worthwhile if difficult excursion is to travel to the ancient village of Sukur right on the border with Cameroon in the Mandara Mountains. It's Nigeria's only UNESCO World Heritage Site, proclaimed in 1999 for its cultural landscape. It's a beautiful settlement of perhaps 2,000 people, high up in the mountains with tremendous views of the valleys below dotted with villages and herdsmen, and terraced hillsides. The word Sukur means 'vengeance' in Margi and Kilba, and *ta sukur* means 'feuding' in the Bura language, so presumably the Sukur people settled in their mountain stronghold after a local spat centuries ago. Sukur's existence was kept from the British until 1927, and not much has changed here for a very long time – people still go about their daily rural lives in much the same way as their ancestors did. It's a small chieftaincy consisting of kin groups of various origins, with one chiefly lineage headed by the *xidi* or chief. The settlement is divided into 'Sukur Sama' and 'Sukur Kasa', referring to upper Sukur and to lower Sukur, and the Palace of the *xidi*, a large stone enclosure with its various gates and niches, is in the top part on a hill dominating the village below. You are more than welcome to visit the chief and he will happily tell visitors in broken English a little of the history of the Sukur people. Since it has gained worldwide interest, in recent years it's been visited by a number of curious researchers, anthropologists and archaeologists, so these days the people are a little more used to the sight of *batauris*, and they have even set up a small museum and a simple house for visitors where you can sleep on a mat on the floor. There's no charge for this but a small donation of a few naira, or, better still, food, would be most appreciated. This is a delightful experience and you will feel most welcome. Since its inclusion on the World Heritage list a festival is held here each year on February 2.

## Getting there and away

To get here is seriously challenging, but if you make it this far you will be well rewarded. If you are not in your own vehicle, from Maiduguri you need to set off early and be equipped with ready-prepared food to last a day or two, since how long it takes depends on the availability of transport and how quickly you can hike. Firstly get a bush taxi from the Bama Motor Park to Bama, than swap on to another one to Madagali, 82km to the south on the A13. From here it is customary to go to the Madagali Local Government Office, a short distance from the motor park (just jump on an *achaba*), where you should ask permission to visit Sukur (they can also organise a guide to take you there). Sukur is way up in the mountains to the southeast of Madagali and your only option is to walk. It's fairly steep so you need to be reasonably fit for the round trip. From Madagali you should be able to get public transport as far as Chambula, a small settlement roughly 12km beyond on the A13. Then get someone to point you in the direction of the Mildo Market; the track is clearly marked out. Once here it's another 5km to the village of Mydlau, and the final part of the walk is on an ancient set of 500 stone steps that climb the mountain from behind the school at Mydlau. If you are driving, ask at the school if you can park your vehicle there. Once at the top the views are fabulous and the steep terraced valleys fall away in every direction. It is possible to return by a different route to Mefir Suku, the village on the plain further down the hill, which every Tuesday holds a market visited by the people of Sukur.

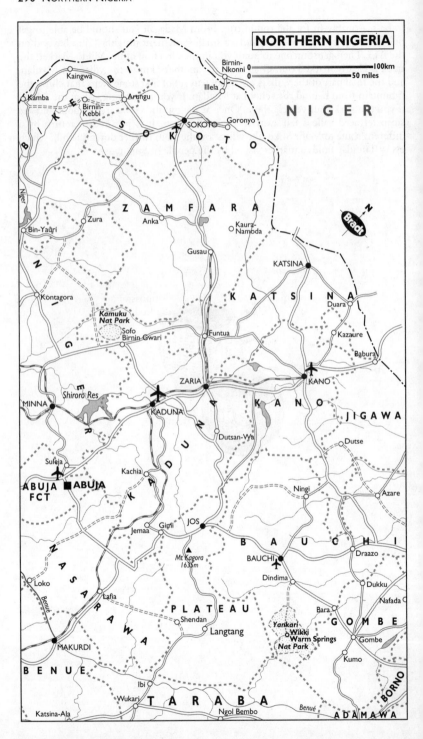

# Northern Nigeria

Parts of the north, such as Lake Kainji National Park, Maiduguri and Lake Chad, have been covered in earlier chapters, simply because of their accessibility from the south, but it is the northern ancient emirates of Kano, Katsina and Zaria that hold perhaps Nigeria's most evocative atmospheres. These are cities steeped in Islam, with prolific mosques, ancient city walls, and old Hausa architecture. In Kano, today a city of perhaps ten million people, there's a market where trade in the impossibly congested lanes has been going on for a millennium, and less than a hundred years ago it was still the West African hub for camel caravans arriving from North Africa and Arabia across the Sahara. Sokoto is still ruled by a sultan, and each of the cities have grand emir's palaces in which trumpeters still herald the presence of the emir. Away from the cities and in the far north, the stark and arid savanna of the Sahel region is an area dotted with mango and gum trees that is still frequented by camels and nomadic Fulani herdsmen with their sheep and goats, as it has been for thousands of years. You'll see farmers using hand hoes or ox-driven ploughs, ancient villages of low mud houses with no windows to keep them cool, beehive huts used as grain containers topped with straw roofs balanced on rocks and logs, curling smoke from charcoal burners, and women and children collected around wells with clay water pots on their heads. Here it is sandy and dusty and blindingly hot, and when it rains there are violent electrical storms and the region is littered with burning trees. Although barren, the region surprisingly produces a variety of fruit and vegetables not seen so readily in the south, and in all the cities you will see pineapples, watermelons, bananas, mangos and oranges for sale on the side of the road, and in restaurants you'll find salads with lettuce and tomatoes on the menu. The north is of course dominated by Islam, and most of the states operate to a certain degree under Sharia law. The very essence of the religion gives the north a very different personality than the south, where millions of Muslim men pray several times a day, and hundreds of thousands of little girls go to school cloaked head to foot. The implications of Sharia are not as intrusive to the traveller in this region as you might expect, and because of the presence of many Christians in the cities, who are mostly living in the Sabon Gari districts (Hausa for 'foreigner's town'), as a non-Muslim visitor you will encounter no problems. This is not the case on a local level however, and the north has famously been known over recent years as the region for violent religious spats between the two religions, and tension amongst the communities is high. The Sahel roads are littered with police checkpoints where policemen in faded uniforms stand on the hot road all day collecting dash, and it's not uncommon to see lorry-loads of robed men carrying AK47s. When visiting the north, always keep your ear to the ground for possible disturbances.

# KADUNA

Kaduna is a relatively modern city on the Kaduna River and is the capital of Kaduna State, and is usually regarded as the first city of the north, but as a new city, it doesn't hold the same appeal or charm as the older emirates. The city was founded by the British in 1913 and was the capital of Nigeria's former Northern Region from 1917 to 1967. After the British government took control of the colony in 1900 from the Royal Niger Company, Lord Lugard first settled in Lokoja, which he made his capital, but he found it too far south in the territory for effective control and moved to a more favourable site, where the Lagos–Kano railway crossed the Kaduna River, known then as Mile 570. It was of strategic importance and in easy reach of the emirates, and as a new town it also had the advantage of being free from the clamours of local chiefs and traditional leaders. In the early days it was only inhabited by government agencies and officials and was dubbed then simply Government Town before being renamed Kaduna after the river. (*Kadduna* means crocodile in a local language and there was once an abundance of them in the river.) The transfer of 366 British officers and around 5,000 African troops to Kaduna in 1913 marked the birth of the town. Clerks, labourers, railway workers, staff of colonial companies and a good deal of immigrant Nupe, Yoruba, Hausa, Igbo, Edo and Fulani followed in their wake, building urban Kaduna into a multi-cultural city. As the capital of the Northern Region, Kaduna was a nerve centre for politics, and Lugard's policy of indirect rule during the colonial period. It was also at the centre of the de-colonisation period from 1951 to 1960, as it was also the home of Ahmadu Bello, the leader of the Nigerian People's Congress party (NPC) who became premier of the Northern Region at independence. The British town planners built an expansive and well laid-out Government Reservation Area that today is still home to Kaduna's elite, and many of the roads are named after British governors and administrators. In 1967, with the creation of 12 states, Kaduna ceased to be the capital of the whole of Northern Nigeria and became instead the capital of North Central State. Then again in 1976, with the carve up of the country into even more states, it became the capital of Kaduna State. Today it remains northern Nigeria's political centre and there are a number of training colleges for teachers, police, and the military, and two universities. It's a busy commercial and industrial centre and has a pipeline that connects the city's oil refinery and petrochemical plant to the oil fields in the Niger Delta, and a large Peugeot assembly plant. Kaduna's recent history has been one of violent riots and religious clashes, most notably in 2000 when 400 people were killed, and again in 2002 when 200 people were killed over the Miss World controversy (see page 37). There are Christians that have lived in Kaduna their entire lives, migrating here from the south decades ago to work in the factories, but since the adoption of Sharia law by Kaduna State in 2000, the tension between Muslims and Christians is almost palpable. The bloody riots have left both physical and emotional scars on the city; there are churches and mosques everywhere, though some are little more than burnt-out wrecks, and you will notice more of a police presence here than in other cities, with armoured vehicles and armed police at the junctions and roundabouts.

## Getting there and away

The **airport** is some way out of the city, roughly 40km to the north, and the only option is to take a drop taxi for around N2,500. Chanchangi Airlines has an office in the city at 8 Ahmadu Bello Way; tel: 062 249949 – there's another desk at the Hamdala Hotel, and a desk at the airport; tel: 062 234595. There are two flights a day from Kaduna and Lagos Monday to Friday at 07.30 and 12.30, and one at 08.00

on Saturdays and Sundays. From Lagos to Kaduna there are flights at 10.00 and 17.00, and 14.45 on Saturdays and Sundays, and the flight takes one hour. From the city office, which is open daily 09.00–18.00, they can organise a taxi to the airport. The **motor parks** are a few kilometres out of the city in several directions. From the Abuja Junction Motor Park, on the expressway linking Kano with Abuja, vehicles arrive and depart for all places south, including Abuja and Suleja, and Zaria and Kano to the north. 'Luxury' buses also go from here overnight to Onitsha, Aba and Port Harcourt. A bus to Abuja is N350, and one to Zaria costs N160, and there are also direct minibuses to Zaria, only one hour away from the city centre on the corner of Ahmadu Bello Way and Ibrahim Taiwo Road. Vehicles also arrive and depart from the Kawo Motor Park at the top of Ali Akilu Road to the north of the city, for Sokoto, Kano and Katsina. Kaduna was built on the railway, and in the event that a train ever turns up again, the **train station** is just south of the Kaduna River on Constitution Road.

## Getting around

The city is fairly spread out but is bisected neatly by one major straight road that runs south to north, but rather confusingly it changes its name frequently. In the south, from the Junction–Constitution road roundabout, which has a huge concrete football on it, it's called Junction Road, before changing names to Ahmadu Bello Way through the guts of the city, and then Ali Akilu Road in the north of the city. **Minibuses** and **shared taxis** run up and down the main drag for N20, and to get to any of the motor parks is a N20 ride on a minibus, all of which are probably too far on an *achaba*. You will find drop taxis at the major hotels.

## Where to stay
### Moderate: US$25 and above

**Command Guest House** 10 Mohammed Buhari Way (formerly Waff Road) tel: 062 242918/21. Easily Kaduna's nicest hotel with over 200 modern rooms in a three-storey block surrounded by established gardens and with tennis and squash courts. The garden bar is a great place to enjoy a sundowner even if you're not staying here. The rooms, whilst being exceptionally good by Nigerian standards, with DSTV, constant power and hot water, and sparkling bathrooms, are very plain, with bare white walls, but they are very comfortable. You can arrange car hire here, there's a functional business centre, and a good restaurant serving a range of Western food with changing daily menus. You'll be charged the higher non-resident rate here of N11,000 (N12,500 deposit) for a standard double, N13,000 (N15,000 deposit) for a luxury double and US$185–295 (US$210–360 deposit) for a suite, plus the 15%. There are a couple of other hotels a few doors along but they are pretty dire and overpriced.

**Hamdala Hotel** 26 Mohammed Buhari Way; tel: 062 245440/7. This huge complex was built in 1961 and opened by Ahmadu Bello, so as you can imagine it is very dated, but it's busy, so has a lived-in feel with good service and a 24-hour gen. The excellent bookshop in the lobby stocks *Newsweek*, *Time* and the like, European glossies, and somewhat of a surprise for a Sharia State, *Penthouse* and *Playboy*. The restaurant in the hotel itself is not bad, though a little shabby, but it is consistently busy – some of the Western dishes on the menu include braised beef and grilled prawns from N700, and fresh fruit for dessert, and there's a comfy bar serving alcohol. At the hotel entrance is also the Unicorn Chinese Restaurant (open daily 11.30–15.00, 18.30–22.30) with a basic menu of mostly chop suey. At the back of the complex is a huge laned pool with diving boards, and despite there being water in it, the gates were locked on our visit and the terrace was very overgrown. In the car park are curio shops and bureaux de change. There is a confusing array of over 200 different-sized rooms here, so it's just a case of looking at them until you find something that suits. Apart from the rooms in the main hotel block and in its extension block, at the back are some chalets, and another 'motel' block (that doesn't look anything like a motel). The cheapest is a double in the motel for N6,000 (N8,000 deposit) or a standard double in the main hotel is N6,500 (N9,000 deposit), plus the 15%.

## Budget: under US$25

**Gloria Moria Hotel** 222 Ahmadu Bello Way/Zaria Rd; tel: 062 240720. This is the best of the budget options, with its nice tiled lobby and it's all newly refurbished with new blinds, wrought iron furniture in the restaurant, and there's a fridge in reception selling juice and cold drinks. There's no car park though, and only parking space for about four cars on the street with a security guard. The small rooms have DSTV and working bathrooms and go for N2,830 (N3,500 deposit) including the 15%, and tea-bread-and-eggs for one person.
**Mussafir Hotel** 15 Constitution Rd; tel: 062 213578, 214023. Small but clean and comfortable rooms with a TV and bucket, some with balconies overlooking the horrendous traffic on Constitution Road and the football stadium opposite, and food and beer is brought to your room. There's a small parking bay out front that is locked at night. Adequate doubles which all have AC go for N1,800, and the gen stays on all night.
**Traveller's Rest** 19 Argungu Rd; tel: 062 217912. Also a good budget option and cheap, but it's unashamedly run-down, with a filthy lobby and corridors; it's also on a noisy street and there's no parking. The rooms, however, are very clean, with two enormous beds and a bucket in the bathroom and tea-bread-and-eggs for N150 and plates of fried rice for dinner at N250 are brought to the room. On another plus side it's across the street from the lively Safari Bar. A room with a fan costs N1,200, with AC N1,600.
**Duncan Hotel** 6 Katsina Rd; tel: 062 240947. Efficient, friendly and popular, though there's no booze or parking and meals are cheap but very ordinary, and you're not going to get much more than a plate of rice or semovita. There are about 20 small and old-fashioned rooms with buckets on two stories, and a double with AC is N1,500, and with a fan N1,200.

# Where to eat and drink

If you are not eating in your hotel, Kaduna has a fair amount of excellent alternative places selling non-Nigerian food thanks to there being a large expat community here. Starting in the north, the **French Café** 2 Ali Akilu Road (open daily 11.00–23.00), is a very lovely, if expensive, restaurant and bakery run by French expats. The bakery out front sells delectable chocolate éclairs and black forest gateaux, and the AC café to the back has a huge menu of sandwiches with fillings such as salmon, smoked turkey, shaved beef, and Italian mozzarella for about N750, real salads with shrimps and avocado for about N900, pastas from N900, and burgers, steaks and chicken from N1,200. There's a huge range of imported spirits and French wine, and finally, the toilets are fabulous. Just around the corner is **Food Palace Restaurant at** 1 Alkali Road, next door to the International Trust Bank, which is nice and new with immaculate plastic chairs and one room with mats to eat sitting on the floor, which is the traditional rural Hausa way of eating. Traditional food is on offer such as pepper soup and garri, and unusual local items such as waina, ground rice soaked in yoghurt and then steamed. **Shagalinku Modern Supermarket** at 7 Ali Akilu Road (open Monday–Friday 09.00–21.00; Saturday–Sunday 10.00–22.00) is a new white building set in a compound with a red and yellow sign selling everything from washing machines and babies' cots to sacks of American par-boiled rice, all imported and all expensive. There's a good cosmetic selection of deodorants, razors and even suntan lotion, and you can pick up imported food items and chocolate upstairs.

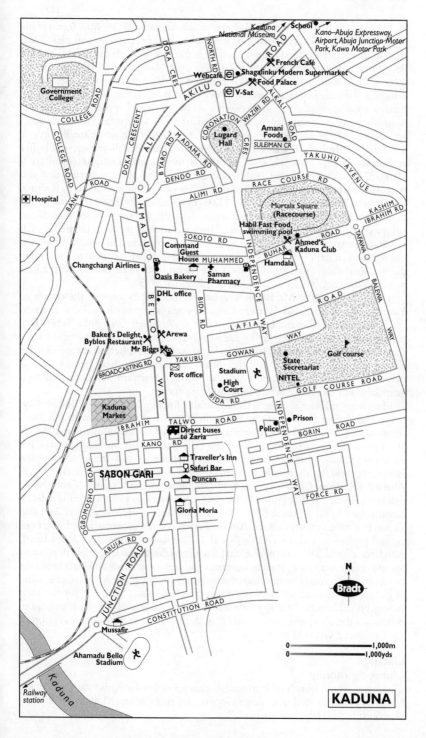

KADUNA

Further south is the **Oasis Bakery** at 22 Ahmadu Bello Way (open daily 07.00–22.00) for cold drinks, tubs of ice-cream, fresh bread, cakes and pies. Then next to the defunct Nigeria Airways office is the **Arewa Chinese Restaurant** at 28 Ahmadu Bello Way (tel: 062 240088; open daily 12.00–15.00 for lunch, 19.00–22.00 for dinner) with a big car park and sparkly lights outside a pagoda-like building, with the restaurant on the upper floor. It offers very authentic Chinese food, a good atmosphere, and a cosy bar serving beer and spirits. The extensive menu has mostly meat dishes, so vegetarians may need to ask for something special, and nearly all the dishes except for seafood cost the same; small portions are N550, medium N700, and large N1,000, and there's an all-you-can-eat buffet at Sunday lunch. More or less opposite is the **Bakers Delight** (open daily 10.00–22.00), a supermarket with some Lebanese and other imported tins and packets and a bakery counter. Behind here is one of the best restaurants in Kaduna, the **Byblos Restaurant** (open daily 12.00–15.00 lunch; 19.00–23.00 dinner). It's pricey, but has a full bar of imported spirits, liqueurs and some wines, nice décor, subdued lights and background music. There are unusual items on the menu such as Chateaubriand, Champignon de Paris (mushrooms baked in wine with melted cheese), lots of delicious steaks and sauces, and pizzas on Wednesday and Friday nights. Meat dishes start from N1,000, vegetarian pasta from N600, and the best value are the tasty omelettes with lots of fillings for N450.

There's a branch of **Mr Biggs** with an internet café behind on the corner of Yakubu Gowon Road and Ahmadu Bello Way near the post office. Further south off Ahmadu Bello Way and in the Sabon Gari on Argungu Road is the **Safari Bar** packed to the gills with men (and some Muslims I think) getting labouredly drunk. But it's a lively spot and women will feel quite comfortable here as it appears to be run by women who flap around the sottish men and help them out the door if necessary. Tables are arranged around an outside courtyard; it's decorated with beer flags, and hawkers do the rounds selling popcorn.

Elsewhere in Kaduna, around the Hamdala Hotel on Mohammed Buhari Way, is the **Habil Fast Food** opposite the main entrance of the hotel, with fast food, boxes of rice, chips and fried chicken in a spotless AC environment, and there's also a swimming pool behind the restaurant that you can use for N200 per day. It's clean with a shaded bar area, but is very busy and women may feel a little exposed swimming here as it's mostly frequented by young men. A few doors along is **Ahmed's/Kaduna Club** (open daily 09.00–midnight), with plenty of cold beers, fish/steak/chicken and chips for N500, and snacks such as pies and spring rolls all accompanied by CNN on the TV. There is a members-only lounge next door and a couple of tennis courts outside. **Amani Foods**, a small supermarket (though not as well stocked as Baker's Delight), is at 17 Sulelman Crescent off Alkali Road, which runs around the race course, and has a few tables outside for cold drinks and tea and coffee and snacks such as hummus and Lebanese salads and pitta bread for N300, and good roast chicken from the rotisserie machine. Across the road is a line of booze shops, some selling wine. For very cheap chop, look out for the men selling grilled chicken on the side of the road; it's freshly cooked and quite delicious – there's a particularly dense crop along Mohammed Buhari Way, around the Command Guest House.

## Listings
### Changing money
There is a whole bunch of bureaux de change in kiosks in the car park at the Hamdala Hotel, as well as money changers, and more across Mohammed Buhari Way outside the Habil restaurant.

## Communications
**Post offices** are located opposite the train station to the south of the city, and on Yakubu Gowon Road to the northeast of the market. The **NITEL** office is on Golf Course Road, and there's a branch of **DHL** at 16 Ahmadu Bello Way. The most reliable **internet** café with several terminals is Webcafé, 11 Ali Akilu Road, just round the corner from the French Café – for both of these it is worth the effort of catching a bus the 1km or so to the north of the city. Webcafé (open daily 09.00–21.00; N150 per hour) is next to an ISP, so email access is consistently good, as it's right under the satellite aerial and dish. It's very popular so you may have to queue. Just south of here is another internet joint, V-Sat at 20 Ali Akilu Road in the Zadina Plaza (open daily 09.00–22.00; N120 per hour).

## Pharmacy
**Saman Pharmacy** is at 3 Mohammed Buhari Way, a block to the east of the Command Guest House (open daily 08.00–22.00). It's in a sort of prefabricated shed but inside is a huge range of imported medical items and lots of recognisable brand names, and the pharmacist in the office next door acts as a general doctor (no charge) for minor complaints.

## Travel agents
**Eminence Travel Agency** 18–19 Ahmadu Bello Way; tel: 062 210034, 235432. The agent for Lufthansa, British Airways and Swissair. It's in a brown office block next to the Oasis Bakery.
**Satellite Travel Services** Tel: 062 240232, 249387. Next door and above the Oasis Bakery; also deals with the major airlines.

# What to see and do
Kaduna has limited sights, but you are very likely to pass through here, as it's an important transport hub to other points in the north, and there are a couple of worthwhile distractions. **Kaduna National Museum** is on Ali Akilu Road about 300m north of the French Café (open daily 09.00–17.00; N100 entry). It's not one of the better Nigerian museums and there are only two dusty rooms with a few replicas of Benin brass plaques, and carved ivory from the old Benin Palace. Again the pieces of Nok terracotta are disappointingly also replicas. The collection is mostly bits and pieces from southern Nigeria, though there is a small display of Islamic tablets and Koran writing, some especially evil-looking Epa cult masks and an elaborate knitted and raffia masquerade costume, and the usual collection of calabashes and pots. The best reason for coming here is the reproduction of a mud-walled **Hausa Village** with about ten buildings covered in corrugated tin roofs, and some open courtyards and gardens under the shade of flowering jacaranda and flame trees. It's outside and at the back of the museum and not obvious, so get someone to show you the gate. This is a popular spot for many Kaduna families, and you can wander around the huts, and the people inside will be happy to talk to you. In one is a ladies' hairdresser; leaving your shoes at the door, go in and chat to the women and young girls sitting on mats or traditional Hausa ten-legged stools as they have their hair done. Once braids are unleashed some of their hair is very long and bushy until it is tamed again by straighteners, perms, or plaiting. In the other huts are weavers and painters, and at the far end is a long hut with a brass maker, blacksmith and silver craftsman. Here you can buy brass rings fashioned out of bullets! Try and be here on Thursday–Sunday when at 17.00 there is a display of drumming and dancing that lasts about an hour. Basically this is performed by a local troupe including dancers, midgets, drummers and Hausa

story tellers, and families bring their children to listen to and watch a traditional story being told. Everything is in Hausa but you can enlist a guide to sit next to you to try and explain what is going on. Ask one of the museum staff or a trader in the huts. The chances are you still won't have any idea what's going on as the tales are of mythical escapades, but it's very musical and atmospheric, with the graceful dancers with hennaed feet and hands, deep decorative scars on their faces and vibrant drumming, and as far as I am aware it's the only performance of its kind in Nigeria. Each performance attracts about a hundred people who sit on basic wooden benches or on the mud floor, and a dash is rightly expected afterwards.

Back in the city centre off Ibrahim Taiwo Road, **Kaduna Market** sells the usual assortment of manufactured plastic goods and clothes, though the fruit and vegetable section at the back is particularly colourful, and again it comes as a surprise to find so much variety of produce in such a barren region. The only other attraction in Kaduna is **Lugard Hall** on Independence Way, built by Lord Lugard and used by the colonial government as their headquarters when they administered northern Nigeria. Today it is the State House of Assembly and an impressive example of colonial architecture, painted green and white in dramatic well-tended grounds, but you can only peek through the gate.

## KAMUKA NATIONAL PARK

Kamuka National Park lies some 125km west of Kaduna on the A125 near the town of Birnin Gwari, and the park gate is 23km to the south of here off the Lagos–Kaduna road near the village of Dagara. Kamuka covers 1,121km$^2$ of savanna woodland marshes and was gazetted as a national park in 1999 from an older forest reserve and named after a local ethnic group, but the park has only ever received a handful of visitors and it's poorly protected. It reputedly has some elephants, roan antelope, western hartebeest, a number of species of duikers, warthog and baboon and jackal, and a variety of birds including guinea fowl and ground hornbill. The park is supposedly open from December to June, and if you manage to gain access and find anyone to pay, the entry fee is supposed to be N300. There's no accommodation and you'll need to be in a self-sufficient vehicle and be prepared for camping, and remember that none of the tracks within the park have been maintained.

## ZARIA

The ancient walled city of Zaria to the north of Kaduna retains much of its old character and has a fine mosque and Emir's Palace, and is one of the most pleasant of the northern cities and is an exceptionally friendly place. First known as Zazzau, it was founded in about AD1000 and became one of the 15th-century Hausa states (see box on page 304). It was once an important city in the trans-Saharan trade route, where camel caravans from the north exchanged salt for slaves, cloth, leather and kola nuts. With them came Arabian influences, and the court of Zazzau increasingly became interested in the teachings of Islamic scholars, and like their contemporaries in Kano and Katsina, the Sarkis (kings) of Zazzau converted to Islam in the 15th century. The jihad of the early 19th century (see page 33) was successful in Zaria, and an emirate was established in 1808 under control of the wider Sokoto Caliphate. A century later it was incorporated into the British Protectorate and cotton, groundnuts, leather and tobacco from the region were sent by rail to Lagos for export. The old walled city is still there, inhabited by mainly Hausa-Fulani – the main market is on the original site where the camel caravans used to stop from the Sahara, and where there are still many Islamic schools. The population is perhaps around two million, of which about three-

## ZAZZAU

The older name for Zaria is Zazzau, and the inhabitants are called Zage-zage or Zazzagawa. Oral tradition has it that the name Zazzau is derived from a famous sword which was honoured by the Zazzagawa and which helped to give a kind of ethnic identity in the years before the recognition of any king. One of the earliest rulers of Zazzau was Bakwa Turunku (it's not certain whether they were a king or queen), who had two daughters. The older daughter was called Amina, after whom the original 15km perimeter wall of Zazzau is named. Zaria, the younger daughter, gave her name to the modern emirate and its capital. Queen Amina ruled Zaria and was known as a great warrior, her territories stretching as far as Bauchi in the east and extending as far south as the River Niger, and she built a walled town wherever she conquered. Tradition also maintains that Queen Amina never married a full-time husband, but instead took a temporary husband for the night, usually one of her bodyguards, and had him killed the following morning so that he would never tell tales of his experiences with her. Queen Amina died near Bida in the present-day Niger State after she chased one lover who managed to get away. He had hidden in a river and Amina jumped in after him to catch him but drowned. There is a portrait of her inside the Emir's Palace. Zaria, Queen Amina's sister, did marry and succeeded Amina as queen, but later became bored with married life, and presumably with being queen, and ran away to the north.

quarters are Muslim. Western education has gained much ground here, with the establishment of the Ahmadu Bello University, the first university in northern Nigeria, located on the northern approach to town, which has witnessed some violent clashes in recent years between the more radical students and the security forces. The Nigerian Aviation College, with its own airfield, is also on this road.

## Getting there and around

Zaria's **motor park** is under and around the bridge of the Kaduna–Kano Expressway on Sokoto Road to the north of the city between the river and university, and here are rows of vehicles parked up on either side of the road going to Kaduna, Kano, Gusau, Sokoto, Katsina and Jos. A bush taxi from Kaduna, only 83km or one hour to the south, costs around N160. The defunct **train station** is near the Union Bank, just to the north of Queen Elizabeth II Road.

From south to north, the old walled city overflows into Tudun Wada, the newer part of the city built after the British came. There is then a big overgrown gap of around 500m of undeveloped land where maize is grown and rubbish thrown, around the swampy Kubani River, to the GRA to the north of the river. Sokoto Road then continues north past the golf course for another kilometre or so to the Sabon Gari and the motor park, before heading out for another couple of kilometres to the university campus. From the motor park it's easy enough to jump on an *achaba* or any of the constant stream of shared taxis and minibuses that run up and down the Sokoto–Kaduna road, the main artery of the city (that in parts is also confusingly known as Hospital Road), for little more than N40.

## Where to stay and eat

The **Zaria Hotel**, Sokoto Road; tel: 069 333092; email: zaho@yahoo.com, is the city's principal hotel. It is set in nice grounds with an empty swimming pool, but you can get alcohol here and it's obviously run by Christians as the signs on the toilets are for Adam and Eve. The bookshop here sells mostly law and medical books for the university students. Bizarrely for a Muslim city, there is actually a functioning nightclub here on Wednesdays, Friday and Saturday nights, an additional big comfy bar, and a very neat restaurant with a daily changing menu of mostly Nigerian food and one continental dish such as fish and chips, and attentive service. The 52 rooms have satellite TV with CNN, and a double is N3800 (N4,000 deposit) and a suite is N9000 (N12,000 deposit) plus the 15%. The **Aiffias Motel**, 9 Sokoto Road; tel: 069 332033, 335399, is a lovely hotel decorated with roses and pot plants, with old-fashioned décor, but it is spotlessly clean and comfortable, and the rooms have hot water and satellite TV, and the suites have tea and coffee in the rooms. Doubles are a very reasonable N3,450 (N3,800 deposit) and suites start from around N5,000 (N7,000 deposit) depending on size. The nice restaurant serves meals from N500, and you may get the likes of chicken with soy sauce or spag bol, and good breakfasts for N400. There's no alcohol served – instead the bar very, very bizarrely sells a selection of sanitary pads (?!). Outside is a kiosk in an old Portakabin serving doughnuts, spring rolls, samosas, pre-cooked toasted sandwiches, moin moin, and meat pies, and there's a shady outside seating area in a little garden. Look in the freezer for imported tubs of ice-cream.

**Teejay Palace Hotel**, 6 Western Way Close, GRA; tel: 069 333303, 335640, is very nice, with comfortable and cool rooms arranged around tiled courtyards, with TV (which only shows CNN), an all-night generator, established gardens, a mosque and no booze. It's well signposted off the Sokoto Road in the peaceful GRA. The restaurant serves stews, soups and starch, but ask the chef for something different such as Spanish omelette or spaghetti. Meals cost in the region of N400–600. There are 50 rooms and a standard double is N3,000 (N3,800 deposit) and suites with an extra lounge start from N4,600 (N5,500 deposit). The **Kongo Conference Hotel**, Old Jos Road, on the right-hand side roughly 1.5km from the junction of Kaduna Road; tel: 069 332872/4, is a large, dated hotel and another 1970s concrete eyesore in a big three-storey block. The restaurant here is the oddest, most kitsch inter-galactic building I have ever seen, with a few tables dotted around, miles away from each other. Architecture buffs should come here just to look at the place. The old-fashioned 80 rooms, however, have reasonable bathrooms with running water, Saudi Arabian satellite TV, and there's an all-night gen. But the rooms are very musty and stuffy and perhaps are not used that often – the one we were in spat all sorts of rubbish out of the AC unit when it was switched on. Doubles start from N3,000 (N4,000 deposit) plus the 15%.

**Zaria Motel**, off Queen Elizabeth II Road, in the GRA opposite the Sharia Court; tel: 069 332451, is a government-run motel in shady, tree-filled grounds – it is unashamedly shabby but it's friendly with a great atmosphere. It's non-Muslim (as attested to by the Gideon Bibles in the rooms), and this is the place where people come for illicit drinking – there are some raucous parties going on in the rooms and car park (despite its proximity to the Sharia Court across the road!). Quite delightfully, after you have checked in the 'light bulb man' will take you to your room, put in the light bulbs and fetch and install the TV, and he also sets up plastic tables in dark corners of the grounds for groups of men arriving in Mercedes chatting about America and playing with their cell phones who come to drink beer in relative anonymity. There's a small restaurant, or they will deliver food to your room such as plates of tasty eggs, chips and baked beans, or not-so-hot *jollof* rice, for little more than N300, and there's excellent *suya* available in the car park. Rooms are N2,000 for a double (N3,300 deposit) plus the 15%, and there are slightly cheaper rooms with no running water (instead a bucket is delivered to

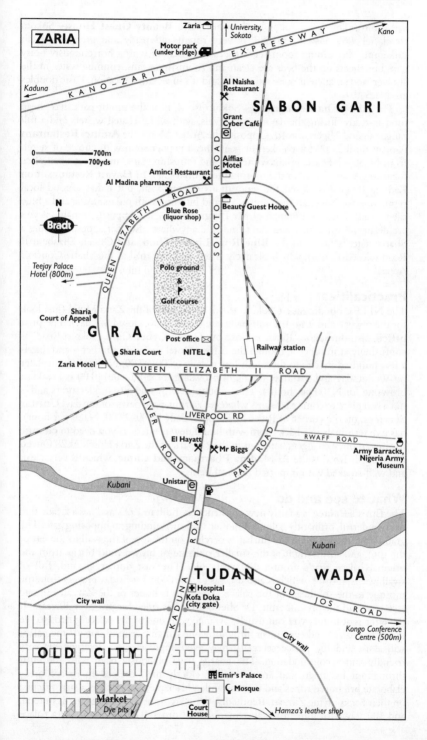

ZARIA

Zaria
Motor park
(under bridge)

University,
Sokoto

Kano

KANO – ZARIA EXPRESSWAY

Kaduna

0 ——— 700m
0 ——— 700yds

Al Naisha
Restaurant

SABON GARI

Grant
Cyber Café

Aminci Restaurant
Al Madina pharmacy

SOKOTO ROAD

Aiffias
Motel

Blue Rose
(liquor shop)

Beauty Guest House

QUEEN ELIZABETH II ROAD

Bradt

N

Teejay Palace
Hotel (800m)

Polo ground
&
Golf course

Sharia
Court of Appeal

G R A

Post office

Railway station

Sharia Court

NITEL

Zaria Motel

QUEEN ELIZABETH II ROAD

LIVERPOOL RD

RIVER ROAD

El Hayatt

Mr Biggs

PARK ROAD

RWAFF ROAD

Army Barracks,
Nigeria Army
Museum

Unistar

Kubani

Kubani

KADUNA ROAD

TUDAN WADA

OLD JOS ROAD

City wall

Hospital
Kofa Doka
(city gate)

City wall

Kongo Conference
Centre (500m)

OLD CITY

Market
Dye pits

Court
House

Emir's Palace

Mosque

Hamza's leather shop

the room). The generator is kept on all night. **Beauty Guest House**, Sokoto Road, tel: 069 334038, 331688, is very rough and ready and grotty, with an unkempt, tatty dining room serving Nigerian staples with a horrendously noisy gen, but sheets on the beds are clean and rooms have fans, running water in the shower, and an ancient one-station TV, and it's in a central location. Basic doubles are N1,500.

The **Al Naisha Restaurant**, 4 Sokoto Road, near the motor park, has cheap food-is-ready during the day on two levels, with white-coated waiters and a full range of good Nigerian food. Opposite the Aiffias Motel, the **Aminci Restaurant** is open until 21.00 for chicken or goat's head pepper soup with choice of starch from N250 – it boasts bright white tiles and refreshing fans, and is not a bad place for tea-eggs-and-bread in the morning for only N200. **El Hayatt Restaurant** on Kaduna Road was closed for renovations on our visit, but it has a good local reputation for Nigerian food and is a grand building with pillars inside and a blue tiled façade. There's a branch of **Mr Biggs** more or less opposite. Finally, if you are desperate for a beer and can't find one anywhere else, Zaria, despite being a Sharia state, is home to the **Blue Rose Liquor Shop**, at 2 Queen Elizabeth II Road (closed Friday), which bizarrely is on the same road as the Sharia Court of Appeal.

## Practicalities
The **NITEL** building is on Sokoto Road, to the east of the Zaria Motel (just look for the tower), and it's open unusually late (until 21.00, closed Sunday). The **post office**, also on Sokoto Road, is close by. **Grant Cyber Café** (Sokoto Road) is confusingly at number 9, though the Aiffias Motel is also at number 9 and that is a few hundred metres to the south (open daily 08.00–22.00; N180 per hour; later on Wednesday and Saturday for night browsing, N350; 08.00–10.00 is breakfast browsing for N100 per hour!). This is popular with students and lecturers and is not a bad place to come to discuss whatever is front-page news for the day. **Unistar Services,** on the corner of River Road (open daily 08.00–22.00; N180 per hour), has two terminals in a back room with brand new printers. If you need to **change money**, money changers hang out in the car park of the Zaria Hotel. At 28 Queen Elizabeth II Road is the **Al Madina Pharmacy and Clinic**, which is very clean and well-stocked with imported medical items.

## What to see and do
The **Emir's Palace** is a fairly new construction, built in 1995, and has a façade that is a wonderful, brilliantly coloured mosaic wall surrounding an imposing gate. The grandstand for watching the durbar is perched on the top of the wall to the left of the gate, and to the right is the smaller old gate of brown mud bricks from the original palace that's around 100 years old. The vast durbar ground, full of swallows, is in front, which is also used as the overflow for Friday prayers from the mosque to the southeast of the palace. The emir is leader of the Zazzau Emirate (see box) and the present emir, Dr Shehu Idris, has ruled for just over 30 years. If the emir is at home, you can usually arrange with one of the palace guards to see inside the palace and even meet him. Someone hanging around outside the palace will assist and the palace secretary may even approach you. Everyone is very friendly and accommodating. The guards have obviously been with the emir throughout his reign and are incredibly elderly men dressed in marvellously elaborate bright red robes and turbans with a black piece of cloth as a sign stitched on their backs saying Zazzau. Reputedly, there are some 350 palace guards in total, and 100 stay with him in his apartments at all times. The old name for a palace

guard is Dogarin, and they once used to collect taxes from the townsfolk of Zaria on behalf of the emir. To the left of the palace is a busy primary school where the teachers and pupils will happily show you around, and a *batauri* will be received with much excited enthusiasm by the children. Again, as in many places in Nigeria, some of these kids may never have seen a white face before. In the streets around the school, look out for the old, double-storied mud buildings that are good examples of the old Hausa mud-brick architecture, with carvings around the door posts and windows that could feasibly be centuries old. They are practically falling down, but you can still see the geometric patterns and frescos in yellow, green, blue and red, shuttered windows, tin roofs, and high, small windows.

The **central mosque**, a few metres to the southeast of the palace, is an unremarkable modern building with concrete monolith minarets surrounded by trees, built on the site of the old mosque. Parts of the old mosque, such as the original internal vaulted ceiling, can still be seen inside, and a reproduction of the old mosque can be seen in the Museum of Traditional Nigerian Architecture in Jos (see page 264). At Friday prayers the mosque holds around 3,000 people, with another 2,000 in the square outside, and it is quite a spectacular event to watch. You could go to watch Friday prayers but be very discreet and stay well in the background – women, of course, are not welcome and even the local women melt away during prayer time. It's a spectacular event when many thousands of beautifully dressed men in their brightly coloured and multi-layered robes, with extravagant turbans and headdresses, simultaneously pray. They stand and bow in lines towards Mecca and despite the thousands of people, the silence is deathly at the most intense time of prayer – it's an extraordinary spectacle. All the northern emirs traditionally wear white robes and a lacy white or black turban that is tied under the chin and that covers the chin up to the mouth. At Friday prayers you may see the emir, who is heralded by trumpeters playing long thin trumpets, as he walks to and from the palace and the mosque, when a cannon goes off. He walks with his entourage to the mosque, shaking hands as he goes with all the men who greet him. As a female, I unfortunately did not witness any of the Friday prayers in northern Nigeria, so here is an account from Darren who watched Friday prayers in Zaria: 'Lizzie and I decided, ultimately correctly, that perhaps Friday prayers wasn't the right place for Lizzie to be present. As I passed through the old city's gate on the back of my *achaba*, the road was just chock-a-block with worshippers, young, old, and extremely old, walking up to the mosque – so much so that I had to get off the motorbike and walk the last couple of hundred metres. The buzz was all-encompassing, but the actual prayers only went on for a relatively short time, and the silence was deafening. The 'after-prayer session' was even more interesting, as the emir of Zaria wandered back to his palace. His path was preceded by trumpeters, bodyguards and by many assorted hangers-on. I stood at the gateway to his palace with hundreds of others waiting to get a look at him, just like some teeny-bopper waiting to get a glimpse of one of the Backstreet Boys as they run from the back of the concert hall into a waiting limousine. He was brilliantly robed in about 20m of the whitest cloth, with red slippers and Ray Ban sunglasses. I thought he gave me a slight wave and nod of acknowledgement, but he may well have been swatting one of the 50 million flies that were present. Following along behind him was a large variety of majestically robed gentlemen looking very important, shaking hands with those offered and doing the old after-Friday prayer business deals and perhaps even collecting debts. I enjoyed it immensely and didn't feel too overwhelmed.'

Another worthwhile visit in Zaria is **Hamza's Leather Shop** on Kaura Road (you will have to enlist the help of a guide to find this – ask outside the Emir's

## THE FORMATION OF THE SEVEN HAUSA KINGDOMS

Duara, a town that is today a tiny dot on the map some 82km west of Katsina and 145km north of Kano, in Katsina State on the Niger border, is an important place in Hausa history, as it is generally believed to be the founding town of the Seven Hausa States, one of the most powerful of West Africa's dynasties. It was first created in the 10th century by a woman called Daurama, who was the queen of her kingdom Daura. Meanwhile, a character called Bayajidda, who was a son of the king of Baghdad, left his homeland after a spat with his father and came to West Africa. He first settled in Borno, but after falling out with his father-in-law he fled Borno, and abandoned his pregnant wife, and arrived in Daura where he sought water for his horse. The Kusugu Well in the town was occupied by a notorious and terrifying snake called Sarki (the word later became a word for king) that was terrorising people and that only allowed them to fetch water once a week, on a Friday. Bayajidda asked the way to the well where he laid his calabash down, and the snake seized it. He then pulled the snake to the surface and cut off its head with his sword. He returned to his lodgings with his calabash of water and the snake's head and the next morning, which was a Friday, the townspeople were amazed to find the snake's body next to the well, and Queen Daurama proclaimed that she would give half of her town to the man that killed the snake. Bayajidda presented the head of the snake to the queen but he replied that he would rather marry her than have half the town, which she promptly agreed to. They had a son called Bawo, who later became king of Daura himself and had six sons; Gazaure succeeded Bawo as the king of Daura, Kumayo was sent to Katsina where he overthrew the Durbawa dynasty, Bagauda was sent to Kano where he overthrew the Tsunburbuwa people, whilst Duma, Gunguma and Zamnakogi went to Gobir, Zazzau and Rano respectively, and established their own dynasties. Together with Bayajidda's son by the other woman in Borno, who ruled Biram in Hadejia, this completed the list of Seven Hausa States, all descended from Bayajidda. By linking these seven kingdoms through trade, and with trade routes to North Africa across the Sahara that also brought Islam, they grew into powerful states and melting pots of new ideas and knowledge, great international markets, and seats of scholarly learning. For centuries, the Hausa dynasty ruled what was to become northern Nigeria, until the Fulani jihad in 1804, led by Usman dan Fodio, who overthrew one after the other of the Hausa kingdoms and appointed an emir in each. Today, the water from the Kusugu Well in Daura is still drinkable and it is believed to cure many ailments.

Palace and you should find someone). It's a shop and tannery for goat, lizard, snake, and crocodile leather and there's a variety of good-quality bags, briefcases and duffel bags on offer, though you may balk at the material being used, and to purchase some of these items could present a problem when taking them home. Crocodile hides come from the Maiduguri River, and there are also monitor lizard briefcases, cobra wallets, and iguana cell phone covers! Instead, go for the items made from soft goatskin. This is a treasure chest of quality leather items and the designs of the women's handbags in particular would give Louis Vuitton a run for his money. Hamza and his staff have been trading and working for over 40 years.

The **Queen Amina Walls** of Zaria, which circumnavigate the old city, are between 14 and 16km long and are pierced by eight gates. The gates are concrete reconstructions, though startlingly and rather magically, the gates are still manned by palace guards carrying bows and arrows. The walls are thought to be about 1,000 years old, and are perhaps the best preserved among the cities of northern Nigeria, but the need for defensive walls has disappeared since the occupation by the British at the beginning of this century. Moreover, the rains of over 50 wet seasons have battered down the mud walls, and like many other walls in the north, today it's a crumbling mound of brown earth with piles of plastic rubbish and goats on top.

Like the more famous ones in Kano, Zaria has its **dye pits,** but again you'll need a guide to take you there as they are off Zage Dantse Road, to the south of the main market. The family operating the pits has been here for over 200 years – today they are run by the one-eyed cloth-dyer O Yummar Idib, who has more dye pits in his nearby house. Art students from all over Nigeria still come to Zaria to discuss with him the ancient method of dyeing. It's a similar set-up as in Kano, but only a few dye pits are in operation, and they use red, green and yellow natural dyes as opposed to just the indigo blue used in Kano. Cloth is dyed to order and is used for ceremonial purposes for the emir and his staff. The old **market** nearby is very clean and organised, very friendly and a pleasure to walk around. Despite the modern produce and manufactured clothes, looking at the herbs, spices, fresh produce, pulses, grains and various dried grasses, flowers, and roots, it's easy to imagine things have not changed much here for hundreds of years.

Outside of the old city, at the Chindit army barracks, is the small **Nigeria Army Museum**. To get there follow RWAFF Road to the end, and you will have to seek permission from the army guards at the gate to enter the barracks (a small dash will probably be expected). There are no set opening hours – it's more a case of someone being there that can show you the museum. Inside is a collection of medals, weapons, army uniforms, maps, and many faded but interesting photographs of the colonial years and the major wars that Nigeria has been involved in during the last century, notably the civil or Biafran War and the Burma Campaign during World War II, where most of the Nigerian forces were sent.

# KANO

Kano is the oldest city in West Africa, and today is the capital of Kano State and is by far the largest city in the north of Nigeria. At the 1991 census the population was put at three million, but it could plausibly be nearer ten million. The city is teeming and vibrant, and there's a variety of interesting things to see. Kano is probably Nigeria's second-largest city after Lagos, and it's generally believed to have outgrown Ibadan. The majority of the population is Muslim, though migration from the south has increased the Christian population over the years, and it has also attracted fame as a hotbed for religious tension in recent years. It is a huge commercial city founded on the trade of the ancient Sahara routes, and it's in the centre of a major agricultural region where cotton, cattle, and about half of Nigeria's peanuts are raised. The traffic is especially chaotic here, and the pollution in the city is palpable, especially at the end of the dry season from April to May, when hot fumes scorch your throat. Kano has several districts, including the old city, which is walled and which contains many clay houses, giving Kano a medieval atmosphere. The parts of the wall that can still be seen today were built in the 15th century, though like in other northern cities, most of it is seriously dilapidated and eroded. Kano is popular for its traditional arts and crafts, including weaving and indigo cloth-dyeing, and it has long been known for its leatherwork; its tanned goatskins were sent to North Africa from about the 15th century, and were known in Europe as Morocco leather. Kano is also recognised as a centre of learning, being the seat of Bayero University and the Kano State Institute for Higher Education, and the British Council Library and the Kano State Library are also located in the city. If you are in town at the end of Ramadan, then the traditional horse-riding celebrations are not to be missed. The emirs of Kano and Katsina both hold colourful durbars during the Muslim festival of Eid-el-Kabir and Id Al Malud. Performances include charges on horseback, knife-swallowers, camels, acrobats, snake charmers, drummers and horn blowers. The city has many good restaurants and accommodation options, and you'll welcome the coffee and cake shops and Western food, though nightlife here is under something of a threat, as in 2004 Kano State issued a decree to ban all alcohol in the state and as it's a Sharia state this is likely to come into force.

## Brief history

Kano was the largest of the Seven Hausa States (see box on page 304) and Kano's written history dates back to AD999, when the city was already several hundred years old. Legend has it that it was founded by a character called Bagauda, one of the six sons of Bawo, the founder of the Hausa States, who was sent here by his father to form a dynasty and monarchy based on the trans-Saharan trade routes when the region was of strategic importance to the trade route, and had wide contacts with North Africa. Many people from Arab North Africa, Mali, and Songhai migrated here and were absorbed into the city – skilled traders and artisans mainly concerned with the gold trade and Islam, and city walls and ditches were built extending out to the surrounding villages and settlements. The walls and ditches were considerably extended during the reign of Mohammed Rumfa between 1463 and 1499. Islam was adopted probably between the 12th and 14th centuries from visiting sheiks from North Africa and Mali, and it was practised by almost all the city's occupants by the 16th century, when Kano was a centre for Islamic learning which attracted scholars from all over the Muslim world. Kano's traders went as far as the Mediterranean, Gonja (modern Ghana) and to what is now Gabon to the south. They exchanged Hausa leather, pottery, metal works and particularly cloth – Kano is still famous for its indigo dye pits and the bright blue cloth was once worn by the Tuaregs and other peoples of the Sahara – and groundnuts (sacks of groundnuts stored in pyramids were still a feature of Kano until the 1970s). In return they took back to Kano salt from Lake Chad, kola nuts from Yorubaland and Ghana, and weapons, silk, spices, perfume and Islamic books from across the Sahara. Kano reached the height of its power in the 17th and 18th centuries, when Kano traders reputedly sent 300 camel-loads of cloth at a time to Timbuktu. The European explorer Captain Clapperton, who went to Kano in 1826, reported seeing a caravan arriving from the north with over 3,000 camels. Kano market was laden with commodities, and in German traveller Heinrich Barth's book *Travels and Discoveries in North and Central Africa* (1857) he describes a list of imports to the city in 1850, which he called 'the great emporium of Negroland'. 'Cotton prints from Manchester, silk and sugar from France, articles of Arab dress from Egypt and Tunis, embroidery from Tripoli, common paper, reading glasses, beads from Venice, copper, sword blades, needles and razors.' Kano was traditionally described as *Tumbi Giwa* – 'the capacious stomach of an elephant'.

Like the rest of northern Nigeria, the Kano region was taken during the Fulani jihad in 1809 and held by them under the Sokoto Caliphate until 1903. But it soon regained its leading commercial position before being taken by the British in 1903, when it became part of northern Nigeria. Lugard, the British governor-general, appointed a new emir, Mohammed Abbas, in place of Emir Aliyu, who was exiled and later died in Lokoja, and Kano became a laboratory for Lugard's experiment in indirect colonial rule. The railway arrived in 1911, and with this development and the road-building by the British, the trade routes across the Sahara began to die. The first international flight arrived in Kano in 1937 and it became Nigeria's second international airport after Lagos. Today Kano remains the most important commercial city in northern Nigeria, attested to by the frantic market that has stood on the same spot for perhaps a thousand years.

## Getting there and away

Aminu Kano (KAN) **Airport** is 8km or 25 minutes' driving time north of the central Sabon Gari area of the city. Buses from the airport leave for the city every ten minutes between 06.00 and 22.00, taxis are available and you can also hire a car and driver. There are direct flights to and from Kano and Amsterdam with KLM, and daily flights to and from Lagos (see listings below). By bush taxi and minibus the furthest you can get to on any one trip from Kano is Maiduguri, 615km away, and the journey takes around seven hours and costs between N800 and N1,500 depending on what type of vehicle you take. Vehicles also go to Katsina (two hours) for around N400 in a bush taxi and N250 in a minibus, and there are other vehicles to Zaria, a little less than two hours and roughly the same price, where you can change for transport to Sokoto, and Kaduna and Jos. Kano's main Nai Bawa **Motor Park** is on Zaria Road about 5km south of the centre and it costs roughly N150 on an *achaba* from here into the centre of the city, though this will vary depending on what part of the city you are heading to. From Katsina, you are likely to arrive at the Kofar Ruwa Motor Park on the Katsina Road north of the city. There are other motor parks on all the main roads leading into the city, so where you arrive rather depends on where you have come from. '**Luxury' overnight buses** to Lagos and Port Harcourt arrive on New Road in the Sabon Gari and it's a huge compound of big coaches and easy enough to find during the day to book a ticket. There are touts at the gate and they will lead you to a number of buses including the Young Shall Grow and Bestway Transport companies, and an overnight bus to Lagos should cost in the region of N2,550. The **train station** is south of the Sabon Gari area on Fagge Road.

## Getting around

Kano heaves with hundreds of thousands of *achaba*s, more than perhaps even Lagos, and whilst we had no problems we were warned that the *achaba* drivers of Kano were especially reckless and ducked and weaved through the traffic, and accidents were very common. When there are accidents in Nigeria between *achabas/okadas* and cars or buses, all hell breaks loose and there are fierce arguments when often the car is completely surrounded by other *okada* drivers who instantly appear to join in the ruckus. If you are uncomfortable with the way your driver is driving, ask him to slow down. Minibuses and shared taxis ply the main roads from the motor parks into the city centre, though you may feel more comfortable in a drop taxi as the traffic is horrendously bad. If you want to tour Kano's sights, a half-day with a hire car and driver should be sufficient.

## Orientation

The city has several districts, including the old city that is dominated by the sandstone Dala Hill and the heaving Kurmi Market, which is where most of the sights are, but it's also the most congested area of the city with narrow lanes and hundreds of thousands of people, so be wary of getting lost here. To the northeast of the old city is the Sabon Gari, generally known as the Christian quarter, which is the only place in the city you can get an alcoholic drink. If you follow Murtala Muhammed Way to the east of the city, you'll reach the GRA – which is much more spacious and peaceful than the old city, with wider streets and bigger houses – where some of the better hotels are located. In the industrial centre, Bompai, in the middle of the city, the main focus is Bompai Road, where you will find the best and most useful shops and restaurants, as well as the Tourist Camp, which is where the helpful Kano State Tourism Board is located. You can hire a guide here but it's expensive, and Kano can easily be explored on your own if you have some experience of travelling in the bigger cities of Nigeria. If you don't, then a guide might be a good idea. They charge roughly N2,000 per two hours and organise a drop taxi to take you around the city for N1,500 (let them do the negotiation for this as they'll get a cheaper price). The office is open daily 08.30–18.00, but if there is no-one around (the staff could be at the mosque) just ask and they will locate someone.

## Where to stay

At the time of research in Kano in 2004, a bill had been passed through the Kano State government banning all sales and consumption of alcohol within the state. Although it hadn't been implemented at the time of writing and these listings include information on where you might be able to find a drink in Kano, the new law may come into force by the time you read this. The bill proposed that the ban on alcohol will not only cover Muslims in the state but also non-Muslims. The punishments bandied about the newspapers at the time for getting caught selling or consuming alcohol was put at 80 lashes for a Muslim and a N50,000 fine or a year in prison, or both, for non-Muslims.

### Mid-range: over US$25

**Prince Hotel** Court Close, Tamandu Rd off Audu Bako Way; tel: 064 639402, 633393. Easily the best hotel in Kano, it's very modern and professionally run, with a bar and 24-hour power. The décor in the 51 rooms is all dark wood and blue rugs, and they generally look like international hotel rooms with working bathrooms and DSTV. It's popular with expats and international journalists, and pre-booking is advised, but in reality this is almost impossible as they require the full deposit for advance booking. Rates are N9,000 (N15,000 deposit) for a single, N10,000 (N15,000 deposit) for a twin – a very unusual concept in Nigeria – N11,000 (N15,000 deposit) for a double, and N13,000–17,000 (N20,000–25,000 deposit) for a suite or executive chalet (plus the usual 15%, which of course goes on everything else you purchase in the hotel as well). Car hire is available and the Calypso Restaurant is here (see under *Where to eat and drink*).

**Tahir Guest Palace** 4 Ibrahim Natsugune Rd, off Ahmadu Bello Way; tel: 064 632057, 649710, 646988; email: tahir@ecnx.net. The first thing you will notice here are the armed guards in the car park. Wealthy Nigerians and expats stay here, though it's very reasonably priced. The Tahir has its own power source and water tower (though I saw kids outside the premises filling buckets up from it). It also boasts a huge breezy lobby, tiled hallways with nice fresh décor, and in the rooms your feet will sink into the thick carpets, and the modern pink bathroom suites have gold-coloured fittings. The restaurant serves a good range of food and the service is attentive, there's a small, inviting swimming pool between the giant satellite dishes, and outside awaits a line of newish cars with knowledgeable drivers if you require transport. There are 130 rooms and a deluxe room costs N7,900 (N13,000 deposit) and a larger suite, N11,000 (N17,000 deposit) plus the 15%.

**Nimah Guest Palace** 8B Sulaiman Crescent; tel: 064 642946, 644557. This is very similar to the Tahir in appearance and is popular with wealthy Muslim families, and it has its own mosque. Cordoned off at the back and behind tall walls is a swimming pool for non-Muslims. The rooms are luxurious, though the décor is very Arabic, with lots of gilt mirrors and marble. Nigerian meals are served in the rooms (but watch for those extra charges) and there's a separate breakfast restaurant upstairs, with booths and a TV, which is open from 05.00–11.00 and where breakfast items go from N200. There's a whole range of rooms here, starting with the smallest double for N5,600 (N8,000 deposit) through to N12,000 (N16,000) for a suite, plus the 15%.

**Durbar Hotel** 11B Ahmadu Bello Way; tel: 064 641657, 641465. Well past its sell-by date, this was once quite a grand place, but today the carpets are worn, the paintwork is peeling and the rooms are scruffy, with buckets in the bathrooms, grubby plastic tables and chairs, and very little in the way of food. But there's DSTV and a workable gym with a few machines. Doubles are N5,000 (N6,000 deposit) and then rates jump to N20,000 for a suite with four bedrooms, plus the 15%.

**Royal Tropicana Hotel** 17–19 Niger St; tel: 064 639350, 639352/3. Fairly modern hotel with a busy informal lobby with a few shops and a bakery, and a bar downstairs serving booze in what was once the hotel disco, an eerie mirrored dungeon that's pitch black if there is no NEPA. The rooms are very ordinary, but there are good views of the city from the top floors. Rates are N4,500 for a standard room and N5,500 for a double and the more expensive suites go from N6,000–16,000 (the deposit on all rates is only a very reasonable N500 more).

## Budget: under US$25

**Central Hotel** Bompai Rd; tel: 064 630000/9. Hopelessly run-down and a 1970s inter-galactic eyesore, with very weird-looking lost-in-space architecture and a hideous concrete courtyard. However, the pool does have water in it and the receptionists advised that whilst local guests could not swim, foreigners were allowed to, and at the bar tucked away at the back of the pool area you can buy cold beer and have an illicit drink on a plastic chair on the bare pool deck. The rooms are dreary and terribly old fashioned, with cracked windows and broken furniture, and rates start from N3,200 (N4,000 deposit).

**Daula Hotel** 150 Murtala Muhammed Way; tel: 064 640010–19. There are 200 (tiny) rooms spread throughout quite nice and established gardens in blocks of double-storey peaceful chalets, with DSTV, and rates start from N3,500 (N4,000 deposit) for a double, N4,100 (N5,000 deposit) for a twin, and N7,000 (N10,000 deposit) for a multi-roomed suite inclusive of the 15%. It's on the expensive side for what you get, but the service is good, you can organise a car and driver, and there's a bureau de change in the car park. The restaurant serves three-course set Nigerian and continental meals such as braised beef and vegetables or omelette and chips, plus a dessert and tea for around N1,200, and there's an empty pool, derelict bar and operational internet café on site.

**Hotel-de-France** 54 Tafawa Balewa Rd; tel: 064 646416. This hotel is run by a friendly but conservative manager called Mustapha who was educated in the USA. Here is a surprising oasis of flowering shrubs and trees and green lawns next to the Toyota plant and opposite the Mercedes plant, with very nice rooms refurbished in 1994 with spotless cool tiles, newish furniture, and modern bathrooms. Sadly, a back block of rooms had burned down in an electrical fire at the time of writing, but there are six rooms still functioning and the owner plans to refurbish the rest. The whitewashed and airy restaurant serves Nigerian food and good green salads, plus fish or steak and chips for N500, but no alcohol. It's a historical 1920s building and was once French-owned. Charles de Gaulle stayed here on his way to Fort Lymeé to check on his troops. A good-value double is N3,000 (N7,000 deposit).

**Tourist Camp** 11A Bompai Rd; tel: 064 642017. The rooms here are small, with minuscule bathrooms, but they have a fridge and local TV, there's usually water in the taps, and it's cheap, at N2,000 a room with no deposit. The gen goes off here at night and it's

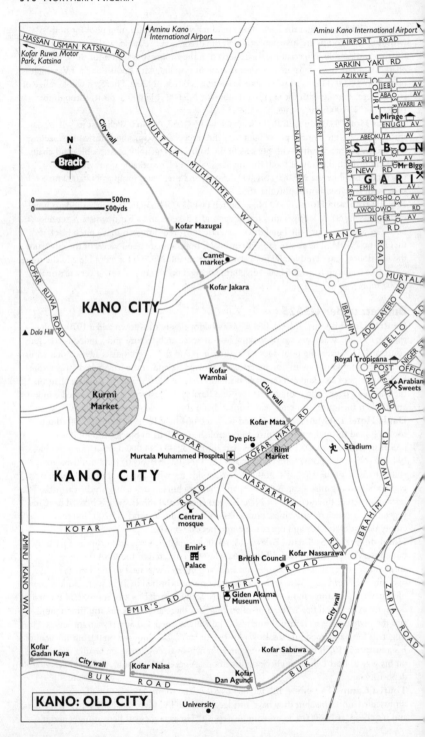

KANO: OLD CITY

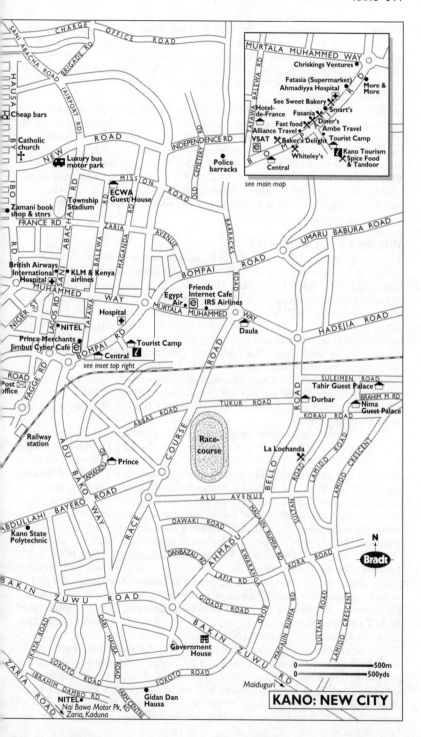

**KANO: NEW CITY**

unbearably hot, with no AC. The compound has a large lit car park with a security guard, and is an ideal spot for camping and for overlanders, and they have actually received the odd truck and vehicle before in the past. There's also a ten-bed dorm with sheets and pillows and a communal bathroom block out at the back. Spice Food and Tandoor restaurant is located here, as is the Kano State Tourist Office and bureau de change, and you can also get laundry done.

**Le Mirage** 27 Enugu St; tel: 064 637788, 640037. A seedy and cheap spot in the rather salubrious Sabon Gari, with no parking or food, but it's close to the drinking joints, and the rooms have AC and DSTV, though the bathrooms have no toilet seats or taps (instead a bucket of hot or cold water is brought to your room). It's popular though, so you may have to arrive early in the day to get a room. A single is N1,200, and a double is N1,550.

**ECWA Guest House** Mission Rd; tel: 064 631410. A large leafy mission compound with spacious rooms, but you have to be on your best behaviour here (no smoking), as this is a church guest house – if they like the look of you, you might get a spartan but clean room with a bucket and loo for under N1,000.

## Where to eat and drink

The best restaurant in the city is the **Calypso Restaurant** at the Prince Hotel (see above for location; open to all daily 07.00–11.00 for breakfast; 12.00–16.00 for lunch; and 19.00–23.00 for dinner). Here you'll find fine dining and fine wines aimed at the international community of expats and the press corps, with a full bar of imported alcohol and an extensive menu of Lebanese starters from N400–600, salads from N600, and main meat dishes from N1,200–1,400, all set amongst starched white table cloths and besuited waiters, so you'll need to dress up a bit. Another highly rated place is **La Lochanda** (40 Sultan Road, off Ahmadu Bello Way; open Monday–Saturday 12.00–15.00 for lunch; daily 19.00–22.00 for dinner). It's an excellent Italian restaurant with good pizzas, lasagnes and pasta, and mixed grill, where a meal for two will cost in the region of N2,500, and there's a bar with beers and some wines. It is set in a private house with shady palms and parking inside the gates.

There are many restaurants located on Bompai Road near the Tourist Camp, as well as *suya* stands and craft stalls on the street. **Baker's Delight** (3 Bompai Road; open daily 10.00–22.00) is a supermarket with some Lebanese and other imported tins and packets and a bakery counter. Next up is **Fast Food Bakery** (open daily 07.30–22.30) with a big range of delicious snacks such as meat pies, pizzas, cakes, biscuits, spring rolls, proper French bread, tea, coffee and fresh juice, simple formica tables, and (oddly) it's run by a Chinese man who also makes birthday cakes. Next door is **Diner's Restaurant** which has a limited selection of food-is-ready but in pleasant surroundings, with red and white checked tablecloths, fans and a TV, and it's dirt cheap. Then there is the **Fasania Chinese Restaurant** run by Chinese people who cook up reasonably priced authentic dishes, followed by **Smart's Indian Restaurant** for Indian sweets and pickles, falafel, *shawarmas* and burgers. Opposite here is the Lebanese-run **Whiteley's** ice-cream shop for a variety of flavours. **Spice Food and Tandoor**, within the grounds of the Tourist Camp (open daily 12.00–15.30 for lunch; 18.00–23.00 for dinner; closed Friday lunch; last orders 22.00), is an excellent Indian restaurant with a charming and chatty owner serving Chapmans and soft drinks, and a full menu of delicious food which is popular with Indians, which is always a good sign. Among the dishes on offer are mutton, chicken and beef jalfrezi, biriyani or korma, plus lots of vegetarian dishes using spinach and cottage cheese, all from around N400 a dish, plus an assortment of nans and rotis or a whole tandoori chicken for N1,000. On our visit the owner was talking about opening a take-away venture outside the complex on the main road. More or less opposite the Tourist Camp is **Fatasia Supermarket** (open daily 09.00–23.00) which has a huge but expensive range of imported goods, a deli counter with olives, feta cheese and good hams, British magazines, well-known products like Heinz Tomato Ketchup and HP Sauce, and a whole aisle of chocolate…! Continue along Bompai Road to the east of the Tourist Camp and on the same side of the road is **See Sweet and Bakery**. There are lots of treats on offer here, starting with biscuits and cream cakes, delicious sorbets and ice-cream for about N150 a cup, a fresh juice bar, thick shakes, proper sandwiches and tasty *shawarmas* for around N400 (all the bread is baked freshly in the in-house bakery). Upstairs is an enormous and modern pool and table-football hall with a giant flat-screen TV for watching sports and music channels, and a bar serving non-alcoholic drinks, and an outside terrace with chairs. The whole set-up is open daily from 09.00–midnight. Next door is the **More & More** supermarket (open daily 09.00–22.00) which is a brand new Lebanese place selling a very broad range of imported and expensive food and household items.

Elsewhere in the city **Arabian Sweets** at 4 Beirut Road serves cheap pastries and burgers but in grimy surroundings, with dirty plastic tables out front. According to the locals the best Nigerian restaurant in the city is **No 1** on Zoo Road, which is off Zaria Road to the south of the city, which serves a full range of authentic Nigerian dishes from all over the country from N800 per plate. There's a branch of **Mr Biggs** on New Road in the Sabon Gari, just north of the Zamani Bookshop. Also in the Sabon Gari is a whole bunch of illicit taverns and bars around Enugu Road in the Sabon Gari district; remember this is Hausa for 'foreigner's town', and as this is the city's non-Muslim quarter, beer and hard liquor are sold from numerous establishments with names such as the **Merry Guest Cool Spot** and the **Be Kind Cool Spot** – just look for the fluttering flags advertising beer. It's a lively and atmospheric place in the evening and you can watch with interest what goes on in the street, but be very wary in this area and stick to the busy and well-lit bars, and if possible make sure the mamma in charge takes you under her wing and looks after you. There are also a few hotels in these streets, but with the notable exception of Le Mirage, dealt with under *Where to stay*, most of the other establishments are fleapits frequented by prostitutes.

## Listings
### Airlines
**Bellview** Tel: 064 311462, airport desk. Has one flight a day between Kano and Lagos (1½ hours) at 10.30 on weekdays, and at 11.30 at weekends. From Lagos to Kano the flight departs Lagos at 06.50 on weekdays and 08.00 at weekends.
**British Airways** Nasimatume Investments Ltd, F1 Airport Rd; tel: 064 637310, 637320, 632230
**Egypt Air** 14c Murtala Muhammed Way, third floor; tel: 064 630759
**IRS Airlines** 16C Murtala Muhammed Way; tel: 064 637939. Daily flights to Lagos and Abuj.
**KLM and Kenya Airways** 17 Sani Abacha Way; tel: 064 632632, 630061

### Books and maps
**Zamani Bookshop** is at 84 Awolowo Road in Sabon Gari (open Monday–Saturday 08.00–12.30, 14.00–17.30), where you can pick up a map of Kano, and some local novels from the well-known Nigerian writers. Because of

Nigeria basing their school curriculum on that of the UK, you'll also find Chekhov and Shakespeare on the shelves. This is the best of a whole bunch of book and stationery shops on this road.

## Changing money

The government bureau de change at the Tourist Camp is the best place to change money, but you have to give them notice if you want to change a large sum. There's another bureau de change close by called Prince Merchants, at 1A Bompai Road behind the Jimbut Cyber Café; both are closed on Sunday and Friday. You'll also find money changers in the car park of the Central Hotel.

## Communications

The main **NITEL** office is some way out of town on Zoo Road, but there's a more convenient one on Lagos Road. The post office is very central, on Post Office Road near the train station (open Monday–Friday 08.00–17.00; Saturday 09.00–13.00).

**Jimbut Cyber Café** Block 1, Bompai Road (open daily 08.30–21.00) has cheap email access at N100 per hour, and you can also make international telephone calls and local GSM calls from here.

**VSAT Networks** further along the street (open daily 09.00–23.00) charges N150 per hour with NEPA, N200 with gen, at four brand new terminals with quick access. AC and cold drinks are also available. I liked the sign here 'Sharia in force – porn prohibited'.

**Chrisking Ventures,** a few doors along (open daily, 08.00–18.00), charges N130 per hour, but there are only four terminals and often the internet is down.

**Friend's Internet Café** 7c Murtala Muhammed Way, opposite the Golf Club (open daily 08.30–23.00) is a fabulous spot. This is a super-quality patisserie and one of the best places to eat in Kano, for coffees and soft drinks, the finest of cakes and pastries, and a huge variety of ice-cream. There's even a pizza oven outside. The gen works all day and there are 18 hi-tech terminals on state-of-the-art office furniture for browsing the internet in glamorous style for N100 per hour, and there's a scanning and printing service.

**SasilNET Café** at the Duala Hotel (open daily 08.30–22.00) is at the back of the hotel property near the empty swimming pool and enormous hotel gens.

## Cultural centres

**British Council** 10 Emir Palace Rd; tel: 064 646652, 643489 (open Mon–Fri 09.00–18.00; Sat 09.00–14.00). The British Council has been in Kano since 1943 and is housed in a historical building of similar architecture to the Gidan Dan Hausa (below). The library here is only open to members, but if you ask nicely you should be able to browse the British newspapers and magazines.

## Hospitals

**Ahmadiyya Musum Hospital** Bompai Rd, opposite the See Sweet and Bakery. Has a laboratory for testing malaria.
**International Hospital** Corner of Airport Rd and Murtala Muhammed Way; tel: 064 649533, 643093. Has 24-hour emergency clinic and a dentist.

## Pharmacies

**Baker's Delight** 3 Bompai Rd (open daily 10.00–22.00). This is a supermarket, but there is also an excellent and knowledgeable pharmacy here that imports drugs from Europe, including Cotexin (a malarial cure also found in East Africa).

## Travel agents

**Alliance Travel and Tours** Next door to Baker's Delight on Bompai Rd; tel: 064 634970. Useful for international flights.

**Ambe Travel and Tours** On the road off Bompai Rd leading to the tourist camp; tel: 064 649399. Again agents for many international airlines.

# What to see and do

Most of Kano's worthwhile sights are in the old city, and you may want to consider hiring a guide to see some of them, though the guides at each of the places are good enough, and you don't really need an additional one to drive around with you in a taxi. If you find a good taxi driver, he will be sufficient to take you into the Kurmi Market, the Emir's Palace and perhaps the city walls unguided. Entry to the old city is through one of the city gates (not the originals but concrete reconstructions).

## Dye pits

Kano's dye pits are still in use and are some of the oldest in Africa, and are located along the road beyond Kofar Mata Gate, and the cloth market is behind a breeze-block wall on the other side of the street. They are privately owned and have been in the same family for over 500 years, and at the entrance the manager will meet you and give you a tour. Expect to pay dash all around, especially for photographs, so have plenty of small notes to hand. Here cloth is soaked in indigo dye in large vats, and the process starts with mixing various natural dyes with water in a calabash before mixing these ingredients with ash in the dye pits and leaving them to ferment for three days. Then the indigo sticks are added and it's again left for three days, before potassium is added, then another three days, before stirring, and another three days, when the ash and indigo sticks are removed. After another two weeks of fermentation the dye is ready to use, and repeatedly used for one year, or longer for the deeper pits that are one to six metres in depth. The indigo provides the brilliant blue colour, the ash the brightness, and the potassium the colour-stay. The depth of colour depends on how long fabric is soaked for – if it is soaked for several hours the blue colour is so dark it becomes almost black. The dyers continually dip the cloth as the oxygen helps seal the colour. The residue that comes out of the pits, the ash, indigo sticks and potassium, is made into mud bricks that are burned until only the potassium is left, and this is then recycled back into the dye pits.

After the cloth is dry it's ironed by charcoal irons or pressed in the traditional way by pounding the cloth over a smooth tree trunk with a wooden mahogany pound. You can go inside the 'ironing shed' and watch the men pounding the cloth and expertly spitting water on the cloth. It takes about 20 minutes to pound one piece of cloth and the pounding gives it a lovely sheen; people pay extra for cloth that has been pounded on both sides, and Kano cloth is often used for ceremonial robes of the most important local leaders. Patterns are created by tying and stitching with raffia or cotton thread, or by using chicken feathers to paint on cloth. This acts as a resist to the dye, much as the wax method on batiks. The indigo cloth is for sale in sheets of a couple of metres long and perhaps a metre wide; the machine-made cotton is roughly N1,300 a sheet, whilst the hand-woven cotton is N2,500 and these are some of the best souvenirs to take home from Nigeria. They have various abstract patterns on them with names such as 'zebra in the bush', 'widow's eye', star in the sky' or 'Emir's Palace'.

## Grand Mosque and Emir's Palace

Kano's Grand Mosque, further down Kofar Mata Road from the dye pits, is one of the largest in Nigeria, attracting up to 50,000 worshippers on a Friday, and is

## KANO DURBAR

Durbars are held in Katsina and Zaria, but the Kano durbar is considered the biggest and the best. It is usually held some time in November, but this depends on the dates of the Muslim calendar. It celebrates the culmination of the two great Muslim festivals, Eid-el-Fitir (commemorating the end of the holy month of Ramadan) and Eid-el-Kabir (commemorating the Prophet Ibrahim sacrificing a ram instead of his son). Durbars are lively and colourful festivals and are known for their horsemen who wear bright red turbans and copper armour, and their accompanying musicians, who wear feathered headdresses decorated with cowrie shells. They date back to the time when the northern emirate states used horses in warfare, and each town, district and nobility household was expected to contribute a regiment to the defence of the emirate. Once or twice a year, the emirate military chiefs invited the various regiments for a durbar (military parade) for the emir and his chiefs. Regiments would showcase their horsemanship, their preparedness for war, and their loyalty to the emirate. During the ceremony the participants are dressed in colourful gowns called *babanringa*, meaning big gowns in Hausa, and the horses are clad in tartan-like regalia. Of all the modern-day durbar festivals, the Kano durbar is the most magnificent and spectacular, and begins with prayers outside town, followed by a colourful procession of gaily dressed riders on horses and camels accompanied by drumming, dancing and singing. They get to the public square in front of the Emir's Palace, where each village group, district, and noble house takes their assigned place. Last to arrive is the Emir and his splendid entourage and trumpeters, who take their place in front of the palace to receive the *jahi*, or homage, of their subjects. The festival begins with each column of seven to ten horsemen racing across the square at full gallop, swords glinting in the sun, who then stop abruptly to salute the emir with raised swords. At this moment the arena will be full of clouds of dust and cheering spectators. The last and most fierce riders are those of the emir's household and regimental guard, known as the Dogari. After the show, celebrations continue well into the night.

located at the back of the Emir's Palace near the servants' entrance. The building itself is not of any architectural value and is a fairly modern structure, and outside is a huge arena where many men pray outside that can't gain access to the mosque. If you are here on a Friday, it's well worth coming here to watch Friday prayers, when these thousands of men dressed in elaborately colourful robes kneel and fall deathly silent at the most intense section of the prayers, and when the *khatib* and *imam* talk to them over the loudspeaker. Unfortunately women will not be appreciated at the event, and non-Muslim men should stay discreetly in the background.

The Emir's Palace is next to the central mosque and you'll need to follow the wall around to the south of the vast complex to get to the front gate. Notice the emir's horses stabled around the walls. The present emir is Emir Dabon Kano, who has reigned since 1963. Again, there is a vast arena at the front of the main gate where the annual durbar takes place (see box), and there's a royal grandstand on top of the wall to the right of the gate. Today, both here and at other Emir's Palaces in the north, the flag of Islam is raised if the emir is in, and is pulled down when he is out. It's a fairly grand building, though it's of little architectural interest, as although it's old, it has been renovated out of all recognition, and houses a number of administrative blocks, but you can peek through the main gate and see the series of courtyards and inner gates beyond, each manned by the traditional and elderly palace guards in their colourful and heavy robes. The best time to come here is to watch the durbar, when many expats from Lagos come up, including embassy staff and international business people, and all the dignitaries from the emir's local councils and governments. Queen Elizabeth II watched the durbar on a visit to Nigeria in 1958, and obviously enjoyed the spectacle, as on a visit in 2003 she requested that it be held in her honour once again. Unfortunately the British security services considered that it would be too high a security risk, which disappointed many Nigerians.

## Gidan Makama Museum
Across the square from the Emir's Palace is the Gidan Makama (the Makama's House) Museum (open daily 08.00–18.00; N100 entry fee plus dash for the guide), which was the first palace of the emir, before he moved across the road to the newer and larger premises. It's now a good museum with examples of local art, including photographs retracing Kano's history. The museum, with a small mosque next door, was built in the 15th century, and was completely restored in 1986, and is now a national monument. It's an old mud building today painted a dark chocolate brown, and there are 11 galleries, and thankfully there's a gen so there's light most of the time and the guides are excellent. There's the old door on display from one of Kano's city gates, Kofa Dukauuyam, some very old photographs of jihad warriors and important members of the Sokoto Caliphate before the arrival of the British, an elephant-skin shield and other items from the jihad wars in the 18th century, and pictures of the old pyramids that were formed from sacks of groundnuts which used to be a feature around Kano up until the 1970s. Outside is a craft shop and drinks stall, and in the grounds a reconstruction of a madobi (women's) hut, with a display of the items she may need in the preparation of a marriage. Look out for the similar houses that are about the same age as the museum in various states of repair in the nearby streets.

## The city wall
The old city had approximately 25km of city walls with 15 gates (kofars) which were first built about 900 years ago, but which were extended and enlarged in the 15th century. When the British arrived in Kano on February 3 1903, through the Kofar Kabuga, the emir at the time escaped through the Kofar Waika, and even today out of superstition the emir does not pass through this gate. South of the museum and between Kofar Saburwar and Kofar Dan Agundi is the 6km section of the city wall that is being rebuilt, thanks to funding from the German government, and it should look very impressive when it's finished. The method used is the traditional mud and straw 'plugs'; rounded bricks made from a combination of mud, water and straw to bind them. Once the wall is built from the plugs, the outer surface is covered with a smooth layer of the same mixture. The rest of the walls are in a sorry state and are covered with rubbish, and you will have to look hard to imagine what the now small piles of brown earth with goats perched on top once looked like, though if the restored section brings more interest in preserving the wall, perhaps other parts will be rebuilt.

## Kurmi Market
The ancient Kurmi Market is in the centre of the old city and it's hugely atmospheric, and is one of the most exotic and colourful places in the Sahel. The

market has been trading on this very spot for perhaps a thousand years, and was first visited by European explorers in the 19th century. Captain Clapperton in *Travels and Discoveries of Northern and Central Africa* describes his visit there in 1826:

> The slave market is held in the long sheds, one for males, the other females, where they are seated in rows, and carefully decked out for the exhibition. Young or old, plump or withered, beautiful or ugly, are sold without distinction; but, in other respects, the buyer inspects them with the utmost attention, and somewhat in the same manner as a surgeon on entering the Navy: he looks at the tongue, eyes, teeth and limbs, and endeavours to detect rupture by forced cough…Slavery here is so common, or the minds of slaves so constituted; that they always appear much happier than their masters: the women, especially, who sing with greatest of glee all the time.

You might get totally overwhelmed and claustrophobic here (and most certainly sweaty) and will have to patiently and politely decline the continual entreaties from the traders. In any case you will get hopelessly lost and any sense of direction will be seriously challenged, so you will really have to go there with a guide. It's not for the faint-hearted, and the passages are very narrow and congested, and the gap between some of the stalls is little more than a few centimetres. You'll probably be taken to the craft section where carved calabashes, leather and beads are for sale, and nearby is the section for the horse attire worn at the durbars, including the richly embroidered Fulani horse blankets and decorations used at festivals. Possibly you'll be taken to the meat section which is so old the walls are falling down – it's covered in flies and the dismembered animal carcasses will send your senses reeling. At all times watch where you are stepping – if you look down you'll sometimes find yourself walking on rickety slats over running drains some metres below.

### Dala Hill
You'll see the flat-topped, red sandstone Dala Hill clearly on the horizon above the market, and it's more or less in the middle of the old city. From the top there are fine views of Kano spreading endlessly in every direction, but to get here you are going to have to find a knowledgeable taxi driver or take a guide from the tourist office, as it's a mind-boggling area of choking alleyways, and the 100 or so steps up to the top are obscured behind a mass of houses. The views are spectacular, and you can see as far as the airport roughly 8km away to the north of the city, with the jets parked up on the apron, which is the only open space visible. In every other direction to the horizon the city is an unbroken vista of densely packed urban buildings; the old mud-brown low-rise houses of the old city immediately around Dala Hill, the congested alleyways and the vast Kurmi Market to the southeast, and beyond are Kano's modern tower blocks, and NITEL and TV aerials. This is one of the best opportunities apart from flying in over Lagos to witness what is the essence of Nigeria – its mass of humanity. Look out for the roof of the Central Mosque and the Emir's Palace. The best time to go up here is in the late afternoon when the sun is behind you, and the glow of the red houses and brown rusty roofs of the ancient city are at their most intense.

### Gidan Dan Hausa
Away from the old city, Kano's other attraction is the Gidan Dan Hausa (gidan means house in Hausa) on Dan Hausa Road (open Monday–Thursday 08.00–16.00; Friday 08.00–13.00; N50 entry fee plus a dash for the guide). The

## THE DEADLY ROAD

Hanns Vischer was a Swiss-born teacher who worked for the British colonial service in Kano at the turn of the 20th century. He is best remembered for being the pioneer of a revolutionary education system that gave due regard to the religion and background of the Hausa people in northern Nigeria, a system that was later copied throughout much of Britain's colonial empire, and for which he was subsequently knighted. He is somewhat less well known for an incredible journey he took in 1906. Vischer became intrigued about the 'deadly road', the centuries-old route across the Sahara that the camel caravans used to follow to transport goods and slaves between West and North Africa. It was referred to as the deadly road because of the amount of skeletons that littered the desert, from slaves and camels that perished on the march north. In 1906, the 30-year-old Vischer undertook an audacious journey through the heart of the Sahara Desert from Tripoli in Libya to Lake Chad in northern Nigeria by camel, through what are today Libya, Niger and Nigeria. Accompanied by religious pilgrims and newly freed slaves, he travelled the route combating torrid heat and tribal raiding parties, and where no water could be found for days. He completed the journey successfully with no loss of life in his party, many of which were freed slaves that had attached themselves to the caravan for protection, going back to their homes in Nigeria. Vischer wrote a book of his journey in 1910, *Across the Sahara*, and he says of the Sahara, 'I had entered it frivolously, like a fool...I left it as one stunned, crushed by the deadly majesty I had seen too closely.' Having completed the journey, and from his post in Kano, Vischer asked his boss in England if he could repeat the journey in reverse. He received this frosty reply: 'Dear Vischer, I prefer my staff to do the work they are paid for, rather than seek personal kudos or geographical advancement in foreign territory...If you are bent on the journey, you should resign and make room for a man who is satisfied with his job. Plain speaking but I like to run my own show. Yours Sincerely, W P Hewby.' Nearly a century later the same route was followed by John Hare, a modern-day Swiss explorer and founder of the Wild Camel Protection Foundation (www.wildcamels.com). In 2001, Hare followed Vischer's wishes and did the journey in reverse, beating Vischer's time across the Sahara thanks to shorter oasis stops and a GPS. In 1906 Vischer travelled 1,581 miles over 5½ months, with 40 camels and 40 men, whilst Hare travelled 1,462 miles over 3½ months, with 25 camels and 12 men. In his party, Hare took a Chinese zoologist – the first Chinese man to cross the Sahara in recorded history. To read John Hare's full account of his journey, try and get a back copy of the December 2002 *National Geographic*, or check out the website www.nationalgeographic.com. His book of the journey is *Shadows across the Sahara* (2003, Constable & Robinson).

Kano State History and Culture Bureau (tel: 064 632385) is located here in a new building next door to the house itself. The house, built in 1905, is an outstanding example of Hausa mud-walled architecture, and was used by the British until independence in 1960, and was Kano's first colonial residency. First built by the emir of Kano as a residence for a local chief, Hanns Vischer became the first British resident from 1908 and was the director of education for northern Nigeria. Vischer arrived in Nigeria in 1906 after travelling by caravan from Tripoli (see box) and first stayed at the Emir's Palace with Lord Lugard before moving to the house. His wife Isabella joined her husband in Kano from 1912, where they lived until World War I broke out in 1914. Vischer was known locally as Dan Hausa, the 'son of the Hausa' because he spoke the language so well. The house was originally the house of a local chief who was responsible for managing the emir's farmland, and some of the rooms are over 150 years old. Vischer extended it in 1907 and by 1909 it was partly a school, and the lessons were taken outside beneath the arms of some tamarind trees, and by 1914 blocks of classrooms had been built in the grounds. Other similar buildings in Kano include the British Council building near the Emir's Palace. If you are at all interested in the Vischer history, ask the director in the Culture Bureau (mostly a line of portrait photographs of past emirs and dignitaries), next to the house if you can look at the documents and photographs donated to the house by the Vischer Family Trust in the UK.

You enter the house through the waiting room as is Hausa tradition, and then go into the visitors' rooms, where there is a collection of pots, stone tools, and other bits and pieces from the Iron Age, plus some of Vischer's china pots from England. There are two pots roughly 1m high and 1m across that are thought to be from 800–500BC – one was apparently used for mixing cement. There is also a copy of the Koran on display that was presented to Ahmadu Bello by the Egyptian president, Abdul Nasser, when Bello visited Egypt in 1963. The Vischers' dining room now houses a very grand horse's durbar costume, some musical instruments, and various celebration gowns and staffs used by previous emirs. Upstairs is a display of local crafts, including an ancient pot with a slot in the top (that must have been the very first piggy bank in northern Nigeria!) and a skin from an unfortunate python that killed two goats in Kano in 1984. In the Vischers' bathrooms you can also view the original 1907 toilets, with (rather comically) newer loos erected alongside. They don't look that different actually. On the roof of the house you will see what was once Vischer's radio room, and the flat roof where his guests used to sleep outside. Rather delightfully, Vischer's gramophone in the master bedroom still works – ask the guide to play it for you. The scratchy tunes instantly cloak the house with a huge amount of atmosphere, especially as you get here at the end of the tour, and have already heard all the stories about Vischer and the house.

## KATSINA

Capital of Katsina State, the city of Katsina is in the extreme north, only a few kilometres from the border with Niger. The city was once surrounded by a 21km wall with seven gates, built in the 11th century, but little of it remains today. From the 14th century, Katsina was a centre for Islamic teachings and like Kano and the other northern cities, a caravan hub for the Hausa States. At the end of the 16th century Katsina replaced Timbuktu as the main centre for Islamic study in West Africa, and back then the city was made up of sections inhabited by various immigrants, traders or professions, and there were quarters for the people of Mali and Borno, students, and Islamic scholars. In the 17th and 18th centuries, Katsina was one of the seven Hausa kingdoms, before being conquered by the Fulani jihad in 1804, when emirs were put in place under the Sokoto Caliphate. When the British took northern Nigeria a century later, the emirate system was upheld by the British as part of Lugard's system of indirect rule. The Katsina College was established in the early years of the colonial era in 1922. The college provided education to the elite of northern Nigeria and was modelled on the British public school system, which subsequently provided educated administrators for the colonial bureaucracy. Many northern political key players attended Katsina College, including Abubakar Tafawa Balewa, the first prime minister of Nigeria, and Ahmadu Bello, the first premier of the Northern Region, as well as many prominent ministers and emirs. In 1938 the college was moved from Katsina to Kaduna, when Kaduna was capital of northern Nigeria, and where it is now known as Barewa College. There's little to see or do in Katsina, but like the other northern cities, it is steeped in ancient atmosphere, and unlike Kano, which is an older city but has some trappings of the Western world, life in Katsina, with its markets, frenetic street life and old mud buildings, hasn't changed much for hundreds of years. Domestic animals roam the alleyways, robed and turbaned men do deals on the street, cloaked women carry vegetables on their heads, and children in Islamic uniforms chant passages from the Koran and write on wooden scripture boards in the many outdoor schools.

## Getting there and away

A highway links Katsina to Kano and to Maradi over the border in Niger (for details on crossing the border see the *Getting there* section in *Chapter 2*). From Kano to Katsina it costs roughly N400 in a bush taxi and around N300 in a minibus for the 173km or two-hour trip. From Zaria it's N450 in a bus and N600 in a bush taxi on a back road via Funtua. There is no direct road or transport link between Katsina and Sokoto to the west, but it's possible to swap vehicles in Funtua – give yourself all day for this journey as it's a big distance. It's also possible to head into Niger, 45km north of Katsina, and follow the highway from Maradi through to Birnin-Nkonni, and cross back into Nigeria, where it's 85km to Sokoto. Local people use this route and there is public transport, as there is trade between Nigeria's Hausa people and the markets of Maradi, but foreigners will require a multi-entry visa for Nigeria and a visa for Niger, so although it involves a shorter distance, it's not terribly practical. The roads up here from Kano and Zaria are fairly potholed, but there are fabulous views of mud villages and the arid landscapes as you head into the Sahel proper. On arrival, vehicles will drop you somewhere along IBB Way, the road that runs the entire length of Katsina in a north–south direction. On departure you'll need to get to the **motor park** on the Kano Road. If you need to **change money** the Limited Bureau de Change is on the corner of IBB Way and the road that goes towards the Gobarau Minaret, and the **post office** and the **NITEL** building are centrally located on IBB Way opposite the Bank of the North.

## Where to stay and eat

**Liyafa Palace Hotel** (tel: 065 431165) is on the road to Kano, on IBB Way roughly 3km outside of town; there's a sign but look hard as all the paint has worn off. This is easily one of the nicest hotels in all of Nigeria, with 108 rooms in three spacious blocks of chalets, real hotel furniture, all-night air-conditioning, great bathrooms with hot water, and DSTV. It was opened by General Ibrahim Babangida in 1991 and has been well looked after since. Facilities include a tennis court and mosque, but the swimming pool is empty and of course there is only a selection of Fanta available in the bar. In the very good restaurant you can get snacks such as burgers and omelettes, and there's a choice of daily specials of main dishes. Ignore the tariff that says foreigners must pay in US$ – the reception staff wouldn't know what to do with a dollar bill if they saw one. Given the standards, rates are not bad at N5,000 for a double (N7,000 deposit) plus the 15%.

The **Katsina Motel** is at 1 Mohammed Bashir Road (tel: 065 430017). To get here, from the first roundabout on the Kano Road as it enters the town and turns into IBB Way, turn right (if coming from Kano) until you reach Yar'adua Road after about 2km. Then turn left and then take the first right, then the first right and you should be on Mohammed Bashir Road. You'll have to arrive early to get a room as it's deservedly popular, and the only choice for those on a budget, though it's not especially cheap. There is a standard restaurant serving a variety of bland food, but they are good at dealing with late arrivals and if you speak to the chef in advance he can come up with something vegetarian or vaguely non-Nigerian. The chalets are set in established gardens, with a few gazebos to sit in the shade, and there's a mosque. A double costs N3,000 (N3,500 deposit). The **Katsina City Restaurant** (115 IBB Way), in the centre of town, serves big and filling Nigerian meals and the likes of spaghetti with tomato sauce, and exceptionally good salads with eggs and tinned baked beans for around N500 a plate. It's consistently packed, with loads of tables decorated with fake roses, fans and blaring TVs, and the service is instant. Similar fare can be found at **Al-Amin Restaurant** (174 IBB Way), further north up the same road, and both are lit up like Christmas trees at night. Also at night along the length of IBB Way are night-time chop stalls selling prepared fruit such as pineapple, and very good hot-and-spicy *suya* cooked over charcoal under paraffin lamps.

## What to see and do
The centre of activity spreads around IBB Way, Katsina's main thoroughfare between the concrete Kofar Kaura, one of the city gates built on the site of an older mud brick one, and the domed **central mosque**. Just beyond the mosque and to the left is the Kangiwa Square that serves as the overflow for the mosque during Friday prayers, and where the **Emir's Palace** flanks the eastern side. It's relatively traffic free and is a pleasant place to wander around. On top of one of the green, yellow and white palace walls covered in faded bill posters is the emir's grandstand, to watch the occasional durbars that take place in the square, and a modern breeze-block clocktower and a flagpole indicating if the emir is in or out. The façade of the palace is fairly modern, but inside the compound are myriad older, squat mud buildings, and if you want to look around you can approach one of the palace guards. Around the square are some colonial buildings with flat roofs built of grey and white blocks of stone, one of which is the police station and another the Sharia Court.

The **Gobarau Minaret,** to the northwestern corner of the Kangiwa Square, is a wonderful example of traditional architecture – to get there follow IBB Way 100–200m and take the first right-hand turn along an unnamed street, and the minaret is easily seen about 100m on the right. The imposing minaret is built of mud and palm timbers, and is all that remains of a mosque constructed in the heyday of the dynasty of the Seven Hausa States. It is thought to have been built between 1348 and 1398, though it has been refurbished a few times since then. Today the remaining 15m tower is the tallest mud-built structure in Nigeria, and a national monument. There's a guide at the bottom, and for a small dash you can climb almost to the top, and there are some fabulous views of the old rooftops of the city, and if you look to the north, you'll look into Niger. You can also see parts of the city wall, though you may have to ask the guide to point these out as the walls are little more than mounds of earth. To the west you can see Katsina's army barracks. The guide at the minaret lives in a compound at the bottom and you can wave to his wife and kids from the top! Also at the bottom of the tower is a Muslim school with only six classrooms, but with over 1,000 pupils. If you make it as far north as Katsina, this is yet another region of Nigeria where few white people have ever been. The chances are you will be completely mobbed by the school children, as was our experience, the little girls cloaked and their hands and feet covered in henna tattoos. It was a delightful experience and they all wanted to touch our skin and hair, and hundreds of children followed us pied-piper style, mimicking everything we said until we had to make a polite escape by *achaba*.

Katsina's **old market** spreads around the streets opposite the minaret and is worth a wander, but be warned about the abattoir and meat section almost directly opposite the minaret behind the first few rows of stalls, as the reeling smells here will somewhat stop you in your tracks. Elsewhere in the packed and sandy lanes are traditional blacksmiths at work at smithies over charcoal burners, Fulani women selling milk and yoghurt from calabashes, piles of grains, cereals and pulses on perilously overloaded stalls, and livestock herded into pens for easy inspection, including long-haired, chocolate-brown goats, and the odd camel.

## GUSAU

Gusau is the capital of Zamfara State, and is located on the Sokoto River, which is an important source of water during the dry season. Once a leper colony, the city is Hausa-Fulani and strictly Muslim, and of all the northern states, Sharia law is followed to the letter here and even public minibuses and shared taxis are designated for women only, and women are not allowed to ride *achaba*s. You are only likely to find yourself here en route to Sokoto, and if it gets too late to continue the 219km to Sokoto you may need to stop in Gusau as there is nowhere else after here. The **Du Ludeo Hotel** (no phone), on Bypass Road to the south of town on the Zaria road, is adequate. It's a new brown and yellow building with a restaurant in a compound with secure parking, and comfortable doubles with fan and working bathrooms cost N,2200, and they will be able to rustle up something in the restaurant. The gen is only on for a few hours in the evening though.

## SOKOTO

Sokoto, the capital of Sokoto State, is situated near to the confluence of the Rima and Sokoto rivers in the extreme northwest of Nigeria, and with an average annual temperature of 28.3°C, it is one of the hottest cities in the world. Sokoto is in the dry Sahel, surrounded by sandy savanna and isolated hills, where camels are used throughout the area, and there's a camel market in Sokoto. The region's lifeline is the floodplains of the Sokoto-Rima River system, which are covered with rich alluvial soil (deposited by running water) for the growing of crops. In dry and drought seasons, power and water are a particular problem this far north, and generator use is restricted. Sokoto is a sprawling city of perhaps five million people and is an important centre of Nigerian Islam – there are dozens of mosques all over the city, and new ones being built all the time. It's not a particularly attractive city, and I think I saw more rubbish here than in the other northern cities, though it is surprisingly green, and the roads are lined with neem trees. Despite having a long history, it lacks the Sahel atmosphere of Katsina and the friendly charm of Zaria.

### Brief history

Originally the capital of the Hausa kingdom of Gobir, established around the 10th century, Sokoto was one of the seven walled Hausa Kingdoms, and in the 13th century, Islam arrived from the north by way of the trans-Saharan caravan routes. In the early 19th century, Fulani chief and Islamic leader Usman dan Fodio chose Sokoto as the capital of his caliphate and a base for the spread of Islam and the expansion of the Fulani Empire. 'Caliph', or 'Khalifa' in Arabic, is a leader of Islam and literally means 'successor of Mohammed', the Islamic prophet. From Sokoto, Usman and his followers administered the holy war known as the Fulani jihad, which lasted from 1804 to 1830 (see page 33). The jihad took control of most of

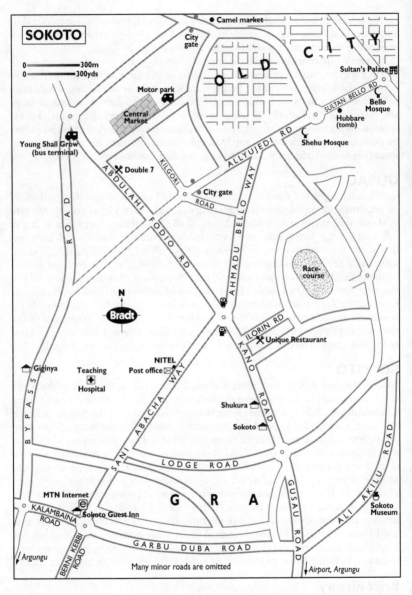

northern Nigeria and adjacent parts of Cameroon and Niger and succeeded in spreading the Islamic faith throughout West Africa. They were attracted to Sokoto for its strategic position and its steep escarpments protecting it from any surprise cavalry attacks. From humble beginnings as a war camp, Sokoto grew in leaps and bounds into a haven for supporters and followers of the jihad, with most of the early inhabitants being jihad warriors and their families. The erection of city walls in 1809 led to increased security in the town, but with an ever-increasing population there came a need to fortify these with another outer city wall 20 years later. Dan Fodio died in 1817 and his tomb in Sokoto is still an important place of pilgrimage for many Nigerian Muslims. He was succeeded by his son, Muhammadu Bello, who was made the first sultan of Sokoto, and who built up the city in the 1820s as the capital of all the new emirates. He was the spiritual leader to whom all the other emirs of the Fulani Empire answered, and the presence of many mosques, Koran schools and religious scholars made Sokoto the centre for Islam in West Africa. This political system still exists today and the sultan of Sokoto is effectively the spiritual leader of Muslim Nigeria. The caliphate continued to be successful through a series of sultans, when the emirs in all parts of the caliphate were expected to shuttle to and from Sokoto to pay homage, to take counsel on state matters or to partake in Islamic learning, until the arrival of the British in 1903. Frederick Lugard conquered the caliphate relatively easily with weapons that included rocket launchers and newly invented machine guns against a Sokoto cavalry equipped with bows and arrows and the odd barrelled pistol. All of the emirates of the Sokoto Caliphate were absorbed into the colonial Protectorate of Northern Nigeria, and by 1914 into one Nigeria. Thanks to Lugard's policy of indirect rule, the sultan of Sokoto and the northern emirs were quickly appeased by the British, who allowed indirect rule through the sultanate and network of emirs, with colonial officers overseeing their governments. After independence, the assassination of the sultan of Sokoto in 1966 was a major cause of the outbreak of the Nigerian civil war (see page 20).

## Getting there and around

Sokoto is located at the junction of two highways connecting the city to Zaria along the A218, and to Jega on the A1, a road that eventually goes all the way to Lagos. Give yourself plenty of time to get here by public transport, as these are not roads you want to be travelling along after dark. They run through remote regions, are badly potholed, and domestic animals on the road may cause accidents. Sokoto's enormous **motor park** is to the north of town, next to the central market from where bush taxis go to Jos, Abuja, Gusau, Zaria, Kaduna, Kano and Argungu (see box below), though you would be advised to initially head for Zaria as any journey beyond there may be after dark. It's N600 by minibus to Zaria. There's also plenty of transport to Illela, the border with Niger 85km to the north, costing N250. The Young Shall Grow terminal is at the roundabout on Abdulahi Fodio Road, near the Ibro International Hotel, and **'luxury' overnight buses** depart daily for Lagos for roughly N2,500, and as far as Aba in the southeast (though not as far as Port Harcourt) for around N3,000. This is probably the longest bus journey you can take in Nigeria, a distance of some 1,200km or 20 hours by road (though again I advise you not to take these buses, as they travel at night). The **airport** is 9.5km to the south of the city and the only transport to and from the airport is a drop taxi for roughly N1,500, which you can pick up in the hotel car parks. ADC airlines has a desk at the Shukura Hotel (tel: 060 230006), and they have a Sokoto–Kano flight at 11.00 on Monday–Friday, Abuja daily at 13.00, except for Wednesday and Sunday when it departs at 11.00, but check as times change frequently and the flights will be cancelled if there are not enough people to make it worthwhile. Getting around Sokoto is easy enough and shared taxis and minibuses ply Kano Road. Motorbike taxis here are just little scooters and are called *kabuskis*.

## Where to stay and eat

Sokoto has a huge number of hotel rooms for such a remote city and most of the hotels each have over 200 rooms. Top of the range is the **Giginya Hotel** on By-Pass Road; tel: 060 231263, 231466. Completely refurbished in 2003, everything here is very fresh and functioning, with 200 newly painted rooms with new hotel

## ARGUNGU FISHING FESTIVAL

The annual Argungu (pronounced 'ar-goon-goo') Fishing Festival is a major week-long event, and one of the leading festivals in West Africa. It takes place near the town of Argungu, 99km southwest of Sokoto. This festival originated in 1934 when Sultan Dan Mu'azu of Sokoto made a visit to the region, and a grand fishing festival was organised in his honour on the Argungu River. Hundreds of men and boys dived into the water and the biggest fish caught was presented to the sultan. Since then, it's become a celebrated yearly event held during February or March, and it marks the end of the growing season and the harvest. Events include art and craft exhibitions, cultural dances and music, local drama, traditional boxing and wrestling, archery competitions, bicycle races, donkey and camel races, and a motor rally. On the river itself are canoe and swimming races, deep-diving competitions, bare-hand fishng, and wild-duck hunting. The festival's grand finale is the fishing show, when thousands of men and boys enter the water, armed with large fishnet scoops. They are joined by canoes filled with drummers, plus men rattling huge seed-filled gourds to drive the fish to shallow waters. During the allotted time, they fight for the fish in the river and a wealth of fish are harvested, including giant Nile perch reaching weights of over 60kg. A 1.6km stretch of the Argungu River is protected throughout the year, so that the fish will be plentiful for this 45-minute fishing frenzy. It's all finished off with singing and dancing well into the night. Unfortunately, because of ethnic tensions in the region over recent years, the festival has been cancelled on some years, and it was last successfully held in March 2004.

furniture imported from Italy, thick carpets, balconies, spotless, brand-new pressed bedding, DSTV, and fridge. There's an all-night generator, spacious tiled lobby with coffee bar and lounge area, an empty swimming pool, and a restaurant which is a bit hit-and-miss with continental food – chicken chasseur is no different to chicken pepper soup, for about N500 a plate. Doubles start from N4,500 (N8,000 deposit) plus the 15% and there's a whole range of more expensive suites. The **Sokoto Hotel**, Kano Road; tel: 060 232126, is a vast concrete block of 244 rooms with broken windows and big car park, and is very tired-looking and dirty, though it's often surprisingly full, despite there being much better places to stay for the money. Doubles with local TV start from N3,000 (N3,500 deposit) plus the 15%. A better option is the **Shukura Hotel** next door on Kano Road; tel: 060 230006. Again it's very popular, with good service and scuffed but adequate rooms with bucket and sometimes working showers, new AC units and reliable power. The restaurant has only four tables so presumably most people eat in their rooms. Other than food-is-ready you may get chips, omelettes and spaghetti for around N400. There is a good source of water here, as attested to by the local women and children collecting water from the taps in the car park. There are 230 rooms, and a standard room is N3,500 (N4,500 deposit) plus the 15%. A standard room has a double bed, so you don't need to pay more for the bigger rooms. The excellent value **Sokoto Guest Inn** is on Kalambaina Road; tel: 060 233205, 232672. Here are 122 rooms in big chalets painted hospital green in pleasant grounds, offering basic but spotlessly clean and cheap accommodation with bucket, fan and local TV. A double is N1,500 inclusive of the 15%, more for a bigger room/bed, and there's a 20% discount on Friday and Saturday nights.

Apart from the *suya* stands in the old city that serve all the bits of a sheep, eating out in Sokoto is really limited to the hotels and the **Double 7**, 9 Abdullahi Fodio Rd; tel: 060 234709, run by one of only three Lebanese families in Sokoto and lit up like a Christmas tree at night, with strings of coloured flashing lights leading from the building to the road. We managed to change money here with the manager. Downstairs is a supermarket (open daily 07.00–23.00) selling imported goods, with a snack bar outside for schwarmas and burgers, and a counter in the back selling fresh bread, good meat pizza slices, cakes and cold drinks. Upstairs is the formal Lebanese restaurant (open daily 08.00–23.00) with a huge menu of mixed grills, pizzas, falafels, schwarmas, steaks, and chicken dishes from N600. The dishes are not necessarily authentic, but they make a change from Nigerian food and they're not too expensive. During weekdays the **Unique Restaurant**, 2 Ilorin Road, behind the Zenith Bank, serves cheap and filling food-is-ready to bank workers from a number of banks in this area during lunchtime, but it is closed evenings and weekends.

## Communications
There's a branch of **DHL** at 16 Fodio Road. The MTN shop around the corner from the Sokoto Guest Inn on Sani Abacha Way has sporadic **internet access** and opening times, as it's NEPA dependent. The **NITEL** office is on Sani Abacha Way and there's no sign, but you'll see the tower, and it's next door to the green and white **post office**, where there's an EMS Speedpost service and, oddly, a laundry service at counter number six!

## What to see and do
The **Sokoto Museum** is on Ali Akilu Road to the east of Kano Road (open Monday–Friday 09.30–16.00; entry N200, plus dash for the guide) and is also dubbed locally as the History and Culture Bureau. It houses an excellent collection of local exhibits telling the story of Usman dan Fodio's jihad, though what you see at the museum rather depends on NEPA. Many of Usman dan Fodio's personal items are on display, such as original Islamic scriptures, maps, weapons, and copies of the Koran. One exhibit is devoted to the colonial era, and includes a wooden throne given to the sultan of Sokoto by Queen Elizabeth II during her visit to Nigeria in the 1950s. Rather crudely and insensitively of the British at the time, the throne has a carving of a naked boy on it, and reputedly the sultan had the boy's head removed before he would sit on it. Another exhibit of note are the original carved city doors that once were erected in the old gates. The Sokoto **central market** is next to the motor park and is a surprisingly clean and modern site, with a highly organised network of neat stalls. It doesn't quite have the same atmosphere as the old Kano and Katsina markets, but it's pleasant enough to wander around under the shade of the neem trees. Look out for the reams of brightly coloured cloth, the male tailors bent over ancient black Singer sewing machines, and the abundant arrangements of fruit and vegetables. By contrast, the **old city** around Sultan Bello Road is very run down and congested, and could feasibly be described as a slum, with its intense rubbish problem and rank drains. Little remains of the city's walls, which are concealed beneath haphazard housing, and the only remaining gates, the Kofar Alivu Jedi on Aliyu Jedi Road, and the Kofar Kade on Old Market Road, are concrete replicas. The **Sultan's Palace** is a huge modern complex built from 1970s concrete, and is not as impressive as some of the other Emir's Palaces of the north, and is nothing more than a simple compound of office buildings with a line of fat-cat councillors' Mercedes and some horses tethered in the car park, though you may see one of the elderly palace guards in their heavy red

and white robes. The main gate is beyond a green and white roundabout on Sultan Bello Road. Two of Sokoto's greatest **mosques** can still be seen near the Sultan's Palace, the Sultan Bello and Shehu mosques, and whilst their golden domes and minarets are impressive to look at on the outside, non-Muslims or women are not allowed inside. Just before the Shehu Mosque, a dirt alleyway leads off to the **Hubbare**, a squat one-storey mud building that was once the home of Usman dan Fodio, and where he is buried along with most of his family and his *imam*; the spot still attracts pilgrims who come to pay homage, but again non-Muslims are highly unwelcome here. There is a **camel market** in this area though, that could have perhaps been trading in camels for a thousand years or more, and here we were reliably informed that these days the starting price for an adult camel is N80,000 and for a youngster N10,000, which of course is negotiable. On one ancient tourism leaflet, I found a listing for sights in Sokoto that said: 'There is a camel market that is well attended by both Nigerians and camels.'

# Appendix 1

## LANGUAGE

English is the official language of Nigeria and is widely spoken and understood just about everywhere except for some of the more rural areas and distant northern towns. In all the cities that have universities, English is used for education, so all younger people speak it. Generally you'll find that English is often spoken rather formerly – 'good afternoon madam', 'you are welcome sir', etc. You may struggle to understand some of the quirky Pidgin-English sayings and phrases, though you just might find yourself peppering your own speech with some of them. 'O' is the classic example which is added on to all sorts of words – I would imagine that an former expat of Nigeria would continue to say *Sorry-o* for the rest of their lives. Pidgin or 'broken' English is a mixture of English and indigenous Nigerian words often used in casual conversation, and has been spoken and understood by almost all Nigerians for more than a century. It's spoken with a lot of spirit and gesticulation. Many English words are used differently in Pidgin English and it can be confusing, and the many misspellings and mispronunciations are so popular that they have entered colloquial use. Some of my favourites include: *chop* – meal; *small chop* – snack; *sistah or brudda* – anyone from the same village; *take leg* or *with feet* – walk; *on it* – switch on; *off it* – switch off; *tossed* – out of order; *move for front small* – go forward a little; *hello* – I can't hear you; *easy yourself* – go to the toilet; and the very best: *raincoat* – condom (also see *Glossary of Nigerian Phrases* on pages 332–3).

Of the 400 or so Nigerian languages and dialects (in some areas such as the Niger Delta, someone in the next village will speak a different language), the most common are Yoruba, spoken in the southwest, Igbo, spoken in the southeast, and Hausa, spoken in the north. In the north, only the educated people speak English, and for the visitor, it can be a problem finding an *okada* driver, chop seller, or a stall keeper who speaks English, though they will usually find someone around who can. Whilst you will get by with English, it is, as always, considered polite to learn a few local greetings, and all Nigerians will be delighted if you make the effort to say a few words in their own tongue. Once in Nigeria, look out for a small pamphlet *Teach Yourself Yoruba, Hausa & Igbo*, by J O Odetunde. Try the bookshops in Lagos (see page 141) This is quite a humorous little book containing all sorts of useful phrases such as 'on the way to school I saw a snake' and 'where can I barb my hair?' There are also a few pages of Nigerian proverbs. My favourites are: 'The sky is large enough for all birds to fly without obstructing their feathers to one another' and 'A man who puts anti-infested faggot into his knee should not be annoyed when lizards begin to pay him a visit'!

## Basic words and phrases

| | Yoruba | Hausa | Igbo |
|---|---|---|---|
| **Greetings** | | | |
| Good morning | Ekuojumo | Ina kwana | Igbolachi |
| Good afternoon | Ekaasan | Ina wuni | Ezigbo ehihie |
| Good evening | Ekuirole (Ekaale from 7pm) | Ina wuni | Mgbede oma |
| Good night | Odaaro | Said a safe | Kachifo |

| | Yoruba | Hausa | Igbo |
|---|---|---|---|
| How are you? | Se daadaa ni? | Kana Lafiya? | Kedu ka idi? |
| I'm fine | Adupe | Lafiya lau | Odi mma |
| My friend | Ore mi | Aboki na | Enyim |
| Thank you | Rse/Aagbabire | Na gode | Dalu |
| Please | E joo | Faranta zuciya | Biko |
| You're welcome | E kaabo | Sannu da zuwa | Nno |
| What's your name? | Kini oruko re? | Yaya sunanka? | Kedu afa gi? |
| My name is... | ...ni oruka mi | Suna sa... | Aham bu... |
| Where is the toilet? | Nibo ni ile igbe yin wa? | Ina bayin ku? | Ebeka ulo nsi unudi? |
| I don't understand | Ko ye mi | Ban fahimta ba | A ghota ghim |
| White person | Oyibo | Bature | Ncha |

## Shopping

| | | | |
|---|---|---|---|
| How is the market? (a greeting to any trader) | Bawo loja? | Ya ya kasuwa? | Kedu maka ahai? |
| I want to buy bread | Mo f era buredi | Zan sayi biredi | Achorom igote ach icha |
| How much is it? | Elo ni? | Nawa ne? | Ego ole ka obu? |
| How much do you want to pay? | Elo lo fe san? | Nawa ne kake so ka biya? | Ego ole ka ichoro ikwu? |
| How much is it last? (literally 'what is your final price?') | Elo ni jale? | Nawa ne gaskiya? | Gini bu ezigbo onu ya? |
| Bring 30 naira last | Mu ogbon naira wa jale | Kawo naira talatin gaskiya | Weta iri naira ato |

## Travelling

| | | | |
|---|---|---|---|
| Is it far? | Se o jinna ni? | Akwai nisa? | O tere aka? |
| Please, show me the way | Ejoo efi ona han mi | Yana jan saniya | O n'adokpu ehi |
| I want to go to Lagos | Mo fe lo si Lagos | Ina so in je Lagos | A choro I ga Lagos |
| Please, where can I get a vehicle going to Lagos? | Ejoo, ni bo ni moti leeri oko Lagos? | Dan allah ina zan samu mota zuwa Lagos? | Biko, ebe ka m ga-enweta ugbo ala na-aga Lagos? |
| Where is the way to the motor park? | Nibo ni oju ona de ibudo iwoko? | Ina hanyar zuwa tashar mota? | Ebe ka esi aga na odu ugbo ala? |
| Take me to the motor park | Gbe mi de ibudo iwoko | Ka kai ni tashar mota | Buru m ga na odu ugbo ala |
| What is your fare? | Elo le fe gba? | Nawa za ka, karba zuwa tasha? | Ego ole ka ina ana? |
| Driver, you're going too fast | Direba ere re ti poj | Mai tuki, gudun ka ya yi yawa! | Okwougboala, ina-agbasi ike nnukwu |

## Eating

| | | | |
|---|---|---|---|
| Do you have...? | Se o ni...? | Kana da...? | Inwere...? |
| Which type of food do you have? | Iru onje wo lo wa? | Wane irin abinci ne kuke dashi? | Kedu udi nri inwere? |

|  | **Yoruba** | **Hausa** | **Igbo** |
|---|---|---|---|
| The food is ready | Onje ti setan | Abinci ya yi | Nri adigo |
| vegetable | efa | ganye | ugu |
| fruit | eso | ya yan itatuwa | mkpuru osisi |
| meat | eran | nama | nwere |
| fish | eja | kifi | azu |
| egg | eyin | kwai | akwa |
| yam | isu | doya | ji |
| plantain | ogede | ayaba | ogede |
| pepper | ata | yaji | ose |
| rice | iresi | shinkafa | osikapa |
| potato | anomo | dankali | nduku |
| tomato | tomati | tumatur | tomanto |
| water | omi | ruwa | mmiri |
| OK, give me rice | Fun mi ni iresi | To, ku ba ni Shinkafa | O dimma, niye m osikapa |

## Days of the week

| | | | |
|---|---|---|---|
| Monday | Ojo aje | Luttinin | Monde |
| Tuesday | Ojo isegun | Talata | Tuzde |
| Wednesday | Ojo ru | Laraba | Wenesday |
| Thursday | Ojo bo | Alhamis | Tosde |
| Friday | Ojo eti | Jumma'a | Fraide |
| Saturday | Ojo abameta | Asabar | Satude |
| Sunday | Ojo aiku | Lahadi | Uka |

## Numbers

**Note**: There are regional dialects within the languages for numbers

| | | | |
|---|---|---|---|
| 1 | okan/meni | daya | otu |
| 2 | eij/meji | biyu | abou |
| 3 | eta/meta | uku | ato |
| 4 | erin/merin | hudu | ano |
| 5 | arun/marun | biyar | ise |
| 6 | efa/mefa | shida | isii |
| 7 | eeje/meje | bakwai | asaa |
| 8 | ejo/mejo | takwas | asato |
| 9 | esan/mesan | tara | iteghete/itolu |
| 10 | ewe/mewa | goma | in |
| 11 | mokanla | goma sha daya | iri na otu |
| 12 etc | mejila etc | goma sha biyu etc | iri na abuo etc |
| 20 | oogun | ashirin | iri abuo |
| 30 | ogbon | talatin | iriato |
| 40 | ogoji | arbain | iri ano |
| 50 | edegbeta | dari biyar | puku ise |
| 60 | ogota | sittin | iri isii |
| 70 | adorin | sabain | iri asaa |
| 80 | ogorin | tamanin | iri asato |
| 90 | adorun | casain | iri iteghete |
| 100 | ogorun | dari | out puku |
| 1000 | egberunkan | dubu | out nnari |

# Appendix 2

## GLOSSARY OF NIGERIAN PHRASES

| | |
|---|---|
| 419 | Any type of fraud, though it originally means financial fraud after the number of the section of the Nigerian penal code that addresses fraud schemes |
| Area Boys | Lagos hoodlums who steal from people using intimidation |
| *batauri* | White person (Hausa); you'll hear this in the northern cities |
| black shirt | Policeman |
| chop | A meal; a restaurant or café is referred to as a 'chop house' |
| dash | Bribe, tip; used as both a noun and a verb as in 'what will you dash me?' |
| drop | Can mean to get off a bus or taxi, but if you want a taxi to yourself (ie: with no other passengers), then you want a drop taxi. You're more likely to use the phrase 'no drop' as it is assumed that all *batauris* or *oyibos* want their own vehicle. |
| easy yourself | Go to the toilet |
| emir | Northern Muslim leader |
| expat | Foreign expatriate worker; there are an estimated 25,000 expats in Nigeria working in sectors such as oil or telecommunications, and as embassy staff |
| food-is-ready | Where you'll see this sign, it means that there is some kind of food ready. Stalls cook up pots of pounded yam, eba etc, with some kind of soup from the morning and keep them going all day. You will have limited choice towards the end of the day, when the food-is-ready starts to run out. |
| go-slow | Traffic jam |
| GRA | Government Reserved Area; mostly created by the British in the colonial years as the residential district for the British officers, but in more recent years it has been the area where governors, councillors and civil servants live. The GRA is invariably the poshest or nicest part of a city, with the biggest houses. |
| moto | Any kind of vehicle, but usually used to refer to a car or bush taxi |
| NEPA | Nigerian Electric Power Agency; Never Expect Power Again (Nigerian slang) |
| NITEL | Nigerian telephone company |
| oba | Traditional Yoruba king and leader, also referred to as an *alafin* |
| off | The verb to switch something off, as in 'off the light' |
| off seat | Out of the office |
| *okada* | Motorbike taxi named after a defunct airline; called *achaba* in the north |
| on | The verb to switch something on, as in 'on the AC' |
| on seat | Meaning in the office |
| *oyibo* | White person (Yoruba slang); you will hear this everywhere |
| pijott | Peugeot car commonly used as a bush taxi that usually has three rows of seats and that can carry nine passengers plus the driver |
| pure water | Half-litre plastic bags of (not always good) drinking water sold everywhere |

| | |
|---|---|
| Sabon Gari | This is Hausa 'for foreigners' town'; often meaning the Yoruba or Igbo, or sometimes the Christian, quarter of a northern city |
| small chop | Snack |
| sorry-o | Expression of sympathy |
| *suya* | Barbecued meat, often served on sticks |
| take leg | Walk |
| *wahalla* | Trouble; 'no wahalla' means no trouble or no worries |
| welcome | Hello |
| with feet | walk |

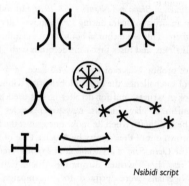

Nsibidi script

# Appendix 3

## FURTHER READING
### History and background

For history I consulted a number of books and found the following most useful, but all are out of print today:

Bradley K, *The Living Commonwealth*, Hutchinson & Co Ltd, 1961
Hallett R, *Africa to 1875*, Heinmann Educational Books Ltd, 1974
Oliver R and Atmore A, *Africa since 1800*, Cambridge University Press, 1972

For information about the Biafran War, I consulted:

Draper M, *Airlift and Airwar in Biafra and Nigeria 1967–1970*, Howell Press Inc, 2000. The author was involved in an airlift to Biafra during 1968 and was later involved with an attempt to ferry other aircraft there. This is a technical book about the military aircraft used by both the Nigerian and the Biafrans, and fuses first-hand accounts with original documentation.

There are a number of prolific Nigerian writers who have, over the last few decades, used their medium as a tool to challenge the state. Nobel-prize winner Wole Soyinka is one of Nigeria's most outspoken writers, and for decades he has used his voice to protest against Nigerian authoritarianism in plays, novels, newspaper articles and poetry. His activism landed him in jail in the late 1960s, when he spoke out against the Nigerians attacking Biafra, and in 1994 he was thrown out of the country by Abacha. One of his most important critical books of Nigeria is *The Open Sore of a Continent: A Personal Narrative of the Nigerian Crisis* (Oxford University Press, 1997) written during the Abacha term of the mid-1990s, when Soyinka said that Nigerians were 'primed for a campaign of comprehensive civil disobedience'. In the book he covers the two decades of military rule and the strife between the ethnic groups, condemns the country's leadership, which he calls illegitimate, and muses about questions of nationalism and international intervention.

Another author who wrote dozens of novels is Ken Saro-Wiwa, Nigeria's foremost environmentalist and literary writer, who is best known for *A Month and a Day: A Detention Diary* (Penguin Books, 1996) which he wrote and smuggled out of jail during his detention by Abacha before being executed on trumped-up charges in 1995. Wiwa led his Ogoni people in the Niger Delta to challenge the environmental degradation of their environment by Shell through gas flaring, oil spillage and soil degeneration, and the various military regimes that exploited the oil wealth. Wiwa called this 'environmental racism'. The book promotes the idealism that all ethnic nationalities must be allowed to shape their destiny and control their resources. Ike Okonta and Oronto Douglas discuss the same subject in *Where Vultures Feast: Shell, Human Rights, and Oil in the Niger Delta* (Lub Books, 2001) which describes the efforts of the people in the Niger Delta to battle the devastation of their homeland by Shell, who have colluded with a series of corrupt and repressive Nigerian governments.

A good contemporary book on Nigeria is *This House Has Fallen: Midnight in Nigeria* (Public Affairs Press, 2000) written by Maier K, *The Independent* newspaper journalist stationed in Lagos for more than a decade. It's generally a historical account, but he also covers the civil disorder and poverty of recent years, and includes first-hand discussions with Nigerians themselves, from taxi drivers and religious leaders, to businessmen and military men. It's an excellent assessment of Nigeria's chaotic state, but he gives dire warnings that Nigeria is quite simply a time bomb ready to go off.

## Fiction and biography

Nigerian-born Ben Okri has published many books including *The Famished Road*, which won the Booker Prize in 1991, *Songs of Enchantment*, *Astonishing the Gods*, *Infinite Riches* and *Dangerous Love*. He has also published two books of poems, the most recent being *Mental Fight*, and a collection of non-fiction, *A Way of Being Free*. His first book, *Stars of the New Curfew* (Secker & Warburg, 1988) is a collection of African short stories about greed and violence. They are vivid tales about the gritty desperation of his characters, hanging on to life by hook or by crook in the slums of Lagos and provincial towns. *The Famished Road* (1st Anchor Books, 1993) tells the story of Azaro, a spirit-child who in the Yoruba tradition of Nigeria exists between life and death, and who maintains ties to the supernatural world. Survival in his chaotic African village is difficult and Azaro and his family must contend with hunger, disease, and violence, as well as the boy's spirit-companions, who are constantly trying to trick him back into their world. *Infinite Riches* and *Songs of Enchantment* follow on from *The Famished Road* with other adventures of Azaro.

Elspeth Huxley's *Four Guineas* (Chatto and Windus Ltd, 1954) is as far as I am aware out of print, but it may possibly be found in a secondhand bookshop. It's a journal of her travels around West Africa in the early 1950s, and is penned in a terribly colonial, old-fashioned way (as was the style of the time). She travelled around Nigeria by chauffeur-driven car and had tea with emirs and government ministers wherever she went. But I found a lot of her descriptions of places and events in the 1950s to be still quite accurate today.

Another famous Nigerian author is Chinua Achebe, who wrote *Things Fall Apart* (1st Anchor Books, first published in 1958, reprinted in 1994), a gripping study of the problem of European colonialism in Africa. The introduction states that the story is about 'a clan which once thought like one, spoke like one, shared a common awareness and acted like one. The white man came and his coming broke this unity. In the process many heads rolled: new words, new usages and new applications gained entrance into men's heads and hearts and the old society gradually gave way.' The story is about an African tribe that lived in an African village called Umuofia at the turn of the 20th century, led by a character called Okonkowo. The white missionaries arrived and started to convert Africans to Christianity. Okonkowo's self-dignity and power were taken away and his life and beliefs began to fall apart. Although a work of fiction, the novel very specifically mirrors the way in which the Igbo in the southeast first encountered the European missionaries and colonialists at the beginning of the 20th century, and how this changed the very essence of their society. Achebe took the phrase *Things Fall Apart* from a poem penned by the Irish poet W B Yeats entitled *The Second Coming* – 'Things fall apart; the centre cannot hold. Mere anarchy is loosed upon the world.'

A new Nigerian novelist is Chris Abani, whose debut novel, *Graceland* (Farrar, Straus and Giroux, 2004), is the story of an innocent child growing into a hardened young man in Nigeria during the late 1970s and early 1980s. The main character is Elvis Oke, who impersonates the American rock-and-roll singer he is named after. The story alternates between Elvis's early years in the 1970s, when his mother dies of cancer and leaves him with a drunk and disapproving father, and his life as a teenager in a Lagos ghetto, a place one character in the book calls 'a pus-ridden eyesore on de face of de nation's capital.'

*Waiting for an Angel* by Helon Habila (W W Norton, 2002). Winner of the Caine Prize for African Writing 2001, and voted fifth-best debut novel by the UK's *Observer* newspaper in 2002. Lomba is a young journalist living under Sani Abacha's military rule in Lagos in the 1990s. He is trying to write a novel in his shabby apartment on Morgan Street (dubbed Poverty Street) and covering arts for a city newspaper, the *Dial*. His life changes drastically after his room-mate is brutally attacked by soldiers, his first love is forced to marry a wealthy old man, journalists are arrested all over the city and the *Dial* offices are set on fire. Lomba decides to take part in a pro-democracy demonstration but is arrested and imprisoned for three years with no access to lawyers or friends. Powerful and vivid, the story moves backwards in a series of closely connected incidents that show Lomba's life before his incarceration. Helon paints an extraordinary picture of life on Poverty Street which he calls 'one of the many decrepit, disease-ridden quarters that dotted the city of Lagos like ringworm on a beggar's body', bringing their sounds, sights and smells to life.

Chimamanda Ngozi Adichie's first novel, *Purple Hibiscus* (Harper Perennial, 2005), offers an intensely personal account of growing up in Nigeria in the early 1990s. Shortlisted for the Orange Prize, it is set in the context of social extremes, political upheaval and religious intolerance. Yet its real strength is in the minutiae of Nigerian family life through the eyes of a 15-year-old girl slowly moving towards maturity.

After his father's death in 1995, Ken Saro-Wiwa's son, Ken Wiwa, wrote an extraordinary book *In the Shadow of a Saint* (Spectrum Books Ltd) about what happened to his father, and about his own personal journey of accepting his loss and of being the son of a martyr. In it he describes the remarkable meetings he had after his father's death with one of Nelson Mandela's daughters, the son of another South African activist who was killed, Steven Biko, and Aung San Suu Kyi, the daughter of another martyr and the founder of Burma. It also describes in detail how he campaigned for his father's release from prison with the world's leaders, who didn't take Abacha's threats of execution seriously and who were as surprised as anyone when Ken Saro–Wiwa was murdered.

For anyone interested in Nigerian music, I recommend Michael Veal's *Fela: The Life & Times of an African Musical Icon* (Temple University Press, 2000). Fela Kuti was Nigeria's greatest musician and the inventor of Afro-beat, a fusion of African music and jazz. He studied music in London and went on to discover James Brown and black politics in the US in the 1960s, and when he returned to Nigeria he created songs and music with a strong protest element that attacked such targets as corrupt politicians and businessmen. Fela's complete rejection of governmental authority, his promiscuity and his flagrant marijuana use were other challenges to the establishment, and the government unleashed a series of attacks on Fela, his family and property. Fela died of AIDS in 1997. The book surveys Fela's life at home and worldwide, detailing his imprisonments and physical abuse, and his performances and song writing. Here are a few lines from one of his songs that serve as a fitting end to a book about Nigeria.

> Why black people suffer today
> Why black people don't have money today
> Why black people haven't travelled to the moon today
> THIS is the reason why:
> We were in our homeland, without troubles
> We were minding our own business
> Some people came from a faraway land
> They fought us and took our land
> They took our people as slaves and destroyed our towns
> Our troubles started at that time
> Our riches they took away to their land
> In return they gave us their colony
> They took our culture away from us
> They gave us their culture which we don't understand
> Black people, we don't know ourselves
> We don't know our ancestral heritage
> We fight each other every day
> We are never together at all –
> THAT is why black people suffer today

# Health and safety

*Bugs, Bites, and Bowels* by Dr Jane Wilson-Howarth, Cadogan

*Expedition Medicine* edited by David Warrell and Sarah Anderson. Handbook of the Royal Geographical Society covering tropical medicine

*The Department of Health's Advice for Travellers on Avoiding the Risks of HIV and AIDS (Travel Safe)*, available from the Department of Health, PO Box 777, London SE1 6XH

*The Traveller's Good Health Guide* by Dr Ted Lankester

*The World's Most Dangerous Places* by Robert Young Pelton, Coskun Aral, and Wink Dulles. Nigeria is listed.

*Travellers' Health: How to Stay Healthy Abroad* by Richard Dawood. A comprehensive book that was completely updated in 2002.

*Your Child Abroad: A Travel Health Guide* by Dr Jane Wilson-Howarth and Dr Matthew Ellis, 2005. Bradt Travel Guides

# Websites

There are dozens of websites produced in Nigeria that cover mostly news, sport or discussion, but most are badly designed, many of the links or pages don't work, and they produce dozens of those infuriating pop-ups. There are, however, some good news sites that are updated regularly:

**www.nigeriaworld.com** is one of the better ones, covering up-to-date news and sport in detail, and it appears that the site is supported by the massive populations of Nigerians living overseas. Freedom of speech certainly does not seem to be a problem on the Nigerian net, and the site features lots of online discussions, forums and opinions.

**www.nigeria.gov.ng** is the formal government website listing government departments, with a few patchy and outdated pages on tourism.

**www.nigeriabusinessinfo.com** has the same repeated tourism blurb and some economic information.

**www.motherlandnigeria.com** has fairly good country information and general features, but it has not been updated for a couple of years.

**www.deltastate.gov.ng** is the new site of the Delta State government, covering political issues and investment opportunities, and some of the tourism sites in the Delta State, but it doesn't give any indication of accessibility or if they are functional.

**www.kanoonline.com** is another state website covering local issues, as is **www.abujacity.com**, but this is especially patchy, with mostly empty pages. While it promises information on culture, film and fashion, it doesn't deliver.

**www.nigeriaunlimited.com** There's not much here except news, but very usefully the site has lifted whole chapters from *Lagos Easy Access* about being an expat in Nigeria, such as the sections on culture-shock and hiring domestic staff, so if you haven't got a copy of the book itself this is worth a visit.

**www.nigeria.com** is probably the most comprehensive site for general information, and has a good selection of features and news covering not just politics but sport and environmental issues.

**www.supereagles.com** has up-to-date information on the national football team.

**www.nigerianoil-gas.com** Industry news and links to all the major corporations in Nigeria.

## Health

See also pages 98–100.

**Blood Care Foundation (UK)** www.bloodcare.org.uk. A charity 'dedicated to the provision of screened blood and resuscitation fluids in countries where they are not readily available'. Says it all really.

**British Travel Health Association (UK)** www.btha.org. Official site for the organisation of travel health professionals.

**Department of Health Travel Advice (UK)** www.doh.gov.uk/traveladvice. Advice on immunisations and requirements for each country. The site is also available as a leaflet, the T6, available free from UK post offices.

**Foreign and Commonwealth Office (UK)** www.fco.gov.uk. Up-to-date general travel advice with a full list of UK embassies/consulates and a link to the Department of Health Travel Advice site (above).

**Medic Alert (UK)** www.medicalert.co.uk. Site for the foundation that issues internationally recognised bracelets and necklaces for those with an existing medical condition or allergy. The bracelet/necklace holds key medical information in the event of you passing out and not being able to tell your doctor what your condition is.

**Public Health Laboratory Service (UK)** www.phls.org.uk. General malaria advice and detailed information about specific drugs. Useful for travellers who are pregnant, have epilepsy, or who have small children.

**World Health Organization** www.who.int. Advice on malarial risks and vaccination requirements, with a link to the WHO Blue Book that lists diseases around the world.

# Index

*Page numbers in bold indicate major entries;*
*those in italics indicate maps*